MATHEMATICS AND
STATISTICS
FOR ECONOMISTS

MATHEMATICS AND STATISTICS FOR ECONOMISTS

SECOND EDITION

GERHARD TINTNER

Distinguished Professor
of Economics and Mathematics
University of Southern California

CHARLES B. MILLHAM

Associate Professor of Mathematics
Washington State University

Holt, Rinehart and Winston, Inc.

New York   Chicago   San Francisco

Atlanta   Dallas   Montreal

Toronto   London   Sydney

Copyright 1953 by Gerhard Tintner
Copyright © 1970 by Holt, Rinehart and Winston, Inc.
All rights reserved
Library of Congress Catalog Card Number: 70-94350
SBN: 03-079510-9
Printed in the United States of America
9 8 7 6 5 4 3 2 1

Tables 1–5 in the appendix are from *Rinehart Mathematical Tables, Formulas and Curves*, Enlarged Edition, compiled by Harold D. Larsen. Copyright 1948, 1953 by Harold D. Larsen. Reprinted by permission of Holt, Rinehart and Winston, Inc. Table 6 is taken from the "X's Probability Scale" table of R. A. Fisher: *Statistical Methods for Research Workers* published by Oliver & Boyd Limited, Edinburgh, and by permission of the author and publishers. Table 7 is reproduced by permission from *Calculation and Interpretation of Analysis of Variance* by George W. Snedecor, © 1934 by The Iowa State University Press.

To Léontine, Phillip, Cindy, and Heidi;
and to Betty and Mike.

PREFACE
to the Second
Edition

This book is a revision of a work originally published in 1953. In the revision we have drawn freely upon the enlarged French translation (*Mathématiques et statistiques pour les économistes*, Paris: Dunod, 1962) and have also incorporated some material taken from the Tintner German *Handbuch der Oekonometrie* (Berlin, Springer, 1960). A Russian translation of this book has also appeared, *Vvednie v ekonometriu* (Izdatel'stvo Statistika, Moscow, 1965). The preface to the Japanese translation (Tokyo, 1961) is reproduced below. A Korean translation also appeared in 1965.

The following sections have been added to the original revised text: 1. Elementary Set Theory; 2. Ordered Pairs and Cartesian Products; 3. Permutations and Combinations, Binomial Theorem; 4, Relations; 19. The Crout Method for the Numerical Solution of a System of Linear Equations; 33. Inequalities; 34. Linear Programming: Graphic Solution; 35. Linear Programming: General; 36. The Simplex Method; 37. Input-Output Analysis; 38. Square Matrices: Addition and Subtraction, Multiplication by a Scalar; 39. Multiplication of Two Square Matrices; 40. Vectors, Inverse Matrices, Crout Method; 42. Computation of Determinants by the Crout Method; 43. Imaginary and Complex Numbers; 44. Finite Difference Equations of Second Order; 93. Differential Equations; 94. Elements of the Calculus of Variations; 100. Some Simple Inventory Problems; 105. Poisson Process; 106. Elements of Queuing Theory; 123. Multiple Regression and Correlation; 124. Identification; 125. Linear Aggregation. In addition, many of the old sections have been revised, and new problems have been added in the exercise sections.

From this list the reader can see that an effort has been made to bring the book up to date, as far as modern mathematical methods of mathematical economics, operations research, and econometrics are concerned.

The book originally grew out of teaching experience at Iowa State

University (Ames Iowa), the University of Pittsburgh, and the University of Southern California (Los Angeles). It is addressed to the general student of economics, undergraduate or graduate, who nowadays requires some knowledge of mathematics in order to follow modern developments in economic theory and knowledge of mathematics and statistics to understand the empirical results derived in econometrics. This book has been written in order to meet this specific need. *Mathematics and Statistics for Economists* includes some applications of elementary mathematics to economics, as well as specific topics in calculus, probability, and elementary statistics. All the examples are taken from economics. It is felt that the economics student who wants to learn mathematics and statistics often has not the time to study topics which are far from his field. Little mathematical preparation is required of the student. It is believed that some knowledge of algebra and elementary trigonometry will be sufficient. But familiarity with elementary economics is required. It is to be hoped that *after* mastering this text the student or reader will possess sufficient knowledge in mathematics and statistics to understand most of the articles published in such journals as *Econometrica, International Economic Review*, the *Journal of the American Statistical Association, American Economic Review*, and others of this type.

It is evident that a book which is planned not for the future professional mathematician but for the future economist cannot be entirely rigorous in the proofs of the mathematical theorems involved. Intuitive proofs and demonstrations are frequently substituted for mathematical rigor, where the more adequate proof is beyond the scope of the book and also beyond the powers of most readers and students. Rigorous treatment is already available elsewhere. Some references are quoted in Appendix A, Suggestions for Further Study.

Many empirical examples are included in the exercise sections of the book. They represent the efforts of econometricians in utilizing statistical methods to obtain theoretically meaningful economic relationships on the basis of concrete statistical data. It should be emphasized that empirical relationships given in the examples are to be interpreted with some caution. They merely represent efforts to estimate some kind of average relationship between the variables indicated. It is to be hoped that these examples, indicative of the great theoretical interest and practical potentialities of econometrics, will make the study of mathematics and statistics more interesting to the economist and will inspire him to further study in the field.

Some of the examples in the text require use of mathematical tables, which are provided at the end of the book. Also recommended is Harold D. Larsen's *Rinehart Mathematical Tables, Formulas and Curves*, Enlarged Edition (New York: Holt, Rinehart and Winston, Inc. 1953).

In connection with the writing of this book we are obliged to a number of colleagues: E.S. Allen, the late D.L. Holl, B. Vinograde, W.G. Murray, the late E.R. Smith, K. Fox of Iowa State University (at Ames); B. Chinitz (University of Pittsburgh), and A. Morgner (University of Southern California). A former student, F. Jarred (University of Adelaide in Australia) helped with the answers to some problems.

Los Angeles, California   —G. T.
November 1969   —C. B. M.

PREFACE
to the Japanese
Edition

It is particularly gratifying to the author to have his book appear in a Japanese edition* because Japanese scholars have recently made many important contributions in the fields of mathematical economics, probability theory, mathematical statistics, and econometrics. All these fields are intimately related to the subject matter of this book. As a matter of fact, the present book endeavors to present a simple introduction to these fields for economists who have some acquaintance with a few elementary aspects of mathematics.

The main purpose of the book is to give the economist who is somewhat familiar with modern economic theory some preparation for the understanding of the econometric method which has become very important in recent years.

According to the definition of Professor Oskar Lange, "Economics is the science of administration of scarce resources in human society."[1]

Econometrics is a specific method in the field of economics. It involves the combination of mathematical economic theory and mathematical statistics with the purpose of obtaining numerical results and verifying economic laws and propositions.[2]

I would like to take advantage of the occasion to point out the importance of econometrics for economic policy. It should be emphasized that

* Preface to the Japanese translation of the book, Gerhard Tintner: *Mathematics and Statistics for Economists*, 2d printing (New York: Rinehart and Co., 1954), English edition: Constable Shiga University, Hikone City, Shiga-Ken Japan. Published by Chikura-shobo Publishing Company, c/o Daiichisogokan, 3chome-1 Kyobashi Chuo-ku Tokyo, Japan. Journal Paper No. J. 2901 of the Iowa Agricultural Experiment Station, Ames, Iowa, Project 1200.

[1] O. Lange: "The Scope and Method of Economics," *Review of Economic Studies*, 1945, vol. 13, p. 19.

[2] G. Tintner: "The Definition of Econometrics," *Econometrica*, 1953, vol. 21, pp. 31–40. Japanese translation: *Bulletin of the Bureau of Statistics, Office of the Prime Minister*, March 1954, vol. 3, no. 6, pp. 57–69.

economics is a positive science and that normative statements are foreign to economics and econometric research. The principles which goven economic policy cannot possibly be derived from economic theory mathematically or nonmathematically. They come from ethical and moral considerations or are derived from the political ideas of the worker in the field. Econometrics can only make a contribution to questions of economic policy in the following sense: Sometimes we are able to derive numerical relationships which hold approximately in the field investigated. Then we might consider the result of various measures of economic policy and point out the approximate consequences which hold if our empirical relationships are valid.

As an example, let us consider the case of an empirically derived demand function, that is, a relationship between the price of a given commodity and the quantity taken on a given market (Section 11). Under certain circumstances which are discussed in this book we are able to derive an approximation to this demand function from data collected in the market by the use of certain statistical procedures (Section 122).

Economic theory tells us that in general this demand function should be downward-sloping. This is to say, the higher the price of this commodity the less will be the quantity taken on the market, other things being equal. An exception to this rule is found only for inferior goods, which are commodities having the property that with increasing income and constant prices, less is consumed rather than more. All these properties of demand functions can be demonstrated by the method of mathematical economics (Section 87).

Econometrics can go one step further, and under certain circumstances may derive an approximation to the demand function as it presumably exists in the given market (Section 122). This econometric relationship should be of interest to producers of the given commodity and to consumers. It would also be of interest to trade associations and cooperatives working in this field. It should be noted that the persons and organizations described up to now do not include the government. So, even if we have an ideal laissez-faire economy, without any government intervention of any kind, econometric relationships might be of interest to the persons concerned, for instance in relation to market research.

If we consider government intervention, for example, price-fixing, the results of econometric research, if reliable, may also be of some importance. Suppose the government fixes the price of a given commodity. The statistically derived econometric relationship, namely the demand function, will then give an approximate answer to the following question: Given the fixed price, how much will be sold on the market, other things being equal?

Such considerations may be of importance, because the price might be fixed so high that very little of the commodity would be sold, and this might have a detrimental influence on the health of the population.

It should be emphasized that it is not the business of econometricians to advocate price-fixing or to argue against price-fixing, but only to point out the approximate results which follow from a given policy if the derived econometric relationship holds, at least approximately.

Government intervention into economic life may take various forms, reaching from protective tariffs and the control of public utilities to the total or almost total control of economic life under collectivist economic planning. Again it should be emphasized that it is not the business of the econometrician to advocate any of those measures or argue against them but only to point out the results of a given economic policy on the basis of the econometric relationship derived. So, for instance, if various fiscal and monetary policies are proposed, then econometric models of the Keynesian type might be useful. (Exercises 42, nos. 8–11). For more comprehensive economic planning, for example the purpose of a war economy, or for collective economic planning, models like Leontief's input-output analysis might be useful (Exercises 18, no. 10). Many more examples which are illustrated on the subsequent pages of this book might be quoted.

It has sometimes been held that mathematics cannot be applied in the social sciences and more specifically in economics because the fundamental relationships are not quantitative. I would doubt this statement in general but would be willing to concede it inasmuch as a static theory of utility or choice is concerned. Mathematics, especially modern mathematics, concerns itself very frequently with nonquantitative relationships. An example for a successful treatment of purely ordinal relationships is given in section 87 (Exercises 87, no. 13), where a short introduction to the problem of the modern theory of choice or indifference analysis is given. Of course, an introductory text like this one cannot go very deeply into these problems. I would like to refer the reader to the literature quoted in Appendix A, "Suggestions for Further Study."

It should be pointed out that much of the known mathematical literature of economics from the political arithmeticians and Quesnay to the present day uses artificial numerical examples which are quantitative and at least in intent mathematical. I would like only to quote the famous labor theory of value in *Das Kapital* by Karl Marx and the subsequent discussion in mathematical terms by Von Bortkiewics[3] and later by P.M. Sweezy.[4] Other aspects of the Marxist theory of capital have been presented in mathematical form by Shigeto Tsuru.[5] Another example is the celebrated *Positive Theorie des Kapitals* by Von Boehm-Bawerk

---

[3] L. von Bortkiewics: *Wertrechnung und Preisrechnung in Marx'schen System*, "Archiv fuer Sozialwissenschaft und Sozialpolitik," 1906, vol. 23, pp. 445–488.

[4] P.M. Sweezy: *The Theory of Capitalist Development*, New York: Oxford University Press, 1942, pp. 123–125.

[5] Shigeto Tsuru: "On Reproduction Schemes," Appendix A of P.M. Sweezy: *op. cit.*, pp. 365–374.

which has been discussed and clarified by Knut Wicksell in mathematical terms in his *Uber Wert, Kapital und Rente*.[6] I don't believe that there is in principle any difference between the nonmathematical presentation of the theories of those famous economists and the mathematical models developed later by their disciples, but it is my feeling that the logic and underlying assumptions have been clarified by the mathematical writers.

Many modern philosophers and logicians hold that mathematics is actually a branch of logic; and nobody will deny that there is a very close relationship between modern mathematical logic and mathematics. Hence I do not see how anybody who uses logical, that is, deductive, methods in constructing economic models could consistently deny the use of mathematics in economics.

This would not be true for consistent followers of the extreme historical or institutionalist school, but it should be remarked that the influence of those schools has recently declined.

There is, of course, no way of proving a priori that the mathematical and econometric methods are successful, but the same would be true for any scientific method. All that is wanted of the reader or student is an open mind toward the possible usefulness of those methods. Only a careful use of econometric methods in the field of economics can eventually give us a pragmatic justification of econometrics. It is to be hoped that this book will perhaps contribute something toward this goal by interesting students of economics in these modern methods and thus stimulate econometric research.

[6] K. Wicksell: *Uber Wert, Kapital und Rente nach den neuren nationaloekonomischen Theorien*, Jena: Gustav Fischer, 1893.

CONTENTS

PART ONE
SOME APPLICATIONS OF ELEMENTARY MATHEMATICS TO ECONOMICS

Chapter 1

Sets, Functions, and Graphs

1 ELEMENTARY SET THEORY

Intuitively we shall define a set S to be a collection of definite, distinguishable objects or entities. We shall say that a set S is determined when we either list the entities that belong to S or give a rule by which we can decide whether or not a given object or entity belongs to S. As a notational convention, if an entity x is a member of the set S, we write, $x \in S$, which reads, "x belongs to S," while if x is not a member of S, we write, $x \notin S$.

For example, we might say, "the set S consists of the elements a, b, and c"; we write, $S = \{a, b, c\}$. Here we have specified the set S by listing its members. Or we could say, "S consists precisely of the first three letters of the Roman alphabet." In this case S was specified by stating a rule by which we can determine whether or not a given entity is a member of S. The letter z is not in S, nor is the number 3.

Suppose now that we are considering two sets, say S and T, and that every element belonging to S also belongs to T. We then say that S is a *subset* of T; we write, $S \subset T$. If S and T have the properties that $S \subset T$ and $T \subset S$, we see that every element in S is in T, and vice versa, and that therefore S and T must be the same set; we express this by writing, $S = T$.

For example, let $S = \{1, 3, 5, a\}$ and $T = \{1, 5, a\}$. Clearly, S is not a subset of T (written, $S \not\subset T$), because $3 \in S$ and $3 \notin T$. However, every element in T is also in S, so $T \subset S$.

As another example, let $S = \{a, b, c\}$ and $T = \{b, c, d\}$. $S \not\subset T$ because $a \in S$ and $a \notin T$. Also, $T \not\subset S$ because $d \in T$ but $d \notin S$. S and T do, however, have some elements in common, and we can see

NOTE: Problems marked by * contain important ideas and theorems which will be required later. Problems and sections marked ** are somewhat more difficult and may be omitted.

3

that the set $R = \{b, c\}$ has the property that $R \subset S$, $R \subset T$ and that no set containing R (except for R) has this property. This motivates the notion of *intersection:* For any two sets S and T, R is said to be the *intersection* of S and T, written, $R = S \cap T$, if R consists precisely of those elements belonging to both S and T.

For example, let $S = \{1, 2, 3\}$ and $T = \{2, 3, 4\}$; then $S \cap T = \{2, 3\}$. If $V = \{3, 4, 5\}$, $S \cap V = \{3\}$ and $T \cap V = \{3, 4\}$.

Clearly, for any two sets S and T, $S \cap T = T \cap S$.

The notion of intersection, however, introduces a difficulty. If $S = \{a, b, c\}$ and $T = \{d, e, f\}$, what is $S \cap T$? If we want $S \cap T$ to be a set, as are S and T, we must extend somewhat our earlier intuitive notion of set. To do this we define the set ϕ, the *empty set*, to be that unique set *having no members.*

A few examples demonstrate that it is indeed sensible to allow such a concept. Consider the set of all English-speaking fish; the set of all angora goats in your desk drawer; the set of all real numbers whose square is negative.

Incidentally, unlike the symbols S, T, R, and so on, which we have assigned to sets at will, we shall reserve the symbol ϕ, and only that symbol, to refer to the empty set.

Another set theoretic relationship is that of *union:* let S and T be sets. We say that R is the *union* of S and T, written, $R = S \cup T$, if R consists of precisely those elements belonging to either S or T (our use of the word "or" is *not* intended to exclude from the union those elements belonging to *both* S and T). For example, suppose $S = \{a, b, c\}$ and $T = \{c, d, e\}$; then $S \cup T = \{a, b, c, d, e\}$. As other examples, if $S = \{a, b, c\}$ and $T = \{d, e\}$, then $S \cup T = \{a, b, c, d, e\}$. If $S = \{a, b, c\}$ and $T = \{b, c\}$, then $S \cup T = \{a, b, c\} = S$.

For our last set theoretic relationship again suppose that S and T are sets. We define R to be the *complement of S relative to T*, written $R = T - S$, if R consists of precisely those elements that belong to T but not to S. For example, let $S = \{a, b, c\}$ and $T = \{c, d, e\}$; then $T - S = \{d, e\}$, as only d and e belong to T and not to S. Similarly, $S - T = \{a, b\}$.

Suppose, further, that $S = \{a, b, c\}$ and $T = \{e, f\}$. Then $S - T = S$, since no element of S is an element of T; for the same reason, $T - S = T$. On the other hand, if $S = \{a, b, c\}$ and $T = \{b, c\}$, then $S - T = \{a\}$ but $T - S = \phi$.

A comment on notation

A standard notation convention, found in the literature of economics as well as in that of mathematics, can be introduced; this will allow us a considerable economy of words in discussing sets whose members are

too numerous to list and for which rules for determining membership
are necessarily lengthly. That convention is as follows: if S is described
by a rule, "____," we can express S by writing, $S = \{x|x\_\_\_\_\}$. We
read, "S equals the set of all elements x such that x____." Thus, if S
consists of all real numbers between 1 and 10, inclusive, we can write
$S = \{x|1 \leq x \leq 10\}$. If $T = V \cap W$ for any two sets V and W, we can
say, $T = \{x|x \in V$ and $x \in W\}$. If $R = V \cup W$, we can say, $R =$
$\{x|x \in V\}$ or $\{x \in W\}$; if $R = V - W$, we can say that $R = \{x|x \in V$
and $x \notin W\}$.

EXERCISES 1

1   *Venn diagram* is the name given to a particular type of pictorial illustration of some set theoretic relationship and is perhaps best described
by example. If S and T are sets and we have no further information
about them, we can "draw" them as follows:

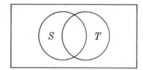

Then $S \cup T$ has as its Venn diagram the hatched region:

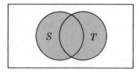

and $S \cap T$:

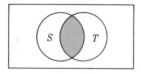

(a) Draw the Venn diagram for $S - (S \cap T)$. (b) Diagram $S - T$ and
$T - S$. (c) Indicate, by demonstrating that the Venn diagrams are
identical, that $S - (S \cap T) = S - T$. (d) Diagram the *symmetric
difference* R of S and T: $R = (S - T) \cup (T - S)$.

2   Let $V = \{1, 2, 3, 4, 5, 6, 7, 8, 9\}$. (a) Find S if $S = \{x|x \in V, x \neq 6,$
$x \neq 9\}$. (b) Find T if $T = \{x|x \neq V\}$ and $x \notin S$. What relationship
exists between T and S?

3   If $S = \{a, b, c\}$, list all subsets of S. Is ϕ a subset of S? Is ϕ a subset of *any* set?

4   If A and B are each sets of real numbers, let $C = \{x | x = Y + Z, Y \neq A, Z \neq B\}$. Find C if $A = \{1, 2, 3, 4\}$ and $B = \{2, 4, 5\}$.

5   Let S, T, and V be sets such that $S \subset T \subset V$. What can you say about the relationship between $V - T$ and $V - S$?

2   ORDERED PAIRS AND CARTESIAN PRODUCTS

We now want to consider a particular sort of set, which we shall call an *ordered pair*. Intuitively, we shall think of an ordered pair (a, b) as being defined by two properties: the set $\{a, b\}$ of elements that go into the ordered pair and the one-element set $\{a\}$, designating which of the two elements $\{a, b\}$ is considered as first in the ordered pair.

Thus, the ordered pair (x, y) is defined by the set $\{y, x\}$ and the set $\{x\}$, while the ordered pair (y, x) is described by the set $\{y, x\}$ together with the set $\{y\}$. Similarly, the set $\{1, 2\}$ together with the set $\{2\}$ defines the ordered pair $(2, 1)$, while the set $\{1, 2\}$ together with the set $\{1\}$ defines the ordered pair $(1, 2)$.

We can infer (correctly), then, that the ordered pair (a, b) is equal to the ordered pair (c, d) if and only if $a = c$ and $b = d$. Thus, even though $\{1, 2\} = \{2, 1\}$, $(1, 2) \neq (2, 1)$; but $(1, 2) = (\frac{3}{3}, \frac{4}{2})$, because $1 = \frac{3}{3}$ and $2 = \frac{4}{2}$.

Having thus considered ordered pairs, we can extend our thinking to the idea of an ordered *n-tuple;* an ordered n-tuple $(a_1, a_2, \cdots, a_n)$ consists of a set $\{a_1, a_2, \cdots, a_n\}$ together with a stipulation stating the order of appearance of the elements a_i. (Rigorously, this is done by assuming that the ordered $(n - 1)$-tuple $(a_1, a_2, \cdots, a_{n-1})$ has been defined, then defining the ordered n-tuple $(a_1, \cdots, a_n)$ as the ordered *pair* $[(a_1, \cdots, a_{n-1}), a_n]$. Thus, the ordered n-tuple $(a_1, a_2, \cdots, a_n)$ is equal to the ordered n-tuple $(b_1, b_2, \cdots, b_n)$ if and only if $a_1 = b$, $a_2 = b_2, \cdots, a_n = b_n$; as before, the sets $\{1, 2, 3, 4\}$ and $\{2, 3, 4, 1\}$ are equal, but $\{1, 2, 3, 4\} \neq \{2, 3, 4, 1\}$.

It is intuitively clear that if S is a set of n members, there are $n(n - 1)(n - 2) \cdots 2 \cdot 1$ ways of forming an ordered n-tuple using the members of S, each one once.

Now suppose that S and T are sets. The Cartesian product $R = S \times T$ (read, "S cross T") of S with T is given by $R = \{(x, y) | x \in S$ and $y \in T\}$.

Thus, R is the set of all ordered pairs we can obtain by choosing each element of S and order pairing it, in turn, with each element of R, always having the element from S as the first member of the ordered pair.

As an example, let $S = \{1, 2, 3\}$. $T = \{a, b\}$. Then $S \times T = \{(1, a),$

$(1, b)$, $(2, a)$, $(2, b)$, $(3, a)$, $(3, b)\}$, while $T \times S = \{(a, 1), (a, 2), (a, 3),$ $(b, 1), (b, 2), (b, 3)\}$.

Is $S \times T$ equal to $T \times S$? The answer is no. Remember, $S \times T$ and $T \times S$ are each sets, and if they are to be equal each member of $S \times T$ must be a member of $T \times S$, and conversely. But $(1, a) \in S \times T$, $(1, a) \notin T \times S$, and we see that $S \times T \neq T \times S$. When *could* we expect equality of $S \times T$ and $T \times S$ for sets T and S?

EXERCISES 2

1   What ordered pairs are defined by the following pairs of sets? (a) $\{x, y\}$, $\{x\}$. (b) $\{1, 2\}$, $\{2\}$. (c) $\{1, 2\}$, $\{1\}$.

2   Let $S = \{a, b, c\}$. How many ordered pairs can we form using the members of S if each is to appear only once in a given ordered pair? if each can appear more than once in a given ordered pair?

3   Which of the following pairs are equal? (a) $(\{1, 2\}, \{2, 1\})$ and $(\{2, 1\}, \{2, 1\})$. (b) $\{(1, 2), (2, 1)\}$ and $\{(2, 1), (1, 2)\}$. (c) $\{(1, 2), (1, 2)\}$ and $\{(2, 1), (1, 2)\}$. (d) $\{(1, 2), (2, 1)\}$ and $\{(1, 2), (1, 2)\}$.

4   Find $A \times B$ and $B \times A$ if (a) $A = \{a, b, c\}$ and $B = \{d, e\}$. (b) $A = \{(1, 2), (1, 3), (2, 4)\}$ and $B = \{d, e\}$.

5   What Cartesian product is indicated by Figure 1?

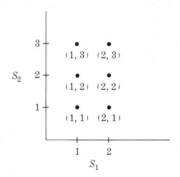

Figure 1

3   PERMUTATION AND COMBINATIONS. BINOMIAL THEOREM

It will be recalled that in our discussion of ordered n-tuples we observed that, given a set $S = \{a_1, a_2, \cdots, a_n\}$ it is possible to form $n(n - 1)$ $\cdots 3 \cdot 2 \cdot 1 = n!$ (read, "n-factorial") distinct ordered n-tuples, each of which contains each element of S once. That is, there are $n!$ distinct *arrangements* of the members of S. We want to pursue this idea of the *number of arrangements* of the members of a set a little further.

Suppose, that we have a set S of n distinguishable objects (cards, chairs, blocks of wood, and so on), and that we have r slots to fill, choosing one of the members of S for each slot until all r slots are occupied.

Clearly, if $r > n$ (more slots than objects), the situation is impossible and the number of ways of filling these slots using the members of S is zero. If $r = 0$, there is one way of filling up the 0 slots. If $0 < r \leq n$, the situation is more involved, but we can reason as follows:

Suppose the slots are numbered 1 through r and we fill each of them in turn, starting with the first. We can choose any one of the n members of S to fill the first slot, clearly. Having filled the first slot, we have $n - 1$ elements of S remaining, any one of which we can choose for the second slot. Hence, the first two slots can be filled in $n(n - 1)$ ways. Continuing, we have $n - 2$ objects to choose from for the third slot and $n(n - 1)(n - 2)$ ways of filling the first three slots. By the time we have filled the $(r - 1)$st slot and are ready for the rth, we have used $r - 1$ members of S and have $n - r + 1$ members of S left to choose from, so that the r slots can be filled, using the n members of S, in $n(n - 1)(n - 2) \cdots n - r + 1 = n!/(n - r)!$ ways.

It should be noted that the operation just described is equivalent to two processes: (1) choosing an object from S and (2) deciding on a slot for it until all slots are filled. In other words, we have discovered that there are $n!/(n - r)!$ ways of choosing r objects out of $n (0 \leq r < n)$ and arranging them. (This formula is valid also for $r = n$ if we first establish the convention that $0! = 1$.)

The number of ways of choosing and arranging r distinguishable objects out of n is called the number of *permutations* of n objects taken r at a time, denoted by $_nP_r$.

EXAMPLE 1

How many ways are there of arranging 6 people in a line for a picture?

This is equivalent to asking for the number of ways of choosing 6 objects out of 6 and then arranging them:

$$_6P_6 = \frac{6!}{(6 - 6)!} = \frac{6!}{0!} = \frac{6!}{1} = 6! = 720.$$

EXAMPLE 2

Ron's camera is only large enough to take a picture of 3 people at 6 feet and is incapable of resolving features at over 6 feet. How many pictures are possible if there are 10 people present (and 2 pictures are different if they are photographs of the same 3 people arranged differently, as well as if the pictures are *not* photographs of the same 3 people)?

This question asks essentially for the number of ways of choosing 3 people out of 10 and arranging the chosen 3. It is therefore answered by

$$_{10}P_3 = \frac{10!}{(10-3)!} = \frac{10!}{7!} = 10.9.8 = 720.$$

Now suppose we want merely to count the number of ways of *choosing r* elements out of the n in a given set S without regard to arrangement of the chosen elements. That is, we want to determine the number of r-element subsets of S that we can form. Let us denote this number by $_nC_r$ and call it the number of combinations of n objects taken r at a time. To find $_nC_r$, recall that in finding $_nP_r = n!/(n-r)!$ we divided the process of constructing a permutation into two parts, choosing the r elements to go into the permutation and then arranging the r chosen elements. The first part is that in which we are now interested, and by definition it can be done in $_nC_r$ ways. As we have seen, the second part, that of arranging the r chosen objects, can be done in $r!$ ways. But this means that $_nC_r(r!) = _nP_r$, or $_nC_r = n!/[r!(n-r)!]$: the number of r-element subsets of a set S with n distinguishable elements is $_nC_r = n!/[r!(n-r)!]$.

EXAMPLE 3

In how many ways can a 9-man work crew be formed from 15 men?

This problem asks only for the number of ways of selecting 9 men out of 15: $_{15}C_9 = 15!/[9!(15-9)!]$, a number we shall not evaluate further.

EXAMPLE 4

A bookstore has a display window capable of holding 8 books. The owner wants to display 2 books each in mathematics, economics, physics, and paleontology, and he regards order as significant in the display in that he can make different displays out of the same 8 books simply by rearranging them.

If he has 4 math, 5 economics, 3 physics, and 6 paleontology books, how many different displays can he make?

This problem is most easily worked by first selecting the texts and then arranging all of them. The store owner can choose texts in each field as follows: $_4C_2$ in math, $_5C_2$ in economics, $_3C_2$ in physics, and $_6C_2$ in paleontology. Having chosen his 8 books, he can arrange them in any of 8! different ways. Hence, the total number of displays available to him are:

$$_4C_2 \cdot {}_5C_2 \cdot {}_3C_2 \cdot {}_6C_2 \cdot 8! = (2 \cdot 3)(5 \cdot 2)(3)(3 \cdot 2)8!$$

One might be tempted to work the problem as follows: select *and* arrange the texts in each field, that is, treat the problem as composed of four distinct permutation problems. But this would be incorrect, for one would be ignoring the displays obtained by mixing texts from different fields.

EXAMPLE 5

How many bridge hands can be dealt from an ordinary deck of 52 cards?

A bridge hand contains 13 cards. Since there are no other stipulations on this bridge hand, we need only choose 13 cards out of 52: $_{52}C_{13}$.

EXAMPLE 6

How many bridge hands contain 3 aces, 2 kings, 1 queen, and 3 jacks?

We want to choose 3 aces out of the 4 in the deck, 2 kings out of the 4 in the deck, and so on. But having chosen the 9 cards stipulated, we still have 4 left to select. These 4 can be any cards in the deck, *except* that none may be an ace, king, queen, or jack. There are 36 such cards in the deck (that is, cards that are none of the above); hence our hand can be chosen in $_4C_3 \cdot {}_4C_2 \cdot {}_4C_1 \cdot {}_4C_3 \cdot {}_{36}C_4$ ways.

Binomial theorem

As a last illustration of combinations we present the binomial theorem: For any numbers x, y, and any positive integer n,

$$(x + y)^n = {}_nC_0x^n + {}_nC_1x^{n-1}y + {}_nC_2x^{n-2}y^2 + \cdots$$
$$+ {}_nC_rx^{n-r}y^r + \cdots + {}_nC_{n-1}xy^{n-1} + {}_nC_ny^n.$$

For example,

$$(x + 2y)^3 = {}_3C_0x^3 + {}_3C_1x^2(2y) + {}_3C_2x(2y)^2 + {}_3C_3(2y)^3$$
$$= x^3 + 6x^2y + 12xy^2 + 8y^3.$$

To obtain an intuitive feeling for the source of this theorem note that, by definition, $(x + y)^n = (x + y)(x + y) \cdots (x + y)$, a product of n identical factors. Ask, then, where the term $x^{n-r}y^r$ in the binomial expansion comes from. It comes from choosing $n - r$ of the n factors to contribute x and having the remaining r factors contribute x. How many ways are there of choosing r out of the n factors, from each of which we take a y to go into $x^{n-r}y^r$? There are obviously $_nC_r$ ways of doing this.

EXERCISES 3

1 How many baseball teams can be formed out of 15 men if each man can play any position but we consider the same group of men to constitute different teams if the same men do not play the same position?

2 A car dealer has 8 new cars on hand, 3 of which are identical in appearance, with the remaining 5 distinct. His showroom has room for 4 cars at a time. How many different displays can be make if the same 4 cars arranged differently (assuming all are distinct) constitute different displays?

3 How many bridge hands contain 4 aces, 4 kings, and 4 queens?

4 How many bridge hands contain 1 ace, 3 queens, 2 4's, and 2 3's?

5 How many "full house" hands are there in poker? (A poker hand consists of 5 cards; a "full house", 3 cards of the same numerical value together with 2 of one numerical value, such as 3 kings and 2 4's.)

6 Find the coefficient of x^3x^4 in the binomial expansion of $(x + y)^7$.

7 Find the coefficient of x^2y^3 in the binomial expansion of $(2x + y)^5$.

8 Show that $2^n = {}_nC_0 + {}_nC_1 + {}_nC_2 + \cdots + {}_nC_r + \cdots + {}_nC_n$.

4   RELATIONS

A binary relation is simply any set of ordered pairs. For example, the set $S = \{(1, 2), (a, b), (3, c)\}$ is a relation: we say, moreover, that if (x, y) belongs to a relation R, then x is R-related to y, or, equivalently, that xRy. Thus, in S above, 1 is S-related to 2, a is S-related to b, and 3 is S-related to c, or, equivalently, $1S2$, aSb, and $3Sc$.

Other examples of relation: let $S = \{(x, y)|x, y \text{ real numbers}, x \leq y\}$. S is a relation, since it is a set of ordered pairs, and some of its members are $(1, 1)$, $(1, 2)$, $(1, 3)$, $(0, 3)$, and $(-3, -2)$. Note that $(2, 1)$ is not a member of S.

Let $T = \{(x, y)|x, y \text{ real numbers}, x - y \text{ even}\}$. Then $(1, 3) \in T$ and $(3, 1) \in T$ and $(1, 2) \notin T$ and $(2, 1) \notin T$.

Since any relation R is a set of ordered pairs, it is clear that a relation R is some subset of a Cartesian product $A \times B$ of two sets A and B. Suppose that we consider relations R that are subsets of $A \times A$, that is, of the Cartesian product of some set A with itself. In this case R is frequently called a relation *in* the set A, and such relations can have several properties not possessed by relations in general.

For example, the relation $T = \{(x, y)|x - y \text{ even}, x \text{ and } y \text{ real numbers}\}$

has the property that if $(x, y) \in T$, then $(y, x) \in T$ also. This property is that of *symmetry*. The relation R is *symmetric* in the set A if $(y, x) \in R$ whenever $(x, y) \in R$. Thus, the relation $S = \{(x, y)|x, y$ real numbers, $x \leq y\}$ is not symmetric because it is false that $y \leq x$ whenever $x \leq y$. For example, $1 \leq 2$ but $2 \nleq 1$.

S has another property, however, that of transitivity. A relation R in a set A is said to be *transitive* if when $(x, y) \in R$ and $(y, z) \in R$ then $(x, z) \in R$. Since if $x \leq y$ and $y \leq z$ we have $x \leq z$, we see that S is transitive.

Is the relation $T = \{(x, y)|x, y$ real numbers, $x - y$ even$\}$ transitive?

Finally, we are interested in the property of reflexivity. A relation R in a set A is *reflexive* if $(x, x) \in R$ whenever $(x, y) \in R$ for some $y \in A$.

For example, $\{(x, y)|x - y$ even, x, y real numbers$\}$ is a reflexive relation because $x - x = 0$ is even for any real number x. The relation $\{(x, y)|x < y, x, y$ real numbers$\}$ is transitive, since if $x < y$ and $y < z$, then $x < z$, but it is not symmetric, since having $x < y$ precludes $y < x$, and it is not reflexive, since $x < x$ for no real number x.

5 FUNCTIONS

A *function* is a relation R, that is, a set of ordered pairs such that no two ordered pairs have the same first element.

For example, let $f = \{(1, 2), (2, 2), (3, 4)\}$. f satisfies the definition of function because no two of these ordered pairs have the same first element. As another example, let $h = \{(x, y)|x, y$ real, $y = 3x\}$. h is a function, as we see in the following argument: suppose (x_0, y_0) and (x_1, y_1) are two ordered pairs in h, and suppose $x_0 = x_1$. Then $3x_0 = 3x_1 = y_0 = y_1$, and the ordered pairs (x_0, y_0) and (x_1, y_1) are identical.

With each function we associate two sets, called the *domain* and *range* of the function. The domain consists of all elements x that appear as first elements in the ordered pairs making up the function, and the range consists of all elements that appear second in the ordered pairs. Thus, in the function $f = \{(1, 2), (2, 2), (3, 4)\}$, the domain of f is $D = \{1, 2, 3\}$, while the range of f is the set $R = \{2, 4\}$. In the function $h = \{(x, y)|y = x^2, x$ a real number$\}$ the range R consists of all nonnegative real numbers, while for $g = \{(x, y)|y = x^2, x \geq 1\}$ the domain D consists of all real numbers $x \geq 1$ and the range R consists of all real numbers $y \geq 1$.

6 EXAMPLES AND DISCUSSION OF FUNCTIONS

Suppose we are considering a function f and that $x \in D$, where D is the domain of f. If (x, y) is the ordered pair in f whose first element is x, it is a notational convention to write $y = f(x)$; if the name x is allowed to indicate any member of D, it is not uncommon to call x the *independent* variable and $y = f(x)$ the *dependent* variable.

For example, suppose $D = \{x|5 \geq x \geq 1\}$ and $f = \{(x, y)|x \in D$ and $y = x^2 + 1\}$. Then R, the range of f, is given by $R = \{y|26 \geq y \geq 2\}$; further, we would say that $f(2) = 5$, $f(1) = 2$, and $f(5) = 26$. More commonly we might say that for $1 \leq x \leq 5$, $y = f(x) = x^2 + 1$.

More often than not functions are designated by only a "formula," such as $f(x) = x^2 + 1$; if no mention is made of the domain of the function, one assumes it to hold for all x for which the formula is meaningful. Given the domain, either explicitly or by implication, and a rule for determining the second member of the ordered pairs (the dependent variable), we can find the range of the function.

For example, if we describe a function f^1 by saying, "$f^1(x) = x^2 + 1$," we are actually saying, "for all x in the domain D of the function f^1, $f^1(x) = x^2 + 1$, and the domain consists of all real numbers." This is *not* the same function as that described earlier, in which D was given to be $\{x|1 \leq x \leq 5\}$. For example, $(6, 37)$ is a member of f^1 but not of f.

Further, suppose a function g is specified only by $g(x) = 1/(x^2 - 4)$. One assumes, then, that g consists of all ordered pairs of the form $(x, 1/(x^2 - 4))$ except for $x = \pm 2$, since the specified formula $g(x) = 1/(x^2 - 4)$ is not defined at $x = \pm 2$. If, moreover, we define the function h by $h(x) = 1/(x^2 - 4)$, $x \neq \pm 2$, $h(2) = 1$, $h(-2) = 2$, we observe that $h(x) = g(x)$ except at $x = \pm 2$, but that for no y does $(2, y) \in g$ or $(-2, y) \in g$, while $(2, 1) \in h$ and $(-2, 2) \in h$. h is thus defined and meaningful for all real numbers while $g(2)$ and $g(-2)$ are without meaning.

EXERCISES 6 (RELATIONS AND FUNCTIONS)

1 Which of the following relations are transitive? reflexive? symmetric? functions? (a) $\{(a, b)\ (a, c), (b, c), (a, a), (b, b)\}$. (b) $\{(1, 1), (2, 2), (3, 3), (1, 2), (2, 3), (1, 3)\}$. (c) $\{(1, a), (2, b), (1, 2), (1, b)\}$. (d) $\{(1, a) (2, b), (b, b)\}$.

2 Which, if any, of the three properties of transitivity, reflexivity, and symmetry can no function possess? How many reflexive functions are there? How many reflexive functions has $\{x|0 \leq x \leq 1\}$ as domain?

3 Let $y = f(x) = 3 - 2x + x^2$. Find $f(0)$, $f(-2)$, $f(5)$, $f(-1)$.

4 Let $y = f(x) = 2x/(x^2 - 1)$. What is the (implied) domain of f? Find $f(0)$, $f(2)$, $f(-2)$.

5 Let $f(x) = a + bx$, where a and b are fixed real numbers. Find $D(0)$; $f(a)$; $f(-a)$; $f(a/b)$; $f(-a/b)$.

6 Let $f(x) = 2x^2 - 1$. Find $f(2x)$; $2f(x)$; $f(2 + x)$.

7   RECTANGULAR COORDINATES

The graphical representation of theoretical or statistical relationships between two variables is very important in economics. To represent a pair of related numbers x and y, which may be positive or negative, we must first draw a system of two *axes*, one horizontal and one vertical. The point of intersection of the axes is labeled O and is called the *origin*. The horizontal axis is called the X axis and the vertical axis the Y axis. The positive directions are to the right and upward, respectively.

Convenient units of x and y are chosen. These units need not be the same, since x and y may represent entirely different types of quantities. The units chosen will depend on the ranges of the values of x and y that are to be included.

A pair of related numbers x and y is designated by (x, y). The geometric representation of such a pair upon an axis system is a point. The x number is said to be the x *coordinate*, or *abscissa*, of the point, and the y number is the y *coordinate*, or *ordinate*, of the point. To plot a point we proceed as follows:

EXAMPLE 1

To plot the point (2, 3) we note that $x = +2$, $y = +3$. We proceed from the origin 2 units to the right (positive direction) and then 3 units upward (positive direction). This gives the required point (2, 3). This point is labeled A in Figure 2.

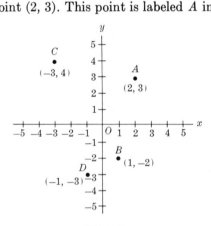

Figure 2

EXAMPLE 2

To plot the point (1, −2) we note that $x = 1$, $y = -2$. We proceed from the origin 1 unit to the right (positive direction) and then 2 units downward (negative direction). This gives the point (1, −2). The point is designated by B in Figure 2.

EXAMPLE 3

To plot the point $(-3, 4)$ we note that $x = -3$, $y = 4$. We proceed from the origin 3 units to the left (negative direction). Then we go 4 units upward (positive direction). This gives the point $(-3, 4)$ as required. This is point C in Figure 2.

EXAMPLE 4

To plot the point $(-1, -3)$ we note that $x = -1$, $y = -3$. We proceed from the origin 1 unit to the left (negative direction) and then 3 units down (negative direction). This gives the required point $(-1, -3)$. This is point D in Figure 2.

EXERCISES 7

1 Plot the following points in a system of rectangular coordinates: (a) $(1, 6)$; (b) $(\frac{1}{2}, 2)$; (c) $(1, \frac{1}{4})$; (d) $(-1, 6)$; (e) $(-3, 4)$; (f) $(3, -7)$; (g) $(2, -5)$; (h) $(-1, -1)$; (i) $(-4, -\frac{1}{2})$.

2 Plot the points $(0, 0)$; $(1, 1)$; $(2, 2)$; $(3, 3)$. Show that they lie on a straight line.

3 Plot the points $(-3, -5)$; $(-2, -3)$; $(-1, -1)$; $(0, 1)$; $(1, 3)$; $(2, 5)$. Show that they are all located on a straight line.

4 Plot the points $(0, -2)$; $(0, -1)$; $(0, 0)$; $(0, 1)$; $(0, 2)$.

5 Plot the points $(-3, 0)$; $(-2, 0)$; $(-1, 0)$; $(0, 0)$; $(1, 0)$; $(2, 0)$; connect consecutive points by straight-line segments.

6 Measure the distance from the origin to the following points: (a) $(0, 4)$; (b) $(5, 0)$; (c) $(1, 2)$; (d) $(-2, 1)$; (e) $(0, -5)$.

7 Locate the points $(1, 1)$; $(-1, 1)$; $(1, -1)$; $(-1, -1)$. Show that they are symmetrically located with respect to the two axes. What is the distance from each axis?

8 Find the distance between the points $(0, 2)$ and $(4, -1)$.

9 Find the distance between $(1, 1)$ and $(5, 5)$.

10 Find the distance between $(-2, 3)$ and $(2, 6)$.

8 GRAPHS OF EQUATIONS

Suppose that a function defined by $y = f(x)$ is given by means of a formula.

The set of all points (x, y) in the line such that x is in the domain of f and $y = f(x)$ is called the *graph* of f.

EXAMPLE 1

Let $y = f(x) = 5x - 2$. We would like to know something about the behavior of x and y for the interval $x = -3$ to $x = +3$. Therefore we construct a table for the choices, $x = -3, -2, -1,$ 0, 1, 2, 3, along with the corresponding values of y:

x	$y = f(x) = 5x - 2$
-3	$5(-3) - 2 = -17$
-2	$5(-2) - 2 = -12$
-1	$5(-1) - 2 = -7$
0	$5(0) - 2 = -2$
1	$5(1) - 2 = 3$
2	$5(2) - 2 = 8$
3	$5(3) - 2 = 13$

The related values of x and y from this table, namely, $(-3, -17)$, $(-2, -12)$, $(-1, -7)$, and so forth, determine a set of points that are plotted on the same graph and connected. The points appear to be on a straight line (Figure 3).

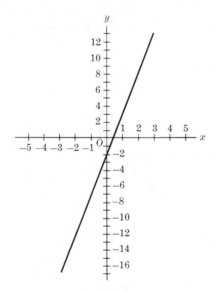

Figure 3

EXAMPLE 2

Assume that $y = f(x) = 2x^2$. Make a graph indicating the behavior of the function from $x = -4$ to $x = +4$.

x	$y = f(x) = 2x^2$
-4	32
-3	18
-2	8
-1	2
0	0
1	2
2	8
3	18
4	32

The graph determined by the resulting collection of points is shown in Figure 4. If more points are determined in the prescribed range, it is found that a smooth curve, known as a *parabola*, is determined.

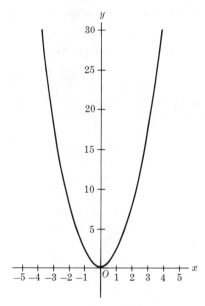

Figure 4

EXERCISES 8

1 Graph the function $y = f(x) = 4 - 3x$ for the range $x = -3$ to $x = 5$.

2 Plot the function $y = f(x) = 5x - 3$ for the range $x = -10$ to $x = 10$.

3 Graph the function $y = 20 + 3x$ for the range $x = 0$ to $x = 5$ where x denotes the amount of labor (in weeks) and y the amount of product (in tons). (a) How many tons can be produced with 2 weeks of labor

$(x = 2)$? (b) How many weeks of labor are necessary to produce 23 tons of the product $(y = 23)$?

4 Plot the function $y = 2x^2 - 5x + 1$ for the range $x = -5$ to $x = 5$. Obtain sufficient points to gain an idea of the smooth curve.

5 Plot a smooth curve representing the function $y = 24/x$ for the range $x = 1$ to $x = 10$. Assume that x is the price (in cents) and y the quantity demanded (in pounds). (a) What is the quantity demanded if the price is 6 cents $(x = 6)$? (b) Which price will cause a demand of 4 pounds $(y = 4)$?

6 Plot the function $y = x^4$ from $x = -3$ to $x = 3$.

7 Plot the two functions, $y = 2x - 5$ and $y = 10 - x$ on the same coordinate system from $x = -6$ to $x = 6$ and determine graphically their intersection.

8 Plot on the same coordinate system the functions $y = x^2$ and $y = 1 - x$ from $x = -4$ to $x = 4$ and find graphically their intersection.

9 Plot on the same coordinate system the functions $y = x^4$ and $y = 2x - 1$ from $x = -4$ to $x = 4$ and determine graphically their intersection.

10 The following production function has been estimated by Nichols for certain operations in the Chicago meat-packing industry: $y = -2.05 + 1.06x - 0.04x^2$. In this equation y is the weekly total live weight of hogs (in millions of pounds) and x is the weekly total of man-hours (thousands). (a) Plot the function between $x = 10$ and $x = 15$. (b) Estimate from the graph the y that corresponds to $x = 11$. (c) What x corresponds to $y = 4.7$?

11 Nichols estimated the relation between weekly payrolls (y, in millions of cents) and weekly total live weight of hogs (x, in millions of pounds) for a Chicago meat-packing house as follows: $y = 0.32 - 0.007x + 0.02x^2$. (a) Plot the function between $x = 1,500$ and $x = 6,000$. (b) What y corresponds to $x = 3,500$? (c) What x corresponds to $y = 500,000$?

Chapter 2
Linear Equations in One Unknown. Quadratic Equations

9 LINEAR EQUATIONS

A statement of equality between two quantities is an equation. For example, $2(a - b) = 2a - 2b$ is an equation. This particular equation is an identity, since the statement is true for all possible values of a and b. We have, for example, if $a = 1, b = 3, 2(1 - 3) = 2 - 6 = -4$; that is, each side of the equation is equal to -4. By making $a = 10$ and $b = 5$ we have $2(10 - 5) = 20 - 10 = 10$; here each side of the identity is equal to 10. The statement remains true regardless of the values assigned to a and b.

Consider now the equation

$$2x - 1 = 7.$$

This equation differs in nature from the previous one, for it is true for $x = 4$ and only for $x = 4$. We have $2(4) - 1 = 8 - 1 = 7$. This is an illustration of an equation in one unknown, x. Only the first power of the unknown x appears in the equation, so we call it a *linear equation*.

By solving a linear equation we mean the determination of the particular value of x that satisfies the equation. Certain basic rules pertaining to equalities are employed in the process of solving; for example (1), the same quantity may be added to or subtracted from both sides of an equality; and (2) both members of the equation may be multiplied or divided by any arbitrary quantity (except zero). These methods are combined frequently to solve linear equations.

EXAMPLE

Solve the equation

$$5x - 3 = 12.$$

Add 3 to both sides:

$$5x - 3 + 3 = 12 + 3,$$
$$5x = 15.$$

19

Divide both sides by 5:

$$\frac{5x}{5} = \frac{15}{5},$$
$$x = 3.$$

To check such a solution in the original equation we write,

$$5(3) - 3 = 12,$$
$$15 - 3 = 12.$$

This is true. Evidently the solution $x = 3$ is correct.

EXERCISES 9

Solve the following equations and check:

1   $-x + 6 = 5x + 10.$

2   $3x - 7 = 19x + 1.$

3   $9(-x + 1) + 5(3x - 5) - (x + 1) = 0.$

4   $(2x - 1)/(3 - 5x) = 10.$

5   $1/(2x - 3) = -5.$

6   $10/(1 - 5x) = 5.$

7   $10 - (1/x) = 4.$

8   $2 - 1/(x + 4) = 4.$

10   GRAPHS OF LINEAR FUNCTIONS

A function of the form $y = ax + b$ is said to be a *linear function*. The graph corresponding to a linear function is a *straight line*.

EXAMPLE 1

In Figure 5 is sketched the graph of the function $y = f(x) = -1 + 2x$. To obtain this graph we construct the following table:

x	$y = f(x)$
-3	-7
-2	-5
-1	-3
0	-1
1	1
2	3
3	5

Connecting the points, which are obtained by reference to the table, we get the straight line in Figure 5.

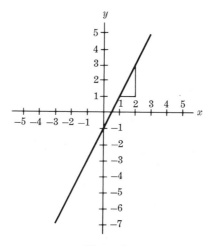

Figure 5

Consider now a line that is supposed to *go through two given points*. This condition determines the particular line without ambiguity. The equation of a line, which goes through the two fixed points (x_1, y_1) and (x_2, y_2), is given by

$$y - y_1 = \frac{y_2 - y_1}{x_2 - x_1} (x - x_1).$$

It is confirmed readily that such a line goes through the two points (x_1, y_1) and (x_2, y_2) by substituting the pair $x = x_1$, $y = y_1$ and also the pair $x = x_2$ and $y = y_2$ into the equation.

EXAMPLE 2

Consider, for example, the straight line that goes through the points (1, 1) and (3, 5). We have

$$x_1 = 1, y_1 = 1, x_2 = 3, y_2 = 5.$$

The above equation becomes

$$y - 1 = \frac{5 - 1}{3 - 1} (x - 1).$$

Simplying this, we get

$$y = 2x - 1.$$

This is the equation of the line shown in Figure 5. It will be observed that this line passes through the points (1, 1) and (3, 5). The expression

$$m = \frac{y_2 - y_1}{x_2 - x_1}$$

is known as the *slope of the line*.

The geometric significance of the slope may be shown as follows: From any point on the line proceed horizontally by 1 unit to the right. Then from the new point proceed vertically upward by m units, if $m > 0$. The point determined in this way is also on the line. If the slope is negative, proceed downward $|m|$ units. The construction, as just described, is shown in Figure 5. From the point (1, 1) we moved 1 unit horizontally to the right to the point (2, 1). Since the slope $m = 2$ is positive, we go up 2 units from (2, 1) to the point (2, 3). This point is again on the line. The equation

$$y - y_1 = m(x - x_1)$$

gives a straight line, which passes through the point (x_1, y_1), with slope m. This fact follows immediately from the definition of slope and the equation of a straight line just considered.

EXAMPLE 3

Consider, for example, the construction of a line that goes through the point $(-4, 2)$ and has the slope $m = -2$. To construct this line we proceed from the point $(-4, 2)$ 1 unit horizontally to the right and reach the point $(-3, 2)$. Since the slope is negative, we move 2 units vertically downward to the point $(-3, 0)$. We then draw a straight line through the 2 points $(-4, 2)$ and $(-3, 0)$. This is the required line. The construction is shown in Figure 6.

The equation of the line shown in Figure 6 is

$$y - 2 = -2(x + 4).$$

This equation can be simplified to

$$y = -2x - 6.$$

It is verified easily that this is the function corresponding to the graph in Figure 6.

It is verified readily that the coefficient a in the function $y = ax + b$ is the slope m. So, let us write the equation of a straight line in the form

$$y = f(x) = mx + b.$$

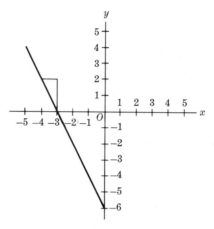

Figure 6

By taking $x = 0$, we find that

$$f(0) = b.$$

Hence b is the value of y that corresponds to $x = 0$, that is, it is the ordinate of a point on the y axis. It is called the *y-intercept*. The above equation of a straight line is called the *slope-intercept* equation.

EXAMPLE 4

Let us, for example, construct the graph of the equation $y = 3x - 5$. We know that the y intercept is -5. Hence we find $y = -5$ on the y axis. Then to construct the slope $m = 3$ we proceed 1 unit horizontally to the right and from there 3 units vertically upward, since the slope is positive. This determines the point $(1, -2)$. So, the straight line passes through the points $(0, -5)$ and $(1, -2)$, as shown in Figure 7.

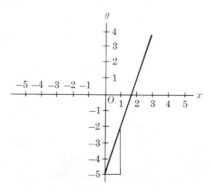

Figure 7

EXERCISES 10

1   Find the equations and graphs of the straight lines that pass through the following pairs of points: (a) $(-1, 4)$, $(1, 0)$; (b) $(-1, -2)$, $(-5, -2)$; (c) $(0, 0)$, $(1, 5)$; (d) $(1, 4)$, $(2, 3)$.

2   Make a graph and find the equation of the straight line with slope -4 that passes through the points: (a) $(0, 1)$; (b) $(-3, 2)$; (c) $(-3, 7)$; (d) $(-5, -2)$.

3   Find the equation and the graph of the straight line that passes through the point $(-1, 3)$ and has the slope (a) -1; (b) 2; (c) 5; (d) 0.

4   Plot each of the following linear equations, using the slope-intercept method: (a) $y = 4x - 6$;   (b) $y = 2 - 5x$;   (c) $y = -5 - 7x$;   (d) $y = 3x$; (e) $y = 8$; (f) $y = 2x + 6$.

5   What is the slope and intercept of each of the following equations: (a) $y = -x$;   (b) $y = -4x - 3$;   (c) $y = 3x - 7$;   (d) $y = 4x + 6$. Plot these equations.

11   LINEAR DEMAND FUNCTIONS

We will deal in this book mainly with *market* or *collective demand functions*. Each of these demand functions shows the relationship between the quantity demanded D and the price p charged on a given market. In general, the higher the price, the lower the demand, though there may be exceptions to this rule.

Collective or market demand functions can be constructed by adding the *individual demand functions* for all individuals in a market. The quantities demanded at a given price by all individuals are added.

EXAMPLE 1

The comments on demand functions may be illustrated in the case of a market consisting of 5 individuals, designated A, B, C, E, and F:

Price	Quantity Demanded by					Market Demand
p	A	B	C	E	F	D
$1	6	10	20	5	12	53
$2	5	6	15	4	11	41
$3	4	2	10	3	10	29

The demand functions of the individuals A, B, C, E, and F can be derived from their utility functions or indifference maps. This will be demonstrated later (see especially Section 87 and problems 6 and 7 in Exercises 87).

The above table tells us that at a price of $1 individual A will demand 6 units of the commodity. At the same price the demand of B will be 10 units, the demand of C 20 units, the demand of E 5 units, and the demand of F 12 units. There are, by assumption, only these 5 individuals in the market. Adding up all the quantities demanded at the price $1, we obtain the collective or market demand D of 53 units. The process is repeated for a price of $2 and for a price of $3.

Now the assumption is made for the sake of simplicity that the market or collective demand function is linear. In other words, if plotted, the graph will show a straight line. Probably this is never strictly true with empirical market demand curves. Linear demand functions must be considered as approximations to the true demand functions, which may be much more complicated.

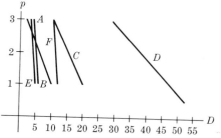

Figure 8

We have represented graphically in Figure 8 the individual demand curves of A, B, C, E, and F, as well as the market or collective demand curve D. It should be noted that by convention we always put the quantities D on the horizontal axis and the prices p on the vertical axis.

Linear demand functions can be derived by statistical methods from actual market data, that is, by using the prices and quantities recorded at various times on the market. These methods will be discussed in Section 122.

EXAMPLE 2

Assume a collective demand curve $D = f(p) = 25 - 5p$. (a) What is the quantity demanded if the price is $3? We have $D = f(3) = 25 - (5)(3) = 10$. (b) Assume the demand is 18 units. What is the corresponding price? We have $18 = 25 - 5p$, and, by solving this equation it is found that $p = \$1.40$. (c) What would be the demand if the commodity in question were a *free good*, that is, if $p = 0$? We have $D = 25 - (5)(0) = 25$. (d) What is the highest price anybody will pay for the commodity? Put $D = 0 = 25 - 5p$. Then $p = 5$. Actually, $D =$

$f(5) = 0$. The price must be *less* than 5 in order for any of the commodity to be sold on the market.

EXERCISES 11

1 A collective demand curve is $D = 100 - 5p$. Find the price if the quantity demanded is (a) 50; (b) 16; (c) 5 units. Find the quantity demanded if the price is (d) 19; (e) 10; (f) 1. (g) Find the demand if the commodity is a free good. (h) What is the highest price anybody would pay for this commodity? (i) Plot the curve.

2 Given the collective demand curve $D = 36 - 3p$, find the price if the quantity demanded is (a) 18; (b) 2. Find the quantity demanded if the price is (c) 11; (d) 5. (e) What is the highest price anybody would pay for this commodity? (f) How much of the commodity would be demanded if it were a free good? (g) Plot the curve.

3 Given the collective demand curve $D = 10 - p/4$, find the quantity demanded if the price is (a) 4; (b) 16; (c) 25. What is the price if the quantity demanded is (d) 9; (e) 7; (f) 2? (g) What is the highest price anybody would pay for this commodity? (h) How much would be demanded if the commodity were a free good? (i) Plot the curve.

4 Given the collective demand curve $D = 1 - p$, find the price if the quantity demanded is (a) 0.9; (b) 0.7; (c) 0.2. Find the quantity demanded that corresponds to a price of (d) 0.75; (e) 0.125; (f) 0.0025. (g) What would be the demand if the commodity were a free good? (h) What is the highest price anybody would pay for this commodity? (i) Plot the curve.

5 The collective demand curve for a commodity is $D = 12.5 - 2.25p$. Find the price if the quantity demanded is (a) 11.75; (b) 10; (c) 1.125. What is the quantity demanded if the price is (d) 3.5; (e) 1; (f) 0.5? (g) Find the highest price anybody would pay for this commodity. (h) How much would be demanded if it were a free good? (i) Plot the curve.

6 The demand curve for sugar in the United States for 1915–1929 was approximately $D = 135 - 8p$, where D and p are suitably defined (Schultz). Find the quantity demanded if the price is (a) 3; (b) 10; (c) 5. What is the price corresponding to a demand of (d) 80. (e) 95; (f) 35? (g) What is the highest price anybody will pay for sugar? (h) How much sugar will be consumed if it is a free good? (i) Plot the demand curve.

7 The demand for cotton in the United States for 1915–1929 was estimated as $10D = 64 - 3p$ (Schultz). Find the quantity demanded if the price is (a) 10; (b) 12.25; (c) 5. What is the price corresponding to a demand of (d) 5; (e) 2.44; (f) 3.36? (g) What would be the demand for cotton if it were a free good? (h) What is the highest price anybody would pay for cotton? (i) Plot the demand curve.

8 The demand curve for barley in the United States for the period 1915–1929 was estimated as $100D = 207 - p$ (Schultz). Find the demand for a price of (a) 55; (b) 160; (c) 85. What is the price if the demand is (d) 1.50; (e) 0.90; (f) 0.85? (g) What is the highest price anybody will pay for barley? (h) How much barley would be consumed if it were a free good? (i) Plot the demand curve.

9 The demand curve for rye in the United States for the period 1915–1929 was estimated as $100D = 88 - p$ (Schultz). Find the demand if the price is (a) 20; (b) 35; (c) 42.5. What is the price if the demand is (d) 0.40; (e) 0.50; (f) 0.60? (g) What would be the consumption of rye if it were a free good? (h) What is the maximum price anybody will pay for rye? (i) Plot the demand curve.

10 The demand for a commodity is $D = A - Bp$, where A and B are positive constants. (a) Find the price if the demand is $A/3$. (b) Find the demand if the price is $A/2B$. (c) Find the demand if the commodity is a free good. (d) What is the highest price anybody will pay for it?

11 Given the relationship $2D + 3p = 5$, (a) find the highest price anybody will pay for this commodity. (b) Find the demand if the commodity is a free good. (c) Express D in terms of p in the form of an ordinary linear demand curve. (d) Plot the demand curve.

12 The demand function for rice in India has been estimated for the period 1949–1964 by Tintner and Patel. Let P be the real price of rice and Q the per capita consumption of rice: $P = 0.96 - 6.77Q$. (a) What is the per capita consumption of rice if rice is a free good $(P = 0)$? (b) What is the highest price anybody will pay for rice $(Q = 0)$?

12 LINEAR SUPPLY FUNCTIONS

The individual supply function of a firm or of an individual shows the amount of a commodity that will be offered on the market at a given price. The collective or market supply function is the sum of the amounts supplied by various individuals or firms at a given price.

EXAMPLE 1

As an example let us consider a market in which a commodity is supplied by three firms (or individuals), A, B, and C:

Price p	Quantity Supplied			Market Supply S
	A	B	C	
$1	0	1	3	4
$2	1	3	6	10
$3	2	5	9	16

At a price of $1 firm A does not supply any of the commodity. Firm B supplies 1 unit and C offers 3 units of the commodity. Adding all these quantities, we have 4 units, as the market or collective supply, S, of the commodity at a price of $1.

If the market price is $2, firm A supplies 1 unit, firm B 3 units, and firm C 6 units. Adding these quantities, we have a market supply S of 10 units if the price is $2. In a similar way we add up all the quantities supplied by firms A, B, and C at a price of $3 and we obtain a market supply of 16 units.

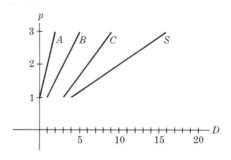

Figure 9

Figure 9 shows the individual supply functions of the individuals (or firms) A, B, and C as well as the market supply curve S.

We assume that the market supply function is linear; that is, if plotted in a graph it appears as a straight line. Such a function must be considered as an approximation of the actual situation.

Supply functions are derived from production theory, which will be considered in Section 88. Statistically they are obtained from market data, that is, from the record of prices and quantities sold on a market at various dates. The problem of deriving statistical supply curves from market data is discussed in Section 122.

EXAMPLE 2

Let $S = f(p) = 3p - 2$ be the supply curve for some commodity. Given $p = 5$, what is the supply? We have $S = f(5) = (3)(5) - 2 = 13$. What price will cause a supply of 10? The equation $10 = 3p - 2$ has the solution $p = 4$. What is the lowest price at which the commodity will be supplied? We put $S = 0 = 3p - 2$, which gives $p = \frac{2}{3}$. Actually, $S = f(\frac{2}{3}) = 0$. At a price of $\frac{2}{3}$ nothing will be supplied. Hence the price must be *greater* than $\frac{2}{3}$ in order that any of the commodity be supplied.

EXERCISES 12

1 Let the supply curve for some commodity be $S = 2p - 1$. Find the supply if the price is (a) 2; (b) 10; (c) 100. Determine the price if the supply is (d) 10; (e) 25; (f) 100. (g) What is the lowest price at which any of the commodity will be supplied? (h) Plot the curve.

2 The supply of a commodity is $S = 3p$. Find the supply if the price is (a) 5; (b) 10; (c) 25. Assume that the supply is (d) 90; (e) 25; (f) 2; determine the price. (g) What is the lowest price at which the commodity will be supplied? (h) Plot the curve.

3 The supply of a commodity is $S = 5p - 10$. Find the price if the supply is (a) 10; (b) 20; (c) 100; (d) 150. Find the supply if the price is (e) 3; (f) 5.50; (g) 10. (h) What is the lowest price at which any of the commodity will be supplied? (i) Plot the curve.

4 Let the supply curve of a commodity be $S = 3p - 10$. Determine the price if the supply is (a) 160; (b) 13; (c) 40. (d) What is the lowest price at which the commodity will be supplied? (e) Plot the curve.

5 Schultz estimates the supply curve for sugar (imported) for the United States in 1903–1913 as $S = 1.1p - 0.1$, where supply and price are measured in convenient units. Find the price if the supply is (a) 1.00; (b) 0.80; (c) 0.50. Determine the supply if the price is (d) 8; (e) 6; (f) 4.10. (g) What is the lowest price that will cause any sugar to be supplied? (h) Plot the supply curve.

6 The supply of a commodity is $S = ap - b$, where a and b are positive constants. Find the price if the supply is (a) $5a - b$; (b) $a + 2b$. Determine the supply if the price is (c) $3b/a$; (d) $5b/a$. (e) What is the lowest price that will cause any supply of the commodity?

7 Let the supply curve of a commodity be $S = mp$, where m is a positive constant. Find the supply if the price is (a) 1; (b) 10; (c) m; (d) $1/3m$. Determine the price if the supply is (e) 8; (f) 6; (g) m; (h) $5/m$. (i) What is the lowest price at which anything will be supplied on the market?

8 Let the supply curve of a commodity be $S = 8p - 10$. Find the quantity supplied if the price is (a) 11; (b) 10; (c) 39. Find the price if the supply is (d) 1; (e) 6; (f) 100. (g) What is the lowest price at which this commodity will be supplied on the market?

9 The supply function of a commodity is $S = 15p - 75$. (a) Find the supply if the price is 10; (b) if it is 6. Determine the price if the supply is (c) 7; (d) if it is 90. (e) What is the lowest price at which any of the commodity will be supplied on the market? (f) Plot the curve.

10 The supply of agricultural commodities in the United States for the period 1920–1943 has been estimated as $Q = -49.375 + 1.721P$, where Q is the quantity supplied and P the price (Tintner). Make a graph of this supply function.

13   MARKET EQUILIBRIUM

Under free competition no individual or firm can by itself influence the market price. There is free movement in and out of various industries.

Market equilibrium exists under free competition if the quantity of a commodity demanded is equal to the quantity supplied. This fact determines the equilibrium price and the quantity exchanged.

It is demonstrated in elementary economics how the equilibrium price is established. If the actual price were higher than the equilibrium price, where demand and supply are equal, then the quantity demanded would be less than the quantity supplied. Some of the sellers would not be able to sell their products at the prevailing price but would be willing to sell at a lower price rather than not sell at all. Competition among the sellers will reduce the price until it is established at the level where demand is equal to supply.

Assume, on the other hand, that the actual price is lower than the equilibrium price. Then the quantity demanded will exceed the quantity supplied. This means that some buyers will not be able to satisfy their demand at the prevailing price. Hence they will be willing to pay higher prices rather than forgo the satisfaction of their demand. Competition among the buyers will drive the price up until it is established at the equilibrium level where demand is equal to supply.

These propositions are demonstrated in problem 8, Exercises 13. Market equilibrium under monopoly will be discussed in Section 73.

It should be noted that we deal here with partial equilibrium (Marshall). We analyze the market of one commodity in isolation and assume that the prices of all other commodities are constant.

EXAMPLE

Let the demand for a commodity be $D = 2 - p$ and the supply be $S = p - 1$ (Figure 10). We must have demand equal to supply, that is, $S = D$, or $p - 1 = 2 - p$. Solving this equation, we get for the equilibrium price $p = \frac{3}{2}$. Inserting this value of p into the demand equation, we have $D = 2 - \frac{3}{2} = \frac{1}{2}$. Substituting the same value into the supply equation, we have $S = \frac{3}{2} - 1 = \frac{1}{2}$. Hence the equilibrium price is $\frac{3}{2}$ and the quantity exchanged is $\frac{1}{2}$.

Let us assume for the given D and S that the actual price is lower than the equilibrium price, for example, that $p = 1$. Then we would have $S = 0$ and $D = 1$. Hence demand is larger than supply, and bidding among the buyers will force the price up.

Assume, on the contrary, that the actual price is higher than the equilibrium price, for example, that $p = 2$. Then we have $S = 1$ and $D = 0$. Now the supply is larger than the demand.

Competition among the sellers will force the price down until the equilibrium level is reached. Such is the case only if $p = \frac{3}{2}$, which is the very point of intersection between the demand and the supply function in our example.

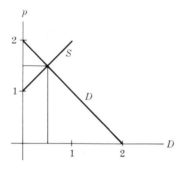

Figure 10

Figure 10 presents a graphic representation of the demand and the supply curves used in this example. The intersection of the demand and the supply curves determines the price established on the market ($1.50) and the quantity sold (0.5).

EXERCISES 13

1   Let the demand curve for a commodity be $D = 10 - 3p$ and the supply curve be $S = 2p - 1$. (a) Find the equilibrium price. (b) Find the quantity exchanged on the market. (c) Make a graph of the demand and supply curves.

2   The demand curve for a commodity is $D = 25 - 2p$. The supply curve is $S = p - 2$. (a) Find the equilibrium price; (b) the equilibrium quantity. (c) Make a graph of the demand and supply curves.

3   The demand for a commodity is $D = 35 - 7p$. The supply curve is $S = 2p - 5$. (a) Find the equilibrium price. (b) Find the quantity exchanged on the market. (c) Graph the demand and supply curves.

4   The demand curve for a commodity is $D = 15 - 2p$. The supply curve is $S = 3p$. (a) Find the equilibrium price; (b) find the equilibrium quantity. (c) Make a graph of the demand and supply curves.

5   The demand curve for a commodity is $D = 35 - 3p$. The supply curve is $S = 2p$. (a) Find the equilibrium price; (b) find the equilibrium quantity. (c) Graph the demand and supply curves.

6   Let the demand for a commodity be $D = 10 - 2p$ and the supply curve be $S = 4p$. (a) Find the equilibrium price. (b) Find the equilibrium quantity exchanged. (c) Plot the demand and supply curves.

7   The demand curve for a commodity is $D = 10 - 3p$ and the supply curve is $S = 5$ (perishable commodity). (a) Determine the equilibrium price. (b) Find the quantity exchanged. (c) Plot the demand and supply functions.

8   Let the demand curve for a commodity be $D = 1 - p$ and the supply curve be $S = 2p$. (a) Determine the equilibrium price. (b) What is the quantity exchanged in equilibrium? (c) Assume that the government fixes the price at $\frac{1}{2}$; show that the supply is greater than the demand. (d) Assume that the government fixes the price at $\frac{1}{5}$; show that the supply is smaller than the demand. (e) Plot the demand and supply curves.

9   Let the demand curve for a commodity be $D = A - Bp$ and the supply curve be $S = Mp - N$, where A, B, M, and N are positive constants. (a) Find the equilibrium price on the market. (b) Determine the quantity exchanged.

10   Schultz estimated the demand for buckwheat for the United States during 1915–1929 as $100D = 234 - 2p$. Assume that the supply of buckwheat is $S = 1.85$. (a) Find the equilibrium price. (b) Find the equilibrium quantity exchanged. (c) Plot the demand and supply curves.

11   The demand and the supply of sugar for the United States during 1890–1915 is estimated, according to Schultz, as $D = 1.6 - 0.5p$ and $S = 0.7p + 0.4$, respectively. (a) Determine the equilibrium price. (b) Find the equilibrium quantity exchanged on the market. (c) Make a graph of the demand and supply curves.

12   For agricultural products in the United States during 1920–1943 the estimated demand was $D = 224.125 - 0.097p$ and the supply was $S = -49.375 + 1.721p$ (Tintner). (a) Find the equilibrium price and quantity. (b) Make a graph of the demand and supply functions.

13   Let S be the per capita supply, D the per capita demand, and P the price of rice in India for the period 1949–1964. Demand and supply functions have been estimated as follows (Tintner and Patel): $P = 0.964 - 6.772D$ and $S = 0.09$. Find the equilibrium price and quantity.

14   Let S be the per capita supply and D the per capita demand of wheat in India for the period 1949–1964. Demand and supply functions are $P = 0.710 - 12.171D$ and $S = 0.025$. (Tintner and Patel). Find the equilibrium price and quantity.

14   TAXATION

Suppose that a specific tax is imposed on sales. That is, for each unit of a commodity sold a certain fixed amount of money has to be paid to the government. This is equivalent to an upward shift of the supply function by the amount of the tax.

EXAMPLE 1

Consider the following supply function:

Price	Quantity Supplied	Price after Tax	Price after Subsidy
1	3	3	0
2	5	4	1
3	7	5	2

For example, before the imposition of the tax 3 units were supplied at a price of $1. If the tax is $2 per unit, the consumer has to pay $3 if $1 is to be left for the supplier. Hence with the tax it takes a price of $3 to bring forth a supply of 3 units on the market. Similarly, before imposition of the tax, 5 units were supplied if the price of the commodity was $2. Now a tax of $2 per unit is imposed. Hence it takes an actual price of $4 (of which $2 goes to the government and $2 to the supplier) to bring forth a supply of 5 units. In the same fashion we can argue that, after imposition of the tax of $2 per unit, it takes a price of $5 (instead of $3 as before the imposition of the tax) to bring about a supply of 7 units on the market. Hence we can say that the supply curve has shifted upward by the amount of the tax (in this case $2).

Next consider a subsidy. The government pays the sellers of a commodity a certain fixed amount per unit. We assume a subsidy of $1 per unit. Consider the above table again. If the original price without subsidy is $1, then 3 units are supplied on the market. But since the government pays a subsidy of $1, the price to be charged to the public to bring about a supply of 3 units is now $0. Similarly, before the institution of the subsidy it took a price of $2 to obtain a supply of 5 units; of this amount the subsidy $1 is paid by the government. Hence the consumers have only to pay $1 to obtain a supply of 5 units on the market, and so forth. It appears that the supply curve has shifted downward by the amount of the subsidy (in this case $1).

EXAMPLE 2

Let the demand curve of a commodity be $D = 10 - p$ and let the supply curve be $S = -2 + 2p$ before taxation. By setting supply equal to demand we get the following equilibrium values: $p = 4$ and $D = S = 6$.

This situation is presented in Figure 11. S_1 is the supply curve before imposition of a tax or subsidy.

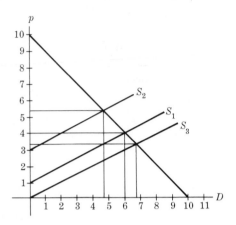

Figure 11

Assume now that a tax of \$2 per unit is imposed. The new supply curve becomes $S = -2 + 2(p - 2) = -6 + 2p$. This is the curve S_2 in Figure 16. Again putting demand equal to supply, we find that $p = 16\frac{2}{3} = 5\frac{1}{3}$, $D = S = 14\frac{2}{3} = 4\frac{2}{3}$. The total amount of the tax is $2(14\frac{2}{3}) = 28\frac{2}{3} = 9\frac{1}{3}$. This is the revenue of the government from the tax.

The price realized by the entrepreneur is now only $16\frac{2}{3} - 2 = 10\frac{2}{3} = 3\frac{1}{3}$.

Now let us assume a subsidy of \$1 per unit. The new supply curve becomes $S = -2 + 2(p + 1) = 2p$. This is now the curve S_3 in Figure 16. Equilibrium is established if demand is equal to supply. This gives $p = 10\frac{2}{3} = 3\frac{1}{3}$; $D = S = 20\frac{2}{3} = 6\frac{2}{3}$. The total amount of the subsidy is $(20\frac{2}{3})(1) = 6\frac{2}{3}$. This is the amount the government has to pay. The price realized by the sellers is now $10\frac{2}{3} + 1 = 13\frac{2}{3} = 4\frac{1}{3}$.

EXERCISES 14

1   Given the demand curve $D = 20 - 2p$ and the supply curve $S = -4 + 3p$, (a) find the equilibrium amount sold and the price before the imposition of a tax or subsidy. Find the price, the quantity sold, and the total amount of the tax or subsidy after the imposition of a tax of (b) \$1; (c) \$2; (d) \$0.50; a subsidy (e) of \$1; (f) of \$0.25.

2   Find the equilibrium price, the quantity sold, and the total amount of the tax or subsidy for the demand and supply curve in problem 1, Exercises 13, after the imposition of (a) a tax of \$1; (b) of \$0.50; (c) of \$0.10; (d) a subsidy of \$1; (e) of \$0.60. (f) Plot the original demand and supply curves and the supply curves after the imposition of the taxes and subsidies.

3   Find the equilibrium price, the quantity sold, and the total amount of the tax or subsidy for the demand and supply curves in problem 2, Exercises 13, after the imposition of (a) a tax of \$0.05; (b) of \$0.10; (c) of \$0.50; (d) a subsidy of \$0.02; (e) of \$0.25.

4   Consider the data in problem 5, Exercises 13. What amount of tax or subsidy would have to be imposed (a) to double the equilibrium price without the tax? (b) to halve the equilibrium price? (c) to make the commodity a free good (price \$0)?

5   Consider the data in problem 6, Exercises 8. What amount of tax or subsidy must be imposed in order to bring about (a) an increase by $\frac{1}{8}$ of the equilibrium amount sold before imposition of the tax; (b) a decrease by half the amount sold; (c) no sale effected at all?

6   Problem 11, Exercises 13, gives demand and supply curves for sugar in the United States. Find the equilibrium price, the quantity sold, and the total amount of the tax or subsidy after the imposition of (a) a tax of \$0.01; (b) of \$0.05; (c) a subsidy of \$0.03; (d) of \$0.05. Plot the original demand and supply curves and the supply curves after the imposition of taxes and subsidies.

7   The demand curve is $D = a - bp$ and the supply curve is $S = -m + np$, where a, b, m, and n are positive constants. (a) Find the equilibrium price and the amount sold on the market before the imposition of a tax or subsidy. (b) Repeat (a) if we assume the imposition of a specific tax or a subsidy t (if t is negative). Also establish (c) the new equilibrium quantity and price and (d) the total amount of the tax or subsidy.

8   Consider the data in problem 12, Exercises 13. What is the effect on price and quantity sold if there is (a) a specific tax of 10; (b) a subsidy of 10 for agricultural products?

9   Consider the demand and supply curves in problem 4, Exercises 13. Consider the effect (a) of the imposition of a specific tax of 1.5; and (b) of a subsidy of 2 on equilibrium price and quantity. Analyze the situation graphically.

10   Let the demand curve be $D = 1 - p$ and the supply curve be $S = p$. Consider the equilibrium quantity and price (a) before and (b) after the imposition of a specific tax of t per unit.

15   QUADRATIC DEMAND AND SUPPLY CURVES

Assume a demand curve $D = 2 - p^2$ and a supply curve $S = p$. Putting demand equal to supply to obtain equilibrium, we get an equation in which the highest power of the variable is 2, namely, $p^2 + p - 2 = 0$. Such an equation is said to be of *second degree* and is described frequently as a *quadratic equation*.

In general, the quadratic has as its equation $ax^2 + bx + c = 0$ and its solutions are given by the formula

$$x = \frac{-b \pm \sqrt{b^2 - 4ac}}{2a}.$$

In the case of the equation $p^2 + p - 2 = 0$, where the unknown is p, the coefficient a is 1, $b = +1$, $c = -2$; thus

$$p = \frac{-1 \pm \sqrt{1 + 8}}{2} = \frac{-1 \pm 3}{2} = -2 \text{ or } +1.$$

We discard the first solution, since price cannot be negative. The equilibrium quantity is then found to be $D = S = 1$. This checks our solution.

EXERCISES 15

1   The demand curve of a commodity is $D = 20 - 3p - p^2$ and the supply curve is $S = 5p - 1$. Find the equilibrium price and the quantity exchanged. Plot both curves.

In the following exercises, given the demand curve and supply curves, find the equilibrium price and quantity and plot both curves:

2   Demand curve: $D = 100 - p^2$; supply curve: $S = p + 5p^2$.

3   Demand curve: $D = 20 - p$; supply curve: $S = 4p + p^2$.

4   Demand curve: $D = 25 - p - p^2$; supply curve: $S = 10$.

5   Demand curve: $D = 250 - 10p - 2p^2$; supply curve: $S = 5p + 6p^2$.

6   Demand curve: $D = 10 - 2p$; supply curve: $S = 5p^2$.

7   Demand curve: $D = 250 - 3p^2$; supply curve: $S = p^2 + 2p^4$. (HINT: Consider p^2 as the unknown.)

8   Demand curve: $D = 10,000 - p^3$; supply curve: $S = 2p^6$. (HINT: Consider p^3 as the unknown.)

9   Demand curve: $D = 100/p$; supply curve: $S = 4p$.

10   Demand curve: $D = 24/p$; supply curve: $S = 5p - 1$.

11   Demand curve: $D = 100/(3p^2)$; supply curve: $S = 4p^2/3$.

Chapter 3

Systems of Linear Equations

16 LINEAR EQUATIONS IN MORE THAN ONE UNKNOWN

Assume that we have a system of n linear equations in n unknowns. When such a system has a solution, that is, a value for each unknown so that each equation is satisfied, the given system may be reduced to a system of $n - 1$ equations in $n - 1$ unknowns. This can be accomplished by eliminating one of the n original variables. We can carry out this elimination by combining the n equations two by two, by adding or subtracting, after first multiplying them by suitable constants. This leaves a system of $n - 1$ linear equations in $n - 1$ unknowns.

This new system can be treated in the same fashion. We combine the $n - 1$ linear equations two by two after multiplying by appropriate constants. Thus we can eliminate another unknown. This leaves a system of $n - 2$ linear equations with $n - 2$ unknowns.

This process may be continued until we have one linear equation in one unknown. This equation can be solved by methods discussed in Section 9, thereby providing the value of one unknown. Using one equation of the system of two equations with two unknowns, we may derive the necessary value for another unknown. The third is found from an equation of the system of three equations with three unknowns, and so forth.

The complete solution should be checked by substituting into the equations of the original system. If the original system has no solution, this process of elimination will ultimately result in a contradiction.

EXAMPLE 1

Assume that we have the following system of two equations in two unknowns:
$$2x + 6y = 9,$$
$$3x + y = 1.$$

Multiply the members of the first equation by 3 and those of the second by 2 in order to eliminate x:

$$6x + 18y = 27,$$
$$6x + 2y = 2.$$

Subtract the second of these equations from the first, thereby obtaining

$$16y = 25.$$

Dividing both sides of this equation by 16, we have immediately

$$y = \frac{25}{16}.$$

We obtain from the first of the original equations

$$2x + 6\left(\frac{25}{16}\right) = 9,$$

$$2x + \frac{150}{16} = 9,$$

$$2x = 9 - \frac{150}{16},$$

$$2x = \frac{144 - 150}{16},$$

$$2x = -\frac{6}{16} = -\frac{3}{8},$$

$$x = -\frac{3}{16}.$$

The solution of our original system of equations is therefore $x = -\frac{3}{16}$ and $y = \frac{25}{16}$. This solution is checked by substitution into the original equations:

$$2\left(-\frac{3}{16}\right) + 6\left(\frac{25}{16}\right) = \frac{144}{16} = 9,$$

$$3\left(-\frac{3}{16}\right) + \frac{25}{16} = \frac{16}{16} = 1.$$

It is possible, of course, that a system of n equations in n unknowns may have no solution.

EXAMPLE 2

Consider the system of equations

$$x + 2y = 3,$$
$$2x + 4y = 1.$$

If we multiply the first equation by 2, we obtain

$$2x + 4y = 6.$$

Hence the two equations are not compatible and the system has no solution

On the other hand, a system of equations may be indeterminate. Then there exists an infinity of solutions.

EXAMPLE 3

Consider the system of equations

$$x + 2y = 3,$$
$$2x + 4y = 6.$$

Evidently the second equation is simply twice the first equation and therefore is not independent of the first equation. Hence we have really only one independent equation. We may assign an arbitrary value to one of the unknowns, say $y = a$, where a is any number. Then the solution is $x = 3 - 2a$, $y = a$. It is easily seen that these solutions satisfy the given two equations:

$$3 - 2a + 2a = 3,$$
$$2(3 - 2a) + 4a = 6.$$

We may also have systems of equations with more variables than the number of equations. After carrying out as many eliminations as possible, we may assign arbitrary numbers to the excess variables and obtain the solution in terms of these quantities.

EXAMPLE 4

Consider the system of equations

$$2x + y + z = 1,$$
$$x + y + z = 0.$$

Since we have two equations in three unknowns, we can assign an arbitrary value to one unknown, say $z = b$. The solution of this system of equations is then $x = 1$, $y = -b - 1$, $z = b$, where b is arbitrary. We see that these values satisfy the original equations:

$$2 - b - 1 + b = 1,$$
$$1 - b - 1 + b = 0.$$

In systems with more equations than variables, the process of elimination will, again, lead us to a solution or, more likely, to the conclusion that the system has no solution.

EXERCISES 16

Solve the following systems of equations and check:

1　$2x + 5y = -1$ and $x + 2y = 9$.

2　$-x + 5y = 10$ and $3x + y = 0$.

3　$4x + 19y = 10$ and $x - y = 1$.

4　$9x - y = 10$ and $5x + 4y = 1$.

5　$-3x - 5y = 0$ and $x + y = 0$.

Solve each of the four systems of equations that follow:

6　$2x - y = 0$,
　　$y + z = 0$,
　　　　$z = 1$.

7　$2x + 3y + 5z = -9$,
　　$x + 10y + 6z = -13$,
　$-5x + y + 10z = 14$.

8　$5x + 4y + 3z = 7$,
　　$x + y + 2z = 4$,
　　$3x + 5y + z = 0$.

9　$5x + 6y + z = 1$,
　　$2x + 7y - z = -1$,
　　$3x + 10y + 2z = 2$.

17　MARKET EQUILIBRIUM FOR SEVERAL COMMODITIES

The demand for and the supply of a commodity depend frequently not only on the price of the particular commodity but also upon the prices of other related commodities. Again we can determine the equilibrium quantities exchanged and the prices of all commodities concerned. The condition for equilibrium is that for all commodities the supply be equal to the demand.

If we had information about the demand and supply functions of *all* commodities in the economy, we could determine the *Walrasian general equilibrium*, that is, *all prices and all quantities exchanged in the economy.*

EXAMPLE

Denote by p_A the price of commodity A and by p_B the price of commodity B. Let D_A and D_B be the demand, respectively, for A and B, and S_A and S_B the supply of A and B. Let the demand function for A be $D_A = 5 - p_A + p_B$ and the demand function for B be $D_B = 7 - p_A - p_B$. The respective supply functions are $S_A = -5 + p_A + 5p_B$ and $S_B = -1 + 3p_A + p_B$. By putting $D_A = S_A$ and $D_B = S_B$ we get the two linear equations

$$10 = 2p_A + 4p_B \quad \text{and} \quad 8 = 4p_A + 2p_B.$$

By solving this system of equations we compute the equilibrium prices $p_A = 1$ and $p_B = 2$. Substituting back into the original equations, we have for the equilibrium quantities

$$D_A = S_A = 6 \quad \text{and} \quad D_B = S_B = 4.$$

EXERCISES 17

1   $D_A = 10 - p_A - 2p_B$; $D_B = 6 - p_A - p_B$; $S_A = -3 + p_A + p_B$; $S_B = -2 + p_B$. (a) Find the equilibrium prices. (b) Determine the equilibrium quantities exchanged on the market.

2   $D_A = 10 - 2p_A + p_B - p_C$; $D_B = 12 + p_A - 4p_B + p_C$; $D_C = 20 - p_A - p_B - 5p_C$; $S_A = 4$; $S_B = 13$; $S_C = 2$. (a) Find the equilibrium prices. (b) Determine the equilibrium quantities exchanged on the market.

3   $D_A = 10 - 3p_A + p_B$; $D_B = 20 + 4p_A - 5p_B$; $S_A = 9$; $S_B = 14$. (a) Find the equilibrium prices. (b) Find the equilibrium quantities.

4   $D_A = 100 - 2p_A - p_B - 2p_C$; $D_B = 200 - 10p_A - 2p_B - 3p_C$; $D_C = 150 - 2p_A - 3p_B - 5p_C$; $S_A = 40$; $S_B = 70$; $S_C = 10$. Find the equilibrium prices and quantities.

5   Let A represent beef, B pork, and C mutton. Schultz estimated the demand functions for beef, pork, and mutton in the United States in 1922–1933 to be, respectively, $D_A = 63.3 - 1.9p_A + 0.2p_B + 0.5p_C$, $D_B = 71.0 + 0.4p_A - 1.2p_B - 0.1p_C$, $D_C = 10.3 + 0.1p_A + 0.1p_B - 0.3p_C$. Assume that $S_A = 60$, $S_B = 70$, $S_C = 7$. (a) Determine the equilibrium prices. (b) Find the quantities exchanged on the market.

6   Let A, B, C, and D designate barley, corn, hay, and oats. Schultz has estimated the demand functions for the Unites States in 1896–1914 as follows: $D_A = 2.24 - 0.01p_A - 0.01p_B + 0.01p_D$; $D_B = 49.07 - 0.02p_A - 0.36p_B - 0.03p_C + 0.03p_D$; $D_C = 1.30 - 0.05p_C + 0.01p_D$; $D_D = 24.16 + 0.03p_A + 0.07p_B - 0.61p_C - 0.30p_D$. Determine the equilibrium prices if $S_A = 2.24$, $S_B = 48.92$, $S_C = 1.29$, $S_D = 23.92$.

7   Let $D_A = a + bp_A + cp_B$; $D_B = e + fp_A + gp_B$; $S_A = h + kp_A$; and $S_B = m + np_B$. Find the equilibrium prices on the market.

8   Let the demand functions for 2 commodities A and B be $D_A = 10 - 2p_A + p_B$, $D_B = 20 + p_A - 5p_B$. The supply functions of A and B are $S_A = 4p_A$ and $S_B = -1 + 6p_B$. Find the equilibrium prices and quantities exchanged on the markets.

9   The demand functions of 3 commodities, A, B, and C, are $D_A = 20 - 3p_A + p_B + p_C$; $D_B = 30 + p_A - 5p_B$; $D_C = 15 + p_A - 3p_C$. The corresponding supply functions are $S_A = 9p_A$, $S_B = 30p_B - 3$, $S_C = 3p_C - 1$. Find the equilibrium prices and quantities exchanged on the markets.

10   If y denotes disposable income, c consumers' expenditure, r gross business savings, and x gross investments, the following simple model of general equilibrium has been established by Haavelmo for the United States for the years 1929–1941:

$$c = 0.712y + 95.05,$$
$$r = 0.158(c + x) - 34.30,$$
$$y = c + x - r,$$
$$x = 93.53.$$

(a) Solve for the unknowns y, c, r, and x and check. (b) Assume $x = 200$ rather than $x = 93.53$, as in the last equation in the above system. Solve for the unknowns and check. What are the estimated disposable income, consumer expenditure, and gross business savings if the gross investment is 300? (HINT: Substitute $x = 300$ for the last equation in the above system, solve for the unknowns, and check.)

18   IMPUTATION

The *theory of economic imputation* deals with the question, *In what way is the value (price) of a final product divided among the various factors of production* (that is, land, labor, and capital) *that have collaborated in the production?*

We assume static conditions; that is, the basic conditions of production and demand remain the same. We also assume free competition. Under free competition, the action of no one individual in the economy is important enough to influence, by itself, the workings of the market. There are a great number of independent firms. No firm can make profits in excess to normal returns. Normal returns are just sufficient to keep the firm in the industry.

Under free competition we have free movement of the factors of production. If the compensations for the use of the factors is not the same in the production of all commodities, the factors will tend to move away from the poorly paid occupations into the better paid ones until the compensation is the same in all lines.

We make also the unrealistic assumption that there are fixed coefficients of production. This would be the case if the various factors of production had to be combined in fixed proportions in order to produce a given product. For example, a certain product A can be produced only by combining 1 unit (acre) of land with 2 units (weeks) of labor. If, on the other hand, 2 units of land are combined with 3 units of labor we get another product B; and so on.

Under these very simplified and artificial conditions the problem of imputation reduces itself to the solution of a system of linear equations.

EXAMPLE

Assume that 1 unit of commodity A is produced by using 1 unit of land and 2 units of labor; and 1 unit of commodity B is produced by using 2 units of land and 3 units of labor. Let the price of commodity A be $p_A = 25$ and of commodity B be $p_B = 40$. Designate the wage rate by W and the rent per acre by R. The sum of the shares of the factors must be added to give the price, since there is no profit. The two equations are

$$R + 2W = 25 \quad \text{and} \quad 2R + 3W = 40.$$

We solve these two equations by elimination and obtain for the wage rate and the rent the values $W = 10$ and $R = 5$.

EXERCISES 18

1   Let a unit of commodity A be produced by combining 5 units of land and 6 units of labor. A unit of B is produced by using 10 units of land and 1 unit of labor. Let $p_A = 23$ and $p_B = 13$. Find the wage W and the rent R.

2   Let 3 units of land, 2 units of labor, and 10 units of capital be combined to produce 1 unit of commodity A. If 1 unit of land, 3 units of labor, and 5 units of capital are used, 1 unit of commodity B is produced. By using 2 units of land, 2 units of labor, and 3 units of capital we get a unit of commodity C. The prices are $p_A = 62$, $p_B = 36$, $p_C = 25$. Determine the rent R, wage W, and interest I. Show that the sum of the shares of all factors equals the price of each commodity. Hence there is no profit.

3   One unit of commodity A is produced by combining 1 unit of land, 2 units of labor, and 5 units of capital. One unit of commodity B is produced by 2 units of land, 3 units of labor, and 1 unit of capital. One unit of commodity C results if we use 3 units of land, 1 unit of labor, and 2 units of capital. Assume that the prices are $p_A = 27$, $p_B = 16$, $p_C = 19$. Find the rent R, wage W, and rate of interest I.

4   Commodity A is produced by combining 2 acres of land, 3 weeks of labor, and 5 units of capital. Commodity B is produced by combining 1 acre of land, 1 week of labor, and 1 unit of capital. Commodity C is produced by combining 2 acres of land, 5 weeks of labor, and 10 units of capital. The prices are $p_A = 78$, $p_B = 23$, $p_C = 135$. Determine the rent R, wage W, and interest I.

5 Commodity A is produced by combining 1 acre of land, 2 weeks of labor, and 3 units of capital; B is produced by combining 2 units of land, 1 unit of labor, and 2 units of capital; C results from a combination of 5 units of land, 2 units of labor, and 1 unit of capital. Given the prices $p_A = 84$, $p_B = 56$, $p_C = 108$, find the rent R, wage W, and interest rate I.

6 Assume that a units of labor and b units of land are combined in order to produce 1 unit of commodity A. By combining c units of land and d units of labor we get 1 unit of commodity B. Let the prices be $p_A = m$ and $p_B = n$; the quantities a, b, c, d, m, and n are constants. Find the wage W and the rent R.

7 A unit of commodity A is produced by combining 1 acre of land and 2 days of labor. A unit of B requires 2 acres of land and 4 days of labor. Let the prices be $p_A = 20$ and $p_B = 40$. Show that it is impossible to determine the rent R and the wage W. Why?

8 A product that is produced by combining 1 week of labor, 3 acres of land, and 10 units of capital sells for \$14 per unit. Another product produced by combining 2 weeks of labor, 4 acres of land, and 20 units of capital sells for \$24 for each unit. A third product is produced by combining 9 acres of land, 20 weeks of labor, and 30 units of capital and sells for \$49. Determine, under conditions of perfect competition, the wage, rent, and interest rate.

9 Let us distinguish between four factors of production: skilled labor, unskilled labor, land, and capital. By combining 1 week of skilled labor, 10 weeks of unskilled labor, 2 acres of land, and 100 units of capital we produce a unit of commodity A, which sells for \$420. Using 3 weeks of skilled labor, 20 weeks of unskilled labor, 1 acre of land, and 200 units of capital we produce a unit of commodity B, which sells for \$835. Using 5 weeks of skilled labor, 20 weeks of unskilled labor, 1 acre of land, and 100 units of capital we produce a unit of commodity C, which sells for \$555. If we use 1 week of skilled labor, 100 weeks of unskilled labor, 3 acres of land, and 500 units of capital we produce a unit of D, which sells for \$2,525. Assuming free competition, determine the compensation of the four factors of production, namely, the wage of skilled labor, W_1, the wage of unskilled labor, W_2, the rent for land, R, and the interest for capital, I. Show that the shares of the factors in the products add up to the prices of the commodities. Hence there is no profit.

10 Using data given by Leontief for the United States in 1939, we assume constant coefficients of production. By using 0.242 units of labor and 5.461 units of capital, we get a unit of agricultural products, which sells for \$1. By using 0.282 units of labor and 5.191 units of capital, one unit of industrial products is produced, which sells for \$1. Assume free competition and compute the compensations for labor and capital.

**19 THE CROUT METHOD FOR THE NUMERICAL SOLUTION OF A SYSTEM OF LINEAR EQUATIONS

We present an example in order to illustrate this method, which is particularly adapted for the use of desk calculators.

EXAMPLE

The following system of linear equations is given:

$$2x_1 - 2x_2 + 3x_3 + 2x_4 = 10,$$
$$4x_1 + x_2 + 2x_3 - x_4 = 0,$$
$$3x_1 + 2x_2 + x_3 + 3x_4 = 5,$$
$$x_1 + x_2 + 4x_3 + x_4 = 1.$$

From this system we derive the following table, which consists of three sections:

(1)	(2)	(3)	(4)	(5)	(6)
			I		
2.000000	−2.000000	3.000000	2.000000	10.000000	15.000000
4.000000	1.000000	2.000000	−1.000000	0.000000	6.000000
3.000000	2.000000	1.000000	3.000000	5.000000	14.000000
1.000000	1.000000	4.000000	1.000000	1.000000	8.000000
			II		
2.000000	−1.000000	1.500000	1.000000	5.000000	7.500000
4.000000	5.000000	−0.800000	−1.000000	−4.000000	−4.800000
3.000000	5.000000	0.500000	10.000000	20.000000	31.000000
1.000000	2.000000	4.100000	−39.000000	2.000000	3.000000
			III		
1.000000	−2.000000	0.000000	2.000000		
2.000000	−1.000000	1.000000	3.000000		

In part I of this table we copy simply the coefficients of the equations (columns 1 to 4) and the constants on the right-hand side of the equations (column 5). The last column provides a check and is simply the sum of all elements in each line:

$$2 - 2 + 3 + 2 + 10 = 15,$$
$$4 + 1 + 2 - 1 + 0 \ = 6,$$
$$3 + 2 + 1 + 3 + 5 \ = 14,$$
$$1 + 1 + 4 + 1 + 1 \ = 8.$$

Note that the diagonal elements are underlined.

Part II of the table is constructed by copying column 1 of the first part of the table. The elements diagonally to the right from the first element of the first line are computed by dividing the corresponding elements of the first line of the first part of the table by the diagonal element (column 2). This results in the following elements line 1, part II right from the diagonal element:

$$\frac{-2}{2} = -1; \qquad \frac{3}{2} = 1.5; \qquad \frac{2}{2} = 1; \qquad \frac{10}{2} = 5; \qquad \frac{15}{2} = 7.5.$$

The last element of line 1 of part II of the table gives a check. The sum of all elements in the first line right from the diagonal element excluding the last must be one less than the last element in this line:

$$-1 + 1.5 + 1 + 5 = 6.5; \qquad 6.5 + 1 = 7.5.$$

This calculation shows that the elements of line 1 of part II of the table are correct.

We compute the diagonal element of line 2 of part II as follows: From the corresponding element in part I of the table (column 1) we deduct the product of the symmetrically located elements in part II, $(4, -1)$, which have already been computed; thus:

$$1 - (4)(-1) = 5.$$

Similarly, we compute the remaining elements of column 2 of part II of the table: From the corresponding elements in part I we subtract the products of the symmetrically located elements in part II, which have already been computed:

$$2 - (3)(-1) = 5; \qquad 1 - (-1)(1) = 2.$$

Now the remaining elements in line 2 of part II are similarly computed, but we also divide the result by the diagonal element (5):

$$\frac{2 - (1.5)(4)}{5} = -0.8,$$

$$\frac{-1 - (1)(4)}{5} = -1,$$

$$\frac{0 - (5)(4)}{5} = -4,$$

$$\frac{6 - (7.5)(4)}{5} = -4.8.$$

The last element in line 2 of part II is again used for a check: The sum of all elements right from the diagonal excluding the last must be one less than the last element in line 2:

$$-0.8 - 1 - 4 = -5.8; \qquad -5.8 + 1 = -4.8.$$

The diagonal element in line 3 of part II of the table is computed as follows: From the corresponding element in part I (column 1) we subtract the products of the symmetrically located elements in part II, (3, 1.5 and 5, −0.8), which have already been computed:

$$1 - (3)(1.5) - (5)(-0.8) = 0.5.$$

Similarly, we compute the remaining element in column 3 of part II:

$$4 - (1)(1.5) - (2)(-0.8) = 4.1.$$

The remaining elements in line 3 of part II of the table are computed in a similar way, except that we also divide though the diagonal element (0.5):

$$\frac{3 - (3)(1) - (5)(-1)}{0.5} = 10,$$

$$\frac{5 - (3)(5) - (5)(-4)}{0.5} = 20,$$

$$\frac{14 - (3)(7.5) - (5)(-4.8)}{0.5} = 31.$$

For a check we have again

$$10 + 20 = 30; \qquad 30 + 1 = 31.$$

The diagonal element in line 4 of part II of the table is computed in the same way:

$$1 - (1)(1) - (2)(-1) - (4.1)(10) = -39,$$

as are the remaining elements in line 4 of part II:

$$\frac{1 - (1)(5) - (2)(-4) - (4.1)(20)}{-39} = 2,$$

$$\frac{8 - (1)(7.5) - (2)(-4.8) - (4.1)(31)}{-39} = 3.$$

Again we have for a check

$$2 + 1 = 3.$$

Part III of the table forms the solution and is computed backwards. First we write the two last elements of line 4 of part II below as the elements of the last (fourth) column (2, 3).

For a check we had already

$$2 + 1 = 3.$$

The first element of column 3 of part III of the table is computed as follows: We subtract from the penultimate element of line 3 of part II (20) the product of the fourth element in the same line in part II (10) and the fourth element of line 1 of part III (2):

$$20 - (10)(2) = 0.$$

For a check we have: Take the last element in line 3 of part III of the table (31) and subtract the product of the third element in the same line (10) times the corresponding element in line 2 of part III (3):

$$31 - (10)(3) = 1.$$

For a check we have again: The element in line 1 must be one less than the element in line 2:

$$0 + 1 = 1.$$

Similarly, we compute the two entries in column 2 of part III of the table:

$$-4 - (-1)(2) - (-0.8)(0) = -2,$$
$$-4.8 - (-1)(3) - (-0.8)(1) = -1.$$

A check gives

$$-2 + 1 = -1.$$

Now we derive from line 1 of part III our solutions:

$$x_1 = 1, \qquad x_2 = -2, \qquad x_3 = 0, \qquad x_4 = 2.$$

This result must be verified with the help of the original system of equations:

$$(2)(1) - 2(-2) + 3(0) + 2(2) = 10,$$
$$4(1) + 1(-2) + 2(0) - 1(2) = 0,$$
$$3(1) + 2(-2) + 1(0) + 3(2) = 5,$$
$$1(1) + 1(-2) + 4(0) + 1(2) = 1.$$

EXERCISES 19

1   Solve the following system of equations:

$$3x_1 - 2x_2 + 5x_3 = -1,$$
$$x_1 + 5x_2 - 2x_3 = 11,$$
$$5x_1 + 3x_2 + 2x_3 = 11.$$

2 Solve the following system of equations:

$$x_1 + x_2 + x_3 + 2x_4 = 4,$$
$$2x_1 - x_2 + x_3 + 3x_4 = 3.$$
$$x_2 + 2x_3 - 2x_4 = 1$$
$$x_1 + x_3 + x_4 = 2$$

3 Solve problem 5, Exercises 12, by the Crout method.

4 Solve problem 5, Exercises 11, by the Crout method.

5 Solve problem 9, Exercises 11, by the Crout method.

Chapter 4
Logarithms

The Italian economist Vilfredo Pareto indicated the following empirical law for the distribution of incomes: If N denotes the number of people who have an income x *or higher*, then $N = A/x^\alpha$, where A and α are constants and α is approximately 1.5. This function fits the data rather well for relatively high incomes.

The statistical fitting of Pareto distributions by the method of least squares will be considered later. (See Section 119, especially problems 22–25, Exercises 119.)

EXAMPLE

Let the Pareto distribution of incomes in a community be given by $N = 2{,}000{,}000{,}000/x^{1.5}$. (1) How many people have an income of \$100,000 or higher? (2) What is the lowest income of the 100 richest people in the community?

The solution of the two parts of this problem is facilitated by the use of logarithms. The following definitions and principles pertaining to the use of logarithms are recalled at this point. In the various statements that follow the symbol log is the abbreviation of logarithm, $b > 0$, $b \neq 1$.

1. $\log_b N = x$ is equivalent to $b^x = N$. If $b = 10$, the logarithms are said to be common logarithms. When the subscript b is omitted it is understood in this book that $b = 10$. Logarithms obey the following properties:

2. $\log 10 = 1$.
3. $\log N^t = t \log N$.
4. $\log MN = \log M + \log N$.
5. $\log M/N = \log M - \log N$.

6. By reference to Table 1, Appendix D, the common logarithm of any number between 1 and 10 may be found. In this table a decimal point is to be understood after the first digit of each number in the N column and a decimal point is to be understood before each 4-digit array within the body of the table. Thus, to obtain log 4.67 the first 2 digits, namely, 4.6, are located in the N column; the third digit, 7, is a column heading; so the desired value, that is, log 4.67 = 0.6693, is the number opposite the 46 and appearing in the column headed by 7. Similarly, log 2.72 = 0.4346 and log 2.00 = 0.3010.

7. It is possible to obtain the common logarithm of any number greater than 10 or less than 1 by the use of Table 1, Appendix D, and Principles 2, 3, 4, and 5, page 50. Thus

$$\begin{aligned}
\log 4.67 &= 0.6693, \\
\log 46.7 &= \log (4.67)(10) = \log 4.67 + \log 10 \\
&= 0.6693 + 1, \qquad \text{or} \qquad 1.6693. \\
\log 467 &= \log (4.67)(10^2) = \log 4.67 + \log 10^2 \\
&= \log 4.67 + 2 \log 10 = 0.6693 + 2, \qquad \text{or} \qquad 2.6693. \\
\log 0.467 &= \log (4.67)(10^{-1}) = \log (4.67) + \log 10^{-1} \\
&= \log 4.67 - 1 \log 10 = 0.6693 - 1.
\end{aligned}$$

In summary,

$$\begin{aligned}
\log 0.00467 &= 0.6693 - 3. \\
\log 0.0467 &= 0.6693 - 2. \\
\log 0.467 &= 0.6693 - 1. \\
\log 4.67 &= 0.6693. \\
\log 46.7 &= 1.6693. \\
\log 467 &= 2.6693. \\
\log 4670 &= 3.6693.
\end{aligned}$$

Let us return to a consideration of question (1) in the example, which involves a study of $N = 2{,}000{,}000{,}000/x^{1.5}$, where $x = 100{,}000$. We may take the common logarithm of each member, thereby obtaining the following sequence of equations:

$$\log N = \log \frac{2{,}000{,}000{,}000}{100{,}000^{1.5}},$$

$\log N = \log 2{,}000{,}000{,}000 - \log (100{,}000)^{1.5},$
$\log N = \log 2{,}000{,}000{,}000 - 1.5 \log 100{,}000,$
$\log N = 9.3010 - 1.5(5) = 9.3010 - 7.5 = 1.8010.$

It is apparent that N is about 63.2, or roughly 63, since log 63.2 = 1.8007.

Question (2) involves a study of the Pareto equation when

$N = 100$. Thus

$$100 = \frac{2,000,000,000}{x^{1.5}}.$$

The solution of this equation for x leads to the following sequence of equations:

$$100x^{1.5} = 2,000,000,000,$$
$$x^{1.5} = 20,000,000.$$
$$\log x^{1.5} = \log 20,000,000,$$
$$1.5 \log x = 7.3010,$$
$$\log x = 4.8673.$$

So x is about 73,700, since $\log 73,700 = 4.8675$.

A graph of the above equation is given in Figure 12. The graph, as shown, is the result of plotting the logarithm of N (number of people having a given income x or larger) against the logarithm of the income x. It is apparent that the result is a straight line.

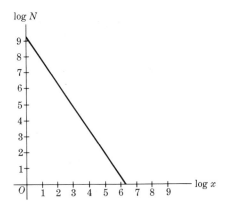

Figure 12

EXERCISES 20

1   Assume that in a city the Pareto distribution is $N = 50,000,000,000/x^{1.2}$. Find the number of people who have an income of (a) over \$500,000; (b) over \$2,500,000; (c) over \$3,000; (d) over \$125,400. What is the lowest income of (e) the 10 richest people? (f) the 250 richest people? (g) the 10,000 richest people? (h) the 15 richest people? (k) the 2 richest people? (l) Plot the distribution in terms of $\log N$ and $\log x$.

2   The Pareto distribution in a community is $N = 3,000,000,000/x^{\frac{2}{3}}$. Find the number of people who have an income of (a) \$150,000 or larger; (b) \$2,125,500 or larger; (c) \$5,500,000 or larger; (d) \$10,000,-000 or larger; (e) \$2,500 or larger; (f) \$5,275 or larger. Find the lowest income of (g) the 10 richest people; (h) the 150 richest people; (i) the

255 richest people; (j) the richest man in the community. (k) Plot the distribution, using log x and log N as coordinates.

3   Assume the Pareto distribution of a community to be $N = 1,236,000,-000/x^{1.1}$. Find the number of people who have an income of (a) $125,200 or higher; (b) $236,567 or higher; (c) $5,234,125 or higher; (d) $1,567 or higher; (e) $12,345,789 or higher. Find the lowest income of (f) the 11 richest people; (g) the 124 richest people; (h) the 10,000 richest people in the community. (i) Plot the distribution, using log x and log N as coordinates.

4   The income distribution of the United States for 1918 has been estimated by Von Szeliski to be $N = 813,000,000,000/x^{1.48}$. Estimate the number of people who had an income (a) of $100,000 or higher; (b) of $2,000,000 or higher; (c) of $150,000 or higher; (d) of $5,000 or higher; (e) of $2,500 or higher. Find the lowest income of (f) the 10 richest people; (g) the 3 richest people; (h) the 125 richest people; (i) the 40 richest people. (j) How many people had an income between $12,500 and $20,000? (k) Plot the distribution using log x and log N.

5   Davis estimated the Pareto distribution of income for the United States in 1918 as follows: $N = 1,926,000,000,000/x^{1.7}$. Find the number of people who had an income of (a) $100,000 or higher; (b) $5,000 or higher; (c) $2,125 or higher; (d) $2,125,000 or higher; (e) $500,000 or higher. Find the lowest income of (f) the 12 richest men; (g) the 100 richest; (h) the 1,200 richest; (i) the 2 richest. (j) How many people had an income between $20,000 and $25,000? (k) between $100,000 and $250,000? (l) Plot the distribution in terms of log x and log N.

6   Davis estimated the Pareto distribution for salaries paid by General Motors in 1936 to be $N = 67,620,000,000/x^2$. Find the number of employees who had an income of (a) $100,000 or over; (b) $50,000 or over; (c) $12,500 or over; (d) $4,000 or over. What was the lowest income of (e) the 100 best-paid employees? (f) the 5 best-paid employees? (g) the 125 best-paid employees? (h) How many people had an income between $7,500 and $10,000? (i) Plot the distribution in terms of log x and log N.

7   Assume the Pareto distribution of a community to be $N = a/x^b$, where a and b are constants. (a) How many people have an income larger than K? (b) larger than $100,000? (c) What is the lowest income of the 100 richest people? (d) of the 10 richest people? (e) How many people have incomes between s and t? (f) between $500,000 and $1,500,000?

8   Let the Pareto distribution in a community be $N = 1,000/\sqrt[3]{x^4}$. NOTE: $\sqrt[3]{x^4} = x^{4/3}$. How many people have an income of (a) $10 or higher? (b) of $100 or higher? (c) What is the lowest income of the 10 richest people? (d) of the 100 richest people? (e) How many people have incomes between 15 and 20?

9   Let the Pareto distribution in a community be $N = 100,000/x^2$. How many people have an income of (a) 10 or higher? (b) 15 or higher? What is the lowest income of (c) the 100 richest people? (d) the 5 richest people? (e) How many people have incomes between 100 and 120? (f) between 50 and 75?

10   Assume that the income distribution in a city is $N = 1,000,000,000/x^{1.5}$. How many people have an income of (a) more than \$100,000? (b) more than \$250,000? (c) What is the lowest income of the 1,500 richest people? (d) of the 3,000 richest people? (e) How many people have incomes between \$500,000 and \$750,000?

11   Klein has estimated the Pareto distribution of income in the United Kingdom for the period 1953–1954 for incomes over £2,000. Let P be the proportion of people having income y or higher; $P = (2,000/y)^{1.9}$ (a) Find the proportion of people having an income of £6,000 or more; (b) of £9,500 or more; (c) between £3,000 and £4,500.

21   DEMAND CURVES WITH CONSTANT ELASTICITY

A demand curve of the general form $D = A/p^B$, where A and B are constants, has constant elasticity, as will be proved later (see Section 66). The statistical fitting of demand curves with constant elasticity is discussed in problem 1, Exercises 122.

By a demand curve with constant elasticity B we understand the following property: If the price increases by 1 percent, the demand will decrease approximately by B percent.

EXAMPLE 1

Assume a demand curve in the form $D = 25/p^3$. (1) What is the demand if the price is 0.5? We have $D = 25/(0.5)^3 = 200$. (2) What price causes a demand of 65 units? Inserting $D = 65$ into the above equation, we get

$$65p^3 = 25,$$
$$p^3 = 5/13.$$
$$3 \log p = \log 5 - \log 13,$$
$$3 \log p = 0.5851 - 1,$$
$$\text{or} \quad 2.5851 - 3.$$
$$\log p = 0.8617 - 1,$$
$$p = 0.727.$$

EXAMPLE 2

In the special case of $B = +1$ in the formula $D = A/p^B$ we have demand curves with unit elasticity. An approximate decrease of 1 percent in the quantity sold corresponds to a 1 percent increase in price. Price times quantity is constant. That is, the total outlay of the buyers or the total receipts of the sellers are the same whatever the price and quantity sold. Consider, for example, the demand curve

$$D = \frac{24}{p}.$$

The curve is shown in Figure 13; since D and p are positive, only the positive branch of the curve is drawn. This type of mathematical curve is called a *rectangular hyperbola*. We have, for

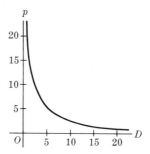

Figure 13

instance, if $p = 2$, $D = {}^{24}\!/_2 = 12$. The total outlay or revenue $pD = (2)(12) = 24$. On the other hand, if $p = 8$, we have $D = 3$. Hence again $pD = (3)(8) = 24$, as before. This constancy is true for any price.

EXERCISES 21

1   Assume a demand curve in the form $D = 100/p^5$. Find the demand if the price is (a) 4; (b) 2.5; (c) 0.60; (d) 0.002. Find the price that will cause a demand of (e) 10; (f) 250; (g) 0.5; (h) 0.003 units. (i) Plot the demand curve.

2   Assume a demand curve in the form $D = 1{,}245/(p)\sqrt[3]{p}$. Find the price that will cause a demand of (a) 20,000; (b) 1,500; (c) 600; (d) 1. Find the demand if the price is (e) 2; (f) 0.85; (g) $\frac{1}{32}$; (h) 1. (i) Plot the demand curve. (NOTE: $\sqrt[3]{p} = p^{1/3}$.)

3   A demand curve is given by $D = 0.657/p^{1.57}$. Find the price that will cause a demand of (a) 10; (b) 3; (c) 0.6; (d) 0.0012. Given the price of (e) 1; (f) 35; (g) 0.86; (h) 0.00065, find the corresponding quantity demanded. (i) Plot the demand curve.

4   The demand curve for sugar in the United States has been estimated by Schultz to be $D = 157.8/p^{0.3}$ for the period 1915–1929. Find the demand for sugar if the price is (a) 5; (b) 8; (c) 11; (d) 12. What price will

call forth a demand of (e) 60? (f) 30? (g) 55? (h) 42? (i) Plot the demand curve.

5   The demand curve for corn in the United States for the period 1915–1929 has been estimated by Schultz to be $D = 172.8/p^{0.49}$. Find the demand if the price is (a) 30; (b) 42; (c) 75; (d) 81. What is the price if the demand is (e) 20; (f) 35; (g) 41; (h) 50. (i) Plot the demand curve.

6   The demand curve for cotton in the United States for the period 1915–1929 has been estimated by Schultz to be $D = 0.59/p^{0.12}$. Find the demand if the price is (a) 30; (b) 50; (c) 75; (d) 51; (e) 32. What is the price if the demand is (f) 0.20; (g) 0.25; (h) 0.30; (i) 0.32. (j) Plot the demand curve.

7   The demand for wheat in the United States for the period 1915–1929 has been estimated by Schultz to be $D = 12.03/p^{0.21}$. Find the price if the demand is (a) 6; (b) 5; (c) 4.5; (d) 2.1; (e) 3.3. Find the demand if the price is (f) 100; (g) 120; (h) 150; (i) 85; (j) 67. (k) Plot the demand curve.

8   The demand for potatoes in the United States for the period 1915–1929 has been estimated by Schultz to be $D = 12.05/p^{0.3}$. Find the demand if the price is (a) 30; (b) 45; (c) 25; (d) 33; (e) 37; (f) 40. Find the price if the demand is (g) 3; (h) 4; (i) 4.5; (j) 5; (k) 7. (l) Plot the demand curve.

9   Let the demand curve for a commodity be $D = a/p^b$, where a and b are positive constants. Determine the price if the demand is (a) $5a$; (b) 1. Find the demand if the price is (c) 1; (d) if the price is a.

**10   Assume that the demand curve of a commodity is $D = a/p^b$, where a and b are positive constants. The supply curve is $S = p$. Find the equilibrium price and quantity on the market.

11   Assume a demand function of the form $D = 100/p$. (a) Find the demand if $p = 5$. (b) Compute the total outlay and revenue pD. (c) Compute the demand if $p = 25$. (d) Compute the total outlay or revenue. (e) Compute the quantity demanded if the price is $p = 2$. (f) Compute the total outlay or revenue. (g) Plot the demand curve.

12   Fox computed the following model for the cattle market in the United States for the period 1922–1941. Denote by p the price, by y the disposable income, by q_D the quantity demanded, by q_s the quantity supplied, and by z the production of cattle. The demand function is $p = Aq_D^{-1.14}y^{0.9}$ and the supply function is $q_s = Bp^{-0.07}z^{0.77}$. Here A and B are constants. State the equilibrium price and quantity in terms of disposable income (y) and production (z).

13   The demand and supply functions for pork in Austria for the years 1948–1955 are $q_D = 75.6p^{-1.02}$ and $q_s = 6.43p^{0.74}$ (Tintner). Find the equilibrium price and quantity.

Chapter 5
Progressions

Progressions. In algebra we define a *sequence* as a *function whose domain is the set of positive integers.* For example, the numbers 1, 2, 3, $\cdots$ constitute the sequence of positive integers in natural order. Or the numbers 1, 4, 9, 16, $\cdots$ are the squares of the integers in their natural order. Again the numbers 1, $\frac{1}{2}$, $\frac{1}{3}$, $\cdots$ form what is called *a harmonic sequence in descending order of magnitude,* and so on.

As a notational convention, if the sequence is given as $f(i)$, $i = 1$, $\cdots$, it is common to "suppress" the functional notation and write u_i or a_i, and so on, for $f(i)$.

The numbers in a sequence are called *terms.* For example, in the last sequence 1 is the first term, $\frac{1}{2}$ is the second term, $\frac{1}{3}$ the third term, and so on.

We are concerned frequently with the *sums* of the terms of sequences, when these sums exist. Let u_1 be the first term of a sequence, u_2 the second term, u_3 the third term, and in general u_i the ith term. The sum of the first n terms of the sequence can be written,

$$S_n = u_1 + u_2 + u_3 + \cdots + u_n = \sum_{i=1}^{n} u_i.$$

The Greek sigma (Σ) is used as the summation sign. The series $\Sigma_{i=1}^{n} u_i$ denotes a summation of terms from the lower limit $i = 1$, that is, u_1, to the upper limit $i = n$, that is, u_n. The limits are sometimes omitted if they are clear from the context. We may write then Σu_i.

EXAMPLE 1

Consider the sequence $u_1 = 1$, $u_2 = \frac{1}{2}$, $u_3 = \frac{1}{3}$, $u_4 = \frac{1}{4}$. The general term is $u_i = 1/i$. The sum of the four terms of the sequence is

$$S_4 = u_1 + u_2 + u_3 + u_4$$
$$= \sum_{i=1}^{4} 1/i$$
$$= 1 + \tfrac{1}{2} + \tfrac{1}{3} + \tfrac{1}{4}$$
$$= {}^{25}\!/_{12}.$$

An *arithmetic progression* is formed by stating the first term and obtaining the nth term by adding a number d to the $(n - 1)$st term, $n = 2, 3, \cdots$. The number that is added is called the *common difference*.

EXAMPLE 2

Consider the sequence 2, 5, 8, 11. The first term is 2. The second term is $5 = 2 + 3$. The third term is $8 = 5 + 3$. Each term is formed by adding the common difference 3 to the preceding term.

EXAMPLE 3

Another example is the sequence 20, 18, 16, 14. The first term is 20. The second term is $18 = 20 - 2$. The third term is $16 = 18 - 2$. The fourth term is $14 = 16 - 2$. Hence each term is formed by adding to the preceding term the common difference -2.

Let a be the first term and d the common difference. Denoting by $x_1, x_2, x_3, \cdots, x_n$, respectively, the first, second, third, and nth terms of the arithmetic progression, we have

$$x_1 = a,$$
$$x_2 = x_1 + d = a + d,$$
$$x_3 = x_2 + d = (a + d) + d = a + 2d,$$
$$x_4 = x_3 + d = (a + 2d) + d = a + 3d.$$

We see that the first term x_1 is a. The second term is formed by adding $1d$ to a. The third term is obtained by adding $2d$ to a. The fourth term results if we add $3d$ to a. We may deduce the general rule: to find the nth term we have to add $(n - 1)d$ to a, that is, $x_n = a + (n - 1)d$.

EXAMPLE 4

In the first arithmetic progression given above the first term is $a = 2$ and the common difference $d = 3$. The third term is

$$x_3 = a + 2d = 2 + 2 \cdot 3 = 8.$$

EXAMPLE 5

Consider the arithmetic progression 10, 8, 6, $\cdots$. Find the fifth term x_5. We have $a = 10$, $d = -2$, $n = 5$. Hence,

$$x_5 = 10 + 4(-2) = 10 - 8 = 2.$$

EXERCISES 22

1 Consider the arithmetic progression 5, 8, 11, $\cdots$. Find (a) x_4; (b) x_7; (c) x_{150}.

2 Consider the arithmetic progression -8, -6, -4, $\cdots$. Find (a) x_6; (b) x_{10}; (c) x_{80}.

3 Consider the arithmetic progression 100, 90, 80, $\cdots$. Find (a) x_7; (b) x_{10}; (c) $x_{1,000}$.

4 Consider the arithmetic progression 3, 6, 9 $\cdots$. Find (a) x_7; (b) x_{12}. (c) For what value of n is $x_n = 81$?

5 An arithmetic progression has $x_2 = 10$ and $x_4 = 30$. (a) Find a and d; (b) x_{10}; (c) x_{25}.

6 An arithmetic progression has $a = 50$ and $x_6 = 0$. Find (a) d; (b) x_{10}; (c) x_{15}.

7 An arithmetic progression has $a = 10$, $x_5 = 0$. Find (a) d; (b) x_2. (c) For what n is $x_n = -25$?

8 An arithmetic progression has the difference $d = (\frac{1}{2})a$. Which term of the series will reach the value $10a$?

9 An arithmetic progression has the difference $d = -a/3$. Which term will be equal to 0?

10 An arithmetic progression has $a = -5d$. Which term will be equal to 0?

23 SUMS OF ARITHMETIC PROGRESSIONS

Denote by S_n the sum of the first n terms of an arithmetic progression; that is,

$$S_n = x_1 + x_2 + x_3 + \cdots + x_n = \sum_{i=1}^{n} x_i.$$

We can write this sum as follows:

$$S_n = a + (a + d) + (a + 2d) + (a + 3d) + \cdots + x_n.$$

This can also be written in the reverse order:

$$S_n = x_n + (x_n - d) + (x_n - 2d) + (x_n - 3d) + \cdots + a.$$

Adding the members of these two equalities, term by term, all d's cancel and we have

$$2S_n = (a + x_n) + (a + x_n) + \cdots + (a + x_n) = n(a + x_n).$$

The general formula for the sum of terms of an arithmetic progression is

$$S_n = \frac{n(a + x_n)}{2}.$$

EXAMPLE

Take the previous example, namely, the progression 10, 8, 6, $\cdots$. We have $a = 10$, $d = -2$. Find S_5, the sum of the first five terms.

We have from the previous formula $x_5 = 2$. So the sum is given by $S_5 = 5(10 + 2)/2 = 30$.

EXERCISES 23

1   Given the arithmetic progression 50, 40, 30, $\cdots$, find (a) S_4; (b) S_6; (c) S_{20}.

2   Given the arithmetic progression -5, -3, -1, $\cdots$, find (a) S_5; (b) S_7; (c) S_{50}.

3   Given the arithmetic progression 19, 22, 25, $\cdots$, find (a) S_4; (b) S_{10}; (c) S_{100}.

4   An arithmetic progression has $a = 100$, $S_{10} = 550$. Find (a) d; (b) x_{12}; (c) S_{15}.

5   Express S in terms of a, d, and n only. (HINT: Use the definition of x_n.)

6   In a certain arithmetic progression $S_5 = 100$ and $S_7 = 140$. Find (a) a and d; (b) x_6; (c) S_{10}.

7   In a particular arithmetic progression $x_2 = 80$, $S_4 = 240$. Find (a) a and d; (b) x_{10}; (c) S_6.

8   In a certain arithmetic progression $S_3 = 33$, $S_5 = 50$. Find (a) a and d; (b) x_8; (c) S_7.

9   Assume in an arithmetic progression that we know that $S_n = A$ and $S_m = B$. Determine a and d.

10   In an arithmetic progression we know that $x_n = C$, $S_m = D$. Determine a and d.

24   GROWTH OF ENTERPRISE

We assume that an enterprise grows over short periods in an arithmetic progression. This means that the output of the enterprise increases (or decreases) each year by the same number of units. This assumption is not strictly true but frequently is a fair approximation to the truth.

EXAMPLE

An enterprise starts by producing 100 units in its first year and the production increases by 20 units each year. How much will the firm produce in the fourth year? We use the formula $x_n = a + (n - 1)d$, where x_n is the production in the nth year, n the number of the year, and d the increase or decrease. We know that $a = 100$, $n = 4$, $d = 20$. The formula gives $x_4 = 160$. What will be the sum total of the whole production in the first three years? The sum of an arithmetic progression is given by $S_n = (a + x_n)(n/2)$. Since $x_3 = 140$, we have $S_3 = 360$.

EXERCISES 24

1 An enterprise produces 200 units in the first year and increases production by 50 units each year. How much will it produce (a) in the fifth year? (b) in the 10th year? (c) What is the sum total of its production in the first seven years? (d) the first four years?

2 An enterprise starts by producing 10,000 units in the first year. It decreases its production by 500 units each year. How much will it produce (a) in the third year? (b) the fifth year? (c) What is the total production in the first four years? (d) When will it produce 0? (e) What is the sum total of the firm's production until it produces 0?

3 An enterprise starts by producing 700 units in the first year. It produced 1,500 units in its fifth year. (a) By how much does production increase each year? (b) When will the enterprise produce 2,100 units? (c) What is the sum total of the firm's production during the first three years of its existence?

4 An enterprise produced 600 units in the third year of its existence and 700 units in its seventh year. (a) What was the initial production in the first year? (b) What was the production in the fifth year? (c) the total production during the first four years?

5 A firm produced 500 units in its first year. The sum total of its production in the first four years of its existence was 2,300 units. (a) By how much did production increase or decrease each year? (b) How much will the firm produce in its fifth year? (c) in its 10th year?

6 A firm produced 0 in its sixth year. The sum total of its production during the first five years was 3,000 units. (a) What was the firm's original production during the first year? (b) By how much did production increase or decrease each year? (c) How much was produced in the second year? (d) What was the sum total of production in the first four years?

7   A firm produced 0 in its fifth year. Its total production during the first four years was 2,400 units. (a) Find the initial production in year 1; (b) the yearly increase or decrease. (c) What was the production in year 4? (d) What was the sum total of its production in the first three years?

8   Firm *A* starts producing 1,000 units and decreases production by 100 units yearly. Firm *B* starts by producing 500 units and increases production by 25 units each year. (a) In what year will *A* and *B* produce the same amount? (b) When will firm *A* produce 0? (c) What is the production of firm *B* in the same year?

9   An index of industrial production in the United States was 91 in 1930 and 125 in 1940. Assuming an arithmetic progression, predict the index for 1950.

10   An index of agricultural production in the United States was 98 in 1930 and 126 in 1950. Assuming an arithmetic progression, predict agricultural production for 1960.

25   GEOMETRIC PROGRESSION

In a geometric progression each term after the first one is formed by multiplying the preceding term by a constant: $a_n = a_{n-1}r$, $n = 2, 3, \cdots$. The number is called the *common ratio*.

Consider, for example, the sequence 3, 6, 12, 24. The first term is 3; the second term is $3 \cdot 2 = 6$; the third term is $6 \cdot 2 = 12$; the fourth term is $12 \cdot 2 = 24$. The common ratio of two consecutive terms is 2; that is, each term in the sequence is formed by multiplying the preceding one by 2.

As another example, consider the sequence 27, 9, 3, 1, $\frac{1}{3}$, $\frac{1}{9}$. The first term is 27; the second term is $27 \cdot \frac{1}{3} = 9$; the third term is $9 \cdot \frac{1}{3} = 3$; the fourth term is $3 \cdot \frac{1}{3} = 1$; the fifth term is $1 \cdot \frac{1}{3} = \frac{1}{3}$; the sixth term is $\frac{1}{3} \cdot \frac{1}{3} = \frac{1}{9}$. The common ratio is $\frac{1}{3}$. Each term is formed by multiplying the preceding one by $\frac{1}{3}$.

Let us denote the first term of a geometric progression by a and the common ratio by r. Let $y_1, y_2, y_3, y_4, \cdots, y_n$ be the first, second, third, fourth, and nth terms, respectively, of a geometric progression. Then

$$y_1 = a,$$
$$y_2 = y_1 \cdot r = ar,$$
$$y_3 = y_2 \cdot r = (ar)r = ar^2,$$
$$y_4 = y_3 \cdot r = (ar^2) \cdot r = ar^3, \quad \text{and so forth.}$$

We see that the first term is a. The second term is formed by multiplying a by r raised to the first power. The third term results if a is multiplied by the second power of r. The fourth term is computed by multiplying a by the third power of r. In general, the nth term of a geometric progression is given by multiplying a (the first term) by the $(n - 1)$ power of r (the common ratio).   Thus,

$$y_n = ar^{n-1}.$$

EXAMPLE

Consider the geometric progression 2, 6, 18, $\cdots$. We have $a = 2$, $r = 3$. Find the fifth term.

$$y_5 = 2(3)^4 = 2 \cdot 81 = 162.$$

EXERCISES 25

1   Consider the geometric progression 10, 20, 40, $\cdots$. Find (a) y_4; (b) y_{10}; (c) y_{15}.

2   Take the geometric progression 6, 2, $\frac{2}{3}$, $\cdots$. Find (a) y_5; (b) y_6; (c) y_{10}.

3   Take the geometric progression 1, 5, 25, $\cdots$. Find (a) y_4; (b) y_6; (c) y_{10}.

4   Consider the geometric progression 12, 6, 3, $\cdots$. Find (a) y_{10}; (b) y_{100}. (HINT: use logarithms.)

5   A geometric progression has $a = 10$ and $y_3 = 1,000$. (a) Find r; (b) y_5; (c) y_{10}.

6   The second term of a geometric progression is $y_2 = 8$ and the fourth term is $y_4 = 4$. (a) Find a and r. (b) What is y_3? (c) Find y_5.

7   Find a general expression for a and r if $y_n = A$, $y_m = B$.

8   Take the geometric progression 1, $(a - b)$, $(a - b)^2$, $\cdots$. (a) Find the general expression for y_n. (b) Find y_6.

9   Find the geometric progression whose second term is 8 and whose fifth term is 8. Find a and r.

10   The second term of a geometric progression is 100 and the fourth term is 1. Find a and r.

26   SUMS OF GEOMETRIC PROGRESSIONS

Let S_n be the sum of the first n terms of a geometric progression: that is,

$$S_n = y_1 + y_2 + y_3 + \cdots + y_n = \sum_{i=1}^{n} y_i.$$

This may be rewritten in the form

$$S_n = a + ar + ar^2 + \cdots + ar^{n-2} + ar^{n-1}.$$

After multiplying the two members by r, there results

$$rS_n = ar + ar^2 + \cdots + ar^{n-2} + ar^{n-1} + ar^n.$$

By subtracting the two members just obtained from those of the previous expression for S_n, we obtain

$$S_n - rS_n = a - ar^n,$$

and, hence,

$$S_n = \frac{a(1 - r^n)}{1 - r} \quad \text{or} \quad \frac{a(r^n - 1)}{r - 1}, \text{ for } r \neq 1.$$

EXAMPLE

Given the geometric progression 2, 6, 18, $\cdots$, find S_4. We have $a = 2, r = 3, n = 4$. Hence,

$$S_4 = \frac{2(3^4 - 1)}{3 - 1} = \frac{2(81 - 1)}{2} = 80.$$

EXERCISES 26

1　Given the geometric progression 1, 4, 16, $\cdots$, find (a) S_3; (b) S_5; (c) S_8.

2　Given the geometric progression 24, 12, 6, $\cdots$, find (a) S_2; (b) S_5; (c) S_{10}.

3　Given the geometric progression 5, 10, 20, $\cdots$, find (a) S_3; (b) S_5; (c) S_7.

4　A geometric progression has the first term $a = 1$, and the sum of the first two terms is $S_2 = 6$. (a) Find r; (b) y_7; (c) S_3.

5　A geometric progression has the ratio $r = \frac{1}{2}$. Assume that $S_3 = 10$. Find (a) a; (b) y_6; (c) S_6.

6　Assume that a geometric progression has $a = 1$. Let $S_2 = A$, where A is a positive constant. Find r.

7　Find a general expression for the difference of the sum of a geometric series with $(n + 1)$ terms and the sum of n terms, that is, $S_{n+1} - S_n$. Interpret.

8　As in problem 7, find $S_{n+m} - S_n$, where n and m are positive integers.

9　Assume that in a geometric progression we have $S_m = A$, $S_{2m} = B$, where A and B are positive constants. (a) Find r; (b) a. (c) Check.

10　Use the formula for the sum of a geometric progression to investigate the sum of the progression 1, -1, 1, -1, $\cdots$. Investigate the sum for various values of n.

27   POPULATION

It was the contention of Malthus that population develops like a geometric progression. The assumption is that each year the population of a given area increases by the same percentage. This is not strictly true, since it is probable that population follows a more complicated law, namely, the logistic. But a geometric series can be used for purposes of interpolation or extrapolation over relatively short periods.

EXAMPLE

A population is 100,000 in the first year and increases by 3 percent each year. What will it be in the fifth year? The formula for $y_n = ar^{n-1}$, where y_n is the value of the term in the nth year, n is the number of the year, and r is the common ratio.

We have $a = 100,000$, $n = 5$, and $r = 1.03$. Thus, $y_n = 100,000 \ (1.03)^4$. Taking logarithms, we get log y_5 = log 100,000 $+ \ 4$ log 1.03. This gives log $y_5 = 5.0512$, so y_5 is about 112,500.

EXERCISES 27

1   The population of a city was 1,000 in year 1. It increases by 6 percent each year. How much will it be (a) in year 2? (b) in year 3? (c) in year 10? (d) When will it reach 1,500? (e) 1,100? (f) 2,000?

2   A population is 185,000 in year 1. It decreases by 5 percent each year. How much will the population be (a) in year 3? (b) in year 10? (c) in year 13? When will it decline to (e) 100,000? (f) 184,500?

3   A population of a city is 250,000 in year 3 and 300,000 in year 7. (a) How much was it in year 1? (b) What is the yearly percent of increase or decrease? (c) What will be the population in year 12? (d) in year 20? (e) When will it reach 350,000? (f) 500,000? (g) When was it 275,000?

4   The population of a country was 6,000,000 in year 5 and 7,150,000 in year 15. (a) How much was it in year 1? (b) What is the yearly percent of increase or decrease? (c) When will the population reach 8,000,000? (d) 10,000,000? When did it amount to (e) 6,500,000? (f) 7,000,000? (g) What will it be in the year 20? (h) in the year 35?

5   The population of the United States was 123,000,000 in 1930 and 132,000,000 in 1940. (a) Find the yearly percent of increase. Determine approximately the population for (b) 1932; (c) 1936; (d) 1939. Determine the approximate population for (e) 1950; (f) 1965.

6   The population of the United States was 4,000,000 in 1790 and 63,000,000 in 1890. (a) Estimate the yearly percent of increase. (b) Obtain an approximate value for the population in 1900; (c) 1930; (d) 1940.

7   The population of the United States was 76,000,000 in 1900. Estimate the population in 1940 under the assumption of an increase each year of

(a) 10 percent; (b) 5 percent; (c) 2.5 percent; (d) 1 percent; (e) 0.5 percent.

8   The population of the United States was 131,670,000 in 1940. Predict the population in 1960, assuming (a) an increase of 6 percent yearly; (b) 3 percent yearly; (c) 1 percent yearly; (d) a decrease of 2 percent each year.

9   The population of New York City was 79,000 in 1800 and 3,437,000 in 1900. (a) Find the annual percent of increase. Determine a value for the population in (b) 1955; (c) 1960.

10   The population of New York City was 6,930,000 in 1930 and 7,835,000 in 1950. (a) Find the annual percent of increase or decrease. According to the law of Malthus, determine the population for (b) 1960; (c) 2000.

11   The population of the United States has been estimated as 131,940,000 in 1940 and as 133,060,000 in 1941. From these data, and assuming growth that follows a geometric progression, predict the population for 1960.

28   COMPOUND INTEREST

The principle of compound interest is well known. Let i be the interest rate and let P be the principal. As a convenience, let $r = 1 + i$. Then *after* 1 year we have the amount

$$A_1 = P + Pi = Pr;$$

after two years

$$A_2 = A_1 r = Pr^2, \quad \text{and so forth.}$$

After n years

$$A_n = Pr^n.$$

The amounts for $n = 1$, $n = 2$, and so forth, are the terms of a geometric progression.

EXAMPLE

Assume $100 is invested at 5 percent interest. What is the total amount after 5 years? We have $P = 100$, $i = 0.05$, $r = 1 + 0.05 = 1.05$. Hence, $A_5 = (100)(1.05)^5$. Solving by logarithms, $\log A_5 = \log 100 + 5 \log 1.05 = 2.00000 + 5(0.0212) = 2.1060$. Hence A_5 is about $127.60.

EXERCISES 28

1   Find the total amount if $10 is invested at compound interest at 4 percent for (a) 2 years; (b) 10 years; (c) 50 years.

2 Find the total amount if $1,000 is invested at compound interest at 3 percent for (a) 3 years; (b) 10 years; (c) 100 years.

3 A sum of $500 is invested at compound interest. Find the total amount after 5 years at (a) 1 percent; (b) 5 percent; (c) 10 percent; (d) 0 percent.

4 How long will it take $100 at 3 percent, compound interest, to amount to (a) $105? (b) $150? (c) $1,000?

5 What rate of interest will cause $50 invested at compound interest to amount to $75 after (a) 10 years? (b) 25 years? (c) 100 years?

6 A sum of $25,000 has been invested at compound interest. At what rate of interest will this sum accumulate to $30,000 after (a) 2 years? (b) 10 years? (c) 50 years?

7 A sum of $1,000,000 is invested at compound interest. Find the total amount after 10 years at (a) 1 percent; (b) 2.5 percent; (c) 5 percent.

8 A certain amount of money was invested at compound interest at 4 percent. After five years the accumulated amount is $2,356,089. What was the original investment?

9 At a 2 percent rate of interest how long will it take an original amount of $100 to accumulate to (a) $200? (b) $500? (c) $1,000?

10 What is the rate of compound interest that will triple an amount of money in five years?

11 The total public debt of the United States was $257,400,000,000 in 1950. How much will this debt be in 1960, assuming a compound interest rate of (a) 1 percent? (b) 2 percent? (c) 5 percent?

Chapter 6
**Determinants

Let us consider the solution of the following general system of 2 linear equations in 2 unknowns:

$$ax + by = h,$$
$$cx + dy = k,$$

where a, b, c, d, h, and k are constants.

By the usual process of elimination, $x = (hd - kb)/(ad - cb)$ and $y = (ka - hc)/(ad - cb)$.

It is now helpful to consider the following idea: An $m \times n$ matrix $A =$

$$\begin{pmatrix} a_{11} & a_{12} & \cdots & a_{1n} \\ a_{21} & a_{22} & \cdots & a_{2n} \\ \text{---} & \text{---} & & \text{---} \\ a_{m1} & a_{m2} & \cdots & a_{mn} \end{pmatrix}$$

is an array of numbers having m rows and n columns; the number appearing in row i and column j is then a_{ij}. For example, if $A = \begin{pmatrix} 1 & 2 & 3 \\ 4 & 5 & -1 \end{pmatrix}$, $a_{11} = 1$, $a_{23} = -1$, and so on.

Having defined *matrix*, note that the system of equations $\begin{array}{l} ax + by = h \\ cx + dy = k \end{array}$ can be nicely summarized in the 2 × 3 matrix $\begin{pmatrix} a & b & h \\ c & d & k \end{pmatrix}$ in which the first column contains the coefficients of the unknown x, the second consists of the coefficients of the unknown y, and the third consists of the right-hand side of the system.

Finally, we define the determinant $\begin{vmatrix} p & q \\ r & s \end{vmatrix}$ of a 2 × 2 matrix (also called a second-order determinant) to be the number given by $\begin{vmatrix} p & q \\ r & s \end{vmatrix} = ps - rq$.

Note the vertical-bar notation in the representation of the determinant. (Determinants, incidentally, are defined only for square matrices; we will consider determinants of 3 × 3 and large square matrices later.)

With these definitions, it follows that the solution of our system of equations can be written

$$x = \frac{\begin{vmatrix} h & b \\ k & d \end{vmatrix}}{\begin{vmatrix} a & b \\ c & d \end{vmatrix}} \quad \text{and} \quad y = \frac{\begin{vmatrix} a & h \\ c & k \end{vmatrix}}{\begin{vmatrix} a & b \\ c & d \end{vmatrix}}.$$

Note that the elements of the determinant in the denominators comprise the array of coefficients of x and y in the two equations. We get the determinant, which appears in the numerator for x, by substituting for the coefficients of x (a and c) the constants (h and k) on the right side of the equations. For y we substitute the constants h and k for the coefficients of y (b and d) in the determinant of the coefficients.

EXAMPLE

Let us take the example considered previously (Section 16):

$$2x + 6y = 9,$$
$$3x + y = 1.$$

The solutions are

$$x = \frac{\begin{vmatrix} 9 & 6 \\ 1 & 1 \end{vmatrix}}{\begin{vmatrix} 2 & 6 \\ 3 & 1 \end{vmatrix}} = \frac{9 \cdot 1 - 1 \cdot 6}{2 \cdot 1 - 3 \cdot 6} = \frac{9 - 6}{2 - 18} = \frac{3}{-16} = -\frac{3}{16}.$$

$$y = \frac{\begin{vmatrix} 2 & 9 \\ 3 & 1 \end{vmatrix}}{\begin{vmatrix} 2 & 6 \\ 3 & 1 \end{vmatrix}} = \frac{2 \cdot 1 - 3 \cdot 9}{2 \cdot 1 - 3 \cdot 6} = \frac{-25}{-16} = \frac{25}{16}.$$

EXERCISES 29

1   Solve the equations in problem 1, Exercises 16, by determinants.

2   Solve the equations in problem 2, Exercises 16, by determinants.

3   Solve the equations in problem 3, Exercises 16, by determinants.

4   Solve the equations in problem 4, Exercises 16, by determinants.

5   Solve the equations in problem 5, Exercises 16, by determinants.

6   Consider the solution of the system $x + y = 10$ and $2x + 2y = +5$ by determinants. Why is no solution possible?

7   Consider the conditions under which a second-order determinant becomes 0. (HINT: expand $\begin{vmatrix} a & b \\ c & d \end{vmatrix}$.)

**8   State generally the conditions under which a system of two linear equations has no solution. (HINT: use the results of problem 7.)

9   State the conditions under which the solutions of a system of two linear equations in two unknowns are 0.

10   Get the general solution of the following system by determinants.
$$a_1 x + b_1 y = m_1,$$
$$a_2 x + b_2 y = m_2.$$

**11   Consider the system
$$2x + 4y = 0,$$
$$x + 2y = 0.$$

(a) Show that the determinant of the coefficients is 0. (b) Assume that $x = k$ (an arbitrary number). Solve for y and show that there is an infinite number of solutions to the given system.

**12   Consider the system
$$(1 - \lambda)x + 2y = 0,$$
$$3x + y = 0.$$

Determine λ from the condition that the determinant of the coefficients should be 0. Proceed as in problem 11.

**13   Consider the system
$$(2 - \lambda)x + y = 0,$$
$$2x + (3 - \lambda)y = 0.$$

Proceed as in problem 12.

**30   DEVELOPMENT OF DETERMINANTS BY MINORS

The determinant
$$\begin{vmatrix} a_1 & a_2 & a_3 \\ b_1 & b_2 & b_3 \\ c_1 & c_2 & c_3 \end{vmatrix}$$
of a 3 × 3 matrix
$$\begin{pmatrix} a_1 & a_2 & a_3 \\ b_1 & b_2 & b_3 \\ c_1 & c_2 & c_3 \end{pmatrix}$$

can be defined in terms of the already defined 2 × 2 determinant in the following way: First, the *minor* of any element in a third-order determinant is the second-order determinant obtained by striking out the row and columns containing the particular element. Thus, the minor of a_1 is the second-order determinant obtained by striking out the first row and column:

$$\begin{vmatrix} b_2 & b_3 \\ c_2 & c_3 \end{vmatrix}.$$

The minor of b_1 is obtained by striking out the second row and first column:

$$\begin{vmatrix} a_2 & a_3 \\ c_2 & c_3 \end{vmatrix}.$$

The minor of the element c_1 is the second-order determinant obtained by striking out the third row and first column:

$$\begin{vmatrix} a_2 & a_3 \\ b_2 & b_3 \end{vmatrix}.$$

The value of the determinant is then defined to be

$$\begin{vmatrix} a_1 & a_2 & a_3 \\ b_1 & b_2 & b_3 \\ c_1 & c_2 & c_3 \end{vmatrix} = a_1 \begin{vmatrix} b_2 & b_3 \\ c_2 & c_3 \end{vmatrix} - b_1 \begin{vmatrix} a_2 & a_3 \\ c_2 & c_3 \end{vmatrix} + c_1 \begin{vmatrix} a_2 & a_3 \\ b_2 & b_3 \end{vmatrix},$$

and we say the 3 × 3 determinant has been evaluated by *expansion by minors*.

Note the alternating signs in the development. The complete expansion is $a_1(b_2c_3 - c_2b_3) - b_1(a_2c_3 - c_2a_3) + c_1(a_2b_3 - b_2a_3)$.

EXAMPLE

Find the value of

$$\begin{vmatrix} 1 & -4 & 3 \\ 2 & 0 & 1 \\ 0 & 5 & -4 \end{vmatrix}.$$

We expand in terms of the elements of the first column. This gives

$$1 \begin{vmatrix} 0 & 1 \\ 5 & -4 \end{vmatrix} - 2 \begin{vmatrix} -4 & 3 \\ 5 & -4 \end{vmatrix} + 0 \begin{vmatrix} -4 & 3 \\ 0 & 1 \end{vmatrix}.$$

By developing the second-order determinants we get

$$(1)(-5) - (2)(1) + (0)(-4) = -5 - 2 + 0 = -7.$$

EXERCISES 30

1   Expand the following determinants in terms of the elements in the first column and find their values:

(a) $\begin{vmatrix} 1 & 3 & 1 \\ 4 & 6 & 0 \\ 0 & -1 & 7 \end{vmatrix}$;   (b) $\begin{vmatrix} 0 & 1 & -6 \\ 1 & 0 & 8 \\ 4 & -2 & 1 \end{vmatrix}$;   (c) $\begin{vmatrix} 1 & 4 & 8 \\ 3 & 1 & -5 \\ 1 & 0 & 1 \end{vmatrix}$.

2   Find the value of the following determinant:

$$\begin{vmatrix} a & -1 & 0 \\ 0 & 0 & a \\ 1 & a & 0 \end{vmatrix} \cdot$$

3   Expand the following determinant:

$$\begin{vmatrix} x & 2 & -1 \\ 1 & 0 & 6 \\ 5 & -1 & 8 \end{vmatrix} \cdot$$

4   Equate the determinant in problem 3 to 0. Find x. Check by substituting the value of x back into the determinant.

5   Find the value of the determinant

$$\begin{vmatrix} a & 0 & 0 \\ 0 & b & 0 \\ 0 & 0 & c \end{vmatrix} \cdot$$

6   Find the value of the determinant

$$\begin{vmatrix} 5 & -1 & 4 \\ 0 & -2 & 1 \\ 4 & 1 & 0 \end{vmatrix}$$

by developing the minors (a) in terms of the first column; (b) in terms of the second column (HINT: when expanding according to the elements of the second column, the alternating signs start with a negative); according to the third column.

7   Compute the value of the following determinants:

$$\begin{vmatrix} 1 & 3 & 1 \\ 2 & 5 & 4 \\ 6 & 1 & 0 \end{vmatrix} ; \quad \begin{vmatrix} 1 & 2 & 6 \\ 3 & 5 & 1 \\ 1 & 4 & 0 \end{vmatrix} \cdot$$

Note that the rows of the first determinant are the same, respectively, as the columns of the second determinant.

**31   SOLUTIONS OF SYSTEMS OF LINEAR EQUATIONS IN THREE UNKNOWNS BY DETERMINANTS

To solve a system of three linear equations in three unknowns we proceed in a manner analogous to the procedure for two linear equations in two unknowns.

We form first the determinant of the coefficients of the unknowns of the equations; this gives the denominator determinant. Then, to obtain the value for x, for example, we form the numerator determinant by replacing the coefficients of x in the denominator determinant by the constants on the right side of the equations.

To find the value for y we replace the coefficients of y in the same denominator determinant by the column of the constants. This determinant divided by the determinant of the coefficients gives the value of y. In a similar fashion we get the value for z. Usually all third-order determinants are developed by minors.

EXAMPLE

Solve the following system of equations by determinants:

$$x + 2y - z = 0,$$
$$2x + 5y + 2z = 14,$$
$$y - 3z = -7.$$

We form first the determinant of the coefficients of the unknowns in the system; it is

$$\begin{vmatrix} 1 & 2 & -1 \\ 2 & 5 & 2 \\ 0 & 1 & -3 \end{vmatrix}.$$

To find the value of x we replace the column of the coefficients of x (first column) in the above determinant by the column of constants on the right side of the equations. This is divided by the determinant of the coefficients as follows:

$$x = \frac{\begin{vmatrix} 0 & 2 & -1 \\ 14 & 5 & 2 \\ -7 & 1 & -3 \end{vmatrix}}{\begin{vmatrix} 1 & 2 & -1 \\ 2 & 5 & 2 \\ 0 & 1 & -3 \end{vmatrix}}.$$

Both determinants are developed in terms of minors, and there results the value $x = -1$. The value of y is given by

$$y = \frac{\begin{vmatrix} 1 & 0 & -1 \\ 2 & 14 & 2 \\ 0 & -7 & -3 \end{vmatrix}}{\begin{vmatrix} 1 & 2 & -1 \\ 2 & 5 & 2 \\ 0 & 1 & -3 \end{vmatrix}}.$$

Again we develop these determinants in terms of minors. We get $y = 2$. Similarly,

$$z = \frac{\begin{vmatrix} 1 & 2 & 0 \\ 2 & 5 & 14 \\ 0 & 1 & -7 \end{vmatrix}}{\begin{vmatrix} 1 & 2 & -1 \\ 2 & 5 & 2 \\ 0 & 1 & -3 \end{vmatrix}}.$$

We develop this again by the method of minors and get the value $z = 3$.

The three values, constituting the desired solution of the system, ought to be checked by substituting into the system of the original linear equations.

EXERCISES 31

1 Consider the following system of linear equations:

$$x - 2y = 6,$$
$$y - z = 5,$$
$$x + y - z = 0.$$

(a) Solve by the use of determinants. (b) Check by substituting back into the equations.

2 Solve the system of equations in problem 8, Exercises 16, by determinants. Check.

3 Solve the system of equations in problem 9, Exercises 16, by determinants. Check.

4 Consider the following system of equations:

$$x + y = 2,$$
$$y + z = 2,$$
$$x + z = 2.$$

Solve by determinants. Check.

5 Solve the following system of equations by determinants:

$$-x + 2y + z = 2,$$
$$x - y + 3z = 16,$$
$$2x + 2y = -11.$$

Check.

6 Solve by determinants the general system of three equations in three unknowns, namely,

$$a_1x + a_2y + a_3z = k_1,$$
$$b_1x + b_2y + b_3z = k_2,$$
$$c_1x + c_2y + c_3z = k_3.$$

7 Show that the value of a second-order determinant is not altered if rows are exchanged, respectively, for columns. Prove for the general second-order determinant.

8 Show that the value of a second-order determinant is 0 if two rows or two columns are equal. Prove for the general second-order determinant.

**32   COMPUTATION OF DETERMINANTS BY THE CROUT METHOD

The computation of determinants by the method just described is lengthy if the determinant is of a high order. Hence, we indicate here with the help of an example a quicker way of computing determinants.

EXAMPLE 1

Suppose we have the square matrix

$$A = \begin{bmatrix} 1 & 0 & 0 \\ 1 & 2 & 1 \\ 1 & 1 & 1 \end{bmatrix}$$

and we desire to compute the determinant

$$A = \begin{vmatrix} 1 & 0 & 0 \\ 1 & 2 & 1 \\ 1 & 1 & 1 \end{vmatrix}.$$

The Crout method, which we have illustrated repeatedly, leads to the following table:

I			
$\underline{1}$	0	0	0
1	$\underline{2}$	1	4
1	1	1	3

II			
$\underline{1}$	0	0	1
1	2	½	3½
1	1	$\underline{½}$	1

In part I we write the matrix whose determinant we want to compute. The last column in part I is used for a check:

$$1 + 0 + 0 = 1,$$
$$1 + 2 + 1 = 4,$$
$$1 + 1 + 1 = 3.$$

Part II of the table is computed by the following method: The first column of Part I is simply copied. The elements of the first line right from the diagonal element (1, underlined) are the corresponding elements in part I divided by its diagonal element:

$$\frac{0}{1} = 0; \qquad \frac{0}{1} = 0; \qquad \frac{1}{1} = 1.$$

The check is again:

$$0 + 0 = 0; \qquad 0 + 1 = 1.$$

The diagonal element in line 2, part II, of the table is the corresponding element in part I (2) minus the product of the symmetrically located elements in part II, already computed:

$$2 - (1)(0) = 2.$$

The other element in column 2 of part II is similarly computed:

$$1 - (1)(0) = 1.$$

The elements in line 2, part II, are computed in a similar way, except that the result is also divided by the diagonal element (2, underlined):

$$\frac{1 - (1)(0)}{2} = \frac{1}{2},$$

$$\frac{4 - (1)(1)}{2} = \frac{3}{2}.$$

For a check we have

$$\frac{1}{2} + 1 = \frac{3}{2}.$$

The diagonal element in line 2, part II, is computed similarly. From the corresponding diagonal element in part I (1) we subtract the symmetrically situated products of the elements in part II already computed:

$$1 - (1)(0) - (1)(\tfrac{1}{2}) = \tfrac{1}{2}.$$

Also, we compute the remaining element in line 3 of parts II as follows:

$$\frac{3 - (1)(1) - (1)(3/2)}{1/2} = 1.$$

For a check we have again

$$0 + 1 = 1.$$

The determinant A is simply the product of the (underlined) diagonal elements in part II:

$$A = (1)(2)(\tfrac{1}{2}) = 1.$$

EXAMPLE 2

We shall compute the value of the determinant of the coefficients of the linear system of equations in Section 19, Example 1. We multiply again the (underlined) diagonal elements in part II of the table in Section 19:

$$\begin{vmatrix} 2 & -2 & 3 & 2 \\ 4 & 1 & 2 & -1 \\ 3 & 2 & 1 & 3 \\ 1 & 1 & 4 & 1 \end{vmatrix} = (2)(5)(0.5)(-39) = -195.$$

EXERCISES 32

1 Find the values of the determinants of the matrices in Exercises 30, problem 1.

2 Find by the Crout method the values of the following determinants:

$$\text{(a)} \begin{vmatrix} 1 & 0 & 0 \\ 0 & 5 & 2 \\ 0 & 0 & -4 \end{vmatrix} \quad \text{(b)} \begin{vmatrix} 3 & 1 & 1 \\ 1 & 2 & -1 \\ 0 & 1 & 1 \end{vmatrix} \quad \text{(c)} \begin{vmatrix} 5 & -1 & -1 & 1 \\ 0 & 2 & 1 & 1 \\ 0 & -1 & 2 & 1 \\ 0 & 0 & 1 & -2 \end{vmatrix}.$$

Chapter 7

Inequalities, Linear Programming, Input-Output Analysis

We will assume that we all know, intuitively, the meaning of the word "positive" in the sense that we can tell the difference between positive numbers and real numbers that are not positive. For short, if a is a positive number, we write $a > 0$, while if a is negative, we write $a < 0$.

Given that, we will say that a is greater than b, written $a > b$, if and only if $a - b > 0$. Thus, $3 > 2$ because $3 - 2 = 1$ is a positive number; similarly, $-2 > -3$ because $-2 - (-3) = 1$ is positive.

Correspondingly, a is less than b, written $a < b$, if $a - b$ is negative $(a - b < 0)$.

The following properties of inequalities can be established:

1. If $a > b$, then $a + c > b + c$ for any number c: $a + c - (b + c) = a - b + c - c = a - b > 0$ by the definition of $a > b$.

2. Since the product of two positive numbers is positive, if $a > b$ and $c > 0$, $ac > bc$: $ac - bc = c(a - b) > 0$ because $a - b > 0$ if $a > b$ and $c > 0$.

3. If $a > b$ and $b > c$, then $a > c$: $a - c = a - b + b - c = (a - b) + (b - c) > 0 + 0 = 0$.

4. If $a > b$ and $c < 0$, $ac < bc$.

One final notational convention: we write $a \geqq b$ if either $a > b$ or $a = b$. For example, $3 \geqq 2$ and $2 \geqq 2$ are both true statements. $3 \geqq 2$ holds because $3 > 2$, and $2 \geqq 2$ is correct because $2 = 2$.

We can use all this to solve inequalities in one variable, as indicated by the following examples.

EXAMPLE 1

For what x does $-3x \geqq 2$ hold? We can answer this by multiplying both sides of this inequality by $-\frac{1}{3}$, since $(-3)(-\frac{1}{3}) = 1$.

This will "reverse" the direction of the inequality, as in (4) above: $(-\frac{1}{3})(-3)x \leq (-\frac{1}{3})(2)$, or $x \leq -\frac{2}{3}$, which is the desired solution.

EXAMPLE 2

For what x is $-2x \geq -4x + 2$ true? Adding $4x$ to both sides of the inequality, we have $-2x + 4x \geq 2$, or $2x \geq 2$, or $\frac{1}{2}(2x) \geq \frac{1}{2}(2)$, giving $x \geq 1$ as the solution.

EXAMPLE 3

For what x is $3x - 2 \leq 1$ and $2x - 1 \geq 0$ valid? There may be no x satisfying both inequalities simultaneously, but if there is such an x, then $3x \leq 3$ or $x \leq 1$ and $2x \geq 1$ or $x \geq \frac{1}{2}$. Hence all x such that $\frac{1}{2} \leq x \leq 1$ satisfy the system.

EXAMPLE 4

For what x is $2x \leq -3$ and $2x + 1 \geq 1$ valid? Any x satisfying these inequalities would need to satisfy $x \leq -\frac{3}{2}$ and $2x \geq 0$, or $x \leq -\frac{3}{2}$ and $x \geq 0$. Clearly, there is no such x, and the given system has no solution.

Of more interest are inequalities in two variables, of the form $ax + by \geq c$. At the outset note that the equation $ax + by = c$ is a line dividing the plane into two "half spaces." On one side of the line are all points (x, y) such that $ax + by > c$, while on the other are all points such that $ax + by < c$. For example, consider the line $2x + 3y = 6$ (Figure 14). Above the line are all

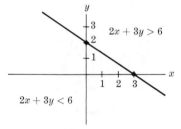

Figure 14

points (x, y) such that $2x + 3y > 6$ while all (x, y) such that $2x + y < 6$ lie below the line.

With any line $ax + by = c$ it is easy to decide which half space consists of those (x, y) such that $ax + by > c$ and which consists of those (x, y) such that $ax + by > c$: choose any point (x', y') *not* on the line. It lies in one or the other of the two half spaces. If $ax' + by' > c$, the half space containing (x', y') is that described by $ax + by > c$; similarly, if $ax' + by' < c$, the half space containing (x', y') is that given by $ax + by < c$.

EXAMPLE 5

Indicate on a graph those points (x, y) such that $3x + y < 4$. First, graph the line $3x + y = 4$: choose any point not on the line, such as $(3, 3)$ (Figure 15), $3(3) + 3 = 9 + 3 = 12 > 4$.

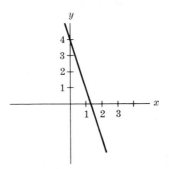

Figure 15

But since $(3, 3)$ lies in the half space $3x + y > 4$, we want the half space *not* containing $(3, 3)$ (Figure 15A).

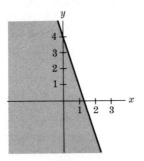

Figure 15A

We may similarly find the solutions to systems of inequalities in two variables.

EXAMPLE 6

Indicate on a diagram all (x, y), if any, that satisfy $3x + y \geqq 2$ and $x + y \leqq 1$.

We can graph both inequalities, and we do so, separately (Figures 16 and 16A).

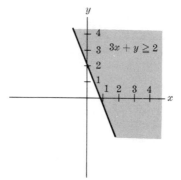

Figure 16

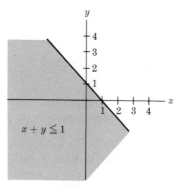

Figure 16A

Graphing both together, we have

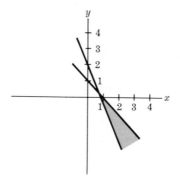

Figure 16B

Since both inequalities are $\geqq$, the lines are included in the solutions.

EXERCISES 33

Solve the inequalities or systems of inequalities in one variable. Diagram the points satisfying the given systems in two variables. If a given system has no solution, produce an example to show that it does not.

1 $2x - 3 \geq 3x + 2$.

2 $2x - 1 \leq 3x + 1$ together with $x + 2 \geq -6$.

3 $3x - 2y \geq 12$.

4 $-x + y \geq 0, x \geq 2$.

5 $y < x, x + y < 1$.

6 $2x + 3y \leq 6, 3x - 2y > 12$.

7 $3x + y \leq 2, x + y \geq 1, x \geq 0, y \geq 0$.

8 $y - x \geq 1, 2x + y \leq 1, x \geq 0, y \geq 0$.

34   LINEAR PROGRAMMING: GRAPHIC SOLUTION

A linear program is the maximization or minimization of a linear function on a set defined by a system of linear inequalities that frequently, but not necessarily, require the variables to be nonnegative. Thus, the problem maximize $3x + 2y$ subject to

$2x + 3y \leq 6$.
$x + 2y \leq 3, x \geq 0, y \geq 0$,   is a linear program in two variables.

Such two-dimensional linear programs can be solved by graphing, using the following information.

It can be shown that a linear function (of the form $ax + by$) defined on a set determined by a system of linear inequalities will achieve both its maximum and its minimum (if, indeed, it *has* both a maximum and a minimum) at a "corner point" of the set. These corner points can be found by noting which of the lines bounding the set intersect to form the corner point in question, then solving simultaneously the equations of the lines. Evaluating the function to be maximized (or minimized) at each such corner point will then, sooner or later, yield the maximum or minimum.

EXAMPLE 1

Maximize $3x + 2y$ subject to

$$2x + 3y \leq 6,$$
$$2x + y \leq 3,$$
$$x \geq 0, y \geq 0.$$

To solve this linear program we first graph the inequalities defining the constraints (Figure 17). The shaded region in the figure gives the desired solution set. Next, we note the corner points, which are circled. There are four corner points, and three

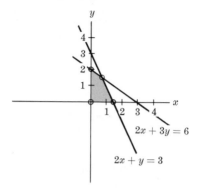

Figure 17

are apparent: one is at $(0, 0)$, another is at $(0, 2)$, and a third is at $(\frac{3}{2}, 0)$. The fourth is at the intersection of the lines

$$2x + 3y = 6,$$
$$2x + y = 3.$$

The solution is $x = \frac{3}{4}$, $y = \frac{3}{2}$, as one can easily verify.

Finally, we evaluate the function to be maximized, $3x + 2y$, at each of the four corner points: we get 0 at $(0, 0)$, 4 at $(0, 2)$, $\frac{9}{2}$ at $(\frac{3}{2}, 0)$, and $2\frac{1}{4}$ at $(\frac{3}{4}, \frac{3}{2})$. The largest of these, $2\frac{1}{4}$, is the desired answer.

Not all linear programs have solutions. The set defined by the inequalities can be empty, or the set can be unbounded, so that the function to be maximized or minimized might fail to have a maximum or minimum.

EXAMPLE 2

Minimize $3x + 2y$ subject to

$$x + y \leqq 1,$$
$$\tfrac{1}{2}y - x \leqq 1,$$
$$x \geqq 0,$$
$$y \geqq 0.$$

The graph of the constraint set is as given in Figure 18. It is clear that no point (x, y) satisfies all four inequalities. Hence this linear program has no solution.

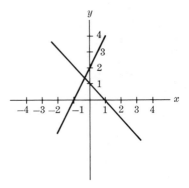

Figure 18

EXAMPLE 3

Maximize $3x + 2y$ subject to

$$y \leq 1,$$
$$y - x \leq 0,$$
$$x \geq 0,$$
$$y \geq 0.$$

The set of points (x, y) satisfying the constraints is the hatched region in Figure 19. One can make $3x + 2y$ as large as desired

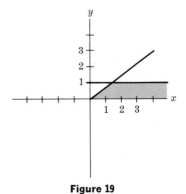

Figure 19

by making x as large as desired, since one may choose x arbitrarily large without violating the constraints so long as $0 \leq y \leq 1$. Thus, here is another linear program with no solution.

EXERCISES 34

1   Maximize $2x_1 + 3x_2$ subject to

$$x_1 + x_2 \leq 5,$$
$$2x_1 + x_2 \leq 6,$$
$$x_1 \geq 0, x_2 \geq 0.$$

2 Maximize $x_1 + x_2$ subject to

$$2x_1 + 3x_2 \leq 6,$$
$$x_1 \leq 2, \ x_2 \leq 1,$$
$$x_1 \geq 0, \ x_2 \geq 0.$$

3 Minimize $x_1 - 2x_2$ subject to

$$x_1 + x_2 \leq 1,$$
$$-x + x_2 \leq 1,$$
$$x \geq 0, \ x_2 \geq 0.$$

Discuss the constraints set.

4 Minimize $x + y$ subject to

$$y \leq 1,$$
$$y + x \leq 2,$$
$$y \leq x,$$
$$x \geq 0,$$
$$y \geq 0.$$

5 Maximize $x + y$ subject to the constraints in problem 4.

35 LINEAR PROGRAMMING: GENERAL

From a mathematical viewpoint linear programming solves the following problem: Given a number of unknowns that are subject to linear inequalities, find the nonnegative values of the unknowns that maximize (or minimize) a linear function of the unknowns (objective function).

Given the objective function

$$Z = c_1x_1 + c_2x_2 + \cdots + c_nx_n, \tag{1}$$

where the c_i are the known constants and the x_i the unknowns (activities), find its maximum under the following conditions (inequalities):

$$a_{11}x_1 + a_{12}x_2 + \cdots + a_{1n}x_n \leq b_1,$$
$$a_{21}x_1 + a_{22}x_2 + \cdots + a_{2n}x_n \leq b_2,$$
$$\cdots$$
$$a_{m1}x_1 + a_{m2}x_2 + \cdots + a_{mn}x_n \leq b_m. \tag{2}$$

In these inequalities the a_{ij} and b_j are known constants. The solutions x_i cannot become negative:

$$x_1 \geq 0, \quad x_2 \geq 0, \quad \cdots, x_n \geq 0. \tag{3}$$

It ought to be pointed out, at least parenthetically, that a linear program can have its constraints stated as equations or inequalities in either direction or as a mixture of these; however, it is always possible to convert a maximization problem to the above form, so we consider only this formulation.

In order to find a solution we first transform the inequalities (2) into equalities by introducing the slack variables $y_1, y_2, \cdots, y_m$, which are also nonnegative. Now the problem is: Maximize the objective function (1) under the following conditions:

$$a_{11}x_1 + a_{12}x_2 + \cdots + a_{1n}x_n + y_1 = b_1,$$
$$a_{21}x_1 + a_{22}x_2 + \cdots + a_{2n}x_n + y_2 = b_2, \qquad (4)$$
$$\cdots$$
$$a_{m1}x + a_{m2}x_2 + \cdots + a_{mn}x_n + y_m = b_m.$$

Now we have $m + n$ inequalities:

$$x_1 \geq 0, \quad x_2 \geq 0, \quad \cdots, \quad x_n \geq 0, \quad y_1 \geq 0, \quad y_2 \geq 0,$$
$$\cdots, \quad y_m \geq 0. \quad (5)$$

We simplify our notation by defining

$$x_1 = z_1, \quad x_2 = z_2, \quad \cdots, \quad x_n = z_n, \quad y_1 = z_{n+1}, \quad y_2 = z_{n+2},$$
$$\cdots, \quad y_m = z_{n+m}. \quad (6)$$

Now our problem is in the new notation. Maximize the objective function

$$z = c_1z_1 + c_2z_2 + \cdots + c_nz_n + 0 \cdot z_{n+1} + 0 \cdot z_{n+2} + \cdots + 0 \cdot z_{n+m} \quad (7)$$

under the conditions

$$a_{11}z_1 + a_{12}z_2 + \cdots + a_{1n}z_n + z_{n+1} = b_1,$$
$$a_{21}z_1 + a_{22}z_2 + \cdots + a_{2n}z_n + z_{n+2} = b_2, \qquad (8)$$
$$\cdots$$
$$a_{m1}z_1 + a_{m2}z_2 + \cdots a_{mn}z_n + z_{n+m} = b_m$$

and also under the nonnegativity conditions:

$$z_1 \geq 0, \quad z_2 \geq 0, \quad \cdots, \quad z_n \geq 0, \quad z_{n+1} \geq 0, \quad z_{n+2} \geq 0,$$
$$\cdots, \quad z_{n+m} \geq 0.$$

The system (8) is a system of m linear equations in $m + n$ unknowns. If we put n of these unknowns equal to zero, we can (in general) solve the system for the remaining m unknowns, or establish that the system in question has no solution. This is called the method of selections.

We have altogether

$$_{m+n}C_n = \frac{(n + m)(n + m - 1) \cdots (n + 1)}{1 \cdot 2 \cdots m}$$

selections (bases). A selection is called feasible if the selected variables are not negative.

We can show that the maximum of the objective function is obtained for solutions to one of the selections. However, this method is not practical for actual calculations. We shall later present the simplex method, which is more adapted for calculations.

EXAMPLE: THE METHOD OF SELECTIONS

Let us consider the problem of a firm in the short run. Here the amounts of certain factors of production are fixed; the firm can employ not more but certainly less than the available quantity of a factor.

Let the number of activities be two ($n = 2$); that is, the unknown quantities of two commodities to be produced, x_1 and x_2.

Let the constant cost of the first commodity be 2 and of the second 3. Let the price of the first commodity be 3 and of the second 5. Then we have $c_1 = 3 - 2 = 1$, $c_2 = 5 - 3 = 2$, so that the profit z is given by $z = x_1 + 2x_2$.

This objective function should be maximized under certain conditions, which represent the conditions of production in the short run.

We assume that there are two factors of production utilized ($m = 2$). In the short run the quantity of these factors is given and is $b_1 = 4$ and $b_2 = 3$.

Now we assume constant coefficients of production. Assume that $a_{11} = 1$; that is, it takes one unit of the first factor to produce one unit of commodity one. The total number of units of the first factor utilized for the production of the first commodity is then x_1. Also, let $a_{12} = 1$; that is, it takes one unit of the first factor to produce one unit of the second commodity. Hence the amount of the first factor utilized for producing the second commodity is x_2. The sum $x_1 + x_2$ cannot be greater than 4, the total amount of the first factor available in the short run.

Now assume that it takes two units of the second factor to produce one unit of the first commodity ($a_{21} = 2$). Hence the total amount of the second factor utilized in producing the first commodity is $2x_1$. Assume, further, that one unit of the second factor is necessary in order to produce one unit of the second commodity ($a_{22} = 1$). Hence the amount of the second factor utilized in producing the second commodity is x_2. The sum $2x_1 + x_2$ cannot be greater than 3, the amount of the second factor available in the short run. Hence our conditions of production are:

$$x_1 + x_2 \leq 4,$$
$$2x_1 + x_2 \leq 3.$$

Further, it is not possible to produce negative amounts of any commodity:

$$x_1 \geq 0, \qquad x_2 \geq 0.$$

As before, we convert the inequalities into equalities. We introduce the following slack variables: y_1, the amount of the first factor that is not used, and y_2, the amount of the second factor that is not used. These slack variables can also not be negative. The problem is now to maximize

$$z = x_1 + 2x_2$$

under the conditions

$$x_1 + x_2 + y_1 = 4,$$
$$2x_1 + x_2 + y_2 = 3.$$

The first equation has the following meaning: The sum of the amount of the first factor used by the first commodity (x_1) plus the amount of the same factor used by the second commodity (x_2) plus the amount left over (y_1) equals the total quantity of the first factor available (4). The second equation means: The amount of the second factor used by the first commodity ($2x_1$) plus the amount of the same factor used by the second commodity (x_2) plus the amount of the second factor not utilized (y_2) equals the total amount available (3).

Also, we have the nonnegativity conditions:

$$x_1 \geq 0, \qquad x_2 \geq 0, \qquad y_1 \geq 0, \qquad y_2 \geq 0.$$

The amounts of the two commodities produced (x_1, x_2) and also the quantities of the two factors left over (y_1, y_2) cannot become negative.

Now we change our notation as follows: $x_1 = z_1$, $x_2 = z_2$, $y_1 = z_3$, $y_2 = z_4$. Our problem is in the new notation. Maximize

$$z = z_1 + 2z_2$$

under the conditions

$$z_1 + z_2 + z_3 = 4,$$
$$2z_1 + z_2 + z_4 = 3,$$
$$z_1 \geq 0, \qquad z_2 \geq 0, \qquad z_3 \geq 0, \qquad z_4 \geq 0.$$

We use the method of selection. Since $m + n = 4$, $m = 2$, we have

$$_4C_2 = \frac{4 \cdot 3}{1 \cdot 2} = 6$$

possible selections.

In each selection we choose $m = 2$ variables, putting the others equal to zero. We denote a given selection by an upper index $^{(k)}$, the objective function as $z^{(k)}$.

For $k = 1$ we choose z_1 and z_2; that is, put $z_3 = z_4 = 0$. Economically this means that each factor of production is completely utilized ($z_3 = y_1 = 0$; $z_4 = y_2 = 0$). Now we have from our system of equations

$$z_1^{(1)} + z_2^{(1)} = 4,$$
$$2z_1^{(1)} + z_2^{(1)} = 3.$$

But this gives the solutions $z_1^{(1)} = -1$ and $z_2^{(1)} = 5$. Since $z_1^{(1)}$ (or x_1) is negative, this solution is not feasible. It is not possible to produce a negative amount of the first commodity.

The second selection, $k = 2$, consists of z_1 and z_3. Also $z_2 = z_4 = 0$. We assume here that the second commodity is not produced ($z_2 = x_2 = 0$) and also that the second factor is completely utilized ($z_4 = y_2 = 0$).

Solving our system of equations, we have:

$$z_1^{(2)} + z_3^{(2)} = 4,$$
$$2z_1^{(2)} = 3.$$

Hence $z_1^{(2)} = 1.5$, $z_3^{(2)} = 2.5$. Both solutions are positive and hence the selection is feasible. We can produce to use 1.5 units of the first commodity and leave 2.5 units of the first factor unused. The objective function becomes

$$z^{(2)} = z_1^{(2)} + 2z_2^{(2)} = 1.5.$$

For $k = 3$ we select z_1 and z_4. We put $z_2 = z_3 = 0$. This means that the second commodity is not produced and the first factor of production is completely utilized. The system of equations is

$$z_1^{(3)} = 4,$$
$$2z_1^{(3)} + z_4^{(3)} = 3.$$

Since $z_1^{(3)} = 4$, $z_4^{(3)} = -5$, this selection is not feasible. It is impossible to leave -5 units of the second factor unused.

For $k = 4$ we have as selection z_2 and z_3. We put $z_1 = z_4 = 0$. The first commodity is not produced and the second factor is completely utilized. Our equations are

$$z_2^{(4)} + z_3^{(4)} = 4,$$
$$z_2^{(4)} = 3.$$

The solutions are $z_2^{(4)} = 3$ and $z_3^{(4)} = 1$. This is a possible solution since none of the values are negative. It tells us to produce 3 units of the second commodity and to leave 1 unit of the first factor unused. The objective function is now

$$z^{(4)} = z_1^{(4)} + 2z_2^{(4)} = 6.$$

The next selection, $k = 5$, uses z_2, and z_4. We put $z_1 = z_3 = 0$. This means that the first commodity is not produced and the first factor of production is fully utilized. We have

$$z_2^{(5)} = 4,$$
$$z_2^{(5)} + z_4^{(5)} = 3.$$

Hence $z_2^{(5)} = 4$ and $z_4^{(5)} = -1$. This selection is not feasible. It is impossible to leave -1 unit of the second factor unused.

The last selection, $k = 6$, uses the base z_3 and z_4. Hence $z_1 = z_2 = 0$; nothing is produced at all ($x_1 = x_2 = 0$). We have

$$z_3^{(6)} = 4,$$
$$z_4^{(6)} = 3.$$

This means that the amount available of the first factor ($y_1 = 4$) and the amount available of the second factor ($y_2 = 3$) are both unutilized. The solution is feasible, but the objective function $z^{(6)} = 0$.

Finally, we have to find the maximum objective function among the feasible selections. We have

$$z^{(2)} = 1.5, \qquad z^{(4)} = 6, \qquad z^{(6)} = 0.$$

Hence it is best to choose $z^{(4)} = 6$. This implies the situation described above under the fourth selection: Produce 0 units of the first commodity and 3 units of the second commodity. Leave 1 unit of the first factor unutilized and use all of the second factor. The resulting net profit is then 6.

The dual

Given the maximization problem, maximize

$$c_1 x_1 + \cdots + c_m x_m$$

subject to

$$a_{11} x_1 + a_{21} x_2 + \cdots + a_{m1} x_m \leqq b_1,$$
$$a_{12} x_1 + a_{22} x_2 + \cdots + a_{m2} x_m \leqq b_2,$$
$$\cdots$$
$$a_{1n} x_1 + a_{2n} x_2 + \cdots + a_{mn} x_m \leqq b_n,$$
$$x_1 \geqq 0, \qquad x_2 \geqq 0, \qquad \cdots, \qquad x_m \geqq 0.$$

We define the dual linear program to be: Minimize $b_1 y_1 + b_2 y_2 + \cdots + b_n y_n$ subject to

$$a_{11} y_1 + a_{12} y_2 + \cdots + a_{1n} y_n \geqq c_1,$$
$$a_{21} y_1 + a_{22} y_2 + \cdots + a_{2n} y_n \geqq c_2,$$
$$\cdots$$
$$a_{m1} y_1 + a_{m2} y_2 + \cdots + a_{mn} y_n \geqq c_m,$$
$$y_1 \geqq 0, \qquad y_2 \geqq 0, \qquad \cdots, \qquad y_m \geqq 0.$$

EXAMPLE

Find the dual of maximize

$$2x_1 + 3x_2 + x_3$$

subject to

$$x_1 + 2x_2 + x_3 \leqq 5,$$
$$2x_1 + x_2 - 3x_3 \leqq 7,$$
$$x_1 \geqq 0, \quad x_2 \geqq 0, \quad x_3 \geqq 0.$$

The dual will have two variables, say y_1 and y_2, and three constraints, plus, of course, the nonnegativity conditions. Minimize

$$5y_1 + 7y_2$$

subject to

$$y_1 + 2y_2 \geqq 2,$$
$$2y_1 + y_2 \geqq 3,$$
$$y_1 - 3y_2 \geqq 1,$$
$$y_1 \geqq 0, \quad y_2 \geqq 0.$$

The very well-known *duality theorem* states that if a maximization problem and its dual have, respectively, numbers x_1, x_2, $\cdots$, x_m and y_1, y_2, $\cdots$, y_n that satisfy the constraints (including the nonnegativity conditions), then both problems have optimal solutions $\bar{x}_1$, $\bar{x}_2$, $\cdots$, $\bar{x}_m$ and $\bar{y}_1$, $\bar{y}_2$, $\cdots$, $\bar{y}_n$, respectively. Moreover, $c_1\bar{x}_1 + c_2\bar{x}_2 + \cdots + c_m\bar{x}_m = b_1\bar{y}_1 + b_2\bar{y}_2 + \cdots + b_n\bar{y}_n$.

In addition, it is easy to show that if x_1, x_2, $\ldots$, x_m and y_1, y_2, $\cdots$, y_n are any numbers satisfying the constraints of the respective problem, then $c_1x_1 + c_2x_2 + \cdots + c_mx_m \leqq b_1y_1 + b_2y_2 + \cdots + b_ny_n$ and that $\bar{x}_1$, $\bar{x}_2$, $\ldots$, $\bar{x}_m$ and $\bar{y}_1$, $\bar{y}_2$, $\cdots$, $\bar{y}_n$ are optimal solutions for the respective problems if and only if $\bar{x}_i = 0$ for all i such that

$$a_{i1}\bar{y}_1 + a_{i2}\bar{y}_2 + \cdots + a_{in}\bar{y}_n > c$$

and $\bar{y}_j = 0$ for all j such that

$$a_{1j}\bar{x}_1 + a_{2j}\bar{x}_2 + \cdots + a_{mj}\bar{x}_m < b_j.$$

EXERCISES 35

1 Solve the following linear programming problem: Maximize the objective function $z = 2x_1 + 3x_2$ under the conditions

$$x_1 + x_2 \leq 10,$$
$$3x_1 - 4x_2 \leq 24,$$
$$x_1 \geq 0, \quad x_2 \geq 0.$$

2 Solve the linear programming problem: Maximize the objective function $z = x_1 + x_2 + x_3$ under the condition

$$x_1 + 2x_2 + 4x_3 \leq 16,$$
$$x_1 \geq 0, \qquad x_2 \geq 0, \qquad x_3 \geq 0.$$

3 The following data are taken from farms in Hancock county, Ellswood township, Iowa, for the period 1928–1952. There are two activities, growing corn (x_1) and growing flax (x_2). The price of corn is 1.56 and the price of flax is 3.81. Assume there are no restrictions of capital or labor. The input coefficient of land is 0.023 for corn and 0.092 for flax. Find the activities that yield maximum profit if the total land available is 148.

4 Assume the same data as in problem 3. There are no restrictions on land and labor, but the input coefficient of capital in corn production is 0.318 and in flax production 0.970. The available capital is 1800. Again find the activities that give maximum profit.

5 Combine the data in problems 3 and 4 and find the activities that maximize profit.

**6 *Dual of linear programming.* Consider our example. We introduce shadow prices u_1 and u_2 for the two factors of production. Note that these are bookkeeping and not market prices. The entrepreneur will *minimize* the imputed cost, $z^* = 4u_1 + 3u_2$, since he has 4 units of the first factor and 3 units of the second. Since each activity must yield at least as much as the price (in the objective function), the conditions are $u_1 + 2u_2 \geq 1$ and $u_1 + u_2 \geq 2$. Also, since the shadow proces cannot be negative, $u_1 \geq 0$ and $u_2 \geq 0$. Introduce slack variables v_1 and v_2. The problem becomes: Minimize $z^* = 4u_1 + 3u_2 + 0v_1 + 0v_2$ under the conditions

$$u_1 + 2u_2 - v_1 = 1, \qquad u_1 + u_2 - v_2 = 2; \qquad u_1 \geq 0,$$
$$u_2 \geq 0, \qquad v_1 \geq 0, \qquad v_2 \geq 0.$$

Define the new variables: $u_1 = w_1$, $u_2 = w_2$, $v_1 = w_3$, $v_2 = w_4$. (a) State the minimum problem in terms of the new variables. (b) Solve with the method of selection. (c) Show that maximum $z =$ minimum z^* and interpret this result. (d) Interpret zero shadow prices. (Note the solution of the example.)

36   THE SIMPLEX METHOD

The method of selections is not practical for large linear programming problems. If n and m are even somewhat large numbers, the number of selections, $n + mCn$, becomes exceedingly large.

A method that quickly leads to the optimal solution is the simplex method. We will illustrate it with the help of the above simple example.

We state it immediately in its final form. Maximize

$$z = c_1 z_1 + c_2 z_2 + c_3 z_3 + c_4 z_4 = z_1 + 2z_2 + 0 \cdot z_3 + 0 \cdot z_4$$

under the conditions

$$z_1 + z_2 + z_3 = 4,$$
$$2z_1 + z_2 + z_4 = 3.$$

We note for later reference the coefficients of the objective function (Table 1) and also the coefficients of the equations (Table 2).

Table 1

Variable	z_1	z_2	z_3	z_4
c_i	1	2	0	0

Table 2

Variable	z_1	z_2	z_3	z_4
First equation	1	1	1	0
Second equation	2	1	0	1

Now we construct the simplex Table 3 by a method to be explained below.

Table 3

		I			
	z_i	z_1	z_2	z_3	z_4
	c_i	1	2	0	0
$z_3 = 4,$ $c_3 = 0$		1	1	1	0
$z_4 = 3,$ $c_4 = 0$		2	1*	0	1
g_i		0	0	0	0
$c_i - g_i$		1	2*	0	0
		II			
$z_2 = 3,$ $c_2 = 2$		2	1	0	1
$z_3 = 1,$ $c_3 = 0$		−1	0	1	−1
g_i		4	2	0	2
$z_i - g_i$		−3	0	0	−2

We write on top of the simplex Table 3 the variables z_i and the corresponding coefficients of the objective function from Table 1.

In the simplex we have to start from a feasible selection. Certainly since z_3 and z_4 are slack variables, we can use them as selection variables and the result will be feasible. We have from the equations

$$1 \cdot z_3 + 0 \cdot z_4 = 4,$$
$$0 \cdot z_3 + 1 \cdot z_4 = 3.$$

This gives $z_3 = 4$ and $z_4 = 3$. We write this result in the part I of the simplex table. We also note for further use the corresponding coefficients in the objective function, $c_3 = 0$, $c_4 = 0$. Now the simplex method leads us to another feasible selection with different selection variables, which will improve the value of the objective function, which now is $z = 0 \cdot z_3 + 0 \cdot z_4 = 0$. To do this we proceed as follows: We express all variables, z_1, z_2, z_3, z_4, in terms of the variables z_3 and z_4. In order to do this we use the coefficients in Table 2. For z_1 we have the system of equations

$$1 \cdot a_3{}^1 + 0 \cdot a_4{}^1 = 1,$$
$$0 \cdot a_3{}^1 + 1 \cdot a_4{}^1 = 2,$$

where the coefficients of the equations correspond to the selection variables z_3 and z_4 and the right-hand side of the equation to z_1. The solution is $a_3{}^1 = 1$, $a_4{}^1 = 2$, and it is written under z_1 in part I of Table 3.

Next we express z_2 in terms of the selection variables z_3 and z_4. We have the system of equations

$$1 \cdot b_3{}^1 + 0 \cdot b_4{}^1 = 1,$$
$$0 \cdot b_3{}^1 + 1 \cdot b_4{}^1 = 1.$$

The coefficients of these equations are the same as before. The right-hand side is taken from the data under z_2 in Table 2. The solutions, $b_3{}^1 = 1$, $b_4{}^1 = 1$, are written under z_2 in part I of Table 3.

Also we express z_3 in terms of z_3 and z_4. The equations are

$$1 \cdot c_3{}^1 + 0 \cdot c_4{}^1 = 1,$$
$$0 \cdot c_3{}^1 + 1 \cdot c_4{}^1 = 0,$$

where the right-hand side is again taken from Table 2 under z_3. The solutions, $c_3{}^1 = 1$, $c_4{}^1 = 0$, is written under z_3 in part I of Table 3.

Finally, we express z_4 in terms of our selection variables z_3 and z_4. Our equations are

$$1 \cdot d_3{}^1 + 0 \cdot d_4{}^1 = 0,$$
$$0 \cdot d_3{}^1 + 1 \cdot d_4{}^1 = 1.$$

The solutions, $d_3{}^1 = 0$, $d_4{}^1 = 1$, are again written under z_4 in part I of Table 3.

Now we must decide which variable to include in a new selection. In order to determine this we multiply in each column of part I of Table 3 the figures with the corresponding c_i $(0, 0)$ and sum. We then obtain the quantities g_i. For the column corresponding to z_1 we have $g_1 = 1 \cdot 0 + 2 \cdot 0 = 0$. This is written below z_1. Also, $g_2 = 1 \cdot 0 + 1 \cdot 0 = 0$, which goes below z_2. Then $g_3 = 1 \cdot 0 + 0 \cdot 0 = 0$, which goes below z_3. Finally, $g_4 = 0 \cdot 0 + 1 \cdot 0 = 0$, entered below z_4.

Then for each i we compute $c_i - g_i$ by deducting the quantities just computed from the second line of Table 3.

$$c_1 - g_1 = 1 - 0 = 1,$$
$$c_2 - g_2 = 2 - 0 = 2,$$
$$c_3 - g_3 = 0 - 0 = 0,$$
$$c_4 - g_4 = 0 - 0 = 0.$$

These quantities are entered in the last line of part I of Table 3. If they all were negative or zero, we would have achieved the final answer. This is not the case. The *largest* of the quantities $c_i - g_i$ determines the variable that becomes a variable in the next selection. This is 2 and corresponds to z_2. It is starred. Hence z_2 must be included in the next selection.

In economic terms, what we are doing is the following: Suppose our problem represents an effort to maximize income from a production process, so that c_1 and c_2 represent unit income from each of two activities, activity 1 and activity 2, respectively, where activity 1 requires 1 unit of input 1 and 2 units of input 2, and so on. g_1 then represents an "income" figure available to us by using inputs 1 and 2 in slack activity. Forgoing 1 unit of activity 1 allows us to allocate 1 unit of input 1 and 2 units of input 2 to slack activity, so that, if c_3 and c_4 represent the income per unit of slack activities 1 and 2, respectively, we earn $c_3(1) + c_4(2)$ by doing without this 1 unit of activity 1. In this case, of course, $c_3 = c_4 = 0_1$, as in any slack situation, so we derive no income in this manner. It is now clear, however, that $c_1 - g_1$ represents the difference in incomes available from engaging in 1 unit of activity 1 or forgoing the 1 unit of activity 1 and allocating its needed inputs to slack activity.

The same reasoning holds in general: If z_i is not a selection variable, $c_i - g_i$ represents the income difference determined by engaging in a unit of activity i and foregoing the unit of activity i to allocate the inputs needed for a unit of activity i to those activities that *have* been selected. It is thus a measure of opportunity cost.

It follows, then, that we will change our income the *most* if we find the largest $c_i - g_i$ associated with an activity i that has not been selected, and select it now. When all $c_i - g_i \leq 0$ no further improvement is possible, and we stop the simplex process.

But which variable should be omitted? In order to answer this question we utilize the column in part I of Table 3 corresponding to z_2, the variable to be included. We divide the values of z_i (4, 3) in the first column of part I by the elements of the column corresponding to z_2 (1, 1). Hence we have: $\frac{4}{1} = 4$ for z_3 and $\frac{3}{1} = 3$ for z_4. The *smallest* of these is 3. Hence z_4 is omitted in the next selection. This means of choosing the variable to be omitted guarantees that the variables in the new selection will be nonnegative.

Now, we write the new results in part II of Table 3. Our selection variables are now z_2 and z_3.

Using our original equations, we solve first for the selection variables:

$$1 \cdot z_2 + 1 \cdot z_3 = 4,$$
$$1 \cdot z_2 + 0 \cdot z_3 = 3.$$

Hence $z_2 = 3$ and $z_3 = 1$. These results are noted in part II, as well as the corresponding coefficients in the objective function,

$$c_2 = 2, \qquad c_3 = 0.$$

Now we must express all variables in terms of the new selection variables z_2 and z_3. We derive for z_1

$$1 \cdot e_2^1 + 1 \cdot e_3^1 = 1,$$
$$1 \cdot e_2^1 + 0 \cdot e_3^1 = 2.$$

The coefficients of the equations are taken from Table 2 for z_2 and z_3. The right-hand side corresponds to z_1. The result, $e_2^1 = 2$, $e_3^1 = -1$, is written under z_1 in part II of Table 3.

In order to express z_2 in terms of our new base variables we have

$$1 \cdot f_2^1 + 1 \cdot f_3^1 = 1,$$
$$1 \cdot f_2^1 + 0 \cdot f_3^1 = 1.$$

This gives $f_2^1 = 1, f_3^1 = 0$, which is entered under z_2 in part II of Table 3. For z_3 our equations become

$$1 \cdot g_2^1 + 1 \cdot g_3^1 = 1,$$
$$1 \cdot g_2^1 + 0 \cdot g_3^1 = 0.$$

Hence $g_2^1 = 0$, $g_3^1 = 1$, and this is entered under z_3 in Table 3, part II. Finally, we have for z_4

$$1 \cdot h_2^1 + 1 \cdot h_3^1 = 0,$$
$$1 \cdot h_2^1 + 0 \cdot h_3^1 = 1.$$

Hence $h_2^1 = 1$, $h_3^1 = -1$, which is entered under z_4 in part II. The next step is the computation of the g_i. Each column in part II of Table 3 is multiplied by the corresponding c_i $(2, 0)$ on the left-hand side and added. We compute

$$g_1 = 2(2) - 1(0) = 4,$$
$$g_2 = 1(2) + 0(0) = 2,$$
$$g_3 = 0(2) + 1(0) = 0,$$
$$g_4 = 1(2) - 1(0) = 2.$$

These values are entered in part II of Table 3. We also compute with the help of the coefficients c_i in line 2 of Table 3

$$c_1 - g_1 = 1 - 4 = -3,$$
$$c_2 - g_2 = 2 - 2 = 0,$$
$$c_3 - g_3 = 0 - 0 = 0,$$
$$c_4 - g_4 = 0 - 2 = -2.$$

These values are entered in the last line of part II of Table 3. Since they are all negative or zero, we have achieved the maximum of the objective function.

We have already the activities $z_2 = 3$, $z_3 = 1$. The optimum objective function is $z = c_2 z_2 + c_3 z_3 = 2 \cdot 3 + 0 \cdot 1 = 6$. It should be noted that this result was achieved in just two steps (parts I and II of Table 3) out of six possible selections.

EXERCISE 36

1 Find with the help of the simplex method the solution of problem 1, Exercises 35.

2 Solve the following linear program with the simplex method: $z = x_1 + x_2 + x_3 =$ maximum.

$$x_1 + 2x_2 + x_3 \leq 10,$$
$$2x_1 + x_2 + 3x_3 \leq 20,$$
$$x_1 + 3x_2 + 2x_3 \leq 15,$$
$$x_1 \geq 0, \qquad x_2 \geq 0, \qquad x_3 \geq 0.$$

3 The following is the result of a sample survey in Hancock County, Ellsworth township, Iowa. Let x_1 be the production of corn and x_2 the production of flax, in bushels. The profit function is $z = 1.56x_1 + 3.81x_2$.

The following conditions of production refer to land (148 acres) and capital (1800):

$$0.023x_1 + 0.092x_2 \leq 148,$$
$$0.318x_1 + 0.970x_2 \leq 1800,$$
$$x_1 \geq 0, \qquad x_2 \geq 0.$$

Solve the linear program with the help of the simplex method.

4 Maximize with the help of the simplex method the linear function $z = x_1 + x_2$ under the conditions

$$2x_1 + 3x_2 \leq 6,$$
$$x_1 \leq 3,$$
$$3x_1 + 2x_2 \leq 5,$$
$$x_1 \geq 0, \qquad x_2 \geq 0.$$

5   Use the simplex method to maximize the function $z = 2x_1 + x_2 + x_3$ under the conditions

$$x_1 + x_2 \leq 10,$$
$$x_2 + x_3 \leq 12,$$
$$x_1 + 2x_2 + 3x_3 \leq 20,$$
$$x_1 \geq 0, \qquad x_2 \geq 0, \qquad x_3 \geq 0.$$

37   INPUT-OUTPUT ANALYSIS

We first analyze a *closed model* of a given economy. We divide the economy into n sectors. Let X_1, X_2, $\cdots$, X_n be the net output of the n sectors, where we neglect internal transactions within the sectors. Let x_{i1}, x_{i2}, $\cdots$, $x_{i,i-1}$, $x_{i,i+1}$, $\cdots$, x_{in} be the sales of sector i, the other sectors in the economy. These are the inputs in the other sectors. The total exchange in a given economy might be described by the following system of equations:

$$x_{12} + x_{13} + \cdots + x_{1,n-1} + x_{1,n} = X_1$$
$$x_{21} + x_{23} + \cdots + x_{2,n-1} + x_{2,n} = X_2,$$
$$\cdots$$
$$x_{n,1} + x_{n,2} + x_{n,3} + \cdots + x_{n,n-1} = X_n.$$

Each line indicates that the total net output of a given sector is the sum of the inputs from this sector to all other sectors.

EXAMPLE 1

Consider an economy that is divided into $n = 3$ sectors. The net output of the first sector is $x_1 = 5$. But this sector sells 2 to sector 2 ($x_{12} = 2$) and 3 to sector 3 ($x_{13} = 3$). The net product of the second sector is $x_2 = 6$. Of this, 3 goes to the first sector ($x_{21} = 3$) and 3 to the third sector ($x_{23} = 3$). Finally, the net product of the third sector is $4(x_4 = 4)$. Of this output, 2 is delivered to the first sector ($x_{31} = 2$) and 2 to the second sector ($x_{32} = 2$). This situation might be represented in an input-output table (Table 1).

Table 1

		To the sector			
		1	2	3	Net output
	1		2	3	5
From the sector	2	3		3	6
	3	2	2		4

The transactions in this economy might be described by the following equations:

$$2 + 3 = 5,$$
$$3 + 3 = 6,$$
$$2 + 2 = 4.$$

These equations tell us that in a closed economy the sum of all inputs coming from a given sector must be equal to the net output of this sector.

In order to analyze the situation further, we assume now constant technical coefficients of production. The amount of goods and services delivered from sector i to sector j (x_{ij}) is directly proportional to the net output of sector j:

$$x_{ij} = a_{ij}X_j.$$

The constant proportionality factor a_{ij} is the technical coefficient of production. We compute it by the formula

$$a_{ij} = \frac{x_{ij}}{X_j}.$$

EXAMPLE 2

Using the data in Example 1, we derive the following coefficients of production: $a_{12} = x_{12}/X_2 = \frac{2}{6} = \frac{1}{3}$; $a_{13} = x_{13}/X_3 = \frac{3}{4}$; $a_{21} = x_{21}/X_1 = \frac{3}{5}$; $a_{23} = x_{23}/X_3 = \frac{3}{4}$; $a_{31} = x_{31}/X_1 = \frac{2}{5}$; $a_{32} = x_{32}/X_2 = \frac{2}{6} = \frac{1}{3}$. They are presented in Table 2.

Table 2

		Consuming sector		
		1	2	3
	1		$\frac{1}{3}$	$\frac{3}{4}$
Originating sector	2	$\frac{3}{5}$		$\frac{3}{4}$
	3	$\frac{2}{5}$	$\frac{1}{3}$	

The meaning of the technical coefficients of production is as follows: If we want an additional unit of the product of the first sector, we need $a_{21} = \frac{3}{5}$ units of the product of the second sector and $a_{31} = \frac{2}{5}$ units of the third sector. If we desire to increase the output of sector 2 by 1 unit, we need $a_{12} = \frac{1}{3}$ units from sector one and $a_{32} = \frac{1}{3}$ units of the output of sector 3. If we desire to increase the output of sector 3 by 1 unit, we need $a_{13} = \frac{3}{4}$ units of the output of sector 1 and $a_{23} = \frac{3}{4}$ units of the product of sector 2.

Now we may state the conditions of general equilibrium between the n sectors of our economy by the following system of linear equations:

$$X_1 - a_{12}X_2 - \cdots - a_{1n}X_n = 0,$$
$$-a_{21}X_1 + X_2 - \cdots - a_{2n}X_n = 0,$$
$$\cdots$$
$$-a_{n1}X_1 - a_{n2}X_2 - \cdots + X_n = 0.$$

EXAMPLE 3

We use the data from Example 1 in order to express the equilibrium of the three sectors of our economy:

$$X_1 - (\tfrac{1}{3})X_2 - (\tfrac{3}{4})X_3 = 0,$$
$$-(\tfrac{3}{5})X_1 + X_2 - (\tfrac{3}{4})X_3 = 0,$$
$$-(\tfrac{2}{5})X_1 - (\tfrac{1}{3})X_2 + X_3 = 0.$$

This is a system of linear homogeneous equations in the unknowns X_1, X_2, X_3. It has a trivial solution, namely, $X_1 = X_2 = X_3 = 0$. This evidently makes no economic sense. Since the determinant of the coefficients of the variables is zero,

$$\begin{vmatrix} 1 & -(\tfrac{1}{3}) & -(\tfrac{3}{4}) \\ -(\tfrac{3}{5}) & 1 & -(\tfrac{3}{4}) \\ -(\tfrac{2}{5}) & -(\tfrac{1}{3}) & 1 \end{vmatrix} = 0$$

we might solve the system of equations in terms of the ratios of the unknowns, for example, X_2/X_1 and X_3/X_1.
From the first two equations we obtain now

$$-\left(\frac{1}{3}\right)\left(\frac{X_2}{X_1}\right) - \left(\frac{3}{4}\right)\left(\frac{X_3}{X_1}\right) = -1,$$
$$\left(\frac{X_2}{X_1}\right) - \left(\frac{3}{4}\right)\left(\frac{X_3}{X_1}\right) = \frac{3}{5}.$$

This gives us the solution $X_2/X_1 = \tfrac{6}{5}$; $X_3/X_1 = \tfrac{4}{5}$. It is easy to verify that these results also satisfy the third equation.

The interpretation of these results is: In static equilibrium, with fixed coefficients of production, the net output of the second sector must be $\tfrac{6}{5}$ of the net output of the first sector; and under similar conditions, the net output of the third sector should be $\tfrac{4}{5}$ of the output of the first sector.

We assume now free competition in our economy. Then there are no profits; that is, total revenue is equal to total cost. We denote by p_1, p_2, $\cdots$, p_n the prices of the products of the n sectors. We have the following equilibrium system for the prices:

$$p_1 - p_2 a_{21} - \cdots - p_n a_{n1} = 0,$$
$$-p_1 a_{12} + p_2 - \cdots - p_n a_{n2} = 0,$$
$$\cdots$$
$$-p_1 a_{1n} - p_2 a_{2n} - \cdots + p_n = 0.$$

The first equation, for example, tells us that the price of one unit of goods and services produced in the first sector must be equal to the cost of producing this unit.

EXAMPLE 4

We use again the data of the previous example. Denote by p_1, p_2, p_3 the prices of the various sectors. They are given by the following system of linear homogeneous equations:

$$p_1 - (\tfrac{3}{5})p_2 - (\tfrac{2}{5})p_3 = 0,$$
$$-(\tfrac{1}{3})p_1 + p_2 - (\tfrac{1}{3})p_3 = 0,$$
$$-(\tfrac{3}{4})p_1 - (\tfrac{3}{4})p_2 + p_3 = 0.$$

Since the determinant of the system of equations

$$\begin{vmatrix} 1 & -(\tfrac{3}{5}) & -(\tfrac{2}{5}) \\ -(\tfrac{1}{3}) & 1 & -(\tfrac{1}{3}) \\ -(\tfrac{3}{4}) & -(\tfrac{3}{4}) & 1 \end{vmatrix} = 0$$

is zero, there is a nontrivial solution for the price ratios, for example, p_2/p_1 and p_3/p_1. We have from the first two equations of our system

$$-\left(\frac{3}{5}\right)\left(\frac{p_2}{p_1}\right) - \left(\frac{2}{5}\right)\left(\frac{p_3}{p_1}\right) = -1,$$
$$\left(\frac{p_2}{p_1}\right) - \left(\frac{1}{3}\right)\left(\frac{p_3}{p_1}\right) = \frac{1}{3}.$$

The solutions are $p_2/p_1 = \tfrac{7}{9}$; $p_3/p_1 = \tfrac{4}{3}$. If, for example, we put the price of products of the first sector $p_1 = 100$, then we have $p_2 = 78$ and $p_3 = 133$. It is easy to verify that the third equation of our system is also satisfied by these values.

The assumption of constant coefficients of production for industry and agriculture is a reasonably good assumption, at least for the short run. But one might doubt the validity of this assumption for the sector of consumption. It is not likely that labor would be produced under conditions of constant coefficients of production. Also, it is unlikely that the products of other sectors would be used by the households in fixed proportions.

Assume now that the last $(n - \text{th})$ sector in our closed system represents households. We suppress this sector and obtain the *open Leontief model*. Denote now by $y_1, y_2, \ldots, y_{n-1}$ the final demand of consumers for the products of the sectors $1, 2, \cdots,$ $n - 1$. We assume that these are now given quantities. The open Leontief system is now

$$X_1 - a_{12}X_2 - \cdots - a_{1,n-1}X_{n-1} = y_1,$$
$$-a_{21}X_1 + X_2 - \cdots - a_{2,n-1}X_{n-1} = y_2,$$
$$\cdots$$
$$-a_{n-1,1}X_1 - a_{n-1,2}X_2 - \cdots + X_{n-1} = y_{n-1}.$$

This new system has one less linear equation than the closed Leontief model. But now we have $n - 1$ nonhomogeneous equations in $n - 1$ unknowns: the net outputs $X_1, X_2, \cdots, X_{n-1}$. In general, we might solve this system and express the net outputs in terms of the consumers' final demands, $y_1, y_2, \cdots, y_{n-1}$. The solution is

$$X_1 = c_{11}y_1 + c_{12}y_2 + \cdots + c_{1,n-1}y_{n-1},$$
$$X_2 = c_{21}y_1 + c_{22}y_2 + \cdots + c_{2,n-1}y_{n-1},$$
$$\cdots$$
$$X_{n-1} = c_{n-1,1}y_1 + c_{n-1,2}y_2 + \cdots c_{n-1,n-1}y_{n-1}.$$

EXAMPLE 5

We use again the data in the previous examples in order to construct an open Leontief system. Assume that the third sector represents consumption. We obtain then the following open system:

$$X_1 - (\tfrac{1}{3})X_2 = y_1,$$
$$-(\tfrac{3}{5})X_1 + X_2 = y_2.$$

Here y_1 and y_2 represent the final demand of consumers for products of sectors 1 and 2. This system of linear equations is not homogeneous and we might solve it for the net outputs of the first two sectors, X_1 and X_2:

$$X_1 = \left(\frac{5}{4}\right) y_1 + \left(\frac{5}{12}\right) y_2,$$

$$X_2 = \left(\frac{3}{4}\right) y_1 + \left(\frac{5}{4}\right) y_2.$$

The interpretation of these equations is as follows: Assume that, *ceteris paribus*, the final demand of consumers for products of the first sector (y_1) increases by 1 unit. Then the net output of the first sector (X_1) should increase by $\frac{5}{4}$ and that of the second sector by $\frac{3}{4}$ units.

Assume now that *ceteris paribus* the final demand of consumers for products of the second sector (y_2) increases by 1 unit. The consequence is that the net output of the first sector (X_1) increases by $\frac{5}{12}$ and that of the second sector (X_2) by $\frac{5}{4}$ units.

EXERCISE 37

1 Assume an economy that is divided into three sectors. The transactions between the sectors are as follows: $x_{12} = 1$, $x_{13} = 2$, $x_{21} = 2$, $x_{23} = 2$, $x_{31} = 1$, $x_{32} = 3$. (a) Find the net outputs of the three sectors, X_1, X_2, X_3. (b) Construct the input-output table for a closed economy. (c) Find the technical coefficients of production. (d) Establish the equilibrium system for the net outputs and solve for the relative outputs X_2/X_1 and X_3/X_1. (e) Suppose that the third sector represents comsumption. Given the final demand of consumers for products of the first two sectors, y_1 and y_2, determine the open Leontief system. (f) Solve the open Leontief system by expressing the net outputs X_1 and X_2 in terms of the final demands y_1 and y_2. What are the net outputs X_1 and X_2 of the two first sectors for $y_1 = \frac{3}{2}$, $y_2 = 2$?

2 The following data refer to the United States for 1954. Let 1 be agriculture, 2 industry, 3 consumption. The following are the transactions (billions of dollars): $x_{12} = 25$, $x_{13} = 5$, $x_{21} = 13$, $x_{23} = 281$, $x_{31} = 17$, $x_{32} = 269$. Answer (a–d) and (f) as 1. (g) Find the net products X_1 and X_2 if the final demands are $y_1 = 4$, $y_2 = 285$.

3 The following data are for the Austrian economy for 1955 (Tintner). (All values in billions of Austrian shillings.) The sectors are: (1) enterprises, (2) government, (3) foreign trade, (4) consumption. The transactions are: $x_{12} = 16.4$, $x_{13} = 25.8$, $x_{14} = 76.9$, $x_{21} = 14.3$, $x_{23} = 0$, $x_{24} = 11.6$, $x_{31} = 22.1$, $x_{32} = 0.7$, $x_{34} = 0$, $x_{41} = 65.6$, $x_{42} = 15.6$, $x_{43} = 0$. (a) Find the net outputs of the four sectors and construct the input-output table. (b) Compute the technical coefficients of production. (c) Find the equilibrium system for the net outputs and solve for X_2/X_1, X_3/X_1, X_4/X_1. (d) Omit the consumption sector and establish the open Leontief system where y_1, y_2, y_3 are the final demands of consumers for the products of the first three sectors. (e) Find the net outputs of the sectors X_1, X_2, X_3 if we have $y_1 = 80$, $y_2 = 12$, $y_3 = 0$.

4 The following data refer to the Portuguese economy for 1957 (Tintner and Murteira). The sectors are as in problem 3. (All transactions in millions of escudos) $x_{12} = 3.49$, $x_{13} = 10.97$, $x_{14} = 45.34$, $x_{21} = 2.14$, $x_{23} = 1.79$, $x_{24} = 3.08$, $x_{31} = 15.14$, $x_{32} = 0$, $x_{34} = 0$, $x_{41} = 48.83$, $x_{42} = 2.85$, $x_{43} = 0$. Answer the same questions as in problem 3. Find

the net outputs X_1, X_2, X_3 in the open Leontief system if the final demands are $y_1 = 46$, $y_2 = 4$, $y_3 = 0$.

5   In the open Leontief system let y be the cost of labor. (a) Show that $y = a_{n1}X_1 + a_{n2}X_2 + \cdots + a_{n,n-1}X_{n-1}$. (b) Use the above results concerning the open Leontief system in order to express the cost of labor, y, in terms of the final demands, $y_1, y_2, \cdots , y_{n-1}$. (c) Find numerical values for (b) for problems 1–4.

Chapter 8

Matrices

You will remember that a square matrix of order n is a table of n^2 numbers in the following form:

$$A = \begin{bmatrix} A_{11} & A_{12} & \cdots & A_{1n} \\ A_{21} & A_{22} & \cdots & A_{2n} \\ & & \cdots & \\ A_{n1} & A_{n2} & \cdots & A_{nn} \end{bmatrix}.$$

An element A_{ij} is identified by the index of the (row) (i) and the column (j).

EXAMPLE 1

A square matrix of order two is, for example,

$$A = \begin{bmatrix} 3 & -1 \\ 0 & 2 \end{bmatrix},$$

and its elements are $A_{11} = 3$, $A_{12} = 1$, $A_{21} = 0$, $A_{22} = 2$.

Two $n \cdot n$ matrices A and B are equal if $A_{ij} = B_{ij}$, $i, j = 1, \cdots n$, $A_{11} = B_{11}$, $A_{12} = B_{12}$, and so on. If the elements that are symmetric with respect to the principal diagonal ($A_{11}, A_{22}, \cdots, A_{nn}$) are equal, $A_{ij} = A_{ji}$, the matrix is *symmetric*.

EXAMPLE 2

The matrix

$$A = \begin{bmatrix} 2 & -1 & 0 \\ -1 & 3 & 1 \\ 0 & 1 & 1 \end{bmatrix}$$

is a symmetrical matrix of order three. We have indeed

$$A_{12} = A_{21} = -1, \qquad A_{13} = A_{31} = 0, \qquad A_{23} = A_{32} = 1.$$

If all elements of a matrix except those in the principal diagonal $(A_{11}, A_{22}, \cdots, A_{nn})$ are zero, the matrix is called *diagonal*.

EXAMPLE 3

The matrix

$$A = \begin{bmatrix} 2 & 0 \\ 0 & 1 \end{bmatrix}$$

is a diagonal matrix of order two. Its elements are $A_{12} = A_{21} = 0$, $A_{11} = 2, A_{22} = 1$.

A $n \cdot n$ diagonal matrix, in which all elements in the principal diagonal are one, is called the *nxn unit matrix* or the *$n \cdot n$ identity matrix*.

EXAMPLE 4

The matrix

$$I = \begin{bmatrix} 1 & 0 & 0 \\ 0 & 1 & 0 \\ 0 & 0 & 1 \end{bmatrix}$$

is the unit matrix of order three.

A matrix in which all elements are zero is called a null matrix.

EXAMPLE 5

The matrix

$$A = \begin{bmatrix} 0 & 0 \\ 0 & 0 \end{bmatrix}$$

is the null matrix of order two.

If we exchange lines and columns in a matrix A, we obtain the *transposed* matrix A'. Each element of the transposed matrix A'_{ij} is equal to the element A_{ji} of the original matrix.

EXAMPLE 6

The transpose of the matrix

$$A = \begin{bmatrix} 1 & -1 & 3 \\ -2 & 4 & 0 \\ 0 & 2 & 5 \end{bmatrix}$$

is the matrix

$$A' = \begin{bmatrix} 1 & -2 & 0 \\ -1 & 4 & 2 \\ 3 & 0 & 5 \end{bmatrix}.$$

A symmetrical matrix is equal to its own transposed matrix.

The sum of two matrices of the same order is obtained by summing the corresponding elements of the two matrices.

EXAMPLE 7

$$\begin{bmatrix} 2 & -1 \\ 1 & 6 \end{bmatrix} + \begin{bmatrix} 0 & 4 \\ -5 & 3 \end{bmatrix} = \begin{bmatrix} 2+0 & -1+4 \\ 1-5 & 6+3 \end{bmatrix} = \begin{bmatrix} 2 & 3 \\ -4 & 9 \end{bmatrix}.$$

Similarly, the *difference* of two matrices of the same order is obtained by subtracting the elements of the second matrix from the elements of the first.

EXAMPLE 8

$$\begin{bmatrix} 2 & -1 & 0 \\ 1 & -2 & 0 \\ 2 & 1 & 1 \end{bmatrix} - \begin{bmatrix} 3 & -2 & -1 \\ 1 & -1 & -2 \\ 2 & -2 & -1 \end{bmatrix} =$$

$$\begin{bmatrix} 2-3 & -1-(-2) & 0-(-1) \\ 1-1 & -2-(-1) & 0-(-2) \\ 2-2 & 1-(-2) & 1-(-1) \end{bmatrix} = \begin{bmatrix} -1 & 1 & +1 \\ 0 & -1 & +2 \\ 0 & 3 & 2 \end{bmatrix}.$$

The *product of a matrix and a scalar* (number) is obtained by multiplying each element of the matrix by the scalar.

EXAMPLE 9

$$A = \begin{bmatrix} 2 & -1 & 0 \\ 1 & 0 & -1 \\ 5 & 0 & 1 \end{bmatrix}; \qquad B = 3. \qquad BA = \begin{bmatrix} 6 & -3 & 0 \\ 3 & 0 & -3 \\ 15 & 0 & 3 \end{bmatrix}.$$

EXAMPLE 10

$$A = \begin{bmatrix} 2 & -1 \\ -1 & 0 \end{bmatrix}; \qquad B = -2. \qquad BA = \begin{bmatrix} -4 & 2 \\ 2 & 0 \end{bmatrix}.$$

EXERCISES 38

1 Given the matrices

$$A = \begin{bmatrix} 1 & 0 & -1 \\ -1 & 0 & 2 \\ 3 & 0 & -1 \end{bmatrix}, \qquad B = \begin{bmatrix} 9 & -5 & -1 \\ 0 & 1 & -2 \\ 5 & -5 & 0 \end{bmatrix},$$

find (a) $A + B$; (b) $A - B$; (c) $2A$; (d) $-3B$; (e) $2A + 3B$; (f) $B = 5A$.

2 Given the matrices

$$A = \begin{bmatrix} 2 & 1 \\ 1 & 2 \end{bmatrix}, \qquad B = \begin{bmatrix} 3 & -1 \\ -1 & 1 \end{bmatrix},$$

$$X = \begin{bmatrix} X_{11} & X_{12} \\ X_{21} & X_{22} \end{bmatrix}, \qquad O = \begin{bmatrix} 0 & 0 \\ 0 & 0 \end{bmatrix},$$

solve the following matrix equations: (a) $X = 2A$; (b) $X = -3B$; (c) $X + A = B$; (d) $2X - B = 5A$; (e) $A + X + B = 0$.

39   MULTIPLICATION OF TWO SQUARE MATRICES

We define the multiplication of two square matrices of the same order as follows:

$$A \cdot B = C, \text{ where}$$

$$C_{ij} = A_{i1}B_{1j} + A_{i2}B_{2j} + \cdots + A_{in}B_{nj}.$$

We obtain the element C_{ij} by summing the products of the ith row of matrix A and the jth column of matrix B. The order of multiplication is important. In general, $A \cdot B$ is not the same as $B \cdot A$.

EXAMPLE 1

$$\begin{bmatrix} 1 & 2 \\ -1 & 0 \end{bmatrix} \cdot \begin{bmatrix} 0 & -1 \\ 3 & 1 \end{bmatrix} = \begin{bmatrix} (1)(0) + (2)(3) & (1)(-1) + (2)(1) \\ (-1)(0) + (0)(3) & (-1)(-1) + (0)(1) \end{bmatrix}$$

$$= \begin{bmatrix} 6 & 1 \\ 0 & 1 \end{bmatrix}.$$

If we multiply in the opposite order we obtain a different result:

$$\begin{bmatrix} 0 & -1 \\ 3 & 1 \end{bmatrix} \cdot \begin{bmatrix} 1 & 2 \\ -1 & 0 \end{bmatrix} = \begin{bmatrix} (0)(1) + (-1)(-1) & (0)(2) + (-1)(0) \\ (3)(1) + (1)(-1) & (3)(2) + (1)(0) \end{bmatrix}$$

$$= \begin{bmatrix} 1 & 0 \\ 2 & 6 \end{bmatrix}.$$

EXERCISES 39

1   Given the matrices

$$A = \begin{bmatrix} 2 & -1 & 0 \\ 0 & 1 & 1 \\ 6 & -5 & 0 \end{bmatrix}, \quad B = \begin{bmatrix} 4 & 1 & -1 \\ 0 & 1 & -1 \\ 1 & 2 & 0 \end{bmatrix}, \quad C = \begin{bmatrix} 2 & 3 & 0 \\ 0 & -1 & 4 \\ 5 & 0 & 0 \end{bmatrix},$$

compute the following products: (a) $A \cdot B$; (b) $B \cdot A$; (c) $A \cdot C$; (d) $C \cdot A$; (e) $B \cdot C$; (f) $C \cdot B$.

**2   Show that one can define the product of three $m \times n$ matrices as follows: $A \cdot B \cdot C = (A \cdot B) \cdot C = A \cdot (B \cdot C)$. Apply this definition to the matrices in problem 1.

3   Given the matrices

$$A = \begin{bmatrix} 2 & 1 \\ 1 & 3 \end{bmatrix}, \quad B = \begin{bmatrix} 1 & 0 \\ 0 & 2 \end{bmatrix}, \quad X = \begin{bmatrix} X_{11} & X_{12} \\ X_{21} & X_{22} \end{bmatrix},$$

solve the following matrix equations: (a) $A \cdot X = B$; (b) $B \cdot X = A$; (c) $X \cdot A = B$; (d) $X \cdot B = A$.

**4   Define $A^2 = A \cdot A$; $A^3 = A \cdot A^2$; $A^4 = A^2 \cdot A^2$. Given the matrix

$$A = \begin{bmatrix} 2 & -1 \\ -1 & 1 \end{bmatrix},$$

find (a) A^2; (b) A^3; (c) A^4.

40   VECTORS. INVERSE MATRICES. CROUT METHOD

An n-dimensional column vector

$$x = \begin{bmatrix} x_1 \\ x_2 \\ \cdot \\ \cdot \\ \cdot \\ x_n \end{bmatrix}$$

is an $n \cdot 1$ matrix. Using matrix multiplication, we might write a system of n linear equations in n unknowns, $x_1, x_2, \cdots, x_n$ as follows:

$$A \cdot x = b,$$

where A is a square matrix of order n and b is a column vector of constants of order n.

EXAMPLE 1

The system of linear equations

$$2x_1 + x_2 = 5,$$
$$x_1 + x_2 = 3$$

might be written as follows:

$$A = \begin{bmatrix} 2 & 1 \\ 1 & 1 \end{bmatrix}, \qquad x = \begin{bmatrix} x_1 \\ x_2 \end{bmatrix}, \qquad b = \begin{bmatrix} 5 \\ 3 \end{bmatrix};$$

$A \cdot x = b$.

$$\begin{bmatrix} 1 & 2 \\ 1 & 1 \end{bmatrix} \cdot \begin{bmatrix} x_1 \\ x_2 \end{bmatrix} = \begin{bmatrix} 2x_1 + x_2 \\ x_1 + x_2 \end{bmatrix} = \begin{bmatrix} 5 \\ 3 \end{bmatrix}.$$

We would like to find the solution of a system of linear equations in this form: $x = C \cdot b$ for some matrix C. Consider the following definition: An $n \cdot n$ matrix A has an inverse A^{-1} and is called nonsingular if there is a matrix C, $n \cdot n$, such that $AC = CA = I$, where I is the $n \cdot n$ identity matrix. A^{-1} is then the matrix C.

EXAMPLE 2

We want to find the inverse matrix of the matrix of Example 1:

$$A = \begin{bmatrix} 2 & 1 \\ 1 & 1 \end{bmatrix}.$$

Call the inverse of this matrix

$$A^{-1} = C = \begin{bmatrix} C_{11} & C_{12} \\ C_{21} & C_{22} \end{bmatrix}.$$

Since

$$C \cdot A = I, \qquad \begin{bmatrix} C_{11} & C_{12} \\ C_{21} & C_{22} \end{bmatrix} \cdot \begin{bmatrix} 2 & 1 \\ 1 & 1 \end{bmatrix} = \begin{bmatrix} 1 & 0 \\ 0 & 1 \end{bmatrix}.$$

By matrix multiplication,

$$\begin{bmatrix} C_{11} \cdot 2 + C_{12} \cdot 1 & C_{11} \cdot 1 + C_{12} \cdot 1 \\ C_{21} \cdot 2 + C_{22} \cdot 1 & C_{21} \cdot 1 + C_{22} \cdot 1 \end{bmatrix} = \begin{bmatrix} 1 & 0 \\ 0 & 1 \end{bmatrix}.$$

This gives the following equations for the determination of the elements of the inverse matrix C_{ij}:

$$2C_{11} + C_{12} = 1,$$
$$C_{11} + C_{12} = 0,$$
$$2C_{21} + C_{22} = 0,$$
$$C_{21} + C_{22} = 1.$$

The solutions are $C_{11} = 1$, $C_{12} = -1$, $C_{21} = -1$, $C_{22} = 2$. Hence the inverse matrix is

$$A^{-1} = C = \begin{bmatrix} 1 & -1 \\ -1 & 2 \end{bmatrix}.$$

We check this result:

$$A \cdot C = \begin{bmatrix} 2 & 1 \\ 1 & 1 \end{bmatrix} \cdot \begin{bmatrix} 1 & -1 \\ -1 & 2 \end{bmatrix}$$
$$= \begin{bmatrix} (2)(1) + (1)(-1) & (2)(-1) + (1)(2) \\ (+1)(+1) + (1)(1) & (1)(-1) + (1)(2) \end{bmatrix}$$
$$= \begin{bmatrix} 1 & 0 \\ 0 & 1 \end{bmatrix}.$$

Now we may find the solution of our linear system of equations:

$$x = A^{-1} \cdot b = C \cdot b = \begin{bmatrix} 1 & -1 \\ -1 & 2 \end{bmatrix} \cdot \begin{bmatrix} 5 \\ 3 \end{bmatrix} = \begin{bmatrix} (1)(5) + (-1)(3) \\ (-1)(5) + (2)(3) \end{bmatrix}$$
$$= \begin{bmatrix} 2 \\ 1 \end{bmatrix} = \begin{vmatrix} x_1 \\ x_2 \end{vmatrix}.$$

For a check we have from the original system of equations

$$2x_1 + x_2 = (2)(2) + 1 = 5,$$
$$x_1 + x_2 = 2 + 1 = 3.$$

Since the computation of the inverse matrix A^{-1} becomes very complicated for large matrices, we give below the Crout method for computing inverse matrices.

The solution of large systems of equations is best accomplished by electronic computers, but in case such computers are not easily accessible we present in what follows numerical methods of computation that may be used in order to solve problems of moderate size. Our aim here is not necessarily to present the most efficient computing methods but to familiarize the student with methods that have wide applicability.

We note that an $n \cdot n$ matrix is nonsingular and has an inverse A^{-1} if and only if the determinant $|A|$ of A is not 0. Thus, in our example $\begin{vmatrix} 2 & 1 \\ 1 & 1 \end{vmatrix} = 1$. Also, if A is nonsingular, there is one and only one matrix C such that C is the inverse of $A = C = A^{-1}$.

EXAMPLE 3

Consider the matrix

$$A = \begin{bmatrix} 2 & 1 & 0 \\ 1 & 3 & 1 \\ 0 & 0 & 2 \end{bmatrix}.$$

We compute the inverse matrix $A^{-1} = C$ as follows:

Table 1

		I				
2	1	0	1	0	0	4
1	3	1	0	1	0	6
0	0	2	0	0	1	3

		II				
2	$\frac{1}{2}$	0	$\frac{1}{2}$	0	0	2
1	$\frac{5}{2}$	$\frac{2}{5}$	$-\frac{1}{5}$	$\frac{2}{5}$	0	$\frac{8}{5}$
0	0	2	0	0	$\frac{1}{2}$	$\frac{3}{2}$

	III	
$\frac{3}{5}$	$-\frac{1}{5}$	0
$-\frac{1}{5}$	$\frac{2}{5}$	0
$\frac{1}{10}$	$-\frac{1}{5}$	$\frac{1}{2}$
$\frac{3}{2}$	1	$\frac{3}{2}$

The principles for the computation of this table are the same as those explained on page 111. In the first part of Table 1 we write the matrix A:

$$A = \begin{bmatrix} 2 & 1 & 0 \\ 1 & 3 & 1 \\ 0 & 0 & 2 \end{bmatrix}$$

and beside it the unit matrix:

$$I = \begin{bmatrix} 1 & 0 & 0 \\ 0 & 1 & 0 \\ 0 & 0 & 1 \end{bmatrix}.$$

The last column is the sum of the preceding elements of each line and serves for a check:

$$2 + 1 + 0 + 1 + 0 + 0 = 4,$$
$$1 + 3 + 1 + 0 + 1 + 0 = 6,$$
$$0 + 0 + 2 + 0 + 0 + 1 = 3.$$

The first column of the second part is simply copied from the first part. The elements in the first line right from the diagonal element (2, underlined) are copied by dividing the corresponding elements in the first part by this diagonal element, 2. The last figure in line 1 gives a check:

$$\tfrac{1}{2} + 0 + \tfrac{1}{2} + 0 + 0 = 1; \qquad 1 + 1 = 2.$$

The diagonal element of the second line is computed as follows: The corresponding element in the first part (3) minus the product of the symmetrically located elements in the second part, already computed:

$$3 - (1)\left(\frac{1}{2}\right) = \frac{5}{2}.$$

The element in the second column below the diagonal is computed in a similar way:

$$(0)(\tfrac{1}{2}) = 0.$$

The elements in the second line of part two are computed in the same fashion, except that we divide by the diagonal element $\tfrac{1}{2}$:

$$\frac{1 - (1)(0)}{5/2} = \frac{2}{5},$$

$$\frac{0 - (1)(1/2)}{5/2} = -\frac{1}{5},$$

$$\frac{1 - (1)(0)}{5/2} = \frac{2}{5},$$

$$\frac{0 - (1)(0)}{5/2} = 0,$$

$$\frac{6 - (1)(2)}{5/2} = \frac{8}{5}.$$

For a check we have again

$$\frac{2}{5} - \frac{1}{5} + \frac{2}{5} = \frac{3}{5}; \quad \frac{3}{5} + 1 = \frac{8}{5}.$$

Now we compute the diagonal element of the third line in part two Table 1. We take the corresponding diagonal element from part one (2) and subtract from it the symmetrically located elements in part two, already computed:

$$2 - (0)(0) - (0)\left(\frac{2}{5}\right) = 2.$$

The remaining elements in line 3 right of the diagonal are computed in the same way, except that we divide also by the (underlined) diagonal element (2):

$$\frac{0 - (0)(1/2) - (0)(-1/5)}{2} = 0,$$

$$\frac{0 - (0)(0) - (0)(0)}{2} = 0,$$

$$\frac{1 - (0)(0) - (0)(0)}{2} = \frac{1}{2},$$

$$\frac{3 - (0)(2) - (0)(8/5)}{2} = \frac{3}{2}.$$

For a check we have again

$$0 + 0 + \frac{1}{2} = \frac{1}{2}; \quad \frac{1}{2} + 1 = \frac{3}{2}.$$

The third part of Table 1 gives the solution. We work it out backwards and write the elements of the third line of part two beginning with the fourth, in the third column of part three:

$$0, 0, \quad \frac{1}{2}, \quad \frac{3}{2}.$$

The elements in column two of part three of Table 1 are computed as follows: From the element $3 + i$ of the second line of part two we subtract the product of the third element of the second line of part two and the element of column 3 of part three situated in the same line:

$$\frac{1}{2} - (0)(0) - \left(\frac{1}{2}\right)\left(-\frac{1}{5}\right) = \frac{3}{5},$$

$$0 - (0)(0) - \left(\frac{1}{2}\right)\left(\frac{2}{5}\right) = -\frac{1}{5},$$

$$0 - (0)\left(\frac{1}{2}\right) - \left(\frac{1}{2}\right)\left(-\frac{1}{5}\right) = \frac{1}{10},$$

$$2 - (0)\left(\frac{3}{2}\right) - \left(\frac{1}{2}\right)(1) = \frac{3}{2}.$$

For a check we have again:

$$\frac{3}{5} - \frac{1}{5} + \frac{1}{10} = \frac{1}{2}; \quad \frac{1}{2} + 1 = \frac{3}{2}.$$

In the first three lines of part three of the table we obtained the transposed matrix A'^{-1} of the inverse matrix A^{-1}. Line 4 is just for checking:

$$A'^{-1} = \begin{bmatrix} \frac{3}{5} & -\frac{1}{5} & 0 \\ -\frac{1}{5} & \frac{2}{5} & 0 \\ \frac{1}{10} & -\frac{1}{5} & \frac{1}{2} \end{bmatrix}.$$

We obtain the inverse matrix $A^{-1} = C$ by exchanging rows and columns of the above matrix:

$$A^{-1} = C = \begin{bmatrix} \frac{3}{5} & -\frac{1}{5} & \frac{1}{10} \\ -\frac{1}{5} & \frac{2}{5} & -\frac{1}{5} \\ 0 & 0 & \frac{1}{2} \end{bmatrix}.$$

We check by computing the product $A \cdot A^{-1} = I$:

$$A \cdot A^{-1} = \begin{bmatrix} 2 & 1 & 0 \\ 1 & 3 & 1 \\ 0 & 0 & 2 \end{bmatrix} \cdot \begin{bmatrix} \frac{3}{5} & -\frac{1}{5} & \frac{1}{10} \\ -\frac{1}{5} & \frac{2}{5} & -\frac{1}{5} \\ 0 & 0 & \frac{1}{2} \end{bmatrix} = \begin{bmatrix} 1 & 0 & 0 \\ 0 & 1 & 0 \\ 0 & 0 & 1 \end{bmatrix} = I.$$

1 Find by the direct method $(C \cdot A = I)$ the inverse matrices and check $(A \cdot A^{-1} = A \cdot C = I)$:

$$\begin{bmatrix} 2 & 3 \\ 1 & 4 \end{bmatrix}, \quad \begin{bmatrix} -1 & 2 \\ 2 & -3 \end{bmatrix}, \quad \begin{bmatrix} 4 & 0 \\ 0 & 1 \end{bmatrix}, \quad \begin{bmatrix} -1 & 0 \\ 0 & -5 \end{bmatrix}.$$

2 Find by the Crout method the inverses of the following matrices and check:

$$\begin{bmatrix} 2 & 0 & 1 \\ 1 & 1 & 1 \\ 1 & 2 & -1 \end{bmatrix}, \quad \begin{bmatrix} -1 & 0 & 0 \\ 0 & 2 & 1 \\ 0 & 1 & 2 \end{bmatrix}, \quad \begin{bmatrix} 1 & 1 & 1 \\ 0 & 2 & 1 \\ 0 & 0 & 5 \end{bmatrix}, \quad \begin{bmatrix} 8 & 3 & 1 & 1 \\ 0 & 1 & 2 & 1 \\ 0 & 1 & 1 & 1 \\ 0 & 0 & 0 & 6 \end{bmatrix}.$$

3 Given the system of equations

$$2x_1 + x_2 = 3,$$
$$-x_1 + 3x_2 = 18,$$

(a) Write the equations in matrix form. (b) Find the inverse matrix. (c) Solve the system of equations, and check.

**4 The following data refer to Austria for 1955 (Tintner). The economy is divided into three sectors: (1) enterprises, (2) government, and (3) foreign trade. The matrix of the coefficients of production is as follows:

$$A = \begin{bmatrix} 0.00 & 0.63 & 1.13 \\ 0.12 & 0.00 & 0.00 \\ 0.19 & 0.03 & 0.00 \end{bmatrix}.$$

(a) Compute the matrix $B = I - A$. Here I is the unit matrix of order three. B is called the *technology matrix*. (b) Find the inverse of the matrix B and verify. (c) Given the column vector of the final demand of consumers for the products of various sectors,

$$y = \begin{bmatrix} 77 \\ 12 \\ 0 \end{bmatrix},$$

and the vector of net outputs of the sectors,

$$X = \begin{bmatrix} X_1 \\ X_2 \\ X_3 \end{bmatrix},$$

solve the system of equations $B \cdot X = y$ using the inverse matrix B^{-1}.

5 The following model has been estimated for the German Republic for the period 1950–1959 (Menges). Let C_t be private consumption. I_t investment, M_t imports, Y_t^B social product, D_t depreciation, K_t capital stock, Y_t net social product, U_t rate of interest, and L_t employment in the year t. The consumption function is $C_t - 0.317Y_t = 4.278 + 0.507C_{t-1}$; the

investment function is $I_t - 0.224Y_t = -10.780 - 0.625U_t$; the import function is $M_t - 0.078Y_t{}^B = -5.873 + 0.902M_{t-1}$; the production function is $Y^B - 0.0195K_t = -299.691 + 0.0195K_{t-1} + 19.741L_t$; the depreciation function is $D_t - 0.0173K_t = -5.526 + 0.0173K_{t-1}$; the definition of capital stock is $K_t - I_t = K_{t-1}$; the definition of net social product is $Y_t - Y_t{}^B + D_t = 0$. Given (data from 1959) $C_{t-1} = 128.600M_{t-1} = 54.582$, $K_{t-1} = 702.740$, $U_t = 3.03$, $L_t = 24.555$, find by the Crout method C_t, I_t, M_t, $Y_t{}^B$, D_t, K_t, Y_t.

Chapter 9

Linear Difference
Equations with Constant
Coefficients

41 FIRST-ORDER HOMOGENEOUS DIFFERENCE EQUATIONS

If we subtract the value of $y = y(x)$, at the point x, from the value of the same function at the point $x + 1$, we obtain *the first difference:*

$$\Delta y = y(x + 1) - y(x).$$

Equations that involve values of $y(x)$ and $y(x + k)$, where k is an integer, are called difference equations. As illustrations, we might observe $ay(x + 1) + by(x) = 0$, or $y(x + 1) = (-b/a)y(x)$.

If a and b are constant, this equation is said to be a linear homogeneous difference equation of the first order with constant coefficients. To find its solution we need to know the value of the function at one point, say at $x = 0$. Let us say that $y(0) = K$. Then we can construct step by step the general solution $y(x)$ when x is an integer:

$$y(1) = \left(-\frac{b}{a}\right) y(0) = \left(-\frac{b}{a}\right) K,$$

$$y(2) = \left(-\frac{b}{a}\right) y(1) = \left(-\frac{b}{a}\right)^2 K,$$

$$y(3) = \left(-\frac{b}{a}\right) y(2) = \left(-\frac{b}{a}\right)^3 K,$$

$$\cdots$$

$$y(x) = \left(-\frac{b}{a}\right)^x K.$$

To check this result we substitute it into the original equation and obtain

$$a\left(-\frac{b}{a}\right)^{x+1} + b\left(-\frac{b}{a}\right)^x = \left(-\frac{b}{a}\right)^x \left[a\left(-\frac{b}{a}\right) + b\right] = 0.$$

Hence our solution satisfies the original difference equation.

117

EXAMPLE

Let the difference equation be

$$y(x + 1) - 2y(x) = 0.$$

In terms of the general equation just considered, we have $a = 1$, $b = -2$, $(-b/a) = +2$. Let us assume that the initial value $y(0) = K = 5$. Hence we have as a general solution: $y(x) = (5)2^x$. So, for $x = 3$, we have

$$y(3) = (5)(2)^3 = (5)(8) = 40.$$

EXERCISES 41

1   Consider the difference equation $y(x + 1) - 5y(x) = 0$ and the condition that $y(0) = 10$. Find (a) the general solution; (b) $y(4)$; (c) $y(6)$.

2   Given the difference equation $y(x + 1) - (\frac{1}{2})y(x) = 0$ and the initial condition $y(0) = 16$, find (a) the general solution; (b) $y(5)$; (c) $y(10)$.

3   Given the difference equation $y(x + 1) - y(x)/10 = 0$ and the condition $y(0) = 10,000$, find (a) the general solution of the equation; (b) $y(2)$; (c) $y(5)$.

4   Using the notation given in Section 28 for compound interest, show that the amount $A(x)$ paid in year x satisfies the difference equation

$$A(x + 1) - rA(x) = 0,$$

where $r = 1 + i$ and i is the rate of interest. Solve the difference equation with $A(0) = P$ (principal), and show that it is identical with the result given in the section quoted.

5   Establish the difference equation for the example in Section 28.

6   Find the difference equation corresponding to the population law of Section 27.

**7   Under what conditions will a linear homogeneous difference equation have fluctuating solutions, that is, solutions that change sign from term to term?

**8   Solve the difference equation $y(x + 1) + 2y(x) = 0$, where $y(0) = 1$, and show that it has a fluctuating solution, as described in Problem 7.

**9   What is the condition under which the solution of a linear homogeneous equation diminishes from term to term?

**10   Consider the difference equation $ay(x + 1) + by(x) = 0$. Assume the solution in the form $y(x) = km^x$, where k and m are constants. (a) Show that m can be derived from the equation $am + b = 0$. (b) Show also that the constant k can be determined from the initial condition $y(0) = K$. Exemplify with the data given in the above example.

11 The first-order difference equation for British industrial production for the period 1869–1939 is given by $x_{t+1} = 1.01x_t$ (Tintner and Thomas). Assume $x_t = 100$ for 1900 and predict national income for 1914; 1939.

42 FIRST-ORDER NONHOMOGENEOUS DIFFERENCE EQUATIONS

A nonhomogeneous linear first-order difference equation is an equation of the form $ay(x + 1) + by(x) = c$, where a, b, and c may or may not be constant; in this treatment they will be taken as constant. The equation as given may be written in the form $y(x + 1) = (-b/a)y(x) + (c/a)$. Again let the initial value $y(0) = K$. Then we have by successive application of the difference equation itself

$$y(1) = K\left(-\frac{b}{a}\right) + \frac{c}{a},$$

$$y(2) = K\left(-\frac{b}{a}\right)^2 + \frac{c}{a}\left[\left(-\frac{b}{a}\right) + 1\right] = K\left(-\frac{b}{a}\right)^2 + \frac{c}{a}\left[\frac{(-b/a)^2 - 1}{(-b/a) - 1}\right],$$

$$y(3) = K\left(-\frac{b}{a}\right)^3 + \frac{c}{a}\left[\left(-\frac{b}{a}\right)^2 + \left(-\frac{b}{a}\right) + 1\right]$$

$$= K\left(-\frac{b}{a}\right)^3 + \frac{c}{a}\left[\frac{(-b/a)^3 - 1}{(-b/a) - 1}\right],$$

$$\cdots$$

$$y(x) = K\left(-\frac{b}{a}\right)^x + \frac{c}{a}\left[\frac{(-b/a)^x - 1}{(-b/a) - 1}\right].$$

This last result is premised on the assumption that x is an integer.

EXAMPLE

Let the difference equation be

$$y(x + 1) - 3y(x) = 10.$$

We have $a = 1$, $b = -3$, $c = 10$. Assume that $y(0) = 12$. The general solution is

$$y(x) = (12)(3)^x + 10\left(\frac{3^x - 1}{3 - 1}\right) = (17)(3^x) - 5.$$

For instance, for $x = 2$ we have $y(2) = 148$.

EXERCISES 42

1 Solve the difference equation $y(x + 1) - (\frac{1}{2})y(x) = 4$, if $y(0) = 8$. Find (a) the general solution; (b) $y(3)$; (c) $y(5)$. (d) Check by substituting back into the difference equation.

2   Solve the difference equation $y(x + 1) - 10y(x) = 1$, if $y(0) = 1$. (a) Find the general solution. (b) Find $y(2)$; $y(4)$. (c) Check by substituting back into the difference equation.

3   Solve the difference equation $y(x + 1) + 2y(x) = 3$, if $y(0) = 16$. (a) Find the general solution. Find (b) $y(2)$; $y(3)$.

*4   Use the notation in Section 28 to show the following: If i is the rate of interest, $r = 1 + i$, P is the principal, and $A(x)$ is the amount in year x, and if B is a bonus paid every year, we obtain the difference equation $A(x + 1) - rA(x) = B$, and the amount is given by $A(x) = Pr^x - (B/i)(1 - r^x)$.

5   A principal $P = \$10,000$ is invested at 5 percent interest, and the firm pays a yearly bonus of $100. What is the total amount after (a) 5 years? (b) 10 years?

6   A principal sum of $P = \$100,000$ is invested at 2 percent. The firm pays a yearly bonus of $5,000. What is the total amount after (a) 3 years? (b) 12 years?

**7   Consider the difference equation $ay(x + 1) + by(x) = c$. Assume the solution in the form $y(x) = km^x + n$, where k, m, n are constants. (a) Show that, in order to make the equation homogeneous, we must have $n = c/(a + b)$. (b) Show that, if $n = c/(a + b)$, m can be determined from the equation $am + b = 0$. Show that the constant k can be determined from the initial condition $y(0) = K$. (d) Demonstrate these propositions with the help of the above example.

*8   Assume an economy in which all income is consumed. Let the extra consumption at the point in time $x + 1$ be a constant multiple a of the income (consumption) at time x. Let the initial consumption (income) be A, where A is constant. Then we have the difference equation $Y(x + 1) = aY(x) + A$, $Y(0) = A$, where Y is income. (a) Show that the solution of the difference equation is

$$Y(x) = \frac{A}{1 - a} - \frac{aAa^x}{1 - a}.$$

(b) Show that if $a < 1$, then as x increases Y approaches nearer and nearer to $A/(1 - a)$.

9   Use the notation of problem 8. Assume $a = \frac{1}{2}$, $A = 100$. Find $Y(2)$; $Y(10)$.

10   In the notation of problem 8, let $a = 0.712$ (estimate of Haavelmo for the United States, 1930–1944). Find $Y(x)$ (a) if $A = 1,000,000,000$; (b) if $A = 5,000,000,000$. (c) Find $Y(3)$, $Y(10)$ under assumptions (a) and (b).

11   The quantity a of problem 8 was estimated as 0.56 for the United States in 1921–1931 (Samuelson). Assume $A = 500,000,000$. Find (a) $Y(5)$; (b) $Y(10)$.

*12 Denote by $p(x)$ the price and by $D(x)$ the quantity of a commodity at time x. Assume that the demand function is $p(x) = A + BD(x)$ and the supply function is $D(x) = C + Ep(x - 1)$; A, B, C, E are constants. The supply depends upon the price a period before, because of a constant period of production. (a) By eliminating $D(x)$, show that the price $p(x)$ satisfies the difference equation $p(x + 1) - BEp(x) = A + BC$. (b) Solve the difference equation under the condition that $D(0) = H$, where H is a constant. (c) Find $D(x)$ and check the two original equations.

13 Given the demand function $p(x) = 70 - (\frac{1}{2})D(x)$, the supply function $D(x) = (\frac{1}{3})p(x - 1)$, and the condition that $D(0) = 10$, (a) find the values of price and quantity for all points in time x. (b) Verify the solution by substituting into the equations. (c) Plot price and quantity against time and show that the fluctuations diminish as time increases. What is the ultimate limit? (d) Plot the demand and supply functions in one diagram. Connect successive points of equilibrium, and show that the diagram has the appearance of a *cobweb* (see Figure 59, Section 122).

14 Given the demand function $p(x) = 6 - D(x)$, the supply function $D(x) = p(x - 1)$, and the initial condition $D(0) = 2$, (a) find the values of price and quantity for all points in time x. (b) Check the solution by substituting into the equations. (c) Plot prices and quantities against time and show that there are constant fluctuations. (d) Plot the cobweb diagram (problem 13d).

15 Given the demand function $p(x) = 12 - D(x)$, the supply function $D(x) = 2p(x - 1)$, and the condition $D(0) = 6$, (a) find the values of price and quantity at all points in time. (b) Check the solutions by substituting into the equations. (c) Plot prices and quantities against time and show that there are increasing fluctuations. (d) Plot the cobweb diagram (problem 13d).

16 The demand for sugar in the United States has been estimated as $p(x) = 2.34 - 1.34D(x)$, and the supply of sugar as $D(x) = 0.5 + 0.6p(x - 1)$ (Schultz). (a) Find the course of price and quantity at all points in time, assuming $D(0) = 1.25$. (b) Verify the results with the help of the previous equations. (c) Plot price and quantity against time. (d) Make a cobweb diagram (problem 13d).

17 Denote by Q_t the ratio between the investment sector and the consumption sector in Great Britain (Sengupta and Tintner). We find empirically for 1700–1940: $Q_t = 0.2 + 0.9Q_{t-1}$. Find Q_{10} if $Q_0 = 1$.

18 Let Y_t be the real national income per capita in the United States (Meneses). The following difference equation has been estimated for the period 1869–1953: $Y_t = 0.178 + Y_{t-1}$. Solve the equation.

43   COMPLEX NUMBERS

We shall define complex numbers to be ordered pairs (x, y) of real numbers, together with the following properties: a complex number (x, y)

is equal to (u, v), $(x, y) = (u, v)$ if and only if $x = u$ and $y = v$; the sum $(x, y) + (u, v)$ of two complex numbers is given by $(x, y) + (u, v) = (x + u, y + v)$; finally, the product $(x, y)(u, v)$ of two complex numbers is given by $(x, y)(u, v) = (xu - yv, xv + yu)$.

From the definition of product of complex numbers comes a way to relate complex numbers to real numbers: If we take the product $(0, 1)(0, 1) = (-1, 0)$ and identify the complex number $(x, 0)$ with the real number x, we see that $(0, 1)^2 = -1$ and that the operations of sum and product of complex numbers as defined reduce to the sum and product of real numbers when restricted to complex numbers of the form $(x, 0)$. If we let $i = (0, 1)$, we then have $i^2 = -1$, or $i = \sqrt{-1}$.

Thus, we find it customary to write $(x, y) = x + iy$, and to call x the real component of the complex number and iy the imaginary component. Addition $(x, y) + (u, v) = (x + iy) + (u + iv)$, then, is accomplished by adding the real components and adding the imaginary components: $(x + iy) + (u + iv) = (x + u) + i(y + v)$. Using the fact that $i^2 = -1$, the product is handled as though multiplying two sums of real numbers: $(x + iy)(u + iv) = xu + ixv + iyu + i^2yv = (xu - yv) + i(xv + yu)$, which is precisely that which was given earlier as the definition of product.

If $z = x + iy$, the conjugate $\bar{z}$ of z is given by $z = x - iy$. Use of the conjugate allows for division $(x + iy)/(u + iv)$ of one complex number by another as follows. Noting that $(u + iv)(u - iv) = u^2 + v^2$, a real number, multiply $(x + iy)/(u + iv)$ above and below by the conjugate $u - iv$ of the denominator:

$$\frac{x + iy}{u + iv} \cdot \frac{u - iv}{u - iv} = \frac{(xu + yv)}{u^2 + v^2} + i(yu - xv) = \frac{xu + yv}{u^2 + v^2} + \frac{(yu - xv)i}{u^2 + v^2}.$$

EXAMPLE 1

Find $(2 + 3i)(1 - 2i)$ and $(2 + 3i)/(1 - 2i)$. Taking the product first,

$$(2 + 3i)(1 - 2i) = (2 + 6) + (-4 + 3)i = 8 - i.$$

Taking the quotient,

$$\frac{2 + 3i}{1 - 2i} = \frac{2 + 3i}{1 - 2i} \cdot \frac{1 + 2i}{1 + 2i} = \frac{(2 - 6) + i(4 + 3)}{1 + 4} = \frac{-4}{5} + i\frac{7}{5}.$$

Geometric representation of complex numbers

The set $\{(x, y)\}$ of all complex numbers $(x, y) = x + iy$ is called the complex plane, and it is natural to associate the complex plane with the rectangular Cartesian coordinates of the $x - y$ plane. Thus, we graph the complex number $(x, y) = x + iy$ as though we were locating the point (x, y) in the real Cartesian plane.

EXAMPLE 2

Locate in the complex plane the points $(2, -1) = 2 - i$ and $(3, 2) = 3 + 2i$ (Figure 20).

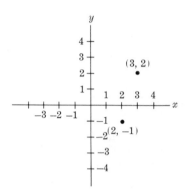

Figure 20

Just as we associate with a real number x its *distance* $|x|$ from the origin 0, or absolute value, so we can determine the distance of a complex number $(x, y) = x + iy$ from the origin in the complex plane, $(0, 0)$. Motivated by the fact that the distance formula of high school geometry gives $\sqrt{x^2 + y^2}$ as the distance of the point (x, y) from $(0, 0)$ in the $x - y$ plane, we define the *magnitude* or norm or *absolute value* of the complex number $(x, y) = x + iy$ to be $|x + iy| = \sqrt{x^2 + y^2} = \sqrt{(x + iy)(x - iy)}$. Geometrically, this is the length of the line segment from the origin $(0, 0)$ to the point (x, y). Thus, $|(3, 2)| = \sqrt{9 + 4} = \sqrt{13}$, and this is the length of the line segment between $(0, 0)$ and $(3, 2)$, while $|(2, -1)| = \sqrt{4 + 1} = \sqrt{5}$.

Polar form of complex numbers

In the study of the trigonometry of the right triangle, the so-called trigonometric functions of an angle such as θ, shown in Figure 21, are the sine of θ (sin θ), the cosine of θ (cos θ), the tangent of θ (tan θ), the cosecant of θ (csc θ), the secant of θ (sec θ), and the cotangent of θ (ctn θ).

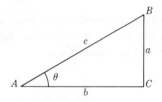

Figure 21

These functions are defined as follows:

$$\sin \theta = \frac{a}{c}, \qquad \csc \theta = \frac{c}{a},$$

$$\cos \theta = \frac{b}{c}, \qquad \sec \theta = \frac{c}{b},$$

$$\tan \theta = \frac{a}{b}, \qquad \operatorname{ctn} \theta = \frac{b}{a}.$$

Of course each definition fails when the denominator is 0.

The values of four of these functions for angles from 0° to 90° are listed in Table 2, Appendix D. By suitable modifications in the definitions, as given, the concept of the trigonometric functions may be extended to angles greater than 90°. In particular, $\tan(180° - \alpha) = -\tan \alpha$; that is, for instance, $\tan 120° = \tan(180° - 60°) = -\tan 60° = -1.7321$, by reference to Table 2.

The tangent function is of special significance in many studies, for the tangent of the angle of inclination that a straight line makes with the horizontal is known as *the slope of the line*. The increase in slope as an angle increases in size from 0 to 90 degrees may be observed by an examination of the tangent column in Table 2.

It is well known in high school algebra classes that it frequently is more convenient to operate with points in the polar coordinate system than with the rectangular coordinate system. Thus, in Figure 22, with a point

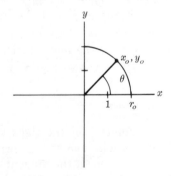

Figure 22

(x, y) in the rectangular Cartesian plane, we associate the point $(r \cos \theta, r \sin \theta)$ in the polar system, where r and θ are determined as follows: If (x_o, y_o) is a point in the real plane, (x_o, y_o) lies on the circle centered at the origin with radius $r_o = x_o{}^2 + y_o{}^2$, that is, (x_o, y_o) satisfies the equation of the circle $x^2 + y^2 = r_o{}^2$. We further note that if θ is the angle between the positive x-axis and the line from $(0, 0)$ to the point (x_o, y_o), moving in a counterclockwise direction, then

$$\tan \theta = \frac{y_o}{x_0}, \quad \sin \theta = \frac{y_o}{x_o{}^2 + y_o{}^2}, \quad \cos \theta = \frac{x_o}{x_o{}^2 + y_o{}^2},$$

so that the point (x_o, y_o) can be determined completely by specifying the radius r_o of the circle on which it lies [centered at $(0, 0)$] and the angle θ formed by moving in a counterclockwise direction from the positive x-axis along the circumference of the circle to the point (x_o, y_o).

So it is with complex numbers: the complex number $x_o + iy_o$ has as its polar form $r_0(\cos \theta + i \sin \theta)$, where $r_o = \sqrt{x_o{}^2 + y_o{}^2}$ and where θ is given by $\cos \theta = x_o/r_o$ and $\sin \theta = y_o/r_o$. The angle θ is called the argument of (x_o, y_o).

EXAMPLE 3

What is the polar form of $(0, -1) = i$? Here $r = 0^2 + (-1)^2 = 1$, $\sin \theta = -1/1 = -1$, $\cos \theta = 0/1 = 0$. A check in a table of trigonometric functions shows that the only angle having $\cos \theta = 0$ and $\sin \theta = -1$ is $\theta = 270° = 3\pi/2$. Thus, $(0, -1) = 1(\cos 270° + i \sin 270°)$.

EXAMPLE 4

Find the rectangular form of $\sqrt{2} (\cos \pi/4 + i \sin \pi/4)$. Cos $\pi/4 = \sqrt{2/2}$, $\sin \pi/4 = \sqrt{2/2}$. Hence $\sqrt{2} (\cos \pi/4 + i \sin \pi/4) = \sqrt{2/2} + i \sqrt{2/2} = 2/2 + i(2/2) = 1 + i$ (Figure 23).

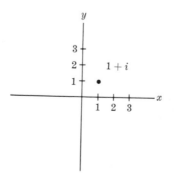

Figure 23

EXERCISES 43

1   Find the sums, product, and quotient $(x + iy)/(u + iv)$: (a) $(3, -2) =$ (x, y), $(u, v) = (1, 2)$. (b) $(1, -1) = (x, y)$, $(u, v) = (2, 3)$. (c) $(5, 0) =$ (x, y), $(u, v) = (0, 5)$. (d) $(x, y) = (3, 2)$, $(u, v) = (1, 1)$.

2   Find the polar form of the complex numbers (x, y) given in problem 1.

3   Use the identities $\cos \theta \cos \phi - \sin \theta \sin \phi = \cos (\theta + \phi)$, $\sin \theta \cos \phi + \cos \theta \sin \phi = \sin (\theta + \phi)$ to show that if $(x, y) = r(\cos \theta + i \sin \theta)$ and $(u, v) = s(\cos \phi + i \sin \phi)$, then

$$(x, y)(u, v) = rs[\cos (\theta + \phi) + i \sin (\theta + \phi)].$$

(*De Moivre's theorem*) Can you generalize this to the product of n complex numbers? What technique of proof would you use?

4   Solve the following systems of equations for z. Where z is not real express it in polar form. (a) $2z^2 - 9 = 0$, (b) $2z^2 + 9 = 0$, (c) $z^2 + 2z + 2 = 0$, (d) $z^2 - 6z + 36 = 0$, (e) $4z^2 - 8z + 5 = 0$.

44   FINITE DIFFERENCE EQUATIONS OF SECOND ORDER

We consider first the homogeneous equation

$$a_2 y_{t+2} + a_1 y_{t+1} + a_0 y_t = 0.$$

It can be shown that a solution to this equation is of the form $y_t = A \cdot m^t$, where A and m are constants.
We have also

$$y_{t+2} = A \cdot m^{t+2}, \qquad y_{t+1} = A \cdot m^{t+1}.$$

Our equation becomes

$$a_2 A \cdot m^{t+2} + a_1 m^{t+1} + a \cdot A m^t = 0.$$

We factor out the expression $A \cdot m^t$. Hence

$$a_2 m^2 + m_1 m + a_0 = 0.$$

This is a quadratic equation. It is called the characteristic equation. Let m_1 and m_2 be its roots. Assume at first that these roots are different. Then the solution is

$$y_t = A_1 m_1{}^t + A_2 m_2{}^t,$$

where A_1 and A_2 are constants, to be determined by the initial conditions.

EXAMPLE 1

Consider a homogeneous second-degree linear difference equation with constant coefficients:

$$y_{t+2} + y_{t+1} - 6y_t = 0.$$

The characteristic equation is

$$m^2 + m - 6 = 0,$$

and its roots are $m_1 = 2$, $m_2 = -3$.
Hence the general solution is

$$y_t = A_1 2^t + A_2(-3)^t.$$

The initial conditions are $y_0 = 15$, $y_1 = 5$. These serve to determine the constants A_1 and A_2. Thus,

$$y_0 = A_1 2^0 + A_2(-3)^0 = A_1 + A_2 = 15,$$
$$y_1 = A_1 2^1 + A_2(-3)^1 = 2A_1 - 3A_2 = 5.$$

The solution is $A_1 = 10$, $A_2 = 5$. Hence the complete solution of our homogeneous equation, which satisfies the intial conditions, is

$$y_t = (10)2^t + (5)(-3)^t.$$

Consider now the case where the characteristic equation

$$a_2 m^2 + a_1 m + a_0 = 0$$

has a double root, $m_1 = m_2$. It can be shown that in this case the solution is

$$y_t = (B_1 + B_2 t)m_1^t.$$

EXAMPLE 2

A homogeneous linear difference equation is

$$y_{t+2} - 4y_{t+1} + 4y_t = 0.$$

Our characteristic equation is now

$$m^2 - 4m + 4 = (m - 2)^2 = 0,$$

and the double root is $m = 2$.
The general solution is

$$y_t = (B_1 + B_2 t)2^t.$$

Assume for initial conditions $y_0 = 10$, $y_1 = 24$. We determine the constants B_1, B_2 as follows:

$$y_0 = (B_1 + B_2 0)2^0 = B_1 = 10,$$
$$y_1 = (B_1 + B_2 1)2^1 = 2B_1 + 2B_2 = 24.$$

Hence $B_1 = 10$, $B_2 = 2$. The solution is finally

$$y_t = (10 + 2t)2^t.$$

Now assume that the characteristic equation has the following complex conjugate roots:

$$m_1 = a + ib, \qquad m_2 = a - ib.$$

The solution is given by

$$y_t = A_1 m_1{}^t + A_2 m_2{}^t.$$

But it is better to use the polar form of the two roots:

$$\zeta = \sqrt{a^2 + b^2},$$

$$\cos \theta = \frac{a}{\zeta},$$

$$\sin \theta = \frac{b}{\zeta},$$

$$m_1 = \zeta(\cos \theta + i \sin \theta),$$
$$m_2 = \zeta(\cos \theta - i \sin \theta).$$

The solution can be written as follows:

$$y_t = \zeta^t(B_1 \sin \theta t + B_2 \cos \theta t),$$

where the constants B_1 and B_2 are again determined by the initial conditions.

EXAMPLE 3

The homogeneous second-order difference equation is

$$y_{t+2} - 4y_{t+1} + 5y_t = 0.$$

The characteristic equation is now

$$m^2 - 4m + 5 = 0.$$

The two conjugate complex roots are

$$m_1 = 2 + i, \qquad m_2 = 2 - i.$$

We write this in polar form:

$$\zeta = \sqrt{2^2 + 1^2} = \sqrt{5} = 2.236068,$$

$$\cos \theta = \frac{2}{\sqrt{5}} = 0.894427,$$

$$\sin \theta = \frac{1}{\sqrt{5}} = 0.447214,$$

$$\theta = 26°34'.$$

The solution is given as

$$y_t = (\sqrt{5})^t[B_1 \sin (26°24')t + B_2 \cos (26°24')t].$$

Assume the initial values $y_0 = 2$ and $y_1 = 5$. We determine the constants B_1 and B_2 as follows:

$$y_0 = (\sqrt{5})^0(B_1 \sin 0^\circ + B_2 \cos 0^\circ) = 1(0 + B_2) = B_2 = 2,$$
$$y_1 = (\sqrt{5})^1[B_1 \sin (26^\circ 34') + B_2 \cos (26^\circ 34')$$
$$= \sqrt{5}\left(\frac{B_1}{\sqrt{5}} + \frac{2B_2}{\sqrt{5}}\right) = B_1 + 2B_2 = 5.$$

It follows that $B_1 = 1$ and $B_2 = 2$. Hence the solution is

$$y_t = (2.236068)^t[\sin (26^\circ 34')t + 2 \cos (26^\circ 34')t].$$

We consider now a simple type of *nonhomogeneous* equation of the second order:

$$a_2 y_{t+2} + a_1 y_{t+1} + a_0 y_t = L,$$

where a_0, a_1, a_2, and L are constants. Suppose we know that z_t is a solution of the corresponding homogeneous equation

$$a_2 z_{t+2} + a_1 z_{t+1} + a_0 z_t = 0.$$

Then we might try to find the solution of the nonhomogeneous equation in the form

$$y_t = z_t + K,$$

where K is a constant. We have

$$a_2(z_{t+2} + K) + a_1(z_{t+1} + K) + a_0(z_t + K) = L.$$

Hence,

$$(a_2 z_{t+2} + a_1 z_{t+1} + a_0 z_t) + (a_2 + a_1 + a_0)K = L.$$

Since the first term of the last equation is zero, we have

$$(a_2 + a_1 + a_0)K = L.$$

Hence the constant K is given by

$$K = \frac{L}{a_2 + a_1 + a_0}.$$

The solution of the nonhomogeneous equation appears as

$$y_t = z_t + \frac{L}{a_2 + a_1 + a_0},$$

where z_t is the solution of the corresponding homogeneous equation.

EXAMPLE 4

We have the following nonhomogeneous linear second-order difference equation with constant coefficients:

$$y_{t+2} - 5y_{t+1} + 6y_t = 10.$$

Since $a_2 = 1$, $a_1 = -5$, $a_0 = 6$, and $L = 10$, the constant K is given by

$$K = \frac{10}{1 - 5 + 6} = \frac{10}{2} = 5.$$

Now we seek the solution of the corresponding homogeneous equation:

$$z_{t+2} - 5z_{t+1} + 6 = 0.$$

The characteristic equation is

$$m^2 - 5m + 6 = 0.$$

Its roots are $m_1 = 2$, $m_2 = 3$. The solution of the nonhomogeneous equation is given by

$$y_t = A_1 2^t + A_2 3^t + 5.$$

The two constants A_1 and A_2 are determined by the initial conditions. Assume $y_0 = 17$ and $y_1 = 31$. Then we have

$$y_0 = A_1 2^0 + A_2 3^0 + 5 = A_1 + A_2 + 5 = 17,$$
$$y_1 = A_1 2^1 + A_2 3^1 + 5 = 2A_1 + 3A_2 + 5 = 31.$$

We have for the determination of the two constants A_1 and A_2

$$A_1 + A_2 = 12,$$
$$2A_1 + 3A_2 = 26.$$

Hence $A_1 = 10$ and $A_2 = 2$. The solution of the nonhomogeneous equation that satisfies the initial conditions is

$$y_t = 10 \cdot 2^t + 2 \cdot 3^t + 5.$$

EXERCISES 44

1   Solve the following finite difference equations with the initial values $y_0 = 1$, $y_1 = 2$: (a) $y_{t+2} - 7y_{t+1} + 10y_t = 0$, (b) $y_{t+2} - 9y_t = 0$. (c) $y_{t+2} - 4y_{t+1} + 8y_t = 0$. (d) $y_{t+2} - 2y_{t+1} - 8y_t = 14$. (e) $y_{t+2} - 4y_{t+1} + 13y_t = 20$. (f) $y_{t+2} + 25y_t = 13$.

2   Define y_t as national income, a as the marginal propensity to consume, and b as the ratio between investment and increase of production (accel-

eration principle). Solve the following difference equation (Samuelson):

$$y_{t+2} - a(1 + b)y_{t+1} + aby_t = 1$$

with the given initial conditions y_0 and y_1.

3 y_t is national income, c the marginal propensity to consume, v_0 constant net investment (Metzler). Assume also $0 < c < 1$. Solve the following difference equation:

$$y_{t+2} - 2cy_{t+1} + cy_t = v_0$$

given the initial conditions y_0 and y_1.

4 The marginal propensity to consume for the United States for the period 1930–1940 was estimated as $c = 0.712$ (Haavelmo). Solve the equation in problem 3 for this value.

5 Klein estimated the marginal propensity to consume for the United States for the period 1921–1941 as $c = 0.58$. Solve the difference equation of problem 3 for this value.

6 Tintner estimated the marginal propensity to consume for Austria for the period 1948–1956 as $c = 0.781$. Solve the equation in problem 3 for this value.

**7 Consider the general linear second-order homogeneous difference equation with constant coefficients. Show that in the case of two distinct real roots that lie between -1 and $+1$ $\lim\limits_{t \to \infty} y_t = 0$. In the case of complex roots, show that $\lim\limits_{t \to \infty} y_t = 0$ if the modulus of the roots is less than 1.

8 Define y_t as the per capita national income in the United States for the years 1869–1953 (Meneses). The following second-order difference equation has been estimated:

$$y_t = 50.720 + 0.191y_{t-1} + 0.062y_{t-2}.$$

Solve the equation.

9 Let y_t be the real per capita national income in the United States for the years 1912–1932 (Meneses). The following difference equation has been estimated:

$$y_t = 154.237 + 1.199y_{t-1} - 0.441y_{t-2}.$$

Solve the equation.

PART TWO
CALCULUS

Chapter 10
Functions, Limits, and Derivatives

45 MORE ABOUT FUNCTIONS

Many times an equation, say $h(x, y) = k$, (k a constant) will be satisfied by all points (x, y) such that $y = f(x)$ for some function f, so that $h(x, f(x)) = k$. Thus, the equation $x^2 + y^2 = 4$ is satisfied by the function $y = \sqrt{4 - x^2}$, $-2 \leq x \leq 2$, and also by the function $y = -\sqrt{4 - x^2}$, $-2 \leq x \leq 2$. In such a case the equation $h(x, y) = k$ is said to define $y = f(x)$ *implicitly*.

Given such an equation, it is often desirable to determine what function, or functions, the equation thus defines. In such a case the procedure is to attempt to solve the equation for one variable in terms of the other, being careful to make whatever statements may be necessary about the domain of the function this determined, so that it is well defined.

EXAMPLE 1

Find all functions, if any, defined implicitly by $x^2 - y^2 = 4$. This equation is equivalent to $y^2 = x^2 - 4$, which is satisfied by the two functions $y = f(x) = \sqrt{x^2 - 4}$, $x \geq 2$ or $x \leq -2$, and $y = g(x) = -\sqrt{x^2 - 4}$, $x \geq 2$ or $x \leq -2$. These functions are graphed in Figures 24 and 25.

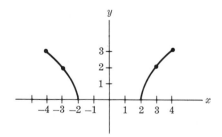

Figure 24

135

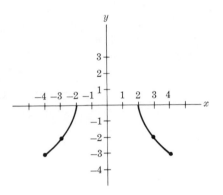

Figure 25

EXAMPLE 2

Find all functions $y = f(x)$ determined implicitly by the equation $y^2 + yx + y = x^2 + 1$, x, y real.

The key to this problem is to recognize that this is a quadratic in y, and we rewrite it as $y^2 + y(x + 1) - (x^2 + 1) = 0$. The solution for y is then

$$y = -\frac{(x + 1) + \sqrt{(x + 1)^2 - 4(x^2 + 1)}}{2}$$

$$= \frac{-(x + 1) + \sqrt{x^2 + 2x + 1 - 4x^2 - 4}}{2}$$

$$= \frac{-(x + 1) + \sqrt{2x - 3x^2 - 3}}{2}.$$

There are two functions, $y = f(x)$, $y = g(x)$, defined as

$$f(x) = -\frac{(x + 1) + \sqrt{2x - 3x^2 - 3}}{2}$$

$$\text{and} \quad g(x) = -\frac{(x + 1) - \sqrt{2x - 3x^2 - 3}}{2},$$

defined where $2x - 3x^2 - 3 \geqq 0$. However, we can easily verify that for *no* x is $2x - 3x^2 - 3 \geqq 0$, x real, so that the given equation defines *no* functions implicitly. Then we see that the given equation is satisfied by *no* points (x, y): for no (x, y) is $y^2 + y(x + 1) - (x^2 + 1) = 0$.

Inverses of functions

If f is a function, that is, a set of ordered pairs $\{(x, y) | y = f(x),$ x in domain of $f\}$, the *inverse* of f, f^{-1}, is given by $f^{-1} = \{(y, x) | y = f(x)\}$.

We see that f^{-1} is a relation, and f^{-1} may or may *not* be a function itself. f^{-1} will, in fact, be a function if and only if for each y in the range of f there is one and only one x in the domain of f such that $y = f(x)$.

EXAMPLE 3

Let $y = f(x) = x^2$, x real. Find f^{-1}.

$$f^{-1} = \{(y, x)|y = x^2\}.$$

Now, $y = x^2$ if and only if either $x = \sqrt{y}$ or $x = -\sqrt{y}$. Hence, $f^{-1} = \{(y, x)|x = \sqrt{y}$ or $x = \sqrt{-y}\}$. The domain of f^{-1} is the set of all nonnegative reals; the range is the set of all reals. f^{-1} is not a function.

It follows from the definition of f^{-1} that we can find f^{-1} by noting that $f[f^{-1}(x)] = x$, x in the range of f. Hence, if one evaluates $f[f^{-1}(x)]$ and solves $f[f^{-1}(x)] = x$ for $f^{-1}(x)$, formally, and operating as though $f^{-1}(x)$ were a variable in an equation, the relation $f^{-1}(x)$ can be found provided we can do the necessary algebra.

EXAMPLE 4

Let $f(x) = x^2 - 2x + 1$. Find $f^{-1}(x)$ and state whether or not f^{-1} is a function.

$$f[f^{-1}(x)] = (f^{-1}(x))^2 - 2f^{-1}(x) + 1 = x,$$
$$\text{or} \quad (f^{-1})^2 - 2f^{-1} + 1 - x = 0.$$
$$f^{-1} = \frac{2 \pm \sqrt{4 - 4(1 - x)}}{2} = 1 \pm \sqrt{x}.$$

Thus, associated with every z in the range of f there are two numbers y in the domain of f: $f^{-1} = \{(z, y)|y = 1 + \sqrt{z}$ or $y = 1 - \sqrt{z}, z \geqq 0\}$. f^{-1} is not a function.

EXAMPLE 4

Let $f(x) = 3x^3 + 2$. Find f^{-1} and determine whether or not f^{-1} is a function. $f[f^{-1}(x)] = 3(f^{-1})^3 + 2 = x$, so that $(f^{-1})^3 = (x - 2)/3$. There is only one solution to this: $f^{-1} = [(x - 2)/3]^{1/3}$. Hence, for z in the range r_f of f, where r_f is the set of all real numbers, there is one and only one y in the domain d_f of f such that $z = f(y)$. Hence $f^{-1}(z) = [(z - 2)/3]^{1/3}$ is a function, with domain and range all real numbers.

EXERCISES 45

1   What, if any, functions f are defined by the following equation that give $y = f(x)$? State the domain and range of any functions thus determined.

(a) $2y^2 - 5x - 5 = 0$. (b) $3xy - 24 = x$. (c) $\dfrac{x + y}{x - y} = 2$. (d) $\dfrac{x^2}{4} +$

$\dfrac{y^2}{9} = 1$. (e) $x^2 + 2xy + y^2 = 1$. (f) $x^3 - 2x^2y + xy^2 = 0$.

2 For the following functions f, find the relation f^{-1} and state whether or
not f^{-1} is a function, and give the domain and range of f^{-1}. (a) $f(x) =$
$3x^3 - 9$. (b) $f(x) = \dfrac{1}{x} + 1$. (c) $f(x) = x$. (d) $f(x) = \sqrt{x - 1}$. (e)
$f(x) = \sqrt{x - 1}$, $x \geq 3$. (f) $f(x) = ln\ x$. (g) $f(x) = 2x^2 - x + l$.

46   DEMAND FUNCTIONS AND TOTAL REVENUE FUNCTIONS

A general market demand functions is given in the form $p = p(D) =$
$f(D)$, where p is the price of the commodity and D is the quantity demanded. This is a generalization of the linear demand functions, quadratic
demand functions, and demand functions with constant elasticity, which
were introduced earlier.

The inverse function is $D = D(p) = g(D)$. Implicity, the relation can
be written $h(p, D) = 0$. All these expressions are equivalent and describe
the same economic relationship between the quantity demanded D and
the price per unit p.

If we multiply price of a commodity by the quantity sold we get the
total receipts of the seller or the total outlay of the consumers. This is
called the *total revenue function;* then the revenue function R may be
written in functional language as

$$R(D) = pD = f(D) \cdot D = h(D).$$

The total-revenue function is considered as a function of the *quantity*
sold, rather than of the price. The total revenue function gives the total
receipts of the sellers, or the total money outlay of the buyers, if a certain
quantity D of the commodity is sold.

We show in Figure 26 the graph of a linear demand function and of the

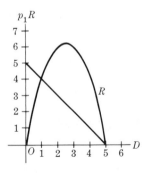

Figure 26

corresponding total revenue function R. Also the demand function is called sometimes the *average revenue curve*.

EXAMPLE

Assume the implicit function, $p + D = 1$. (a) Make it explicit for p; it is $p = 1 - D$. This is said to be the *demand curve*. (b) Find the total revenue curve; it is $R = pD = D - D^2$. (c) Find the price if $\frac{1}{2}$ unit is sold. The result is $p(\frac{1}{2}) = 1 - \frac{1}{2} = \frac{1}{2}$. (d) Find the total revenue if $\frac{1}{3}$ unit is sold. We obtain $R(\frac{1}{3}) = \frac{1}{3} - \frac{1}{9} = \frac{2}{9}$.

EXERCISES 46

1 Given the relationship $2p + 3D = 10$, (a) find the demand curve; (b) the total-revenue curve; (c) find $p(1)$; (d) $p(2.5)$; (e) $p(0.755)$; (f) $R(0.75)$; (g) $R(1.125)$; (h) $R(3)$; (i) $R(0)$. (j) Plot the demand curve and the total revenue curve.

2 Given the relationship $3p + D = 60$, (a) find the demand curve; (b) the total revenue curve. (c) Find $p(0)$; (d) $p(1)$; (e) $p(6)$; (f) $R(7)$; (g) $R(1.5)$; (h) $R(5.25)$. (i) Plot the demand curve and total revenue curve.

3 Given the relationship $p^2 + 5D = 100$, (a) find the demand curve. (b) Find the total revenue curve. (c) Find $p(10)$; (d) $p(2)$; (e) $p(17)$; (f) $R(2.50)$; (g) $R(3.25)$; (h) $R(0.125)$, (i) Plot the demand curve and the total revenue curve.

4 Given the relationship $p^D = 100$. (a) find the demand curve; (b) the total revenue curve. (c) Find $p(1)$; (d) $p(5)$; (e) $R(3)$; (f) $R(10)$; (g) $R(5)$; (h) $R(7.125)$. (i) Plot the demand curve and the total revenue curve.

5 Given the relationship, $p \log D = 24$, (a) find the demand curve; (b) the total revenue curve. (c) Find $p(10)$; (d) $p(2)$; (e) $p(18.5)$; (f) $R(10)$; (g) $R(5)$; (h) $R(7.125)$. (i) Plot the demand curve and the total revenue curve.

6 Let $10pD^2 = 1,000$. (a) Find the demand curve; (b) the total revenue curve. (c) Find $p(2)$; (d) $R(1)$; (e) $R(25)$. (f) Plot the demand curve and the total revenue curve.

7 Given the relationship $p^2 - 2p + D = 10$, (a) find the demand curve; (b) the total revenue curve. (c) Find $p(0.5)$; (d) $p(0.1)$; (e) $p(0.001)$; (f) $R(0.98)$; (g) $R(6.33)$; (h) $R(0.25)$. (HINT: Take the radical positive.)

8 The implicit demand curve for sugar in the United States (1915–1929), according to Schultz, is estimated by $p + 0.1D = 12$. (a) Find the demand curve; (b) the total revenue curve. (c) Find $p(60)$; (d) $p(75)$; (e) $p(85)$; (f) $R(50)$; (g) $R(45)$; (h) $R(62)$. (i) Plot the demand curve and the total revenue curve.

9   The implicit demand curve for cotton, 1914–1929, for the United States, according to Schultz, is estimated by $pD^{1.4} = 0.11$. (a) Find the demand curve; (b) the total revenue curve. (c) Find $p(15)$; (d) $p(20)$; (e) $p(12)$; (f) $R(10)$; (g) $R(12)$; (h) $R(15)$. (i) Plot the demand curve and the total revenue curve.

10 The implicit form of the demand function for potatoes in the United States, 1915–1929, according to Schultz, is estimated by $100D + 2p = 440$. (a) Find the demand curve; (b) the total revenue curve. (c) Find $p(2)$; (d) $p(3)$; (e) $p(4)$; (f) $R(2.5)$; (g) $R(3)$; (h) $R(3.5)$. (i) Plot the demand curve and the total revenue curve.

11 The demand for barley in the United States, 1915–1929, according to Schultz, is estimated by $D = 6.39/p^{0.39}$. (a) Find the demand curve; (b) the total revenue curve. (c) Find $p(1)$; (d) $p(2)$; (e) $p(3)$; (f) $R(4)$; (g) $R(3)$. (h) Plot the demand curve and the total revenue curve.

12 The demand for hay in the United States for the period 1915–1929, according to Schultz, is estimated by $10D = 53 - 2p$. (a) Find the demand curve $p(D)$; (b) the total revenue curve. (c) Find $p(0.2)$; (d) $p(0.35)$; (e) $p(0.4)$; (f) $R(0.5)$; (g) $R(0.3)$; (h) $R(0.55)$. (i) Plot the demand curve and the total revenue curve.

13 The demand for butter in Stockholm (1925–1937) has been estimated as $D = 38/p^{1.2}$ (Wold). Find (a) the demand curve; (b) the total revenue curve; (c) $p(2)$; (d) $R(2)$.

47   TOTAL AND AVERAGE COST FUNCTIONS

We understand by total cost the sum total of *all* monetary expenditures incurred in order to produce a given amount of the commodity. We deal here only with short-term cost functions. These functions are constructed under the assumption that there is a certain fixed capital equipment.

Denote the amount produced by D and the total cost by C. We have a functional relationship between total cost and amount produced; that is,

$$C = f(D).$$

Average cost is cost per unit of the commodity produced. In order to compute average cost we divide the total cost by the number of units produced. We denote the average cost by A; thus, in the language of functional relationships,

$$A = \frac{C}{D} = \frac{f(D)}{D} = g(D).$$

On the other hand, if the average cost is known, we get the total cost by multiplying average cost by the number of units produced; that is,

$$C = AD.$$

Figure 27 shows a total cost curve C and an average cost curve A, which have the typical shapes generally assumed in economic theory for short-term cost curves. Note that average costs are high for small amounts produced, then decrease to a minimum, and later increase again as large quantities of the commodity are produced.

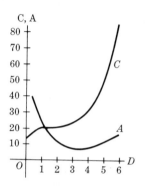

Figure 27

EXAMPLE

Given the implicit relationship $3D^2 - C = 0$, (a) find the total cost curve; it is $C = 3D^2$. (b) Find the average cost curve; it is $A = C/D = 3D$. (c) Find the total cost if 10 units are produced. There results $C(10) = 3(10)^2 = 300$. (d) Find the average cost if 3 units are produced. We have $A(3) = (3)(3) = 9$.

EXERCISES 47

1   Given the relationship $C - 2D - D^2 = 0$, (a) find the total cost curve; (b) the average cost curve. (c) Find $C(12)$; (d) $C(4)$; (e) $C(3)$; (f) $A(6)$; (g) $A(11)$; (h) $A(5)$. (i) Plot the total cost curve and the average cost curve.

2   Given the relationship $D = C^3$, (a) determine the total cost curve; (b) the average cost curve. (c) Find $C(1)$; (d) $C(0)$; (e) $C(5)$; (f) $C(4)$; (g) $A(1)$; (h) $A(6)$; (i) $A(11)$; (j) $A(9)$. (k) Plot the total cost curve and the average cost curve.

3   Given the relationship $5C - 3D = 100$, (a) find the total cost curve; (b) the average cost curve. (c) Find $C(0)$; (d) $C(3)$; (e) $C(6)$; (f) $A(1)$; (g) $A(10)$. (h) Plot the total cost curve and the average cost curve.

4   Given the relationship $D = -80 + C^2$, (a) find the total cost curve; (b) the average cost curve. (c) Find $C(1)$; (d) $C(10)$; (e) $C(3)$; (f) $C(12)$; (g) $A(10)$; (h) $A(5)$; (i) $A(6)$; (j) $A(7)$. (k) Plot the total cost curve and the average cost curve.

5   Given the relationship $C^2 - D - 5D^2 = 45$, (a) find the total cost curve; (b) the average cost curve. (c) Find $C(0)$; (d) $C(10)$; (e) $C(100)$; (f) $A(1)$; (g) $A(5)$; (h) $A(15)$; (i) $A(3)$. (j) Plot the total cost curve and the average cost curve.

6   Given the relationship $D = \log C - 5$, (a) establish the total cost curve; (b) the average cost curve. (c) Find $C(0)$; (d) $C(10)$; (e) $C(150)$; (f) $A(10)$; (g) $A(100)$; (h) $A(50)$. (i) Plot the total cost curve and the average cost curve.

7   Given the relationship $C^2/D^3 = 8$, (a) find the total cost curve; (b) the average cost curve. (c) Find $C(4)$; (d) $C(80)$; (e) $C(100)$; (f) $A(1)$; (g) $A(25)$.

8   Given the relationship $5 \log C - 4 \log D = 2$, (a) find the total cost curve; (b) the average cost curve. (c) Find $C(1)$; (d) $C(10)$; (e) $C(32)$; (f) $C(100)$; (g) $A(2)$; (h) $A(10)$; (i) $A(25)$; (j) $A(5)$.

9   Given the relationship $C/\log D = 24$, (a) find the total cost curve; (b) the average cost curve. (c) Find $C(1)$; (d) $C(2)$; (e) $C(100)$; (f) $C(10,000)$; (g) $C(500)$; (h) $A(100)$; (i) $A(25)$; (j) $A(100,000)$.

10   Yntema has estimated a relationship between the total cost C and the quantity produced D of the United States Steel Corporation, 1928–1938, to be $C - 56D = 182$. (a) Find the total cost curve; (b) the average cost curve. (c) Find $C(5)$; (d) $C(10)$; (e) $C(15)$; (f) $C(9.25)$; (g) $C(6.5)$; (h) $A(10)$; (i) $A(12.5)$; (j) $A(19.5)$; (k) $A(6.75)$. (l) Plot the total cost curve and the average cost curve.

11   The total cost function of a hosiery mill was estimated by Dean as follows: $C = -10,485 + 6.75D - 0.0003D^2$. (a) Find the average cost curve; (b) $C(4,400)$; (c) $C(6,000)$; (d) $C(8,550)$; (e) $C(6,895)$; (f) $A(5,000)$ (g) $A(8,200)$; (h) $A(4,575)$. (i) Plot the total cost curve and the average cost curve.

12   Dean estimated the total cost function of a leather belt shop as follows: $C = 3,000 + 0.8D$. (a) Find the average cost curve; (b) $C(50,000)$; (c) $C(120,000)$; (d) $C(95,000)$; (e) $A(50,000)$; (f) $A(65,000)$; (g) $A(25,560)$. (h) Plot the total cost curve and the average cost curve.

48   DIFFERENCE QUOTIENTS

If $y = f(x)$, the difference quotient is defined as

$$\frac{\Delta y}{\Delta x} = \frac{f(x + \Delta x) - f(x)}{\Delta x},$$

where Δx is an increment of x and Δy is the increment or change of y corresponding to the change Δx to $f(x)$. The ratio $\Delta y/\Delta x$ shows the average *rate of change* in y with respect to x. To x corresponds a y given by $y = f(x)$. To $x + \Delta x$ corresponds $y + \Delta y = f(x + \Delta x)$. This latter value is computed by substituting $x + \Delta x$ in place of x in the equation $y = f(x)$. We have, therefore, the relations

$$y + \Delta y = f(x + \Delta x), \qquad y = f(x),$$

from which it follows immediately that

$$\Delta y = f(x + \Delta x) - f(x).$$

To obtain the difference quotient, this has to be divided by the increment in the independent variable Δx; hence

$$\frac{\Delta y}{\Delta x} = \frac{f(x + \Delta x) - f(x)}{\Delta x}.$$

It is a matter of considerable interest to note that the difference quotient as defined above is the slope of a line through the two points (x, y) and $(x + \Delta x, y + \Delta y)$ on the curve corresponding to the function $y = f(x)$. This will be made clear in the examples that follow.

EXAMPLE 1

Figure 28 shows the function $y = f(x) = x^2$. Let us select $x = 2$ and $\Delta x = 1$; of course, $y = f(2) = 4$; as already indicated, $\Delta y = f(x + \Delta x) - f(x) = f(3) - f(2) = 9 - 4 = 5$. So the difference

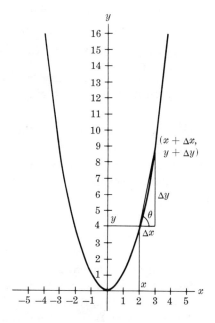

Figure 28

quotient at the point $x = 2$, $y = 4$ is

$$\frac{\Delta y}{\Delta x} = \frac{5}{1} = 5.$$

This difference quotient is tan θ in Figure 28, that is, the slope of the straight line connecting the points (2, 4) and (3, 9). By reference to Table 2, Appendix D, it is found that $\theta = 78.7°$, approximately.

EXAMPLE 2

Let $y = f(x) = 5x^3 + 3x - 1$. Determine the difference quotient. By substituting $x + \Delta x$ for x into the above formula we get

$$y + \Delta y = 5(x + \Delta x)^3 + 3(x + \Delta x) - 1.$$

This can be expanded as follows:

$$y + \Delta y = 5[x^3 + 3x^2(\Delta x) + 3x(\Delta x)^2 + (\Delta x)^3] + 3(x + \Delta x) - 1,$$
$$y + \Delta y = 5x^3 + 15x^2(\Delta x) + 15x(\Delta x)^2 + 5(\Delta x)^3 + 3x + 3(\Delta x)$$
$$- 1.$$

But
$$y = 5x^3 \qquad\qquad\qquad\qquad + 3x \qquad - 1.$$

By subtracting the members in the second line from those in the first, we get

$$\Delta y = 15x^2(\Delta x) + 15x(\Delta x)^2 + 5(\Delta x)^3 + 3(\Delta x).$$

To obtain the difference quotient $\Delta y / \Delta x$, we divide the last expression term by term by Δx and obtain

$$\frac{\Delta y}{\Delta x} = 15x^2 + 15x(\Delta x) + 5(\Delta x)^2 + 3.$$

This expression may be evaluated for any given x and Δx to obtain the desired difference quotient. For instance, for $x = 1$ and $\Delta x = 0.1$, we have

$$\frac{\Delta y}{\Delta x} = 15(1)^2 + 15(1)(0.1) + 5(0.1)^2 + 3 = 19.55.$$

This means that for an increment $\Delta x = 0.1$ the average rate of change of y relative to x, when $x = 1$, is 19.55. This value is also the slope of the line connecting the points (1, 7) and (1.1, 8.955) on the curve. Since tan $\theta = 19.55$, we find from our tables that $\theta = 87.1°$, approximately.

EXAMPLE 3

Let $y = f(x) = 2x^2 - x$. What is the difference quotient?

$$y + \Delta y = 2(x + \Delta x)^2 - (x + \Delta x).$$

$$y + \Delta y = 2x^2 + 4x(\Delta x) + 2(\Delta x)^2 - x - \Delta x.$$

$$y = 2x^2.$$

$$\Delta y = \qquad 4x(\Delta x) + 2(\Delta x)^2 - \Delta x.$$

$$\frac{\Delta y}{\Delta x} = \qquad 4x \quad + 2(\Delta x) - 1.$$

For instance, let $x = 10$ and $\Delta x = 2$. Then the difference quotient $\Delta y/\Delta x$ is $(4)(10) + (2)(2) - 1 = 43$. So the slope of the straight line through the two points on the curve is 43. Hence, $\tan \theta = 43$ and $\theta = 88.7°$, approximately.

EXERCISES 48

1   Given $y = f(x) = x^3 + 2x^2 - 5$, (a) find the general formula for the difference quotient. (b) Compute the difference quotient for $x = 4$, $\Delta x = 2$. (c) What is the angle θ? (d) Make a graph and indicate the quantities given.

2   Given the function $y = 3x - 5$, (a) compute the general expression for the difference quotient. (b) Find the difference quotient for $x = 5$, $\Delta x = \frac{1}{2}$. (c) What is the angle θ? (d) Make a graph and indicate the various quantities.

3   Given the function $y = x^2 + 3x - 6$, (a) find the general expression for the difference quotient. (b) Assume that $\Delta x = 3$; find the x for which the angle θ is $45°$.

4   Let the function be $y = f(x) = 24/x$. (a) Find the general expression for the difference quotient. (b) Compute the difference quotient for $x = 6$, $\Delta x = 1$. (c) Make a graph and indicate Δx and Δy.

5   Let $y = f(x) = x^3$. (a) Find the general expression for the difference quotient. (b) Assume that $\Delta x = 1$, and find the x for which the angle $\theta = 30°$.

6   Consider the function $y = 10$. (a) Graph. (b) Find the general expression for the difference quotient.

7   Consider the function $y = f(x) = x^3$. (a) Plot. (b) Find the general expression for the difference quotient. (c) Find the difference quotient and angle θ if $x = 2$; if $\Delta x = 1$; if $\Delta x = 0.1$; if $\Delta x = 0.01$; if $\Delta x = 0.0001$.

**8 Is there a function whose difference quotient $(\Delta y)/(\Delta x)$ is k, where k is constant? (HINT: Consider the general linear function $y = a + bx$.) What is the interpretation of k?

**9 Consider the function $y = f(x) = x^2$. Let $\Delta x = 1$. Insert numerical values in the following table of differences Δy:

x	$y = f(x)$	$\Delta y = f(x + 1) - f(x)$
0	$f(0)$	
1	$f(1)$	$f(1) - f(0)$
2	$f(2)$	$f(2) - f(1)$
3	$f(3)$	$f(3) - f(2)$

**10 Use the scheme indicated in problem 9 to compute the differences Δy for the function $y = 2x^3 - x + 1$ for $\Delta x = 1$; use integral values of x in the range $x = 0$ to $x = 5$.

**11 Use the method indicated in problem 9 to find the differences Δy of the function $y = 2x - 1$ for $\Delta x = \frac{1}{2}$; employ values of x in the range $x = -2$ to $x = 2$.

**12 Use the method indicated in problem 9 to find the differences Δy of the function $y = x^4 - 2x^2$ with $\Delta x = 2$ for integral values of x in the range $x = 0$ to $x = 6$.

49 LIMITS

The concept of limit of a function is, without doubt, one of the most ticklish that must be dealt with at an elementary level. On the one hand, a rigorous definition and exposition will strike most nonmathematicians as needlessly complicated, overly difficult, and unnecessary, while a less than rigorous development might lull the student into a false sense of understanding. It could lead, at worst, to a misapplication of the notion in the student's major work that would have grave consequences.

There seems to be no good middle ground. We shall, therefore, give an intuitive presentation, but augment this with the slightest bit of rigor and the statement of a few theorems, without proof, with many examples.

Suppose, then, that f is a function whose domain and range are intervals of the real line or perhaps the entire real line. Suppose x_0 is a point in the domain of f, A is a point in the range of f, and that we can make the distance between $f(x)$ and A, $|f(x) - A|$, as small as we wish by requiring that the distance between x and x_0, $|x - x_0|$, be sufficiently small. We then say that the limit of f as x approaches x_0 is equal to A, and write $\lim_{x \to x_0} f(x) = A$.

Note that no mention is made of $f(x_0)$. In particular, $f(x_0)$ need not be A, and, in fact, there is no need at all to require that x_0 be in the domain of f or that A be in the range of f. All that is needed for us to be able to discuss $\lim_{x \to x_0} f(x)$ is that *any* interval $(x_0 - \delta, x_0 + \delta)$, $\delta > 0$, containing x_0, must also contain points of the domain of f. Our definition, then, is the following: We say $\lim_{x \to x} f(x) = A$ if when $(A - \epsilon, A + \epsilon)$ is an interval containing A there is then some interval $(x_0 - \delta, x_0 + \delta)$ containing x_0 such that $f(x)$ is in $(A - \epsilon, A + \epsilon)$ whenever x is a point in $(x_0 - \delta, x_0 + \delta)$ that is also in the domain of f.

EXAMPLE 1

Use the definition of limit to show that $\lim_{x \to 1} 2x + 1 = 3$.

Suppose, then, that we are given an interval $(3 - \epsilon, 3 + \epsilon)$ containing 3. Can we find an interval $(1 - \delta, 1 + \delta)$ containing 1 such that $f(x) = 2x + 1$ is in $(3 - \epsilon, 3 + \epsilon)$ whenever x is in $(1 - \delta, 1 + \delta)$?

We will start with what we wish to have and work backwards. We want $3 - \epsilon < 2x + 1 < 3 + \epsilon$ for x in $(1 - \delta, 1 + \delta)$, or, $2 - \epsilon < 2x < 2 + \epsilon$, so that $1 - \epsilon/2 < x < 1 + \epsilon/2$. But this is precisely what we need, for reversing our steps we see that whenever $1 - \epsilon/2 < x < 1 + \epsilon/2$, we have $3 - \epsilon < 2x + 1 < 3 + \epsilon$, and this is true for any $\epsilon > 0$. Thus, $\delta = \epsilon/2$.

EXAMPLE 2

Let $f(x) = (x^2 - 1)/(x - 1)$, $x \neq 1$. Show that $\lim_{x \to 1} f(x) = 2$. Note that 1 is not in the domain of f. Nonetheless, we can certainly do as we are asked. Suppose $(2 - \epsilon, 2 + \epsilon)$ is some interval containing 2. We wish to find an interval $(1 - \delta, 1 + \delta)$ containing 1 such that $2 - \epsilon < (x^2 - 1)/(x - 1) < 2 + \epsilon$ whenever $1 - \delta < x < 1 + \delta$, $x \neq 1$. Again we start with what we wish to conclude. Suppose $2 - \epsilon < (x^2 - 1/(x - 1) < 2 + \epsilon$. Then $2 - \epsilon < x + 1 < 2 + \epsilon$ (using the facts that $x^2 - 1 = (x - 1)(x + 1)$ and $x \neq 1$), so that $1 - \epsilon < x < 1 + \epsilon$. Thus, retracing our steps, if $(1 - \epsilon < x < 1 + \epsilon$, then $2 - \epsilon < (x^2 - -1)/(x - 1) < 2 + \epsilon$. Hence, our sought-after δ is given by $\delta = \epsilon$.

There are certain theorems concerning the behavior of limits that can be obtained from the definition. It is essential for the student of economics to have some proficiency with them, and the rest of this section is devoted to this end. Let A and B be real numbers. Then

$$\lim_{x \to a} x^n = a^n. \tag{1}$$

If $\quad \lim_{x \to a} f(x)] = A \quad$ and $\quad \lim_{x \to a} g(x) = B, \quad$ then $\quad$ (2)

$$\lim_{x \to a} [f(x) + g(x)] = \lim_{x \to a} f(x) + \lim_{x \to 0} g(x) = A + B; \tag{a}$$

$$\lim_{x \to a} [f(x) \cdot g(x)] = \lim_{x \to a} f(x) \cdot (\lim_{x \to a} g(x)) = A \cdot B; \tag{b}$$

if $\quad \lim_{x \to a} g(x) = B \neq 0, \quad$ then $\quad \lim_{x \to a} \dfrac{f(x)}{g(x)} = \dfrac{\lim\limits_{x \to a} f(x)}{\lim\limits_{x \to a} g(x)} = \dfrac{A}{B}.$ (c)

$$\lim_{x \to a} C = C \text{ for any real number } C. \tag{3}$$

EXAMPLE 3

Find $\lim_{x \to 2} (3x^2 - 2)/(x + 1)$. We first ascertain that $\lim_{x \to 2} x + 1$
$\neq 0$. $\lim_{x \to 2} x + 1 = \lim_{x \to 2} x + \lim_{x \to 2} 1 = 2 + 1 = 3$ [using
(1), (2a), and (3)]. Then

$$\lim_{x \to 2} \frac{3x^2 - 2}{x + 1} = \frac{\lim\limits_{x \to 2} 3x^2 - 2}{\lim\limits_{x \to 2} x + 1} = \frac{3 \lim\limits_{x \to 2} x^2 + \lim\limits_{x \to 2} (-2)}{\lim\limits_{x \to 2} x + 1} = \frac{3 \cdot 4 - 2}{3}$$

$$= \frac{10}{3}.$$

EXAMPLE 4

Find $\lim_{x \to 1} (x - 1)/(x^3 - 1)$. Sadly, $\lim_{x \to 1} x^3 - 1 = 0$, as does
$\lim_{x \to 1} x - 1$. However, $x^3 - 1 = (x - 1)(x^2 + x + 1)$, and,
moreover, for $x \neq 1$,

$$\frac{x - 1}{x^3 - 1} = \frac{x - 1}{(x - 1)(x^2 + x + 1)} = \frac{1}{x^2 + x + 1}, \quad \text{so that}$$

$$\lim_{x \to 1} \frac{x - 1}{x^3 - 1} = \lim_{x \to 1} \frac{1}{x^2 + x + 1} = \frac{1}{3}.$$

There are two more sorts of limit we wish to consider. First,
suppose that for some function $f(x)$, as x becomes larger and is in
fact allowed to exceed any given real number, $f(x)$ approaches
some real number A. We then say that $\lim_{x \to \infty} f(x) = A$. More
formally, $\lim_{x \to \infty} f(x) = A$ if, given $\epsilon > 0$ there is some real num-

ber M such that $f(x)$ is in $(A - \epsilon, A + \epsilon)$ whenever $x > M$ and x is in the domain of f.

EXAMPLE 5

Show that $\lim_{x \to \infty} \dfrac{2x - 1}{x} = 2$. We wish to show that if $(2 - \epsilon,$ $2 + \epsilon)$ is any interval, we can find some real number M such that $2 - \epsilon < (2x - 1)/x < 2 + \epsilon$ if $x > M$. We can assume $x > 0$ because we are interested only in what happens to $(2x - 1)/x$ as x becomes large without bound. Hence, $2 - \epsilon < (2x - 1)/x < 2 + \epsilon$ if and only if $2x - \epsilon x < 2x - 1 < 2x + \epsilon x,$

or if $\qquad\qquad -\epsilon x < -1 < \epsilon x.$

Since $-1 < x$ for all relevant x and $\epsilon > 0$, $-1 < \epsilon x$ is no restriction at all on x. $-\epsilon x < -1$ holds, however, if and only if $x > 1/\epsilon$. $1/\epsilon$ is the number M sought after.

One can similarly define $\lim_{x \to -\infty} f(x) = A$: We say $\lim_{x \to -\infty} f(x) = A$ if, given any interval $(A - \epsilon, A + \epsilon)$ containing A there is a negative number M such that $f(x)$ is in $(A - \epsilon, A + \epsilon)$ if $x < M$ and x is in the domain of f.

The theorems stated previously also hold for $\lim_{x \to \pm\infty} f(x) = A$, A a real number.

Finally, let a be a real number or $\pm \infty$. If $f(x)$ can be made to exceed any real number by taking x sufficiently close to a [or by making x sufficiently small or large in the case of $\lim_{x \to -\infty} f(x)$ or $\lim_{x \to \infty} f(x)$, respectively], we say $\lim_{x \to a} f(x) = \infty$, while a corresponding statement serves to say what is meant by $\lim_{x \to a} f(x) = -\infty$ or $\lim_{x \to \pm\infty} f(x) = -\infty$.

It is easy to show that $\lim_{x \to \infty} x^n = \infty$ and that $\lim_{x \to \infty} 1/x^n = 0$. By using these results together with the theorems stated earlier, one can calculate many limits frequently encountered in the literature of economics.

The theorems, however, were stated only for real limits and are not generally applicable for infinite limits. In particular, such limit forms as $\infty - \infty$, $0 \cdot \infty$, $0/0$, ∞/∞ are not capable of evaluation with the techniques presented here. Should they be encountered in one's work, more advanced texts should be consulted for these indeterminate forms.

One can, however, use the definition of ∞ and $-\infty$ to note that if $\lim_{x \to a} f(x) = A$ and $\lim_{x \to a} g(x) = \infty$, then $\lim_{x \to a} [f(x) + g(x)] = \infty$, and that $\lim_{x \to a} f(x) \cdot g(x) = \infty$ if $A > 0$, while $\lim_{x \to a} f(x) \cdot g(x) = -\infty$ if $A < 0$.

EXAMPLE 6

Find

$$\lim_{x \to -2} \frac{x^2 - 1}{(x + 2)^2}.$$

Note that $\lim_{x \to -2} x^2 - 1 = 3$, while $\lim_{x \to -2} (x + 2)^2 = 0$. Hence, one can make $(x - 1)/(x + 2)^2$ as large as desired by taking x sufficiently close to -2; we conclude that $\lim_{x \to -2} (x^2 - 1)/(x + 2) = \infty$.

This problem also serves to illustrate a previous statement, that the previous theorems hold in general only for finite limits. If one tries to consider

$$\lim_{x \to -2} \frac{x^2 - 1}{x + 2} = \lim_{x \to -2} \frac{x^2}{x + 2} - \lim_{x \to -2} \frac{1}{x + 2}$$

one arrives at the conclusion that

$$\lim_{x \to -2} \frac{x^2 - 1}{x + 2} = \infty - \infty,$$

an indeterminate form.

EXAMPLE 7

Find $\lim_{x \to \infty} (3x^2 + x)/(x^2 - 1)$. One can divide both the numerator and the denominator by x^2 to obtain

$$\lim_{x \to \infty} \frac{3x^2 + x}{x^2 - 1} = \lim_{x \to \infty} \frac{3 + 1/x}{1 - 1/x^2} = \frac{\lim_{x \to \infty} (3 + 1/x)}{\lim_{x \to \infty} (1 - 1/x^2)} = \frac{3 + 0}{1 - 0} = 3.$$

EXAMPLE 8

Find

$$\lim_{x \to \infty} \left(\frac{3x^2 + x}{x^2 - 1} \right) e^x.$$

Since

$$\lim_{x \to \infty} \frac{3x^2 + x}{x^2 - 1} = 3, \qquad \frac{3x^2 + x}{x^2 - 1} e^x$$

can be made to differ from $3e^x$ by as little as desired by taking x to be sufficiently large. Since $3e^x \to \infty$ as $x \to \infty$,

$$\lim_{x \to \infty} \left(\frac{3x^2 + x}{x^2 - 1} \right) e^x = \infty.$$

EXERCISES 49

1   Find the following limits:

(a) $\lim\limits_{x \to 5} \dfrac{2x + 5}{4x}$.   (b) $\lim\limits_{x \to \infty} \dfrac{100}{x}$.   (c) $\lim\limits_{x \to 2} \dfrac{x^2 - 4}{x - 2}$.

(d) $\lim\limits_{x \to \infty} \dfrac{3x^2 + 2x + 1}{x^2 - 1}$ (e) $\lim\limits_{x \to 1} \dfrac{(2x^2 + 3)(x - 1)^2}{x^2 - 1}$.

(f) $\lim\limits_{x \to a} \dfrac{1/(x - 1)/a}{x - a}$.   (g) $\lim\limits_{x \to -\infty} \dfrac{x - 2}{(x - 4)(x - 5)}$.

2   Use the definition of limits to show:

(a) $\lim\limits_{x \to 1} x^2 + 2 = 3$.   (b) $\lim\limits_{x \to 2} \dfrac{x - 1}{x + 1} = \dfrac{1}{3}$.

(c) $\lim\limits_{x \to \infty} \dfrac{2x - 1}{x + 1} = 2$.

3   The trend of agricultural income in India for the period 1901–1960 is given by the logistic function (Tintner, Narashima, Patil, Raghavan).

$$y_t = \frac{4406}{1 + 0.51e^{-0.11t}}.$$

Show that $\lim_{t \to \infty} y_t = 4406$.

50   DERIVATIVES

The difference quotient $\Delta y/\Delta x$ has been introduced in a previous section for $y = f(x)$.

The limit, if it exists, of this difference quotient as $\Delta x \to 0$ is known as the derivative. The derivative of $y = f(x)$ is denoted by such symbols as y', $f'(x)$, $D_x y$, $df(x)/dx$, or dy/dx. Thus

$$y' = f'(x) = D_x y = D_x f(x) = \frac{df(x)}{dx} = \frac{dy}{dx} = \lim_{\Delta x \to 0} \frac{\Delta y}{\Delta x}$$

$$= \lim_{\Delta x \to 0} \frac{f(x + \Delta x) - f(x)}{\Delta x}.$$

As pictured in Figure 29, the closer to 0 Δx becomes, the closer together will be the two points having the abscissas x and $x + \Delta x$ and the ordinates y and $y + \Delta y$, respectively. The straight line joining the points (x, y) and $(x + \Delta x, y + \Delta y)$, which cuts the curve in at least two points, approaches the position of the tangent to the curve $y = f(x)$ at (x, y) as $\Delta x \to 0$. This latter conclusion follows from the fact that as $\Delta x \to 0$ the point $(x + \Delta x, y + \Delta y)$ approaches the point (x, y), so that the line joining them approaches the tangent to the curve $y = f(x)$ at the point (x, y).

The limit of the difference quotient is by definition the derivative $f'(x)$.

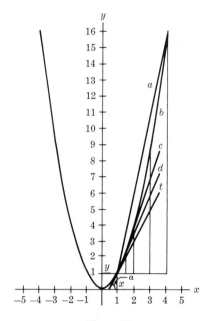

Figure 29

Hence $f'(x)$ is the slope of the straight line which is tangent to the curve $y = f(x)$ at the point (x, y); by the slope of the tangent line is meant the tangent of the angle α between the tangent line and the x axis. In symbols,

$$y' = f'(x) = \lim_{\Delta x \to 0} \frac{\Delta y}{\Delta x} = \tan \alpha.$$

EXAMPLE 1

Figure 29 shows the behavior of $\Delta y/\Delta x$ as $\Delta x \to 0$, if $y = f(x) = x^2$, and if the point (x, y) is chosen as $(1, 1)$. The lines labeled a, b, c, and d are the lines of slope $\Delta y/\Delta x$, drawn for the increments $\Delta x = 3, 2, 1, \frac{1}{2}$. They converge more and more toward the line t which is tangent to the curve $y = x^2$ at the point $(1, 1)$. The angle α made by the tangent line t with x axis is as shown.

EXAMPLE 2

Find the derivative at the point (x, y) if

$$y = f(x) = 3x^4 - 2x^2 + 1.$$

First we derive the difference quotient by methods described previously:

$$y + \Delta y = 3(x + \Delta x)^4 - 2(x + \Delta x)^2 + 1.$$

This is evaluated by the binomial theorem as follows:

$$y + \Delta y = 3[x^4 + 4x^3(\Delta x) + 6x^2(\Delta x)^2 + 4x(\Delta x)^3 + (\Delta x)^4]$$
$$- 2[x^2 + 2x(\Delta x) + (\Delta x)^2] + 1.$$
$$y + \Delta y = 3x^4 + 12x^3(\Delta x) + 18x^2(\Delta x)^2 + 12x(\Delta x)^3$$
$$+ 3(\Delta x)^4 - 2x^2 - 4x(\Delta x) - 2(\Delta x)^2 + 1.$$
$$y = 3x^4 \qquad\qquad\quad - 2x^2 \qquad\qquad\qquad\quad + 1.$$
$$\Delta y = 12x^3(\Delta x) + 18x^2(\Delta x)^2 + 12x(\Delta x)^3 + 3(\Delta x)^4$$
$$- 4x(\Delta x) - 2(\Delta x)^2.$$

Next we divide term by term by Δx, thereby obtaining

$$\frac{\Delta y}{\Delta x} = 12x^3 + 18x^2(\Delta x) + 12x(\Delta x)^2 + 3(\Delta x)^3 - 4x - 2(\Delta x).$$

By definition, the derivative $f'(x)$ is $\lim\limits_{\Delta x \to 0} \Delta y/\Delta x$. As $\Delta x \to 0$, $(\Delta x)^2 \to 0$ and $(\Delta x)^3 \to 0$. The only terms not containing Δx or powers of (Δx) in the difference quotient are $12x^3 - 4x$. All the other terms become 0. Hence

$$f'(x) = 12x^3 - 4x.$$

This is the desired derivative, which is the slope of the tangent line at some point (x, y) on the curve. For instance, let $x = \frac{1}{2}$; then

$$f'(\tfrac{1}{2}) = (12)(\tfrac{1}{2})^3 - 4(\tfrac{1}{2}) = -\tfrac{1}{2}.$$

Hence, at the point on the curve where $x = \frac{1}{2}$, the slope of the tangent line is $-\frac{1}{2}$. In other words, this is the angle α between the tangent line to the curve at the point in question and the x axis; thus

$$\tan \alpha = -\tfrac{1}{2}.$$

We see from Table 2, that the angle α is 153.4°.

EXERCISES 50

All derivatives in the following exercises are to be computed by obtaining $\lim\limits_{\Delta x \to 0} \Delta y/\Delta x$.

1 Let $y = f(x) = 3x^2 - 5x + 10$. (a) Find the difference quotient.(b)Find the derivative. (c) Find $f'(5)$. (d) What is the angle the tangent line to the curve at the point $x = 5$ makes with the x axis? (e) Make a graph of the curve and the tangent.

2 Let $y = f(x) = 3x^2$. (a) Find the difference quotient. (b) Find the derivative. (c) Find $f'(3)$; (d) the angle α. (e) Compute the difference quotient

and the angle θ for $x = 3$; $\Delta x = 1$. (f) For $x = 3$; $\Delta x = \frac{1}{2}$. (g) For $x = 3$; $\Delta x = 0.1$. (h) For $x = 3$; $\Delta x = 0.002$. Note that the difference between the difference quotient, the derivative, and the angles θ and α becomes smaller and smaller as Δx decreases. (i) Make a graph of the curve and the tangent.

3   Let $y = f(x) = x^3$. (a) Find the difference quotient. (b) Find the derivative. (c) Find $f'(2)$. (d) Find the angle α. (e) For what value of x does the angle α have the measure $60°$?

4   Let $y = x^4 - 2x^2 + 6$. (a) Find the difference quotient. (b) Find the derivative. (c) Find $f'(0)$ and the corresponding angle α. (d) Find $f'(-2)$ and the corresponding angle α. (e) Plot the function.

5   Let $y = f(x) = 3x^2 - 6x + 8$. (a) Find the difference quotient; (b)the derivative; (c) $f'(0)$ and the corresponding angle α; (d) $f'(-5)$ and the corresponding angle α; (e) $f'(2)$ and the corresponding angle α. (f) Where is the angle $\alpha = 15°$? (g) For what x is $\alpha = -30°$? (h) Make a graph of the curve and the tangent lines.

6   Let $y = f(x) = 1 + 2x + 3x^2 - x^3$. (a) Find the difference quotient; (b) the derivative; (c) $f'(0)$ and the angle α; (d) $f'(-5)$ and the angle α; (e) the values of x and y for which the angle α is $45°$.

7   Let $y = f(x) = -x^3$. (a) Find the difference quotient; (b) the derivative; (c) $f'(1)$ and the angle α; (d) the x and y where the angle α is $-60°$.

8   Consider the function $y = f(x) = 3 - 2x + 5x^2 - x^3 + x^4$. (a) Find the difference quotient. (b) Determine the derivative. (c) Find the value of $f'(-4)$ and the corresponding angle α.

9   Consider the function $y = f(x) = 6x^2$. Find the values of x and y where the angle α is (a) $45°$; (b) $-45°$. (c) Plot the function and check.

**10   Is there a function whose derivative is $y' = k$, where k is a constant? (HINT: Consider the derivative of the general linear function $y = a + bx$, where a and b are constants.) What is the interpretation of k?

11   (Tintner and Davila) Using Ecuadorian data for the period 1950–1961, we found the following consumption function: $c = 497 + 0.57x$, where c is real per capita consumption and x is real per capita income. Find the marginal propensity to consume, dc/dx.

12   (Johnston) Denote by C_t consumption and by Y_t gross domestic product. The following relations have been estimated for the United Kingdom for the period 1948–1958: $C_t = 0.49Y_t + 3800$. Find the marginal propensity to consume, dC_t/dY_t.

51   MARGINAL COST

Marginal cost is defined as the quotient of the increment of total cost, resulting from an increment in the amount produced, divided by the latter increment. More precisely, it should be defined as the limit of the ratio

$$\frac{increment\ in\ total\ cost}{increment\ in\ output},$$

as the increment in output tends to 0.

If $C = C(D)$ is the total cost of producing D units, by definition,

$$\text{Marginal cost } C' = \lim_{\Delta D \to 0} \frac{\Delta C}{\Delta D} = \frac{dC}{dD}.$$

EXAMPLE 1

Figure 30 presents the graph of the total cost curve

$$C = f(D) = 10 + 15D - 6D^2 + D^3.$$

From this we derive the marginal cost curve

$$C' = f'(D) = 15 - 12D + 3D^2$$

by the process of differentiation, outlined above. It should be noted that the typical short-term marginal-cost curve, like the

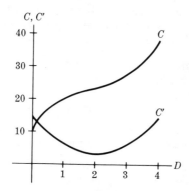

Figure 30

one shown in the graph labeled C', first decreases, reaches a minimum, and finally increases as more and more units of the commodity are produced.

EXAMPLE 2

Let the total cost curve be $C = D^2$. Then

$$\Delta C = (D + \Delta D)^2 - D^2 = D^2 + 2D(\Delta D) + (\Delta D)^2 - D^2$$
$$= 2D(\Delta D) + (\Delta D)^2.$$

Thus

$$\frac{\Delta C}{\Delta D} = 2D + \Delta D.$$

Evidently

$$C' = \lim_{\Delta D \to 0} \frac{\Delta C}{\Delta D} = 2D.$$

This is the *marginal cost curve*. For example, for 3 units produced, $C'(3) = 6$.

EXERCISES 51

1   Given the total cost curve $C = 2 + D$, (a) find the marginal cost curve. (b) Find $C'(0)$; (c) $C'(5)$; (d) $C'(10)$. (e) Make a graph of the total cost curve and the marginal cost curve.

2   Given the total cost curve $C = 1 + 2D + 3D^2$, (a) find the marginal cost curve. (b) Find $C'(1)$; (c) $C'(6)$; (d) $C'(10)$; (e) $C'(20)$. (f) Make a graph of the total cost curve and marginal cost curve.

3   Given the total cost curve $C = D^2 + 2D$, (a) find the marginal cost curve. (b) Find $C'(10)$; (c) $C'(0)$; (d) $C'(2)$; (e) $C'(15)$; (f) $C'(3)$. (g) Plot the total cost curve and the marginal cost curve.

4   Given the total cost curve $C = 10 + 2D + 3D^2 + 4D^3$, (a) find the marginal cost curve. (b) Find $C'(0)$; (c) $C'(1)$; (d) $C'(5)$; (e) $C'(10)$; (f) $C'(15)$. (g) Plot the total cost curve and the marginal cost curve.

5   Find the marginal cost curve for the total cost curve in problem 1, Exercises 47. Also find (a) $C'(1)$; (b) $C'(5)$; (c) $C'(10)$. (d) Plot the total cost curve and the marginal cost curve.

6   Find the marginal cost curve belonging to the total curve in problem 3, Exercises 30. Also calculate (a) $C'(1)$; (b) $C'(10)$; (c) $C'(5)$; (d) $C'(2.35)$. (e) Plot the total cost curve and the marginal cost curve.

7   Given the total cost curve from problem 10, Exercises 47, find the marginal cost of steel. Also find (a) $C'(1)$; (b) $C'(100)$. (c) Plot the total cost curve and the marginal cost curve.

8   Given the total cost curve $C = m + nD$, (a) find the marginal cost curve. (b) Find $C'(0)$; (c) $C'(10)$; (d) $C'(5)$.

9   Given the total cost curve $C = mD + nD^2$, (a) find the marginal cost curve. (b) Find $C'(1)$; (c) $C'(0)$; (d) $C'(5)$; (e) $C'(m)$; (f) $C'(n)$.

10   Take the total cost curve from problem 11, Exercises 47, and find the marginal cost of hosiery. Also find (a) $C'(5,000)$; (b) $C'(3,500)$; (c) $C'(6,568)$; (d) $C'(7,500)$. (e) Plot the total cost curve and the marginal cost curve.

11   Take the total cost curve from problem 12, Exercises 47. Find the marginal cost curve for leather belts. Also find (a) $C'(60,000)$; (b)

$C'(100,000)$; (c) $C'(75,000)$; (d) $C'(45,500)$; (e) $C'(20,000)$. (f) Plot the total cost curve and the marginal cost curve.

12   The total cost function of a light plant has been estimated as $C = 16.68 + 0.125D + 0.00439D^2$ (Nordin). C is the total fuel cost for an 8-hour period in dollars; D is percent of capacity. Find the marginal cost curve. (a) Find $C'(50)$; (b) $C'(30)$; (c) $C'(90)$. (d) Plot the total cost curve and the marginal cost curve.

52   MARGINAL REVENUE

Total revenue R has been defined (Section 46) as the product of price and the quantity sold. Thus R is the total receipts of the sellers or the total outlay of the buyers.

Marginal revenue is the ratio of the increment in total revenue and the increment in the quantity sold. More precisely, it is the limit of the ratio

$$\frac{increment\ in\ total\ revenue}{increment\ in\ sales},$$

as the increment in sales tends to 0. Thus

$$R = pD$$

and

$$R'(D) = \lim_{\Delta D \to 0} \frac{\Delta R}{\Delta D}.$$

EXAMPLE

Let the demand function for a commodity be given by

$$p = f(D) = 10 - 2D.$$

The total revenue function is $R = g(D) = pD = (10 - 2D)D = 10D - 2D^2$. We get $R + \Delta R$ by replacing D in the last formula by $D + \Delta D$; that is,

$$R + \Delta R = 10(D + \Delta D) - 2(D + \Delta D)^2,$$
$$= 10(D + \Delta D) - 2[D^2 + 2D(\Delta D) + (\Delta D)^2],$$
$$= 10D + 10(\Delta D) - 2D^2 - 4D(\Delta D) - 2(\Delta D)^2.$$

We subtract $R = 10D - 2D^2$ to obtain ΔR; thus

$$\Delta R = 10(\Delta D) - 4D(\Delta D) - 2(\Delta D)^2.$$

To compute the difference quotient we divide by ΔD, thereby obtaining

$$\frac{\Delta R}{\Delta D} = 10 - 4D - 2(\Delta D).$$

As $\Delta D \to 0$, the last term approaches 0, so

$$R'(D) = g'(D) = \lim_{\Delta D \to 0} \frac{\Delta R}{\Delta D} = 10 - 4D.$$

This is the marginal revenue function. We have, for example, when $D = 2$,

$$R'(2) = 10 - (4)(2) = 2 \quad \text{and} \quad R'(4) = 10 - (4)(4) = -6.$$

In Figure 31 the demand function is labeled p where $p = 10 - 2D$. The total revenue function $R = p \cdot D$ is denoted by R, where

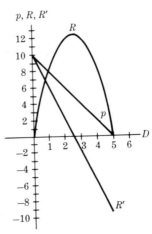

Figure 31

$R = 10D - 2D^2$. Finally the marginal revenue function is labeled R', where $R' = 10 - 4D$.

It should be noted that the marginal revenue function can become negative. This is obvious, since the increment of the total revenue can become negative.

It is apparent from the graph that the demand function p is a straight line. Note that the marginal revenue curve, which is also a straight line, cuts the D axis at half the distance from the origin to the point of meeting of the demand curve p and the D axis.

EXERCISES 52

1 Given the demand curve $p = 10 - 3D$, (a) find the total revenue curve; (b) the marginal revenue curve; (c) $R'(1)$; (d) $R'(0)$; (e) $R'(3)$; (f) $R'(10/3)$. (g) Make a graph of the demand curve; the total revenue curve; the marginal revenue curve.

2 Given the relationship $2D + 3p = 15$, (a) find the demand curve; (b) the total revenue curve; (c) the marginal revenue curve; (d) $R'(0)$; (e) $R'(1)$; (f) $R'(4)$; (g) $R'(2.5)$.

3 Given the demand curve $p = 16 - D^2/2$, (a) find the total revenue curve; (b) the marginal revenue curve; (c) $R'(1)$; (d) $R'(5)$; (e) $R'(1.125)$. (f) Make a graph of the demand curve; the total revenue curve; the marginal revenue curve.

4 Given the relationship in problem 1, Exercises 46, (a) determine the demand curve; (b) the total revenue curve; (c) the marginal revenue curve; (d) $R'(0)$; (e) $R'(0.5)$; (f) $R'(2.35)$.

5 Given the relationship in problem 8, Exercises 46, (a) find the demand curve for sugar; (b) the total revenue curve; (c) the marginal revenue curve; (d) $R'(55)$; (e) $R'(40)$; (f) $R'(70)$. (e) Make a graph of the demand curve; the total revenue curve; the marginal revenue curve.

6 Given the relationship in problem 10, Exercises 46, (a) find the demand curve for potatoes; (b) the total revenue curve; (c) the marginal revenue curve; (d) $R'(1)$; (e) $R'(2)$; (f) $R'(1.5)$; (g) $R'(3)$. (h) Make a graph of the demand curve; the total revenue curve; the marginal revenue curve.

7 Given the relationship in problem 12, Exercises 46, (a) find the demand curve for hay; (b) the total revenue curve; (c) the marginal revenue curve; (d) $R'(3)$; (e) $R'(4)$; (f) $R'(3.5)$; (g) $R'(2.1)$.

8 Take the demand curve for rye from problem 9, Exercises 11. (a) Find the total revenue curve; (b) the marginal revenue curve; (c) $R'(0.1)$; (d) $R'(0.2)$; (e) $R'(0.3)$; (f) $R'(0.4)$; (g) $R'(0.5)$.

9 Given the relationship $aD + bp = k$, where a, b, and k are constants, (a) find the total revenue curve; (b) the marginal revenue curve; (c) $R'(0)$; (d) $R'(1)$; (e) $R'(a)$; (f) $R'(k)$.

**10 Assume a demand function $p = a - bD$, where a and b are positive constants. (a) Find R. (b) Find R'. (c) Find the intercept of p with the D axis by solving the equation $p = 0$ for D. (d) Find the intercept of R' with the D axis by solving the equation $R' = 0$ for D. (e) Establish a relationship between the two intercepts.

Chapter 11
Rules of Differentiation

Let us consider the derivative of $y = f(x) = x^n$, where n is a positive integer. An extension of the result obtained to any arbitrary, rational, positive or negative exponent will be given later (problems 5 and 10, Exercises 59).

By definition of the derivative, we have

$$y' = f'(x) = \lim_{\Delta x \to 0} \frac{\Delta y}{\Delta x} = \lim_{\Delta v \to 0} \frac{f(x + \Delta z) - f(x)}{\Delta x}.$$

From the formula $y = f(x) = x^n$, we obtain $f(x + \Delta x)$ by substituting $x + \Delta x$ for x. Thus

$$f(x + \Delta x) = (x + \Delta x)^n.$$

This can be developed by the binomial theorem as follows:

$$f(x + \Delta x) = x^n + \frac{n}{1} x^{n-1}(\Delta x) + \frac{n(n-1)}{1 \cdot 2} x^{n-2}(\Delta x)^2 + \cdots + (\Delta x)^n.$$

From this expression we subtract $y = x^n$ to obtain the increment Δy, which gives

$$\Delta y = \frac{n}{1} x^{n-1}(\Delta x) + \frac{n(n-1)}{1 \cdot 2} x^{n-2}(\Delta x)^2 + \cdots + (\Delta x)^n.$$

To compute the difference quotient $\Delta y/\Delta x$, we divide term by term by Δx, thereby obtaining

$$\frac{\Delta y}{\Delta x} = \frac{n}{1} x^{n-1} + \frac{n(n-1)}{1 \cdot 2} x^{n-2}(\Delta x) + \cdots + (\Delta x)^{n-1}.$$

The first term does not involve the increment Δx. All other terms involve Δx or powers of Δx.

160

Passing to the limit as $\Delta x \to 0$, we have

$$f'(x) = \lim_{\Delta x \to 0} \frac{\Delta y}{\Delta x} = nx^{n-1}.$$

So we have the following rule: If $y = f(x) = x^n$, where n is a positive integer, the derivative is

$$y' = f'(x) = nx^{n-1}.$$

EXAMPLE

For example, the derivative of $y = f(x) = x^5$ is $f'(x) = 5x^4$. If $x = 2$, the derivative is $f'(2) = (5)(2^4) = 80$.

Let us consider an important special case if the function $y = f(x) = x$, where $n = 1$. We have $f'(x) = 1 \cdot x^0 = 1$, since any number raised to the power 0 is 1. It follows that the derivative of x itself with respect to x is 1.

EXERCISES 53

1 (a) Find the derivative of $y = f(x) = x^5$. (b) Find $f'(-1)$.

2 (a) Find the derivative of $y = f(x) = x^3$; (b) find $f'(1)$; (c) $f'(-5)$. (d) Find the x and y for which the angle of inclination of the tangent to the curve is $60°$.

3 Find the derivative of $y = f(x) = x^7$.

4 Find the derivative of $y = f(x) = x^2$.

5 (a) Find the derivative of $y = f(x) = x^6$. (b) Find $f'(0)$. (c) Where is the slope of the tangent line equal to -1?

6 Find the derivative of $y = f(x) = x^8$.

7 Find the derivative of $y = f(x) = x^{20}$.

8 Find the derivative of $y = f(x) = x^{13}$.

9 (a) Find the derivative of $y = f(x) = x^4$. (b) Find $f'(-2)$ and the angle of inclination when $x = -2$.

10 (a) Find the derivative of $y = f(x) = x^{10}$. (b) Find $f'(0)$ and the angle of inclination.

54 DERIVATIVE OF A CONSTANT TIMES A FUNCTION

Recall: If the function $f(x)$ approaches a certain limit L, as x approaches a, then the function $cf(x)$, where c is a constant, approaches cL, as x approaches a, due to consequences 2b and 3 of Section 49.

EXAMPLE 1

Consider the function $f(x) = (5 + 2x)/(3 - x)$. We have $\lim_{x \to 0} f(x) = \frac{5}{3}$.

Now consider the function $g(x) = 3f(x) = (15 + 6x)/(3 - x)$. Evidently $\lim_{x \to 0} g(x) = 3$ times the previous limit, or $(3)(\frac{5}{3}) = 5$.

We can apply this result about limits to the problem of finding the derivative of a constant times a function. Let $u = f(x)$ be a function of x. Now introduce a new function,

$$y = g(x) = cu = cf(x),$$

where c is a constant.

We have, from the definition of a derivative,

$$u' = f'(x) = \lim_{\Delta x \to 0} \frac{\Delta u}{\Delta x}.$$

It follows from the theorem about limits at the beginning of this section that

$$y' = g'(x) = \lim_{\Delta x \to 0} \frac{\Delta y}{\Delta x} = c \lim_{\Delta x \to 0} \frac{\Delta u}{\Delta x} = cu'.$$

In words, the derivative of a function of x multiplied by a constant is the constant times the derivative of the function.

EXAMPLE 2

Suppose we have $y = f(x) = 3x^4$. The derivative of the function $u = x^4$ (from the rule for the derivative of a power) is $u' = 4x^3$. Since x^4 is multiplied by 3, $4x^3$ must be multiplied by 3 to give the derivative of y; thus

$$y' = f'(x) = (3)(4x^3) = 12x^3.$$

For example, at the point $x = 2$, we have

$$f'(2) = (12)(2^3) = 96.$$

EXAMPLE 3

Let $y = 2x^3$. The derivative of x^3 is $3x^2$. Hence $y' = 2 \cdot 3x^2 = 6x^2$.

EXERCISES 54

1 (a) Differentiate $y = f(x) = 4x^6$. (b) Find $f'(-1)$; (c) $f'(0)$.

2 (a) Differentiate $y = f(x) = 10x^3$. (b) Find $f'(1)$; (c) $f'(-2)$.

3 (a) Differentiate $y = f(x) = 4x^4$. (b) Find $f'(0)$. (c) Find the x and y where the slope is -1.

4 (a) Find the derivative of $y = f(x) = -5x^2$. (b) Find $f'(0)$; (c) $f'(1)$; (d) $f'(-2)$.

5 Find the derivative of $y = f(x) = -3x^4$.

6 Find the derivative for $y = f(x) = 6x^2$.

7 Find the derivative of $y = f(x) = -5x^6$.

8 Consider the function in problem 7. Find the values of x and y where the angle of inclination is (a) $-15°$; (b) $-45°$.

9 Find the derivative of the function $y = -4x^2$ for $y = -3$; find the angle of inclination.

10 (a) Find the derivative of the function $y = f(x) = -5x^2$. Find the point on the curve where the slope of the tangent line is (b) -6; (c) 4. (d) Plot the curve and the tangent lines.

55 DERIVATIVES OF SUMS AND DIFFERENCES OF FUNCTION

Recall that if $\lim_{x \to a} f(x) = L$ and $\lim_{x \to a} g(x) = M$, then $\lim_{x \to a} [f(x) + g(x)] = \lim_{x \to a} f(x) + \lim g(x) = L + M$, as stated in Section 49.

Now, let $u = f(x)$ and $v = g(x)$ be functions of the same independent variable x. Their derivatives are

$$u' = f'(x) = \lim_{\Delta x \to 0} \frac{\Delta u}{\Delta x},$$

$$v' = g'(x) = \lim_{\Delta x \to 0} \frac{\Delta v}{\Delta x}.$$

Then introduce a new function $y = h(x) = u + v$. We have for its derivative

$$y' = h'(x) = \lim_{\Delta x \to 0} \frac{\Delta y}{\Delta x} = \lim_{\Delta x \to 0} \frac{\Delta u + \Delta v}{\Delta x} = \lim_{\Delta x \to 0} \frac{\Delta u}{\Delta x} + \lim_{\Delta x \to 0} \frac{\Delta v}{\Delta x} = u' + v'.$$

This follows from the fact, discussed above, that the limit of the sum of two functions is the sum of the limits. An analogous theorem holds for the difference.

We can summarize as follows: The derivative of a sum of functions is the sum of the derivatives. The derivative of a difference of functions is the difference of the derivatives.

EXAMPLE

Assume that $y = f(x) = 2x^2 - 5x$. The derivative of $2x^2$ is $4x$, the derivative of $5x$ is 5. Hence, $y' = f'(x) = 4x - 5$.

EXERCISES 55

1 (a) Find the derivative of $y = f(x) = 4x - 2x^2$. (b) Find $f'(0)$.

2 (a) Find the derivative of $y = f(x) = x - x^4$. (b) Find $f'(3)$.

3 (a) Find the derivative of $y = f(x) = 2x^2 - 5x^3 + x^4$. (b) Find $f'(0)$; (c) $f'(-2)$.

4 (a) Find the derivative of $y = f(x) = 2x - x^2$. (b) Find $f'(-1)$ and the corresponding angle of inclination of the tangent line. (c) Find the x and y where the angle of inclination is $-30°$.

5 (a) Find the derivative of $y = f(x) = x^4 - 3x^2$. (b) Find $f'(-2)$ and the corresponding angle of inclination.

6 Given the demand curve $p = 10 - 3D$, (a) find the total revenue curve R; (b) the marginal revenue curve R'; (c) $R'(2.5)$; (d) $R'(1)$.

7 Given the demand curve $p = 1,000 - 2D - 3D^2$, (a) find R; (b) R'; (c) $R'(1)$; (d) $R'(12)$; (e) $R'(6)$; (f) $R'(5.8)$.

8 Consider the demand for sugar in the United States for the period 1915–1929 (Schultz): $p = 14.7 - 0.1D$. (a) Find R; (b) R'; (c) $R'(80)$; (d) $R'(100)$; (e) $R'(65)$.

9 Consider the demand for cotton in the United States for the period 1915–1929 (Schultz): $p = 8 - D$. (a) Find R; (b) R'; (c) $R'(5)$; (d) $R'(1)$; (e) $R'(4)$; (f) $R'(6.5)$.

10 Consider the demand for barley in the United States for the period 1915–1929 (Schultz): $p = 86 - 25D$. (a) Find R; (b) R'; (c) $R'(1.5)$; (d) $R'(0.75)$; (e) $R'(0.85)$; (f) $R'(0.55)$; (g) $R'(0.725)$. (h) Plot the demand curve and the total revenue curve.

11 Consider the demand for rye in the United States for the period 1915–1929 (Schultz): $p = 76 - 73D$. (a) Find R; (b) R'; (c) $R'(0.40)$; (d) $R'(0.55)$; (e) $R'(0.365)$; (f) $R'(0.255)$. (g) Plot the demand curve and the total revenue curve.

12 Consider the demand for buckwheat in the United States for the period 1915–1929 (Schultz): $p = 101 - 294D$. (a) Find R; (b) R'; (c) $R'(0.2)$; (d) $R'(0.1)$; (e) $R'(0.25)$; (f) $R'(0.05)$. (g) Plot the demand curve and the total revenue curve.

13 Consider the demand for hay in the United States for the period 1915–1929 (Schultz): $p = 15 - 2D$. (a) Find R; (b) R'; (c) $R'(0.5)$; (d) $R'(1)$; (e) $R'(0.2)$; (f) $R'(0.75)$; (g) $R'(0.95)$. (h) Plot the demand curve and the total revenue curve.

56   DERIVATIVE OF A CONSTANT

Let $y = f(x) = c$, where c is a constant. Since c is independent of x we have

$$y + \Delta y = c,$$

$$y \qquad = c,$$

$$\Delta y = 0,$$

$$\frac{\Delta y}{\Delta x} = 0.$$

Hence

$$y' = \lim_{\Delta x \to 0} \frac{\Delta y}{\Delta x} = 0.$$

In general, the derivative of a constant is 0.

EXAMPLE

Let $y = 5x + 1$. We shall use the formula for the derivative of a sum. The derivative of $5x$ is 5. The derivative of 1 (which is a constant) is 0. Hence $y' = 5$.

EXERCISES 56

1   Find the derivative of the function $y = -10 - 2x + 5x^2$.

2   (a) Find the derivative of the function $y = f(x) = x^5 - 10x^4 + 2x^3 - x + 10$. (b) Find $f'(0)$; (c) $f'(-2)$; (d) $f'(5)$.

3   (a) Find the derivative of $y = f(x) = 1 + 2x + x^2$. (b) Draw its graph. (c) Find $f'(1)$; (d) $f'(-4)$. (e) Find the x and y for which the angle of inclination of the tangent becomes 20°; (f) $-60°$.

4   Let c be the consumption expenditure in dollars, y the deflated disposable income. From data in the United States for 1922–1941, we have the estimated relationship $c = 0.672y + 113.1$ (Haavelmo). (a) Find the derivative dc/dy, which is the marginal propensity to consume. (b) Compute $1/[1 - (dc/dy)]$. This is the so-called multiplier. (See problem 11, Exercises 49) NOTE: c is here the dependent variable and not a constant.

5   Take the demand curve $p = 10/D$. (a) Find R; (b) R'; (c) $R'(0)$; (d) $R'(1)$; (e) $R'(2)$; (f) $R'(3)$.

6   Let the total cost curve of a commodity be $C = 2 + 5D + 3D^4$. (a) Find the marginal cost curve; (b) $C'(0)$; (c) $C'(3)$.

7   Let the total cost curve of a commodity be $C = 10 + 3D$. (a) Find the marginal cost curve; (b) $C'(4)$; (c) $C'(100)$. (d) Plot the total cost curve and the marginal cost curve.

8   Consider the total cost curve of steel (Yntema) as $C = 182 + 56D$. (a) Find the marginal cost curve; (b) $C'(10)$; (c) $C'(15)$; (d) $C'(20)$. (e) Plot the total and marginal cost curves.

9   Take as the total cost of hosiery (Dean) $C = -10,485 + 6.75D - 0.0003D^2$. (a) Find the marginal cost curve; (b) $C'(5,000)$; (c) $C'(7,000)$; (d) $C'(6,500)$. (e) Plot the total and marginal cost curves.

10   Given the total cost of leather belts (Dean) $C = 3,000 + 0.8D$, (a) find the marginal cost curve; (b) $C'(100,000)$; (c) $C'(50,000)$; (d) $C'(75,000)$. (e) Plot the total and marginal cost curves.

11   Take as the total sales cost in a department store $C = 16.8 + 1.052D - 0.002D^2$ (Dean). (a) Find the marginal cost curve; (b) $C'(30)$; (c) $C'(150)$; (d) $C'(100)$; (e) $C'(75)$. (f) Plot the total and marginal cost curves.

57   DERIVATIVE OF A PRODUCT

To find the derivative of a product of two functions we proceed as follows: Assume that we have two functions of the independent variable x, namely, $u = g(x)$ and $v = h(x)$. Their derivatives are defined as

$$u' = g'(x) = \lim_{\Delta x \to 0} \frac{\Delta u}{\Delta x},$$

$$v' = h'(x) = \lim_{\Delta x \to 0} \frac{\Delta v}{\Delta x}.$$

We form a new function y, which is the product of the two functions u and v; that is, $y = f(x) = uv$.

The derivative of y, by definition, is $y' = f'(x) = \lim_{\Delta x \to 0} \Delta y/\Delta x$.

To compute the derivative of a product of two functions we note first that u, v, and y are by definition all functions of the same independent variable x. Hence, as x changes from x to $x + \Delta x$, at the same time u changes to $u + \Delta u$, v to $v + \Delta v$, and y to $y + \Delta y$. As $\Delta x \to 0$, also $\Delta y \to 0$, $\Delta u \to 0$, and $\Delta v \to 0$. This statement is made on the assumption that all the functions are well behaved in the intervals under consideration; it is possible to create functions for which the assertion is not true.

We have

$$y + \Delta y = (u + \Delta u)(v + \Delta v) = uv + (\Delta u)v + (\Delta v)u + (\Delta u)(\Delta v),$$
$$y \qquad\qquad = \qquad\qquad\qquad uv.$$

Subtracting the members of the second equation from those of the first,

$$\Delta y = (\Delta u)v + (\Delta v)u + (\Delta u)(\Delta v).$$

To find the difference quotient $\Delta y / \Delta x$, we divide the last expression, term by term, by Δx, thereby obtaining

$$\frac{\Delta y}{\Delta x} = \frac{(\Delta u)v}{\Delta x} + \frac{(\Delta v)u}{\Delta x} + \frac{(\Delta u)(\Delta v)}{\Delta x}.$$

To compute the derivative, we let $\Delta x \to 0$. Moreover, we must use the rules already discussed for computing limits: in particular, the limit of a sum is the sum of the limits, and the limit of a product is the product of the limits. Consequently,

$$y' = f'(x) = \left(\lim_{\Delta x \to 0} \frac{\Delta u}{\Delta x} \right) v + \left(\lim_{\Delta x \to 0} \frac{\Delta v}{\Delta x} \right) u + \left(\lim_{\Delta x \to 0} \frac{\Delta u}{\Delta x} \right) [\lim_{\Delta x \to 0} (\Delta v)].$$

We note that $\lim_{\Delta x \to 0} (\Delta v) = 0$. Hence the last term in the above expression becomes 0, since one factor is 0 and the other is assumed to exist.

The limits appearing in the first two terms are derivatives, so we have as a result:

$$y' = f'(x) = u'v + v'u.$$

In words, the derivative of the product of 2 functions is the derivative of the first factor times the second factor plus the derivative of the second factor times the first factor.

EXAMPLE

To illustrate, consider the expression $y = f(x) = (x^2 + 5)(3x - 1)$. Here $u = x^2 + 5$ and $v = 3x - 1$. The derivatives are $u' = 2x$, $v' = 3$. Hence $y' = f'(x) = u'v + v'u = (2x)(3x - 1) + (3)(x^2 + 5) = 9x^2 - 2x + 15$.

EXERCISES 57

1   Find the derivative of $y = (x - 6)(2x^2 + 2x + 1)$.

2   (a) Find the derivative of the function $y = f(x) = (x^2 + 1)(2x^3 - 3x + 1)$. (b) Find $f'(0)$; (c) $f'(-2)$; (d) $f'(4)$.

3   Find the derivative of the function $y = f(x)$ that is the product of $(1 - 2x + x^2 + 4x^3)$ and $(2 - x - x^2)$.

4   (a) Find the derivative of $y = f(x) = (x - 2)(3 - 4x)$. (b) Find $f'(0)$; (c) $f'(-4)$. (d) Find the x and y where the angle of inclination of the tangent is $45°$; (e) $-60°$; (f) $0°$.

5   Find the derivative of $y = (x^3 - 4x^2 + 5x - 10)(x^4 - 7x^2 + 6)$.

6   Use the formula of the derivative of a product to find the derivative of $y = x^2$. (HINT: $x^2 = x \cdot x$.)

7   (a) Find the derivative of $y = f(x) = (x^3 - 2x^2 + 4x - 1)(-x^4 + 6x^3 - x^2 + 5x - 7)$. (b) Find $y'(1) = f'(1)$, and the corresponding angle of inclination. (c) Find $y'(-2) = f'(-2)$, and the corresponding angle of inclination.

8   (a) Use the formula for the derivative of a product to find the derivative of $y = f(x) = 3x(1 - x)$. Is there a point on the curve where the slope of the tangent line is (b) -1; (c) 5; (d) 0? (e) Plot the curve and the tangent lines.

9   Consider the demand curve $p = (10 - 2D)(20 - D^2)$. (a) Find R; (b) R'; (c) $R'(4)$; (d) $R'(3)$; (e) $R'(1)$; (f) $R'(2.5)$.

10   Given the demand curve $p = (1 - D)(2 - 3D)$, (a) find R; (b) R'; (c) $R'(0.5)$; (d) $R'(0.3)$; (e) $R'(0.25)$. (f) Plot the demand curve and the marginal revenue curve.

58   DERIVATIVE OF A QUOTIENT OF FUNCTIONS

To find the derivative of the quotient of two functions we proceed as follows: Let $u = g(x)$ and $v = h(x)$ be functions of the independent variable x. A new function $f(x)$ is defined as their quotient; that is,

$$y = f(x) = \frac{u}{v} \quad \text{where } g(x) \neq 0.$$

The derivatives of the three dependent variables u, v, and y with respect to the independent variable x are defined as follows:

$$u' = g'(x) = \lim_{\Delta x \to 0} \frac{\Delta u}{\Delta x},$$

$$v' = h'(x) = \lim_{\Delta x \to 0} \frac{\Delta v}{\Delta x},$$

$$y' = f'(x) = \lim_{\Delta x \to 0} \frac{\Delta y}{\Delta x}.$$

Note again that as x changes to $x + \Delta x$, the three dependent variables change also: u to $u + \Delta u$; v to $v + \Delta v$; y to $y + \Delta y$. Hence we have

$$y + \Delta y = \frac{u + \Delta u}{v + \Delta v}.$$

From this expression we subtract y in order to compute Δy; there results

$$\Delta y = \frac{u + \Delta u}{v + \Delta v} - \frac{u}{v}.$$

The common denominator is $v(v + \Delta v)$, so

$$\Delta y = \frac{(u + \Delta u)v - (v + \Delta v)u}{(v + \Delta v)v} = \frac{(\Delta u)v - (\Delta v)u}{(v + \Delta v)v}.$$

To find the difference quotient, we divide the latter expression in the numerator, term by term, by Δx; that is,

$$\frac{\Delta y}{\Delta x} = \frac{(\Delta u / \Delta x)v - (\Delta v / \Delta x)u}{(v + \Delta v)v}.$$

To find the derivative, we let $\Delta x \to 0$. We recall the rules for limits, such as the limit of a difference is the difference of the limits, and the limit of a quotient is the quotient of the limits. We obtain

$$y' = f'(x) = \frac{[\lim_{\Delta x \to 0} \Delta u / \Delta x]\, v - [\lim_{\Delta x \to 0} (\Delta v)/(\Delta x)]u}{\lim_{\Delta u \to 0} (v + \Delta v)v}.$$

We have noted previously that as $\Delta x \to 0$, also $\Delta v \to 0$. Hence

$$\lim_{\Delta x \to 0} (v + \Delta v) = v.$$

It follows that the derivative is

$$y' = f'(x) = \frac{u'v - v'u}{v^2}.$$

In words, the derivative of a quotient of functions is the derivative of the numerator times the denominator minus the derivative of the denominator times the numerator, divided by the square of the denominator.

EXAMPLE

This rule may be exemplified by the following problem:

$$y = f(x) = \frac{3x^2}{4x - 1}.$$

The numerator is $u = 3x^2$ and the denominator is $v = 4x - 1$. The derivatives are $u' = 6x$ and $v' = 4$. Hence the derivative of y is

$$y' = f'(x) = \frac{(6x)(4x - 1) - (4)(3x^2)}{(4x - 1)^2} = \frac{12x^2 - 6x}{(4x - 1)^2}.$$

EXERCISES 58

1   Find the derivative of $y = 6x^2/(2x + 1)$.

2   (a) Find the derivative of $y = f(x) = (2x^2 - 3x + 1)/(x^2 + 5x + 6)$.
    (b) Find $f'(0)$; (c) $f'(1)$; (d) $f'(-5)$.

3 Find the derivative of $y = (1 - x^2)/(x^3 + 2x)$.

4 (a) Find the derivative of $y = f(x) = (x + 1)/(3x - 2)$. (b) Find $f'(1)$; (c) $f'(4)$ and the corresponding angle of inclination of the tangent.

5 Consider the function $y = (5x + 1)/(2x + 1)$. Find the value of x and y where the angle of inclination is (a) 45°; (b) 0°; (c) 26°.

6 Find the derivative of $y = (ax + b)/(cx + d)$, where a, b, c, and d are constants.

7 Take the demand curve $p = 10/(1 + 5D)$. (a) Find R; (b) R'; (c) $R'(1)$; (d) $R'(10)$. (e) Plot the demand curve and the marginal revenue curve.

8 Consider the demand curve $p = 6/(2 + 3D)$. (a) Find R; (b) R'; (c) $R'(1)$; (d) $R'(4)$; (e) $R'(10)$. (f) Plot the demand curve and the marginal revenue curve.

9 Consider the total cost function as $C = 2D/(20 - 3D)$. (a) Find the marginal cost curve; (b) $C'(1)$; (c) $C'(5)$; (d) Plot the total cost curve and the marginal cost curve.

10 Let the total cost curve for a commodity be $C = 5D/(25 - 5D^2)$. (a) Find the marginal cost curve; (b) $C'(1)$; (c) $C'(2)$.

59 DERIVATIVE OF A FUNCTION OF A FUNCTION

A very useful formula gives the derivative of a function of a function. For example, suppose we want to find the derivative of

$$y = f(x) = (x^3 - 3x^2 + 5)^4.$$

We can regard the expression in brackets, $x^3 - 3x^2 + 5$, as a new function of x, which will be designated by u. So

$$u = g(x) = x^3 - 3x + 5.$$

Then y can be written as

$$y = u^4.$$

The function y is said to be a function of a function. It is a function of u; but u itself is a function of x.

The derivative of u with respect to x is

$$\frac{du}{dx} = \lim_{\Delta x \to 0} \frac{\Delta u}{\Delta x}.$$

The derivative of y with respect to u is

$$\frac{dy}{du} = \lim_{\Delta u \to 0} \frac{\Delta y}{\Delta u}.$$

The derivative of y with respect to x is

$$\frac{dy}{dx} = \lim_{\Delta x \to 0} \frac{\Delta y}{\Delta x}.$$

It has been noted previously that as $\Delta x \to 0$, also $\Delta u \to 0$ and $\Delta y \to 0$. This follows from the fact that both y and u are functions of x assumed to have derivations with respect to x.

Consider now the difference quotient $\Delta y / \Delta x$. This is a fraction. The numerator and denominator can be multiplied by the same quantity $\Delta u \neq 0$ without changing the value of the fraction. It is also permitted to rearrange the terms in the following order:

$$\frac{\Delta y}{\Delta x} = \left(\frac{\Delta y}{\Delta u}\right)\left(\frac{\Delta u}{\Delta x}\right).$$

The derivative of y with respect to x is computed by letting $\Delta x \to 0$, hence

$$\frac{dy}{dx} = \lim_{\Delta x \to 0} \left(\frac{\Delta y}{\Delta u}\right)\left(\frac{\Delta u}{\Delta x}\right) = \left(\lim_{\Delta u \to 0} \frac{\Delta y}{\Delta u}\right) \cdot \left(\lim_{\Delta u \to 0} \frac{\Delta u}{\Delta x}\right).$$

The justification of the expression on the right is that the limit of a product is the product of the limits. Since $\Delta u \to 0$ as $\Delta x \to 0$, we can replace Δx by Δu in the first limit.

The two limits in the last expression are, by definition, dy/du and du/dx. Hence

$$\frac{dy}{dx} = \frac{dy}{du} \cdot \frac{du}{dx}.$$

In words, to find the derivative of y with respect to x when y is a function of u, which is itself a function of x, proceed as follows: Multiply the derivative of y with respect to u by the derivative of u with respect to x.

EXAMPLE 1

Let us continue our consideration of

$$y = (x^3 - 3x + 5)^4.$$

We put

$$u = x^3 - 3x + 5,$$

and y becomes a function of u, namely,

$$y = u^4.$$

The derivative of y with respect to u is

$$\frac{dy}{du} = 4u^3.$$

The derivative of u with respect to x is

$$\frac{du}{dx} = 3x^2 - 3.$$

Hence the derivative of y with respect to x is the product

$$\frac{dy}{dx} = (4u^3)(3x^2 - 3) = 4(x^3 - 3x + 5)^3(3x^2 - 3).$$

The final result is achieved by substituting for u its expression in terms of x.

EXAMPLE 2

Let $y = (x^2 - 2x + 5)^3$. We have $u = x^2 - 2x + 5$ and $du/dx = 2x - 2$. In terms of u we have $y = u^3$ and $dy/du = 3u^2$. Hence, $dy/dx = (dy/du)(du/dx) = 3u^2(2x - 2) = 3(x^2 - 2x + 5)^2(2x - 2)$.

EXERCISES 59

1   Find the derivative of $y = (3x - 2)^5$.

2   Find the derivative of $y = (2 - 3x + 4x^3)^5$.

3   Take as the total cost $C = (1 + 5D^2)^5$. (a) Find the marginal cost curve; (b) $C'(1)$; (c) $C'(2)$; (d) $C'(3)$.

4   Take as the total cost $C = (1 + 3D)^3$. (a) Find the marginal cost curve; (b) $C'(1)$; (c) $C'(25)$; (d) $C'(16)$.

*5 Prove that the formula for the derivative of a power holds for fractional n. Let $u = x^{p/q}$, where p and q are positive integers. Hence, $n = p/q$ is a rational number. Let $y = u^q = x^p$. Differentiate this expression with respect to x, using the formula for the derivative of a function of a function. Simplify and prove that $du/dx = (p/q)x^{(p/q)-1} = nx^{n-1}$.

6   Use the result of problem 5 to find the derivatives of (a) $\sqrt{x}$; (b) $\sqrt[3]{x}$; (c) $\sqrt[4]{x^3}$; (d) $\sqrt[5]{x^7}$. (Note that $\sqrt{x} = x^{1/2}$, $\sqrt[3]{x} = x^{1/3}$, $\sqrt[4]{x^3} = x^{3/4}$, and so forth.)

7   Let the total cost curve be $C = \sqrt{1 + 2D}$. (a) Find the marginal cost curve; (b) $C'(1)$; (c) $C'(1.5)$; (d) $C'(4)$.

8   Let the total cost curve of a commodity be $C = 100 + 5\sqrt[3]{D}$. (a) Find the marginal cost curve; (b) $C'(1)$; (c) $C'(8)$; (d) $C'(27)$.

9   Take as the demand curve $p = \sqrt{10 - 2D}$. (a) Find the total revenue R; (b) R'; (c) $R'(3)$; (d) $R'(4.5)$.

*10   Consider the derivative of $y = x^{-n}$, where n is a positive constant. Prove that the general rule for the derivative of a power holds also for negative exponents. (HINT: Let $u = x^n$, so that $y = 1/u$. Differentiate, remembering that y is a function of x. Simplify and demonstrate that $dy/dx = (-n)x^{-n-1}$.)

11   Use the result of problem 10 to find the derivative of each of the following functions: (a) $y = 1/x$; (b) $y = 1/x^7$; (c) $y = 10/(2x + 1)$; (d) $y = 24/\sqrt{x}$.

12   Consider the demand for sugar in the United States for 1915–1929 (Schultz): $p = 6,570,000/D^3$. (a) Find R and R'; (b) $R'(60)$; (c) $R'(50)$; (d) $R'(5)$; (e) $R'(35)$; (f) $R'(30)$.

13   Consider the demand for corn in the United States for 1915–1929 (Schultz): $p = 12,800/D^{1.3}$. (a) Find R and R'; (b) $R'(20)$; (c) $R'(35)$; (d) $R'(45)$; (e) $R'(50)$; (f) $R'(30)$.

14   Consider the demand for cotton in the United States for 1915–1929 (Schultz): $p = 0.756/D^{0.8}$. (a) Find R and R'; (b) $R'(20)$; (c) $R'(15)$; (d) $R'(35)$; (e) $R'(50)$; (f) $R'(35)$.

15   Consider the demand for wheat in the United States for 1922–1934 (Schultz): $p = 2,180/D^2$. (a) Find R and R'; (b) $R'(6)$; (c) $R'(3.3)$; (d) $R'(6.5)$; (e) $R'(2.125)$; (f) $R'(3.33)$.

16   Consider the demand for potatoes in the United States for 1915–1929 (Schultz): $p = 2,630/D^3$. (a) Find R and R'; (b) $R'(3)$; (c) $R'(4.5)$; (d) $R'(3.25)$; (e) $R'(1.25)$; (f) $R'(4)$.

17   Consider the two functions $y = f(x) = x^2$ and $x = g(y) = \sqrt{y}$. (a) Show that g is the inverse of f. (b) Compute $dy/dx = f'(x)$ and $dx/dy = g'(y)$. (c) Show that $f'(4)g'(16) = 1$; (d) $f'(3)g'(9) = 1$; (e) $f'(10)g'(100) = 1$. (f) Show in general that $f'(x)g'(y) = 1$, if $y = f(x)$.

**18   Let $y = f(x)$ and $x = g(y)$ be inverse functions. Show that $f'(x) = 1/g'(y)$, by differentiating $g(y) = x$ on both sides with respect to x and remembering that y is a function of x.

**19   Use the result of the previous example to find the derivative of $y = \sqrt{x}$ by differentiating $x = y^2$ with respect to y and expressing the reciprocal of this derivative in terms of x. Check by finding the derivative of $y = x^{1/2}$.

**20   Find the derivative of $y = \sqrt[3]{x}$ in the same way as in the previous example. Check by finding the derivative of $y = x^{1/3}$.

**21   Find the derivative of $y = \sqrt[n]{x}$ by using the method of example 19. Check by finding the derivative of $y = x^{1/n}$.

Chapter 12

Derivatives of Logarithmic and Exponential Functions

Consider the following sequence:

$$u_1 = (1 + 1)^1 = 2,$$

$$u_2 = \left(1 + \frac{1}{2}\right)^2 = 1 + 2\left(\frac{1}{2}\right) + \left(\frac{1}{2}\right)^2 = 2 + \frac{1}{4},$$

$$u_3 = \left(1 + \frac{1}{3}\right)^3 = 1 + 3\left(\frac{1}{3}\right) + 3\left(\frac{1}{3}\right)^2 + \left(\frac{1}{3}\right)^3 = 2 + \frac{10}{27},$$

$$u_4 = \left(1 + \frac{1}{4}\right)^4 = 1 + 4\left(\frac{1}{4}\right) + 6\left(\frac{1}{4}\right)^2 + 4\left(\frac{1}{4}\right)^3 + \left(\frac{1}{4}\right)^4 = 2 + \frac{113}{256}.$$

It can be shown that u_n, where $u_n = (1 + 1/n)^n$, if n is a positive integer, has the property that

$$2 < u_n < 3.$$

Hence we conjecture that the following limit exists:

$$\lim_{n \to \infty} \left(1 + \frac{1}{n}\right)^n.$$

This limit is called e; its value does not demand that n be integral. The limit can be evaluated by expanding u_n by the binomial theorem, and by letting $n \to \infty$. This procedure gives

$$e = 1 + \frac{1}{1} + \frac{1}{1 \cdot 2} + \frac{1}{1 \cdot 2 \cdot 3} + \frac{1}{1 \cdot 2 \cdot 3 \cdot 4} + \cdots$$

The number e obtained thereby is an irrational number; that is, it cannot be expressed as a ratio of any two integers. Its value to five decimal places is

$$e = 2.71828.$$

If $m = 1/n$, it is evident that as $n \to \infty$, $m \to 0$. Hence, since

$$\lim_{n \to \infty} \left(1 + \frac{1}{n}\right)^n = e,$$

it follows that

$$\lim_{m \to 0} (1 + m)^{1/m} = e.$$

The number e is used frequently in higher mathematics. It is taken as the base of the so-called system of natural logarithms, or logarithms to the base e.

EXERCISES 60

1 Compute: (a) $(1 + \frac{1}{5})^5$; (b) $(1 + \frac{1}{10})^{10}$.

2 Use the expansion for e, namely,

$$e = 1 + \frac{1}{1} + \frac{1}{1 \cdot 2} + \frac{1}{1 \cdot 2 \cdot 3} + \cdots$$

to compute an approximation to e using (a) 2 terms, (b) 4 terms, and (c) 6 terms.

61   NATURAL LOGARITHMS

The logarithm of the number a taken to the base e is written $\log_e a$. This is also called *a natural logarithm*. We recall that the logarithm of a number b to the base 10 is written $\log b$. It should also be remembered that $\log 100 = 2$, since $100 = 10^2$; $\log 1{,}000 = 3$, since $1{,}000 = 10^3$; $\log 0.01 = -2$, since $0.01 = \frac{1}{100} = 10^{-2}$; and so on.

Natural logarithms, or logarithms to the base e, may be interpreted in a similar way; that is, $\log_e a$ is the exponent to which the base e has to be raised in order to get the number a.

EXAMPLE 1

Since $e^2 = 7.3891$, $\log_e 7.3891 = 2$; since $e^3 = 20.086$, $\log_e 20.086 = 3$; and since $1/e = e^{-1} = 0.367879$, $\log_e 0.367879 = -1$; and so on.

Logarithms to the base 10 can be converted into logarithms to the base e by a simple process. Let a be the natural logarithm and b the logarithm to the base 10 of some number N; that is, $\log_e N = a$, and $\log N = b$. Hence $N = e^a$ and $N = 10^b$. After taking the natural logarithm of the two members of the second equality we obtain

$$\log_e N = \log_e 10^b$$

or

$$\log_e N = b \log_e 10.$$

At this point it seems appropriate to call attention to Table 3, Appendix D, namely, a table of 4-place natural logarithms, that is, logarithms to the base e. In this table will be found $\log_e 10 = 2.3026$. It then becomes apparent, if one recalls the definition of b, that

$$\log_e N = 2.3026 \log N.$$

Also, it follows readily that

$$\log N = 0.4343 \log_e N.$$

In conclusion, it has been shown that the natural logarithm of any number may be computed by multiplying the logarithm of this number to the base 10 by the conversion factor 2.3026. Of course, if a table such as Table 3 is available, natural logarithms may be obtained by direct reference to it. Both methods are employed in the examples that follow.

EXAMPLE 2

From Table 1, Appendix D, $\log 17 = 1.2304$. Hence the natural logarithm of 17 is

$$\log_e 17 = (1.2304)(2.3026) = 2.8331.$$

By reference to Table 3, Appendix D,

$$\log_e 17 = \log_e (10)(1.7) = \log_e 10 + \log_e 1.7$$
$$= 2.3026 + 0.5306 = 2.8332.$$

EXAMPLE 3

$$\log 0.5 = 0.6990 - 1, \quad \text{or} \quad -0.3010.$$

Hence

$$\log_e 0.5 = (-0.3010)(2.3026) = -0.6931.$$

By reference to Table 3, noting the value of $\log_e 0.1$ at the bottom of the page,

$$\log_e 0.5 = \log_e (5)(0.1) = \log_e 5 + \log_e 0.1 = 1.6094 + .6974 - 3$$
$$= 2.3068 - 3 = -0.6932.$$

EXERCISES 61

1   Find the logarithms to the base e of the following: (a) e; (b) 1; (c) e^6; (d) $\sqrt[3]{e}$; (e) $\sqrt[4]{e^5}$; (f) $1/e$; (g) $1/e^6$; (h) $1/e^2$; (i) $1/\sqrt[4]{e}$; (j) $1/\sqrt{e^3}$; (k) $1/\sqrt[6]{e^9}$.

2   Using the formula for the conversion of logarithms to the base 10 to logarithms to the base e, compute the natural logarithms of the following: (a) 100; (b) 45; (c) 34.198; (d) 0.189; (e) 1; (f) 0.00001; (g) 0.02347; (h) 0.09872.

3 Check the results obtained in problem 2 by using Table 3.

4 Find the numbers whose *natural* logarithms are (a) 0.6931; (b) 2.3026; (c) 1.7918; (d) 4.0943; (e) 5.0106; (f) 1.9315; (g) 1.2528. (HINT: Convert the natural logarithms into logarithms to the base 10.)

5 Check the results obtained in problem 4 by using Table 3. Give special attention to parts (d) and (e).

62   DERIVATIVE OF THE LOGARITHMIC FUNCTION

To find the derivative of the logarithmic function, we recall that

$$e = \lim_{n \to \infty} \left(1 + \frac{1}{n}\right)^n = \lim_{m \to 0} (1 + m)^{1/m}$$

Let us start our analysis by taking

$$y = f(x) = \log_e x.$$

Then

$$y + \Delta y = \log_e (x + \Delta x).$$

Subtracting y from this expression provides a formula for Δy: hence

$$\Delta y = \log_e (x + \Delta x) - \log_e x.$$

We recall that the logarithm of a fraction is the difference of the logarithms. Hence we can write

$$\Delta y = \log_e \frac{x + \Delta x}{x} = \log_e \left(1 + \frac{\Delta x}{x}\right).$$

To find the difference quotient we divide by Δx; this gives

$$\frac{\Delta y}{\Delta x} = \left(\frac{1}{\Delta x}\right) \log_e \left(1 + \frac{\Delta x}{x}\right).$$

An expression is not changed if it is multiplied and divided by the same quantity. So, multiply and divide the right member of the last equation by x; this gives

$$\frac{\Delta y}{\Delta x} = \left(\frac{1}{x}\right)\left(\frac{x}{\Delta x}\right) \log_e \left(1 + \frac{\Delta x}{x}\right).$$

We remember that the logarithm of a power of a quantity is computed by multiplying the logarithm of the quantity by the power. Hence we can write

$$\frac{\Delta y}{\Delta x} = \left(\frac{1}{x}\right) \log_e \left(1 + \frac{\Delta x}{x}\right)^{(x/\Delta x)}.$$

The derivative is computed by letting $\Delta x \to 0$; this gives

$$v' = f'(x) = \lim_{\Delta x \to 0} \left(\frac{1}{x}\right) \log_e \left(1 + \frac{\Delta x}{x}\right)^{x/\Delta x}$$

Evidently as $\Delta x \to 0$, $(\Delta x/x) \to 0$, since x is taken as fixed. Putting $\Delta x/x = m$, we can write

$$y' = f'(x) = \lim_{m \to 0} \left(\frac{1}{x}\right) \log_e (1 + m)^{1/m}$$

But it is already known that

$$\lim_{m \to 0} (1 + m)^{1/m} = e.$$

Consequently,

$$y' = f'(x) = \left(\frac{1}{x}\right) \log_e e = \frac{1}{x},$$

since $\log_e e = 1$.

Hence we have the rule; the derivative of the natural logarithm of x is the reciprocal of x.

EXAMPLE

Find the derivative of the function

$$y = f(x) = (5x)(\log_e x).$$

We use the formula for the derivative of a product; namely, $y' = u'v + v'u$. In this case, $u = 5x$, $v = \log_e x$. The derivatives are $u' = 5$, $v' = 1/x$. Hence

$$y' = f'(x) = (5)(\log_e x) + \left(\frac{1}{x}\right)(5x) = 5 \log_e x + 5.$$

When $x = 3$, this result yields

$$f'(3) = 5 \log_e 3 + 5 = 5(1.0986) + 5 = 10.4930.$$

EXERCISES 62

1 Find the derivative of the function $y = 10 \log_e x - 5$. Evaluate $f'(1)$; $f'(4)$.

2 Find the derivative of $y = 2x - 3 \log_e x$. Evaluate $f'(2)$; $f'(10)$.

3 Find the derivative of $y = 2x (\log_e x)$. Evaluate $f'(1)$; $f'(e)$; $f'(12)$.

4 Find the derivative of $y = (2 \log_e x)/x^3$. Evaluate $f'(2)$; $f'(8)$.

5 Find the derivative of $y = (\log_e x)^4$. Evaluate $f'(1)$; $f'(e^2)$; $f'(9)$.

6 The demand curve is $p = 100 - 3 \log_e D$. (a) Find R; (b) R'; (c) $R'(1)$; (d) $R'(10)$; (e) $R'(2)$.

7 The demand curve is $p = 100/\log_e D$. (a) Find R; (b) R'; (c) $R'(5)$; (d) $R'(2)$.

8 The total cost function is $C = \log_e D$. (a) Find the marginal cost curve; (b) $C'(1)$; (c) $C'(2)$; (d) $C'(e^3)$.

9 The total cost function is $C = 10 + 5\log_e D$. (a) Find the marginal cost curve; (b) $C'(1)$; (c) $C'(5)$; (d) $C'(e^2)$.

10 The total cost function is $C = (10 + D)\log_e D$. (a) Find the marginal cost curve; (b) $C'(1)$; (c) $C'(e^2)$; (d) $C'(4)$.

11 The total cost function is $C = (\log_e D)/(20 - 3D)$. (a) Find the marginal cost curve; (b) $C'(1)$; (c) $C'(e)$; (d) $C'(5)$.

63 GENERAL LOGARITHMIC DIFFERENTIATION

We use the formula for the derivative of a function of a function to derive the general principle of logarithmic differentiation.

Let $y = f(x) = \log_e u$, where $u = g(x)$ is a function of x. The formula for the derivative of a function of a function is

$$\frac{dy}{dx} = \frac{dy}{du} \cdot \frac{du}{dx}.$$

In our case $y = \log_e u$. Hence

$$\frac{dy}{du} = \frac{1}{u},$$

$$\frac{du}{dx} = u',$$

and, by multiplication,

$$\frac{dy}{dx} = \frac{u'}{u}.$$

This gives the following rule: The derivative of the natural logarithm of any function of x is the derivative of the function with respect to x divided by the function itself.

EXAMPLE 1

Assume that $y = \log_e (3 - 2x^3)$. Find the derivative of the function. We have, evidently,

$$u = 3 - 2x^3,$$
$$u' = -6x^2.$$

Hence

$$\frac{dy}{dx} = \frac{-6x^2}{3 - 2x^3}.$$

EXAMPLE 2

Let

$$y = \frac{(2x - 4)(x^2 + 3x + 1)}{(1 + 2x)^4}.$$

Let us take the logarithm to the base e of both sides; this gives

$$\log_e y = \log_e (2x - 4) + \log_e (x^2 + 3x + 1) - 4 \log_e (1 + 2x).$$

We use the above formula for the derivative of the logarithm of a function for all the terms appearing in this equality and obtain

$$\frac{y'}{y} = \frac{2}{(2x - 4)} + \frac{2x + 3}{(x^2 + 3x + 1)} - \frac{(4)(2)}{(1 + 2x)}.$$

Multiplying the left and right members of this equation by

$$y = \frac{(2x - 4)(x^2 + 3x + 1)}{(1 + 2x)^4}$$

gives

$$v' = \frac{2(x^2 + 3x + 1)}{(1 + 2x)^4} + \frac{(2x + 3)(2x - 4)}{(1 + 2x)^4}$$
$$- \frac{8(2x - 4)(x^2 + 3x + 1)}{(1 + 2x)^5}.$$

EXERCISES 63

Use logarithmic differentiation to find the derivatives of the following functions:

1   $\log_e (1 - 4x)$.

2   $\log_e (1 + 1/x^2)$.

3   $\log_e (x^2 + 3x - 7)$.

4   $(2 + 4x)(1 + 5x^2)$.

5   $(x^2 - 5x + 7)/(5x - 6)$.

6   $(1 - 4x)^2(1 - 2x^2 + x^4)^6$.

7   $[(1 + x)^2(1 - 2x)^3]/[(x^2 - 5)^2]$.

8   The following Engel curves have been estimated for meat for the United Kingdom for the period 1937–1939 (Prais and Houthakker). Denote by v the expenditure on meat and by v_0 total expenditure per head: (a) $\log v = 0.159 + 0.692 \log v_0$;   (b) $\log v = 1.69 - (15.9/v_0)$;   (c) $v = -40.8 + 37.5 \log v_0$;   (d) $v = 12.9 + 0.196v_0$;   (e) $v = 41 - (801/v_0)$. Find the elasticities of the expenditure of meat with respect to total expenditure $(Ev/Ev_0) = (dv/dv_0)(v_0/v)$.

9 Total cost function: $C = 6 \log_e (1 + 3D)$. (a) Find the marginal cost curve; (b) $C'(0)$; (c) $C'(1)$; (d) $C'(6)$.

10 The following result refers to the trend of British industrial production for the period 1700–1940 (Sengupta and Tintner).

$$y = f(t) = \frac{573}{1 + 232e^{-0.06t}}$$

This is a *logistic* trend. (a) Find the inverse function, $t = g(y)$. (b) Find the derivative $dt/dy = g'(y)$. (c) Use the formula $dy/dt = 1/(dt/dy = 1/g'(y)$ and show that the proportional rate of change of production, $(dy/dt)/y$, is a linear function of y. Interpret.

11 Let x_1 be the expenditure on sugar, x_2 on education, and x_3 on medical services, Iyengar has estimated the following Engel curves for the rural population of India for 1955: $\log x_1 = a + 1.33 \log Y$, $\log x_2 = b + 2.43 \log Y$, $\log x_3 = c + 2.62 \log Y$, where Y is total expenditure and a, b, and c are constants. Find the income elasticities Ex_1/Ey, Ex_2/Ey, Ex_3/Ey.

64   DERIVATIVE OF THE EXPONENTIAL FUNCTION

A special application of logarithmic differentiation pertains to the derivative of the exponential function

$$y = e^x.$$

Taking the logarithm to the base e of both members of the equation yields

$$\log_e y = x.$$

After differentiating these two members with respect to x, there results

$$\frac{y'}{y} = 1.$$

Hence,

$$y' = y = e^x.$$

This gives the rule for the derivative of the exponential function e^x: The derivative with respect to x of the exponential function e^x is equal to itself.

EXAMPLE 1

Find the derivative of the function

$$y = (1 + 3e^x)^5.$$

We use the principle of the derivative of a function of a function. Here $u = 1 + 3e^x$ and $y = u^5$. Hence

$$\frac{dy}{du} = 5u^4,$$

$$\frac{du}{dx} = 3e^x.$$

By multiplication,

$$\frac{dy}{dx} = (5u^4)(3e^x) = (15)(e^x)(1 + 3e^x)^4.$$

EXAMPLE 2

Find the derivative of the function

$$y = \frac{1}{3^x}.$$

This is most easily done by the use of logarithms. We have

$$\log_e y = -x \log_e 3,$$

$$\frac{y'}{y} = - \log_e 3,$$

since on the right $(- \log_e 3)$ may be regarded as the constant coefficient of x. Thus

$$y' = -y(\log_e 3) = \frac{- \log_e 3}{3^x} = \frac{-1.0986}{3^x}.$$

EXERCISES 64

Find the derivatives of the following functions:

1 e^{-2x}.

2 e^{5x}.

3 $1/4e^{5x}$.

4 $(2 + 3e^x)^6$.

5 $(1 + 4e^x)/(2 + 3e^x)$.

6 2^x.

7 10^x.

**8 What is the derivative of $y = a^x$, where a is any positive number? (HINT: Take the natural logarithm of each member.)

9 Consider the demand curve $p = 100 - e^D$. (a) Find R; (b) R'; (c) $R'(1)$; (d) $R'(3)$.

10 Consider the demand curve $p = 10e^{-3D}$. (a) Find R; (b) R'; (c) $R'(0)$; (d) $R'(1)$; (e) $R'(4)$.

11 Consider the total cost curve $C = 10e^{5D}$. (a) Find the marginal cost curve; (b) $C'(1)$; (c) $C'(10)$; (d) $C'(7)$.

Chapter 13
Economic Applications
of the Derivative

65 ELASTICITY

We define the elasticity of a function $y = f(x)$ with respect to x as

$$\frac{Ey}{Ex} = \lim_{\Delta x \to 0} \frac{(\Delta y/y)}{(\Delta x/x)} = \left(\frac{x}{y}\right)\left(\frac{dy}{dx}\right).$$

It is apparent that the elasticity is the limit of the ratio of the *relative* increment in y to the *relative* increment in x as the increment of x tends to 0. It is a pure, dimensionless number, independent of the scale employed in the measurement of x and y. The elasticity of y with respect to x is obtained approximately as the percent of increase or decrease in y that will follow if x is increased by 1 percent.

EXAMPLE

Let $y = 3x - 6$. (a) Find the elasticity. We have, by definition,

$$\frac{Ey}{Ex} = \left(\frac{x}{y}\right)\left(\frac{dy}{dx}\right) = \frac{3x}{3x - 6} = \frac{x}{x - 2}.$$

(b) Find the elasticity if $x = 10$. By substituting $x = 10$ into the formula, we have $10/8 = 5/4$. If x is increased by 1 percent, y will increase by about $5/4$ percent.

EXERCISES 65

1 $y = 1 + 2x - x^2$. (a) Find the elasticity of y with respect to x; (b) for $x = 1$; (c) for $x = 0$; (d) for $x = 5$; (e) for $x = 10$.

2 $y = x^2 - 3x + 10$. (a) Find the elasticity Ey/Ex; (b) for $x = 0$; (c) for $x = 10$; (d) for $x = 1$; (e) for $x = 5$.

3 $y = x^3$. (a) Find Ey/Ex; (b) for $x = 1$; (c) for $x = 5$.

4 $y = (1 - 2x)/(2 + 3x)$. (a) Find Ey/Ex; (b) for $x = 0$; (c) for $x = 2$; (d) for $x = 10$; (e) for $x = 3$.

5 $y = e^{5x}$. (a) Find Ey/Ex; (b) for $x = 1$; (c) for $x = 0$; (d) for $x = 1.2$; (e) for $x = 5$; (f) for $x = 2$.

6 $y = 5 \log_e x$. (a) Find Ey/Ex; (b) for $x = 10$; (c) for $x = e$; (d) for $x = 3$; (e) for $x = e^4$.

7 Find the elasticity of $y = a + bx$, where a and b are constants.

8 Find the elasticity of $y = ax^m$, where m is a constant.

**9 Find the elasticity of $y = au$, where a is a constant and u is a function of x.

**10 Find the elasticity of $y = au + b$, where a and b are constants and u is a function of x.

**11 Find the elasticity of $y = u + v$, where u and v are functions of x.

**12 Find the elasticity of $y = u - v$, where u and v are functions of x.

**13 Find the elasticity of $y = au + bv$, where u and v are functions of x, and a and b are constants.

**14 Find the elasticity of $y = uv$, where u and v are functions of x.

**15 Find the elasticity of $y = u/v$, where u and v are functions of x.

**16 The elasticity of $y = f(x)$ is also written

$$\frac{Ey}{Ex} = \left(\frac{dy}{dx}\right)\left(\frac{x}{y}\right) = \frac{(d/dx)(\log_e y)}{(d/dx)(\log_e x)}.$$

Justify this statement.

66 ELASTICITY OF DEMAND

By definition,

$$\frac{ED}{Ep} = \left(\frac{p}{D}\right)\left(\frac{dD}{dp}\right) = \frac{p}{D}\left(\frac{1}{dp/dD}\right).$$

This follows from the fact that $dD/dp = 1/(dp/dD)$. See problem 18, Exercises 59.

The elasticity of demand is the limit of the relative decrease in the quantity demanded, resulting from a relative increment in price, if the increment in price tends to 0. It is approximately the percent of decrease in the quantity demanded resulting from an increase in price of 1 percent.

EXAMPLE

Let the demand curve be $p = 1 - D$. (a) Find

$$\frac{ED}{Ep} = \frac{p}{D}\left(\frac{1}{dp/dD}\right).$$

Substituting, we have

$$\frac{ED}{Ep} = \frac{(1 - D)}{D}\left(\frac{1}{-1}\right) = \frac{1 - D}{-D}.$$

(b) Find the elasticity for $D = \frac{1}{4}$. Substituting into the formula, we have $(1 - \frac{1}{4})/(-\frac{1}{4}) = -3$. This means that if $\frac{1}{4}$ unit is sold, an increment of 1 percent in the price will decrease the amount sold by about 3 percent.

EXERCISES 66

1　Given the demand curve in problem 6, Exercises 55, (a) find the elasticity of demand; (b) for $D = 1$; (c) for $D = 2.5$; (d) for $D = 1.5$; (e) for $D = 0.5$.

2　Given the demand curve in problem 9, Exercises 57, (a) find the elasticity of demand; (b) for $D = 1$; (c) for $D = 4$; (d) for $D = 2.5$; (e) for $D = 1.2$.

*3　Consider the demand curve $Dp^a = b$, where a and b are constants. Prove that this curve has constant elasticity.

*4　Consider the demand curve $Dp = a$, where a is a constant (rectangular hyperbola). Prove that the elasticity of this curve is -1.

5　Show that a demand curve that is a horizontal line $p = a$, where a is a constant, has an "infinite" elasticity. This is the demand curve for the product of a firm under perfect competition.

6　Show that a demand curve that is a vertical line $D = a$, where a is a constant, has an elasticity of 0.

7　Why is the elasticity of demand negative for most demand curves? (HINT: Consider the meaning of dp/dD in the definition of the elasticity of demand.)

8　Find the elasticity of the demand for sugar from the demand curve in problem 8, Exercises 55, (a) for $D = 80$; (b) for $D = 100$; (c) for $D = 50$; (d) for $D = 45$.

9　Find the elasticity of the demand for cotton from problem 9, Exercises 55, (a) for $D = 1$; (b) for $D = 5$; (c) for $D = 7$; (d) for $D = 2$.

10　Find the elasticity of the demand for barley from problem 10, Exercises 55, (a) for $D = 1$; (b) for $D = 0.80$; (c) for $D = 1.25$; (d) for $D = 1.05$; (e) for $D = 2.35$.

11　Find the elasticity of the demand for rye from problem 11, Exercises 55, (a) for $D = 0.50$; (b) for $D = 0.75$; (c) for $D = 0.4$; (d) for $D = 0.45$; (e) for $D = 0.35$.

12　Find the elasticity of the demand for buckwheat from problem 12, Exercises 55, (a) for $D = 0.30$; (b) for $D = 0.25$; (c) for $D = 0.20$; (d) for $D = 0.10$.

13 Find the elasticity of the demand for sugar from Problem 12, Exercises 59.

14 Find the elasticity of the demand for cotton from Problem 14, Exercises 59.

15 Find the elasticity of the demand for wheat from Problem 15, Exercises 59.

16 Find the elasticity of the demand for potatoes from Problem 16, Exercises 59.

17 Find the elasticity of the demand for hay from Problem 13, Exercises 55, (a) for $D = 1$; (b) for $D = 0.80$; (c) for $D = 0.65$.

67   MARGINAL REVENUE AND ELASTICITY OF DEMAND

The total revenue is defined as $R = p \cdot D$, where $p = f(D)$ is the demand curve. Hence, we have for the marginal revenue

$$R' = \left(\frac{dp}{dD}\right) D + p.$$

This follows from the formula for the derivative of a product. The elasticity of demand is, by definition,

$$\frac{ED}{Ep} = \frac{p}{D}\left(\frac{1}{dp/dD}\right).$$

From this last equation we have

$$\frac{dp}{dD} = \frac{p}{D(ED/Ep)}.$$

After substituting this into the formula for marginal revenue, there results

$$R' = \frac{p}{ED/Ep} + p = p\left(1 + \frac{1}{ED/Ep}\right).$$

In words, the marginal revenue is the price times 1 plus the reciprocal of the elasticity.

EXAMPLE

Let the demand function be $p = 1 - D$. We derive from this

$$R = p \cdot D = D - D^2,$$

$$R' = 1 - 2D.$$

To show the interrelationship of our formulas let us take

$$\frac{ED}{Ep} = \left(\frac{p}{D}\right)\left(\frac{1}{dp/dD}\right) = \left(\frac{1-D}{D}\right)\left(\frac{1}{-1}\right) = \frac{1-D}{-D}.$$

Using the formula derived previous to this example, we have

$$R' = p\left(1 + \frac{1}{ED/Ep}\right) = (1 - D)\left(1 - \frac{1}{(1-D)/D}\right)$$

$$= (1 - D)\left(\frac{1 - 2D}{1 - D}\right) = 1 - 2D.$$

This is the same formula for R' as obtained directly.

EXERCISES 67

1   Given the demand curve in problem 7, Exercises 55, demonstrate the relationship between marginal revenue and elasticity of demand.

2   Given the demand curve in problem 9, Exercises 57, show the relationship between the marginal revenue and the elasticity of demand.

3   Given the demand curve in problem 8, Exercises 58, show the relationship between the elasticity of demand and the marginal revenue.

4   Given the demand curve in problem 9, Exercises 59, show the relationship between elasticity of demand and marginal revenue.

5   Given the demand curve in problem 6, Exercises 62, show the relationship between the elasticity of demand and the marginal revenue.

6   What is the elasticity of demand if $R' = 0$?

7   What is the marginal revenue for a demand curve that is a horizontal line and has "infinite" elasticity?

8   Show the relationship between the elasticity of demand and the marginal revenue for the demand for sugar in problem 8, Exercises 55.

9   Show the relationship between the elasticity of demand and the marginal revenue for the demand for rye in problem 11, Exercises 55.

10   Show the relationship between marginal revenue and elasticity of demand for the demand for corn in problem 13, Exercises 59.

11   Show the relationship between the marginal revenue and the elasticity of demand for the demand for wheat in problem 15, Exercises 59.

68   FURTHER GEOMETRIC SIGNIFICANCE OF THE FIRST DERIVATIVE

We recall the definition of the derivative of $y = f(x)$, namely,

$$y' = f(x) = \lim_{\Delta x \to 0} \frac{\Delta y}{\Delta x}.$$

Let us take the increment of x, that is, Δx, to be a positive number. The derivative is positive, then, if Δy is positive. In this case the curve given by the equation $y = f(x)$ must be *rising* at the point (x, y) in question. Moreover, the curve $y = f(x)$ has, at this point, a tangent line with positive slope.

Now consider the case in which Δy is negative. This means that to a positive increment Δx corresponds a negative increment in y. Hence, at the point (x, y), the derivative $f'(x)$ is negative. So the curve given by the equation $y = f(x)$ is falling, and the slope of the tangent line to the curve at the point (x, y) is negative (illustrated in Figure 32). The case where $\Delta y = 0$ will be dealt with in Section 55.

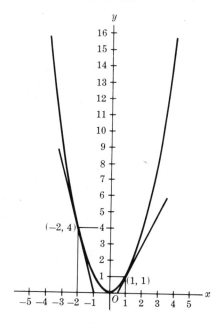

Figure 32

EXAMPLE 1

Figure 32 presents the graph of the function $y = f(x) = x^2$. Thus $y' = f'(x) = 2x$. Consider the situation at the point $x = -2$, $y = 4$. It is determined that $f'(-2) = (2)(-2) = -4$. The curve is evidently falling as one moves to the right in the neighborhood of the point $(-2, 4)$. Moreover, the slope of the tangent line is negative.

Next consider the point $(1, 1)$. We have $f'(1) = (2)(1) = 2$. This is positive; hence the curve is rising as one moves to the right in the neighborhood of the point in question, and the slope of the tangent line is positive.

Consider the point where $x = 2$. We have $f'(2) = 4$. This is positive. Hence, at the point $x = 2$, $y = 4$, the function in question is increasing, and the slope of the tangent line is positive.

Consider the point where $x = -1$. We have $f'(-1) = -2$. Hence the derivative is negative at the point $x = -1$, $y = 1$. The curve is falling, since the slope of the tangent line at the point $(-1, 1)$ is negative.

It is apparent that the derivative $y' = 2x$ is positive for $x > 0$ and negative for $x < 0$. Hence the curve in question will increase for all positive x as one moves to the right and will decrease for all negative x as one moves to the right.

EXAMPLE 2

Is the function $y = 2x^2 - x + 4$ increasing at the point where $x = 2$? We have $y' = f'(x) = 4x - 1$; $f'(2) = 4 \cdot 2 - 1 = 7$. Hence the curve is increasing at the point $x = 2$, $y = 10$ as one moves to the right. The slope of the tangent line is positive at this point.

EXERCISES 68

1   Consider the function $y = f(x) = 2x^3 - x^2$. Is this function increasing or decreasing at the point where (a) $x = 1$; (b) $x = -1$; (c) $x = 5$; (d) $x = -3$? (e) Make a graph of the function for a check.

2   Consider the function $y = f(x) = xe^x$. Can you find the values of x for which this function is always increasing? Where it is always decreasing? (HINT: Find the derivative, then factor, and remember that e^x is always positive.)

3   Where is the function $y = \log_e x$ increasing and where is it decreasing? Remember that $\log_e x$ is only defined for positive x.

4   Consider the behavior of the function $y = f(x) = x^2 e^{-2x}$. Where is it increasing and where is it decreasing? (HINT: $e^{-n} = 1/e^n$.)

5   Let $y = a + bx$, where a and b are constant (straight line). Is this function increasing or decreasing?

6   Consider the behavior of the function $y = f(x) = x - x^2$. Where is it increasing and where decreasing?

7   Given the following *demand* functions, find the amounts sold for which the *total revenue* R increases and decreases: (a) $p = 1 - D$; (b) $p = 10 - 3D$; (c) $p = 20 - 5D$; (d) $p = 100 - 2D^2$; (e) $p = 10D - D^2$.

8   Consider the demand function for sugar in problem 8, Exercises 55. For what amounts sold will the total revenue function be increasing and for what amounts will it be decreasing? Plot the total revenue curve.

9   Consider the demand function for rye in problem 11, Exercises 55. For what amounts sold will the total revenue function be increasing and for what amounts will it be decreasing? Plot the total revenue curve.

10   Consider the demand function for corn in problem 13, Exercises 59. Determine for what amounts sold the total revenue is increasing and for what amounts it is decreasing. Check by plotting the total revenue curve.

11   A logistic trend for Indian agricultural income for the years 1900–1960 has been estimated as follows (Tintner, Narasimham, Raghavan). Let Y be agricultural income and t time.

$$y = \frac{4406}{1 + (0.51)e^{-0.11t}}$$

(a) Find dy/dt and d^2y/dt^2. (b) Determine the inflection point.

Chapter 14
Higher Derivatives

We recall the definition of the first derivative, namely,

$$y' = f'(x) = \lim_{\Delta x \to 0} \frac{\Delta y}{\Delta x}.$$

In general, $y' = f'(x)$ will be another function of x which often can be differentiated. The derivative of the first derivative gives what is called the second derivative; that is,

$$y'' = f''(x) = \lim_{\Delta x \to 0} \frac{\Delta y'}{\Delta x}.$$

To find the third derivative we proceed to differentiate the second derivative, and obtain

$$y''' = f'''(x) = \lim_{\Delta x \to 0} \frac{\Delta y''}{\Delta x}.$$

The fourth derivative y^{IV} is computed by finding the derivative of the third derivative. The fifth derivative y^V is computed by finding the derivative of the fourth derivative, and so on.

In general, to find the nth derivative of a function we differentiate the $(n - 1)$th derivative.

EXAMPLE

Consider the function $y = f(x) = 2 - 3x + 4x^2$. Find the higher derivatives.

The first derivative is

$$y' = f'(x) = -3 + 8x.$$

The second derivative is the derivative of the first derivative

$$y'' = f''(x) = 8.$$

The third derivative is the derivative of the second derivative

$$y''' = f'''(x) = 0.$$

The fourth derivative is the derivative of the third derivative. This is 0, as are all higher derivatives.

To compute the function and its derivatives at the point $x = 2$, we have

$$f(2) = 12,$$
$$f'(2) = 13,$$
$$f''(2) = 8,$$
$$f'''(2) = 0,$$
$$f^{\text{IV}}(2) = 0,$$

and so on.

EXERCISES 69

1   Find the first three derivatives of the following functions: (a) $y = 10x - 6$; (b) $y = 2 + 5x - x^2 + x^5$; (c) $y = xe^x$; (d) $y = (\log_e x)/x$.

2   Consider the function $y = e^x$. (a) Find the first three derivatives. (b) Try to establish a general rule for the mth derivative, $y^{(m)}$.

3   Consider the function $y = \log_e x$. (a) Find the first four derivatives. (b) Try to establish a general rule for the mth derivative, $y^{(m)}$.

4   Consider the function $y = x^a$, where a is a positive integer. (a) Find the first three derivatives. (b) Find the derivatives of order a, $y^{(a)}$. (c) Establish formulas for $y^{(a+1)}$ and $y^{(a+2)}$. (d) What conclusion can be drawn about the lowest order for which all future derivatives become 0? (e) Illustrate with the function $y = x^3$.

5   Find the general form of the derivatives of the function $y = 1/x^m$, where m is a positive integer. (HINT: Express the function first with negative exponent.)

6   Try to establish the general form for the nth derivative of $y = (a + bx)^m$, where a and b are constants and m is a positive integer. What are the values for $y^{(m)}$ and higher derivatives?

7   Try to establish the general form of the nth derivative of the function $y = e^{ax}$, where a is a constant.

8   Find all derivatives of the function $y = f(x) = x^4 - 3x^2 + 1$ which are not 0.

9   Find all derivatives of the function $y = f(x) = x^8 - 2x^7 + x^3 - 6$ which are not 0.

10   Find all derivatives of the function $y = f(x) = 5x^2 - 4x + 1$ which are not 0.

70   GEOMETRIC INTERPRETATION OF THE SECOND DERIVATIVE

A geometric interpretation of the first derivative $y' = f'(x)$ has been given previously; if the first derivative is positive at a certain point, it means that the curve corresponding to the function in question is rising at that point. If it is negative, it means that the curve is falling. It should also be recalled that the first derivative $y' = f'(x)$ gives the slope of the line tangent to the curve at the point (x, y).

We recall that the second derivative is the derivative of the first derivative. Hence a positive second derivative indicates that the first derivative is increasing. This means geometrically that at the point (x, y) the curve must be *concave upward* (see Figure 33).

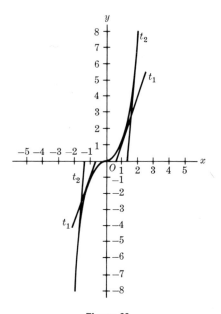

Figure 33

Consider next the case of a negative second derivative. This condition means that the first derivative, the slope of the line tangent to the curve at the point (x,y), decreases. So the curve is *concave downward*.

These results may be summarized as follows:

If $y'' = f''(x) > 0$, then the curve is concave upward.

If $y'' = f''(x) < 0$, the curve is concave downward.

EXAMPLE 1

Figure 33 presents a graph of the function $y = f(x) = x^3$. The first derivative, which gives the slope of the tangent, is $y' =$

$f'(x) = 3x^2$. The second derivative, which indicates the rate of change of the slope of the tangent, becomes $y'' = f''(x) = 6x$.

This is positive for positive x and negative for negative x. Hence our curve is concave upward for positive x and concave downward for negative x. The change in the slope of the tangent lines is illustrated by the value of the slope at the point $x = -2$, -1, 1 and 2:

$$f'(-2) = 12,$$
$$f'(-1) = 3,$$
$$f'(1) = 3,$$
$$f'(-2) = 12.$$

It is seen that the slope of the tangent line decreases for negative x and increases for positive x.

EXAMPLE 2

Let $y = f(x) = 3x^4 - 2x^2$. The first derivative is $y' = f'(x) = 12x^3 - 4x$. The second derivative is the derivative of the first derivative; namely, $y'' = f''(x) = 36x^2 - 4$.

Is the curve in question concave upward or downward at the point $x = 0$? We have $f''(0) = -4 < 0$. This is negative. Hence the curve is concave downward at the point $(0, 0)$.

Is the curve concave upward or downward if $x = 1$? We have $f''(1) = 32 > 0$. This is positive. Hence the curve is concave upward at the point $(1, 8)$. For a general analysis of the situation we note that

$$f''(x) = 36x^2 - 4 = 4(9x^2 - 1).$$

This will be positive for

$$9x^2 - 1 > 0,$$
$$9x^2 > 1,$$
$$x^2 > \frac{1}{9}.$$

Hence the second derivative will be positive if $x^2 > \frac{1}{9}$, that is, $x > \frac{1}{3}$ or $x < -\frac{1}{3}$. Within the interval $-\frac{1}{3} < x < \frac{1}{3}$ the second derivative will be negative. So we conclude that the curve is concave downward in the interval $-\frac{1}{3} < x < \frac{1}{3}$; elsewhere it is concave upward.

EXERCISES 70

1 Investigate the concavity of the graph of the function $y = f(x) = x^3 - 2x$ at the following points: (a) $(1, -1)$; (b) $(2, 4)$; (c) $(-1, 1)$; (d) $(-3, -21)$. (e) Make a general statement about the concavity of the curve. (f) Make a graph for a check.

2   Investigate the concavity of the graph of the function $y = 2x^2 + 3$ at the following points: (a) $(0, 3)$; (b) $(2, 11)$; (c) $(-1, 5)$; (d) $(-5, 53)$. (e) Make a general statement about the concavity of the curve. (f) Make a graph for a check.

3   Investigate the concavity of the curve corresponding to the equation $y = f(x) = 5 - 2x - x^2$ at the following points: (a) $(0, 5)$; (b) $(1, 2)$; (c) $(4, 19)$; (d) $(-1, 6)$; (e) $(-3, 2)$. (f) Make a general statement about the concavity of the curve. (g) Graph the curve in order to check.

4   Investigate the concavity of the curve associated with the function $y = f(x) = x^4$ at the following points: (a) $(1, 1)$; (b) $(2, 16)$; (c) $(3, 81)$; (d) $(5, 625)$; (e) $(-1, 1)$; (f) $(-2, 16)$; (g) $(-3, 81)$. (h) Establish a general rule for the concavity of the graph in question. (i) Graph the curve.

5   Investigate the concavity of the curves corresponding to the following functions: (a) $y = e^x$; (b) $y = 1/e^x$; (c) $y = \log_e x$; (d) $y = x \cdot e^x$.

6   Investigate the concavity of the curve corresponding to the function $y = x^3 - 6x^2 + 5$. Check by graphing the curve.

7   Investigate the concavity of the curve corresponding to the function $y = x^3 - 2x^2 + 10$. Check by graphing the curve.

8   Determine the concavity of the curve corresponding to the function $y = 2x^4 - x^3 + 4x$. Check by making a graph.

71   INCREASING AND DECREASING MARGINAL COSTS

We assume the existence of a total cost function

$$C = f(D),$$

which possesses first and second derivatives. The marginal cost is, by definition, the first derivative

$$C' = f'(D).$$

The sign of the derivative of this marginal cost curve gives information upon the question of whether there is increasing, decreasing, or constant marginal cost under varying conditions of production. If

$$C'' = f''(D) > 0,$$

we have increasing marginal cost. If

$$C'' = f''(D) < 0,$$

we have decreasing marginal cost. Finally, if

$$C'' = f''(D) = 0,$$

we have constant marginal cost.

EXAMPLE

To illustrate this, again consider Figure 32. The total cost function is

$$C = f(D) = 10 + 15D - 6D^2 + D^3,$$

The marginal cost curve is the derivative of C,

$$C' = f'(D) = 15 - 12D + 3D^2.$$

The second derivative, which gives the criterion for increasing or decreasing marginal cost, is

$$C'' = f''(D) = -12 + 6D.$$

This function may be positive or negative. To find the point of constant marginal cost, we put it equal to 0, and obtain

$$f''(D) = -12 + 6D = 0.$$

Hence we have constant marginal cost if $D = 2$.

It is obvious that C'' is negative for D smaller than 2 and positive for D greater than 2. This means that there is decreasing marginal cost up to a production of 2 units and increasing marginal cost if more than 2 units are produced. At a production of exactly 2 units of the commodity we have constant marginal cost. Thus, the total cost curve C is concave downward for quantities smaller than 2 and concave upward for quantities larger than 2.

EXERCISES 71

1 Total cost: $C = 50,000D - 300D^2 + D^3$. (a) Find C'; (b) C''. (c) Investigate the nature of the marginal cost. (d) Make a graph of the total cost curve and the marginal cost curve.

2 Total cost: $C = 100 + 50D - 2D^3 + D^4$. (a) Find C'; (b) C''. (c) Investigate the nature of the marginal cost curve. (d) Make a graph of the total cost curve and the marginal cost curve.

3 Total cost: $C = 50 + 40D - 12D^2 + D^3$. (a) Find C'; (b) C''. (c) Investigate the nature of the marginal cost curve.

4 Total cost: $C = 500D - 48D^2 + 2D^3$. (a) Find C'; (b) C''. (c) Investigate the nature of the marginal cost curve.

5 Total cost: $C = 200 + 1,000D - 24D^2 + 4D^3 + D^4$. (a) Find C'; (b) C''. (c) Investigate the nature of the marginal cost curve.

6 Investigate the nature of the marginal cost curve corresponding to the total cost curve in problem 10, Exercises 62.

7 Investigate the nature of the marginal cost curve of steel in problem 8, Exercises 56. Graph the total cost curve and the marginal cost curve.

8   Investigate the nature of the marginal cost curve of hosiery in problem 9, Exercises 56. Make a graph of the total cost curve and marginal cost curve.

9   Investigate the nature of the marginal cost curve of leather belts in problem 10, Exercises 56. Make a graph of the total cost curve and the marginal cost curve.

10   Investigate the nature of the marginal cost curve of department stores (problem 11, Exercises 56). Make a graph of the total cost curve and the marginal cost curve.

Chapter 15
Maxima and Minima in
One Variable.
Inflection Points

We shall give a purely geometric argument for the use of the derivative in the study of maximum and minimum points on a curve. Roughly speaking, a maximum point on a curve is a point that is higher than its neighbors; a minimum point is lower than its neighbors. Strictly, x_0 is a maximum point if $f(x_0) > f(x)$ for all x in some interval $(x_0 - \delta, x_0 + \delta)$, $x \neq x_0$, and x_0 is a minimum point of f if $f(x_0) < f(x)$ for all $x \neq x_0$ in some interval $(x_0 - \delta, x_0 + \delta)$. In our consideration we will arbitrarily eliminate those maximum or minimum points that result from cusps; that is, we will consider only those cases of maximum or minimum points where the tangent line is horizontal (note Figure 34). But a horizontal tangent need not necessarily imply a maximum or minimum (see, for example, Figure 33). Hence the existence of a horizontal tangent line is a necessary, but not a sufficient, condition for a maximum or minimum if cusps are eliminated from the consideration.

We see from the graph that at a maximum point the curve is concave downward. Also from the graph it appears that at a minimum point the curve is concave upward.

A horizontal tangent line implies that the slope of the line tangent to the curve at the point in question must be 0. The slope is given by the first derivative of the curve whose equation is $y = f(x)$. So the necessary condition for a maximum or minimum is $y' = f'(x) = 0$.

For a maximum we must have concavity downward. The concavity of a curve is indicated by the sign of its second derivative; the curve will be concave downward if $y'' = f''(x) < 0$.

For a minimum we must have concavity upward. This implies that $y'' = f''(x) > 0$.

199

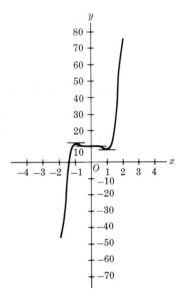

Figure 34

The rules for finding maxima and minima can be summarized in the following way:

For a maximum,
$$f'(x) = 0, \qquad f''(x) < 0.$$
For a minimum,
$$f'(x) = 0, \qquad f''(x) > 0.$$

There are very special functions such that $f''(x) = 0$ when $f'(x) = 0$; further analysis must be employed under such a circumstance to determine whether the graph might have a maximum or a minimum point.

EXAMPLE 1

Figure 34 presents a graph of the function
$$y = f(x) = 3x^5 - 5x^3 + 10.$$
The derivative of this function is
$$y' = f'(x) = 15x^4 - 15x^2.$$

The necessary condition for a maximum or minimum demands that $y' = 0$. We can factor the derivative and write,
$$y' = f'(x) = 15x^2(x - 1)(x + 1) = 0.$$

This has three solutions: $x = -1$, $x = 0$, $x = 1$. The graph shows that at all three points there are horizontal tangent lines, as one would expect. To ascertain which one of these points is a maximum or a minimum depends upon the sign of the second derivative,

$$y'' = f''(x) = 60x^3 - 30x.$$

We have at $x = -1$, $f''(-1) = -30$. This is negative. Hence there is a maximum at the point $x = -1$. The value of the function at $x = -1$ is $f(-1) = 12$.

Next, $f''(0) = 0$. Thus the criteria already established are not valid. However, an examination of the curve indicates that we have neither a maximum nor a minimum. We will see later that we have an inflection point.

Finally, $f''(1) = 30$. This is positive. Hence we have a minimum at $x = 1$. The value of the function is $f(1) = 8$.

EXAMPLE 2

Let us consider the function $y = f(x) = 3x^5 - 10x^3$. The derivative is $y' = f'(x) = 15x^4 - 30x^2$. The second derivative is $y'' = f''(x) = 60x^3 - 60x$. To find the maxima and minima, we put $y' = f'(x) = 0$.

$$f'(x) = 15x^4 - 30x^2$$
$$= (15x^2)(x^2 - 2) = (15x^2)(x + \sqrt{2})(x - \sqrt{2}) = 0.$$

Hence we have three "critical values" for x, namely, $x = 0$, $\sqrt{2} = 1.414$, and $-\sqrt{2} = -1.414$. To find which are maxima and which minima, we substitute these values into the formula for the second derivative and obtain

$$f''(0) = 0,$$
$$f''(\sqrt{2}) = f''(1.414) = 84.84 > 0,$$
$$f''(-\sqrt{2}) = f''(-1.414) = -84.84 < 0.$$

No conclusion can be drawn when $x = 0$; however, it happens to be neither a maximum nor a minimum point. We have a minimum at the point $x = \sqrt{2}$ and a maximum at the point $x = -\sqrt{2}$.

EXAMPLE 3

Consider the curve $y = f(x) = x^3 - 3x + 1$. We have $y' = f'(x) = 3x^2 - 3$ and $y'' = f''(x) = 6x$. For a maximum or a minimum we must have $y' = 3x^2 - 3 = 0$. Hence the so-called critical points are $x = 1$ and $x = -1$. When $x = 1$, $f''(1) = 6 > 0$. Thus at the point $x = 1$, $y = -1$ we have a minimum. For $x = -1$, $f''(-1) = -6 < 0$. Therefore at the point $x = -1$, $y = 3$ we have a maximum.

Up to now we have considered functions that may vary over

an unrestricted interval. If the function is restricted to a given interval $a \leq x \leq b$, then the value of the function $f(a), f(b)$ must also be considered.

EXAMPLE 4

Consider the function $y = f(x) = (x - 1)^2$, where $0 \leq x \leq 3$. We have the condition $f'(x) = 2(x - 1) = 0$ for an extremum (relative maximum or minimum) and this gives $x = 1$; since $f''(x) = 2$, this is a minimum. At this point $f(1) = 0$. Also $f(0) = 1$, $f(3) = 4$. Hence the function has a maximum at $x = 0$, a minimum at $x = 1$, and a maximum at $x = 3$.

EXERCISES 72

1 Investigate the function $y = 2x^3 + 3x^2 - 2x + 1$ for maxima and minima. Make a graph.

2 Investigate the function $y = 10x^3 - 15x^2 + 10$ for maxima and minima. Plot the function.

3 Investigate the function $y = 1 + 2x - x^3$ for maxima and minima. Make a graph.

4 Investigate the function $y = x^2 - 3x + 1$ for maxima and minima. Make a graph.

5 Investigate the function $y = 3x^4 + 16x^3 + 18x^2 + 20$ for maxima and minima. Make a graph.

6 Investigate the function $y = xe^{-x}$ for maxima and minima. Make a graph.

7 Investigate the function $y = x \log_e x$ for maxima and minima.

8 Investigate the function $y = e^{-x^2}$ for maxima and minima.

9 Investigate the function $y = (x^5/5) - (13x^3/3) + 36x - 9$ for maxima and minima. Make a graph.

10 Investigate the function $y = x^2 e^x$ for maxima and minima.

73 MONOPOLY

The profit of the monopolist is $\pi = R - C$, where the total revenue $R = pD$. It will be recalled that p is the demand function and C is the total cost function. The monopolist tries to maximize the profit by producing the amount and charging the price that will make his profit as large as possible.

The necessary condition for a maximum is $\pi' = R' - C' = 0$, or $R' = C'$; that is, marginal revenue equals marginal cost. For maximum profit, $\pi'' < 0$, or $R'' - C'' < 0$, from which we obtain $R'' < C''$. The last condition assures the *stability* of the situation, also $\pi > 0$. There is no incentive to the monopolist to produce more or less or charge a different price. We have a maximum rather than a minimum.

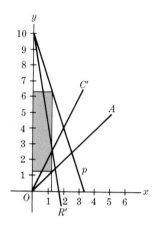

Figure 35

Figure 35 presents the demand function

$$p = 10 - 3D$$

and the average cost curve

$$A = D.$$

From this we derive the total revenue function

$$R = pD = 10D - 3D^2$$

and the marginal revenue function R' shown in the graph

$$R' = 10 - 6D.$$

The total cost curve is

$$C = AD = D^2$$

and from this we obtain the marginal cost curve

$$C' = 2D,$$

which is shown in the graph.

Total profit is given by

$$\pi = R - C = (10D - 3D^2) - D^2 = 10D - 4D^2.$$

For a maximum, the first derivative π' must be 0 and the second derivative π'' must be negative. So

$$\pi' = 10 - 8D = 0.$$

This gives the solution $D = {}^{10}\!/_8 = {}^5\!/_4$. The second derivative is

$$\pi'' = -8 < 0.$$

This is negative. Hence we have maximum profit when $D = {}^5\!/_4$ units are produced.

The price is given by inserting $D = {}^5\!/_4$ in the demand function; that is, $p = 10 - (3)({}^5\!/_4) = {}^{25}\!/_4$.

The average cost is

$$A = \frac{5}{4}.$$

Total revenue is

$$R = pD = \left(\frac{25}{4}\right)\left(\frac{5}{4}\right) = \frac{125}{16}.$$

Total cost is

$$C = AD = \left(\frac{5}{4}\right)\left(\frac{5}{4}\right) = \frac{25}{16}.$$

Hence the maximum profit itself is

$$\pi = R - C = \frac{125}{16} - \frac{25}{16} = \frac{100}{16} = \frac{25}{4}.$$

This is indicated by the shaded area in Figure 35.

Alternatively, we could have found maximum profit by making marginal revenue equal to marginal cost; thus

$$10 - 6D = 2D.$$

The solution of this equation is again $D = {}^5\!/_4$. It is seen from the graph that the intersection of the marginal revenue curve and the marginal cost curve determines the *quantity* produced.

The second derivatives of the total revenue function and total cost function are

$$R'' = -6; \qquad C'' = 2.$$

It is evident that $-6 < 2$. Hence the equilibrium is *stable* and we have a true maximum of profits.

EXERCISES 73

1   Let the demand curve of a commodity be $p = 10 - 5D$. The average cost is $A = 3$. (a) Find C; (b) C'; (c) R; (d) R'; (e) π. (f) Find the necessary condition for a maximum of profits. (g) Find the sufficient condition for a maximum. (h) Make a graph of p, A, R', C'. (i) Show how the inter-

section of R' and C' determines the quantity produced. (j) Find p, R, C, π under conditions of maximum profit and interpret them in the graph.

2   The demand curve of a commodity is $p = 300 - 2D$ and the average cost curve is $A = D$. (a) Find R; (b) C; (c) R'; (d) C'; (e) π. (f) Determine the amount produced that will maximize profits. (g) Show that at this point $R' = C'$. (h) Show the stability of the position. (i) Show that $R'' < C''$. (j) Determine price, total revenue, total cost, and profit of the monopolist.

3   The demand curve for some commodity is $p = 12 - 3D$. The average cost curve is $A = 2D^2$. (a) Find the necessary condition for a maximum of profits; (b) the sufficient condition. (c) Find the price, total revenue, total cost, and profit for the maximum. (d) Make a graph of p, A, R', and C'. Show how the quantity produced, the price, total revenue, total cost, and profit can be determined graphically.

4   The demand curve for a commodity is $p = 36 - 2D^2$. The average cost curve is $A = 15D$. (a) Find the necessary conditions for a maximum of profits. (b) Show the stability of equilibrium. (c) Find the quantity produced, the price, total revenue, total cost, and profit for the maximum. (d) Demonstrate that $R' = C'$ and $R'' < C''$ at the point of equilibrium.

5   The demand curve for a commodity is $p = 10e^{-2D}$. The average cost curve is $A = 1/D$. (a) Find the necessary conditions for a maximum of profits. (b) Show that the equilibrium is stable.

6   The demand curve for a commodity is $p = -\log_e D$. The average cost is 0. (a) Find the necessary condition for maximum profits. (b) Show that the equilibrium is stable.

7   The demand curve for a commodity is $p = 50e^{-3D}$. The average cost is 0. (a) Find the necessary conditions for a maximum of profits. (b) Determine the sufficient conditions.

8   The demand for a commodity is $p = m - nD$. The average cost curve is $A = r + sD$, where m, n, r and s are positive constants. (a) Find R, C, π. (b) Determine the necessary condition for maximum profit; (c) the sufficient condition. (d) Find price, total revenue, total cost, and profit for the maximum position.

9   The demand for sugar in the United States is estimated as $p = 2.34 - 1.34D$ (Schultz). Assume that the average cost curve of sugar is $A = 1/D - 0.83 + 0.85D$. (a) Find R, C, π. (b) Determine the necessary conditions for a maximum of profits, assuming a sugar monopoly. (c) Show that the equilibrium is stable. (d) Find price, total revenue, total cost, and profits under monopoly. (e) Assume the same demand curve and a supply curve on the competitive market: $p = 1.7D - 0.83$. Establish the competitive equilibrium on the sugar market. Determine the quantity produced and the price, and compare with the monopoly solution. (f) Make a graphical comparison by plotting on the same graph the demand curve, the average cost curve, the marginal cost curve (same

as the supply curve), and the marginal revenue curve. Demonstrate the price formation under monopoly and under free competition.

10   The demand for steel in the United States is estimated to be $p = 250 - 50D$ (Whitmann). The estimated average cost of making steel is $A = 182/D + 56$ (Yntema). (a) Find R, C, C', R'. (b) Find the necessary condition for a maximum of steel profits assuming a monopoly in steel. (c) Find the sufficient condition of maximum profits. (d) Establish the quantity produced, price, total revenue, total cost, and profits under monopoly. (e) Assume the same demand curve and a competitive supply curve (marginal cost curve) for steel, $p = 56$, assuming the same cost curve under free competition and monopoly. Find the quantity produced and the price established under conditions of free competition. (f) Plot the demand curve, the average cost curve, the marginal cost curve (same as supply curve), and the marginal revenue curve. Demonstrate the price formation under monopoly and under free competition.

74   AVERAGE AND MARGINAL COST

We denote by C the total cost, by D the quantity produced, by A the average cost. We have, by definition, $A = C/D$.

Using the formula for differentiation of a quotient, we get as a necessary condition for minimum average cost

$$\frac{dA}{dD} = A' = \frac{DC' - C}{D^2} = 0.$$

Hence $DC' - C = 0$ and $C' = C/D = A$. It follows that for minimum average cost the average cost is equal to marginal cost.

EXAMPLE

We start with the total cost curve

$$C = 15D - 6D^2 + D^3.$$

We derive the equation of the average cost curve by writing

$$A = \frac{C}{D} = 15 - 6D + D^2.$$

The marginal cost curve has the equation

$$C' = \frac{dC}{dD} = 15 - 12D + 3D^2.$$

Both the average cost curve and the marginal cost curve are shown in Figure 36.

For the minimum, average cost A we must have

$$A' = 0, \qquad A'' > 0.$$

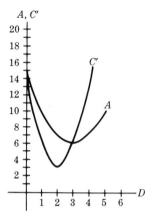

Figure 36

Thus

$$A' = -6 + 2D = 0,$$

which yields $D = 3$. Further,

$$A'' = 2 > 0.$$

This is positive; hence there is a minimum rather than a maximum when $D = 3$.

The value of the minimum average cost, that is, A when $D = 3$, is

$$A = 15 - (6)(3) + (3)^2 = 6.$$

The marginal cost for $D = 3$ is

$$C' = 15 - (12)(3) + (3)(3)^2 = 6.$$

Hence marginal and average costs are equal (both are 6), as was expected, at the point of minimum average cost ($D = 3$).

We see from the graph that the marginal cost curve C' cuts the average cost curve A at its minimum value. It also appears that the marginal cost curve cuts the average cost curve from below.

EXERCISES 74

1 Let $A = 20 - 6D + D^2$. (a) Find the minimum of A. (b) Show that for the minimum $A = C'$. (c) Make a graph of A and C'. Verify that they are equal for the minimum of A.

2 Let $A = 50 - 8D + D^2$. (a) Find the minimum of A. (b) Show that at the minimum $A = C'$. (c) Make a graph of A and C' and verify the previous relationship.

3   Let the average cost curve be $A = 10 - 4D^3 + 3D^4$. (a) Find the minimum of A. (b) Verify that at the minimum $A = C'$.

4   The average cost curve of a commodity is $A = 1 + 120D^3 - 6D^2$. (a) Find the minimum of A. (b) Verify that at the minimum $A = C'$.

5   The average cost curve of a commodity is $A = e^D + e^{-D}$. (a) Find the minimum of A. (b) Verify that at the minimum $A = C'$.

6   The average cost curve is $A = m - nD + kD^2$, where m, n, and k are positive constants. (a) Find the minimum of A. (b) Verify that at the minimum $A = C'$.

7   Let the average cost curve be $A = 1 + D \log_e D$. (a) Determine the minimum of A. (b) Show that at the point of minimum of average cost, average cost equals marginal cost.

8   The total-cost function is $C = 2D - 2D^2 + D^3$. (a) Find the average-cost function A. (b) Establish the minimum of average cost. (c) Find the marginal-cost function C'. (d) Show that, at the minimum of average cost, average cost is equal to marginal cost. (e) Plot the average-cost and marginal-cost functions.

9   The total-cost function is $C = 5D - 3D^2 + 2D^3$. (a) Find the average-cost function A. (b) Establish the minimum of the average cost. (c) Find the marginal-cost function C'. (d) Show that, at the minimum of average cost, average cost is equal to marginal cost. (e) Plot the average-cost and marginal-cost curves.

10   The total-cost function is $C = 4D - D^2 + 2D^3$. (a) Find the average-cost function A. (b) Establish the minimum of the average-cost function. (c) Find the marginal-cost function C'. (d) Show that, at the minimum of average cost, average cost is equal to marginal cost. (e) Plot the average-cost and marginal-cost curves.

75   POINTS OF INFLECTION

We will present a purely geometrical argument for the criteria employed in locating points of inflection. By definition, a point of inflection exists at a point where the concavity of the curve changes. The curve changes either from concave upward to concave downward or from concave downward to concave upward.

When we were discussing the geometric interpretation of second derivatives, we showed that the concavity of a curve is given by considering the sign of the second derivative of the function corresponding to the curve. If the second derivative $y'' = f''(x)$ is positive, the curve is concave upward. If the second derivative of the function is negative, the curve is concave downward.

It is obvious that at the point of change of the concavity of the curve the second derivative has in general to change from positive to negative or from negative to positive. Hence at the point of change the second derivative must, in general, be 0. There are some special functions, rarely encountered in this field, where the argument just given is not appropriate.

The following rule can be derived from these considerations: In general, if $f''(x) = 0$, there is an inflection point on the curve.

One exception to this will be discussed below in problem 5, Exercises 75.

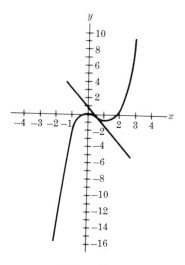

Figure 37

EXAMPLE

Figure 37 presents the graph of the function

$$y = f(x) = x^3 - 2x^2.$$

We want to examine the function for inflection points. The first derivative is

$$y' = f'(x) = 3x^2 - 4x.$$

The second derivative must vanish if there is an inflection point; so let us take

$$y'' = f''(x) = 6x - 4 = 0.$$

The solution of this equation is

$$x = \tfrac{2}{3}.$$

Hence we expect an inflection point at the point $(\tfrac{2}{3}, -\tfrac{16}{27})$ on the curve.

The slope of the tangent line at the inflection or turning point is computed by inserting $x = \frac{2}{3}$ into the formula for the first derivative; this gives

$$f'\left(\frac{2}{3}\right) = (3)\left(\frac{2}{3}\right)^2 - (4)\left(\frac{2}{3}\right) = -\frac{4}{3}.$$

EXERCISES 75

1   Consider the function $y = f(x) = 2x^3 - x^2$ for concavity. (a) Is there an inflection point? (b) What is the slope of the tangent line at the point of inflection? (c) Make a graph of the function.

2   Consider the function $y = e^x$ for concavity. Is there an inflection point?

3   Consider the concavity of the function $y = 2 + 3x - x^2$. Has this curve an inflection point? Make a graph.

4   Consider the concavity of the function $y = 3 + 5x + 4x^2$. Has this curve an inflection point?

**5   Consider the function $y = x^4$. Graph. Compute y', y''. Show that there is *no* inflection point at $x = 0$ in spite of the fact that $y'' = 0$ for this value. Compare the behavior of this function with that of $y = x^5$. Make graphs of both functions.

6   Find the total cost curve for problem 1, Exercises 74. (a) Find the point of inflection of the total cost curve C. (b) Show that the inflection point of the total cost curve is the point of minimum marginal cost. (c) Make a graph of the total cost and marginal cost curves and consider the relationship between the concavity of the total cost curve and the phenomenon of increasing and decreasing marginal cost.

7   Find the total cost function for the case described in problem 2, Exercises 74, and proceed as in problem 6.

8   Consider the total cost function corresponding to the average cost function given in problem 3, Exercises 74. Proceed as in problem 6.

**9   Show that, in general, for any total cost function $C = f(D)$ the point of inflection corresponds to the minimum of the marginal cost curve $C' = f'(D)$.

Chapter 16

Derivatives of Functions
of Several Variables

76 FUNCTIONS OF SEVERAL INDEPENDENT VARIABLES

Up to now we have considered only functions of one (independent) variable. But in economics we have frequently a given quantity depending not just upon one but on several independent variables, for example, the demand for beef depends on the price of beef, the price of pork, and the price of mutton.

If z is a function of two variables x and y, we write

$$z = f(x, y).$$

This means that for every *pair* of values of the independent variables x and y in the domain of f, we can find a number z which corresponds to this pair.

Theoretically, a function of two variables is still a *set* of ordered pairs, no two of which have the same first element, but now the first member of this ordered pair is itself an ordered pair, namely, $f = \{((x, y), z)|z = f(x, y)\}$. Geometrically, a plane is needed to contain the domain, and the function describes a surface over the domain.

EXAMPLE 1

Let us define a function of two variables by the formula

$$z = f(x, y) = x^2 - 2y + 10.$$

We get, for example, for $x = 1$, $y = 3$,

$$f(1, 3) = (1)^2 - 2(3) + 10 = 5.$$

Similarly, by substituting other values for x and y,

$$f(-4, 2) = (-4)^2 - 2(2) + 10 = 22,$$
$$f(2, -5) = (2)^2 - 2(-5) + 10 = 24,$$
$$f(0, 3) = (0)^2 - 2(3) + 10 = 4,$$
$$f(3, 0) = (3)^2 - 2(0) + 10 = 19.$$

If u is a function of three variables x, y, and z, we write

$$u = f(x, y, z).$$

By assigning specific values to the three independent variables x, y, and z, we can compute the number u which is associated with them.

EXAMPLE 2

Define, for example,

$$u = f(x, y, z) = xy - 4z.$$

Substituting first $x = 1$, $y = 3$, $z = 10$, we have

$$f(1, 3, 10) = (1)(3) - 4(10) = -37.$$

By substituting $x = -5$, $y = 2$, $z = -1$, we have

$$f(-5, 2, -1) = (-5)(2) - 4(-1) = -6,$$

and so on.

EXERCISES 76

1   Given the function $z = f(x, y) = (x/2)(x + y)$, find (a) $f(0, 1)$; (b) $f(2, 4)$; (c) $f(1, 2)$; (d) $f(-1, -5)$.

2   Given the function $z = f(x, y) = x^2 + 2xy + 5y^2 - x + 3y + 6$, find (a) $f(0, 0)$; (b) $f(1, 0)$; (c) $f(0, -1)$; (d) $f(-2, -3)$.

3   Given the function $u = f(x, y, z) = 2x + 3y + 5z + 1$, find (a) $f(0, 1, -2)$; (b) $f(1, 1, 1)$; (c) $f(5, 2, -4)$; (d) $f(a, -a, -a)$.

4   Given the function $z = f(x, y) = xe^y$, find (a) $f(0, 0)$; (b) $f(2, 0)$; (c) $f(1, 1)$; (d) $f(-1, -1)$; (e) $f(3, -2)$.

5   Given the function $u = f(x, y, z) = xy/z$, find (a) $f(1, 1, 1)$; (b) $f(0, 1, 2)$; (c) $f(a, a, -a)$.

6   Let $w = f(x, y, z, u) = (x + y)/(z + u)$. Find (a) $f(0, 1, 1, 2)$; (b) $f(-1, 0, 0, 1)$; (c) $f(3, 5, -1, 6)$.

7   Given the function $z = f(x, y) = x^2 - xy + y^2 - 4x$, find (a) $f(0, 0)$; (b) $f(2, 5)$; (c) $f(-a, a)$.

8   Given the function $z = f(x, y) = x/y$, find (a) $f(a, a)$; (b) $f(a, -a)$; (c) $f(-a, -a)$.

9   Let $u = f(x, y, z) = x^2 - 2xy + xz - z^2$. Find (a) $f(1, 1, 0)$; (b) $f(-3, -6, 1)$; (c) $f(a, a, a)$.

77 PARTIAL DERIVATIVES

Let us consider a function of two independent variables,

$$z = f(x, y).$$

The partial derivative of z with respect to x is defined as

$$\frac{\partial z}{\partial x} = \lim_{\Delta x \to 0} \frac{\Delta z}{\Delta x} = \lim_{\Delta x \to 0} \left(\frac{f(x + \Delta x, y) - f(x, y)}{\Delta x} \right).$$

Other symbols used for the partial derivative are

$$\frac{\partial z}{\partial x} = f_x(x, y) = D_x z.$$

Note that the variable x takes on an increment Δx, but the variable y is kept constant if the partial derivative is taken with respect to x. Hence, in practice the partial derivative of $z = f(x, y)$ with respect to x is computed by taking the derivative of z with respect to x, treating y as if it were a constant.

In a similar manner the partial derivative of z with respect to y is defined as

$$\frac{\partial z}{\partial y} = f_y(x, y) = D_y z = \lim_{\Delta x \to 0} \frac{\Delta z}{\Delta y} = \lim_{\Delta y \to 0} \frac{f(x, y + \Delta y) - f(x, y)}{\Delta y}.$$

We note in this case that y takes on an increment Δy, but x is kept fixed. Hence, the partial derivative of $z = f(x, y)$ with respect to y is computed in practice by taking the derivative with respect to y and treating x like a constant.

EXAMPLE 1

Consider the function

$$z = f(x, y) = x^2y + 4x - 2y + 5.$$

To find the partial derivative with respect to x, we treat y as a constant and take the derivative with respect to x.

$$\frac{\partial z}{\partial x} = f_x(x, y) = 2xy + 4.$$

This can be evaluated for various values of x and y. We have, for example, for the partial derivative of z with respect to x at the point $x = 1, y = -2$

$$f_x(1, -2) = (2)(1)(-2) + 4 = 0.$$

At the point $x = 5$, $y = 1$ we have for the same partial derivative

$$f_x(5, 1) = (2)(5)(1) + 4 = 14.$$

To find the partial derivative with respect to y, we differentiate the function with respect to y, treating x as a constant,

$$\frac{\partial z}{\partial y} = f_y(x, y) = x^2 - 2.$$

This can be evaluated for various values of x and y. For example, we have for $x = 6$, $y = 1$

$$f_y(6, 1) = (6)^2 - 2 = 34.$$

We proceed similarly with functions of more than two independent variables. We compute the partial derivative of a function of several variables with respect to one of the independent variables by taking the derivative with respect to the assigned variable, treating all other independent variables as constant.

EXAMPLE 2

Consider, for example,

$$u = f(x, y, z) = x^2 - 2xy + y^3 + yz.$$

The partial derivative with respect to x is computed by differentiating u with respect to x, treating y and z as constants,

$$\frac{\partial u}{\partial x} = f_x(x, y, z) = 2x - 2y.$$

The partial derivative with respect to y is computed by differentiating u with respect to y, holding x and z constant,

$$\frac{\partial u}{\partial y} = f_y(x, y, z) = -2x + 3y^2 + z.$$

The partial derivative with respect to z results by taking the derivative of u with respect to z, holding x and y constant,

$$\frac{\partial u}{\partial z} = f_z(x, y, z) = y.$$

These partial derivatives can be evaluated for any given values of x, y, and z. We have, for example,

$$f_x(1, 2, 6) = (2)(1) - (2)(2) = -2,$$
$$f_y(-1, 4, 2) = (-2)(-1) + (3)(4)^2 + 2 = 52,$$
$$f_z(3, 5, -3) = 5.$$

EXERCISES 77

1 Given the function $z = x^2 + xy^2 - 2x + 5y$, (a) find both partial derivatives; (b) evaluate them for $x = 1$, $y = 2$.

2 Given the function $z = x^3 + 2x^2 + y^2 - y$, (a) find both partial derivatives; (b) evaluate for $x = -1$, $y = 3$.

3 Given the function $u = 2x + 3xy - xz$, (a) find the partial derivatives of u with respect to x, y, and z; (b) evaluate them for $x = 0$, $y = 1$, $z = -2$.

4 Given the function $z = x + ye^{-x}$, (a) find both partial derivatives; (b) evaluate them for $x = 1$, $y = -1$.

5 Given the function $z = x \log_e (xy)$, (a) find both partial derivatives; (b) evaluate them for $x = 1$, $y = 1$.

6 Given the function $u = 2x^2 - xy + z^3 - 4xz + 6z - 8$, (a) find all partial derivatives; (b) evaluate them for $x = 1$, $y = -1$, $z = 0$.

7 The consumption of beer in the United Kingdom has been estimated from data covering the period 1920–1938 to be $q = 177.6Q^{-0.023}p^{-1.040}\pi^{0.939}$, where q is the quantity of beer consumed, Q is the aggregate real income, p the average retail price for beer, and π the average retail price of all other commodities (Stone). (a) Find the partial derivatives $\partial q/\partial Q$; $\partial q/\partial p$; $\partial q/\partial \pi$. (b) Evaluate the partial derivatives for $Q = 100$, $p = 100$, $\pi = 100$.

8 The consumption of spirits in the United Kingdom has been estimated for the period 1920–1938 to be $q = 228Q^{0.538}p^{-0.717}\pi^{0.717}$, where q is the quantity of spirits consumed, Q the aggregate real income, p the average retail price of spirits, and π the average retail price of all other commodities (Stone). (a) Find the partial derivatives $\partial q/\partial Q$; $\partial q/\partial p$; $\partial q/\partial \pi$. (b) Evaluate the partial derivatives for $Q = 90$, $p = 110$, $\pi = 100$.

9 The consumption of tobacco in the United Kingdom has been estimated for the period 1920–1938 to be $q = 750.2Q^{0.072}p^{-0.513}\pi^{0.513}$ (Stone). Here q is the amount of tobacco consumed, Q the aggregate real income, p the retail price of tobacco, and π the average retail price of all other commodities. (a) Find the partial derivatives $\partial q/\partial Q$; $\partial q/\partial p$; $\partial q/\partial \pi$. (b)Evaluate the partial derivatives for $Q = 120$, $p = 100$, $\pi = 150$.

10 The consumption of soap in the United Kingdom has been estimated for the period 1920–1938 to be $q = 28.97Q^{0.317}p^{-0.38}\pi^{0.327}$ (Stone). Here q is the consumption of soap, Q the aggregate real income, p the retail price of soap, and π the average retail price of all other commodities. (a) Find the partial derivatives $\partial q/\partial Q$; $\partial q/\partial p$; $\partial q/\partial \pi$. (b) Evaluate the partial derivatives for $Q = 80$, $p = 110$, $\pi = 95$.

78 MARGINAL PRODUCTIVITY

A production function

$$x = f(a, b)$$

shows the amount x of the product X produced if a units of production A (for example, labor) are used simultaneously with b units of production B (say, land).

Now let us investigate what happens if there is an increment in the amount of A while the amount of B is held constant. The average rate of increase in x with respect to a is given by

$$\frac{f(a + \Delta a, b) - f(a, b)}{\Delta a}.$$

The limit of this ratio as $\Delta a \to 0$ will be the partial derivative

$$\frac{\partial x}{\partial a} = f_a(a, b).$$

This is the marginal productivity of the factor A.

Similarly, if the amount of A is held constant and the amount of B increases, we would be interested in considering

$$\frac{f(a, b + \Delta b) - f(a, b)}{\Delta b}.$$

The limit of this ratio, as the increment Δb tends to 0, will be the partial derivative

$$\frac{\partial x}{\partial b} = f_b(a, b).$$

This is the marginal productivity of the factor B.

EXAMPLE

The production function of a commodity is $x = f(a, b) = 10a + 5b - a^2 - 2b^2 + 3ab$. (a) Find the marginal productivity of A. By partial differentiation, $\partial x / \partial a = f_a(a, b) = 10 - 2a + 3b$. (b) What is the marginal productivity of A if $a = 1$ and $b = 5$? Substituting, we have $f_a(1, 5) = 23$. Thus, on the assumption that b can be held constant, the limit of the ratio between the increment in the product x and the increment in the factor a tends to 23.

EXERCISES 78

1 The production function for a commodity is $x = 10a - a^2 + ab$. (a) Find the marginal productivities of A and B. (b) Find the two marginal productivities if $a = 2$ and $b = 6$.

2 The production function of a commodity is $x = 10a + 20b + 8c - a^2 + 2b^2 - c^2abc$. (a) Find the marginal productivities of A, B, and C. (b) Determine these marginal productivities if $a = 1$, $b = 2$, $c = 3$.

3 The production function of a commodity is $x = 100a + 200b + 50c - a^2 - 2b^2 - 3c^2 - 5ab + 3ac - bc$. (a) Find the marginal productivities of A, B, and C. (b) Determine these productivities if $a = 1$, $b = 2$, $c = 5$.

4 The production function for the United States during the years 1899–1922 was estimated by Douglas to be $x = 1.01L^{0.75}C^{0.25}$, where x is total production, L is labor, and C is capital. (a) Find the marginal productivities of L and C. (b) Establish the marginal productivities for $L = 160$, $C = 130$.

5 The production function for Australia, during 1934–1935 was estimated by Douglas and Gunn as $x = L^{0.64}C^{0.36}$, where x is production, L is labor, and C is capital. (a) Find the marginal productivities of L and C. (b) Determine the marginal productivities for $L = 1.5$, $C = 1.1$.

6 The production function for the United States in 1919 was estimated by Douglas and Gunn as $x = L^{0.76}C^{0.25}$, where x is the product, L is labor, and C is capital. (a) Find the marginal productivities of L and C. (b) Estimate the marginal productivities for $L = 1$, $C = 1$.

7 The production function for Canada in 1937 was estimated by Douglas and Daly as $x = L^{0.43}C^{0.58}$, where x is the product, L is the amount of labor, and C is the capital. (a) Determine the marginal productivities of C and L. (b) Find the marginal productivities if $C = 0.9$, $L = 0.8$.

8 The production function of Iowa farms was estimated for 1942 as $x = a^{0.287}b^{0.156}c^{0.053}d^{0.211}f^{0.158}$, where x is the product, a the land, b the labor, c the improvements, d the liquid assets, f the cash operating expenses (Tintner). (a) Determine the marginal productivities of a, b, c, d, and f. (b) Estimate the marginal productivities for $a = b = c = d = f = 1$.

9 The production function for hogs in Iowa has been estimated for 1942 as $x = 100a^{0.28}b^{0.23}c^{0.04}d^{0.17}f^{0.18}$, where the symbols a, b, c, d, f have the same meaning as in problem 8 and x is the production of hogs (Tintner). (a) Find the marginal productivities for $a = 1$, $b = 2$, $c = 1$, $d = 1.5$, $f = 0.5$.

10 The production function of farms in Iowa in 1939 has been estimated as $x = a^{0.34}b^{0.24}c^{0.04}d^{0.17}e^{0.08}f^{0.11}$, where a, b, c, d, and f have the same meaning as in problem 8 and e is working assets (Tintner and Brownlee). (a) Find the marginal productivities of a, b, c, d, e, and f. (b) Estimate the marginal productivities for $a = 2.37$, $b = 2.4$, $c = 5.134$, $d = 5.171$, $e = 2.685$, and $f = 2.127$.

11 The production function for the United States during 1921–1941 was estimated to be $x = a^{2.13}b^{0.34}$, where x is the total product, a labor, and b fixed capital (Tintner). (a) Find the marginal productivities of labor and capital. (b) Estimate the marginal productivities for $a = 1.7$, $b = 2$.

79   PARTIAL ELASTICITIES OF DEMAND

Let $D_A = f(p_A, p_B)$ be the demand for commodity A which depends upon the prices of commodities A and B, denoted, respectively, by p_A and p_B. We define the partial elasticity of demand to be

$$\frac{ED_A}{Ep_A} = \left(\frac{\partial D_A}{\partial p_A}\right)\left(\frac{p_A}{D_A}\right)$$

and, similarly,

$$\frac{ED_A}{Ep_B} = \left(\frac{\partial D_A}{\partial p_B}\right)\left(\frac{p_B}{D_A}\right).$$

The partial elasticity of the demand for commodity A with respect to the price of A is (approximately) the percent of increase or decrease in the demand for A if the price of A increases by 1 percent and the price of B is constant. The partial elasticity of demand for commodity A with respect to the price of B is (approximately) the percent of increase or decrease in the demand for A if the price of B increases by 1 percent while the price of A remains constant.

EXAMPLE

Let the demand function for commodity A be $D_A = f(p_A, p_B) = 25 - 2p_A + p_B$. (a) Find the partial elasticities. We have the partial derivatives $\partial D_A/\partial p_A = -2$ and $\partial D_A/\partial p_B = 1$. Inserting them into the above formulas we have

$$\frac{ED_A}{Ep_A} = \frac{-2p_A}{25 - 2p_A + p_B} \quad \text{and} \quad \frac{ED_A}{Ep_B} = \frac{p_B}{25 - 2p_A + p_B}.$$

(b) Evaluate the elasticities for $p_A = 3$, $p_B = 1$. We get

$$\frac{ED_A}{Ep_A} = \frac{-6}{20} = -0.3.$$

This means that, as the price of A increases by 1 percent, if the price of B remains constant, the demand for A will decrease by about 0.3 percent. Further,

$$\frac{ED_A}{Ep_B} = \frac{1}{20} = 0.05.$$

If the price of A stays constant and the price of B increases by 1 percent, the demand for A will increase by about 0.05 percent.

EXERCISES 79

1   Let A be beef, B pork, and C mutton. The demand for beef is estimated, according to Schultz, to be $D_A = 63.3 - 1.9p_A + 0.2p_B + 0.5p_C$. (a) Find

the partial elasticities of the demand for beef with respect to the price of beef, the price of pork, and the price of mutton. (b) Estimate the partial elasticities for $p_A = 10$, $p_B = 8$, $p_C = 7$.

2   Using the same notation as in problem 1, we have for the estimated demand for pork $D_B = 71.0 + 0.4p_A - 1.2p_B - 0.1p_C$ (Schultz). (a) Find the partial elasticities of the demand for pork with respect to the prices of beef, pork, and mutton. (b) Determine the partial elasticities for $p_A = 8$, $p_B = 10$, $p_C = 12$.

3   Using the same notation as in problem 1, the demand for mutton is estimated as $D_C = 10.3 + 0.1p_A + 0.1p_B - 0.3p_C$ (Schultz). (a) Find the partial elasticities of the demand for mutton with respect to the prices of beef, pork, and mutton. (b) Determine the partial elasticities for $p_A = 8$, $p_B = 9$, $p_C = 7$.

4   Let A be barley, B corn, C hay, D oats. Schultz estimated the demand for barley in the United States as follows: $D_A = 2.24 - 0.01p_A - 0.01p_B + 0.01p_D$. (a) Find the partial elasticities of the demand for barley with respect to the prices of barley, corn, hay, and oats. (b) Estimate the partial elasticities for $p_A = 1$, $p_B = 1$, $p_D = 1$.

5   Using the same notation as in problem 4, we have for the estimated demand for corn $D_B = 49.07 - 0.02p_A - 0.36p_B - 0.03p_C + 0.03p_D$ (Schultz). (a) Find the partial elasticities of the demand for corn with respect to the prices of corn and hay. (b) Estimate the partial elasticities for $p_A = 1$, $p_B = 2$, $p_C = 3$, $p_D = 1$.

6   Schultz estimated the demand for hay in the United States (notation in problem 5) as $D_C = 1.30 - 0.05p_C + 0.01p_D$. (a) Find the partial elasticities of the demand for hay with respect to the prices of corn, hay, and oats. (b) Estimate the partial elasticities for $p_C = 2$, $p_D = 1$.

7   The demand for oats in the United States is estimated as $D_D = 24.2 + 0.1p_B - 0.6p_C - 0.3p_D$ (the same notation as in problem 4). (a) Find the partial elasticity of the demand for oats with respect to the prices of barley, corn, hay, and oats. (b) Estimate the partial elasticities for $p_B = 1$, $p_C = 1$, $p_D = 1$.

8   Recall the demand function for beer in the United Kingdom, problem 7, Exercises 77. Define in the notation of this problem the income elasticity of the demand for beer as $Eq/EQ = (\partial q/\partial Q)(Q/q)$, and the price elasticities as $Eq/Ep = (\partial q/\partial p)(\partial p/\partial q)$, $Eq/E\pi = (\partial q/\partial \pi)(\pi/q)$. Find the income elasticity and the two price elasticities of the demand for beer.

9   Consider the demand function for spirits in the United Kingdom, problem 8, Exercises 77. Using the definitions in problem 8 above, compute the income elasticity and both price elasticities of the demand for spirits.

10 Consider the demand for tobacco in the United Kingdom, problem 9, Exercises 77. Using the definitions of problem 8 above, find the income elasticity and both price elasticities of the demand for tobacco.

11   Consider the demand for soap in the United Kingdom, problem 10, Exercises 77. Using the definitions of problem 8 above, derive the income elasticity and both price elasticities of the demand for soap.

12   C. F. Roos and V. von Szeliski give the following formula for the estimated demand for passenger automobiles in the United States: $D = 0.92I^{1.07}p^{-0.74}T^{1.10}$, where D denotes replacement sales of automobiles, I is income, p the average price per car, T the index of the scrapping of cars. Find (a) the income elasticity of demand $ED/EI = (\partial D/\partial I)(I/D)$, (b) the price elasticity of demand $ED/Ep = (\partial D/\partial p)(p/D)$.

13   The demand for bicycles in the Netherlands has been estimated from data covering the period 1922–1933 as $V = 11.2K - 8.6P - 379$ (Derksen and Rombouts), where V is the annual total consumption of bicycles, K an index of purchasing power, and P the price of bicycles. (a) Find the income elasticity $EV/EK = (\partial V/\partial K)(K/V)$; (b) the price elasticity $EV/EP = (\partial V/\partial P)(P/V)$. (c) Evaluate the elasticities for $K = 100$, $P = 45$.

14   The demand for shoes in the United States has been estimated for the period 1919–1934 as $v = 0.053i^{0.35}p^{-0.16}$ (von Szeliski and Paradiso). Here v is the number of pairs of shoes per capita, p a price index of shoes and boots, and i national income per capita. (a) Find the price elasticity $Ev/Ep = (\partial v/\partial p)(p/v)$; (b) the income elasticity $Ev/Ei = (\partial v/\partial i)(i/v)$.

15   The following demand function for butter has been estimated for the United Kingdom for the period 1920–1938 (Stone, Rowe, Carlett, Hurstfield, Potter). Denote by Q_1 the quantity of butter demanded, by R real per capita income, by p_1 the price of butter, by p_2 the price of flour, by p_3 the price of cakes and biscuits, by p_4 the price of meat, by p_5 the price of margarine, and by p_6 the price of all other commodities. Let A be a constant: $Q_1 = AR^{0.37}p_1^{-0.43}p_2^{-0.23}p_3^{0.59}p_4^{0.56}p_5^{0.10}p_6^{-0.58}$. Compute the income and price elasticity of demand and all cross elasticities.

16   Denote by Q the per capita demand for tobacco, by p the real price of tobacco, by R real disposable income, by a real advertising cost for tobacco, and by A real advertising cost for all other goods. We obtain for the United States for 1926–1945 the following estimated demand function: $Q = 2.46p^{-0.39}R^{0.371}a^{0.085}A^{-0.036}$. Find (a) the price elasticity of demand; (b) the income elasticity.

17   Denote margarine by A and butter by B. The demand for margarine has been estimated by Pabst for the United States for 1904–1933 as $D_A = p_A^{-1.32}p_B^{0.4}$. Find the partial elasticities of demand.

18   Using the notation of the previous problem, the demand for butter is $D_B = p_A^{0.33}p_B^{-0.1}$ (Pabst). Compute the partial elasticities of demand.

19   Stoikovic has estimated the demand function for potatoes in the United States for the period 1929–1955. Let Q be the per capita demand, P the real price, and Y real disposable income: $Q = 0.097P - 0.236Y +$

0.288. Find the price elasticity of demand, EQ/EP, and the income elasticity of demand, EQ/EY. Note that the income elasticity is negative (inferior good) and the price elasticity positive (Giffen phenomenon).

20   Rhomberg and Boissoneault have derived a demand function for imported automobiles in the United States for the period 1954–1962. Let x be the demand for imported automobiles, y real disposable income, and p a price index of imported automobiles. The demand function is $\log x = 5.91 \log y - 3.34 \log p - 15.5$. Find the price elasticity, Ex/Ep, and the income elasticity, Ex/Ey.

21   Suits and Koizumi have estimated demand and supply functions for the United States onion market for the period 1929–1952. Let p_t be the price, x_t the per capita quantity, Y_t the per capita disposable income, c_t a cost index, and t time. The demand function is $\log p_t = 0.681 - 2.27 \log x_t + 1.31 \log Y_t$. The supply function is estimated as $\log x_t = 0.134 + 0.0123(t - 1924) + 0.324 \log p_{t-1} - 0.512 \log c_{t-1}$. (a) Compute from the demand function the price elasticity of demand, Ex_t/Ep_t, and the income elasticity of demand, Ex_t/EY_t. (b) Compute from the supply function the price elasticity of supply, Ex_t/Ep_{t-1}, and the cost elasticity of supply, Ex_t/Ec_{t-1}.

22   Let Q be the quantity of textiles consumed per capita, R income per capita, P real price of textiles, t time, and S exports (Goreux). The demand for textiles is given by $\log Q = 0.717 + 0.481 \log R - 0.133 \log P - 0.00067 \log t + 0.10 \log S$. Find (a) the price elasticity, EQ/EP; (b) the income elasticity, EQ/ER.

23   Let c be the demand for coffee in France, grams per capita, p the price, and t time (Lenoir). For 1873–1896 the demand function is derived as follows: $c - 1649 = 32.7(t - 1884.5) - 2.75(p - 3.47)$, where t is time. (a) Derive dc/dp. (b) Find Ec/Ep for $c = 1649$, $p = 3.47$, $t = 1884.5$.

**80   DIFFERENTIATION OF IMPLICIT FUNCTIONS

In order to find the various derivatives, we have up to now assumed that one variable is the dependent variable and the other variables are independent variables. But in economics functions appear frequently that cannot easily be expressed in this form. Hence it is of some importance to be able to differentiate implicit functions.

Assume, for example, that we have a function of two variables,

$$f(x, y) = 0,$$

and that this implicitly defines y as a function of x. We want to find the derivative dy/dx without solving first for y, because, for some cases, this may not be possible. Since y is a function of x, it is to be presumed that y will take on an increment Δy as x takes on an increment Δx. Thus, the total increment in the function, as x takes on an increment Δx, is

$f(x + \Delta x, \; y + \Delta y) - f(x, y)$. It follows that

$$\frac{f(x + \Delta x, y + \Delta y) - f(x, y)}{\Delta x} = \frac{f(x + \Delta x, y + \Delta y) - f(x, y + \Delta y)}{\Delta x}$$

$$+ \frac{f(x, y + \Delta y) - f(x, y)}{\Delta x} = 0.$$

As $\Delta x \to 0$, the first term on the right approaches $f_x(x, \; y + \Delta y)$, or, of course, $f_x(x, y)$, since $\Delta y \to 0$ as $\Delta x \to 0$. The second term may be rewritten in the form

$$\frac{f(x, y + \Delta y) - f(x, y)}{\Delta y} \left(\frac{\Delta y}{\Delta x} \right).$$

As $\Delta x \to 0$, this term approaches $f_y(x, y) \, dy/dx$. Consequently, we have

$$f_x(x, y) + f_y(x, y) \left(\frac{dy}{dx} \right) = 0,$$

or

$$\frac{dy}{dx} = - \frac{f_x}{f_y}.$$

The derivation as just made requires special properties of continuity on the part of the functions; however, in general, such conditions are satisfied by the functions employed in economics.

EXAMPLE 1

Find the derivative of y with respect to x for the implicit function

$$y^5 + 2x^2y^2 + xy - 42 = 0$$

at the point $x = 1, \; y = 2$. We have

$$f_x = 4xy^2 + y,$$
$$f_y = 5y^4 + 4x^2y + x.$$

Thus

$$\frac{dy}{dx} = - \frac{4xy^2 + y}{5y^4 + 4x^2y + x}.$$

For $x = 1, \; y = 2$ we have

$$\frac{dy}{dx} = - \frac{18}{89}.$$

Let us now consider an implicit function of three (or more) variables; for example,

$$f(x, y, z) = 0,$$

wherein x and y are regarded as independent variables, but z is treated as a function of both x and y. We want to find $\partial z/\partial x$ and

$\partial z/\partial y$, the two partial derivatives. By an analysis similar to that given above,

$$f_x + f_z \left(\frac{\partial z}{\partial x}\right) = 0,$$

$$f_y + f_z \left(\frac{\partial z}{\partial y}\right) = 0,$$

Hence

$$\frac{\partial z}{\partial x} = -\frac{f_x}{f_z},$$

$$\frac{\partial z}{\partial y} = -\frac{f_y}{f_z}.$$

EXAMPLE 2

Let the implicit function be

$$z^5 - x^2 z^2 + xy + 2 = 0.$$

We want to find the partial derivatives $\partial z/\partial x$ and $\partial z/\partial y$ at the point $x = 3$, $y = 2$, $z = 1$.

$$f_x = -2xz^2 + y,$$
$$f_y = x,$$
$$f_z = 5z^4 - 2x^2 z.$$

Thus

$$\frac{\partial z}{\partial x} = -\frac{(-2xz^2 + y)}{5z^4 - 2x^2 z},$$

$$\frac{\partial z}{\partial y} = -\frac{x}{5z^4 - 2x^2 z}.$$

At the point $x = 3$, $y = 2$, $z = 1$, we have $\partial z/\partial x = -\frac{4}{13}$ and $\partial z/\partial y = +\frac{3}{13}$.

Assume now that we have two quantities y and z which are both functions of x. We have two independent equations defining the relation among the three variables

$$f(x, y, z) = 0,$$
$$g(x, y, z) = 0.$$

In order to find the derivatives dy/dx and dz/dx, we differentiate both relations with respect to x, again extending the analysis considered above, and then solve the resulting system of equations:

$$f_x + f_y \left(\frac{dy}{dx}\right) + f_z \left(\frac{dz}{dx}\right) = 0,$$

$$g_x + g_y \left(\frac{dy}{dx}\right) + g_z \left(\frac{dz}{dx}\right) = 0.$$

Hence we have

$$\frac{dy}{dx} = \frac{f_z g_x - f_x g_z}{f_y g_z - f_z g_y},$$

$$\frac{dz}{dx} = \frac{f_x g_y - f_y g_x}{f_y g_z - f_z g_y}.$$

EXAMPLE 3

Let the relations among the three variables x, y, and z be

$$f(x, y, z) = x^2 + 2xy + z - 4 = 0,$$
$$g(x, y, z) = x^3 - yz + z^3 - 1 = 0.$$

We want to find the derivatives dy/dx and dz/dx at the point $x = y = z = 1$. We have

$$f_x = 2x + 2y,$$
$$f_y = 2x,$$
$$f_z = 1,$$
$$g_x = 3x^2,$$
$$g_y = -z,$$
$$g_z = 3z^2,$$

$$\frac{dy}{dx} = \frac{3x^2 - 6xz^2 - 6yz^2}{6xz^2 + z},$$

$$\frac{dz}{dx} = \frac{-2xz - 2yz - 6x^3}{6xz^2 + z}.$$

At the point $x = y = z = 1$ we have $dy/dx = -\frac{9}{7}$ and $dz/dx = -\frac{10}{7}$.

EXERCISES 80

1 Find the derivative dy/dx of the following implicit functions: (a) $x^4 - 2x^3y^2 + y^3 + 101 = 0$, at the point $x = 2$, $y = 3$; (b) $x^5y^4 - x^3y^2 + xy - 1 = 0$, if $x = y = 1$; (c) $xe^{y^2} - e^y = 0$, if $x = 1, y = 0$; (d) $2^xy^2 + x3^y - 90 = 0$ at the point $x = 2$, $y = 3$.

2 Assume the function $x^2 + y^2 = 4$. Find the derivatives dy/dx and dx/dy, (a) by differentiating the implicit function; (b) by making the function explicit.

3 A demand function is defined implicitly as $D^2p^3 = 1$. Find the elasticity of demand (a) by differentiating the implicit relationship; (b) by making the relation explicit and differentiating it.

4 Find the partial derivatives $\partial z/\partial x$ and $\partial z/\partial y$ of the following implicit functions: (a) $z^5 + y^2z^2 - 2xy = 0$, if $x = y = z = 1$; (b) $xe^z + ze^y - 2e = 0$, if $x = 2$, $y = 0$, $z = 1$; (c) $x^2 \log_e z + ze^{xy} - y - 1 = 0$, for $x = 2$, $y = 0$, $z = 1$; (d) $x^5y^2 - z^3xy = 0$, for $x = y = z = 1$.

5 Let $x^2 + y^2 + z^2 = 16$. Find the partial derivatives $\partial z/\partial x$ and $\partial z/\partial y$, (a) by differentiating the implicit relationship; (b) by making the relationship explicit for z.

6 The implicit form of a production function is $x^2ab = 1$. Find the marginal productivities (a) by differentiating the implicit relationship; (b) by making the relationship explicit for x.

7 A demand function is given by $D_a^2 p_a^3 p_b = 10$. Find the partial elasticities of demand (a) by differentiating the implicit relationship; (b) by making the relationship explicit.

8 Find the derivatives dy/dx and dz/dx from the equations

$$xy^2 + 4zx - 5 = 0,$$
$$xz + y^2z^2 - 2 = 0,$$

if $x = y = z = 1$.

9 Find the derivatives dy/dx and dz/dx of the system

$$xy + z - 5 = 0,$$
$$xz + 2y - 7 = 0,$$

at the point $x = 1$, $y = 2$, $z = 3$.

10 What is the effect of a tax levied on each unit sold by a monopolist? (HINT: the profit after tax is, in the notation of Section 73, $\pi = R(D) - C(D) - tD$, if t is the tax. Hence the necessary condition for a maximum is

$$\pi' = R'(D) - C'(D) - t = 0,$$

and the sufficient condition is

$$\pi'' = R''(D) - C''(D) < 0.$$

Differentiate the necessary condition with respect to t and find dD/dt. Determine the sign from the sufficient condition. What can you say about the sign of dp/dt?)

11 Equilibrium on the market of a commodity is defined by the two equations

$$f(D, a) - p = 0,$$
$$g(D) - p = 0,$$

where D is the quantity, p is the price, f is the demand function, g is the supply function, and a is a shift parameter (for example, signifying change in taste). Let $f_a > 0$, $f_D < 0$, $g_D > 0$ and find the signs of the change in quantity, dD/da, and the change in price, dp/da.

12 Let x be the product, L and C labor and capital. A Cobb-Douglas production function is defined as $x = aL^bC^{1-b}$, where a and b are constants. (a) Assume x is constant and find the marginal rate of substitution, $r = -dC/dL$. Express it in terms of $y = (C/L)$. (b) Prove that the elasticity of substitution $Ey/Er = d\log y/d\log r = (dy/dr)(r/y) = 1$.

13　*The homohyphallic production function* (Arrow, Chenery, Minhas, Solow): $x = (aL^b + aC^b)^{1/b}$; a, b, and c are constants. Proceed as in problem 12 and compute the elasticity of substitution.

**14　The following model for Austria for the period 1948–1956 has been derived by von Hohenbalken and Tintner. Denote by C consumption, by Y nominal national income, by P price level, by X real gross national income, by D employment, by N population, by W money wages, and by K public consumption plus increases in stocks plus investments plus exports minus imports. The estimates are as follows: Consumption function: $C/NP = 2{,}140.9 + 0.492(Y/NP)$; definition of national income: $Y = C + K$; definition of real national income: $X = Y/P$; demand for labor: $0.423(X/D) = W/P$; production function: $X = 182{,}081{,}700D^{0.423}$. Assume K is constant and find $\partial C/\partial W$, $\partial Y/\partial W$, $\partial P/\partial W$, $\partial X/\partial W$, $\partial D/\partial W$.

Chapter 17
Homogeneity

81 HOMOGENEOUS FUNCTIONS

A special type of function which is of importance in many fields of economics is the so-called homogeneous function. Consider the function of two variables,

$$z = f(x, y).$$

This function is said to be a homogeneous function of degree k if the following relationship holds:

$$f(tx, ty) = t^k f(x, y), \, t > 0.$$

In words, a function is said to be homogeneous of degree k if when each of the independent variables is multiplied by a positive constant t the new function is t^k times the original function.

EXAMPLE 1

Let $z = f(x, y) = x^2 + 4xy + 3y^2$. If we multiply x and y by a positive constant t, we get

$$
\begin{aligned}
f(tx, ty) &= (tx)^2 + 4(tx)(ty) + 3(ty)^2 \\
&= t^2 x^2 + 4t^2 xy + 3t^2 y^2 \\
&= t^2 (x^2 + 4xy + 3y^2) \\
&= t^2 f(x, y).
\end{aligned}
$$

We conclude that $f(x, y) = x^2 + 4xy + y^2$ is a homogeneous function of degree $2(k = 2)$.

Let us, for example, double the independent variables x and y. We have immediately

$$f(2x, 2y) = 2^2 f(x, y).$$

227

EXAMPLE 2

Consider the function $z = f(x, y, z) = (3x/z) - (2y/z)$. Multiplying the three independent variables x, y, and z by an arbitrary positive constant t, we have

$$f(tx, ty, tz) = \frac{3(tx)}{(tz)} - \frac{2(ty)}{(tz)}$$

$$= \frac{3x}{z} - \frac{2y}{z}$$

$$= t^0 f(x, y, z).$$

Since $t^0 = 1$, the function $f(x, y, z)$ is said to be a homogeneous function of degree 0. If all independent variables x, y, and z are multiplied by any arbitrary positive constant, the value of the function remains unchanged. As an illustration, if x, y, and z are multiplied by 5, we have merely

$$f(5x, 5y, 5z) = f(x, y, z).$$

EXERCISES 81

1   Establish the degree of homogeneity of the function $y(x, y) = x^3 + 4x^2y - 2xy^2 + y^3$. Check the result by multiplying the variables x and y by 5.

2   Establish the degree of homogeneity of the function $f(x, y, z) = x^2 + 3xy + z^2$. Check by multiplying the independent variables x, y, and z by 4.

3   What is the degree of homogeneity of the function

$$f(x, y, z, u, v) = \sqrt[3]{2x^2 - y^2 + 5z^2 - 3u^2}.$$

Check by multiplying the independent variables by $\frac{1}{8}$.

4   What is the degree of homogeneity of the function $f(x, y, z) = (2x - 3y)/5z$? Check by multiplying the independent variables by $\frac{1}{3}$.

5   Let the price of commodity A be denoted by p_A. The price of another commodity B is denoted by p_B. The demand for A is $D_A = 50p_B/p_A$ and the demand for B is $D_B = 100p_A/p_B$. (a) Show that the two demand functions are homogeneous functions of 0 degree. (b) Check by assuming that the prices p_A and p_B are doubled. (c) Check by assuming that the prices p_A and p_B are halved. (d) What conclusions can you draw for the change in the demand for A and B if all prices increase or decrease by the same percent? (e) Compute the demand for the commodities A and B if $p_A = 5$ and $p_B = 3$. (f) Show that the demand remains the same if the prices given in (e) are tripled.

6   Let p_A, p_B, and p_C be the prices of three commodities, A, B, and C. Assume the demand functions for the three commodities in the following

form:

$$D_A = \frac{2p_C - p_A}{p_C},$$

$$D_B = \frac{5p_C - p_A - 2p_B}{p_C},$$

$$D_C = \frac{10p_A - p_B}{p_C}.$$

(a) Show that the three demand functions are homogeneous functions of 0 degree in the three prices. (b) Check by assuming that all prices increase by 20 percent. (c) Check by assuming that all prices decrease by 40 percent. (d) Compute the quantities demanded of the commodities A, B, and C if $p_A = 2$, $p_B = 1$, and $p_C = 10$. (e) Compute the quantities demanded if the prices given in (d) are doubled.

7 Investigate for homogeneity the production function for the United States given in problem 4, Exercises 78.

8 Investigate for homogeneity the production function for Australia given in problem 5, Exercises 78.

9 Investigate for homogeneity in the prices p and π the consumption function for spirits in the United Kingdom given in problem 8, Exercises 77.

10 Investigate for homogeneity in the prices p and π the consumption function of tobacco given in problem 9, Exercises 77.

11 Murti and Sastry have estimated a production function for Indian industry for 1952. Let x be output, n employment, and k capital (net assests). The relation is estimated as $x = 0.68n^{0.53}k^{0.50}$. Is this production function homogeneous, and of which degree is it?

12 Niitamo has estimated a production function for Finnish industry for 1925–1952. With the notation of the above example, this might be written, $x = an^{0.779}k^{0.221}$, where a is a constant. Is this function homogeneous, and of which degree is it?

13 Hjelm and Sandquist have derived a production function for milk in Sweden for 1950. Let y be the yield of milk, x_1 labor, x_2 feed grain and oil cake, x_3 pasture, x_4 roughage, and x_5 other cost. The estimated relation is

$$2.90x_1^{0.015}x_2^{0.250}x_3^{0.350}x_4^{0.408}x_5^{0.030}.$$

(a) Is this production homogeneous, and of which degree is it? (b) Find the partial elasticities of production with respect to inputs Ey/Ex_1, Ey/Ex_2, Ey/Ex_3, Ey/Ex_4, Ey/Ex_5.

82 EULER THEOREM

An important relationship for differentiable homogeneous functions involving their partial derivatives is as follows: Let $f(x, y)$ be a homogeneous function of the kth degree. Then $xf_x(x, y) + yf_y(x, y) = kf(x, y)$. This identity is called *the Euler theorem*.

**To derive this theorem we differentiate

$$f(tx, ty) = t^k f(x, y)$$

with respect to the parameter t; we obtain

$$xf_{tx}(tx, ty) + yf_{ty}(tx, ty) = kt^{k-1}f(x, y).$$

Since t is arbitrary, we may take $t = 1$. From this follows the Euler theorem:

$$xf_x(x, y) + yf_y(x, y) = kf(x, y).$$

This can be generalized for any number of independent variables.

EXAMPLE 1

We have shown that the function

$$f(x, y) = x^2 + 4xy + 3y^2$$

is a homogeneous function of second degree. We compute the partial derivatives

$$f_x(x, y) = 2x + 4y,$$
$$f_y(x, y) = 4x + 6y.$$

Then

$$xf_x(x, y) + yf_y(x, y) = x(2x + 4y) + y(4x + 6y)$$
$$= 2x^2 + 8xy + 6y^2$$
$$= 2(x^2 + 4xy + 3y^2)$$
$$= 2f(x, y).$$

Since $f(x, y)$ is a homogeneous function of second degree, the sum of the partial derivatives, each times its respective independent variable, is twice the original function $f(x, y)$, as was expected.

EXAMPLE 2

The function

$$f(x, y, z, u) = 3x - 2y + 4z - u$$

is a homogeneous function of first degree, also called a linear homogeneous function. We find the partial derivatives

$$f_x(x, y, z, u) = 3,$$
$$f_y(x, y, z, u) = -2,$$
$$f_z(x, y, z, u) = 4,$$
$$f_u(x, y, z, u) = -1.$$

Thus

$$xf_x(x, y, z, u) + yf_y(x, y, z, u) + zf_z(x, y, z, u) + uf_u(x, y, z, u)$$
$$= 3x - 2y + 4z - u$$
$$= f(x, y, z, u).$$

Hence we see that in this linear homogeneous function the sum of all the partial derivatives, each times its respective independent variable, is equal to the original function $f(x, y, z, u)$.

EXERCISES 82

1 Given the function $u = 2x^4 - 4y^4$, (a) determine whether it is a homogeneous function. (b) Apply the Euler theorem.

2 Given the function $u = x + 2y - 5z$, (a) determine whether it is a homogeneous function. (b) Apply the Euler theorem.

3 Given the function $u = x^2 + y^2$, (a) determine whether it is a homogeneous function. (b) Apply the Euler theorem.

**4 Let $u = ax^b y^c$; a, b, and c are constants. (a) Find the condition under which this is a linear homogeneous function. (b) Apply the Euler theorem if these conditions hold true.

5 Is the production function for the United States in the period 1899–1922, given in problem 4, Exercises 78, linear and homogeneous? Apply the Euler theorem. What would be the resulting production if amounts of labor and capital were doubled?

6 Is the production function for Australia in 1934–1935, given in problem 5, Exercises 78, linear and homogeneous? Apply the Euler theorem.

7 Is the production function for Canada in 1937, given in problem 7, Exercises 78, linear and homogeneous? Apply the Euler theorem.

8 Is the production function for Iowa farms in 1942, given in problem 8, Exercises 78, linear and homogeneous? Apply the Euler theorem.

9 Investigate the homogeneity of the production function for hogs in Iowa, given in problem 9, Exercises 78. Apply the Euler theorem.

10 Investigate the production function of farms in Iowa, given in problem 10, Exercises 78, for homogeneity. Apply the Euler theorem.

11 Is the production function for the United States for 1921–1941, given in problem 11, Exercises 78, linear and homogeneous?

12 The following relation has been estimated for Austria for 1954–1955 (Tintner). X_1 is agricultural production, X_2 land, X_3 labor, X_4 capital. The production function is $X_1 = 9.52X_2^{0.06351}X_3^{0.31931}X_4^{0.61719}$. (a) Compute the marginal productivities of land, labor, and capital. (b) Is the production function homogeneous? (c) Does it satisfy the Euler equation?

Chapter 18
Higher Partial Derivatives and Applications

83 **HIGHER PARTIAL DERIVATIVES**

Assume that we have a function of two independent variables, $z = f(x, y)$. The two first derivatives are

$$\frac{\partial z}{\partial x} = f_x(x, y) = \frac{\partial f(x, y)}{\partial x},$$

$$\frac{\partial z}{\partial y} = f_y(x, y) = \frac{\partial f(x, y)}{\partial y}.$$

As already indicated, the partial derivative $f_x(x, y)$ is the derivative of $f(x, y)$ with respect to x, treating y as a constant. The partial derivative $f_y(x, y)$ is the derivative of $f(x, y)$ with respect to y, treating x as a constant.

We can also define higher derivatives in an analogous manner. For example,

$$\frac{\partial^2 z}{\partial x^2} = f_{xx}(x, y) = \frac{\partial f_x(x, y)}{\partial x}.$$

This means that the second partial derivative with respect to x is computed by differentiating the first partial derivative $f_x(x, y)$ partially with respect to x. That is, we take the derivative of the function $f_x(x, y)$ with respect to x, holding y constant.

Similarly,

$$\frac{\partial^2 z}{\partial y^2} = f_{yy}(x, y) = \frac{\partial f_y(x, y)}{\partial y}.$$

That is, the second partial derivative with respect to y is computed by differentiating partially with respect to y the first partial derivative with respect to y.

Apart from these two second-order derivatives there are also the mixed

232

partial derivatives

$$\frac{\partial^2 z}{\partial x\, \partial y} = f_{xy}(x,\, y) = \frac{\partial f_y(x,\, y)}{\partial x},$$

$$\frac{\partial^2 z}{\partial y\, \partial x} = f_{yx}(x,\, y) = \frac{\partial f_x(x,\, y)}{\partial y}.$$

Under proper conditions of continuity that are found in virtually all functions of interest to us, $f_{xy}(x,\, y) = f_{yx}(x,\, y)$. Hence, in practice, the mixed partial derivative $f_{xy}(x,\, y)$ can be computed in two ways which yield the same result: Either we differentiate the first partial derivative with respect to x, partially with respect to y, or we differentiate the first partial derivative with respect to y, partially with respect to x. The generalization of these methods for functions of more than two independent variables is obvious.

EXAMPLE

Assume a function of two variables,

$$z = f(x,\, y) = 2x^2 - 3xy + 5y^2.$$

The first partial derivatives are

$$\frac{\partial z}{\partial x} = f_x(x,\, y) = 4x - 3y,$$

$$\frac{\partial z}{\partial y} = f_y(x,\, y) = -3x + 10y.$$

The second partial derivative with respect to x is derived by taking the partial derivative of $f_x(x,\, y) = 4x - 3y$ with respect to x; that is,

$$\frac{\partial^2 z}{\partial x^2} = f_{xx}(x,\, y) = 4.$$

The second partial derivative with respect to y is computed by finding the partial derivative of $f_y(x,\, y) = -3x + 10y$ with respect to y. Thus

$$\frac{\partial^2 z}{\partial y^2} = f_{yy}(x,\, y) = 10.$$

The mixed second-order partial derivative $f_{xy}(x,\, y)$ may be computed in two ways. The first is to find the partial derivative of the function $f_x(x,\, y) = 4x - 3y$ with respect to y; this gives

$$\frac{\partial^2 z}{\partial x\, \partial y} = f_{xy}(x,\, y) = -3.$$

The same result is achieved by finding the partial derivative of the function $f_y(x, y) = -3x + 10y$ with respect to x; that is,

$$\frac{\partial^2 z}{\partial x \, \partial y} = f_{yx}(x, y) = -3.$$

EXERCISES 83

1   Given $z = x^4 - 5xy^3 + 6xy - x + 4y + 10$, find all the second-order partial derivatives.

2   Given $z = t = ye^{-x}$, find all the second-order partial derivatives.

3   Given $z = x \log_e y$, find all the second-order partial derivatives.

4   Given $z = e^x \log_e xy$, find all the second-order partial derivatives.

5   Given $u = x^3 - xy + 4xz - z^2$, find all the second-order partial derivatives.

6   Given $z = x^3 - 6x^2y + xy - 7$, (a) find all the second-order partial derivatives. (b) Evaluate for $x = 1$, $y = -1$.

7   Given the function $z = x/y$, (a) find all second-order partial derivatives. (b) Evaluate for $x = 2$, $y = -6$.

8   Given the function $u = x^4xyz - z^6$, (a) find all the second-order partial derivatives. (b) Evaluate for $x = y = z = 1$.

9   Given the function $w = x^3 - xyz + u^4z$, (a) find all the second-order partial derivatives. (b) Evaluate for $x = 1$, $y = -1$, $z = 0$, $u = 2$.

10   Given the function $w = xy/zu$, (a) determine all the second-order partial derivatives. (b) Evaluate for $x = 1$, $y = -1$, $z = 2$, $u = 4$.

84   MAXIMA AND MINIMA IN SEVERAL VARIABLES

We remember that the necessary condition for a maximum or minimum for a function $y = f(x)$ of one independent variable was

$$f'(x) = 0.$$

Assume now that we have a function of two variables,

$$z = f(x, y).$$

What are the necessary conditions for a maximum or minimum of this function?

First, assume that we keep the independent variable y fixed. Let us assign to it the value $y = b$, where b is a constant. Then the function

$$z = f(x, b)$$

is a function of the single variable x, since by assumption b is a constant. The necessary condition for a maximum of this function is, as before, that its derivative (with respect to the single variable x) vanish; that is,

$$f_x(x, b) = 0.$$

Next, in the function $f(x, y)$ let us assign a constant value to x. For example, let $x = a$, where a is a constant. The function now becomes

$$z = f(a, y).$$

This is a function of the single independent variable y. The necessary condition for a maximum is that its derivative (with respect to the single variable y) vanish; that is,

$$f_y(a, y) = 0.$$

From this demonstration, although it is not completely rigorous, we may conclude that the necessary condition for the existence of a maximum or a minimum of a function of two variables is that both first-order partial derivatives become 0:

$$f_x(x, y) = 0,$$
$$f_y(x, y) = 0.$$

By analogy, we can extend this theorem to any number of independent variables and we have the general rule: a necessary condition for the existence of a maximum or minimum of a function of several variables is that all the first-order partial derivatives be 0.

The sufficient conditions for a maximum or minimum of a function of several variables are too difficult to derive here. We will simply state them for the case of two independent variables.

A maximum or minimum exists, in general, if the following condition involving a determinant is fulfilled:

$$\begin{vmatrix} f_{xx}(x, y) & f_{xy}(x, y) \\ f_{xy}(x, y) & f_{yy}(x, y) \end{vmatrix} = f_{xx}(x, y)f_{yy}(x, y) - [f_{xy}(x, y)]^2 > 0.$$

In other words, the determinant given above must be positive in order to have a maximum or minimum. Moreover,

$$f_{xx}(x, y) > 0, \qquad f_{yy}(x, y) > 0 \qquad \text{for a minimum,}$$
$$f_{xx}(x, y) < 0, \qquad f_{yy}(x, y) < 0 \qquad \text{for a maximum.}$$

We need actually consider the sign of only one of the derivatives f_{xx} and f_{yy}, since the other has necessarily the same sign if the determinant is positive.

EXAMPLE

Consider the function

$$z = f(x, y) = 2x + 8y - x^2 - 2y^2.$$

The first-order partial derivatives are

$$f_x(x, y) = 2 - 2x,$$
$$f_y(x, y) = 8 - 4y.$$

The necessary conditions for a maximum or a minimum demand that the two first-order derivatives are 0; that is,

$$f_x(x, y) = 2 - 2x = 0.$$
$$f_y(x, y) = 8 - 4y = 0.$$

The solution of this system of equations is $x = 1$, $y = 2$.

In order to investigate whether there is actually a maximum or minimum at the point $x = 1$, $y = 2$, we compute the second-order derivatives

$$f_{xx}(x, y) = -2,$$
$$f_{xy}(x, y) = 0,$$
$$f_{yy}(x, y) = -4,$$

$$\begin{vmatrix} f_{xx}(x, y) & f_{xy}(x, y) \\ f_{xy}(x, y) & f_{yy}(x, y) \end{vmatrix} = \begin{vmatrix} -2 & 0 \\ 0 & -4 \end{vmatrix} = (-2)(-4) - (0)^2$$
$$= 8 > 0.$$

The determinant is positive; hence we have either a maximum or a minimum.

We note that both second-order derivatives are negative; that is,

$$f_{xx}(x, y) = -2 < 0,$$
$$f_{yy}(x, y) = -4 < 0.$$

Hence we conclude that we have a maximum of the function $z = f(x, y)$ at the point $x = 1$, $y = 2$. The maximum value of the function is computed by substituting the values of $x = 1$ and $y = 2$ into the function $f(x, y)$:

$$f(1, 2) = (2)(1) + (8)(2) - (1)^2 - (2)(2)^2 = 9.$$

This is the maximum value of z.

EXERCISES 84

1   Consider the function $z = x^2 + 2x + y + y^2$ for maxima and minima. Find the corresponding value of z.

2   Consider the function $z = 10 - x^2 - 5y^2 + 3xy - x + 2y$ for maxima and minima. Find the corresponding value of z.

3   Consider the function $z = x^2 - 12x + y^2 - 27y$ for maxima and minima. Find the corresponding value of z.

4   Consider the function $z = xy - x^2$ for maxima and minima.

5   Consider the function $z = xy - x + y$ for maxima or minima.

6   Find the maxima and minima of the function $z = 12 - x^2 + 2y - y^2$.

7   Consider the function $z = xy$ for maxima and minima.

8   Consider the maxima and minima of the function $z = x^3 + y^2 - 3x - 12y + 10$.

**9   Consider the function $z = ax^2 + 2bxy + cy^2$, where a, b, and c are constants. What are the values of the parameters a, b, and c for (a) a maximum; (b) a minimum; (c) neither a maximum nor a minimum of z?

10   Consider the function $z = ax + by + c$ (a, b, and c constants) for maxima and minima.

11   Consider the maxima and minima of the function $w = x^2 + y^2 + z^2 + u^2 + v^2$.

85   JOINT PRODUCTION

Assume that a manufacturer produces two commodities A and B. Denote by D_A the amount of A produced and by D_B the amount of B. The demand curves are $p_A = f(D_A)$ and $p_B = g(D_B)$. The joint cost function is (total cost) $C = h(D_A, D_B)$. The profit is $\pi = p_A D_A + p_B D_B - C$. The entrepreneur endeavors to maximize his profit by producing the appropriate amounts of the commodities and charging the prices that will give largest profits.

The necessary conditions for a maximum of profit is $\partial \pi / \partial D_A = 0$ and $\partial \pi / \partial D_B = 0$. The sufficient conditions for a maximum of profits can also be given.

EXAMPLE

Let the demand curves for two commodities be $p_A = 1 - D_A$ and $p_B = 1 - D_B$. The total cost curve for the joint production is $C = D_A D_B$. The profit function is $\pi = D_A - D_A^2 + D_B - D_B^2 - D_A D_B$. The necessary conditions for maximum profits are

$$\frac{\partial \pi}{\partial D_A} = 1 - 2D_A - D_B = 0 \quad \text{and} \quad \frac{\partial \pi}{\partial D_B} = 1 - D_A - 2D_B = 0.$$

The solution of these two equations is $D_A = \frac{1}{3}$, $D_B = \frac{1}{3}$. Consequently, the prices are $p_A = \frac{2}{3}$ and $p_B = \frac{2}{3}$, and the total cost is $C = \frac{1}{9}$. The total profit is $\pi = \frac{1}{3}$.

The sufficient conditions for maximum profits involve the

second derivatives; thus

$$\frac{\partial^2 \pi}{\partial D_A{}^2} = -2, \qquad \frac{\partial^2 \pi}{\partial D_B{}^2} = -2, \qquad \frac{\partial^2 \pi}{\partial D_A \, \partial D_B} = -1.$$

Since

$$\begin{vmatrix} -2 & -1 \\ -1 & -2 \end{vmatrix} = (-2)(-2) - (-1)(-1) = 3 > 0,$$

we have a maximum or minimum.

However, since

$$\frac{\partial^2 \pi}{\partial D_A{}^2} = -2 \quad \text{and} \quad \frac{\partial^2 \pi}{\partial D_B{}^2} = -2$$

are both negative, the values $D_A = \frac{1}{3}$ and $D_B = \frac{1}{3}$ give maximum profits.

EXERCISES 85

1   The demand curves for two commodities are $p_A = 28 - 3D_A$ and $p_B = 22 - 2D_B$. The joint cost function is $C = D_A{}^2 + 3D_B{}^2 + 4D_A D_B$. (a) Find the necessary and sufficient conditions for maximum profits. (b) Determine the prices, total cost, and profit.

2   The demand curves for two commodities are $p_A = 35 - 4D$ and $p_B = 26 - D_B$. The joint cost function is $C = D_A{}^2 + D_B{}^2 + 3D_A D_B$. (a) Find the necessary and sufficient conditions for maximum profit. (b) Determine the prices, total cost, and profit.

3   The demand curves for two commodities are $p_A = 7$ and $p_B = 20$. The joint cost function is $C = D_A{}^2 + 3D_B{}^2 + D_A D_B$. (a) Find the necessary and sufficient conditions for maximum profits. (b) Find the prices, total cost, and profits.

4   The demand functions of two commodities are $p_A = 80 - 8D_A$ and $p_B = 100 - 2D_B$. The joint cost function is $C = 20D_A + 2D_B + 2D_A{}^2 + 2D_B{}^2 - 2D_A D_B$. (a) Find the necessary and sufficient conditions for maximum profit. (b) Determine the prices, total cost, and profits.

5   The demand curves for three commodities are $p_A = 10 - 3D_A$, $p_B = 20 - 5D_B$, and $p_C = 60 - 7D_C$. The joint cost function is $C = 10 + 5D_A + 2D_B + 6D_C$. (a) Find the necessary conditions for maximum profits. (b) Determine the prices, total cost, and profit.

6   The demand functions for three commodities are $p_A = 21 - 5D_A$, $p_B = 77 - 10D_B$, and $p_C = 30 - 2D_C$. The joint cost function is $C = 2D_A D_B + D_A D_C + 3D_B D_C$. (a) Find the necessary conditions for maximum profit. (b) Determine the prices, total cost, and profit.

7   The demand functions for four commodities are $p_A = 220 - 10D_A$, $p_B = 90 - 5D_B$, $p_C = 60 - 6D_C$, and $p_D = 30 - 2D_D$. The joint cost function is $C = 5D_A + 9D_B + 5D_C + D_D + 2D_AD_B + D_AD_C + D_AD_D + 3D_BD_C + 2D_CD_D$. (a) Find the necessary conditions for maximum profits. (b) Find the prices, total cost, and profit.

8   The demand curves for two commodities are $p_A = 5 - D_A$ and $p_B = 5 - D_B$. The joint cost function is $C = \log_e D_AD_B$. (a) Find the necessary and sufficient conditions for maximum profits. (b) What are the prices, total cost, and profits?

9   The demand curves for two commodities are $p_A = a - bD_A$ and $p_B = c - dD_B$. The joint cost function is $C = mD_A{}^2 + nD_B{}^2 + qD_AD_B$, where a, b, c, d, m, n, and q are constants. (a) Find the necessary and sufficient conditions for maximum profits. (b) What are the prices?

86   CONSTRAINED MAXIMA AND MINIMA

In mathematical economics we meet problems frequently in which certain functions have to be maximized and minimized under side conditions. For instance, in utility theory, utility has to be maximized, but the maximization is subject to the budget equation. In production theory, the profit of the firm has to be maximized, while the existence of a production function has be be taken into account, and so on.

Such problems are called *problems of constrained maxima and minima*, or *maxima and minima subject to side conditions*. The exact theory of these maxima and minima is beyond the scope of this book. We will state only without proof a method by means of which one can derive the necessary conditions for the existence of constrained maxima and minima.

We will state the conditions for problems in two variables. The results can be extended easily to any number of variables. Assume that we have a function of two variables,

$$z = f(x, y).$$

This function $f(x, y)$ has to be maximized or minimized under the condition

$$g(x, y) = 0.$$

We form a new function

$$F(x, y) = f(x, y) + \lambda g(x, y),$$

where λ is a scalar, the so-called *Lagrange multiplier*.

The necessary conditions for a maximum or minimum involve the partial derivatives of the function $F(x, y)$:

$$F_x(x, y) = f_x(x, y) + \lambda g_x(x, y) = 0,$$
$$F_y(x, y) = f_y(x, y) + \lambda g_y(x, y) = 0.$$

These two equations, together with the conditional equation $g(x, y) = 0$, permit us to determine in general all points (x, y) that could constitute a maximum or minimum of z.

EXAMPLE

Assume that the function

$$z = f(x, y) = 10 + x + 3y - \tfrac{1}{2}x^2 - y^2$$

has to be maximized or minimized, under the condition that

$$g(x, y) = 2x + 3y - 13 = 0.$$

First we construct the function

$$F(x, y) = f(x, y) + \lambda g(x, y)$$
$$= 10 + x + 3y - \tfrac{1}{2}x^2 - y^2 + \lambda(2x + 3y - 13),$$

where λ is an undetermined constant (Lagrange multiplier). We find the partial derivatives of $F(x, y)$ as follows:

$$F_x(x, y) = 1 - x + 2\lambda,$$
$$F_y(x, y) = 3 - 2y + 3\lambda.$$

Putting the partial derivatives equal to 0 and using the conditional equation $g(x, y) = 0$, we get three linear equations in three unknowns; thus

$$-x + 2\lambda = -1,$$
$$-2y + 3\lambda = -3,$$
$$2x + 3y = 13.$$

The solution of this system of equations is $x = {}^{43}\!/_{17}$, $y = {}^{45}\!/_{17}$, $\lambda = {}^{13}\!/_{17}$. Hence the values $x = {}^{43}\!/_{17}$ and $y = {}^{45}\!/_{17}$ give a maximum or minimum.

EXERCISES 86

1   Find the maximum of $u = xy$ under the condition that $x + 3y = 5$. What is the maximum value of u?

2   Find the minimum of $u = 2x^2 + 3y^2$ under the condition that $5x + 6y = 10$. Compare it with the unconstrained minimum.

3   Find the minimum of $u = x^2 + 3y^2 + 5z^2$ under the condition that $2x + 3y + 5z = 100$. What is the value of the constrained minimum of u?

4   Find the maximum of $u = 10x + 20y - x^2 - y^2$ under the condition $2x + 5y = 10$. Compare it with the unrestricted maximum.

5   Find the minimum of $u = 3x + 6y$ under the condition that $x^2 + 5y^2 = 25$. What is the value of the constrained maximum?

6 Find the maximum of $u = e^{xy}$ under the conditions that $2x + 5y = 1$. What is the value of the constrained maximum?

7 Find the maximum of $u = xyz$ under the condition that $2x - 3y + z = 10$. What is the value of the constrained maximum?

8 Find the maximum of $u = \log_e xy$ under the condition that $2x + 3y = 5$. What is the value of the constrained maximum?

9 Let $u = ax^2 + bxy + cy^2$. Find the maximum or minimum of u if $mx + ny = k$, where a, b, c, m, n, and k are constants. What is the value of the constrained maximum or minimum?

10 Find the maximum of $u = kxy$ if $mx + ny = r$, where k, m, n, and r are constants. What is the value of the constrained maximum?

**11 Consider the maximum of $z = f(x, y)$ under the condition that $g(x, y) = 0$. Eliminate the Lagrange multiplier λ and show that $f_x/f_y = g_x/g_y$. Show by implicit differentiation (Section 80) that the expressions on both sides of this equation are equal to the slope of the tangent $-dy/dx$.

**12 Show that the result of problem 11 holds for the situation described in Example 1.

87 UTILITY THEORY

Let us consider for the sake of simplicity the case in which an individual spends all his money on just two commodities, X and Y.

There is a function $U = f(x, y)$, which (in a sense) indicates the satisfaction derived by the individual from varying combinations of the amounts of the commodities X and Y. The amounts of these commodities are x and y. We will see later that U need not be measurable (problem 13, Exercises 87).

Assume that the prices of X and Y are p_x and p_y. They are established on the market independent of any actions of the individuals in question. Assume that the individual's income I is also given. Then we have the so-called *budget equation*

$$p_x x + p_y y = I,$$

where p_x, p_y, and I are given constants.

The individual will try to maximize U by choosing appropriate amounts of X and Y while taking the condition represented by the budget equation into account.

This is a problem in restricted maxima. We form the new function

$$F(x, y) = f(x, y) + \lambda(p_x x + p_y y - I).$$

The partial derivatives of F are equated to 0; that is,

$$F_x(x, y) = 0,$$
$$F_y(x, y) = 0.$$

The budget equation should, in general, give enough equations to determine x, y, and λ. Then x and y are the quantities of the commodities X and Y demanded by the individual under the conditions stated above.

EXAMPLE

Let us consider the following equation:

$$U = 4x + 17y - x^2 - xy - 3y^2.$$

Let $p_x = 1$, $p_y = 2$, and $I = 7$. The budget equation is $x + 2y = 7$; U has to be maximized under this condition. We form the function $F(x, y) = 4x + 17y - x^2 - xy - 3y^2 + \lambda(x + 2y - 7)$. λ is a Lagrange multiplier. After differentiating $F(x, y)$ partially and equating both partial derivatives to 0, we have

$$\frac{\partial F}{\partial x} = 4 - 2x - y + \lambda = 0,$$

$$\frac{\partial F}{\partial y} = 17 - x - 6y + 2\lambda = 0.$$

Combining these two equations with the budget equation $x + 2y = 7$ provides $x = 1$ and $y = 3$ for the demand for X and Y.

EXERCISES 87

1   Let the utility index be $U = xy$. Assume that $p_x = 1$, $p_y = 2$, and $I = 10$. Find the demand for X and Y.

2   Assume the utility index to be $U = 58x + 76y - 5x^2 - 2xy + 10y^2$. Let $p_x = 1$, $p_y = 3$, and $I = 14$. Find the demand for X and Y.

3   A utility function for food (x) and nonfood (y) has been derived for American data for 1935–1941 (Nordin). The utility function is $U = -0.000890x^2 + 0.008353y^2 + 0.022401xy + 104.572144x + 96.686771y$. Derive from this the demand for food and for nonfood if we have $p_x = 1$, $p_y = 1.1$, $I = 2500$.

4   A utility index is $U = e^{xy}$. Let $p_x = 1$, $p_y = 5$, and $I = 10$. Find the demand for X and Y.

5   A utility index is $U = x^2 y^3$. Assume $p_x = 1$, $p_y = 4$, and $I = 10$. Find the demand for X and Y.

6   Assume that $U = xy$. Let $p_x = p$ (a constant), $p_y = 2$, and $I = 10$. (a) Find the demand for X and Y. (b) Find the elasticity of demand for X, that is, $Ex/Ep = (dx/dp)(p/x)$. (c) Find the elasticity for $x = 5$.

7   Assume $U = xy$. Let $p_x = 1$, $p_y = q$ (a constant), and $I = 10$. (a) Find the demand for X and Y. (b) Determine the elasticity of the demand for Y, that is, $Ey/Eq = (dy/dq)(q/y)$. (c) Find the elasticity for $y = 10$.

8 Assume $U = xy$. Let $p_x = p$ (a constant), $p_y = q$ (a constant), and $I = 10$. (a) Find the demand for X and Y. (b) Determine the partial elasticities of demand $Ex/Ep = (\partial x/\partial p)(p/x)$, $Ex/Eq = (\partial x/\partial q)(q/x)$, $Ey/Ep = (\partial y/\partial p)(p/y)$, $Ey/Eq = (\partial y/\partial q)(q/y)$. (c) Evaluate the partial elasticities for $x = 5$, $y = 10$.

9 Assume that $U = xy$. Let $p_x = 1$, $p_y = 2$, and $I = J$ (a constant). (a) Find the demand for X and Y. (b) Find the income elasticities of demand $Ex/EJ = (dx/dJ)(J/x)$ and $Ey/EJ = (dy/dJ)(J/Y)$. (c) Evaluate the income elasticities for $J = 10$.

**10 An indifference curve is derived by letting $U = $ constant. Take the utility index of problem 1 and draw indifference curves for $U = 12$, 12.5, 13. Plot the budget equation and show that the point of maximum utility is determined at the point of tangency of the budget equation with an indifference curve.

**11 Marginal utility of X is $\partial U/\partial x$; marginal utility of Y is $\partial U/\partial y$. Show with the help of the data in problem 1 that $(\partial U/\partial x)/p_x = (\partial U/\partial y)/p_y$, if utility is maximized. These are the weighted marginal utilities. They represent the marginal utility of \$1 worth of each commodity.

12 The marginal rate of substitution of X for Y is the amount of X that is necessary to compensate the individual for the loss of a small unit of Y. It is defined as $R = (\partial U/\partial x)/(\partial U/\partial y)$. (a) Show by the elimination of λ from the necessary conditions for maximum utility that we have always $R = p_x/p_y$. (b) Verify for the utility index in problem 1.

**13 Utility theory assumes only the ordering and not the measurability of utility. Show that the new utility indexes $V = U^2$, $W = U^5$, and $Z = \log_e U$ give the same result for the demand for X and Y as the utility index in problem 1 under the same conditions for prices and incomes.

**14 Assume a utility index $V = g(U)$, where $U = f(x, y)$. Show with the help of the theorem for the differentiation of a function of a function that maximization of U and V leads to the same results for the demand for X and Y.

**15 It is important to note that $-\lambda$ is the marginal utility of money. Prove this by using the results of problem 11 and remember that the price of money is 1.

**16 Take an indifference curve defined by $U(x, y) = c$, where c is constant. (a) Find the slope of the indifference curve by partial differentiation. (b) Verify analytically the result of the graphical analysis in problem 10. (HINT: Use the method indicated in Section 80.)

88 PRODUCTION UNDER FREE COMPETITION

Under free competition the individual firm cannot exert an influence upon the price of the product or upon the prices of the factors of production. They are determined independently of the actions of the firm on the markets. On each market there are so many firms that the action of any single one can be neglected.

Consider, for example, a firm that produces a product X and uses two factors, A and B, in the process of production. The production function is

$$x = f(a, b).$$

Here x is the amount of the product and a and b the amounts of the factors. Denote by p_x the price of the product X and by p_a and p_b the prices of the two factors of production. The profit of the firm is

$$\pi = xp_x - ap_a - bp_b.$$

It should be noted that $xp_x = R$, the total revenue, and that $ap_a + bp_b = C$, total cost.

The profit has to be maximized subject to the existence of the production function. We form the function

$$F(x, a, b) = xp_x - ap_a - bp_b + \lambda[x - f(a, b)],$$

where λ is a Lagrange multiplier.

The following equations are, in general, enough for the solution of the problem

$$F_x(x, a, b) = p_x + \lambda = 0,$$
$$F_a(x, a, b) = -p_a - \lambda f_a = 0,$$
$$F_b(x, a, b) = -p_b - \lambda f_b = 0,$$
$$x = f(a, b).$$

An alternative method without the use of the Lagrange multiplier λ is as follows: Substitute $x = f(a, b)$ into the expression for π. Then we have

$$\pi = p_x f(a, b) - ap_a - bp_b.$$

The necessary conditions for maximum profit are

$$\pi_a = p_x f_a(a, b) - p_a = 0,$$
$$\pi_b = p_x f_b(a, b) - p_b = 0.$$

EXAMPLE

Assume a production function of the form

$$x = f(a, b) = 10 - a^{-1} - b^{-1}.$$

The prices are $p_x = 9$, $p_a = 1$, $p_b = 4$. The profit function is $\pi = 9x - a - 4b$. This function has to be maximized under the condition that the relation among x, a, and b described by the production function holds.

We introduce the new function

$$F(x, a, b) = 9x - a - 4b + \lambda(x - 10 + a^{-1} + b^{-1}),$$

where the constant λ is a Lagrange multiplier. To deduce the necessary conditions for a maximum of profits, we find the partial derivatives and put them equal to 0:

$$F_x(x, a, b) = 9 + \lambda = 0,$$
$$F_a(x, a, b) = -1 - \lambda a^{-2} = 0,$$
$$F_b(x, a, b) = -4 - \lambda b^{-2} = 0.$$

We deduce from the first equation that $\lambda = -9$. We substitute this value into the two remaining equations and obtain

$$-1 + 9a^{-2} = 0,$$
$$-4 + 9b^{-2} = 0.$$

Hence, we have for the amounts of the factors, $a = 3$ and $b = \frac{3}{2}$. From the production function we get the amount of the product, $x = 9$. Finally, the profit equation gives $\pi = 72$.

As an alternate procedure, we can substitute the equation for x from the production function into the profit equation. This gives

$$\pi = 90 - 9a^{-1} - 9b^{-1} - a - 4b.$$

We have now to find the unrestricted maximum of the function with respect to a and b. We form the partial derivatives and put them equal to 0 in order to find the necessary conditions for a maximum, thus

$$\pi_a = 9a^{-2} - 1 = 0,$$
$$\pi_b = 9b^{-2} - 4 = 0.$$

These are exactly the same equations as before, and we get the same solutions for x, a, b, and π.

EXERCISES 88

1 The production function of a firm is $x = f(a, b) = 5 - a^{-\frac{1}{2}} - b^{-\frac{1}{2}}$. The prices are $p_x = 2$, $p_a = 1$, $p_b = 8$. Find the amounts of the factors demanded, the amounts of the product produced, and the amount of profits made by the firm.

2 The production function for a firm is $x = f(a, b) = 10 - a^{-2} - b^{-2}$. The prices are $p_x = 4$, $p_a = 27$, $p_b = 1$. Find the amounts of the factors demanded, the amount of the product supplied, and the profit made by the firm.

3   The production function of a firm is

$$x = \frac{12ab - a - b}{ab}.$$

The prices are $p_x = 9$, $p_a = 1$, $p_b = 4$. Find the amounts of the factor demanded, the amount of the product supplied, and the amount of profit made by the firm.

*4   Given the production function $x = f(a, b)$, the profit function becomes $\pi = p_x f(a, b) - p_a a - p_b b$. Find the sufficient conditions for a maximum of profit (see Section 84).

5   Show that the sufficient conditions for profit maximization are fulfilled for the production function given in the example above and for the functions in problems 1 to 3.

6   Assume a production function for a commodity in the form $x = f(a, b)$. Maximize profits. Show that in equilibrium the marginal productivities are $f_a(a, b) = p_a/p_x$, $f_b(a, b) = p_b/p_x$, and also that

$$\frac{f_a(a, b)}{f_b(a, b)} = \frac{p_a}{p_b};$$

that is, the ratio of the marginal productivities, when in equilibrium, is equal to the price ratio. (HINT: Eliminate the Lagrange multiplier λ.) Apply to the data in problem 1.

7   An implicit function of the variables x, a, and b, denoted by $g(x, a, b) = 0$, is called a transformation function. Derive the equilibrium conditions of production under the assumption that profit is being maximized while the transformation function $g(x, a, b) = 0$ is satisfied.

8   The production function of a firm is $x = f(a, b, c) = 20 - a^{-1} - b^{-1} - c^{-1}$. The prices are $p_x = 4$, $p_a = 1$, $p_b = 9$, and $p_c = 16$. Find the amounts of the factors demanded, the amount of the product produced, and the total profit made by the firm.

9   The production function of a firm is $x = f(a, b) = 20 - a^{-1} - b^{-2}$. The prices are $p_x = 5$, $p_a = 20$, and $p_b = 40$. (a) Find the necessary and sufficient conditions for a maximum of profits. (b) Determine the amounts of the factors demanded, the amount of the product produced, and the amount of profit made by the firm.

**10   Use the results of problem 6 to give a geometric interpretation for the first-order conditions of profit maximization. (HINT: Consider da/db for fixed x, the constant product curve.)

*11   Let a Cobb-Douglas production function be given by $x = aL^b K^c$, where a, b, and c are positive constants. Further, denote by p_x, p_L, and p_K the (constant) prices of the product, labor (wages), and capital. (a) Show that the necessary conditions of a maximum of profits $P = p_x x -$

$p_L{}^L - p_K{}^K$ imply $bx/L = p_L/p_x$; $cx/K = p_K/px$. (b) Show that the necessary and sufficient conditions of a maximum of profits imply $0 < b < 1$; $0 < c < 1$; $b + c < 1$.

12 A production function for the manufacturing industry in the United States for the period 1899–1922 has been estimated by Douglas as $x = 1.35L^{0.63}K^{0.30}$. Proceed as in problem 11.

13 A production function for New South Wales for 1901–1927 has been estimated by Douglas as follows: $x = 1.14L^{0.78}K^{0.20}$. Proceed as in problem 11.

14 Niitamo has estimated a production function for Finnish industry for 1925–1952 as follows: $x = 1.011L^{0.779}K^{0.221}w^{0.130}h^{0.545}$, where w is the index of exports and h the ratio of graduating secondary students to working population. (a) Show that the conditions of maximization of profits cannot be fulfilled. (b) Is this production function homogeneous in L and K, and of which degree is it?

Chapter 19

Elements of Integration, Differential Equations, Calculus of Variations

89 ANTIDERIVATIVES

Suppose we have a function $f(x)$ defined on some interval, finite or infinite, of the real line. We can then ask, is f the derivative of any function F? If so, what function, and is there more than one?

The fact is that if f is continuous on any closed subinterval of the domain of f, f is the derivative of some function $F(x)$ on that closed subinterval. Further, many functions that are not continuous will be the derivative of some function F.

In general, if $F(x)$ is differentiable and $F'(x) = f(x)$, we say that $F(x)$ is an antiderivative of f. We say "an" antiderivative of f because if c is any real number, $F(x) + c$ also has $f(x)$ as derivative, so that if f has one antiderivative, it has infinitely many.

Thus, finding an antiderivative of a function is in a sense the reverse of differentiation, and finding antiderivatives is done mostly by applying the rules of differentiation in reverse. The ultimate check as to whether $F(x)$ is an antiderivative of $f(x)$ is to determine that $F'(x) = f(x)$.

EXAMPLE 1

Find the antiderivatives of $f(x) = x^3$. The question is, what functions have x^3 as derivative? Remembering that we differentiate x^n by reducing the exponent to $n - 1$ and multiplying by n, we reverse the process, adding 1 to the exponent and dividing by the new exponent:

$$\frac{x^{3+1}}{3 + 1} = \frac{x^4}{4}.$$

Finally, we want *all* antiderivatives of x^3: they are all functions of the form $x^4/4 + c$.

CHECK: If $F(x) = x^4/4 + c$, $F'(x) = x^3 = f(x)$.
We may infer that the antiderivative of any function ax^p is

$$\frac{a}{p+1} x^{p+1} + c, \qquad p \neq 0,$$

since if

$$F(x) = \frac{a}{p+1} x^{p+1} + c, \qquad F'(x) = ax^p.$$

Recalling also that the derivative of a sum is the sum of the derivatives, we can find the antiderivative of a sum by finding an antiderivative of each term in the sum, adding, and supplying the arbitrary constant c of antidifferentiation.

It is also standard notation to write $F(x) + c = \int f(x)dx$ if $F'(x) = f(x)$.

EXAMPLE 2

Find $\int 2xdx$. We want to find all functions having $2x = f(x)$ as derivative. The exponent p in this case is 1:

$$\int 2xdx = \frac{2x^{1+1}}{1+1} + c = x^2 + c.$$

CHECK: If $F(x) = x^2 + c$ for any real number c, $F'(x) = 2x = f(x)$.

EXAMPLE 3

Find $\int (3x^2 + 2x + 1)dx$.

$$\int (3x^2 + 2x + 1)dx = \int 3x^2dx + \int 2xdx + \int 1dx$$
$$= x^3 + x^2 + x^1 + c = x^3 + x^2 + x + c.$$

(It matters little that in actuality we have three different constants, one for each of the three antiderivatives. Since the constants are arbitrary, we may add them to obtain the single arbitrary constant c.)

CHECK: If $F(x) = x^3 + x^2 + x + c$ for any real number c, $F'(x) = 3x^2 + 2x + 1 = f(x)$.

We also recall that if $F(x) = ke^{ax}$, $F'(x) = ake^{ax}$, and that if $F(x) = \ln x$, $F'(x) = 1/x$. We can then apply these results to obtain some more antiderivatives.

EXAMPLE 4

Find

$$\int \left(2x^3 + \frac{1}{3x} + 2e^{3x} + 1\right) dx.$$

$$\int \left(2x^3 + \frac{1}{3x} + 2e^{3x} + 1\right) dx = \int 2x^3 dx + \int \frac{1}{3x} dx$$

$$+ \int 2e^{3x} dx + \int 1 dx = \frac{2}{4} x^4 + c_1 + \frac{1}{3} \ln x + c_2 + \frac{2}{3} e^{3x}$$

$$+ c_3 + x + c_4 = \frac{1}{2} x^4 + \frac{1}{3} \ln x + \frac{2}{3} e^{3x} + x + c,$$

where $c = c_1 + c_2 + c_3 + c_4$.

EXERCISES 89

Find the following antiderivatives. Check your results by differentiation.

1   $\int (1 - 2x + x^3) dx.$

2   $\int (x - 5x^2 + x^4) dx.$

3   $\int (10/x + e^x) dx.$

4   $\int 15 \sqrt{x} = \int 15 x^{\frac{1}{2}} dx.$

5   $\int 17/\sqrt[3]{x} \, dx.$

6   $\int 4/\sqrt[4]{x} \, dx.$

7   $\int (3e^{2x} + \sqrt[5]{x}) dx.$

8   $\int (3/x + 2e^{\frac{1}{2}x} + 1) dx.$

90   MARGINAL COST, TOTAL COST, AVERAGE COST

Since marginal cost $C' = dC/dD$, we have total cost $C = \int C' dD$ and average cost $A = C/D$. This follows from the definition of marginal cost as the derivative of total cost.

Integration introduces an arbitrary constant. But if, besides the marginal cost function, the value of the total cost at any arbitrary value is also given, we can determine the function completely.

EXAMPLE

The marginal cost curve for some product is $C' = 1 + 2D + 6D^2$.
(a) Find the total cost curve if $C(0) = 100$. By integration,

$$C = \int (1 + 2D + 6D^2) dD = D + D^2 + 2D^3 + c.$$

From the additional condition that $C(0) = 100$, $0 + 0^2 + 2(0^3) + c = 100$. Hence $c = 100$, and $C = 100 + D + D^2 + 2D^3$. (b) Find the average cost curve $A = C/D$. Obviously $A = C/D = 100/D + 1 + D + 2D^2$.

EXERCISES 90

1   The marginal cost function is $C' = 1 + 100D - 5D^2$. (a) Find C if $C(1) = 200$. (b) Find A.

2   $C' = 10/D + 5$. (a) Find C if $C(1) = 20$. (b) Find A. (c) Evaluate C, C', and A for $D = 10$.

3   $C' = 2 + 5e^D$. (a) Find C if $C(0) = 100$. (b) Find A. (c) Evaluate C, C', and A for $D = 60$.

4   $C' = 100 - 2D + 5D^2 + D^4$. (a) Find C if $C(0) = 100$. (b) Find A. (c) Evaluate C, C', and A for $D = 10$.

5   $C' = 100 \sqrt{D}$. (a) Find C if $C(9) = 20$. (b) Find A. (c) Evaluate C, C', and A for $D = 16$.

6   $C' = 10 \sqrt[3]{D}$. (a) Find C if $C(8) = 100$. (b) Find A. (c) Evaluate C, C', and A for $D = 27$.

7   $C' = 100/\sqrt{D}$. (a) Find C if $C(16) = 100$. (b) Find A. (c) Evaluate C, C', and A for $D = 100$.

8   The marginal cost curve of steel is $C' = 56$. Find the total cost curve and the average cost curve if $C(0) = 182$.

9   The marginal cost curve of hosiery is $C' = 6.75 - 0.0006D$. Find the total cost curve and the average cost curve if $C(0) = -10,485$.

10   The marginal cost curve of leather belts is $C' = 0.8$. Find the total cost curve and the average cost curve if $C(10) = 3,008$.

11   The marginal cost curve for sales in a department store is $C' = 1.052 - 0.004D$. Find the total cost curve and average cost curve if $C(0) = 16.8$.

91   THE INTEGRAL

Suppose we have a function f, whose domain includes some interval $[a, b]$, and let us suppose further that f is continuous on $[a, b]$ and that $f(x) \geq 0$ for all x in $[a, b]$. In Figure 38 let us consider the area A of the region R bounded by the graph of f, the x-axis, and the lines $x = a$ and $x = b$.

We could arrive at an underestimate of A in the following manner. Suppose we divide $[a, b]$ into n subintervals by choosing points $a = x_0 < x_1 < x_2 < \cdots < x_{n-1} < x_n = b$ (Figure 39). The ith subinterval $[x_{i-1}, x]$ will then have length $\Delta x_i = x_i - x_{i-1}$. Suppose, further, that we

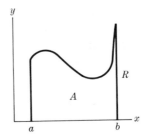

Figure 38

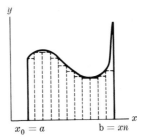

Figure 39

find a point u_i in $[x_{i-1}, x_i]$ that has the property that $f(u_i) \leq f(x)$ for all x in $[x_{i-1}, x_i]$, and consider the rectangle of length $f(u_i)$ and width $\Delta x_i = x_i - x_{i-1}$. It is clear that the region R contains each of these rectangles and that the sum of the areas of the individual rectangles is not greater than A. Since the area of a rectangle is length times width we have

$$\sum_{1=1}^{n} f(u_i)(x_i - x_{i-1}) = \sum_{1=1}^{n} f(u_i)\Delta x_i \leq A.$$

Suppose, further, that we divide $[a, b]$ into more and more subintervals; that is, let n become larger, and do so in such a way that the length of *each* subinterval $[x_{i-1}, x_i]$ becomes smaller as n becomes larger. It is clear that as this is done the sum $\Sigma_{i=1}^{n} f(u_i)\Delta x_i$ certainly does *not* differ more and more from A, and also that $\lim_{n \to \infty} f(u_i)\Delta x_i \leq A$.

Similarly, we can arrive at an overestimate of A by choosing our n subintervals $[x_{i-1}, x_i]$ of length $x_i - x_{i-1}$, and then choosing a point l_i in $[x_{i-1}, x_i]$ such that $f(l_i) \geq f(x)$ for all x in $[x_{i-1}, x_i]$ (Figure 40). We have then *circumscribed* a set of rectangles, the ith one of which has area $f(l_i)(x_i - x_{i-1})$, about the region R, so that $\Sigma_{1=1}^{n} f(l_i)(x_i - x_{i-1}) \geq A$ no matter how the subintervals are chosen. Finally, if we again let n become larger and require that the length of the longest subinterval approach 0 as n becomes larger, we can conclude that $\lim_{n \to \infty} \Sigma_{i=1}^{n} f(l_i)\Delta x_i \geq A$.

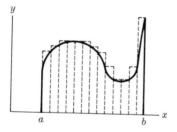

Figure 40

It is then possible to show that $\lim_{n\to\infty} \Sigma_{i=1}^n f(l_i)\Delta x_i = L$ for some number L, and that $\lim_{n\to\infty} \Sigma_{i=1}^n f(u_i)\Delta x_i = V$ for some number V, no matter how the subintervals $[x_{i-1}, x_i]$ are defined so long as $\Delta x_i \to 0$ as $n \to \infty$, and that $V = L$. But since $V \leq A \leq L$, this means that $A = L$, and this serves to motivate the definition of integral.

Let $f(x)$ be defined on a domain including the interval $[a, b]$, and suppose f is continuous on (a, b). Let $[a, b]$ be partitioned into n subinterval $[x_{i-1}, x_i]$ of length Δx_i, and let z_i be any point in $[x_{i-1}, x_i]$. If the length Δx_i of the subinterval $[x_{i-1}, x_i]$ goes to 0 as n becomes arbitrarily large, we define $\lim_{n\to\infty} \Sigma_{i=1}^n f(z_i)\Delta x_i$ to be the integral of f over $[a, b]$ and write $\lim_{n\to\infty} \Sigma_{i=1}^n f(z_i)\Delta x_i = \int_a^b f(x)dx$. This limit will always exist no matter how z_i is chosen or how the x_i are chosen so long as $\Delta x_i \to 0$ for all i as $n \to \infty$.

Note that nothing was said in the definition about requiring $f(x) > 0$ for all x in $[a, b]$. This was done only in the motivation, which was given in terms of area, and the definition of integral is meaningful whether f is nonnegative or not.

Also note that the definition stipulates that z_i can be any point whatsoever in $[x_{i-1}, x_i]$ and that the subintervals can be chosen in any manner whatsoever so long as $\Delta x_i \to 0$ for all i as $n \to \infty$. That being true, one might just as well choose $\Delta x_i = (b - a)/n$, that is, require all subintervals to be of equal length, and choose z_i to be either x_{i-1} or x_i in any computation involving the definition. In fact, if we do this, we have $x_1 = a + (b - a)/n$, $x_2 = a + 2[(b - a)/n]$, $x_3 = a + 3[(b - a)/n]$, and, in general, $x_i = a + i[(b - a)/n]$, so that the ith subinterval is $[a + (i - 1)((b - a)/n], a + i[(b - a)/n)]$. If we choose z_i to be the right endpoint of (x_{i-1}, x_i), we have

$$\lim_{n \to \infty} \sum_{i=1}^{n} f\left[a + i\left(\frac{b - a}{n}\right)\right]\frac{b - a}{n} = \int_a^b f(x)dx.$$

EXAMPLE 1

Calculate $\int_0^2 2x\,dx$. From trigonometry we know the area of this triangle is $\frac{1}{2}(2)(4) = 4$. (Since $f(x) = 2x \geq 0$ for $0 \leq x \leq 2$, an interpretation of $\int_0^2 2x\,dx$ as area is valid.) We can use this as a check on our result (see Figure 41).

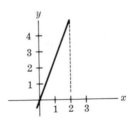

Figure 41

In this case, $(b - a)/n = (2 - 0)/n = 2/n$, the right endpoint of the ith subinterval is $0 + i(2/n) = 2i/n; f(2i/n) = 2(2i/n) = (4i/n)$, and the area of the ith rectangle is $(4i/n)(2/n) = 8i/n^2$. We need one more fact: $\Sigma_{i=1}^n i = n[(n + 1)/2]$: the sum of the first n positive integers is $n[(n + 1)/2]$. Using this, $\int_0^2 2x\,dx = \lim_{n\to\infty} \Sigma_{i=1}^n (8i/n)^2 = \lim_{n\to\infty} 1/n^2 \Sigma_{i=1}^n 8i = \lim_{n\to\infty} 8/n^2 \Sigma_{i=1}^n i = \lim_{n\to\infty} (8/n^2)n[(n + 1)/2] = \lim_{n\to\infty} (4n^2 + 4n)/n^2 = 4 \lim_{n\to\infty} (1 + 1/n) = 4.1 = 4$.

It is probably clear that evaluating $\int_a^b f(x)\,dx$ for an arbitrary continuous function f could present grave difficulties. Fortunately, we do not need to depend on the definition of integral. We recall that any function continuous on a closed interval has antiderivatives on that interval. The following result, known as the fundamental theorem of calculus, relates the antiderivative to the integral.

THEOREM. Let f be a continuous function on a closed interval $[a, b]$ and let $F(x)$ be any antiderivative of f on $[a, b]$. Then $\int_a^b f(x)\,dx = F(b) - F(a)$.

If we use the notation $F(x)|_a^b = F(b) - F(a)$, $\int_0^2 2x\,dx = x^2|_0^2 = 4$.

EXAMPLE 2

Find $\int_1^3 [2e^x + 1/x + 3x^2]\,dx$. $\int_1^3 [2e^x + 1/x + 3x^2]\,dx = 2e^x + \ln x + x^3|_1^3 = 2e^3 + \ln 3 + 3^3 - (2e^1 + \ln 1 + 1) = 2e^3 + \ln 3 + 26 - 2e$.

It follows from the fundamental theorem of calculus and the properties of antiderivatives that $\int_a^b [f(x) + g(x)]\,dx = \int_a^b f(x)\,dx + \int_a^b g(x)\,dx$ and that $\int_a^b cf(x)\,dx = c \int_a^b f(x)\,dx$. It is also possible to show that if $a < c < b$, $\int_a^b f(x)\,dx = \int_a^c f(x)\,dx + \int_c^b f(x)\,dx$.

EXERCISES 91

1   Suppose $f(x) \geqq g(x)$ for x in $[a, b]$. Show that the area between $y = f(x)$, $y = g(x)$, $x = a$, $x = b$ is given by $\int_a^b (f(x) - g(x))\,dx$ for f, g continuous.

2 Use the result of problem 1 to show that if $f(x) \leq 0$ and continuous for x in $[a, b]$, the area bounded by $x = a$, $x = b$, the x-axis, and $y = f(x)$ is given by $\int_a^b [-f(x)]dx$. HINT: What is the equation of the x-axis?

3 Find the area bounded by the x-axis, the lines $x = -2$ and $x = 2$, and the curve $y = x^3$. HINT: Graph, and use problem 2 and the properties of the integral.

4 Give an example to show that, in general, it is not true that $\int_a^b (f(x) \cdot g(x))dx = \int_a^b f(x)dx \int_a^b g(x)dx$.

5 Evaluate each of the following. If the integral given represents an area bounded by the function being integrated and the x-axis, describe the area. (a) $\int_1^5 x^2 dx$; (b) $\int_1^{16} 2x dx$; (c) $\int_0^3 (1 - 2x + x^2)dx$; (d) $\int_0^{27} 5 \sqrt[3]{x}dx$; (e) $\int_{-1}^3 (1 + 3x - x^3)dx$; (f) $\int_0^2 [e^x + 1/x + 1]dx$.

92 CONSUMERS' SURPLUS

A demand curve shows the amount people would buy at a given price. Let the market price be p_0. At this market price D_0 units are sold. Then everyone who would be willing to pay more than the market price gains from the fact that the price is only p_0. The gain is called *consumers' surplus* (Marshall). It represents the total money gain if the situation with a market price p_0 is compared with perfect discrimination. Under perfect discrimination a monopolist would extract from each customer for each unit of the commodity the maximum price he would be willing to pay for it.

If we make the assumption of constant marginal utility of money and also that all people have the same utility function, then the area measured by $\int_0^{D_0} pdD - p_0 D_0$ can be interpreted as *gain in utility*. It is the area under the demand curve minus the total revenue and is called the *consumers' surplus*. In Figure 42, it is the shaded region

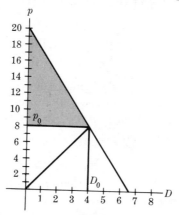

Figure 42

EXAMPLE 1

Assume, for instance, a demand function of the form

$$20 - 3D = p.$$

The quantity demanded is a function of the price

$$D = \frac{20}{3} - \frac{p}{3}.$$

It should be recalled from the definition of a collective demand function that this represents the amount people will buy on the market at various prices. From the graph it appears that the higher the price, the smaller the demand.

Let the supply function on this market be $p = 2D$. The quantity supplied is a function of the price $D = \frac{1}{2}p$. The market equilibrium is established at the point where demand equals supply; that is, where $20/3 - p/3 = \frac{1}{2}p$.

The solution of this equation is $p_0 = 8$, and from the demand or supply function, $D_0 = 4$. At a price of \$8, the demand is equal to the supply, and the quantity exchanged is 4 units.

But it appears from our graph that there are people who are willing to pay as much as \$20 for the commodity in question. All these and others who would have been willing to pay more than the market price $p_0 = \$8$ profit from the fact that they have only the market price to pay.

Their total monetary gain could have been extracted by a clever monopolist who might be able to practice perfect discrimination. It is represented by the shaded area in Figure 42.

This shaded area is the area under the demand curve from 0 to D_0 minus the product $p_0 D_0$, that is, the rectangle which represents the actual outlay of the consumers. We have

$$\int_0^{D_0} p\,dD - p_0 D_0 = \int_0^4 (20 - 3D)\,dD - (8)(4)$$

$$= \left[20D - \frac{3D^2}{2} \right]_0^4 - 32 = 56 - 32 = 24.$$

Hence the consumers' surplus in our case is \$24. This represents the monetary savings of the public because of the existence of a free market on which everybody, rich or poor, can buy at the prevailing market price.

EXAMPLE 2

Let $p = 1 - D$. Assume that $p_0 = \frac{1}{3}$; then $D_0 = \frac{2}{3}$. The consumers' surplus is

$$\int_0^{2/3} (1 - D)\,dD - \frac{2}{9} = \left[D - \frac{D^2}{2} \right]_0^{2/3} - \frac{2}{9} = \frac{2}{9}.$$

EXERCISES 92

1 Let the demand curve be $p = 10 - 2D$. Evaluate the consumers' surplus for (a) $p_0 = 1$; (b) $p_0 = 3$; (c) $p_0 = 5$; (d) $p = 0$ (free good). (e) Make a graph.

2 The demand function for a commodity is $p = 36 - D^2$. Find the consumers' surplus for (a) $p_0 = 11$; (b) $p_0 = 5$; (c) $p_0 = 6$; (d) $p_0 = 0$. (e) Make a graph.

3 The demand function for a commodity is $p = 100 - 2D - D^2$. Find the consumers' surplus for (a) $p_0 = 1$; (b) $p_0 = 5$; (c) $p_0 = 0$ (free good). (d) Illustrate by a graph.

4 The demand function of a commodity is $p = 81 - D^4$. Find the consumers' surplus for (a) $p = 0$ (free good); (b) $p_0 = 10$; (c) $p_0 = 36$. (d) Indicate them graphically.

5 The demand function of a commodity is $p = 100 - 5D - D^2$. Find the consumers' surplus for (a) $p_0 = 0$; (b) $p_0 = 11$; (c) $p_0 = 25$. (d) Illustrate with a graph.

6 Consider the demand curve for sugar in problem 9, Exercises 73. Find the consumers' surplus (a) under monopoly; (b) under free competition; (c) if sugar were a free good. (d) Compare the three situations graphically.

7 Consider the demand curve for steel in problem 10, Exercises 73. Find the consumers' surplus (a) under monopoly; (b) under free competition; (c) if steel were a free good. Compare the three situations graphically.

8 Consider the situation described in problem 1, Exercises 15. Evaluate the consumers' surplus before and after the imposition of various specific taxes and subsidies. Illustrate by a graph.

9 Use the data in problem 2, Exercises 15, to evaluate the consumers' surplus before and after the imposition of various taxes or subsidies. Illustrate by a graph.

10 Use the data in problem 3, Exercises 15, and evaluate the consumers' surplus before and after the imposition of the taxes and subsidies indicated. Show also by a graph the effects of taxes and subsidies on consumers' rent.

11 Use the data in problem 6, Exercises 15, to evaluate the consumers' surplus before and after the imposition of the indicated taxes or subsidies for sugar. Illustrate by a graph.

12 Use the data in problem 8, Exercises 15. Consider the effect on consumers' surplus of the tax or subsidy indicated for agricultural products. Illustrate by a graph.

13 (Tintner and Patel) Let P be the price of rice, Q the quantity of rice, and s the amount of fertilizer used in rice production. Using data for India for 1949–1964 (Tintner and Patel), we find for the per capita demand function for rice $P = 0.964 - 6.773Q$ and for the supply func-

tion $Q = 0.063 + 0.036s$. (a) Find the equilibrium on the rice market if $s = 0.5$. (b) Find the consumers' surplus.

**93   DIFFERENTIAL EQUATIONS

Consider the function $y = f(x) = x^2$. Taking derivatives, we have $dy/dx = f'(x) = 2x$. This is a differential equation:

$$\frac{dy}{dx} = 2x.$$

A solution to a differential equation is any function f that satisfies it. We solve the equation by finding the indefinite integral:

$$y = \int 2x\,dx = x^2 + c = f(x).$$

The constant c might be found if we know the value of the function at a given point x. Assume, for example, that $f(1) = 2$. Then we have

$$f(1) = 1^2 + c = 1 + c = 2,$$

and hence $c = 1$. Hence $f(x) = x^2 + 1$ is the solution of the differential equation $dy/dx = 2x$, with the initial condition

$$f(1) = 2.$$

Sometimes the variables can be separated. Then the differential equation might be written in the form

$$g(x)dx + \int h(y)dy = 0,$$

and the integral is given by

$$\int g(x)dx + \int h(y)dy = c,$$

where c is a constant, to be determined by initial conditions.

EXAMPLE 1

Consider the equation

$$\frac{dy}{dx} = \frac{x^2}{y}.$$

This might be written

$$ydy - x^2dx = 0.$$

Taking antiderivatives, we have

$$\int ydy - \int x^2dx = \frac{y^2}{2} - \frac{x^3}{3} = c,$$

where c is a constant, to be determined by initial conditions. Assume that we know that the solution passes through the point $x = 0$, $y = 1$. Then we have

$$\frac{1^2}{2} - \frac{0^3}{3} = \frac{1}{2} = c.$$

Hence the implicit solution of our differential equation which goes through the given point is

$$\frac{y^2}{2} - \frac{x^3}{3} = \frac{1}{2}.$$

EXAMPLE 2

Consider the differential equation

$$\frac{dy}{dx} = a + by.$$

We separate the variables:

$$\frac{dy}{a + by} - dx = 0.$$

In order to integrate the first term, we multiply by b:

$$\frac{bdy}{a + by} - bdx = 0.$$

It is easily seen that if $u = \log_e (a + by)$ we have $du/dy = b/(a + by)$ (function of a function rule of differentiation). Hence,

$$\log_e (a + by) - bx = c,$$

where c is an arbitrary constant, to be determined by the initial condition. This might be written

$$\log_e (a + by) = c + bx,$$

or,

$$a + by = de^{bx},$$

where $d = e^c$ is another constant. Hence,

$$y = Le^{bx} - \frac{a}{b},$$

where $L = d/b$ is again a constant. Assume, for example, that $y(0) = k$, k given. Then

$$y(0) = Le^{b(0)} - \frac{a}{b} = k.$$

Then it follows that the constant $L = k + (a/b)$ and the complete solution of the differential equation, which fulfills the initial condition that $y(0) = k$, appears as

$$y = 1 + \frac{a}{b} e^{bx} - \frac{a}{b}.$$

Now we consider a second-degree homogeneous differential equation with constant coefficients:

$$a_2 \left(\frac{d^2y}{dx^2} \right) + a_1 \left(\frac{dy}{dx} \right) + a_0 y = 0.$$

This equation is called a second-degree homogeneous differential equation because it involves d^2y/dx^2, has zero on its right side, and the coefficients a_0, a_1, a_2 are constants.

Assume the solution is in this form:

$$y = A e^{mx},$$

where A and m are constants. We have

$$\frac{dy}{dx} = A m e^{mx}, \qquad \frac{d^2y}{dx^2} = A m^2 e^{mx}.$$

Substituting these values into our differential equation, we have

$$a_2 A m^2 e^{mx} + a_1 A m e^{mx} + a_0 A e^{mx} = 0.$$

We factor out the common factor $A e^{mx}$ and derive the *characteristic equation:*

$$a_2 m^2 + a_1 m + a_0 = 0.$$

Here we must distinguish various possibilities. Assume first that there are two distinct real roots of the characteristic equation, m_1 and m_2. Then the solution appears as

$$y = A_1 e^{m_1 x} + A_2 e^{m_2 x},$$

where A_1 and A_2 are constants, to be determined by initial conditions.

EXAMPLE 3

Consider the differential equation

$$\frac{d^2y}{dx^2} - 3 \left(\frac{dy}{dx} \right) + 2y = 0.$$

The characteristic equation is

$$m^2 - 3m + 2 = (m - 1)(m - 2) = 0.$$

Hence the roots of the characteristic equation are $m_1 = 1$, $m_2 = 2$. The solution of our differential equation is

$$y = A_1 e^x + A_2 e^{2x},$$

where we determine the constants A_1 and A_2 from initial conditions. Assume, for example, that we know that $y(0) = 0$, $y(1) = 1$. We have

$$y(0) = A_1 e^0 + A_2 e^{2 \cdot 0} = A_1 + A_2 = 0,$$
$$y(1) = A_1 e + A_2 e^2 = 1.$$

Hence $A_1 = -1/(e^2 - e)$, $A_2 = 1/(e^2 - e)$.

Consider now the case in which the two roots of the characteristic equation coincide: $m_1 = m_2$. The solution is then

$$y = (A_1 + A_2 x)e^{m_1 x}.$$

EXAMPLE 4

Consider the second-order differential equation

$$\frac{d^2 y}{dx^2} - 6\left(\frac{dy}{dx}\right) + 9y = 0.$$

Here we have for the characteristic equation

$$m^2 - 6m + 9 = (m - 3)^2 = 0.$$

Hence the two roots coincide, $m_1 = m_2 = 3$. The solution is

$$y = (A_1 + A_2 x)e^{3x},$$

where we again determine the constants A_1 and A_2 from initial conditions. Assume, for example, that $y(0) = 0$, $y(1) = e^3$. We have

$$y(0) = (A_1 + A_2 \cdot 0)e^{3 \cdot 0} = A_1 = 0,$$
$$y(1) = (A_1 + A_2 \cdot 1)e^{3 \cdot 1} = (A_1 + A_2)e^3 = e^3.$$

Hence $A_1 = 0$, $A_2 = 1$, and the complete solution is

$$y = xe^{3x}.$$

Finally, consider the case in which the roots of the characteristic equation are conjugate complex:

$$m_1 = a + ib, \qquad m_2 = a - ib, \qquad i = \sqrt{-1},$$

where a and b are real numbers. The solution appears now as

$$y = e^{ax}\left(A_1 \cos \frac{360x}{b} + A_2 \sin \frac{360x}{b}\right).$$

EXAMPLE 5

Suppose our differential equation is

$$\frac{d^2y}{dx^2} - 2\left(\frac{dy}{dx}\right) + 5y = 0.$$

The *auxiliary equation* is now

$$m^2 - 2m + 5 = 0.$$

The roots are conjugate complex: $m_1 = 1 + 2i$, $m_2 = 1 - 2i$. Hence the solution is now

$$y = e^x\left(A_1 \cos\frac{360x}{2} + A_2 \sin\frac{360x}{2}\right)$$
$$= e^x(A_1 \cos 180x + A_2 \sin 180x).$$

The constants A_1 and A_2 are determined by the initial conditions. Assume, then, $y(0) = 1$, $y(\frac{1}{2}) = \sqrt{e}$. We have

$$y(0) = e^0(A_1 \cos 0 + A_2 \sin 0) = 1(A_1 \cdot 1 + A_2 \cdot 0) = A_1 = 1,$$
$$y(\tfrac{1}{2}) = e^{\frac{1}{2}}(A_1 \cos 90 + A_2 \sin 90) = \sqrt{e}\,(A_1 \cdot 0$$
$$+ A_2 \cdot 1) = \sqrt{e}\,A_2 = \sqrt{e}.$$

Hence $A_1 = 1$, $A_2 = 1$, and the complete solution is

$$y = e^x(\cos 180x + \sin 180x).$$

EXERCISES 93

1   Solve the following first-order differential equations, assuming that $y(0) = 1$ and that dy/dx is given by (a) x; (b) $2y$; (c) x/y; (d) y/x; (e) $2y + 1$.

2   Let y be national income and t time. Sengupta and Tintner derived the following differential equation for the trend of British national income for 1700–1940: $dy/dt = -0.003y + 0.00304$. Solve this differential equation, assuming $y(0) = 0$.

3   Solve the following second-order differential equations, assuming that $y(0) = 0$ and $y(1) = 1$. (a) $d^2y/dx^2 + 2(dy/dx) - 3y = 0$; (b) $d^2y/dx^2 - 8(dy/dx) + 16y = 0$; (c) $d^2y/dx^2 + 2dy/dx + y = 0$.

4   Solve the inhomogeneous first-order differential equation $a_1(dy/dx) + a_0 y = b$, where a_0, a_1, and b are constants. $y(0) = k$, a constant. HINT: Assume the solution as $y = Ae^{mx} + b$, determine first b in order to make the equation homogeneous, then solve the homogeneous equation.

**94   ELEMENTS OF THE CALCULUS OF VARIATIONS

Consider the following problem. Maximize (or minimize) the integral:

$$u = \int_{t_1}^{t_2} f(t, x, \dot{x})dt,$$

where we denote $\dot{x} = dx/dt$ and require that $x(t_1) = a$, $x(t_2) = b$, a and b given constants.

We consider now a variation in the function f, denoted by ∂f. We have evidently

$$\partial f = \left(\frac{\partial f}{\partial x}\right) \partial x + \left(\frac{\partial f}{\partial \dot{x}}\right) \partial \dot{x}$$

$$= \left(\frac{\partial f}{\partial x}\right) \partial x + \left(\frac{\partial f}{\partial \dot{x}}\right) \left(\frac{d \partial x}{dt}\right),$$

where ∂x and $\partial \dot{x}$ are variations of x and $\dot{x}$.

Then the variation of the integral is

$$\partial u = \int_{t_1}^{t_2} (\partial f) dt = \int_{t_1}^{t_2} \left(\frac{\partial f}{\partial x}\right) (\partial x) dt + \int_{t_1}^{t_2} \left(\frac{\partial f}{\partial \dot{x}}\right) \left(\frac{d \partial x}{dt}\right) dt.$$

Now consider

$$\frac{d}{dt} \left[\left(\frac{\partial f}{\partial \dot{x}}\right) \partial x \right] - \int \frac{d}{dt} \left[\left(\frac{\partial f}{\partial \dot{x}}\right) (\partial x) dt \right] = \frac{d}{dt} \left[\left(\frac{\partial f}{\partial \dot{x}}\right) (\partial x) \right]$$

$$- \frac{d}{dt} \left[\left(\frac{\partial f}{\partial \dot{x}}\right) (\partial x) \right] = \frac{d}{dt} \left[\left(\frac{\partial f}{\partial \dot{x}}\right) (\partial x) \right] + \left(\frac{\partial f}{\partial \dot{x}}\right) \left(\frac{d \partial x}{dt}\right) - \frac{d}{dt}$$

$$\left(\frac{\partial f}{\partial \dot{x}}\right) (\partial x) = \left(\frac{\partial f}{\partial \dot{x}}\right) \frac{d(\partial x)}{dt},$$

where we have used the fact that the derivative of the indefinite integral is the expression under the integral sign as well as the rule of finding the derivative of a product. Hence we have, apart from a constant of integration,

$$\int \left[\left(\frac{\partial f}{\partial \dot{x}}\right) \left(\frac{d \partial x}{dt}\right) \right] dt = \left[\left(\frac{\partial f}{\partial \dot{x}}\right) (\partial x) \right] - \int \frac{d}{dt} \left[\left(\frac{\partial f}{\partial \dot{x}}\right) (\partial x) \right] dt,$$

and going from the indefinite to the definite integral, we have

$$\int_{t_1}^{t_2} \left[\left(\frac{\partial f}{\partial \dot{x}}\right) \left(\frac{d \partial x}{dt}\right) \right] dt = \left[\left(\frac{\partial f}{\partial \dot{x}}\right) (\partial x) \right]_{t_1}^{t_2} - \int_{t_1}^{t_2} \left[\frac{d}{dt} \left(\frac{\partial f}{\partial \dot{x}}\right) (\partial x) \right] dt.$$

Hence the variation of the integral can be written

$$\partial u = \left[\left(\frac{\partial f}{\partial \dot{x}}\right) (\partial x) \right]_{t_1}^{t_2} + \int_{t_1}^{t_2} \left[\left(\frac{\partial f}{\partial x}\right) - \frac{d}{dt} (\partial f \partial \dot{x}) \right] (\partial x) dt.$$

We note that since $x(t_1) = a$ and $x(t_2) = b$ are given the first term on the right is zero. Apart from this condition ∂x is arbitrary. Hence for the expression under the integral to be zero, we derive the Euler equation:

$$\frac{\partial f}{\partial x} = \frac{d}{dt} \left(\frac{\partial f}{\partial \dot{x}}\right),$$

which is the necessary condition for a minimum or maximum of our integral. Note that in general this will be a second-order differential equation.

EXAMPLE 1

Suppose we want to minimize the integral

$$u = \int_0^1 f(t, x, \dot{x})dt = \int_0^1 \frac{1}{2}(x^2 + \dot{x}^2)dt$$

with the conditions $x(0) = (1/e) + e$, $x(1) = 2$. We have

$$f = \frac{1}{2}(x^2 + \dot{x}^2) \qquad \frac{\partial f}{\partial x} = x, \qquad \frac{\partial f}{\partial \dot{x}} = \dot{x}.$$

Hence,

$$\frac{d\dot{x}}{dt} = \frac{d^2x}{dt^2} = x.$$

Assuming the solution in the form $x = Ae^{mt}$, we have

$$\frac{dx}{dt} = Ame^{mt}, \qquad \frac{d^2x}{dt^2} = Am^2e^{mt}.$$

Hence,

$$Am^2e^{mt} = Ae^{mt}.$$

Cancelling Ae^{mt} on both sides, we have the characteristic equation

$$m^2 = 1,$$

with the two roots $m_1 = 1$, $m_2 = -1$. Our solution is

$$x = A_1e^t + A_2e^{-t}.$$

In order to determine the constants of integration A_1 and A_2, we use the initial conditions

$$x(0) = A_1e^0 + A_2e^{-0} = A_1 + A_2 = \frac{1}{e} + e,$$

$$x(1) = A_1e^1 + A_2e^{-1} = A_1e + \frac{A_2}{e} = 2.$$

The solutions are $A_1 = 1/e$, $A_2 = e$, and the function that minimizes our integral is

$$x(t) = \frac{x \cdot e^t}{e} + e \cdot e^{-t} = e^{t-1} + e^{1-t}.$$

EXERCISES 94

1. Minimize the integral $\int_0^1 (x + 2\dot{x})^2 dt$ if $x(0) = (1/\sqrt{e}) + \sqrt{e}$ $x(1) = 2$.

2. Maximize the integral $\int_0^1 (\frac{1}{2}\dot{x}^2 + 5x) dt$ if $x(0) = 10$ and $x(1) = 13\frac{1}{2}$.

3. *Dynamic monopoly.* Assume a monopolist has a linear demand function, $x = a + b\hat{p}$, where x is quantity and $\hat{p}$ is expected price. Assume that further expected price $\hat{p}$ is a linear function of prevailing price p and the time derivative of price, $\dot{p}$: $\hat{p} = c + dp + g\dot{p}$. Assume further that the monopolist's total cost curve is cubic: $C = A + Bx + Dx^2 + Ex^3$. Let him maximize the profit over time: $u = \int_{t_0}^{t_i} (px - C) dt$. Use the methods of the calculus of variations to find the price that gives maximum profit.

4. *Ramsey theory of capital.* Assume a utility function $U(C)$ where C is consumption. Denoting K as capital, and by $g(K)$ a production function, we have $C = g(K) - \dot{K}$, where $\dot{K} = dK/dt$ is capital formation or investment. If we maximize

$$u = \int_0^\infty U(C) dt = \int_0^\infty U[g(K) - \dot{K}] dt$$

show (a) that the Euler equation yields $-d[(dU/dC)]/dt = (dU/dC)(dg/dK)$, or $-d/dt[\log (dU/dC)] = dg/dK$. (b) Assume $U = \log C$, $g(K) = aK$ (a constant), and find optimal capital formation.

PART THREE
PROBABILITY AND STATISTICS

Chapter 20
Probability

Suppose we consider an experiment E which we require to have several attributes. First, we require that E be capable of indefinite repetition, that it can be repeated endlessly under identical conditions. Second, suppose that it is not possible to predict the outcome of E in any single run or trial but that we can determine the set of possible outcomes of E. Finally, suppose that it is possible to observe n repetitions of the experiment and to make assertions about the occurrences of each of the possible outcomes of E. In such a case we say that E is a random experiment.

Such a hazy description of what we have in mind calls for examples. Thus, the tossing of a coin is a random experiment, as is the selection of 4 cards from a well-shuffled deck of 52 or the choice of a car based on the roll of a die.

The set of all possible outcomes of E is called the sample space of E. Thus, the sample space S for the toss of a coin consists of the two outcomes "head and tail," or $S = \{h, t\}$. If E is the roll of a die, $S = \{1, 2, 3, 4, 5, 6\}$. If E is the simultaneous roll of two dice and we are interested in the sum of the numbers appearing, $S = \{2, 3, 4, 5, \cdots, 10, 11, 12\}$.

An event for E is merely any subset of S. Thus, if $S = \{1, 2, 3, 4, 5, 6\}$, the sets $\{1, 3\}$, $\{2, 5, 6\}$, and $\{1, 3, 4, 5, 6\}$ are all events for E. An elementary event for E is an event with one member; thus, if $S = \{1, 2, 3, 4, 5, 6\}$, the events $A = \{1\}$, $B = \{3\}$, $C = \{4\}$ are all elementary events for E. $N = \{4, 5\}$, $E = \varphi$ are not elementary events for E.

Further, given two events A and B, we say A and B are mutually exclusive if $A \cap B = \varphi$, that is, if they have no elementary events in common.

EXAMPLE

Let $A = \{1, 3, 5\}$ and $B = \{2, 6\}$. Then A and B are mutually exclusive.

We say an event $A \subset S$ has *occurred* if the outcome of E is any member of A. Thus, on an intuitive level A and B are mutually exclusive if knowing that A occurred tells us that B did not.

Now suppose that S is the sample space for an experiment E. For all events $A \subset S$, let $P(A)$ be a real number, called the probability of A, with the following properties:

1. $0 \leq P(A) \leq 1$ for all $A \subset S$.
2. $P(S) = 1$, $P(\varphi) = 0$.
3. If A and B are mutually exclusive, $P(A \text{ or } B) = P(A) + P(B)$.

To understand a motivation for probability, we consider the idea of relative frequency. Suppose E is repeated n times, and let m_A be the number of times A occurred in these m repetitions. Then m_A/n is called the relative frequency of the event A. It is easy to show that the relative frequency m_A/n of A has the following properties:

1. $0 \leq \dfrac{m_A}{n} \leq 1$.

2. $\dfrac{m_A}{n} = 1$,

if and only if A occurred on all of the m repetitions, and $m_A/n = 0$ if and only if A *never* occurred.

3. If A and B are mutually exclusive, then

$$\frac{m_{A \cup B}}{n} = \frac{m_A + m_B}{n} = \frac{m_A}{n} + \frac{m_B}{n}.$$

Thus, given this notion, which could come about due to observation of random experiments, it is easy to see, in part at least, what might have motivated the definition of the probability function P.

The foundations of probability, however, are very much disputed. Some identify them with relative frequencies in large samples and some with relative frequencies in the unknown population from which the sample is drawn. Also, there is a school of subjective probability, which identifies probability with subjective strength of belief in a hypothesis based on certain empirical evidence.

We will use relative frequency in Section 96 on the laws of probability.

EXERCISES 95

1   Let E be the experiment of choosing one letter at random from the word "kind." Find the sample space for E and list all elementary events.

2   The experiment E consists of choosing a 5-card poker hand out of a shuffled deck of 52 cards. (a) How many elementary events (poker hands) are there? (b) Let A be the event, "the hand contains 2 aces" and B the event, "the hand contains 2 kings." How many elementary events are in $A \cap B$? (c) How many elementary events are members of A if A is the event, "the hand contains 4 aces"?

3   The experiment E consists of tossing a coin three times. (a) Give the sample space S for E. (b) Give the event, "there are at least 2 heads." (c) Give the event, "there are exactly 2 heads." (d) Give the event, "the first toss is 0 head." (e) Give the event, "the first and third tosses are heads." HINT: What do you need to describe the outcome of E? You must stipulate the results of the first, second, and third tosses, so a 3-tuple is necessary.

4   A skillful gambler rolls a die 30 times. The results are 1,2,3,4,5,6,1,2,3, 4,5,6,1,2,3,4,5,6,1,2,3,4,5,6,1,2,3,4,5,6. He can repeat this sequence indefinitely. (a) What is the relative frequency of 2 in the 30 rolls? (b) What do you expect the limit of this relative frequency to be as the number of rolls becomes arbitrarily large?

96   THE LAWS OF PROBABILITY

Let us consider several properties of the function P.

1. Let $A \subset S$, $\bar{A} = S - A$. Then $P(A) = 1 - P(A)$. For $A \cap \bar{A} = \varphi$, $P(A \cup \bar{A}) = P(S) = 1$. Then $P(A \cup \bar{A}) = 1 = P(A) + P(\bar{A})$.

2. For any two events A and B in S, $P(A \cup B) = P(A) + P(B) - P(A \cap B)$. For $A \cup B = A \cup (B \cap \bar{A})$, $B = (A \cap B) \cup (\bar{A} \cap B)$. Then $P(A \cup B) = P(A) + P(B \cap \bar{A})$, $P(B) = P(A \cap B) + P(\bar{A} \cap B)$. Subtracting, we have $P(A \cup B) - P(B) = P(A) - P(A \cap B)$, or $P(A \cup B) = P(A) + P(B) - P(A \cap B)$.

3. If $A \subset S$, $P(A)$ is given by the sums $\Sigma P(e)$ of the probabilities for the elementary events in A.

EXAMPLE

Toss a die such that

$$P(1) = P(2) = \frac{1}{3}, \qquad P(3) = \frac{1}{6},$$
$$P(4) = P(5) = P(6) = \frac{1}{8}.$$

Let $A = \{1, 4, 3\}$ and $B = \{3, 4, 5\}$. Then $P(A) = P(1) + P(4) = \frac{1}{3} + \frac{1}{18} = \frac{7}{18}$, $P(B) = P(3) + P(4) + P(5) = \frac{1}{6} + \frac{2}{18} = \frac{5}{18}$.

Suppose now that we take $P(A)$ to be $\lim_{n \to \infty} m_A/n$, the limit of the relative frequency of A as the number of repetitions of E becomes arbitrarily large assuming this limit exists. It can be shown that such a $P(A)$ is totally consistent with the properties we desired $P(A)$ to have, and it has the added advantages of intuitive appeal and ease of manipulation. We will use this approach to derive the rest of our results, assuming the existence of all limits.

Multiplication Theorem

Again let us consider n trials. Among the n trials there are m_A trials in which the event A occurs. Hence m_A/n is the relative frequency of A and its limit is the probability of A. Now consider another event B. Among the m_A trials in which the event A occurs, there are $\bar{m}_B$ in which we *also* have B. The relative frequency of the combined event, A and B, is $\bar{m}_B/n$. Its limit is the probability that A and B will happen together.

The relative frequency of A and B can be written

$$\frac{\bar{m}_B}{n} = \frac{\bar{m}_B}{m_A} \cdot \frac{m_A}{n}.$$

On the right side the second fraction is simply the relative frequency of the event A. Its limit is the probability of A. But the first term on the right side is the relative frequency of the event B among the trials in which the event A has occurred. Its limit is the so-called *conditional probability*.

Denote now the probability of A as p_A, the probability of getting A and B by p, and the conditional probability of B, if it is known that A has occurred, by $p_{B(A)}$.

By passing to the limit as $n \to \infty$ in the formula, we obtain

$$p = p_{(B)A} p_A.$$

EXAMPLE 1

Consider an urn in which there are 2 red balls and 3 black balls. The probability of drawing a red ball at random will be denoted by p_A; we have

$$p_A = \frac{2}{5},$$

since there are 2 red balls among the 5 balls in the urn.

Consider now the probability of drawing a black ball, *after a red ball has been drawn* (and not replaced). This conditional probability will be denoted by $p_{(B)A}$. We have

$$p_{B(A)} = \tfrac{3}{4}.$$

When 1 red ball has been drawn, 4 balls are left in the urn; 3 of these 4 balls are black. Hence the conditional probability of the event B, after A is known to have happened, is $\tfrac{3}{4}$.

Consider finally the probability of drawing a red ball (event A) and then a black ball (event B). We have from the above formula

$$p = (\tfrac{2}{5})(\tfrac{3}{4}) = \tfrac{6}{20} = \tfrac{3}{10}.$$

A very important special case of the last consideration is the case of *independent* events A and B. In this case the relative frequency of B is independent of the fact whether A has occurred or not, so we have

$$\frac{\bar{m}_B}{m_A} = \frac{m_B}{n}.$$

Denoting the limit of the relative frequency of the trials with the event B among all the trials by p_B, we have from the above formula

$$p = p_A p_B.$$

The probability that two *independent* events will happen together is the product of their probabilities.

The theorem can be extended to any number of independent events. That is, the probability that a number of independent events will happen together is the product of their probabilities.

EXAMPLE 2

Consider the independent throwing of 2 unbiased coins, say a dime and a nickel. What is the probability of obtaining 2 heads?

The probability of obtaining a head with the dime is $\tfrac{1}{2}$, since the coin is unbiased. The probability of obtaining a head with the nickel is $\tfrac{1}{2}$, since this coin is also unbiased. The coins are thrown independently. It follows that the probability of obtaining 2 heads is the product of the 2 probabilities; that is,

$$(\tfrac{1}{2})(\tfrac{1}{2}) = \tfrac{1}{4}.$$

Consider two exclusive events which exhaust the set of elementary events, A_1 and A_2. Let B be another event, and denote by $P(B|A_1)$ the probability that B happens under the hypothesis that A_1 has happened, and by $P(B|A_2)$ the probability that B happens if A_2 has happened. Let $P(B)$ be the probability of B

and $P(A_1)$ and $P(A_2)$ the probability of A_1 and A_2. We have

$$P(B) = P(B|A_1)P(A_1) + P(B|A_2)P(A_2).$$

Now we have for the event A_1 and B

$$P(A_1 \cap B) = P(A_1)P(B|A_1).$$

Similarly,

$$P(A_1|B)P(B) = P(B|A_1)P(A_1),$$
$$P(A_1|B) = P(B|A_1)P(A_1)/P(B)$$

Since we also have $P(A_1 \cap B) = P(B) \cdot P(A_1|B)$, we obtain

$$P(A_1|B) = P(A_1)P(B|A_1)/[P(A_1)P(B|A_1) + P(A_2)P(B|A_2)].$$

We get a similar formula for A_2. Also this proposition can be generalized for n events: A_1, A_2, $\cdots$, A_n. This is *Bayes' theorem*.

EXAMPLE 4

Consider two urns, A_1 and A_2. Let $P(A_1) = P(A_2) = \frac{1}{2}$. Let urn A_1 contain 2 white and 3 black balls and urn A_2 1 white and 1 black ball. Let the event B be the drawing of a white ball. We have

$$P(B|A_1) = \frac{2}{3}, \qquad P(B|A_2) = \frac{1}{2}.$$

If a white ball has been drawn (the event B occurred), what is the probability that the white ball came from urn A_1? We have from the above formula

$$P(A_1|B) = \frac{(\frac{1}{2})(\frac{2}{3})}{(\frac{1}{2})(\frac{2}{3}) + (\frac{1}{2})(\frac{1}{2})} = \frac{4}{7}.$$

EXERCISES 96

1   A true die is rolled. Find the probabilities of obtaining (a) either 1 or 2; (b) either 2 or 5 or 6; (c) an even number; (d) an odd number; (e) any number but 5; (f) either 1 or 2 or 3 or 4 or 5 or 6.

2   Three exclusive events have the probabilities $p_A = \frac{1}{3}$ for A, $p_B = \frac{1}{6}$ for B, $p_C = \frac{1}{2}$ for C. What are the probabilities of obtaining (a) either A or B? (b) either A or C? (c) either B or C? (d) either A, B, or C?

3   The probability of obtaining a head with a coin is p, the probability of obtaining a tail is q. What is the probability of obtaining either heads or tails? What conclusions can be drawn about the sum of the two probabilities?

4   Three exclusive events have the probabilities $p_A = 0.5$, $p_B = 0.2$, $p_C = 0.3$. Find the probabilities of the following contingencies: (a) either A or B; (b) either A or C; (c) either B or C; (d) either A, B, or C.

5 A perfect die is cast two times. Find the probability of obtaining the sum 8. (HINT: Consider all possible contingencies.)

6 If $A, B, C, \cdots$ are a series of exclusive events that exhaust all possibilities, it follows that $p_A + p_B + p_C + \cdots = 1$. Explain.

7 A half dollar, a dime, and a nickel are thrown independently. All are true coins. Find the probability (a) of obtaining heads with all of them; (b) of getting tails with all of them; (c) of getting heads with the half dollar and tails with the other two coins; (d) of getting heads with the half dollar, tails with the dime, and heads with the nickel in three independent throws of the three coins.

8 Events A, B, C, D are independent. Their probabilities are, respectively, $p_A = \frac{1}{8}$, $p_B = \frac{1}{2}$, $p_C = \frac{1}{4}$, $p_D = \frac{1}{10}$. Find the probabilities that the following events will happen together: (a) A and B; (b) A and C; (c) A and D; (d) B and C; (e) B and D; (f) C and D; (g) $A, B,$ and C; (h) $A, B,$ and D; (i) $A, C,$ and D; (j) $B, C,$ and D; (k) $A, B, C,$ and D.

9 Five perfect coins are thrown independently. What is the probability (a) of obtaining only heads; (b) only tails; (c) heads with the first two coins and tails with the rest; (d) heads with the first coin and tails with the others?

10 Two perfect dice are cast independently. Find the probabilities of obtaining (a) the sum 6; (b) the sum 2; (c) the sum 12. (HINT: Consider all contingencies.)

11 A total of n perfect dice are cast independently. Determine the probability of obtaining as the sum the number (a) n; (b) $6n$.

12 An urn contains 2 red balls, 5 black balls, and 3 white balls. Find the following probabilities assuming that none of the drawn balls is replaced: (a) the conditional probability of obtaining a black ball after a red ball has been drawn; (b) the probability of drawing a red ball and then a black ball; (c) the conditional probability of drawing a white ball after a red ball has been drawn; (d) the probability of drawing a red ball and a white ball in succession; (e) the conditional probability of drawing a black ball after a white ball has been drawn; (f) the probability of drawing a white ball and a black ball in succession; (g) the conditional probability of drawing a red ball after a white ball has been drawn; (h) the probability of drawing in succession a white ball and a red ball.

13 Let A_1 be an urn containing 2 white balls and 3 black balls. A_2 is an urn with 1 white ball and 9 black balls. Let B be the event of the drawing of a white ball. Find $P(B|A_1)$, the probability that the white ball came from the first urn if $P(A_1) = P(A_2) = \frac{1}{2}$.

97 PROBABILITY DISTRIBUTIONS

A random variable is a variable that can assume a number of values with given probabilities. Random variables are also called *stochastic* or *chance variables*. For example, the outcome of the rolls of a die is a random variable, since it can assume the values 1, 2, 3, 4, 5, 6 with certain probabilities. More specifically, a random variable is any real-valued function defined on the sample space of an experiment E. The set of values the random variable can assume is called the range space of the random variable. For example, suppose we toss a die. The sample space has 6 members: 1, 2, 3, 4, 5, 6. For s in the sample space, we could let $x(s) = 2s + 1$. x is then a random variable, with range space $\{3, 5, 7, 9, 11, 13\}$. Similarly, if $y(s) = s^2$, y is a random variable, with range space $\{1, 4, 9, 16, 25, 36\}$.

The probability that a given random variable assumes a specific value in its range space is given by the probability of the event in the sample space that corresponds to this value. Thus, in the above example, with $x(s) = 2s + 1$, if the die is balanced, then the probability that x is either 3, 5, or 13 is given by the probability that s is 1, 2, or 6, which is $\frac{1}{2}$.

The array of the values that the random variable can have together with the probabilities of these values is called *the probability distribution*. It is apparent that the sum of all the probabilities must be 1. This follows from the addition theorem of probabilities.

EXAMPLE 1

Consider a throw with two unbiased coins. The coins are thrown independently. The random variable x is the number of heads. The following contingencies are equally probable:

Coin 1	Coin 2
H	H
H	T
T	H
T	T

The probability of each contingency listed in the previous table is $\frac{1}{4}$. Hence we obtain the following probability distribution for x, the number of heads:

x	p
0	$\frac{1}{4}$
1	$\frac{1}{2}$
2	$\frac{1}{4}$
	1

The sum of probabilities is 1. This follows from the fact that, with two coins, either no heads, 1 head, or 2 heads must come up, so the sum of the probabilities of all these contingencies is certainty: that is, $p = 1$.

Figure 43 is a so-called histogram. This is a graphical representation of the probability distribution given above. Note that

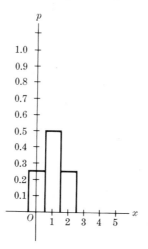

Figure 43

the various rectangles are drawn in such a way that their *centers* are at the values of x given in the table; the height of each rectangle corresponds to the probability associated with its respective value of x.

It should be noted that the sum of the areas of all the rectangles in Figure 43 is 1. This corresponds to the fact that the sum of all the probabilities is 1.

From the above table we can compute the so-called *cumulative probability distribution*. This is derived by adding the probabilities successively:

x	Cumulative Probability
0	$\frac{1}{4}$
1	$\frac{3}{4}$
2	1

The cumulative probability $P(x_0)$ of x gives the probability that $x \leqq x_0$ for all real numbers x_0. Thus, in this example, $P(-3) = 0$, because all values of x are $\geqq 0$. $P(5) = 1$, because every value in the range space of x is at most 2. $P(4) = 1$, $P(\frac{1}{10}) = \frac{1}{4}$, and so on. Here $\frac{1}{4}$ is the probability that x is less than or equal to 0; $\frac{3}{4}$ is the probability that x is less than or equal to 1; 1 is the probability that x is less than or equal to 2.

For a random variable that can vary continuously between the values $x = a$ and $x = b$, we define a *probability density:* $p(x)$. The function $p(x)$ is such that the integral

$$\int_c^d p(x)\, dx$$

(where $c \geq a$, $d \leq b$) gives the probability that x will be somewhere between c and d. Since it is certain that the random variable x must assume values between a and b, we have

$$\int_a^b p(x)\, dx = 1.$$

The cumulative probability is now given by

$$P(x_0) = \int_a^{x_0} p(x)\, dx.$$

This is the probability that x will be smaller than or equal to a given value $x_0 \leq b$.

EXAMPLE 2

Consider a random variable x that can assume all possible values between 2 and 6 with *equal* probability. We have $a = 2$, $b = 6$. This circumstance yields the probability density $p(x) = \frac{1}{4}$, $2 \leq x \leq 6$. This is confirmed by the fact that the integral of the probability density function over the whole range from $x = 2$ to 6 is

$$\int_a^b p(x)\, dx = \int_2^6 \left(\frac{1}{4}\right) dx = \left[\frac{1}{4}x\right]_2^6 = \left(\frac{1}{4}\right) 6 - \left(\frac{1}{4}\right)(2) = 1.$$

This result corresponds to the fact that the area under the curve shown in Figure 44 is 1. Probability distributions of this type are called *rectangular probability distributions*.

The cumulative distribution for the previous illustration is given by

$$\int_a^{x_0} p(x)\, dx = \int_2^{x_0} \frac{1}{4}\, dx = \left[\frac{1}{4}x\right]_2^{x_0} = \frac{x_0}{4} - \frac{1}{2}.$$

For example, the probability that x will be smaller than or equal to 5, $x_0 = 5$, is

$$\frac{5}{4} - \frac{1}{2} = \frac{3}{4}.$$

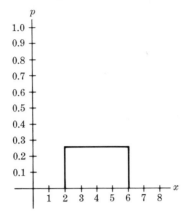

Figure 44

The probability that x will be equal to or smaller than 4 $x_0 = 4$, is

$$\frac{4}{4} - \frac{1}{2} = \frac{1}{2}.$$

By integration, we have also for the probability that $3 \leq x \leq 4$

$$\int_3^4 \frac{1}{4} \, dx = \left[\frac{1}{4} x \right]_3^4 = \frac{4}{4} - \frac{3}{4} = \frac{1}{4}.$$

EXAMPLE 3

The probability distribution of the various results of throws with a true die is as follows:

x	p
1	1⁄6
2	1⁄6
3	1⁄6
4	1⁄6
5	1⁄6
6	1⁄6

The sum of the probabilities is 1.

EXAMPLE 4

The probability density of a rectangular probability distribution is defined by $p(x) = \frac{1}{4}$, $-2 \leq x \leq 2$. This is sometimes said to be the probability that x will fall between x and $x + dx$, where dx

is the differential of x. We have

$$\int_{-2}^{2} \left(\frac{1}{4}\right) dx = \left[\frac{x}{4}\right]_{-2}^{2} = 1.$$

EXERCISES 97

1   The probability distribution of a variable X is

X	p
0	0.5
1	0.2
2	?

Find the probability of $X = 2$. Check. Make a histogram.

2   A rectangular probability distribution is defined as $p(X) = k, 0 \leq X \leq 5$. Determine k. Check. Make a graph of the probability density function. Find the cumulative distribution.

3   A given probability distribution is as follows:

X	p
1	a
2	0.5
3	a

Find (a) the probability of $X = 1$ and $X = 3$. Check. (b) Find the cumulative distribution. (c) Make a histogram.

4   A probability distribution is given by $p(x) = e^{-x}, 0 \leq x < \infty$. (a) Prove that the integral is 1. (HINT: Evaluate $\int_{0}^{u} e^{-x} dx = G(u)$ and consider $\lim_{u \to \infty} G(u)$.) (b) Find the cumulative-probability distribution. (c) What is the probability that $0 \leq x \leq 3$? (d) that $1 \leq x \leq 5$?

5 $p(x) = (\frac{1}{2})(\frac{1}{2})^{x}, x = 1, 2, \cdots$. (a) Prove that the sum of the probabilities is 1. (b) What is $p(3)$? (c) $p(6)$? (d) $p(1)$? (e) Make a graph.

6   Normal distribution follows the law $p(x) = e^{-x^2/2}/\sqrt{2\pi}$, where $\pi = 3.14159$. Make a graph.

7   A probability distribution follows an arithmetic progression for $x = 1, 2, 3, 4$. We are given that $p(1) = 0.4, p(2) = 0.3, \cdots$. (a) Establish the complete distribution. (b) Prove that the sum of the probabilities is 1.

8   Take the normal distribution in problem 6. Where does the probability attain its maximum? The value of x that maximizes the probability is called *the mode*. What is the value of the maximum probability?

9   Consider the probability distribution of throwing x heads independently with three perfect coins. Establish the probability distribution, the cumulative probability distribution, and make a histogram. (HINT: see Example 1.)

10 Consider the probability of throwing x heads independently with four perfect coins. Establish the probability distribution, the cumulative probability distribution, and make a histogram. (HINT: see Example 1.)

**11 Consider the probability of throwing the sum x with two perfect dice. Establish the probability distribution, the cumulative probability distribution, and make a histogram.

Chapter 21
Random Variables

98 MATHEMATICAL EXPECTATION

A random variable has been defined as a function that can assume a number of values with definite probabilities. The values that the random variable can assume together with the probabilities are called the *probability distribution*.

We describe in the following pages a number of ways in which a probability distribution can be characterized. One of the most important characteristics of the probability distribution is the mathematical expectation, or mean value, of the random variable. This is the arithmetic mean of the probability distribution. We will, however, reserve the term "arithmetic mean" for the sample and call the mean value the *mathematical expectation*, or *true mean*, when dealing with probabilities. It is also called the *population mean*.

Assume first that we have a *discrete* random variable, which can assume the values $x_1, x_2, \cdots, x_m$ with the respective probabilities $p_1, p_2, \cdots, p_m$. The mathematical expectation of the random variable x is denoted by $Ex = \mu$, and is computed by the formula

$$\mu = Ex = x_1p_1 + x_2p_2 + x_3p_3 + \cdots + x_mp_m = \sum_{i=1}^{m} x_ip_i.$$

If we have a *continuous variable* x, let us assume that it can vary between a and b; that is, $a \leq x \leq b$. Moreover, let the probability density of the distribution of x be given by $p(x)$. In the formula above obtained for a discrete variable we replace summation by integration and get for the mathematical expectation of the random variable x

$$\mu = Ex = \int_a^b xp(x)dx.$$

EXAMPLE 1

Consider a discrete variable having the following probability distribution:

x	p	xp
0	0.5	0.0
1	0.3	0.3
2	0.2	0.4
μ = Ex =		0.7

Figure 45 presents a histogram of the above probability distribution. We have indicated the mathematical expectation μ by a

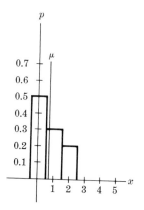

Figure 45

heavy vertical line. It is apparent from the graph that the mathematical expectation, or population mean, is a good way of characterizing the general location, or central tendency, of the probability distribution.

EXAMPLE 2

Consider the case of a continuous variable that possesses the probability density function $p(x) = \frac{1}{3}$, $0 \leq x \leq 3$. We have

$$\mu = Ex = \int_0^3 \left(\frac{x}{3}\right) dx = \left[\frac{x^2}{6}\right]_0^3 = \frac{3}{2}.$$

Figure 46 presents the probability density and the corresponding mathematical expectation, or population mean, μ. It will be obvious again that μ provides a good measure of the general location of the distribution.

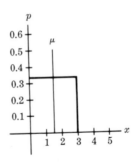

Figure 46

An important proposition which is demonstrated in advanced books on probability is the *law of large numbers*. It may be formulated as follows:

Suppose an experiment E is repeated in n independent trials. Let A be an event in the sample space of E, let $P(A)$ be its probability and n_A/n its relative frequency. Then the difference between $P(A)$ and n_A/n can be made as small as desired if n is taken large enough.

EXERCISES 98

1   Consider the following probability distribution:

x	p
1	0.4
2	0.4
3	0.2

Find $Ex = \mu$. Make a histogram and indicate the population mean.

2   Let $p(x) = \frac{1}{10}$, $-5 \le x \le 5$. Find $Ex = \mu$. Make a graph of the distribution and indicate the population mean.

3   Take the following probability distribution:

x	p
0	0.2
1	0.2
2	0.2
3	0.2
4	0.2

Find $Ex = \mu$.

4 Given the probability distribution $p(x) = 1/a$, $0 \leq x \leq a$, find $Ex = \mu$.

5 Consider the following probability distribution:

x	p
0	¼
1	½
2	¼

Find $Ex = \mu$. Make a histogram and indicate the population mean.

6 Given the probability distribution $p(x) = ½a$, $-a \leq x \leq a$, find $Ex = \mu$.

7 Take the following probability distribution:

x	p
0	⅛
1	⅜
2	⅜
3	⅛

Find $Ex = \mu$.

8 Given the probability distribution $p(x) = 1/(b - a)$, $a \leq x \leq b$, find $Ex = \mu$.

9 Assume the following probability distribution:

x	p
0	1/27
1	2/9
2	4/9
3	8/27

Find $Ex = \mu$.

10 Given the probability distribution $p(x) = 2 - 2x$, $0 \leq x \leq 1$, find $Ex = \mu$. Make a graph of the distribution and indicate the population mean.

99 COMPUTATIONS WITH MATHEMATICAL EXPECTATIONS

The concept of mathematical expectation is important in the derivation of various theorems in modern statistics. We will indicate briefly some rules for employing the notion of mathematical expectation in various computations.

1. The mathematical expectation of a random variable times a constant is the constant times the mathematical expectation of this random variable.

We give the proof for a *discrete* random variable. Let us define a random variable x that can assume the values $x_1, x_2, \cdots, x_m$ with the respective probabilities $p_1, p_2, \cdots, p_m$. Its probability distribution is

x	p
x_1	p_1
x_2	p_2
x_3	p_3
.	.
.	.
.	.
x_m	p_m

As indicated previously, the mathematical expectation, or the population mean, of x is given by

$$\mu_x = Ex = x_1 p_1 + x_2 p_2 + \cdots + x_m p_m = \sum_{i=1}^{m} x_i p_i.$$

Let us introduce a new random variable, say $v = cx$, where c is a constant. The probability distribution of v is

v	p
$v_1 = cx_1$	p_1
$v_2 = cx_2$	p_2
.	.
.	.
.	.
$v_m = cx_m$	p_m

We have for the mathematical expectation of v (which is x times the constant c):

$$\mu_v = Ev = Ecx = v_1 p_1 + v_2 p_2 + \cdots + v_m p_m = \sum_{i=1}^{m} p_i v_i$$

$$= cx_1 p_1 + cx_2 p_2 + \cdots + cx_m p_m = \sum_{i=1}^{m} cx_i p_i.$$

Evidently c can be factored out of the summation, and we have

$$\mu_v = Ev = c(x_1p_1 + x_2p_2 + \cdots + x_mp_m) = c\left(\sum_{i=1}^{m} x_ip_i\right) = cEx = c\mu_x.$$

This establishes our conclusion in the case of a discrete variable: The mathematical expectation of a random variable times a constant is the constant times the mathematical expectation of the random variable.

EXAMPLE 1

Assume the probability distribution of a random variable x given as follows:

x	p
2	0.25
4	0.75

The mathematical expectation of x is

$$\mu_x = Ex = (2)(0.25) + (4)(0.75) = 3.5.$$

Define a new variable, say $v = 5x$. We have for its probability distribution

v	p
10	0.25
20	0.75

Its mathematical expectation is

$$\mu_v = Ev = (10)(0.25) + (20)(0.75) = 17.5.$$

Hence

$$Ev = 17.5 = (5)(3.5) = (5)Ex,$$

which is the conclusion predicted by the rule given.

2. The mathematical expectation of a sum of random variables is the sum of the mathematical expectations.

EXAMPLE 2

Assume two independent random variables whose probability distributions are given below:

x	p	y	q
1	0.5	1	0.25
2	0.5	2	0.5
		3	0.25

The mathematical expectations are

$$\mu_x = Ex = (1)(0.5) + (2)(0.5) = 1.5,$$
$$\mu_y = Ey = (1)(0.25) + (2)(0.5) + (3)(0.25) = 2.$$

Let us find the mathematical expectation of the sum $w = x + y$. Since, by assumption, the random variables x and y are independent, we can construct a table that gives the probability of the simultaneous occurrence of the possible values of x and y. The probabilities are computed by multiplying the probabilities of x and y. The following table represents a *joint probability distribution* of the random variables x and y:

x \ y	1	2	3
1	0.125	0.25	0.125
2	0.125	0.25	0.125

For example, from the original tables we find that the probability that $x = 1$ is 0.5. The probability that $y = 1$ is 0.25. The probability that $x = 1$ and $y = 1$, simultaneously, is $(0.5)(0.25) = 0.125$; this value is found at its appropriate position in the new table.

From the table above we can derive the following probability distribution for $w = x + y$:

w	P
2	0.125
3	0.375
4	0.375
5	0.125

This is derived in the following way: To make the sum $w = x + y = 2$, we must have $x = 1$ and $y = 1$. The probability for this circumstance from the table above is 0.125. To get a sum $w = 3$, we have either $x = 1$ and $y = 2$ or $x = 2$ and $y = 1$. The probability of the first of these two contingencies is 0.25; the probability of the second is 0.125. Now the addition theorem of probabilities applies; that is, the probability of $w = 3$ is $0.25 + 0.125 = 0.375$, and so forth.

By direct calculation, employing the values in the new table, it is determined that the mathematical expectation of the sum

w is 3.5. But this value is

$$Ex + Ey = \mu_x + \mu_y = 1.5 + 2.$$

This emphasizes that the mathematical expectation of the sum of two random variables x and y is the sum of their mathematical expectations.

3. The mathematical expectation of the product of two independent random variables is the product of their mathematical expectations.

EXAMPLE 3

Using the same random variables as in Example 2, we derive from the table of the simultaneous distribution of x and y the distribution of the product $z = xy$

z	Q
1	0.125
2	0.375
3	0.125
4	0.25
6	0.125

The mathematical expectation of z is

$$\mu_z = Ez = (1)(0.125) + (2)(0.375) + (3)(0.125) + (4)(0.25)$$
$$+ (6)(0.125) = 3.000.$$

It is true also that

$$Ez = Exy = 3 = (1.5)(2) = (Ex)(Ey) = \mu_x \cdot \mu_y.$$

This result emphasizes that the mathematical expectation of the product of two independent random variables is the product of their mathematical expectations.

4. The mathematical expectation of a constant is equal to the constant.

We can consider the constant as a random variable which assumes the one particular value c with certainty (probability 1). Hence the mathematical expectation of a constant is equal to the constant itself.

It should be noted that the mathematical expectation μ itself is a constant. Hence we have

$$E(Ex) = Ex = \mu.$$

EXAMPLE 4

Consider the random variables x, y, z. Assume that they are independent and that their mathematical expectations are

$$\mu_x = Ex = 1,$$
$$\mu_y = Ey = -2,$$
$$\mu_z = Ez = 5.$$

What is the mathematical expectation of the function

$$w = 3 + 2x - 4xy + 4yz?$$

From our previous rules we have

$$\mu_w = Ew = 3 + 2Ex - 4(Ex)(Ey) + 4(Ey)(Ez)$$
$$= 3 + 2(1) - 4(1)(-2) + 4(-2)(5) = -27.$$

EXERCISES 99

1   Assume we have two independent random variables x and y. Let $Ex = 6$, $Ey = 8$. Find (a) $E2x$; (b) $E3y$; (c) $E(x + 3)$; (d) $E(3y - 6)$; (e) $E(x + y)$; (f) $E(y - x)$; (g) $E(2x - 4y)$; (h) $E(2x + 5y - 3)$; (i) Exy; (j) $E(5xy)$; (k) $E(xy - 4x + 5y - 6)$; (l) $E(3x + y - xy + 6)$.

2   Assume three independent random variables x, y, and z. Let the mathematical expectations be $Ex = 1$, $Ey = -5$, $Ez = 6$. Find (a) $E2x$; (b) $E4y$; (c) $E5z$; (d) $E(x + y + z)$; (e) $E(x - 2y + z)$; (f) $E(2x - y)$; (g) $E(5y - 3x)$; (h) Exy; (i) Exz; (j) Eyz; (k) $E(3xy - 6yz + 4xz)$.

3   Assume two independent random variables. The probability density of x is $p(x) = \frac{1}{4}$, $1 \le x \le 5$. The probability density of y is $p(y) = \frac{1}{3}$, $3 \le y \le 6$. (a) Find Ex; (b) Ey; (c) $E(x + y)$; (d) $E(x - y)$; (e) $E(2x - 5y)$; (f) $E(3x - y + 8)$; (g) Exy.

4   Assume the following probability distributions of two independent random variables:

x	p	y	q
2	0.25	0	0.25
4	0.25	1	0.5
6	0.25	2	0.25
8	0.25		

(a) Compute the mathematical expectations μ_x and μ_y. (b) Compute the mathematical expectations of $E(x + y)$; $E(x - y)$; Exy by formula and directly by the methods in Examples 2 and 3.

5   Use the data in Example 2 to compute the following: (a) $E(2x - y)$; (b) $E(3x + 2y)$; (c) $E(3x - 2y - 6)$. Use both the formula and the method utilized in the example.

6 Use the data in Example 2 to compute the following expectations: (a) $E(3xy)$; (b) $E(-xy)$; (c) $E(10 - 2xy)$. Use both the formula and the direct method of Example 3.

7 Call the random variable x in problem 1, Exercises 98, and call the random variable y in problem 2, Exercises 98. Find the following expectations, assuming independent distributions: (a) $E(x - y)$; (b) Exy; (c) $E(3x - 5y + 10)$; (d) $E(100 - 5xy)$.

100 SOME SIMPLE INVENTORY PROBLEMS

We shall first consider inventory problems under deterministic conditions. Assume that an enterprise during a time period T sells an amount Q of its product at a constant rate per unit of time. Assume further that the sales are uniform during the interval T.

Production of the commodity takes place during intervals that are separated by time intervals t, which are constants. The fixed cost of production during each production run is c, also constant. We denote by q the amount of the commodity produced in each period of production. Let s be the storage cost of a unit of the commodity for a unit of time.

During the time period T the number of periods of production is Q/q and the time interval between the start of production runs is given by

$$t = \frac{T}{(Q/q)} = \frac{Tq}{Q}$$

if we neglect the period of production.

The average inventory during a period of nonproduction is $q/2$, assuming constant rate of use, and the cost of storage for the interval of nonproduction is $(q/2)(st) = (q/2)[s(Tq/Q)]$; hence the total cost of storage for the time interval T is $(q/2)(sT)$. On the other hand, the cost of the Q/q periods of production is cQ/q. Neglecting variable cost, we find that the total cost of production and sales of Q units of the commodity is

$$C = \left(\frac{sTq}{2}\right) + \frac{cQ}{q}.$$

In this expression T and Q are given. We assume also that c is constant. Then total cost C is only a function of q. In order to make C a minimum we must have

$$\frac{dC}{dq} = 0; \qquad \frac{d^2C}{dq^2} > 0.$$

Hence the optimal value of q is given by

$$q_0 = \sqrt{\frac{2CQ}{sT}}.$$

The corresponding value of the time period of nonproduction is

$$t_0 = \sqrt{\frac{2cT}{sQ}}.$$

The minimum total cost is given by

$$C_0 = \sqrt{2scQT}.$$

EXAMPLE 1

Assume that a certain enterprise produces $Q = 100$ units of a commodity uniformly during $T = 10$ months. The storage cost of the commodity is $S = \$2$ per month and unit of the commodity. The fixed production cost of each period of production is $c = \$5$. This is assumed to be independent of the quantity q produced during each period of production.

The number of periods of production is $Q/p = 100/q$, and the length of the interval of nonproduction is

$$t = \frac{T}{(100/q)} = \frac{10q}{100} = \frac{q}{10}.$$

The total storage cost during 10 months for an average inventory of $q/2$ is $(q/2)sT = 10q$. The cost of the $100/q$ periods of production is $cQ/q = 500/q$. Hence the total cost of production and sales is

$$C = 10q + \left(\frac{500}{q}\right).$$

This becomes a minimum for $q_0 = \sqrt{500/10} = \sqrt{50} = 7.07$ units of the commodity. The length of the intervals of nonproduction is then $t_0 = q_0/10 = 0.707$ months, and the minimum total cost is given by

$$C_0 = \sqrt{(2)(100)(10)(2)(5)} = \sqrt{20,000} = 141.42.$$

Let now i be the shortage cost for each unit of the commodity not delivered. The enterprise has an inventory S at the beginning of a period of nonproduction. It will sell immediately the quantity $q - S$ without incurring inventory cost. Each time interval t of nonproduction is divided into the time interval $t_1 = (S/q)t$, during which orders are immediately filled. The mean inventory during this time interval is $S/2$. In the second time interval $t_2 = (q - S)t/q$ orders cannot be filled, and the mean period of waiting is given by

$$\frac{t_2}{2} = \frac{(q - S)t}{2q}.$$

The selling cost during a time period of nonproduction is then the sum of inventory cost,

$$\left(\frac{S}{2}\right) s \left(\frac{St}{q}\right) = \frac{S^2 st}{2q},$$

and shortage cost,

$$\frac{(q - S)i(q - S)^t}{2q} = \frac{(q - S)^2 it}{2q}.$$

Hence the total selling cost for Q/q periods of nonproduction during the time interval T is

$$\frac{Q}{q}\left[\left(S^2 \frac{st}{2q}\right) + (q - S)^2 \frac{it}{2q}\right] = \frac{T}{2q}[S^2 s + (q - S)^2 i].$$

The total cost of production and sales of Q units during the time interval T is, hence,

$$C = \frac{Qc}{q} + \frac{T}{2q}[S^2 s + (q - S)^2 i].$$

Now Q, T, c, s, and i are given constants. The necessary conditions for a minimum of C are $\partial C/\partial q = 0$, $\partial C/\partial S = 0$. The optimum is given by

$$q_0 = \sqrt{\frac{2Qc(s + i)}{Tsi}},$$

$$S_0 = \sqrt{\frac{2Qci}{Ts(s + 1)}},$$

$$t_0 = \sqrt{\frac{2Tc(s + i)}{Qsi}},$$

and the minimum total cost is

$$C_0 = \sqrt{\frac{2QTcsi}{s + i}}.$$

EXAMPLE 2

Make the same assumptions as in Example 1, also that the shortage cost is $i = \$3$. Hence we have $Q = 100$, $T = 10$, $c = 5$, $s = 2$, $i = 3$. Using the above formulas, we have for minimum total cost

$$q_0 = \sqrt{\frac{(2)(100)(5)(2+3)}{(10)(2)(3)}} = \sqrt{\frac{250}{3}} = 9.13 \text{ units,}$$

$$t_0 = \sqrt{\frac{(2)(100)(5)(2+3)}{(100)(2)(3)}} = \sqrt{\frac{25}{30}} = 0.913 \text{ months,}$$

$$S_0 = \sqrt{\frac{(2)(100)(5)(3)}{(10)(2)(2+3)}} = \sqrt{30} = 5.48 \text{ units.}$$

If this policy is followed, the minimum total cost is given by

$$C_0 = \sqrt{\frac{(2)(100)(10)(2)(3)(5)}{2+3}} = \sqrt{12{,}000} = \$109.54.$$

Comparing this result with Example 1, we see that the total cost is now smaller.

Now we introduce *stochastic* considerations. Assume that a seller buys in a given time interval, say each day, the quantity S of a product. But the daily demand is now a random variable with a probability density $f(r)$. Hence the probability of a demand less than S is given by

$$F(S) = \int_0^S f(r)\,dr,$$

where $F(0) = 0$, $F(\infty) = 1$.

If the inventory S is too large, there is a loss of c_1 per unit of unsold product. If, on the other hand, S is too small, the seller suffers a loss of c_2 per unit. Hence, if the actual demand is r, the loss of the seller is

$$
\begin{array}{lll}
c_1(S - r) & \text{if} & r < S, \\
c_2(r - S) & \text{if} & r > S.
\end{array}
$$

Now the seller wants to minimize losses in the long run. These are represented by the *mathematical expectation* of loss:

$$E = \int_0^S c_1(S - r)f(r)\,dr + \int_S^\infty c_2(r - S)f(r)\,dr.$$

The optimum inventory will be given by the conditions

$$\frac{dE}{dS} = 0, \qquad \frac{d^2E}{dS^2} > 0.$$

In order to find these conditions we must find the rules for differentiation under the integral sign.

The derivative of the integral

$$F(x) = \int_0^x f(u, x)\,du$$

with respect to the upper limit x is given by

$$\frac{dF(x)}{dx} = f(x, x) + \int_0^x \left[\frac{\partial f(u, x)}{\partial x} \right] du.$$

The derivative of the integral

$$G(x) = \int_x^\infty f(u, x) du$$

with respect to the lower limit x is

$$\frac{dG(x)}{dx} - f(x, x) + \int_x^\infty \left[\frac{\partial f(u, x)}{\partial x} \right] du.$$

Now we write the mathematical expectation of loss in this form:

$$E(S) = c_1 \int_0^S g(r, S)f(r)dr + c_2 \int_S^\infty h(r, S)f(r)dr.$$

Using the above rules, we obtain for the derivative

$$\frac{dE(S)}{dS} = c_1 \left[g(S, S)f(S) + \int_0^S \frac{\partial g(r, S)}{\partial Sf(r)} \right] dr$$

$$+ c_2 \left[-h(S, S)f(S) + \int_S^\infty \frac{\partial h(r, S)}{\partial Sf(r)} dr \right].$$

Since

$$g(r, S) = S - r, \qquad h(r, S) = r - S,$$
$$g(S, S) = S - S = 0, \qquad h(S, S) = S - S = 0,$$
$$\frac{\partial g(r, S)}{\partial S} = 1, \qquad \frac{\partial h(r, S)}{\partial S} = -1,$$

we obtain

$$\frac{dE(S)}{dS} = c_1 \left[0 + \int_0^S f(r)dr \right] + c_2 \left[0 - \int_S^\infty f(r)dr \right]$$
$$= c_1[F(S) - (0)] - c_2[F(\infty) - E(S)]$$
$$= c_1[F(S) - 0] - c_2[1 - F(S)].$$

The necessary condition for a minimum of the mathematical expectation of losses is then

$$\frac{dE(S)}{dS} = (c_1 + c_2)F(S) - c_2 = 0.$$

The optimal stock S_0 is given by the equation

$$F(S_0) = \frac{c_2}{c_1 + c_2}.$$

If $c_1 = c_2$, we have $F(S_0) = \frac{1}{2}$; the optimum stock is given by the median of the probability distribution.

EXAMPLE 3

Assume that the loss for one unsold unit is $c_1 = 2$ and the estimated loss for insufficiency of one unit of the product is $c_2 = 3$. Also assume that the probability distribution of demand for the product is rectangular between $r = 0$ and $r = 5$, with probability density $f(r) = \frac{1}{5}$. Hence the cumulative probability is

$$F(S) = \int_0^S \frac{dr}{5} = \frac{S}{5}.$$

Then the optimum inventory is given as

$$F(S_0) = \frac{3}{2 + 3} = \frac{3}{5} = \frac{S_0}{5}.$$

The optimum inventory, which in the long run will minimize the average loss, is $S_0 = 3$.

EXERCISES 100

1 With the notations of this section assume that $Q = 1000$, $T = 20$. Find the optimal q_0, t_0, and C_0 under the following conditions: (a) $c = 10$, $s = 1$; (b) $c = 2$; (c) $c = 1$, $s = 20$.

2 With the notation of this section, assume $Q = 500$, $T = 50$, $c = 10$. Find the optimal q_0, S_0, t_0, and C_0 for (a) $s = 1$, $i = 10$; (b) $s = 3$, $i = 4$; (c) $s = 20$, $i = 1$.

3 Using the notation of this section, assume $c_1 = 1$, $c_2 = 2$. Find the optimal inventory S_0 for the following probability distributions: (a) $f(r) = 1$, $0 \leq r \leq 1$; (b) $f(r) = \frac{1}{4}$, $0 \leq r \leq 4$; (c) $f(r) = \frac{1}{2}$, $1 \leq r \leq 3$; (d) $f(r) = 1/a$, $0 \leq r \leq a$; (e) $f(r) = 1/(b - a)$, $a \leq r \leq b$; (f) $f(r) = 2(1 - r)$, $0 \leq r \leq 1$.

4 Using the notation of this section, assume c_1 and c_2 as given constants. The probability distribution of demand is given by $f(r) = 1$, $0 \leq r \leq 1$. (a) Find the mathematical expectation of loss E as function of the inventory S. (b) Find the minimum of E by computing the first two derivatives. (c) What is the minimum of E?

**5 Make the same assumptions as in problem 3, but the probability distribution is now $f(r) = L \cdot e^{-Lr}$, $L > 0$, $0 < r < \infty$. NOTE: $\int x e^{ax} dx = e^{ax}(ax - 1)/a^2$.

Chapter 22

Moments

101 MOMENTS ABOUT THE ORIGIN

Assume a random variable x and its probability distribution as given. Instead of computing the mathematical expectation of x we can also compute the mathematical expectation of any arbitrary function of x, for example, x^2, $\log x$, e^x, $1/x$, and so forth. A particularly useful class of these functions comprises *the moments*.

In general, the kth moment about the origin of a random variable x is defined as the mathematical expectation of the kth power of x; that is,

$$\mu_k' = Ex^k, \qquad k = 0, 1, 2, \cdots.$$

For a discrete variable x, which assumes the values x_1, x_2, $\cdots$, x_m with the respective probabilities p_1, p_2, $\cdots$, p_m, we define the kth moment about the origin as

$$\mu_k' = Ex^k = \sum_{i=1}^{m} x_i^k p_i, \qquad k = 0, 1, 2, \cdots.$$

Assume that the random variable x varies continuously between a and b. The probability density of x is $p(x)$. The kth moment about the origin is

$$\mu_k' = Ex^k = \int_a^b x^k p(x)dx, \qquad k = 0, 1, 2, \cdots.$$

It should be noted that the summation employed for discrete variables has been replaced by integration.

From the definition of the kth moment about the origin we have

$$\mu_0' = Ex^0 = E1 = 1.$$

This says that the 0th moment about the origin is 1. Also,

$$\mu_1' = Ex^1 = Ex = \mu.$$

Thus the first moment about the origin is μ, the mathematical expectation of the random variable x itself. This is the *mean value of the distribution of* x, *or the mean of the population.*

Higher-order moments about 0 have no immediate interpretation.

EXAMPLE 1

Find the third moment about 0 of the probability distribution

x	p	$x^3 p$
0	0.5	0.0
1	0.3	0.3
2	0.2	1.6

$$\mu_3' = Ex^3 = 0 + 0.3 + 1.6 = 1.9.$$

EXAMPLE 2

Let $p(x) = \frac{1}{3}$, $0 \le x \le 3$. We have

$$\mu_4' = Ex^4 = \int_0^3 \left(\frac{x^4}{3}\right) dx = \left[\frac{x^5}{15}\right]_0^3 = \frac{243}{15} = \frac{81}{5}.$$

EXERCISES 101

1 Given the probability distribution in problem 1, Exercises 98, find $\mu_5' = Ex^5$; $\mu_3' = Ex^3$.

2 Given the probability distribution in problem 2, Exercises 98, find $\mu_2' = Ex^2$; $\mu_3' = Ex^3$.

3 Given the probability distribution in problem 3, Exercises 98, find $\mu_2' = Ex^2$; $\mu_4' = Ex^4$.

4 Given the probability distribution in problem 4, Exercises 98, find $\mu_2' = Ex^2$; $\mu_4' = Ex^4$.

5 Given the probability distribution in problem 5, Exercises 98, find $\mu_2' = Ex^2$; $\mu_5' = Ex^5$.

6 Given the probability distribution in problem 6, Exercises 98, find $\mu_3' = Ex^3$; $\mu_6' = Ex^6$.

7 Given the probability distribution in problem 7, Exercises 98, find μ_2'; μ_3'.

8 A probability distribution is of the form $p(x) = 1/a$, $0 \le x \le a$. Find a if $\mu_1' = Ex = \mu = 2$. Check.

9   Given the probability distribution

x	p
0	a
1	b
2	c
3	d

find the probabilities a, b, c, d, if $\mu_1' = Ex = \mu = 1.5$, $\mu_2' = Ex^2 = 2.9$, $\mu_3' = Ex^3 = 6.3$. Check.

**10   Given the probability distribution $p(x) = 1$, $0 \leq x \leq 1$. Find the formula for the kth moment about the origin.

***11   Given the probability distribution $p(x) = 1/(b - a)$, $a \leq x \leq b$. Find the formula for the kth moment about the origin.

102   MOMENTS ABOUT THE MATHEMATICAL EXPECTATION

A very important class of moments are the moments about the mathematical expectation. The kth moment about the mathematical expectation is the mathematical expectation of the kth power of the deviation of x from its mathematical expectation $Ex = \mu$; that is, for a discrete random variable x,

$$\mu_k = E(x - \mu)^k = \sum_{i=1}^{m} (x_i - \mu)^k p_i.$$

Thus, to obtain μ_k, we compute first the mathematical expectation μ. This is subtracted from the values of x, and the difference thus obtained is raised to the kth power. The result is multiplied in each case by the corresponding probability; then the products are summed.

For a continuous random variable x whose probability density p is $p(x)$. We have for the kth moment about the mathematical expectation

$$\mu_k = E(x - \mu)^k = \int_a^b (x - \mu)^k p(x)dx.$$

Let us now consider the moments about the mathematical expectation for various values of k:

$$\mu_0 = E(x - \mu)^0 = E1 = 1.$$

Thus the moment of order 0 about the mathematical expectation is 1. To study the first moment, we recall that the mathematical expectation of a constant is equal to the constant; moreover, the mathematical expectation $Ex = \mu$ is itself such a constant. Hence, $E(Ex) = Ex = \mu$. So we have as a

conclusion
$$\mu_1 = E(x - \mu) = Ex - E(\mu) = \mu - \mu = 0.$$

It follows that the first moment about the mathematical expectation is 0. Next we consider the second moment:

$$\mu_2 = E(x - \mu)^2 = \sigma^2.$$

The second moment about the mathematical expectation is very important in the field of statistics, and is known as the *dispersion of the distribution*. It shows the manner in which the various items x are distributed about the mean value $Ex = \mu$. It is called also the *population variance*, and designated by σ^2. The square root of the second moment about the mathematical expectation is denoted by σ, and is called the *population standard deviation;* that is,

$$\sqrt{\mu_2} = \sqrt{E(x - \mu)^2} = \sigma.$$

The third moment about the mathematical expectation,

$$\mu_3 = E(x - \mu)^3,$$

provides a measure of the skewness of the distribution. If a distribution is symmetrical about the mean value or mathematical expectation μ, then $\mu_3 = 0$. For instance, the distribution in Figure 46 is symmetrical, so $\mu_3 = 0$; the distribution in Figure 45 is asymmetrical.

The fourth moment about the mathematical expectation,

$$\mu_4 = E(x - \mu)^4,$$

is connected with the flatness or peakedness of the probability distribution. The technical name for this is *kurtosis*.

The normal distribution in Figure 50 has no kurtosis. The distributions in Figure 54 are more peaked than the normal distribution. Formulas for the computation of the second, third, and fourth moments about the mathematical expectation from the moments about the origin will be given in problems 6, 9, and 10, Exercises 102.

EXAMPLE 1

Consider the following probability distribution:

x	p_1	xp	$x - \mu$	$(x - \mu)^2$	$(x - \mu)^2 p_1$
1	⅓	⅓	-1	1	⅓
2	⅓	⅔	0	0	0
3	⅓	³⁄₃	1	1	⅓

We have $\mu = Ex = \tfrac{1}{3} + \tfrac{2}{3} + \tfrac{3}{3} = \tfrac{6}{3} = 2$. From the last column we have also $\sigma^2 = \tfrac{1}{3} + 0 + \tfrac{1}{3} = \tfrac{2}{3}$.

Now consider a second probability distribution:

x	p_2	xp	$x - \mu$	$(x - \mu)^2$	$(x - \mu)^2 p_2$
1	$\frac{1}{6}$	$\frac{1}{6}$	-1	1	$\frac{1}{6}$
2	$\frac{2}{3}$	$\frac{4}{3}$	0	0	0
3	$\frac{1}{6}$	$\frac{3}{6}$	1	1	$\frac{1}{6}$

From the above computations, the mean $\mu = Ex = 2$ and the variance $\sigma^2 = \frac{1}{3}$.

The two probability distributions are represented in Figure 47.

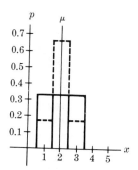

Figure 47

The first distribution is drawn with heavy lines, the second with broken lines. They have the same population mean, $\mu = Ex = 2$. But the variance of the first distribution is twice that of the second; it is apparent from the figure how the variance measures the spread, or dispersion, of the distribution about its mean.

EXAMPLE 2

Consider the probability distribution that follows:

x	p	$x - \mu$	$(x - \mu)^2 p$
0	0.5	-0.7	0.245
1	0.3	0.3	0.027
2	0.2	1.3	0.338

We have $\mu = Ex = 0.7$, $\mu_2 = E(x - \mu)^2 = 0.610 = \sigma^2$. This is the population variance.

EXAMPLE 3

Take the probability distribution $p(x) = \frac{1}{3}$, $0 \leq x \leq 3$. Then $Ex = \mu = 1.5$.

$$\mu_3 = E(x - \mu)^3 = \int_0^3 \left[\frac{(x - 1.5)^3}{3} \right] dx$$

$$= \int_0^3 \frac{1}{3}(x^3 - 4.5x^2 + 6.75x - 3.375)dx = 0.$$

Since the third moment about the mathematical expectation is 0, the distribution is symmetrical.

EXERCISES 102

1   Given the distribution in problem 1, Exercises 98, find μ_2; μ_3; μ_4.

2   Given the probability distribution in problem 2, Exercises 98, find μ_2; μ_3; μ_4.

3   Given the probability distribution in problem 3, Exercises 98, find μ_2; μ_3; μ_4.

4   Given the probability distribution in problem 4, Exercises 98, find μ_2; μ_3; μ_4.

5   Given the probability distribution in problem 5, Exercises 98, find μ_2; μ_3.

*6   Show that the *variance* $\mu_2 = \mu_2' - (\mu_1')^2 = Ex^2 - (Ex)^2 = Ex^2 - \mu^2 = \sigma^2$; where σ is the standard deviation. (HINT: Develop $(x - \mu)^2$ by the binomial theorem and evaluate the expectation.)

7   Use the formula from problem 6 to compute the variance for the probability distribution in problem 1, Exercises 98. Find the standard deviation.

8   Use the formula in problem 6 to compute the variance and standard deviation of the probability distribution of problem 2, Exercises 98.

*9   Prove that $\mu_3 = \mu_3' - 3\mu_2'\mu_1' + 2(\mu_1')^3 = Ex^3 - 3Ex^2Ex + 2(Ex)^3 = Ex^3 - 3\mu Ex^2 + 2\mu^3$.

*10   Prove that $\mu_4 = \mu_4' - 4\mu_3'\mu_1' + 6\mu_2'(\mu_1')^2 - 3(\mu_1')^4 = Ex^4 - 4Ex^3Ex + 6Ex^2(Ex)^2 - 3(Ex)^4 = Ex^4 - 4\mu Ex^3 + 6\mu^2 Ex^2 - 3\mu^4$.

11   Use the formulas in problems 6, 9, and 10 to compute μ_2, μ_3, and μ_4 for the distribution in problem 3, Exercises 98.

12   Use the formulas in problems 6, 9, and 10 to compute μ_2, μ_3, and μ_4 for the distribution in problem 4, Exercises 98.

Chapter 23

Binomial and
Normal Distributions

REPEATED TRIALS AND BINOMIAL DISTRIBUTION

Assume that the probability of an event happening is p. The probability that it does not happen is $q = 1 - p$. We will say we have a success if the event occurs and a failure if it does not happen.

We have altogether n trials in which we observe the event. What is the probability that the event will occur exactly r times in n independent trials?

One way in which this can happen is to have r successes first and then the $(n - r)$ failures. These events are independent and happen simultaneously. Hence by the multiplication theorem of probabilities, the probability of obtaining r successes first and then $(n - r)$ failures is $p^r q^{n-r}$.

But we do not care about the arrangement of the successes and failures as long as there are altogether r successes and $n - r$ failures. For example, we would be equally satisfied if the $n - r$ failures came first and the r successes last. The probability of this particular arrangement would be the same as above. This is also true of any other arrangement of the r successes and the $n - r$ failures. Let us add the probabilities of all these arrangements.

We know from the theory of combinations that the number of arrangements of the r successes and $n - r$ failures is the number of combinations of n things taken r at a time. This number of combinations is given by the binomial coefficient; thus

$$_nC_r = \binom{n}{r} = \frac{n!}{r!(n - r)!} = \frac{n(n - 1)(n - 2) \cdots (n - r + 1)}{1 \cdot 2 \cdot 3 \cdot \cdots \cdot r}.$$

So the probability must be multiplied by this binomial coefficient. Hence the probability of the event happening r times out of n trials is

$$P_r = {}_nC_r p^r q^{n-r}.$$

303

We remember that $_nC_0 = 1$. Furthermore, since the only possible values for r are 0, 1, 2, $\cdots$, n, then $P_0 + P_1 + P_2 + \cdots + P_n = 1$.

EXAMPLE 1

A true coin is tossed 3 times. What is the probability of heads coming up 2 times?

Since we have a true coin, the probability of heads is $p = \frac{1}{2}$. Also, the probability of heads *not* coming up is $q = 1 - p = \frac{1}{2}$. The number of trials is $n = 3$. The number of successes, according to the problem, is $r = 2$. Hence

$$P_2 = {}_3C_2 \left(\frac{1}{2}\right)^2 \left(\frac{1}{2}\right)^1 = \frac{3 \cdot 2}{1 \cdot 2} \left(\frac{1}{2}\right)^2 \left(\frac{1}{2}\right)^1 = \frac{3}{8}.$$

To check this we write down all the possible outcomes of three throws with a true coin. We shall let H denote heads and T tails. Altogether there are 8 possible arrangements of 3 throws. Of these there are only 3 that have 2 heads. Since all these 8 arrangements have the same probability, $\frac{1}{8}$, we have $P_2 = \frac{3}{8}$, as before.

EXAMPLE 2

Let an event have the probability $p = \frac{1}{3}$. Hence the probability that it will not happen is $q = 1 - p = \frac{2}{3}$. There are 4 trials.

Let us construct the whole probability distribution, that is, P_0, P_1, P_2, P_3, and P_4, which is called a *binomial distribution*, because of the binomial coefficients occurring in it. The distribution is

$$P_0 = {}_4C_0 \left(\frac{1}{3}\right)^0 \left(\frac{2}{3}\right)^4 = (1)(1)\left(\frac{16}{81}\right) = \frac{16}{81}.$$

$$P_1 = {}_4C_1 \left(\frac{1}{3}\right)^1 \left(\frac{2}{3}\right)^3 = (4)\left(\frac{1}{3}\right)\left(\frac{8}{27}\right) = \frac{32}{81}.$$

$$P_2 = {}_4C_2 \left(\frac{1}{3}\right)^2 \left(\frac{2}{3}\right)^2 = (6)\left(\frac{1}{9}\right)\left(\frac{4}{9}\right) = \frac{24}{81}.$$

$$P_3 = {}_4C_3 \left(\frac{1}{3}\right)^3 \left(\frac{2}{3}\right)^1 = (4)\left(\frac{1}{27}\right)\left(\frac{2}{3}\right) = \frac{8}{81}.$$

$$P_4 = {}_4C_4 \left(\frac{1}{3}\right)^4 \left(\frac{2}{3}\right)^0 = (1)\left(\frac{1}{81}\right)(1) = \frac{1}{81}.$$

As a matter of interest, and as a check, it is observed that the sum of these probabilities is 1. Figure 48 presents a histogram of this binomial distribution.

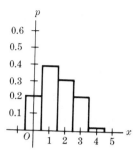

Figure 48

EXAMPLE 3

Let the probability of an event be $p = \frac{1}{4}$. What is the probability that it will happen 2 times in 4 trials? We have $q = 1 - p = \frac{3}{4}$. Then

$$P_2 = {}_4C_2 \left(\frac{1}{4}\right)^2 \left(\frac{3}{4}\right)^2 = \frac{4 \cdot 3}{1 \cdot 2}\left(\frac{1}{16}\right)\left(\frac{9}{16}\right) = \frac{27}{128}.$$

What is the probability that it will happen *at least* 1 time in 3 trials? The event can happen in 3 trials either not at all or 1, 2, or 3 times. Hence the desired probability is $P = P_1 + P_2 + P_3$. Since the sum of all the probabilities is 1, the sum is readily obtained as $1 - P_0 = 37/64$, since

$$P_0 = {}_3C_0 \left(\frac{1}{4}\right)^0 \left(\frac{3}{4}\right)^3 = \frac{27}{64}.$$

What is the probability that it will happen *not more* than 2 times in 3 trials? It is

$$P = P_0 + P_1 + P_2 = 1 - P_3 = \frac{63}{64},$$

since $P_3 = {}_3C_3(\frac{1}{4})^3(\frac{3}{4})^0 = \frac{1}{64}$.

EXERCISES 103

1   An event has the probability $p = \frac{1}{3}$. Find the probability that it will happen (a) 1 time in 3 trials; (b) 2 times in 6 trials; (c) 5 times in 5 trials; (d) 2 times in 4 trials; (e) *at least* 2 times in 7 trials; (f) *not more than* 3 times in 6 trials.

2   A true die is thrown. Find the probabilities that 6 will appear (a) 2 times in 3 trials; (b) 10 times in 10 trials (use logarithms); (c) 3 times in 6 trials; (d) at least 1 time in 5 trials; (e) not more than 2 times in 12 trials.

3   A true coin is thrown. Find the probability that we get heads (a) 1 time in 2 trials; (b) 2 times in 6 trials; (c) 4 times in 4 trials; (d) at least 1 time in 20 trials; (e) not more than 2 times in 15 trials.

4   An event has the probability $p = 0.2$. Find the probability that it happens (a) 2 times in 6 trials; (b) 3 times in 4 trials; (c) 6 times in 12 trials; (d) at least 1 time in 50 trials; (e) not more than 2 times in 200 trials.

5   An event has the probability $p = 0.8$. What is the probability that it will happen (a) 3 times in 6 trials? (b) 5 times in 9 trials? (c) at least 3 times in 4 trials? (d) not more than 9 times in 11 trials?

6   What is the probability of obtaining 10 heads with a true coin in 10 trials?

7   An event has the probability $p = 0.99$. What is the probability that it happens (a) 1 time in 4 trials? (b) 2 times in 7 trials? (c) at least 5 times in 6 trials? (d) not more than 2 times in 3 trials? (HINT: use logarithms.)

8   An event has the probability $p = 0.999$. What is the probability that it happens (a) 1 time in 2 trials? (b) not at all in 10 trials? (c) at least 1 time in 5 trials? (d) not more than 1 time in 100 trials? (HINT: use logarithms.)

9   Two true dice are thrown. What is the probability of obtaining the sum of 12 (a) 6 times in 6 trials? (b) 1 time in 100 trials? (c) at least 1 time in 5 trials? (d) not more than 2 times in 60 trials?

10   A true coin is tossed. What is the probability of obtaining (a) n heads in n trials? (b) 0 heads in n trials? (c) at least 1 head in n trials?

11   An event has the probability $p = \frac{2}{5}$. Compute the complete binomial distribution for the outcomes in the case of 6 trials. Plot the histogram of the distribution.

12   An event has the probability $p = \frac{3}{8}$. Find the complete binomial distribution for $n = 5$ trials. Plot the histogram of the distribution.

*13   *Poisson distribution.* Assume that the mean of the binomial distribution $np = L$, a constant. Then with large n the binomial distribution tends toward the Poisson distribution:

$$P_x = \frac{e^{-L}L^x}{x!}, \quad x = 0,1,2,\cdots$$

(a) Prove that $\Sigma_{x=0}^{\infty} P_x = 1$. (b) Prove that the mean of the Poisson distribution $\Sigma_{x=0}^{\infty} xP_x = L$. (HINT: $1 + (y/1!) + (y^2/2!) + \cdots = e^y$.)

14   Let x be distributed according to the Poisson distribution: $P_x = e^{-5}5^x/x!$. (a) Find P_2. (b) Find $P_0 + P_1$. (c) Find the mean of the distribution.

104   THE NORMAL DISTRIBUTION

As we have seen, the binomial distribution gives the probability that an event with probability p will happen r times in n trials; the formula for the computation is

$$P_r = {}_nC_r p^r q^{n-r}.$$

The computation of the binomial coefficient ${}_nC_r$ becomes very laborious if both n and r are large. Consider, for example, an event whose probability of happening is $p = \frac{1}{3}$. The probability that it will not happen is $q = \frac{2}{3}$. The probability that it will happen 40 times in 100 trials is given by

$$P_{40} = {}_{100}C_{40} \left(\frac{1}{3}\right)^{40} \left(\frac{2}{3}\right)^{60},$$

$$= \frac{(100)(99)(98)(97) \cdots (61)}{(1)(2)(3)(4) \cdots (40)} \left(\frac{1}{3}\right)^{40} \left(\frac{2}{3}\right)^{60}.$$

The computation of the binomial coefficient involves 40 multiplications in the numerator and the same number in the denominator. If n and r are still larger, the computations become even more involved. Hence it is desirable to have a convenient approximation to the binomial distribution for large n and r.

We will show in this section that a good approximation to the binomial distribution for large n is, under certain conditions, the so-called normal distribution. This distribution is also called the *normal error curve*, or the *Gaussian distribution*. A rigorous proof of the fact that as n becomes large the binomial distribution approximates the normal one is beyond the scope of this book. It requires very powerful mathematical methods.

We will compute first some moments of the binomial distribution. We recall that the random variable r, the number of successes in n trials, has the following distribution:

r	p_r
0	${}_nC_0 p^0 q^n$
1	${}_nC_1 p^1 q^{n-1}$
2	${}_nC_2 p^2 q^{n-2}$
3	${}_nC_3 p^3 q^{n-3}$
$\cdots$	
n	${}_nC_n p^n q^0.$

From this we compute the first moment about the origin; this is the mean value of mathematical expectation of r. We obtain

$$\mu_1' = \mu = Er$$

$$= (0){}_nC_0 p^0 q^n + (1){}_nC_1 p^1 q^{n-1} + (2){}_nC_2 p^2 q^{n-2}$$
$$+ (3){}_nC_3 p^3 q^{n-3} + \cdots + (n){}_nC_n p^n q^0$$
$$= (1)\frac{n}{1} p^1 q^{n-1} + (2)\frac{n(n-1)}{1 \cdot 2} p^2 q^{n-2} + (3)\frac{n(n-1)(n-2)}{1 \cdot 2 \cdot 3} p^3 q^{n-3}$$
$$+ \cdots + (n)\frac{n(n-1)(n-2) \cdots 1}{1 \cdot 2 \cdot 3 \cdot \cdots \cdot n} p^n q^0.$$

We can factor out the common factor np and get

$$Er = (np)\left[1 \cdot p^0 q^{n-1} + \frac{(n-1)}{1} p^1 q^{n-2} + \frac{(n-1)(n-2)}{1 \cdot 2} p^2 q^{n-2} + \cdots \right.$$
$$\left. + \frac{(n-1)(n-2) \cdots 1}{1 \cdot 2 \cdots (n-1)} p^{n-1} q^0 \right].$$

Consider now the expression in the square brackets. The coefficients are the binomial coefficients in the expansion

$$(p + q)^{n-1} = {}_{n-1}C_0 p^0 q^{n-1} + {}_{n-1}C_1 p^1 q^{n-2} + \cdots + {}_{n-1}C_{n-1} p^{n-1} q^0.$$

Hence we can write $\mu = Er = np(p + q)^{n-1}$.

But we recall that $p + q = 1$. Thus, $\mu = Er = np$. This is the mean value or mathematical expectation of the binomial distribution.

EXAMPLE 1

Consider an event that has the probability $p = \frac{2}{3}$, $q = \frac{1}{3}$. Let the number of trials be $n = 4$. What is the mean value or mathematical expectation of the number of successes r?

Using the formula for the binomial distribution, we compute the following table:

r	P_r
0	$\frac{1}{81}$
1	$\frac{8}{81}$
2	$\frac{24}{81}$
3	$\frac{32}{81}$
4	$\frac{16}{81}$

By direct computation we have for the mathematical expectation of r

$$\mu = Er = 0\left(\frac{1}{81}\right) + 1\left(\frac{8}{81}\right) + 2\left(\frac{24}{81}\right) + 3\left(\frac{32}{81}\right) + 4\left(\frac{16}{81}\right)$$
$$= \frac{216}{81} = \frac{8}{3}.$$

The same result can also be obtained rather simply by the formula

$$\mu = Er = np = 4\left(\frac{2}{3}\right) = \frac{8}{3}.$$

By a similar method we can compute the second moment about the origin for the binomial distribution

$$\mu_2' = Er^2 = npq + n^2p^2.$$

We recall the formula for computing the variance from the two first moments about the origin (problem 6, Exercises 102):

$$\sigma^2 = \mu_2 = \mu_2' - (\mu_1')^2 = Ex^2 - \mu^2.$$

Hence we have for the variance of the binomial distribution

$$\sigma^2 = \mu_2 = Er^2 - (Er)^2 = npq + n^2p^2 - (np)^2 = npq.$$

The standard deviation is the square root of the variance; so

$$\sigma = \sqrt{\mu_2} = \sqrt{npq}.$$

EXAMPLE 2

Let us use the same binomial distribution as in Example 1. We recall that the mathematical expectation or mean value of the binomial distribution was found to be $\mu = Er = \frac{8}{3}$.

From the table given above we get by direct computation for the variance of the binomial distribution

$$\mu_2 = \sigma^2 = E(r - Er)^2$$

$$= \left(0 - \frac{8}{3}\right)^2 \left(\frac{1}{81}\right) + \left(1 - \frac{8}{3}\right)^2 \left(\frac{8}{81}\right) + \left(2 - \frac{8}{3}\right)^2 \left(\frac{24}{81}\right)$$

$$+ \left(3 - \frac{8}{3}\right)^2 \left(\frac{32}{81}\right) + \left(4 - \frac{8}{3}\right)^2 \left(\frac{16}{81}\right)$$

$$= \frac{648}{729} = \frac{8}{9}.$$

Using the formula just derived, we obtain also

$$\sigma^2 = \mu_2 = npq = 4 \left(\frac{2}{3}\right) \left(\frac{1}{3}\right) = \frac{8}{9}.$$

The standard deviation of our binomial distribution is

$$\sigma = \sqrt{\mu_2} = \sqrt{\frac{8}{9}} = 0.943.$$

We state now, without proof, the following theorem: If, in a binomial distribution, the number of trials n becomes large, and the probabilities p or q are not very small, the binomial distribution can be approximated by the so-called normal distribution, whose probability density is given by

$$p(u) = \frac{1}{\sqrt{2\pi}} e^{-\frac{1}{2}u^2}, \quad -\infty < u < \infty.$$

$$u = \frac{r - \mu}{\sigma}, \quad \text{and} \quad \mu = Er = np, \sigma^2 = npq.$$

The normal distribution is not only a convenient approximation to the binomial distribution. It occurs frequently in empirical distributions of natural and social phenomena because of the *central limit theorem*.

Assume that we have n random variables that are independent. Their distribution is arbitrary. Consider the distribution of their sum. It can be shown that this sum is, under certain conditions, normally distributed if n becomes infinite.

Many empirical statistical distributions are normal. This is especially true of the distribution of errors of observations. A graph of the normal distribution is shown in Figure 50.

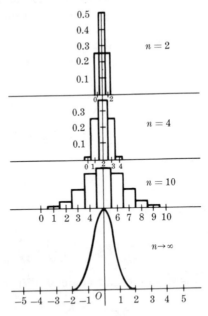

Figure 49

In Figure 49 is shown the convergence of a binomial distribution to the normal, as n becomes larger and larger. This convergence is shown by studying the binomial $(\frac{1}{2} + \frac{1}{2})^n$ for $n = 2, 4, 10$. The curves are so constructed that they all have the same mean and variance. It is apparent that the larger n (the number of trials) becomes, the more the histograms have an appearance not too different from the normal distribution. The normal distribution is shown at the bottom of the figure.

The probability with a normally distributed variable u with mean 0 and variance 1, $a \leq u \leq b$, is given by the integral,

$$\int_a^b \frac{1}{\sqrt{2\pi}} e^{-\frac{1}{2}x^2} dx.$$

The integral of the normal probability distribution is tabulated by exhibiting the area under the normal curve from 0 to u; thus

$$\int_0^u \frac{1}{\sqrt{2\pi}} e^{-\frac{1}{2}x^2} dx.$$

This is the probability that the normally distributed variable will fall between 0 and u.

It is seen from Figure 49 that the normal distribution is symmetrical about its mean $\mu = 0$. Hence, the probability that a normally distributed variable will fall between 0 and u is the same as that it will fall between $-u$ and 0. The normal distribution goes from $-\infty$ to $+\infty$, as seen in Figure 49.

If we have a normal distribution of a random variable x having the mean μ and variance σ^2, we must make the transformation,

$$u = \frac{x - \mu}{\sigma},$$

in order to use our tables (note Table 4, Appendix D). Since the table gives areas between 0 and u, we find the probability that x lies between x_1 and x_2 in the following way. Obtain the values of u_1 and u_2 by use of the following formulas:

$$u_1 = \frac{x_1 - \mu}{\sigma}, \qquad u_2 = \frac{x_2 - \mu}{\sigma}.$$

Then look in the table under u_1 and u_2. If u_1 and u_2 have the same sign, subtract the smaller area from the larger one. If u_1 and u_2 have different signs, add the areas. This will give the probability that the normally distributed variable x with mean μ and variance σ^2 lies between x_1 and x_2.

As an example we show in Figure 50 the area under the normal curve from $u_1 = -1$ to $u_2 = 1.5$. The u's have different signs; hence, we must add the areas obtained from the table; that is, since the area for $u = 1$ is given in Table 4 as 0.3413 and for $u = 1.5$ as 0.4332, we have $0.3413 + 0.4332 = 0.7745$. This is

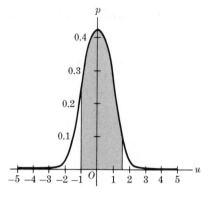

Figure 50

the shaded area shown in the graph. It corresponds to the probability that the normally distributed variable u with 0 mean and unit variance will fall in the interval $-1 \le u \le 1.5$.

EXAMPLE 3

Assume that x is normally distributed. Its population mean is $\mu = 5$ and its population variance is $\sigma^2 = 4$. Hence its population standard deviation is $\sigma = 2$.

(a) Find the probability that $6 \le x \le 8$. We have

$$u_1 = \frac{6 - 5}{2} = 0.5,$$

$$u_2 = \frac{8 - 5}{2} = 1.5.$$

From Table 4, Appendix D, we obtain 0.1915 for the area under the normal curve at $u = 0.5$ and obtain 0.4332 at $u = 1.5$. Since u_1 and u_2 have the same sign, we must subtract. So we obtain $0.4332 - 0.1915 = 0.2417$ for the probability that x will fall between 6 and 8.

(b) Find the probability that $2 \le x \le 3$. This time we have

$$u_1 = \frac{2 - 5}{2} = -1.5,$$

$$u_2 = \frac{3 - 5}{2} = -1.$$

Since the normal distribution is symmetrical, we can neglect the minus signs. We have the area 0.4332 for $u = 1.5$ and the area 0.3413 for $u = 1$. Since we have like signs for u_1 and u_2, we subtract; thus $0.4332 - 0.3413 = 0.0919$ is the probability that x will fall between 2 and 3.

(c) What is the probability that $1 \leq x \leq 7$? We have

$$u_1 = \frac{1 - 5}{2} = -2,$$

$$u_2 = \frac{7 - 5}{2} = 1.$$

We have 0.4773 in the table for the area under the normal curve for $u = 2$ (neglecting again the negative sign because of the symmetry of the normal distribution), and we have 0.3413 for $u = 1$. Since we have unlike signs, we must add the areas. The sum, $0.4773 + 0.3413 = 0.8186$, gives the probability that x will fall between 1 and 7.

(d) What is the probability that $5 \leq x \leq 8$? We have

$$u_1 = \frac{5 - 5}{2} = 0,$$

$$u_2 = \frac{8 - 5}{2} = 1.5.$$

From the table we have 0 area for $u = 0$ and 0.4332 for $u = 1.5$. Hence the probability that x will fall between 1 and 7 is 0.4332.

(e) What is the probability that $9 \leq x \leq 20$? We have

$$u_1 = \frac{9 - 5}{2} = 2,$$

$$u_2 = \frac{20 - 5}{2} = 7.5.$$

We have the area 0.4773 for $u = 2$; $u = 7.5$ is beyond the range of the table. But we note that for u greater than 3.88 the area is 0.5000, correct to four decimals. Hence we take this area for any u beyond the range of the table. Since u_1 and u_2 have like signs, we subtract and obtain $0.5000 - 0.4773 = 0.0227$. This is the probability that x lies between 9 and 20.

(f) What is the probability that $x \geq 11$? This can be thought of as $11 \leq x \leq \infty$. We have

$$u_1 = \frac{11 - 5}{2} = 3,$$

$$u_2 = \infty.$$

For $u = 3$, the area is 0.4987. For $u = \infty$ we take the area as 0.5000. The signs are alike, so we subtract and get $0.5000 - 0.4987 = 0.0013$. This is the probability that x is greater than 11.

EXAMPLE 4

Compute the normal approximation to the binomial distribution in Example 1 for $r = 2$.

Since the normal distribution is continuous, we take the area between $r = 1.5$ and $r = 2.5$. Remember that $\mu = Er = 2.67$ and $\sigma = 0.943$. We have

$$u_1 = \frac{1.5 - 2.67}{0.943} = -1.24,$$

$$u_2 = \frac{2.5 - 2.67}{0.943} = -0.18.$$

We have from the tables the area 0.0714 for $u = 0.18$ and the area 0.3925 for $u = 1.24$. The signs of u_1 and u_2 are the same, so we subtract and get $0.3925 - 0.0714 = 0.3211$.

This is the normal approximation to the value for $r = 2$ in our binomial. This value was $^{24}\!/_{81} = 0.2963$. The error of the normal approximation is $0.3211 - 0.2963 = 0.0248$.

EXERCISES 104

1   An event has the probability $p = 0.4$. What is the probability that it will happen not less than 35 times and not more than 55 times in 100 trials? (HINT: Use the normal approximation to the binomial distribution.)

2   An event has the probability $p = 0.49$. What is the probability that it will happen not less than 30 and not more than 40 times in 50 trials?

3   An event has the probability $p = 0.475$. What is the probability that it will happen not less than 935 times and not more than 945 times in 2,000 trials?

4   An event has the probability $\frac{1}{2}$. Find the probability that it will happen *at least* 6 times in 10 trials (a) by the exact evaluation of the binomial distribution; (b) by the normal approximation. Compare the results.

5   An event has the probability $\frac{1}{3}$. What is the probability in 1,000 trials that it will happen (a) between 300 and 400 times? (b) between 330 and 335 times? (c) between 300 and 320 times? (d) between 350 and 355 times? (e) at least 290 times? (f) at least 370 times? (g) not more than 315 times? (h) not more than 355 times?

6   A variable x is normally distributed with $\mu = Ex = 10$, $\sigma^2 = 9$. Find the probability that x will fall (a) between 10 and 11; (b) between 12 and 19; (c) between 8 and 9.5; (d) between 7 and 8.2; (e) between 0 and 6; (f) between 12.5 and 35; (g) between 9.5 and 11.3.

7   A variable x is normally distributed with $\mu = Ex = 50$, $\sigma^2 = 25$. Find the probability that it will fall between the following limits: (a) 45 and

48; (b) 52 and 60; (c) 0 and 40; (d) 55 and 100; (e) that it is larger than 54; (f) smaller than 57; (g) larger than 43; (h) smaller than 39.

8 An event has the probability $\frac{1}{2}$. Compute the probabilities that it happens 0, 1, 2, 3, 4, 5, 6, 7, 8 times in 8 trials. Compare these probabilities with the normal approximations. Make a histogram and plot the normal curve.

9 Compute the normal approximations to the binomial distribution in problem 11, Exercises 103. Make a histogram of the binomial distribution and plot the normal distribution.

10 Compute the normal approximation to the binomial distribution in problem 12, Exercises 103. Plot the histogram of the binomial and the normal distributions.

**11 Find the value of x which maximizes the probability P of the normal distribution with mean μ and variance σ^2.

$$ P = \frac{1}{\sigma \sqrt{2\pi}} e^{-(x-\mu)^2/2\sigma^2} $$

The value that maximizes the probability is the *mode*. Show that for the normal distribution the mode is equal to the population mean μ.

12 The distribution $p(x) = e^{-(\log x - M)^2/2\sigma^2}/x\sigma \sqrt{2\pi}$ is the *lognormal* distribution. By using the transformation $y = (\log x - M)/\sigma$ it might be transformed into the normal distribution tabulated in Table 4, Appendix D. Assume $M = 2$, $\sigma = 1$ and find $\int_{10}^{50} p(y)dy$ with the help of this transformation.

13 Assume that the logarithm of income is normally distributed. Denote by $f(y, t; x, s)$ the probability that income is y at time t if it was x at time s $(t > s)$ (Tintner and Patel). Empirically we find for Indian real national income for 1948–1962

$$ f(y, t; x, s) = \frac{e^{-[\log y - \log x - 0.03(t-s)]^2/2(0.59)(t-s)}}{y \sqrt{2\pi(0.59)}} $$

Find $f(y, t; x, s)$ for $y = 130$, $t = 14$, $x = 86.5$, $s = 0$.

105   POISSON PROCESS

Consider a random variable x that can assume only nonnegative integral values, $x = 0, 1, 2, \cdots$. Let $P_x(t)$ be the probability distribution of x at time t (t is continuous). Now we consider what may happen in a small time interval between t and $t + \Delta t$. With not negligible probabilities only two possibilities may occur: (1) a transition from x to $x + 1$, whose probability is given by $L(\Delta t)$; for some positive constant L, and (2) no change, with the probability $1 - L(\Delta t)$. All other transitions can occur only with negligible probabilities. Now we have

$$P_x(t + \Delta t) = L(\Delta t)P_{x-1}(t) + [1 - L(\Delta t)]P_x(t).$$

This means that the probability of obtaining x at the point in time $t + \Delta t$ is the sum of two alternatives: either a transition at the point in time t from $x - 1$ to x, with the probability $L(\Delta t)P_{x-1}(t)$, or no change, with the probability $[1 - L(\Delta t)]P_x(t)$.

Now we rearrange the terms of our equation as follows:

$$\frac{P_x(t + \Delta t) - P_x(t)}{(\Delta t)} = L[P_{x-1}(t) - P_x(t)].$$

It is easily seen that as $\Delta t \to 0$, we arrive on the left-hand side at the derivative $dP_x(t)/dt$. Hence in the limit,

$$\frac{dP_x(t)}{dt} = L[P_{x-1}(t) - P_x(t)].$$

This is a mixed differential-difference equation. Its solution is

$$P_x(t) = e^{-Lt}\frac{(Lt)^x}{x!} \qquad x = 0, 1, \cdots,$$

and we recognize this as a Poisson distribution with mean value Lt (problem 13, Exercises 103).

Since the mean of the resulting distribution is Lt, we might determine L by dividing the number of events occurring in a period t by the length of the time interval t.

EXAMPLE

Consider a Poisson process with $L = 3$. Then we obtain a mean value (trend) $Lt = 5t$. For example, for $t = 10$, we have the trend value $Ex = 50$. Also, say for $t = 1$, we have the Poisson distribution,

$$P_x(1) = \frac{e^{-5}5^x}{x!}$$

Hence we get, for example,

$$P_0(1) = \frac{e^{-5}5^0}{0!} = e^{-5}; \qquad P_1(1) = \frac{e^{-5}5^1}{1!} = 5e^{-5};$$

$$P_2(1) = \frac{e^{-5}5^2}{2!} = \frac{25e^{-5}}{2}; \qquad P_3(1) = \frac{e^{-5}5^3}{3!} = \frac{125e^{-5}}{6}, \qquad \text{and so on.}$$

EXERCISES 105

1 Verify that the probability distribution of the Poisson process satisfies the differential-difference equation.

2 Given a Poisson process with $L = 3$, (a) find Ex for $t = 5$; (b) compute $P_0(1)$, $P_1(1)$, $P_2(1)$, $P_3(1)$, $P_4(1)$.

3 The following deals with Pennsylvania manufacturing for the period 1899–1959 (Tintner, Narasimham, Patil, Raghavan). (5-year periods, $t = 0$ corresponds to 1899, $t = 13$ to 1959.) If y is the value of manufacturing in Pennsylvania, let $x = y/913$. We estimate a Poisson process for x as follows: $P_x(t) = e^{-0.7t}(0.7t)^x/x!$. Predict x and y for $t = 16$ (1974).

4 The following refers to Indian national income for the period 1948–1949 ($t = 11$) to 1961–1962 ($t = 14$) (Mukherjee, Tintner, Narayanan). Let y be net national output. Define $x = (y - 78)/1 \cdot 2$. Then we obtain for x a Poisson process: $P_x(t) = e^{-3.56}(3 \cdot 5t)^x/x!$. Predict Ex and Ey for $t = 20$ (1967–1968).

106 ELEMENTS OF QUEUING THEORY

Consider a queue and let n be the number of people waiting, including those being served. Let $p_n(t)$ be the probability that there are n people in one queue. Assume, further, that the probability of a new arrival is approximately $L(\Delta t)$ and the probability that a customer will leave the queue is approximately $K(\Delta t)$, where L and K are constants and Δt is a small time interval. We have for $n = 0$

$$P_0(t + \Delta t) = K(\Delta t)p_1(t) + [1 - L(\Delta t)]p_e(t),$$

and for $n = 1, 2, 3, \cdots$,

$$p_n(t + \Delta t) = L(\Delta t)p_{n-1}(t) + K(\Delta t)p_{n+1}(t) + [1 - L(\Delta t)]p_n(t).$$

Proceeding as we did with the derivation of the Poisson process, we assume that $\Delta t \to 0$ and derive the differential-difference equations:

$$\frac{dp_0(t)}{dt} = Kp_1(t) - Lp_0(t),$$

$$\frac{dp_n(t)}{dt} = Lp_{n-1}(t) + Kp_{n+1}(t) - (L + K)p_n(t).$$

We want to find the equilibrium probability distribution, that is, the distribution for $t \to \infty$. Then the left sides of the equations are zero, and we have

$$0 = Kp_1 - Lp_0,$$
$$0 = Lp_{n-1} + Kp_{n+1} - (L + K)p_n.$$

Hence we derive $p_n = R^n(1 - R)$, where we must have $R = L/K < 1$. R is called the traffic intensity. This is a geometric distribution. It can be shown that the average length of the queue in the limit is given by

$$En = \frac{R}{1 - R}.$$

EXAMPLE

Assume that the probability of the arrival of a customer is $2(\Delta t)$ and that the probability of a customer leaving the queue is $5(\Delta t)$. Hence we have $L = 2$ and $K = 5$; the equilibrium distribution of the length of the queue is

$$p_n = R^n(1 - R),$$

where $R = L/K = \frac{2}{5}$. Hence $p_n = (\frac{2}{5})^n(\frac{3}{5})$. For example, we have $p_0 = (\frac{2}{5})^0(\frac{3}{5}) = \frac{3}{5}$, the probability of no customer in the queue. Also $p_1 = (\frac{2}{5})^1(\frac{3}{5}) = \frac{6}{25}$, the probability of one customer in the queue. Also $p_2 = (\frac{2}{5})^2(\frac{3}{5}) = \frac{12}{125}$, for $n = 2$, and so on. The average length of the queue is $R/(1 - R) = \frac{2}{3}$.

EXERCISES 106

1   Given $L = 1$ and $K = 3$, (a) find the limiting probability distribution of the length of the queue p_n and compute p_n for $n = 0, 1, 2, 3$; (b) find the average length of the queue.

**2   Prove that the mean length of the queue, $\Sigma_{n=0} np_n = R/(1 - R)$. (HINT: Differentiate both sides of the relation $\Sigma_{n=0} R^n = (1 - R)^{-1}$ with respect to R. Multiply the result on both sides by $R/(1 - R)$.)

Chapter 24
Elements of Sampling

107 ESTIMATION

Modern statistics distinguishes between the population and the sample. The sample may be used to gain some information about the unknown population from which it is drawn. We will deal only with *random samples*, but it should be emphasized that under certain conditions other methods of sampling may be more efficient in providing information about the unknown population.

A random sample is constructed in such a way that every item in the population has an equal chance to be chosen in the sample. Suppose, for instance, that we want some idea of the family income in a town of 10,000 families. There is only enough money available to investigate 100 families. We want to construct a random sample of 100 out of the total population of 10,000 families.

One method of constructing the sample is the following: Write the names and addresses of all 10,000 families on slips of paper. The 10,000 paper slips are put into a container and well mixed. Out of the container 100 slips are drawn at random. The 100 families selected in this fashion constitute a random sample of the total population of 10,000 families.

Great caution must be exerted in selecting the random sample. For instance, it may be more convenient to select the 100 families from the families of the faculty of a college located in the city. This, however, would not give a random sample, for not every family in the city has the same chance to be chosen in the sample. Probably the average income estimated from this selection of faculty families would be too high. Or we might be tempted to select the 100 families out of the telephone directory of the city. We could, for example, take the first 100 names in the telephone directory. This would violate an important principle of random sampling. Not all families have telephones, especially the poorer ones. Hence, the postulate of random sampling that every family must have an equal chance to be chosen is violated. Our estimate of the average

319

income from the sample out of the telephone directory would probably overestimate the average income.

Another method of sampling which will not be discussed here at length is the method of *stratified sampling*. Under certain conditions this method may be preferable to random sampling. To sample in this way, we divide our whole population into strata. For instance, the 10,000 families in the city may be classified according to professions. These strata form our subsamples. The size of the random sample to be chosen from each stratum is proportionate to the number of families in the particular stratum. For example, if 25 percent of the families in the city belong to a certain profession, then 25 percent of the sample, that is, 25 families out of a total sample of 100 families, ought to be taken at random from this particular profession. This method of sampling, which has definite advantages, is called *representative sampling*.

In economic statistics we generally do not know all we wish to about the population from which our data are a sample. We may consider the data as random samples of a hypothetically infinite population. For example, if a set of wheat prices is recorded on a market it may be considered as a random sample of all (unrecorded) wheat prices from transactions on the market, or even as a sample of the (hypothetically infinite) population of all possible wheat prices.

Statistical *estimation* is the method by which we extract information about the population from the sample. This is the only object of sampling. We are not, in general, interested in the sample for its own sake.

The estimates derived from the sample are functions of the various observations contained in the sample. Since these observations are random variables, the estimates are themselves also random variables. An estimate is also called a *statistic*.

For instance, in the example given above, we drew a random sample of 100 families from a total (finite) population of 10,000 families in a city in order to learn something about the average income *in the population*, that is, among the 10,000 families.

Various principles have been advanced for estimation. We can state here only a few: One important property is *unbiasedness*.

By an unbiased estimate we understand an estimate whose mean value (mathematical expectation) is equal to the true value in the population. For instance: The sample mean is an unbiased estimate of the population if its mathematical expectation is equal to the population mean. The sample variance is an unbiased estimate of the population variance if the mathematical expectation of the sample variance is equal to the population variance, and so on.

To show that the *sample mean* is an unbiased estimate of the population mean, assume a sample consisting of the items

$$x_1, \ x_2, \ x_3, \ \cdots, \ x_n.$$

All the items in the sample are supposed to have been drawn at random from a population with mean $Ex = \mu$ and population variance σ^2. Since we have a random sample, the random variables $x_1, x_2, \cdots, x_n$ are independent.

We define the sample mean as the arithmetic mean of the n items

$$\bar{x} = \frac{x_1 + x_2 + x_3 + \cdots + x_n}{n} = \frac{\sum\limits_{i=1}^{n} x_i}{n}.$$

We have noted that all observations are drawn from a population with true mean (population mean) μ. Hence the mathematical expectation of all the items $x_1, x_2, \cdots, x_n$ is $Ex = \mu$; that is,

$$Ex_1 = Ex = \mu,$$
$$Ex_2 = Ex = \mu,$$
$$Ex_3 = Ex = \mu,$$
$$\cdots$$
$$Ex_n = Ex = \mu.$$

We want to show that the mathematical expectation of $\bar{x}$ is also equal to μ. Take

$$E\bar{x} = E\left[\left(\frac{1}{n}\right)x_1 + \left(\frac{1}{n}\right)x_2 + \cdots + \left(\frac{1}{n}\right)x_n\right].$$

We use two propositions established earlier when dealing with computations involving mathematical expectations (Section 99); namely, the mathematical expectation of a sum is the sum of the mathematical expectations.

The mathematical expectation of a constant times a random variable is the constant times the mathematical expectation of the random variable.

From these two propositions it follows that

$$E\bar{x} = \left(\frac{1}{n}\right)Ex_1 + \left(\frac{1}{n}\right)Ex_2 + \cdots + \left(\frac{1}{n}\right)Ex_n$$
$$= \left(\frac{1}{n}\right)(Ex + Ex + \cdots + Ex)$$
$$= \left(\frac{1}{n}\right)(n\mu) = \mu.$$

The mathematical expectation of the sample mean $\bar{x}$ is the population mean μ. Hence $\bar{x}$ is an unbiased estimate of the population mean.

By the method of expectations we can also compute the *variance of the sample mean* $\bar{x}$; that is,

$$\sigma_{\bar{x}}^2 = E(\bar{x} - E\bar{x})^2.$$

We have

$$\bar{x} - \mu = \frac{x_1 + x_2 + \cdots + x_n}{n} - \mu$$

$$= \frac{x_1 + x_2 + \cdots + x_n - n\mu}{n}$$

$$= \frac{(x_1 - \mu) + (x_2 - \mu) + \cdots + (x_n - \mu)}{n}.$$

Since the sample $x_1, x_2, \cdots, x_n$ is drawn from the population with mean $Ex = \mu$ and variance σ^2, we have

$$E(x_1 - \mu)^2 = \sigma^2,$$
$$E(x_2 - \mu)^2 = \sigma^2,$$
$$\cdots$$
$$E(x_n - \mu)^2 = \sigma^2.$$

The items $x_1, x_2, \cdots, x_n$ are taken at random. Hence they are independent. We recall that the mathematical expectation of two independent random variables is the product of their mathematical expectations; hence we have, for example,

$$E(x_1 - \mu)(x_2 - \mu) = E[x_1 x_2 - x_1\mu - x_2\mu + (\mu)^2]$$
$$= Ex_1 Ex_2 - (\mu)Ex_1 - (\mu)(Ex_2) + E(\mu)^2 = 0.$$

By a similar argument we have

$$E(x_1 - \mu)(x_3 - \mu) = 0,$$
$$E(x_1 - \mu)(x_4 - \mu) = 0,$$
$$\cdots$$
$$E(x_1 - \mu)(x_n - \mu) = 0.$$

In general, we have

$$E(x_i - \mu)(x_j - \mu) = 0, \quad \text{if } i \neq j.$$

Squaring the expression for $\bar{x} - \mu$ derived previously and taking the mathematical expectation, we have

$$\sigma_{\bar{x}}^2 = E(\bar{x} - \mu)^2$$
$$= E\left[\frac{\begin{array}{c}(x_1 - \mu)^2 + (x_2 - \mu)^2 + \cdots + (x_n - \mu)^2 \\ + 2(x_1 - \mu)(x_2 - \mu) + \cdots + 2(x_i - \mu)(x_j - \mu) + \cdots\end{array}}{n^2}\right],$$

where $i \neq j$ in the product terms. We know that the mathematical expectation of all the products is 0. The mathematical expectation of the n squares is σ^2 for each square. Hence we get for the variance of the sample mean

$$\sigma_{\bar{x}}^2 = E(\bar{x} - \mu)^2 = \frac{n\sigma^2}{n^2} = \frac{\sigma^2}{n}.$$

That is, the variance of the sample mean of a sample of n is the population variance σ^2 divided by n.

If we extract the square root of the variance of the sample mean, we get the so-called *standard error* of the sample mean, namely,

$$\sigma_{\bar{x}} = \frac{\sigma}{\sqrt{n}}.$$

In words, the standard error of the sample mean $\bar{x}$ in a sample of n is the standard deviation of the population σ divided by the square root of n.

Now we consider the *sample variance*. Let us again assume that we have a sample of n, namely,

$$x_1, x_2, \cdots, x_n.$$

All these items are drawn at random from a population with population mean μ and population variance σ^2. Hence we have

$$Ex_1 = \mu, \qquad E(x_1 - \mu)^2 = \sigma^2,$$
$$Ex_2 = \mu, \qquad E(x_2 - \mu)^2 = \sigma^2,$$
$$\cdots \qquad\qquad \cdots$$
$$Ex_n = \mu. \qquad E(x_n - \mu)^2 = \sigma^2.$$

We define the sample variance as follows:

$$V = \frac{(x_1 - \bar{x})^2 + (x_2 - \bar{x})^2 + \cdots + (x_n - \bar{x})^2}{n - 1},$$

$$= \frac{\sum\limits_{i=1}^{n} (x_i - \bar{x})^2}{n - 1}.$$

In words, the sample variance is computed by dividing the sum of squares of the deviations from their arithmetic mean by $n - 1$, that is, by one less than the number of items in the sample. It may be considered as the arithmetic mean of the squares of deviations, which are random variables.

We want to show that the mathematical expectation of the sample variance is equal to population variance; that is,

$$EV = \sigma^2.$$

If this is true, then the sample variance is an unbiased estimate of the population variance.

**Since the mathematical expectation of a sum is the sum of the mathematical expectations, we have

$$EV = \frac{E(x_1 - \bar{x})^2 + E(x_2 - \bar{x})^2 + \cdots + E(x_n - \bar{x})^2}{n - 1}.$$

Let us compute one of the mathematical expectations in the numerator; for instance, $E(x_1 - \bar{x})^2$.

Evidently we can add and subtract the constant $\mu = Ex$ in the parentheses without changing the expression; that is,

$$(x_1 - \bar{x}) = (x_1 - \mu) - (\bar{x} - \mu).$$

Squaring this expression, and obtaining the mathematical expectation, we have

$$E(x_1 - \bar{x})^2 = E[(x_1 - \mu)^2 - 2(x_1 - \mu)(\bar{x} - \mu) + (\bar{x} - \mu)^2]$$
$$= E(x_1 - \mu)^2 - 2E(x_1 - \mu)(\bar{x} - \mu) + E(\bar{x} - \mu)^2.$$

We have from previously derived formulas

$$E(x_1 - \mu)^2 = \sigma^2,$$

$$E(\bar{x} - \mu)^2 = \frac{\sigma^2}{n}.$$

There still is the problem of computing the mathematical expectation of the middle term. Ignoring the factor -2, the mathematical expectation of this term is

$$E(x_1 - \mu)(\bar{x} - \mu)$$
$$= E\left[(x_1 - \mu)\left(\frac{x_1 + x_2 + \cdots + x_n}{n} - \mu\right)\right]$$
$$= E\left[(x_1 - \mu)\left(\frac{x_1 + x_2 + \cdots + x_n - n\mu}{n}\right)\right]$$
$$= E\left[(x_1 - \mu)\left(\frac{(x_1 - \mu) + (x_2 - \mu) + \cdots + (x_n - \mu)}{n}\right)\right]$$
$$= E\left[\frac{(x_1 - \mu)^2 + (x_1 - \mu)(x_2 - \mu) + \cdots + (x_1 - \mu)(x_n - \mu)}{n}\right]$$
$$= \frac{E(x_1 - \mu)^2 + E(x_1 - \mu)(x_2 - \mu) + \cdots + E(x_1 - \mu)(x_n - \mu)}{n}.$$

Since the mathematical expectation of the square $(x_1 - \mu)^2$ is, by definition, σ^2, and since the mathematical expectation of all the other terms is 0 (this has been shown above), this fraction becomes σ^2/n.

Using this result and the previously established formulas, we have

$$E(x_1 - \bar{x})^2 = E(x_1 - \mu)^2 - 2E(x_1 - \mu)(\bar{x} - \mu) + E(\bar{x} - \mu)^2$$
$$= \sigma^2 - \frac{2\sigma^2}{n} + \frac{\sigma^2}{n}$$
$$= \frac{(n - 1)\sigma^2}{n}.$$

By a similar argument we derive also for the other terms in the numerator of EV

$$E(x_2 - \bar{x})^2 = \frac{(n-1)\sigma^2}{n},$$

$$E(x_3 - \bar{x})^2 = \frac{(n-1)\sigma^2}{n},$$

$$\cdots$$

$$E(x_n - \bar{x})^2 = \frac{(n-1)\sigma^2}{n}.$$

Hence we have finally for the mathematical expectation of the variance

$$EV = \frac{E(x_1 - \bar{x})^2 + E(x_2 - \bar{x})^2 + E(x_3 - \bar{x})^2 + \cdots + E(x_n - \bar{x})^2}{n-1}$$

$$= \frac{n(n-1)/n}{n-1}\sigma^2 = \sigma^2.$$

Hence the mathematical expectation of the sample variance is the population variance σ^2. The sample variance as given by the above formula is an unbiased estimate of the population variance.**

It should be noted that in order to compute V we divide the sum of squares of the deviations from the mean by $n-1$. That is, we divide the number of observations by a number which is 1 less than n. The quantity $(n-1)$ is frequently called the *number of degrees of freedom* used for the computation of the variance. This term has a somewhat complicated meaning. Speaking rather loosely, we may express the idea of degrees of freedom as follows: The amount of information available in a sample depends upon its size. A sample of 100 contains more information than a sample of only 10 items, and so on. We use some of this information in a sample of n items to compute the same mean. This uses up 1 degree of freedom. Hence, when we compute the sample variance we have only $(n-1)$ degrees of freedom left, since for the computation of the variance we need to know the sample mean.

The method of maximum likelihood, which is used very frequently to obtain estimates, is illustrated in problem 5, Exercises 107. The method of least squares, which is also used to obtain estimates, is discussed in Section 118.

Consistency is also a desirable attribute for an estimate. A consistent statistic will tend more and more to the population value estimated as the sample increases in size. The sample mean and the sample median (problem 11, Exercises 109) are examples of consistent statistics if the population is normal.

Some estimates tend to be normally distributed as the sample increases in size. They are called *efficient* if they have in the limit the smallest possible variance. The sample mean is an efficient statistic if the population is normal. Its variance is smaller than, for example, the variance of the sample median for large samples.

Finally, there are statistics that include all the relevant information available even in small samples. Such statistics are called *sufficient*. The sample mean of a sample taken from a normal population is such a sufficient statistic.

EXERCISES 107

1   Show that the mathematical expectation of the quantity $z = \Sigma_{i=1}^{n} x_i : Ez = n\mu$, if the random sample $x_1, x_2, \cdots, x_n$ is drawn from a population with true mean $Ex = \mu$.

**2   Let $x_1, x_2, \cdots, x_n$ be a random sample drawn from a population with true mean μ and population variance σ^2. Consider the expression

$$w = \sum_{i=1}^{n} k_i x_i,$$

where the k_i are constants and $\Sigma_{i=1}^{n} k_i = 1$. (a) Show that the mathematical expectation $Ew = Ex = \mu$. (b) Demonstrate that $E(w - Ew)^2 = \sigma^2 \Sigma_{i=1}^{n} k_i^2$. (c) Use the previous results to establish the formulas given above for the mathematical expectation and variance of the sample mean $\bar{x}$. (HINT: Take $k_i = 1/n$.)

*3   Show that the formula for the sample variance, namely,

$$V = \frac{\sum\limits_{i=1}^{n} (x_i - \bar{x})^2}{n - 1},$$

may be simplified to

$$V = \frac{\sum\limits_{i=1}^{n} x_i^2 - n\bar{x}^2}{n - 1}.$$

(HINT: Remember the definition of the sample mean: $\bar{x} = \Sigma_{i=1}^{n} x_i/n$.)

4   Using the results in the last example, show that the sample variance in the case of grouped items is

$$V = \frac{\sum\limits_{i=1}^{m} (x_i - \bar{x})^2 f_i}{N - 1} = \frac{\sum\limits_{i=1}^{m} x_i^2 f_i - N\bar{x}^2}{N - 1},$$

where the symbols have the following interpretation: There are m classes, the frequencies of which are $f_1, f_2, \cdots, f_m$; the x_i is the class mean;

$\sum_{i=1}^{m} f_i = N$ is the total number in the sample, and the sample mean is $\bar{x} = \sum_{i=1}^{m} x_i f_i / N$.

**5 Let the probability density of x_1 be

$$p_1 = \frac{1}{\sqrt{2\pi}} e^{-\frac{1}{2}(x_1 - a)^2};$$

let the probability density of x_2 be

$$p_2 = \frac{1}{\sqrt{2\pi}} e^{-\frac{1}{2}(x_2 - a)^2}$$

$$\cdots;$$

and finally let the probability density of x_n be

$$p_n = \frac{1}{\sqrt{2\pi}} e^{-\frac{1}{2}(x_n - a)^2}.$$

All the x_i are independently, normally distributed with variance 1. (a) Find the probability that the independent events $x_1, x_2, \cdots, x_n$ will happen together. (b) Maximize this probability (*method of maximum likelihood*) by choosing the appropriate value of a. (c) Show that the maximum likelihood estimate is the sample mean $\bar{x}$.

**6 Show that the mathematical expectation of

$$W = \frac{\sum_{i=1}^{n} (x_i - \bar{x})^2}{n}$$

is not equal to the population variance σ^2. What is the mathematical expectation of W?

**7 Show that the mathematical expectation of

$$Z = \frac{\sum_{i=1}^{n} (x_i - \mu)^2}{n}$$

is equal to the population variance. What is the difference between Z and the W in problem 6?

108 FREQUENCY DISTRIBUTIONS

If a sample consists of many items, it is virtually necessary to arrange it in a frequency distribution. The classes of this distribution are given in advance. If an item falls exactly on the limit of two adjacent classes, it ought to be distributed between them evenly; that is, one half ought to be put into the upper class and one half into the lower. The class midpoints are the arithmetic means of the class limits.

EXAMPLE

A sample consists of the following items: 2, 8, 6, 3, 5, 1, 4. Arrange a frequency distribution with the following classes: 0–2, 2–4, 4–6, 6–8, 8–10. Between 0 and 2 there is the item 1, and we will count one half of item 2, since 2 coincides with a limit; so there is a frequency of 1.5. Between 2 and 4 there is the item 3, and we will count one half of item 2 and one half of item 4; so there is a frequency of 2; and so on. This may be displayed in the following table:

Class Limits	Class Midpoint	Frequency
0–2	1	1.5
2–4	3	2
4–6	5	2
6–8	7	1
8–10	9	0.5

The graph of a frequency distribution is called a *histogram*. Figure 51 presents the histogram of the frequency distribution just constructed. Note that the limits of the blocks in the graph are the limits of the classes in the frequency distribution.

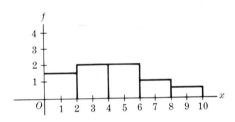

Figure 51

EXERCISES 108

1 Given the following sample of items: 4, 10, 23, 20, 19, 8, 6, 5, 25, 4, 17, 36, arrange the set of values (a) in a frequency distribution with classes 0–4, 4–8, · · · ; (b) with classes 0–5, 5–10, 10–15 · · · ; (c) with classes 0–10, 10–20, · · · . (d) Make histograms.

2 Given a sample consisting of the items 2, 4, 6, 3, 9, 6, 4, 9, 8, 5, 2, 9, 5, 1, 1, arrange the sample in a frequency distribution with (a) classes 0–2, 2–4, · · · ; (b) with classes 0–3, 3–6, · · · . (c) Graph the distributions.

3 Given the data 0, 8, 18, 45, 23, 45, 9, 17, 19, 25, 39, 41, 19, 25, 6, 10, 36, (a) arrange them in a frequency distribution with the classes 0–10, 10–20, · · · . (b) Make a histogram.

*4   Consider the data 1, 4, 10, 17, 5, 6, 10. (a) The *range* is defined as the difference between the largest and the smallest item; find the range. (b) Form a frequency distribution by dividing the range into five parts; (c) by dividing the range into seven parts. (d) Make graphs of the distributions.

5   Use the data in problem 1. (a) Find the range. (b) Form a frequency distribution by dividing the range into three parts; (c) into four parts. (d) Make graphs.

6   Use the data in problem 2. (a) Find the range. (b) Form a frequency distribution by dividing the range into four parts. (c) Make graphs.

7   Use the data in problem 3. (a) Find the range. (b) Form a frequency distribution by dividing the range into six parts. (c) Make a histogram.

8   Use the data in problem 4. (a) Find the range. (b) Form a frequency distribution by dividing the range into three parts. (c) Make a histogram.

109   SAMPLE MEAN AND VARIANCE

Let us set up a table that displays a frequency distribution and certain associated products.

Class Mean	Frequency		
x_i	f_i	$x_i f_i$	$x_i^2 f_i$
x_1	f_1	$x_1 f_1$	$x_1^2 f_1$
x_2	f_2	$x_2 f_2$	$x_2^2 f_2$
. . . . . .	. . . . . .	. . . . . .	. . . . . .
x_m	f_m	$x_m f_m$	$x_m^2 f_m$
Sums:	$N = \sum_{i=1}^{m} f_i$	$\sum_{i=1}^{m} x_i f_i$	$\sum_{i=1}^{m} x_i^2 f_i$

As previously indicated, the class means are the arithmetic means of the class limits.

We have defined earlier the sample mean as $\bar{x} = (1/n)\sum_{i=1}^{n} x_i$. In the frequency distribution under consideration we have m classes with certain frequencies. Under such a circumstance the sample mean becomes

$$\bar{x} = \frac{1}{N} \sum_{i=1}^{m} x_i f_i,$$

if the sum of all the frequencies is

$$N = \sum_{i=1}^{m} f_i.$$

So N is computed as the sum of the second column of the above table, and $\bar{x}$ is computed as the ratio of the sum of the third column and the sum of the second column. The sample mean is an unbiased estimate of the population mean.

We gave earlier a formula for the sample variance of ungrouped data in problem 3, Exercises 107; that is,

$$V = \frac{\sum_{i=1}^{n} (x_i - \bar{x})^2}{n - 1} = \frac{\sum_{i=1}^{n} x_i^2 - n\bar{x}^2}{n - 1}.$$

With grouped data this becomes

$$V = \frac{\sum_{i=1}^{m} (x_i - \bar{x})^2 f_i}{N - 1} = \frac{\sum_{i=1}^{m} x_i^2 f_i - N\bar{x}^2}{N - 1}.$$

The expression $\sum_{i=1}^{m} x_i^2 f_i$ is the sum obtained from column 4 in the above table. The sample variance is an unbiased estimate of the population variance.

The sample standard deviation is the square root of the sample variance; that is, $s = \sqrt{V}$.

EXAMPLE 1

Assume that we have the sample 3, 5, 2. We have three items; hence, $n = 3$. We compute $\sum_{i=1}^{3} x_i = 3 + 5 + 2 = 10$; $\sum_{i=1}^{3} x_i^2 = 9 + 25 + 4 = 38$. From the formulas above

The sample mean is $\qquad \bar{x} = \dfrac{10}{3} = 3.33.$

The sample variance is $\qquad V = \dfrac{38 - (3)(3.33)^2}{2} = 2.37.$

The sample standard deviation is $\quad s = \sqrt{2.37} = 1.54$

EXAMPLE 2

By contrast with Example 1, let us consider an illustration involving grouped data, as follows:

Class Limits	Class Mean	Frequency		
	x	f	xf	x^2f
0–4	2	1	2	4
4–8	6	3	18	108
8–12	10	1	10	100
		$N = 5$	$\Sigma xf = 30$	$\Sigma x^2 f = 212$

We have

$$\bar{x} = \frac{30}{5} = 6; \qquad V = \frac{212 - (5)(36)}{4} = \frac{32}{4} = 8;$$

$$s = \sqrt{8} = 2.83.$$

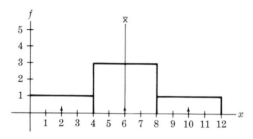

Figure 52

Figure 52 shows a histogram of the frequency distribution given in Example 2. The class means are indicated by arrows. We have also indicated the sample mean by a heavy vertical line. It provides a measure of the general location of the frequency distribution or its central tendency.

EXAMPLE 3

Make the following experiment. Write the name and some characteristic (height, age) of each student in the class on a slip of paper. Make a frequency distribution, if necessary, and establish the average. Mix the slips well in a hat and draw successively samples of 2, 3, 4, · · · items. Find the sample mean and variance of each sample.

EXERCISES 109

1 Consider the following sample:

Class Limits	Frequency
0–10	1
10–20	2
20–30	3
30–40	2
40–50	2

Make a histogram. Find the sample mean, variance, and standard deviation.

2 Consider the following sample:

Class Limits	Frequencies
1–3	10
3–5	50
5–7	40

Make a histogram. Find the sample mean, variance, and standard deviation.

3 Consider the following sample:

Class Limits	Frequencies
0–4	1
4–8	4
8–12	5
12–16	3
16–20	2
20–24	1

Make a histogram. Find the sample mean, variance, and standard deviation.

4 Consider the following sample:

Class Limits	Frequencies
2–5	2
5–8	3
8–11	5
11–14	4
14–17	3
17–20	3

Make a histogram. Find the sample mean, variance, and standard deviation.

5 Consider the following sample:

Class Limits	Frequencies
0–5	1
5–10	3
10–15	4
15–20	1
20–25	1

Make a histogram. Find the sample mean, variance, and standard deviation.

6   Consider the following sample:

Class Limits	Frequencies
0–20	5
20–40	20
40–60	30
60–80	15

Make a histogram. Determine the sample mean, variance, and standard deviation.

7   The distribution of families and single consumers in the United States, by money income levels, 1942, is given by the following table:

Income Class Limits	Frequency
$ 0–500	3,488,000
500–1,000	6,652,000
1,000–1,500	6,601,000
1,500–2,000	6,008,000
2,000–2,500	4,618,000
2,500–3,000	3,372,000
3,000–4,000	2,620,000
4,000–5,000	2,633,000
5,000–7,500	1,901,000
7,500–10,000	628,000

Find the sample mean, variance, and standard deviation.

8   Income tax returns of corporations in the United States, 1942, by total assets are listed in the following table:

Total Assets Class Limits	Number of Returns Frequency
$ 0–50,000	196,642
50,000–100,000	58,338
100,000–250,000	57,365
250,000–500,000	27,300
500,000–1,000,000	18,109
1,000,000–5,000,000	19,582
5,000,000–10,000,000	2,905
10,000,000–50,000,000	2,467

Compute the mean, variance, and standard deviation.

9   The population of the United States, 1945, by ages, is as follows:

Age Class Limits	Frequency (Millions)
0–5	11
5–10	11
10–15	12
15–20	12
20–25	12
25–30	11
30–35	10
35–40	10
40–45	9
45–50	8
50–55	7
55–60	6
60–65	5
65–70	4
70–75	3
75–80	3

(a) Make a histogram. (b) Compute the sample mean, variance, and standard deviation.

10   Compute the sample mean and variance without grouping the data: Exercises 108; (a) problem 1; (b) problem 2; (c) problem 3; (d) problem 4.

**11   The sample median is computed by ordering the items in a sample according to size. The median is the item in the middle (for odd sample numbers) or the arithmetic mean of the two items in the middle (for even sample numbers). Compute the median for (a) the data in problem 2, Exercises 108; (b) the data in problem 1, Exercises 108.

110   SHEPPARD'S CORRECTION

If we compute the sample variance from grouped data, we should correct for grouping. An error is evidently committed by substituting the midpoint for all the items in a given class.

This error of grouping can be corrected quite satisfactorily by subtracting from the variance the square of the class interval, divided by 12. This is called *Sheppard's correction*.

EXAMPLE

In Example 2, Section 109, the class interval was 4 and the uncorrected variance was 8. Using Sheppard's correction, we have for the corrected value of the variance $8 - (4)^2/12 = 8 - 16/12 =$

$8 - 1.33 = 6.67$. The corrected standard deviation is $\sqrt{6.67} = 2.58$. This should be compared with the uncorrected value of 2.83.

EXERCISES 110

1 Using the data in problem 1, Exercises 109, compute the variance and the standard deviation, using Sheppard's correction for grouping.

2 Using the data in problem 2, Exercises 109, compute the variance and the standard deviation, using Sheppard's correction.

3 Using the data in problem 3, Exercises 109, compute the sample variance and the standard deviation, using Sheppard's correction.

4 Using the data in problem 4, Exercises 109, compute the variance and the standard deviation, using Sheppard's correction.

5 Using the data in problem 5, Exercises 109, compute the variance and the standard deviation, using Sheppard's correction.

6 Using the data in problem 6, Exercises 109, compute the variance and the standard deviation, using Sheppard's correction.

7 Using the data in problem 9, Exercises 109, compute the sample variance and the standard deviation, using Sheppard's correction.

8 Using the data in problem 10, Exercises 109, compute the sample variance and the standard deviation using Sheppard's correction.

111 CONFIDENCE LIMITS

We demonstrated in Section 107 that the arithmetic mean of a sample of n items has the mathematical expectation $E\bar{x} = \mu$ and the variance $\sigma_{\bar{x}}^2 = \sigma^2/n$. The following is proved in more advanced books on statistics: If the sample comes from a normal population, the quantity

$$u = \frac{\bar{x} - \mu}{\sigma_{\bar{x}}}$$

is normally distributed with mean 0 and variance 1. It follows the normal distribution described above. If the population is not normally distributed, u will under certain conditions tend to be normally distributed if the sample becomes large.

For large samples we can assume that the square root of the sample variance will provide a reasonably good estimate of the population standard deviation. This follows from the law of large numbers. It is almost certain that the sample variance, which is the mean of certain random variables, differs from the population variance (the mathematical expectation of these variables) as little as desired, if only the sample becomes sufficiently large. Hence, in this case we will compute the quantity

$$s_{\bar{x}} = \sqrt{\frac{V}{n}} = \frac{s}{\sqrt{n}}$$

as an empirical estimate for the standard error of the arithmetic mean $\sigma_{\bar{x}}$. The quantity

$$u = \frac{\bar{x} - \mu}{s_{\bar{x}}}$$

will be approximately normally distributed with mean 0 and variance 1. The larger the sample, the better will be the approximation.

This theorem can be used to establish a large sample pair of confidence limits for the (unknown) true mean of the population from which the sample is taken. Fiducial limits are computed in the same way but have a somewhat different interpretation. From the table of the normal distribution we see that the probability that u lies between -1.96 and 1.96 is 0.05. This gives us the 95 percent confidence interval.

The quantities $\bar{x}$ and $s_{\bar{x}}$ are computed according to the known formulas. Then we compute the limits

$$\bar{x} + 1.96 s_{\bar{x}} \quad \text{and} \quad \bar{x} - 1.96 s_{\bar{x}}.$$

Now consider the statement that the (unknown) true mean of the population μ will be contained within these confidence, or fiducial, limits. This statement will be true in 95 percent of the cases and untrue in 5 percent if the total number of cases is large. It is almost certain that the difference between the empirical relative frequency and the theoretical probability becomes as small as desired in large samples. That is, in the long run, on the average, we will be right in 95 out of 100 cases if we claim that the true or population mean is contained within the limits computed above.

EXAMPLE 1

Assume that we have a sample of 100 items ($N = 100$). Consider that the empirical arithmetic mean in the sample is $\bar{x} = 20$ and the sample variance is $V = 4$. Find a set of confidence limits for the population mean for a confidence coefficient of 95 percent.

We compute the empirical approximation to the standard error of the sample mean; thus

$$s_{\bar{x}} = \sqrt{\frac{4}{100}} = \frac{2}{10} = 0.2.$$

The two limits are

$$\bar{x} + 1.96s_{\bar{x}} = 20 + 1.96(0.2) = 20.392,$$
$$\bar{x} - 1.96s_{\bar{x}} = 20 - 1.96(0.2) = 19.608.$$

These limits have the meaning: The statement that the population mean lies between 19.608 and 20.392 and between similarly computed limits will sometimes be true and sometimes false. But if we use the above formula, then in a large number of samples the chances are that in the long run, on the average, the interval will contain the true mean in about 95 percent of all cases.

EXAMPLE 2

Assume that we have the following sample:

Class Limits	Class Mean	Frequency		
	x	f	xf	x^2f
0–10	5	10	50	250
10–20	15	30	450	6,750
20–30	25	20	500	12,500
		60	1,000	19,500

The number of items N in the sample is 60. We have from the sums indicated in the table

$$\bar{x} = \frac{1,000}{60} = 16.67,$$

$$V = \frac{19,500 - (60)(16.67)^2}{59} = 47.91,$$

$$s = \sqrt{46.89} = 6.92.$$

From this we get an approximation for the standard error of the sample mean; namely,

$$s_{\bar{x}} = \frac{6.92}{\sqrt{60}} = 0.893.$$

We want to establish the 95 percent confidence, or fiducial, limits for the population mean. They are

$$16.67 + (1.96)(0.893) = 18.42,$$
$$16.67 - (1.96)(0.893) = 14.92.$$

Thus, in repeated samples, the (unknown) population mean μ will lie, in the long run, on the average, within similarly computed limits in about 95 percent of the cases.

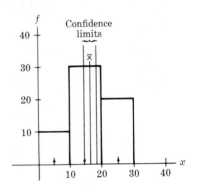

Figure 53

Figure 53 gives the above frequency distribution, the sample mean, and the fiducial, or confidence, limits of the population mean established above.

EXERCISES 111

Compute the 95 percent confidence limits for the population mean of the samples listed below:

1 Problem 1, Exercises 108.

2 Problem 2, Exercises 108.

3 Problem 3, Exercises 108.

4 Problem 4, Exercises 108.

5 Problem 1, Exercises 109.

6 Problem 3, Exercises 109.

7 Problem 4, Exercises 109.

8 Problem 7, Exercises 109.

9 Problem 8, Exercises 109.

10 Problem 9, Exercises 109.

Chapter 25

Tests of Hypotheses

112 TESTS OF STATISTICAL HYPOTHESES (LARGE SAMPLES)

A very important branch of modern statistics deals with the tests of statistical hypotheses. A statistical hypothesis is a hypothesis about a property of the (unknown) population.

Suppose that we have a sample with which we want to test the hypothesis. We compute the probability that the particular sample and its characteristics (mean, and so on) would have arisen if the hypothesis were true. This probability will not in general be 0, but it may be very small.

We will choose a *level of significance*, for example, 5 percent. This means that a hypothesis is to be rejected if our sample could have arisen by pure chance in less than 5 percent of the cases, if the hypothesis is true. If the probability is less than 5 percent, say 0.001 percent, we will reject the hypothesis; if the probability is larger than 5 percent, say 20 percent, we will not reject it.

We give here the large sample theory of tests of hypotheses concerning the population mean μ of a normal population. The small-sample theory is presented in Section 113. We have shown above that for large samples the sample standard deviation s is a good approximation to the population standard deviation σ. This follows from the law of large numbers. Hence the quantity

$$u = \frac{\bar{x} - \mu}{s_{\bar{x}}}$$

will be normally distributed with 0 mean and unit variance, where μ is the hypothetical population mean and

$$s_{\bar{x}} = \frac{s}{\sqrt{n}}$$

is an empirical approximation to its standard error.

339

From these data we can compute the probability that a positive or negative deviation equal to or greater than u might have arisen by pure chance. This probability is

$$P = 1 - 2p,$$

where p is the probability listed for u in Table 4, Appendix D. To be more specific, P is the probability of obtaining the empirical sample mean $\bar{x}$, or another sample mean with the same or greater positive or negative deviation from the hypothetical population mean μ.

Two types of errors are committed in testing hypotheses. The first type occurs if a true hypothesis is rejected. The probability of the error of the first kind is given by the level of significance. If the level of significance is 5 percent, then a true hypothesis will be rejected in about 5 percent of the cases, in the long run, on the average.

But there is another type of error, called the *error of the second kind*. This error occurs if a false hypothesis is not rejected. Statistical procedures ought to be devised in such a way that the probability of committing an error of the second kind is minimized. The following tests have the property of minimizing the probability of errors of the second kind for a given probability of errors of the first kind.

EXAMPLE 1

Let us assume a sample of 400 items. The sample mean is $\bar{x} = 21$, the sample variance $V = 100$. We want to test the hypothesis that the (unknown) population mean $\mu = 20$. The level of significance is 5 percent. We have

$$s_{\bar{x}} = \sqrt{\frac{V}{n}} = \sqrt{\frac{100}{400}} = 0.5,$$

$$u = \frac{\bar{x} - \mu}{s_{\bar{x}}} = \frac{21 - 20}{0.5} = 2.$$

For $u = 2$ we have from Table 4, $p = 0.4773$. Hence the probability of obtaining as large a value, or a larger value, of u (disregarding the sign) by chance is

$$P = 1 - (2)(0.4773) = 0.0454.$$

This value, only about $4\frac{1}{2}$ percent, is less than the level of significance specified (5 percent). Hence the hypothesis that $\mu = 20$ must be rejected.

EXAMPLE 2

In a sample of $N = 100$ take $\bar{x} = 19.5$, $V = 25$, $s = 5$. Test the hypothesis that $\mu = 20$ where the level of significance is 5 percent.

We have $s_{\bar{x}} = \frac{5}{10} = 0.5$; $u = (19.5 - 20)/0.5 = -1$. From Table 4, we have 0.3413 for $u = 1$. The probability of a positive or negative divergence as large as or larger than the one observed is $1 - (2)(0.3413) = 0.3174$. This value is larger than 5 percent so the hypothesis is not rejected.

EXERCISES 112

1 Take the sample $\bar{x} = 25$, $N = 2,500$, $V = 100$. Test the hypothesis that $\mu = 24.3$, level of significance 5 percent.

2 Consider the sample $N = 100$, $\bar{x} = 19.5$, $V = 36$. Test the hypothesis that $\mu = 20$, level of significance 1 percent.

3 Given the frequency distribution in problem 2, Exercises 109, test the hypothesis that $\mu = 4.1$, level of significance 5 percent.

4 Given the sample in problem 6, Exercises 109, test the hypothesis that $\mu = 43$, level of significance 1 percent.

5 Given the sample in problem 5, Exercises 109. Test the hypothesis (a) $\mu = 12$; (b) $\mu = 13$; (c) $\mu = 14$; (d) $\mu = 16$; level of significance 1 percent.

6 A sample of 2,500 items has a sample mean of 41 and a sample variance of 100. Test the hypothesis that the population mean $\mu = 40$, level of significance 5 percent.

7 A sample of 49 items has a sample mean of 8 and a sample variance of 16. Test the hypothesis that the true mean $\mu = 10$, level of significance 1 percent.

*8 Show that the probability that the mean in a sample will fall between $\bar{x} - 2.58s_{\bar{x}}$ and $\bar{x} + 2.58s_{\bar{x}}$ is 0.99. (HINT: Remember that $\bar{x}$ in large samples is normally distributed with mean μ and variance σ^2/N. The limits are called the 99 percent confidence, or fiducial, limits.)

9 Use the results in problem 8 to establish the 99 percent fiducial, or confidence, limits for the mean of the sample in problem 2, Exercises 109.

10 Use the results in problem 8 to establish the 99 percent confidence, or fiducial, limits for the mean of the sample in problem 6, Exercises 109.

113 TESTS OF STATISTICAL HYPOTHESES (SMALL SAMPLES)

The tests of hypotheses given above are valid only for large samples. They are based upon the fact that for large samples the sample variance V is a good approximation for the population variance σ^2. This follows from the law of large numbers. The chances are that the approximation will be closer the larger the sample.

If the sample is small, the above procedures are not adequate. But it can be shown by methods beyond the scope of this book that for small samples from a normal population the quantity

$$t = \frac{\bar{x} - \mu}{s_{\bar{x}}}$$

follows not the normal but the so-called t *distribution*, or *Student's distribution*. The probability density of t is given by

$$p(t) = \frac{[(n - 1)/2]!}{\sqrt{n\pi}\,[(n - 2)/2]![1 + (t^2/n)]^{(n+1)/2}}.$$

This distribution is shown graphically in Figure 54 and has been tabulated. Note Table 5, Appendix D. In this table n is the number of degrees

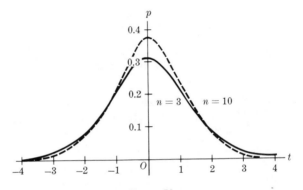

Figure 54

of freedom. Figure 54 shows the t distribution for 3 and 10 degrees of freedom. The area tabulated is the probability that

$$1 - \int_{-t}^{t} p(x)\,dx = P.$$

The quantity P is the probability that the deviation will be numerically equal to or larger than t.

The t distribution may also be used to find confidence limits for the population mean in small samples from a normal population.

The number of degrees of freedom n at which the table of the t distribution has to be entered is $N - 1$, one less than the number of items in the sample.

It appears from Figure 54 that the larger the number of degrees of freedom, the more will the t distribution approximate the normal distribution. Hence, if the number of degrees of freedom becomes as large as or larger than 30, we may use instead of t the quantity u, which is normally distributed with 0 mean and unit variance, tabulated in Table 4, Appendix D.

EXAMPLE

In a sample of $N = 9$ items we have the sample mean $\bar{x} = 13$ and the sample variance $V = 25$. Hence $s = 5$, and $s_{\bar{x}} = s/\sqrt{N} = 5/\sqrt{9} = \frac{5}{3} = 1.67$. Test the hypothesis that the true or population mean is $\mu = 10$. Take the level of significance as 5 percent. Thus $t = (x - \mu)/s_{\bar{x}} = (13 - 10)/1.67 = 3/1.67 = 1.8$. For $n = N - 1 = 8$ degrees of freedom, we have $t = 2.306$ at the 5 percent level of significance. Our empirical t is only 1.8. Hence its probability is greater than 5 percent, and the hypothesis that the true or population mean is 10 is not rejected.

EXERCISES 113

1 Use the sample of problem 1, Exercises 109, to test the hypothesis that $\mu = 24$, level of significance 1 percent.

2 Use the data in problem 2, Exercises 109, to test the hypothesis that $\mu = 4$, level of significance 5 percent.

3 Use the data in problem 3, Exercises 109, to test the hypothesis that $\mu = 10$, level of significance 1 percent.

4 Use the data in problem 4, Exercises 109, to test the hypothesis that $\mu = 11$, level of significance 5 percent.

5 Use the data in problem 5, Exercises 109, to test the hypothesis that $\mu = 10$, level of significance 5 percent.

6 Use the data in problem 6, Exercises 109, to test the hypothesis that $\mu = 38$, level of significance 1 percent.

7 Use the data in problem 7, Exercises 109, to test the hypothesis that $\mu = 2,100$, level of significance 1 percent.

8 Use the data in problem 9, Exercises 109, to test the hypothesis that $\mu = 35$, level of significance 5 percent.

**9 Consider the problem of establishing the 95 percent confidence, or fiducial, limits for the sample mean in small samples. (HINT: The number of degrees of freedom has to be taken into account.)

**10 Use the results of problem 9 to establish the 95 percent confidence, or fiducial, limits for the data in problem 1, Exercises 109.

**11 Use the results of problem 9 to establish the 95 percent and the 99 percent fiducial, or confidence, limits for the sample in problem 3, Exercises 109.

114 TESTS OF SIGNIFICANCE FOR TWO SAMPLES

In a test of significance we test a hypothesis which we call the *null* hypothesis. First, we fix *a priori* a certain level of significance. Then we find the probability that the positive or negative deviation between the empirical results of the sample and the postulated hypothesis should have arisen by pure chance. If the probability is less than the level of significance chosen, we reject the null hypothesis. We say that the quantity we are testing is *significant*.

We will use the test of significance to test the difference between the mean in two samples. Let there be N_1 observations in the first sample and N_2 in the second sample. Let $\bar{x}_1$ and $\bar{x}_2$ be the means in the two samples and V_1 and V_2 their sample variances. Both samples come from normal populations.

We have the null hypothesis that in the population the two population means are equal, that is, that $Ex_1 - Ex_2 = 0$.

To test this hypothesis we compute

$$t = \frac{\bar{x}_1 - \bar{x}_2}{s_{\bar{x}_1-\bar{x}_2}}.$$

The denominator of this fraction can be computed by recalling that

$$s^2_{\bar{x}_1-\bar{x}_2} = \frac{[(N_1 - 1)V_1 + (N_2 - 1)V_2](N_1 + N_2)}{N_1 N_2 (N_1 + N_2 - 2)},$$

which is the square of the standard error of the difference of the means. For large samples, $t = u$, and is normally distributed. For small samples we have t distributed according to the t distribution with $n = N_1 + N_2 - 2$ degrees of freedom.

EXAMPLE 1

Assume that we have two samples with $N_1 = 100$, $N_2 = 400$. Take the sample means as $\bar{x}_1 = 11.5$ and $\bar{x}_2 = 12$ and the sample variances as $V_1 = 9$ and $V_2 = 4$. We want to test the hypothesis that in the populations we have no difference between their means. The level of significance is 1 percent. Since we have large samples, we must evaluate

$$u = \frac{\bar{x}_1 - \bar{x}_2}{s_{\bar{x}_1-\bar{x}_2}}.$$

For the square of the standard error of the difference between the sample means we obtain

$$s^2_{\bar{x}_1-\bar{x}_2} = \frac{[(99)(9) + (399)(4)](100 + 400)}{(100)(400)(100 + 400 - 2)} = 0.0624.$$

Then the standard error of the difference of the means is

$$s_{\bar{x}_1 - \bar{x}_2} = \sqrt{0.0624} = 0.25.$$

Finally,

$$u = \frac{11.5 - 12}{0.25} = -2.$$

From Table 4, Appendix D, we have 0.4773 for $u = 2$; we neglect the sign because of the symmetry of the normal distribution. This is the probability of getting a u *less* than 2. We want the probability of obtaining a u greater in absolute value than 2. Hence our probability is $1 - 2(0.4773) = 0.0454$. This is more than 0.01, the given level of significance. Hence, the null hypothesis cannot be rejected. The difference in the means is not significant.

EXAMPLE 2

Let us illustrate the situation for small samples. Assume in the first sample $N_1 = 9$, $\bar{x}_1 = 5$, $V_1 = 25$; in the second sample $N_2 = 4$, $\bar{x}_2 = 13$, $V_2 = 16$. We want to test the null hypothesis that in the populations there is no difference between the means; that is, we test the significance of $\bar{x}_1 - \bar{x}_2$, level of significance 5 percent.

We have for the standard error of the difference of the two means

$$s_{\bar{x}_1 - \bar{x}_2} = 2.85.$$

Hence,

$$t = \frac{(5 - 13)}{2.85} = -2.81.$$

Because of the symmetry of the t distribution we can neglect the negative sign. For $n = N_1 + N_2 - 2 = 11$ degrees of freedom we have $t = 2.201$ at the level of significance specified. Our empirical t, namely, 2.81, is larger. Hence the null hypothesis that there is no difference in the population between the two means is to be rejected. The two population means are in all probability significantly different.

EXERCISES 114

1   Consider the following two samples:

Sample 1		Sample 2	
Class Limits	Frequencies	Class Limits	Frequencies
0–4	1	0–5	2
4–8	4	5–10	5
8–12	3	10–15	2

Test the significance of the difference of the means, level of significance 5 percent.

2   Consider the following two samples:

Sample 1		Sample 2	
Class Limits	Frequencies	Class Limits	Frequencies
0–10	10	0–20	10
10–20	10	20–40	30
20–30	10	40–60	20
30–40	10		
40–50	10		

Test the significance of the difference of the two sample means, level of significance 1 percent.

3   Consider the following two samples:

Sample 1		Sample 2	
Class Limits	Frequencies	Class Limits	Frequencies
10–20	7	0–20	5
20–30	4	20–40	5

Test the significance of the difference between the sample means, level of significance 1 percent.

4   Consider the following three samples:

Sample 1		Sample 2		Sample 3	
Class Limits	Frequencies	Class Limits	Frequencies	Class Limits	Frequencies
0–2	1	2–6	5	0–4	2
2–4	2	6–10	5	4–8	7
4–6	3				
6–8	3				

Test the significance of (a) $\bar{x}_1 - \bar{x}_2$; (b) $\bar{x}_1 - \bar{x}_3$; (c) $\bar{x}_2 - \bar{x}_3$. Take the level of significance as 5 percent.

5   Consider the following three samples:

Sample 1		Sample 2		Sample 3	
Class Limits	Frequencies	Class Limits	Frequencies	Class Limits	Frequencies
0–10	49	0–7	30	0–12	51
10–20	51	7–14	37	12–24	50
		14–21	35		

Test the significance of (a) $\bar{x}_1 - \bar{x}_2$; (b) $\bar{x}_1 - \bar{x}_3$; (c) $\bar{x}_2 - \bar{x}_3$; the level of significance is 1 percent.

6   Consider the following two samples:

Sample 1		Sample 2	
Class Limits	Frequencies	Class Limits	Frequencies
0–4	1	0–5	1
4–8	0	5–10	4
8–12	3	10–15	3
12–16	3	15–20	2
16–20	1		

Test the significance of the difference between the sample means, level of significance 1 percent.

7   Consider the following three samples:

Sample 1		Sample 2		Sample 3	
Class Limits	Frequencies	Class Limits	Frequencies	Class Limits	Frequencies
0–12	20	0–20	60	0–5	20
10–20	50	20–40	20	5–10	20
20–30	20			10–15	20
				15–20	15
				20–25	10

(a) Test the significance of $\bar{x}_1 - \bar{x}_2$; (b) of $\bar{x}_1 - \bar{x}_3$; (c) of $\bar{x}_2 - \bar{x}_3$, level of significance 5 percent.

8   Consider the following two samples:
Sample 1: 1, 5, 3, 0, 2.
Sample 2: 9, 7, 5, 0, 3, 4, 7.
Test the significance of the difference between the sample means, level of significance 1 percent.

**9   Call the difference between two sample means in large samples d. Establish limits for d such that the probability that d will fall between them is (a) 95 percent; (b) 99 percent; (c) 100 percent; (d) 90 percent.

10   The following table gives family wage or salary for the U. S. in 1939. Test the significance of the difference between the means of these distributions. The level of significance is 1 percent.

Wage	Frequency in Millions of Families		
Class Limits	Urban	Rural Nonfarm	Rural Farm
$ 0–200	4.1	1.8	4.1
200–500	0.5	0.4	0.7
500–1,000	1.4	1.0	1.0
1,000–1,500	3.1	1.4	0.7
1,500–2,000	3.3	1.0	0.3
2,000–2,500	2.9	0.7	0.2
2,500–3,000	2.0	0.4	0.1
3,000–5,000	1.1	0.2	0.0

11 The following table gives the age distribution for the United States for 1940.

Age Class Limits	Frequency in Millions of Persons			
	Male	Female	White	Colored
0–5	5	6	9	1
5–10	5	6	9	1
10–15	6	6	10	1
15–20	6	6	11	1
20–25	6	6	10	1
25–30	5	6	10	1
30–35	5	6	9	1
35–40	5	5	9	1
40–45	4	5	8	1
45–50	4	4	8	1
50–55	4	4	7	1
55–60	3	3	5	
60–65	2	2	4	
65–70	2	2	4	
70–75	1	1	2	

Test the significance of the difference of the means when the level of significance is 5 percent (a) between male and female; (b) between white and colored.

Chapter 26
Fitting of Distributions

**115 FITTING OF THE NORMAL DISTRIBUTIONS

We have reason to believe sometimes that a random sample comes from a normal population. Then we may try to fit the normal curve to the sample values in order to achieve an approximation to the normal distribution of the population.

EXAMPLE

Consider the following sample:

Class Limits	x	f	Upper Limits (Standardized)	Cumulative Probability	p	Np
0–2	1	1	−2.36	0.0091	0.0077	0.39
2–4	3	1	−1.74	0.0409	0.0318	1.59
4–6	5	4	−1.11	0.1335	0.0926	4.63
6–8	7	8	−0.48	0.3156	0.1821	9.11
8–10	9	13	0.15	0.5596	0.2440	12.20
10–12	11	15	0.78	0.7823	0.2227	11.14
12–14	13	5	1.41	0.9207	0.1384	6.92
14–16	15	2	2.04	0.9793	0.0586	2.93
16–18	17	0	2.67	0.9962	0.0169	0.85
18–20	19	1	3.30	0.9995	0.0033	0.17
		$N = 50$				

To fit a normal distribution we convert the upper limits of the various classes in the frequency distribution into standard measure by computing

$$u = \frac{X - \bar{x}}{s},$$

where X is the upper class limit, $\bar{x}$ is the sample mean, and s the sample standard deviation.

349

The probabilities for u are given in Table 4, Appendix D. For negative u, the value of the area under the normal curve has to be subtracted from 0.5. For positive u, 0.5 has to be added to the value given in the table. The probabilities p are computed by taking the differences of two successive items in the column of cumulative probabilities.

As indicated, we find that $N = 50$. The sample mean $\bar{x} = 9.52$, the sample variance $V = 10.09$, and the sample standard deviation $s = 3.18$. The fourth column gives the upper limit in each class in standardized form. We have, for example, for the first class $(2 - 9.52)/3.18 = -2.36$, and so on.

The cumulative probabilities are derived from Table 4. We have, for example, for the third class, corresponding to $u = -1.11$, $0.5 - 0.3665 = 0.1335$, and so on. For positive standardized variables we have, for example, in the seventh class, corresponding to $u = 1.41$, $0.5 + 0.4207 = 0.9207$. By forming the differences we get the actual probabilities; for instance, in the third class, we have $0.1335 - 0.0409 = 0.0926$. Multiplying by $N = 50$, we get the last column.

Figure 55 presents the histogram of the frequency distribution in the above example and also the fitted normal curve.

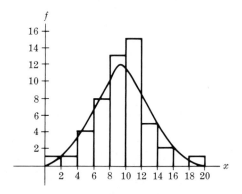

Figure 55

EXERCISES 115

1   Given the data in problem 2, Exercises 109, (a) fit a normal curve; (b) graph the original frequency curve and the fitted normal curve.

2   Given the data in problem 3, Exercises 109, (a) fit a normal curve; (b) graph the original frequency curve and the fitted normal curve.

3   Given the data in problem 4, Exercises 109, (a) fit a normal curve; (b) graph the original frequency distribution and the fitted normal curve.

4 Given the data in problem 5, Exercises 109, (a) fit a normal curve; (b) graph the original frequency distribution and the fitted normal curve.

5 Given the data in problem 6, Exercises 109, (a) fit a normal curve; (b) graph the original frequency curve and the fitted normal curve.

6 Given the data in problem 7, Exercises 109, (a) fit a normal curve; (b) graph the original frequency distribution and the fitted normal curve.

7 Given the data in problem 9, Exercises 109, (a) fit a normal curve; (b) graph the original frequency distribution and the corresponding normal curve.

8 Consider the following data for the United States for 1941:

Acres	No. of Farms
0–3	36,000
3–10	470,000
10–20	559,000
20–50	1,221,000
50–100	1,291,000
100–500	2,225,000

(a) Fit a normal curve. (b) Graph the original frequency curve and the fitted curve.

9 Consider the following data for the United States for 1942:

Income Classes ($)	No. of Families
500–1,000	2,319,000
1,000–1,500	4,604,000
1,500–2,000	4,837,000
2,000–2,500	4,920,000
2,500–3,000	3,953,000

(a) Fit a normal distribution. (b) Graph the data and the normal frequency curve.

10 Consider the following data:

Class Limits	Frequencies
0–2	10
2–4	40
4–6	60
6–8	40
8–10	10

(a) Fit a normal distribution. (b) Graph the data and the fitted normal curve.

**116 TESTS OF GOODNESS OF FIT

To test the goodness of fit for fitting the normal distribution we compute the quantity χ^2, defined by

$$\chi^2 = \sum \frac{(f_i - Np_i)^2}{Np_i}.$$

In this summation we have the squares of the deviations between the empirical relative frequencies and the theoretical probabilities, divided by the latter. If we have a perfect fit, relative frequencies and probabilities are identical, so $\chi^2 = 0$.

The distribution of this quantity has been established. Its probability density is

$$p(\chi^2) = \frac{(\chi^2)^{(k-2)/2}e^{(-\chi^2)/2}}{2^{(k)/2}[(k-2)/2]!},$$

where k is the number of degrees of freedom.

Care must be taken that in all classes the quantity Np_i is at least as large as 5. If this is not the case, neighboring classes have to be combined into one single class.

The number of degrees of freedom is the number of classes upon which the test is based, less 3. The area under the curve has been tabulated. The tabulated probability is

$$P = 1 - \int_0^{\chi^2} p(s) \, ds.$$

We get from Table 6, Appendix D, the probability P that for a given number of degrees of freedom the empirical χ^2 will be equal to or larger than the χ^2 in the table.

The number of degrees of freedom is k. This is the number of classes in the distribution, minus the number of constants used in computing χ^2.

Figure 56 shows the χ^2 distribution for 3 and 6 degrees of freedom. If

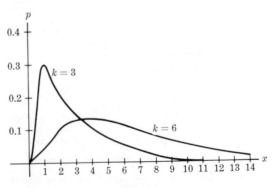

Figure 56

the number of degrees of freedom becomes large, we can assume that the quantity

$$u = \sqrt{2\chi^2} - \sqrt{2k - 1}$$

follows the normal distribution, with mean zero and variance one. (Table 4, Appendix D.)

It is apparent from the graph that the χ^2 distribution for $k = 6$ is nearer to a normal distribution than the one for χ^2 with 3 degrees of freedom. We may use the normally distributed quantity u, defined above, if we have 30 or more degrees of freedom.

The null hypothesis tested in a test of significance for goodness of fit is that we obtain a perfect fit, that is, that in the population the value of χ^2 is 0.

EXAMPLE

We want to test the goodness of fit of the normal curve fitted in the previous example. We assume a level of significance of 5 percent. We have to combine the first three and the last four classes, since for them the values of Np are less than 5. The data are

Class Limits	f	Np	$(f - Np)^2/Np$
Below 6	6	6.61	0.06
6–8	8	9.11	0.14
8–10	13	12.20	0.05
10–12	15	11.14	1.34
Over 12	8	10.87	0.76
			$\chi^2 = 2.35$

The terms in the last column come from the formula $(f - Np)^2/Np$. We get, for instance, in the first class: $(6 - 6.61)^2/6.61 = 0.06$. The sum of all these quantities is χ^2.

To test the significance of χ^2 we note that the number of classes is 5. The number of degrees of freedom is $5 - 3 = 2$, because 3 constants $(N, \bar{x}, V)$ have been estimated from the sample. Hence we lose 3 degrees of freedom. At the 5 percent level, χ^2 can be as large as 5.99 for 2 degrees of freedom. Our empirical χ^2 is much smaller; in fact, it is only 2.35. It is not significant, which means that we get a reasonably good fit.

EXERCISES 116

1 Given the data in problem 1, Exercises 109, (a) fit a normal curve; (b) test the goodness of fit, level of significance 1 percent.

2 Given the data in problem 6, Exercises 109, (a) fit a normal curve; (b) test the goodness of fit, level of significance 5 percent.

3 Given the data in problem 7, Exercises 109, (a) fit a normal curve; (b) test the goodness of fit, level of significance 1 percent.

4 Given the data in problem 8, Exercises 115, test the goodness of fit of the normal curve, level of significance 5 percent.

5 Given the data in problem 9, Exercises 115, test the goodness of fit of the normal curve, level of significance 1 percent.

6 Given the data in problem 10, Exercises 115, fit a normal curve and test the goodness of fit, level of significance 5 percent.

7 Use the data in problem 1, Exercises 114, sample 1, to fit a normal frequency curve. Test the goodness of fit, level of significance 1 percent.

8 Use the data in problem 4, Exercises 114, sample 3, to fit a normal frequency curve. Test the goodness of fit, level of significance 5 percent.

**117 CONTINGENCY TABLES

Assume we have a random sample. The individual items have been classified according to two characteristics, those of A and B, and C and D. We obtain a 2×2 contingency table as follows:

	C	D	Total
A	a	b	$a + b$
B	c	d	$c + d$
Total	$a + c$	$b + d$	$a + b + c + d$

If the sample comes from a normal population, we can test the independence of the classification by computing.

$$\chi^2 = \frac{(ad - bc)^2(a + b + c + d)}{(a + b)(c + d)(a + c)(b + d)}.$$

This is distributed like χ^2 with 1 degree of freedom.

This distribution is only approximate. It will be valid if the expected values, which would prevail under independence, are not less than 5.

EXAMPLE

Consider the following contingency table:

			Total
	11	9	20
	8	12	20
Total	19	21	40

The formula gives

$$\chi^2 = \frac{[(11)(12) - (8)(9)]^2(40)}{(20)(20)(19)(21)} = \frac{120}{133} = 0.902.$$

Suppose we choose for our level of significance 1 percent. For 1 degree of freedom, χ^2 may be as large as 6.63. Since our empirical value is smaller, there is no reason to reject the null hypothesis that the characteristics are independent.

EXERCISES 117

1 Consider the following contingency table:

25	5
15	35

Test for independence, level of significance 5 percent.

2 Consider the following contingency table:

25	25
15	35

Test for independence, level of significance 1 percent.

3 The following data are for the United States for 1940 (in millions):

	White	Colored
Male	59.4	6.6
Female	58.8	6.8

Test the independence of sex and color, level of significance 1 percent.

4 The following data (in millions) were true for the United States for 1930:

	White	Colored
Male	55.9	6.2
Female	54.4	6.2

Test the independence of sex and color, level of significance 5 percent.

5 The following data (in millions), are for the United States' labor force for 1930:

	Employed	Unemployed
Male	35.0	2.0
Female	10.0	0.4

Test the independence of employment status and sex, level of significance 5 percent.

6 The United States' labor force for 1940 (in millions) is characterized as follows:

	Employed	Unemployed
Male	34.0	6.2
Female	11.2	1.8

Test the independence of employment status and sex, level of significance 1 percent.

7 The distribution of the labor force for the United States for 1940 (in millions) was as follows:

	Agriculture Forestry Fisheries	Other Industries
Employed	8.5	36.7
Unemployed	0.6	6.2

Test the independence of employment status and the distribution in industries, level of significance 5 percent.

**8 Show that the expected values in a 2 × 2 table in case of independence are

$$\frac{(a+b)(a+c)}{a+b+c+d} \qquad \frac{(a+b)(b+d)}{a+b+c+d}$$

$$\frac{(a+c)(c+d)}{a+b+c+d} \qquad \frac{(b+d)(c+d)}{a+b+c+d}.$$

Compute the expected values for the Example on pages 354–355.

Chapter 27
Regression and
Correlation

118 METHOD OF LEAST SQUARES

One method of estimation, employing the method of least squares, is particularly appropriate with economic data, where frequently we do not have normal distributions. The method of least squares consists in the choice of an estimate so that the sum of the squares of the deviations of the data from the estimate is a minimum.

The method of least squares gives the best, unbiased linear estimate. The word *best* means here that the least squares estimate has a smaller variance than any other linear estimate. By *unbiased* is meant that the mean value (mathematical expectation) of the estimate is equal to the true population value. That is, the average of a great many least square estimates is likely to differ from the true value as little as we like. The adjective *linear* is employed because the estimates must be linear functions of the parameters estimated. All these results are independent of any assumption of normality of the observations. (Markoff theorem.)

Assume we have a number of observations $x_1, x_2, \cdots, x_n$. Let us use the method of squares in order to estimate the "true" value of x in a sample of n independent observations.

Let a be the quantity we want to find. According to the fundamental principle of least squares, we want to minimize the sum of squares:

$$Q = (x_1 - a)^2 + (x_2 - a)^2 + (x_3 - a)^2 + \cdots + (x_n - a)^2.$$

This is the sum of the squares of the deviations of the observations from the estimate a.

We want to adjust a in such a fashion that Q becomes a minimum. Hence we must have $dQ/da = 0$, $d^2Q/da^2 > 0$. Thus

$$dQ/da = -2(x_1 - a) - 2(x_2 - a) - 2(x_3 - a) - \cdots - 2(x_n - a)$$
$$= 0,$$
$$d^2Q/da^2 = 2 + 2 + 2 + \cdots + 2 = 2n > 0.$$

Simplifying the first equation, we have

$$na = x_1 + x_2 + x_3 + \cdots + x_n$$

$$a = \left(\frac{1}{n}\right) \sum_{i=1}^{n} x = \bar{x}.$$

We see that the least square estimate $a = \bar{x}$ is the arithmetic mean. It follows from the fact that the second derivative is positive (n being the number of observations) that we have a true minimum Q.

EXERCISES 118

1   Let a sample consist of the items 2, 5, 9. (a) Compute the sum of squares of the deviations from the estimated value a, that is, $Q = (2 - a)^2 + (5 - a)^2 + (9 - a)^2$, by squaring the expressions in brackets. (b) Find the derivative of Q with respect to a. (c) Show that the least squares estimate of a is the arithmetic mean of the three numbers given above.

2   Given the 6 numbers 2, 7, 4, 1, 0, −3, proceed as in Example 1.

*3   Use the method of least squares to find the estimate of the true value of $\log x_1$, $\log x_2$, $\cdots$, $\log x_n$. This least squares estimate is $\log G = (1/n)\Sigma_{i=1}^{n} \log x_i$, so G is the geometric mean.

4   Use the formula established in problem 3 to find the geometric mean of (a) 2, 3, 9; (b) 1, 16, 19; (c) 2, 10, 15, 105; (d) 2, 5, 5, 10, 18; (e) 1, 6, 5; (f) 0, 5, 2, 3, 5.5, 7.6, 10.7.

**5   Find the minimum value of Q which is assumed in the example above for $a = \bar{x}$. Interpret it statistically.

6   Use the formula established in problem 3 to find the geometric mean of the data given in problem 1, Exercises 108.

7   Use the result of problem 3 to establish the geometric mean of the data in problem 2, Exercises 108.

8   Use the data in problem 3, Exercises 108, to compute the geometric mean according to the result in problem 3.

9   Compute the geometric mean of the data in problem 4, Exercises 108 according to the results of problem 3.

**10   Consider the situation described in problem 5, Exercises 107. Show that the least squares estimate and the maximum likelihood estimate are the same, namely, $\bar{x}$, which is the arithmetic mean of the observations in the sample.

119   CURVE FITTING

The method of least squares is useful in curve fitting. Assume we have the series of items x_1, x_2, $\cdots$, x_n and the associated series y_1, y_2, $\cdots$,

y_n. We want to estimate or predict y if x is given, and if we assume that there is a linear relationship $\hat{y} = a + bx$, where $\hat{y}$ is the estimated value. It follows that

$$\hat{y}_1 = a + bx_1$$
$$\hat{y}_2 = a + bx_2$$
$$\cdots$$
$$\hat{y}_n = a + bx_n.$$

So the errors are $(y_i - \hat{y}_i) = y_i - (a + bx_i)$.

The sum of squares of errors to be minimized is $F = (y_1 - a - bx_1)^2 + (y_2 - a - bx_2)^2 + \cdots + (y_n - a - bx_n)^2$. This is to be minimized by the appropriate choice of the values of a and b. We have the necessary conditions $\partial F/\partial a = 0$ and $\partial F/\partial b = 0$. These give the two *normal equations* for a and b, namely,

$$\sum y = na + b \sum x,$$
$$\sum xy = a \sum x + b \sum x^2,$$

where Σx, for example, is adopted for purposes of simplicity to denote the sum of all the x's.

If the variable x is time, the fitted line is called a *linear trend*.

EXAMPLE

Assume the development of an economic time series:

Year	x	y	xy	x^2
1910	-3	1	-3	9
1920	-1	2	-2	1
1930	1	2	2	1
1940	3	3	9	9
Sums	0	8	6	20

We have chosen the x so that their sum becomes 0. It is observed that $\Sigma x = 0$, $\Sigma y = 8$, $\Sigma xy = 6$, $\Sigma x^2 = 20$.

Since $n = 4$, the normal equations are

$$8 = 4a + 0 \cdot b = 4a,$$
$$6 = 0 \cdot a + 20b = 20b.$$

This gives the solution $a = 2$ and $b = 0.3$. Thus the equation for prediction is

$$\hat{y} = a + bx = 2 + 0.3x.$$

This result can be used for interpolation, since the relationship is linear. For instance, estimate the value of y in 1935: The corresponding x is 2, and the estimated value of y is $2 + 0.3(2) = 2.6$. If conditions are the same for the future as in the past, we can also use the formula for extrapolation. For example, what under these conditions is the predicted value of y in 1950? Evidently $x = 5$, so $\hat{y} = 2 + 0.3(5) = 3.5$.

This example is illustrated by Figure 57. We show the observations as crosses in their relation to the fitted straight line. The deviations from the fitted line, the sum of the squares of which is minimized, are also indicated.

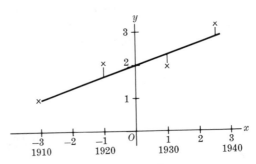

Figure 57

1   Consider the following values for consumption of wheat in the United States:

Year	Consumption
1910	36
1915	43
1920	34
1925	41
1930	47

(a) Fit by the method of least squares the best linear trend. (HINT: Choose $x = -2, -1, 0, 1, 2$.) (b) Interpolate for 1926; (c) for 1927; (d) for 1929. (e) Extrapolate for 1940; (f) for 1945; (g) for 1947.

2   Consider the following data for the price of rye in the United States:

Year	Price
1890	66
1900	56
1910	90
1920	78

(a) Fit a linear trend by the method of least squares. (HINT: Choose $x = -3, -1, 1, 3$.) (b) Interpolate for 1915; (c) for 1916; (d) for 1919. (e) Extrapolate for 1925; (f) for 1932.

3   Consider the following data for consumption of cotton in the United States:

Year	Consumption
1895	25
1900	36
1905	49
1910	45
1915	65
1920	50
1925	61

(a) Fit a linear trend by the method of least squares. (b) Graph the data and the trend. (c) Interpolate for 1921; (d) for 1923; (e) for 1924. (f) Extrapolate for 1930; (g) for 1943.

4   Consider the following data for the price of potatoes in the United States:

Year	Price
1918	120
1921	110
1924	62
1927	97

(a) Fit a linear trend by the method of least squares. (b) Graph the data and trend. (c) Interpolate for 1925; (d) for 1926. (e) Extrapolate for 1930; (f) for 1935.

5   Consider the following data for the consumption of pig iron in the United States:

Year	Consumption
1880	140
1890	121
1900	101
1910	105

(a) Fit a linear trend by the method of least squares. (b) Graph the data and trend. (c) Interpolate for 1905; (d) for 1909. (e) Extrapolate for 1914; (f) for 1916.

6 Consider the following production data for steel in the United States:

Year	Production
1930	12
1932	4
1934	6
1936	11
1938	8

(a) Fit a linear trend by the method of least squares. (b) Graph the data and trend. (c) Interpolate for 1935; (d) for 1937. (e) Extrapolate for 1939; (f) for 1940.

7 Consider the following data on wholesale price indexes, 1929 = 100.

Year	All Commodities	Raw Materials	Semi-manufactured	Manufactured Production
1930	91	86	87	93
1931	77	67	74	82
1932	68	56	63	74
1933	69	58	70	75
1935	84	79	78	87
1937	91	87	91	92
1939	81	72	82	85
1940	82	74	84	86
1941	92	86	92	94
1942	104	103	99	104
1943	108	115	99	106
1944	109	116	100	107

(a) Fit straight-line trends by the method of least squares. (HINT: Call 1930 year 1, 1931 year 2, and so forth.) (b) Graph original data and trends. (c) Interpolate for 1934. (d) Interpolate for 1938. (e) Extrapolate for 1945.

8 Consider the following data pertaining to the cost of living index for the United States, where 1935–1939 = 100:

Year	Index
1930	119
1931	109
1932	98
1933	92
1934	96
1935	98
1936	99
1937	103
1938	101
1939	99
1940	100
1941	105
1942	116

(a) Fit a straight-line trend. (b) Graph the data and trend. (c) Extrapolate for 1943; (d) for 1944; (e) for 1945.

**9 Prove that the normal equations in the example above actually give a minimum of F. Consider necessary and sufficient conditions.

*10 Assume the relationship between x and $\hat{y}$ to be $\hat{y} = a + bx + cx^2$ (parabola), and show that under these conditions the method of least squares leads to the normal equations:

$$\sum y = na + b \sum x + c \sum x^2,$$

$$\sum xy = a \sum x + b \sum x^2 + c \sum x^3,$$

$$\sum x^2y = a \sum x^2 + b \sum x^3 + c \sum x^4.$$

11 Use the results of problem 10 to fit a parabolic trend to the data of the example above.

12 Use the results of problem 10 to establish a parabolic trend for the data in problem 2. Work parts (b) to (f) in problem 2 if a parabolic trend is assumed, and compare the results with the results of the linear trend.

13 Use the results of problem 10 to fit a parabolic trend to the data of problem 5. Use this trend to work (b) to (f) in problem 5 and compare the results with the results of the linear trend.

*14 Establish the normal equations for an exponential trend in the logarithmic form: $\log \hat{y} = a + bx$. (HINT: Substitute $\log y$ for y in the normal equation for a straight-line trend. The normal equations are, then,

$$\sum \log y = an + b \sum x,$$

$$\sum x \log y = a \sum x + b \sum x^2.\Big)$$

Show that the normal equations follow from the necessary conditions of a minimum and that the sufficient conditions are fulfilled.

15 Consider the data:

Year	U.S. Population (millions)
1900	76
1910	92
1920	106
1930	123
1940	132

(a) Fit an exponential trend (problem 14). (b) Graph the data and trend. (c) Interpolate for 1925; (d) for 1937; (e) for 1939. (f) Extrapolate for 1945.

16 Use the results of problem 14 to fit an exponential trend to the data in the example above.

17   Use the results of problem 14 to fit an exponential trend to the data of problem 2. Work parts (b) to (f) of the problem. (HINT: The estimates are now log y and have to be converted into ordinary numbers.)

18   Use the results of problem 14 to fit an exponential trend to the data in problem 5. Work parts (b) to (f) of problem 5 with an exponential trend.

19   Use the results of problem 14 to fit an exponential trend to the data of problem 3. Work parts (b) to (g) of problem 3 with this trend.

**20   Assume that the values $y_1, y_2, \cdots, y_n$ are normally and independently distributed according to

$$p_1 = \left(\frac{1}{\sqrt{2\pi}}\right) e^{-\frac{1}{2}(y_1-a-bx_1)^2}, \qquad p_2 = \left(\frac{1}{\sqrt{2\pi}}\right) e^{-\frac{1}{2}(y_2-a-bx_2)^2}, \cdots,$$

$$p_n = \left(\frac{1}{\sqrt{2\pi}}\right) e^{-\frac{1}{2}(y_n-a-bx_n)^2}.$$

(a) Establish the probability that the independent events $y_1, y_2, \cdots, y_n$ will happen together. (b) Maximize this probability (method of maximum likelihood). Show that the resulting normal equations for a and b are the same as in the method of least squares.

*21   Consider two series, $x_1, x_2, \cdots, x_n$ and $y_1, y_2, \cdots, y_n$. The estimated value of x is $\hat{x} = A + By$. Establish the normal equation for A and B which minimize $G = (x_1 - A - By_1)^2 + (x_2 - A - By_2)^2 + \cdots + (x_n - A - By_n)^2$. Show that the normal equations are the same as in the example above with the role of x and y exchanged.

*22   Let x be income and y the number of people receiving income x or *higher*. Assume a Pareto curve for the cumulative distribution of income (Section 20). Fit this curve in the logarithmic form $\log \hat{y} = a + b \log x$, if the data are $x_1, x_2, \cdots, x_n; y_1, y_2, \cdots, y_n$. (HINT: Show that the normal equations for a and b result from those obtained by fitting $\hat{y} = a + bx$, but with $\log x$ substituted for x and $\log y$ substituted for y; that is,

$$\sum \log y = na + b \sum \log x,$$

$$\sum (\log x)(\log y) = a \sum \log x + b \sum (\log x).^2\Big)$$

Show that the necessary and sufficient conditions for a minimum are fulfilled.

23   Consider the data for income distribution in the United States for 1918:

Income Classes	Frequencies
500–1,000	12,531,000
1,000–3,000	19,875,000
3,000–10,000	1,971,000
10,000–1,000,000	255,000

(a) Find the cumulative distribution. (b) Fit the Pareto distribution using the results of problem 22. (c) Estimate the number of people receiving $5,000 or more; (d) $7,250 or more; (e) $1,785 or more; (f) between $1,100 and $1,250; (g) between $5,000 and $8,000.

24 Take the following income distribution for the United States for 1926:

Income Classes	Frequencies
$1,000–5,000	31,796,000
5,000–25,000	1,111,000
25,000–250,000	111,000
250,000–1,000,000	4,000

(a) Find the cumulative frequency distribution. (b) Fit a Pareto curve (problem 22). (c) Estimate the number of people having an income of more than $4,000; (d) more than $10,000; (e) more than $70,000; (f) more than $2,000; (g) between $4,000 and $4,500; (h) between $500,000 and $750,000.

25 Family wages or salaries in the United States for 1939 were as follows:

Class Limits	Number of Families
$500–1,000	5,169,000
1,000–1,500	4,675,000
1,500–2,000	3,746,000
2,000–3,000	3,684,000
3,000–5,000	1,779,000

(a) Find the cumulative frequency distribution. (b) Fit a Pareto curve. (c) Estimate the number of families having an income of more than $2,500; (d) more than $4,000; (e) between $1,250 and $1,275; (f) between $2,500 and $2,750.

26 Use the data in problem 10, Exercises 114, to estimate the Pareto distributions of incomes of urban, rural farm, and rural nonfarm workers.

27 Use the data in problem 7, Exercises 109, to derive the Pareto distribution of incomes for families.

28 Use the data in problem 8, Exercises 109, to find the Pareto distribution of incomes for corporations.

120 SIMPLE REGRESSION

Assume that we have two series of n values, each of two variables x and y: $x_1, x_2, \cdots, x_n$ and $y_1, y_2, \cdots, y_n$. The variables x and y are both taken as random variables. We have already shown that the best linear equation for the prediction of y, if x is given, is found by the method of least squares. The value of y obtained in this way, namely, $\hat{y} = a + bx$, is called the *regression of y on x*. The normal equations for the determination of a and b are

$$\sum y = na + b \sum x,$$
$$\sum xy = a \sum x + b \sum x^2.$$

On the other hand, if we know y and want to predict x, we use the linear equation $\hat{x} = A + By$, called the *regression of x on y*. The method of least squares this time gives the following normal equations for the determination of a and b:

$$\sum x = nA + B \sum y,$$
$$\sum xy = A \sum y + B \sum y^2.$$

It will be noted that the roles of x and y are exchanged.

EXAMPLE

Consider the following series of observations:

x	y	x^2	xy	y^2
1	4	1	4	16
3	2	9	6	4
0	2	0	0	4
4	4	16	16	16
8	12	26	26	40

If we want to predict y when we know x, we compute the regression of y on x; that is,

$$\hat{y} = a + bx.$$

Using the above formulas, we have the following normal equations from the table:

$$12 = 4a + 8b,$$
$$26 = 8a + 26b.$$

Solving this system of equations, we have $a = 2.6, b = 0.2$. Hence the regression of y on x is

$$\hat{y} = 2.6 + 0.2x.$$

For example, for $x = 2$, we have $\hat{y} = 3$. For $x = 10$, we have $\hat{y} = 4.6$.

Next we compute the regression of x on y:

$$\hat{x} = A + By.$$

The normal equations become, in this case,

$$8 = 4A + 12B,$$
$$26 = 12A + 40B.$$

Solving this system of equations, we have $A = 0.5$, $B = 0.5$. Hence the regression of x on y is

$$\hat{x} = 0.5 + 0.5y.$$

Suppose, for example, we want to estimate x if we know that $y = 1$; we obtain $\hat{x} = 1$. Or, if we want to estimate x if $y = 6$, there results $\hat{x} = 3.5$.

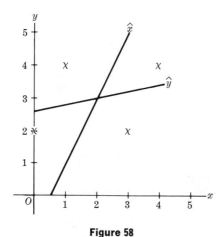

Figure 58

Figure 58 shows the so-called scatter diagram of our two variables x and y. The observations are denoted by points. The two regression lines are also given and labeled $\hat{x}$ and $\hat{y}$.

EXERCISES 120

1 Consider the data:

x	y
1	0
2	1
3	5
0	1

(a) Find both regression lines. (b) Make a scatter diagram. (c) Predict y if $x = 4$. (d) Predict x if $y = 3$.

2 Consider the data:

x	y
1	5
0	0
0	1
2	3
4	5
1	4

(a) Determine both regression lines. (b) Make a scatter diagram. (c) Predict y if $x = 5$. (d) Predict x if $y = 2$.

3 Consider the data:

x	y
1	6
5	1
3	0
2	0
1	1
1	2
7	1
3	5

(a) Find both regression lines. (b) Make a scatter diagram. (c) Predict y if $x = 10$. (d) Predict x if $y = 2.5$.

4 Consider the data:

x	y
8	7
3	0
5	10

(a) Find both regression lines. (b) Make a scatter diagram. (c) Predict y if $x = 6$. (d) Predict x if $y = 4$.

5 The following table gives a wholesale price index (x) and the index of industrial production in the United States (y):

Year	Wholesale Prices x	Industrial Production y
1935	80	87
1936	81	103
1937	86	113
1938	79	89
1939	77	109

(a) Determine both regression lines. (b) Make a scatter diagram. (c) Assuming that conditions remain as in the period under consideration, predict the index of industrial production for a wholesale price index of 90. (d) Under the same conditions as given, predict the wholesale price index if the index of industrial production is 120.

6 The following table gives wheat prices and wheat production in the United States:

Year	Production, Million Bushels x	Price per Bushel y
1932	2.9	0.6
1933	2.4	0.9
1934	1.4	1.2
1935	2.3	1.3
1936	1.5	1.5
1937	2.6	1.3
1938	2.6	0.8
1939	2.6	1.0

(a) Find both regression lines. (b) Make a scatter diagram. (c) Assuming the same fundamental conditions to prevail on the wheat market as during the period of the data, predict the price of wheat if the production is 2 million bushels. (d) Under the same conditions, predict the production of wheat if the price is $1 per bushel.

7 The following table gives the total deposits and the interest rate in the United States for various years:

Year	Total Deposits in Billions of Dollars x	Interest Rates (percent) y
1935	45	3.0
1936	50	2.7
1937	52	2.6
1938	51	2.5
1939	55	2.8

(a) Make a scatter diagram. (b) Determine both regression lines. (c) Assuming the fundamental conditions the same as in the period covered by the data, predict the interest rate if there are 60 billion deposits. (d) Under the same conditions, predict the deposits if the interest rate is 1.5 percent.

8   The following table gives agricultural production and price indexes in the United States:

Year	Index of Production	Index of Prices
	x	y
1937	106	122
1938	103	97
1939	106	95
1940	110	100

(a) Make a scatter diagram. (b) Find both regression lines. (c) Assuming conditions to be the same in agriculture as in the period covered, predict the price index if the index of agricultural production is 100. (d) Under the same conditions, predict the index of production if the price index is 130.

9   The following table gives the total national income and the index of industrial production in the United States:

Year	National Income, in Billions of Dollars	Index of Industrial Production
	x	y
1929	83	110
1930	69	91
1931	54	75
1932	40	58
1933	42	69
1934	49	74
1935	56	87
1936	65	103
1937	72	113
1938	64	89

(a) Make a scatter diagram. (b) Compute both regression lines. (c) Assuming economic conditions to be the same as in the period 1929–1938, predict the index of production if there is a national income of 100 billion. (d) Under the same conditions, predict the national income if the index of industrial production is 50.

10   The following table gives disposable income and gross investment in the United States for certain years:

Year	Disposable Income per Capita, Deflated x	Gross Investment per Capita, Deflated y
1930	$478	$97
1931	440	81
1932	372	45
1933	381	45
1934	419	66
1935	449	78
1936	511	103
1937	520	98

(a) Make a scatter diagram. (b) Find both regression lines. (c) Assuming the same economic conditions to prevail as in the period covered by the data, predict per capita deflated gross investment if the per capita disposable deflated income is $600. (d) Under the same conditions, predict the per capita deflated disposable income if the per capita deflated gross investment is $35.

11   The following table gives information on leather belts:

Year	Output x	Total Cost y
1934	3	234
1935	4	316
1936	11	880
1937	6	670

(a) Find both regression lines. (b) Predict the total cost if the output is 10. (c) Predict the output if the total cost is 1,000. (d) Make a scatter diagram.

12   The following table gives information on steel for the United States:

Year	Production x	Total Cost y
1930	12	84
1932	4	44
1934	6	51
1936	11	82
1938	8	61

(a) Find both regression lines. (b) Predict the cost if production is 10. (c) Predict the production if the cost is 50. (d) Make a scatter diagram with both regression lines.

121   SIMPLE CORRELATION

A measure for the linear relationship between the two variables x and y is described as the *sample correlation coefficient;* it is given by the formula

$$r = \frac{\Sigma(x - \bar{x})(y - \bar{y})}{\sqrt{\Sigma(x - \bar{x})^2 \Sigma(y - \bar{y})^2}}.$$

This may be simplified to

$$r = \frac{\Sigma xy - n\bar{x}\bar{y}}{\sqrt{(\Sigma x^2 - n\bar{x}^2)(\Sigma y^2 - n\bar{y}^2)}},$$

where $\bar{x}$ and $\bar{y}$ are the sample means of x and y. The sample correlation coefficient r provides an empirical estimate of the population correlation coefficient ρ.

If $r = 0$ the variables are said to be uncorrelated. But this does not mean that they are independent in the probability sense, for it is possible, for example, that the variance of y depends on x, and so on.

If we assume that we have a joint-normal distribution of the random variables x and y, we can test the significance of r. We compute the quantity

$$t = \frac{r\sqrt{(n - 2)}}{\sqrt{1 - r^2}}.$$

This statistic t follows Student's t distribution with $n - 2$ degrees of freedom. The null hypothesis is that in the population corresponding to the sample there is no linear relationship between x and y, that is, the population correlation coefficient $\rho = 0$. If this null hypothesis is rejected from the point of view of a given level of significance, we say that r is *significant.*

The number of degrees of freedom is $n' = n - 2$. This follows from the fact that the regression equation involves two constants, a and b, or A and B, which have to be estimated from the data. This uses two degrees of freedom out of a total of n observations.

**To interpret r, the sample correlation coefficient, we start with the identities proved earlier. We have for the two sums of squares:

$$\sum (x - \bar{x})^2 = \sum x^2 - n\bar{x}^2,$$

$$\sum (y - \bar{y})^2 = \sum y^2 - n\bar{y}^2.$$

These sums of squares have been used previously to compute the sample variances. We have a similar relationship for the sum of cross products:

$$\sum (x - \bar{x})(y - \bar{y}) = \sum xy - n\bar{x}\bar{y}.$$

Now consider the two normal equations which give a and b for the regression of y on x, $(\hat{y} = a + bx)$:

$$\sum y = na + b \sum x,$$
$$\sum xy = a \sum x + b \sum x^2.$$

Multiply the members of the first equation by Σx and the second by n, in order to eliminate a; there results

$$\left(\sum x\right)\left(\sum y\right) = na \sum x + b \left(\sum x\right)^2,$$
$$n \sum xy = na \sum x + nb \sum x^2.$$

Subtracting the members of the first equation from the corresponding members of the second to eliminate a, we have

$$n \sum xy - \left(\sum x\right)\left(\sum y\right) = b \left[n \sum x^2 - \left(\sum x\right)^2 \right].$$

After dividing both sides of the equation by n, we have

$$\sum xy - n \left(\frac{\Sigma x}{n}\right)\left(\frac{\Sigma y}{n}\right) = b \left[\sum x^2 - n \left(\frac{\Sigma x}{n}\right)^2 \right],$$

or

$$\sum xy - n\bar{x}\bar{y} = b \left(\sum x^2 - n\bar{x}^2\right).$$

This follows from the definition of the sample means; namely,

$$\bar{x} = \frac{\Sigma x}{n},$$
$$\bar{y} = \frac{\Sigma y}{n}.$$

The term on the left side is the sum of cross products. The term on the right side is the sum of the squares of the deviations of x from its mean $\bar{x}$; thus

$$\sum (x - \bar{x})(y - \bar{y}) = b \sum (x - \bar{x})^2,$$

and, finally,

$$b = \frac{\Sigma(x - \bar{x})(y - \bar{y})}{\Sigma(x - \bar{x})^2}.$$

Now consider the first normal equation,

$$\sum y = na + b \sum x.$$

We may divide by n, and obtain, recalling the values of $\bar{y}$ and $\bar{x}$,

$$\bar{y} = a + b\bar{x}.$$

Hence, deducting the last expression from $\hat{y} = a + bx$, we have

$$\hat{y} - \bar{y} = a + bx - (a + b\bar{x}) = b(x - \bar{x}).$$

So the deviation of y from the fitted line is

$$y - \hat{y} = y - \bar{y} - (\hat{y} - \bar{y}) = (y - \bar{y}) - b(x - \bar{x}).$$

The sum of squares of these deviations is

$$\sum (y - \hat{y})^2 = \sum (y - \bar{y})^2 - 2b \sum (x - \bar{x})(y - \bar{y}) + b^2 \sum (x - \bar{x})^2.$$

Substituting the value of b derived above, this can be simplified to

$$\sum (y - \hat{y})^2 = \sum (y - \bar{y})^2 - \frac{[\Sigma(x - \bar{x})(y - \bar{y})]^2}{\Sigma(x - \bar{x})^2}.$$

Now divide both sides of the last equation by $\Sigma(y - \bar{y})^2$; there results

$$\frac{\Sigma(y - \hat{y})^2}{\Sigma(y - \bar{y})^2} = 1 - \frac{[\Sigma(x - \bar{x})(y - \bar{y})]^2}{\Sigma(x - \bar{x})^2 \Sigma(y - \bar{y})^2}.$$

The last term on the right is the square of the sample correlation coefficient, as defined above. Hence we get the relationship**

$$\frac{\Sigma(y - \hat{y})^2}{\Sigma(y - \bar{y}^2)} = 1 - r^2.$$

In this formula we have on the left the ratio of two sums of squares. In the numerator appears the sum of the squares of the deviation of the variable y from the fitted, or estimated, values $\hat{y}$. In the denominator is the sum of the squares of the deviations of y from its mean $\bar{y}$.

By dividing the numerator and denominator of the fraction on the left by $n - 1$ we get the ratio of two variances; that is,

$$\frac{[\Sigma(y - \hat{y})^2]/(n - 1)}{[\Sigma(y - \bar{y})^2]/(n - 1)} = 1 - r^2.$$

Now we have on the left in the numerator the portion of the variance of y which has not been explained by the regression of y on x. In the denominator we have the variance of y. Hence the square of the correlation coefficient may be interpreted as the proportion of the variance of y which can be explained or accounted for by the regression of y on x. The square of the correlation coefficient is called the *coefficient of determination*.

The expression in the numerator cannot be larger than the expression in the denominator. If there are no deviations from the linear regression line, the expression in the numerator will become 0. In that case we have $r^2 = 1$. We have a perfect linear correlation if either $r = 1$ or $r = -1$. Evidently r cannot be larger than 1 or smaller than -1. The expression on the left, the ratio of two nonnegative quantities (sums of squares), cannot become negative.

Next consider the case in which the numerator in the expression on the left assumes its greatest possible value. In this case all the variability of y remains unaccounted for by the regression of y on x; the expression in the numerator is the same as the one in the denominator. Hence in this case we get 1 on the left side of the equation, and it follows that $r = 0$. A 0 correlation coefficient corresponds to the case when there is no linear relationship between x and y. Of course, there may still be a nonlinear relationship. If $r = 0$, we say that the two random variables x and y are *uncorrelated*.

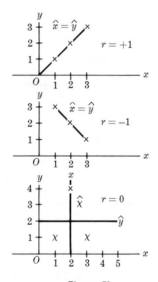

Figure 59

Figure 59 shows 3 scatter diagrams as illustrations for various values of the correlation coefficient. On the top we have the case $r = 1$, so the coefficient of determination is $r^2 = 1$. There are no deviations between the fitted line and the variable. The two regression lines coincide. Thus, there is a perfect positive linear relationship between x and y.

The diagram in the middle shows the case where $r = -1$; the coefficient of determination is 1, as before. The two regression lines coincide again, but now they slope downward. There is a perfect negative linear relationship between x and y.

Finally, the diagram on the bottom shows a case where $r = 0$. The coefficient of determination $r^2 = 0$. This means that there is no linear relationship between the random variables x and y. The regression lines are seen to be perpendicular.

In order to test the significance of the sample regression coefficient b, we compute

$$t = \frac{b \sqrt{(n-2)(\Sigma x^2 - n\bar{x}^2)}}{\sqrt{\Sigma y^2 - n\bar{y}^2 - b^2(\Sigma x^2 - n\bar{x}^2)}}$$

For tests of hypotheses we have

$$t = \frac{(b - \beta) \sqrt{(n-2)(\Sigma x^2 - n\bar{x}^2)}}{\sqrt{\Sigma y^2 - n\bar{y}^2 - b^2(\Sigma x^2 - n\bar{x}^2)}},$$

where β is the hypothetical regression coefficient in the population. Both these quantities t are distributed like Student's t with $n - 2$ degrees of freedom.

EXAMPLE

Consider the following data:

	x	y	x^2	xy	y^2
	1	2	1	2	4
	2	2	4	4	4
	2	1	4	2	1
	1	0	1	0	0
	0	2	0	0	4
Sums:	6	7	10	8	13

We have $n = 5$, $\bar{x} = 1.2$, $\bar{y} = 1.4$. The correlation coefficient is

$$r = \frac{8 - (5)(1.2)(1.4)}{\sqrt{[10 - 5(1.2)^2][13 - 5(1.4)^2]}} = \frac{-0.4}{\sqrt{(2.8)(3.2)}} = \frac{-0.4}{\sqrt{8.96}}$$

$$= \frac{-0.4}{2.99} = -0.134.$$

Since $r = -0.134$, we have a negative relationship between x and y. Thus large values of x are associated with small values of y, and vice versa.

The coefficient of determination $r^2 = (-0.134)^2 = 0.018$. This shows that if we know x we can explain 0.018 (almost 2 percent) of the variance of y. And knowledge of y enables us to explain almost 2 percent of the variance of x.

To make a test of significance let us adopt a level of significance of 5 percent. The statistic

$$t = \frac{(-0.134) \sqrt{(5 - 2)}}{\sqrt{1 - (0.134)^2}} = -0.234.$$

For $5 - 2 = 3$ degrees of freedom we see that t must be at least 3.182 to be significant. Hence the null hypothesis (that ρ in the population is 0) is not rejected and our empirical correlation coefficient of -0.134 is not significant.

To test our empirical regression coefficient $b = -0.143$ on the 1 percent significance level, we compute

$$t = \frac{(-0.143)\ \sqrt{(5 - 2)[10 - (5)(1.2)^2]}}{\sqrt{13 - (5)(1.4)^2 - (-0.143)^2[10 - (5)(1.2)^2]}}$$

$$= -0.234$$

For $n - 2 = 5 - 2 = 3$ degrees of freedom we must have $t = 5.841$ on the 1 percent significance level. Our empirical t (-0.234) is much smaller and not significant. We conclude that it is likely that in the population there is no linear relationship between x and y.

To find confidence limits with a 95 percent confidence coefficient we use the above formula with $t = \pm 3.182$ (5 percent level, 3 degrees of freedom):

$$\frac{(-0.143 - \beta)\ \sqrt{(5 - 2)[10 - (5)(1.2)^2]}}{\sqrt{13 - (5)(1.4)^2 - (-0.143)^2[10 - (5)(1.2)^2]}} = \pm 3.182.$$

This gives the following 95 percent confidence limits for the population regression coefficient β: -2.089 and 1.803.

EXERCISES 121

Compute the correlation coefficient and the coefficient of determination for the following problems. Test the significance of the correlation coefficient, assuming that the data come from a normal population. The level of significance is 5 percent. Compute the 95 percent confidence limits of the regression coefficient.

1 Problem 1, Exercises 120.

2 Problem 2, Exercises 120.

3 Problem 3, Exercises 120.

4 Problem 4, Exercises 120.

5 Problem 5, Exercises 120.

6 Problem 6, Exercises 120.

7 Problem 7, Exercises 120.

8 Problem 8, Exercises 120.

9 Problem 9, Exercises 120.

**10   Show that the two regression lines coincide if $r = 1$, or $r = -1$.

11   Consider the following data for Germany (Menges):

Year	Tourist Consumption C_t	Net Social Product Y_t
1949	1.62	73.2
1950	3.40	87.1
1951	4.38	107.6
1952	6.14	120.9
1953	7.77	130.3
1954	9.72	140.0
1955	11.63	160.2
1956	13.08	175.8
1957	15.33	189.5

(a) Find the regression of C_t on Y_t. (b) Predict C_t if $Y_t = 200$. (c) Test the regression coefficient, level of significance 5 percent. (d) Compute the correlation coefficient. (e) Test the correlation coefficient, level of significance 1 percent.

122   FITTING OF DEMAND AND SUPPLY CURVES

Great care has to be exercised in the fitting of empirical demand and supply curves from time series data. We can deal here only with the simplest possible cases and indicate some of the problems involved.

If we consider the interaction of supply and demand from the point of view of economic theory, we note the following: The price paid and the quantity sold are *both* determined by mutual interaction of the demand and supply functions on the market (see Section 13). The intersection of the supply and demand curves determines the price and the quantity sold.

From these truths follows the fact that we cannot, in general, compute both the demand and the supply function from time series data, frequently called the *problem of identification*. Neglecting more complicated cases, we note three important, special situations:

1. *Stable Demand Function and Fluctuating Supply Function.* This is probably the typical situation for agricultural commodities. It has been observed that the per capita demand for agricultural products is relatively stable in time. But the supply of agricultural commodities fluctuates very violently, especially under the influence of weather conditions. It is apparent from Figure 60 that the successive yearly observations will lie on the demand curve. Hence we can estimate the demand curve but not the supply curve from time series data.

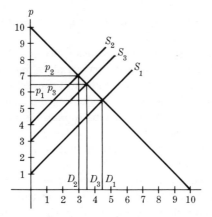

Figure 60

Figure 60 shows a somewhat idealized situation in which the demand curve D is constant; S_1, S_2, S_3 represent supply curves at various points of time, say in three consecutive years. They shift, for example, because of weather conditions.

Assume that we have a very good harvest in year 1, a very bad one in year 2, and a medium one in year 3. Since the demand curve is stable and the supply curve is subject to shifts, all the quantities and prices observed on the market will lie on the demand curve. A statistical regression analysis should in this case reveal the demand curve.

2. *Stable Supply Function and Fluctuating Demand Function.* This may be typical for certain industrial products, such as steel. The supply conditions in old established industries are relatively stable. But the demand for industrial products (for example, steel) fluctuates violently in the business cycle.

It appears from Figure 61 that all the observations will lie on the supply

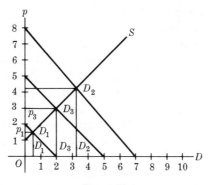

Figure 61

curve. Hence it appears reasonable that we can fit the supply function but not the demand function from time series data.

Figure 61 shows a situation with a stable supply curve and a fluctuating demand curve; S is the stable supply curve. Let D_1 be the demand curve in the depth of the depression, D_2 the demand function at a time of boom and D_3 the demand function at a time of mediocre business. The intersections of the supply curve with the various demand curves lie here on the supply curve. Hence a statistical analysis of the recorded quantities sold and the prices established on the market will reveal the supply curve but not the demand curve.

3. *Neither the Demand nor the Supply Curve Remain Stable.* This is probably the most frequent case in practice. The observed quantities sold on the market and the market prices do not lie either on the demand or on the supply curve. Neither of the two curves can be estimated by statistical analysis of prices and quantities alone.

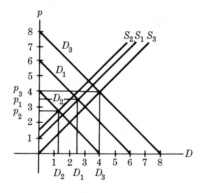

Figure 62

Figure 62 shows the case that is probably most common, in which neither the demand nor the supply curve stay constant. We show three shifting demand and supply curves.

The prices and quantities actually established on the market lie neither on the demand nor on the supply curve. But, since the shifts in demand are more violent than the shifts in supply, a statistical analysis of the quantities sold and bought and the prices charged and paid on the market will give a relationship, which will more nearly represent the supply curve than the demand curve. It should be emphasized that neither the demand nor the supply curve can actually be estimated statistically in this case.

Cobweb theorem: Suppose a commodity has a more or less fixed period of production. That is, a decision about production has to be made for a fixed period (for example, one year) before the final product comes forth. This is the case with many agricultural commodities, for example, hogs.

The demand for this commodity in each year will depend upon the price existing in the particular year. Hence regression analysis of the quantities and prices of the same year will yield an approximation to the demand function.

But the supply of the commodity in any given year will depend upon the price of *last year*. Hence regression analysis of the quantities of any given year and the prices of the year before gives an approximation to the supply function. Such a correlation, where one series lags behind the other, is called a *lag correlation*.

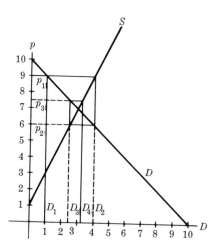

Figure 63

Figure 63 illustrates the cobweb theorem. We assume a fixed demand function and a stable supply curve. If the quantity sold was 3 and the price 7 (at the intersection of the demand and supply curves), then the price and quantity would remain stable. We could not get any data to determine the demand or supply function. Apart from random fluctuations and shifts in the curves, which we have excluded, and apart from outside influences, all the prices recorded at various points in time will be 7. Also, all the quantities recorded as sold on the market will be 3.

But assume that by accident or for some other reason the quantity 1 is produced. We see from the demand curve that with this small quantity the price will be very high, that is, 9.

We have assumed that the period of production of the commodity is fixed, say one year. At a high price of 9 the suppliers of the commodity plan to produce 4 units, as shown on the supply curve. Hence in the next year the quantity 4 is supplied.

But if 4 units are supplied, the buyers will not pay a price of 9 but only of 6. Again, the suppliers take the price of 6 for granted as next year's price and plan to produce only 2.5 units in the third year. But at the low quantity of 2.5 units the consumers will pay a price as high as 7.5 in the third year, and so forth.

It appears from Figure 63 that the points (D_1, p_1), (D_2, p_2), (D_3, p_3) all lie on the demand curve D. Hence the ordinary regression analysis of the quantities sold on the market and the prices that prevail simultaneously should give an estimate of the demand curve.

It also appears from Figure 63 that the points (D_2, p_1), (D_3, p_2), (D_4, p_3) all lie on the supply curve S. Hence a statistical regression analysis of the quantities established on the market, together with the prices that prevailed *a year before*, will yield an estimate of the supply curve. Such a statistical procedure is called *lag correlation*.

Lagged regression

We use the data from the example in Section 121 to compute the lagged regression between x and y. The series of x is shifted one unit back, denoted by x' and we get the data:

x'	y	x'^2	$x'y$	y^2
1	2	1	2	4
2	1	4	2	1
2	0	4	0	0
1	2	1	2	4
6	5	10	6	9

The normal equations are

$$5 = 4a + 6b,$$
$$6 = 6a + 10b.$$

The solution of these two equations is $a = 3.5$, $b = -1.5$; thus, the regression equation is $\hat{y} = 3.5 - 1.5x'$. For example, if $x' = 4$ (that is, $x = 4$ in the previous year), $\hat{y} = -2.5$. The lag correlation coefficient is

$$r' = \frac{6 - (4)(1.5)(1.25)}{\sqrt{[10 - (4)(1.5)^2][9 - (4)(1.25)^2]}} = -0.90$$

Let us test this lag correlation coefficient, level of significance 5 percent; $t = -2.919$. We have for $4 - 2 = 2$ degrees of freedom, $t = 4.303$. Hence our empirical lag correlation coefficient is not significant, since it is smaller. The hypothesis that in the population the lag correlation coefficient $\rho' = 0$ is not rejected.

EXERCISES 122

In the following exercises consider the economic significance of the statistical results. Does the regression line represent a demand or a supply curve?

1

Sugar in the United States

Year	Consumption	Price
1915	43	55
1920	46	110
1925	62	54

(a) Find the two regression lines. (b) Predict the price if the consumption is 50. (c) Predict the consumption if the price is 90. (d) Find the correlation coefficient; (e) the coefficient of determination. (f) Make a scatter diagram with both regression lines. (g) Test the significance of the correlation coefficient (level 1 percent). (h) Test the regression coefficient of consumption on price, level of significance 1 percent. (i) Replace the data by their logarithms and fit a demand curve with constant elasticity. (j) Find the 95 percent confidence limits of the regression coefficient of log consumption on log price (elasticity).

2

Corn in the United States

Year	Consumption	Price
1926	27	64
1927	28	72
1928	28	75
1929	26	78

(a) Find the two regression lines. (b) Predict the price if the consumption is 25. (c) Predict the consumption if the price is 65. (d) Find the correlation coefficient; (e) the coefficient of determination. (f) Make a scatter diagram and indicate both regression lines. (g) Test the significance of the correlation coefficient (level 5 percent). (h) Take the logarithms of the data and fit the two regression lines. (i) Find the correlation coefficient for the logarithms; (j) the coefficient of determination. (k) Test the correlation coefficient for its significance (level 5 percent).

(l) Test the regression coefficient of log consumption on log price (elasticity), level of significance 5 percent.

3

Wheat (world wide)

Year	Consumption	Price
1885	23	77
1890	24	84
1895	27	50
1900	27	62
1905	34	75
1910	36	91
1915	43	96
1920	34	183
1925	41	144
1930	47	67

(a) Find both regression lines. (b) Predict the price if consumption is 40. (c) Predict the consumption if the price is 80. (d) Find the correlation coefficient; (e) the coefficient of determination. (f) Make a scatter diagram with both regression lines. (g) Test the significance of the correlation coefficient (level of significance 1 percent). (h) Find the 95 percent confidence limits for the regression coefficient of consumption on price. (i) Take the logarithms of the data and find both regression lines for such values. (j) Find the correlation coefficient between the logarithms. (k) Test the correlation coefficient, level of significance 5 percent.

4

Rye, United States

Year	Consumption	Price
1880	54	74
1890	77	66
1900	90	56
1910	162	90
1920	162	78

(a) Find both regression lines. (b) Predict the consumption if the price is 60. (c) Predict the price if the consumption is 80. (d) Find the correlation coefficient; (e) the coefficient of determination. (f) Make a scatter diagram with both regression lines. (g) Test the significance of the correlation coefficient (level of significance 1 percent). (h) Take the logarithms of the data and compute both regression lines. (i) Find the correlation coefficient for the logarithms; (j) the coefficient of determination. (k) Test the significance of the correlation coefficient (level of significance 1 percent). (l) Find the 95 percent confidence limits for the regression coefficient of log consumption on log price (elasticity).

FITTING OF DEMAND AND SUPPLY CURVES   385

5   Cotton, United States

Year	Consumption	Price
1875	12	11
1880	18	10
1885	20	8
1890	26	9
1895	25	8
1900	36	9
1905	49	11
1910	45	14
1915	65	11
1920	50	16
1925	61	20

(a) Find both regression lines. (b) Predict the consumption if the price is 5. (c) Predict the price if the consumption is 50. (d) Find the coefficient of correlation; (e) the coefficient of determination. (f) Make a scatter diagram with both regression lines. (g) Test the significance of the correlation coefficient (level of significance 5 percent).

6   Potatoes, United States

Year	Consumption	Price
1915	36	62
1918	41	120
1921	36	110
1924	42	62
1927	40	97

(a) Compute both regression lines. (b) Predict the price if the consumption is 35. (c) Predict the consumption if the price is 50. (d) Find the coefficient of correlation; (e) the coefficient of determination. (f) Make a scatter diagram with both regression lines. (g) Test the significance of the correlation coefficient (level of significance 1 percent). (h) Take the logarithms of the data. (i) Find both regression lines; (j) the correlation coefficient; (k) the determination coefficient. (l) Make a scatter diagram with both regression lines. (m) Test the significance of the correlation coefficient (level of significance 5 percent). (n) Find the 99 percent confidence limits of the regression coefficient of log consumption on log price (elasticity).

7   Pig Iron, United States

Year	Price	Consumption
1880	129	140
1890	103	121
1900	102	101
1910	98	105

(a) Find both regression lines. (b) Predict the consumption if the price is 100. (c) Predict the price if the consumption is 150. (d) Find the correlation coefficient; (e) the coefficient of determination. (f) Make a scatter diagram with both regression lines. (g) Test the significance of the correlation coefficient (level of significance 1 percent). (h) Find the 95 percent confidence limits of the regression coefficient of consumption on price.

8   Hogs, United States

Year	Total Quantity (Millions)	Average Price Wholesale Cents per Pound
1939	67	6.6
1940	78	5.8
1941	71	9.6
1942	78	13.9
1943	95	14.6
1944	97	13.5
1945	69	14.8

(a) Compute both regression lines. (b) Predict the quantity if the price is 5. (c) Predict the quantity if the price is 15. (d) Make a scatter diagram. (e) Compute the correlation coefficient. (f) Test the significance, level 5 percent. (g) Find the coefficient of determination. (h) Tabulate each quantity sold and *last year's price*. Compute the regression of quantity on price of the year before. (i) Predict the quantity if the price in the year before was 10. (j) Predict the quantity sold if the price in the year before was 12. (k) Find the lag correlation coefficient; (l) test its significance, level 5 percent. (m) Compute the coefficient of determination.

9   Sugar, United States

Year	Consumption per Capita Pounds	Retail Price Index, Average 1935–1939 = 100
1929	108	114
1930	104	107
1931	107	99
1932	102	90
1933	99	94
1934	105	98
1935	104	101
1936	102	100
1937	93	101
1938	96	98
1939	107	101

(a) Find the regression line of the quantities on the price. (b) Make a scatter diagram. (c) Predict the quantity if the price index is 120; (d) if it is 85; (e) if it is 105. (f) Find the correlation coefficient; (g) test its significance, level 5 percent. (h) Find the coefficient of determination. (i) Consider the quantity sold and the price index of the year before and compute the regression of quantities on the price of the year before. (j) Make a scatter diagram. (k) Predict the quantity if the price index of the year before was 100; (l) if it was 125; (m) if it was 83. (n) Compute the lag correlation coefficient; (o) test its significance, level 5 percent. (p) Compute the coefficient of determination.

10   Agriculture, United States

Year	Farm Production Index, 1909–1914 = 100	Farm Prices Index, 1909–1914 = 100
1929	99	149
1930	98	128
1931	102	90
1932	96	68
1933	96	72
1934	93	90
1935	91	109
1936	94	114
1937	106	122
1938	103	97
1939	106	95

(a) Find the regression of production on prices. (b) Make a scatter diagram and indicate the regression line. (c) Predict the production if the price is 100; (d) if the index is 150. (e) Find the correlation coefficient; (f) test its significance, level 5 percent. (g) Compute the coefficient of determination. (h) Consider production and the price index of last year and find the linear regression of the index of production on last year's price index. (i) Predict the index of production if the price index of last year was 110; (j) if it was 160. (k) Find the lag correlation coefficient; (l) test its significance, level 5 percent. (m) Find the coefficient of determination. (n) Find the 95 percent confidence limits for the regression coefficient of production on the price of the year before.

123   MULTIPLE REGRESSION AND CORRELATION

We want to find the best estimate of a variable x_{1t} if the variables $x_{2t}, x_{3t}, \cdots, x_{pt}$ are given. Assume that we have a random sample of the variables for $t = 1, 2, \cdots, N$. The number of observations is N.

Confining ourselves to linear estimates, we denote the estimate of $_t x_1$

by $\hat{x}_{1t}$ and write it as follows:

$$\hat{x}_{1t} = k_0 + k_2 x_{2t} + k_3 x_{3t} + \cdots + k_p x_{pt}.$$

The constants k_0, k_2, k_3, $\cdots$, k_p are to be estimated. Assume that the values x_{2t}, x_{3t}, $\cdots$, x_{pt} are known, and that the errors or deviations $x_{1t} - \hat{x}_{1t}$ are independent random variables. They are samples from the same probability distribution with zero mean and finite variance, independent of t.

Under these conditions we might apply the method of *least squares* in order to determine the unknown constants k_0, k_2, k_3, $\cdots$, k_p. We minimize the sum of squares of the deviations:

$$Q = \sum_{t=1}^{N} (x_{1t} - x_{1t})^2.$$

According to the Gauss-Markov theorem, this method will give us under the stated conditions the best linear unbiased estimate of the relation between x_{1t} and x_{2t}, x_{3t}, $\cdots$, x_{pt}.

We note that it is here sufficient that the function we want to estimate be linear in the unknown parameters k_0, k_2, k_3, $\cdots$, k_p. The function need not be linear in the observations, x_{it}. It holds just as well for any function of the observations, for example, x_{it}^2, $1/x_{it}$, $\log x_{it}$.

We mean here by an unbiased estimate that the mathematical expectation of the estimate $\hat{x}_{1t}$ is equal to the (unknown) value of x_{1t} in the population from which our sample is taken.

In order to find the minimum of Q, the sum of squares of deviations, we must have as a necessary condition

$$\frac{\partial Q}{\partial k_0} = 0, \quad \frac{\partial Q}{\partial k_2} = 0, \quad \frac{\partial Q}{\partial k_3} = 0, \cdots \frac{\partial Q}{\partial k_p} = 0.$$

For computational purposes it is convenient to introduce certain transformations of our variables.

Define first the arithmetic mean of the variable x_{it}:

$$\bar{x}_i = \frac{\left(\sum\limits_{t=1}^{N} x_{it} \right)}{N}.$$

Now define the deviations from the arithmetic means:

$$y_{it} = x_{it} - \bar{x}_i.$$

The sums of the squares and products of these deviations are defined as follows:

$$S_{ij} = \sum_{t=1}^{N} y_{it} y_{jt} = \sum_{t=1}^{N} (x_{it} - \bar{x}_i)(x_{jt} - \bar{x}_j) = \sum_{t=1}^{N} x_{it} x_{jt} - N \bar{x}_i \bar{x}_j = S_{ji}.$$

The last form is best suited for computation purposes.

The sum of squares Q can be written as follows:

$$Q = \sum_{t=1}^{N} (x_{1t} - \hat{x}_{1t})^2$$

$$= \sum_{t=1}^{N} [(\bar{x}_1 - k_0 - k_2\bar{x}_2 - k_3\bar{x}_3 \cdots - k_p\bar{x}_p)$$

$$+ (y_{1t} - k_2 y_{2t} - k_3 y_{3t} - \cdots - k_p y_{pt})]^2.$$

If we find the derivative $\partial Q/\partial k_0 = 0$, we have

$$-2 \Big[N(\bar{x}_1 - k_0 - k_2\bar{x}_2 - k_3\bar{x}_3 - \cdots - k_p\bar{x}_p)$$

$$+ \sum_{t=1}^{N} (y_{1t} - k_2 y_{2t} - k_3 y_{3t} - \cdots - k_p y_{pt}) \Big] = 0.$$

But evidently

$$\sum_{t=1}^{N} y_{it} = \sum_{t=1}^{N} (x_{it} - \bar{x}_i) = \sum_{t=1}^{N} x_{it} - N\bar{x}_i = 0$$

from the definition of the arithmetic mean.

Hence it follows that

$$\bar{x}_1 = k_0 + k_2\bar{x}_2 + k_3\bar{x}_3 + \cdots + k_p\bar{x}_p.$$

The best fit must pass through the arithmetic means of all our variables x_{it}.

Now we might calculate the sum of squares Q as follows:

$$Q = \sum_{t=1}^{N} (y_{1t} - k_2 y_{2t} - k_3 y_{3t} - \cdots - k_p y_{pt})^2.$$

By finding the following partial derivatives we secure a minimum:

$$\frac{\partial Q}{\partial k_2} = -2 \sum_{t=1}^{N} y_{2t}(y_{1t} - k_2 y_{2t} - k_3 y_{3t} - \cdots - k_p y_{pt})$$

$$= -2(S_{21} - k_2 S_{22} - k_3 S_{32} - \cdots - k_p S_{p2}) = 0,$$

$$\frac{\partial Q}{\partial k_3} = -2 \sum_{t=1}^{N} y_{3t}(y_{1t} - k_2 y_{2t} - k_3 y_{3t} - \cdots - k_p y_{pt})$$

$$= -2(S_{31} - k_2 S_{23} - k_3 S_{33} - \cdots - k_p S_{p3}) = 0,$$

$$\cdots$$

$$\frac{\partial Q}{\partial k_p} = -2 \sum_{t=1}^{N} y_{pt}(y_{1t} - k_2 y_{2t} - k_3 y_{3t} - \cdots - k_p y_{pt})$$

$$= -2(S_{1p} - k_2 S_{2p} - k_3 S_{3p} - \cdots - k_p S_{pp}) = 0.$$

Hence our system of p normal equations is given by

$$\bar{x}_1 = k_0 + k_2\bar{x}_2 + k_3\bar{x}_3 + \cdots + k_p\bar{x}_p,$$
$$S_{12} = S_{22}k_2 + S_{23}k_3 + \cdots + S_{2p}k_p,$$
$$S_{13} = S_{32}k_2 + S_{33}k_3 + \cdots + S_{3p}k_p,$$
$$\cdots$$
$$S_{1p} = S_{p2}k_2 + S_{p3}k_3 + \cdots + S_{pp}k_p.$$

These are p linear equations in p unknown parameters $k_0, k_2, k_3, \cdots, k_p$. For the solution we have to compute

$$\bar{x}_i = \frac{\sum\limits_{t=1}^{N} x_{it}}{N},$$

$$S_{ij} = \sum\limits_{t=1}^{N} x_{it}x_{jt} - N\bar{x}_i\bar{x}_j = S_{ji}.$$

EXAMPLE 1

Suppose we have the $N = 10$ observations given in Table 1.

Table 1

t	x_{1t}	x_{2t}	x_{3t}
1	1	2	3
2	2	0	3
3	0	4	0
4	1	2	0
5	3	1	1
6	2	1	0
7	1	1	3
8	0	1	6
9	0	2	9
10	0	6	5

We compute first the arithmetic means of our variables:

$$\bar{x}_1 = \frac{\sum\limits_{t=1}^{10} x_{1t}}{10} = \frac{10}{10} = 1,$$

$$\bar{x}_2 = \frac{\sum\limits_{t=1}^{10} x_{2t}}{10} = \frac{20}{10} = 2,$$

$$\bar{x}_3 = \frac{\sum\limits_{t=1}^{10} x_{3t}}{10} = \frac{30}{10} = 3.$$

The sums of squares and products of our variables x_{it} are

$$\sum_{t=1}^{10} x_{1t}^2 = 20, \quad \sum_{t=1}^{10} x_{1t}x_{2t} = 10, \quad \sum_{t=1}^{10} x_{1t}x_{3t} = 15,$$

$$\sum_{t=1}^{10} x_{2t}^2 = 68, \quad \sum_{t=1}^{10} x_{2t}x_{3t} = 64, \quad \sum_{t=1}^{10} x_{3t}^2 = 170.$$

Now we compute the sums of squares and products of the deviations of our variables from their arithmetic means:

$$S_{11} = \sum_{t=1}^{10} x_{1t}^2 - 10\bar{x}_1^2 = 20 - (10)(1)^2 = 10,$$

$$S_{12} = S_{21} = \sum_{t=1}^{10} x_{1t}x_{2t} - 10\bar{x}_1\bar{x}_2 = 10 - (10)(1)(2) = -10,$$

$$S_{13} = S_{31} = \sum_{t=1}^{10} x_{1t}x_{3t} - 10\bar{x}_1\bar{x}_3 = 15 - (10)(1)(3) = -15,$$

$$S_{22} = \sum_{t=1}^{10} x_{2t}^2 - 10\bar{x}_2^2 = 68 - (10)(2)^2 = 28,$$

$$S_{23} - S_{32} = \sum_{t=1}^{10} x_{2t}x_{3t} - 10\bar{x}_3^2 = 170 - (10)(3)^2 = 80,$$

$$S_{33} = \sum_{t=1}^{10} x_{3t}^2 - 10\bar{x}_3^2 = 170 - (10)(3)^2 = 80.$$

For the determination of the unknown parameters of the linear relation

$$\hat{x}_{1t} = k_0 + k_2x_{2t} + k_3x_{3t}$$

we have the following normal equations:

$$\bar{x}_1 = k_0 + k_2\bar{x}_2 + k_3\bar{x}_3,$$
$$S_{22}k_2 + S_{23}k_3 = S_{21},$$
$$S_{32}k_2 + S_{33}k_3 = S_{31}.$$

In our case the last two equations are

$$28k_2 + 4k_3 = -10,$$
$$4k_2 + 80k_3 = -15.$$

Hence $k_2 = -0.332734$, $k_3 = -0.170863$. The constant k_0 is computed from the first equation:

$$1 = k_0 + k_2(2) + k_3(3) = k_0 - 0.332734(2) - 0.170863(3),$$

and the estimate is $k_0 = 2.178057$. Hence the desired linear relation is

$$\hat{x}_{1t} = 2.178057 - 0.332734x_{2t} - 0.170863x_{3t}.$$

Assume, for instance, that we have for t_0: $x_{2t_0} = 3$, $x_{3t_0} = 4$. The estimated value of x_{1t_0} is given by

$$\hat{x}_{it_0} = 2.178057 - 0.332734(3) - 0.170863(4) = 0.496403.$$

This is the most probable value that can be predicted for x_{1t_0} under the circumstances.

This is as far as we can go without making assumptions about specific probability distributions. These are necessary if we want to compute confidence limits, make tests of significance, test hypotheses, and so on. This is frequently desirable in econometric work.

Let us now make the assumption that the deviations $x_{1t} - \hat{x}_{1t}$ come for a *normal* distribution with mean zero and (unknown) variance σ^2. The probability density of $x_{1t} - x_{1t}$ is then

$$p_t = \frac{e^{-\frac{1}{2}(x_{1t}-\hat{x}_{1t})^2}}{\sigma \sqrt{2\pi}}.$$

We assume that our observations form a random sample. Then the probability to obtain a given sample is

$$p = p_1 p_2 \cdots p_N = \frac{e^{-Q/2\sigma^2}}{(2\pi)^{(N/2)}\sigma^N}$$

The principle of *maximum likelihood* tells us to maximize the probability p, that is, the probability of the sample. This is done by choosing the parameters k_0, k_2, k_3, $\cdots$, k_p. But these parameters enter into p only through the sum of squares Q. This sum of squares appears in p in the exponent with a negative sign. Hence p varies inversely with Q, and a minimum of Q corresponds to a maximum p. Hence the method of maximum likelihood leads in this case again to the method of least squares if we assume that the errors or deviations are independent and follow a normal distribution.

In order to test the significance of the linear relation, we compute the *multiple correlation coefficient* R whose square is given by

$$R^2 = \frac{(S_{12}k_2 + S_{13}k_3 + \cdots + S_{1p}k_p)}{S_{11}}.$$

Let us recall the sum of squares,

$$S_{11} = \sum_{t=1}^{N} y_{1t}^2 = \sum_{t=1}^{N} (x_{1t} - \bar{x}_1)^2,$$

where $\bar{x}_1$ is the arithmetic mean:

$$\bar{x}_1 = \frac{\left(\sum_{t=1}^{N} x_{1t}\right)}{N}.$$

Hence under our assumptions of normality the random variable S_{11} has a χ^2 distribution with $N - 1$ degrees of freedom. Also, $S_{11}/(N - 1)$ is the sample variance of the random variable x_{1t}. We shall use two quantities A and B:

$$A = S_{11} - S_{12}k_2 - S_{13}k_3 + \cdots + S_{1p}k_p,$$
$$B = k_2 S_{12} + k_3 S_{13} + \cdots + k_p S_{1p}.$$

Both are sums of squares. A is a sum of squares that follows the χ^2 distribution with $N - p$ degrees of freedom, B an independent sum of squares with the χ^2 distribution with $p - 1$ degrees of freedom.

We have also

$$R^2 = \frac{B}{S_{11}}; \quad A = S_{11} - B. \quad \text{Hence} \quad B = R^2 S_{11};$$
$$A = (1 - R^2)S_{11}.$$

Now we construct an F test. The variable,

$$F = \frac{B/(p - 1)}{A/(N - p)} = \frac{R^2(N - p)}{(1 - R^2)(p - 1)}$$

has Snedecor's F distribution with $p - 1$ and $N - p$ degrees of freedom.

The null hypothesis is that in the unknown normal population, from which our sample is taken, the multiple correlation coefficient is zero. This means that there exists in the population a not linear relationship between the random variables x_{1t} and x_{2t}, x_{3t}, $\cdots$, x_{pt}. Table 7, Appendix D, gives the F distribution for levels of significance of 5 percent, 1 percent, and 0.1 percent. We note also that $s^2 = A/(N - p)$ is an unbiased estimate of the population variance: σ^2.

Let us now consider the matrix of the unknown parameters in the $p - 1$ last normal equations:

$$M = \begin{bmatrix} S_{22} & S_{23} & \cdots & S_{2p} \\ S_{32} & S_{33} & \cdots & S_{3p} \\ & & \cdots & \\ S_{p2} & S_{p3} & \cdots & S_{pp} \end{bmatrix}.$$

Let the inverse of this symmetrical matrix be $C = M^{-1}$:

$$C = \begin{bmatrix} C_{22} & C_{23} & \cdots & C_{2p} \\ C_{32} & C_{33} & \cdots & C_{3p} \\ & & \cdots & \\ C_{p2} & C_{p3} & \cdots & C_{pp} \end{bmatrix}.$$

This is also a symmetrical matrix. The diagonal element of this matrix C_{ii} corresponds to the regression coefficient k_i ($i = 2, 3, \cdots, p$). We might test the significance of this estimate by computing

$$t_i = \frac{k_i}{s\sqrt{C_{ii}}}, \; i = 2, 3, \cdots p.$$

Now k_i is a linear combination of normal variates, which itself is normally distributed. Also, $s^2 = A/(N - p)$ has a χ^2 distribution with $N - p$ degrees of freedom. Hence the variable t_i has Student's t distribution with $N - p$ degrees of freedom. We might, therefore, use t_i for a significance test of k_i. The null hypothesis is now that in the normal population from which our random sample is taken the coefficient k_i is zero.

We can also use the t distribution for tests of hypotheses. Consider the hypothesis that in the unknown normal population the value of k_i is $\bar{k}_i$, a given number. We compute now

$$t_i = \frac{k_i - \bar{k}_i}{s\sqrt{C_{ii}}},$$

and this quantity has again a t distribution with $N - p$ degrees of freedom. These values are tabulated in Table 5, Appendix D. The same table gives us also values of t for a given confidence coefficient, say 95 to 99 percent. Let t^* be the tabulated value for the desired confidence coefficient. The confidence limits, for the given level of significance, are then given by the formula

$$k_i \pm t^* s \sqrt{C_{ii}}.$$

This means that the unknown coefficient k_i in the population might be expected with a given confidence coefficient (95 or 99 percent) to fall within the interval $k_i - t^* s \sqrt{C_{ii}}$ to $k_i + t^* s \sqrt{C_{ii}}$.

We have similar results for the regression constant k_0. The quantity

$$t_0 = k_0 \sqrt{\frac{N - p}{s}}$$

follows a t distribution with $N - p$ degrees of freedom. We might utilize t_0 in order to test a null hypothesis about k_0 in the population.

Given a hypothetical value of k_0, say $\bar{k}_0$ in the population, we have again a t test:

$$t_0 = (k_0 - \bar{k}_0) \frac{\sqrt{N - p}}{s}.$$

This quantity follows Student's distribution with $N - p$ degrees of freedom. Given a value t^* corresponding to a given confidence coefficient, the interval

$$k_0 \pm \frac{t^* s}{\sqrt{N - p}}$$

gives us a confidence interval for k_0 with a given confidence coefficient.

EXAMPLE 2

We utilize again the data from Example 1. But we show how the method of Crout (Section 19) might be employed in order to compute at the same time the regression coefficients and also the quantities necessary for a test of significance.

Table 2

		I			
28.000000	4.000000	−10.000000	1.000000	0.000000	23.000000
4.000000	80.000000	−15.000000	0.000000	1.000000	70.000000

		II		
28.000000	0.142857	−0.357143	0.035714	0.821429
4.000000	79.428572	−0.170863	−0.001798	0.839928
0.612590				

III	
−0.332734	−0.170863
0.035971	−0.001798
−0.001798	0.012590
0.701439	0.839928

In part I of Table 2 we write the coefficients of the last two normal equations in Example 1. In the third column of this part we write the constant terms of these equations. In columns 4 and 5 we write the unit matrix of order two. The last column is the sum of all preceding elements in each line and is used for a check.

Part II of Table 2 is constructed as described in Section 19. We want to obtain the inverse matrix C. In part III of the table we have the solution: The first line gives the regression coefficients k_2 and k_3. Lines 2 and 3 of this part give the inverse matrix and the last line is a check. Hence the inverse matrix is

$$C = \begin{bmatrix} 0.035971 & -0.001798 \\ -0.001798 & 0.012590 \end{bmatrix}.$$

We compute first the multiple correlation coefficient. Its square is given by

$$R^2 = \frac{S_{12}k_2 + S_{13}k_3}{S_{11}} = \frac{(-10)(-0.332734) + (-15)(-0.170863)}{10}$$
$$= 0.589029.$$

Now we test the significance of the linear regression. We compute

$$F = \frac{R^2(N - p)}{(1 - R^2)(p - 1)} = \frac{(0.589029)(10 - 3)}{(1 - 0.589029)(3 - 1)} = 5.027.$$

This quantity follows, under our assumption of normality, Snedecor's F distribution with $p - 1 = 3 - 1 = 2$ and $N - p = 10 - 3 = 7$ degrees of freedom. We find from Table 7, Appendix D, for the significance level 5 percent and $F = 4.74$ for 2 and 7 degrees of freedom. Hence there is a chance greater than 95 percent that in the unknown population the multiple correlation coefficient is not zero. The probability is less than 5 percent that in the (unknown) normal population, from which our sample is taken, there is no linear relation:

$$\hat{x}_{1t} = k_0 + k_2 x_{2t} + k_3 x_{3t}.$$

In order to test the significance of the regression coefficients k_2 and k_3 we note the diagonal elements of the inverse matrix C:

$$C_{22} = 0.035971, \qquad C_{33} = 0.012590.$$

Also we compute an estimate of the variance σ^2:

$$s^2 = \frac{A}{N - p} = \frac{S_{11} - S_{12}k_2 - S_{13}k_3}{N - p}$$

$$= 10 - \frac{(-10)(-0.332734) - (-15)(-0.170863)}{10 - 3} = 0.587102.$$

Hence $s = \sqrt{0.587101}$. We have the following values for Student's t, for $N - p = 10 - 3 = 7$ degrees of freedom:

$$t_2 = \frac{k_2}{s\sqrt{C_{22}}} = \frac{-0.332734}{\sqrt{(0.587102)(0.035971)}} = -2.295,$$

$$t_3 = \frac{k_3}{s\sqrt{C_{33}}} = \frac{-0.170863}{\sqrt{(0.587102)(0.012590)}} = -1.987.$$

Table 5, Appendix D, shows that for 7 degrees of freedom for a level of significance of 5 percent we have $t^* = 2.365$. Hence neither of the two regression coefficients k_2 or k_3 is significant at the level of significance of 5 percent.

Now we want to compute confidence limits at the 5 percent level of significance (confidence coefficient 95 percent). We use the value of t found above: $t^* = 2.365$. We obtain for k_2:

$$k_2 \pm t^* s \sqrt{C_{22}} = -0.332734 \pm (2.365) \sqrt{(0.587102)(0.035971)}.$$

This gives the limits -0.675659 and 0.010191 for k_2.

Similarly, we have for k_3:

$$k_3 \pm t^* s \sqrt{C_{33}} = -0.170836 \pm (2.365) \sqrt{(0.587102)(0.012590)},$$

and the 95 percent confidence limits for k_3 are -0.374226 and 0.032554.

For a test of significance of the constant k_0 we have another t-variable with $N - p = 10 - 3 = 7$ degrees of freedom:

$$t_0 = k_0 \sqrt{\frac{N - p}{s}} = \frac{(2.178057) \sqrt{7}}{\sqrt{0.587102}} = 19.80.$$

The value of t for 7 degrees of freedom for a level of significance of 5 percent is $t^* = 2.365$. Hence the value of k_0 is significant. It is extremely unlikely that in the unknown normal population the value of this constant is zero.

Finally, let us test a hypothesis about k_2, that is, $\bar{k}_2 = -0.5$. Again we obtain Student's t with $N - p = 10 - 3 = 7$ degrees of freedom:

$$t_2 = (k_2 - \bar{k}_2) \frac{\sqrt{N - p}}{s \sqrt{C_{22}}} = \frac{-0.332743 - (-0.5)}{\sqrt{(0.587102)(0.035971)}} = 1.154.$$

Since this empirical t (1.154) is less than t value at the 5 percent level of significance ($t^* = 2.365$), we cannot reject the hypothesis that in the unknown population the value of the regression coefficient $\bar{k}_2 = -0.5$.

EXERCISES 123

1   Consider the following data:

t	1	2	3	4	5	6	7	8
x_{1t}	1	2	3	0	1	2	1	0
x_{2t}	0	0	1	2	0	1	1	0
x_{3t}	1	2	3	1	3	5	2	3

(a) Compute the sums Σx_{1t}, Σx_{2t}, Σx_{3t}. (b) Compute the arithmetic means $\bar{x}_1$, $\bar{x}_2$, $\bar{x}_3$. (c) Compute the sums of squares and products: Σx_{1t}^2, $\Sigma x_{1t}x_{2t}$, $\Sigma x_{1t}x_{3t}$, Σx_{2t}^2, $\Sigma x_{2t}x_{3t}$, Σx_{3t}^2. (d) Compute the sums of squares and products of deviations from the means: S_{11}, S_{12}, S_{13}, S_{22}, S_{23}, S_{33}. (e) Estimate with the help of the method of least squares the linear relation $\hat{x}_{1t} = k_0 + k_2 x_{2t} + k_3 x_{3t}$. (f) Estimate $\hat{x}_{1t}$, given $x_{2t} = 3$, $x_{3t} = 4$. (g) Compute the square of the multiple correlation coefficient R^2. Assume a normal distribution for the errors or deviations $x_{1t} - \hat{x}_{1t}$, which form a random sample, and test the significance of the multiple correlation coefficient at a 1 percent level of significance. (h) Test the significance of the constant k_0 and of the regression coefficients k_2 and k_3 for a level of significance of 5 percent. (i) Compute with a confidence coefficient of 99 percent the confidence limits for k_2 and k_3. (j) Test the hypothesis $\bar{k}_2 = -2$ for a 1 percent level of significance. (k) Test the hypothesis $\bar{k}_3 = 5$ for a 5 percent level of significance.

2 The following data for 1949–1956 come from Austrian economic statistics. All are real values per capita. x_{1t} is real consumption, x_{2t} real disposable income, and x_{3t} real disposable income of the past year:

Year	1949	1950	1951	1952	1953	1954	1955	1956
x_{1t}	10	11	11	11	12	12	14	14
x_{2t}	15	16	17	16	17	18	22	22
x_{3t}	14	15	16	17	16	17	18	22

(a) Compute the sums Σx_{1t}, Σx_{2t}, Σx_{3t}. (b) Compute the following arithmetic means: $\bar{x}_1$, $\bar{x}_2$, $\bar{x}_3$. (c) Compute the following sums of squares and products: Σx_{1t}^2, $\Sigma x_{1t}x_{2t}$, $\Sigma x_{1t}x_{3t}$, Σx_{2t}^2, $\Sigma x_{2t}x_{3t}$, Σx_{3t}^2. (d) Compute the sums of squares and products of deviations from the following arithmetic means: S_{11}, S_{12}, S_{13}, S_{22}, S_{23}, S_{33}. (e) Estimate by the method of least squares the linear relationship $\hat{x}_{1t} = k_0 + k_2 x_{2t} + k_3 x_{3t}$. This is a *dynamic consumption*. (f) Compute the *multiplier* $m = 1/(1 - k_2)$. (g) Make the assumption that the deviations $x_{1t} - \hat{x}_{1t}$ are normally and independently distributed. Compute the square of the multiple correlation coefficient R^2 and test it at the 5 percent level of significance. (h) Test the constant k_0 and the regression coefficients k_2 and k_3 at the 5 percent level of significance. (i) Compute the 95 percent confidence limits for the regression coefficients k_2 and k_3. (j) Test the hypothesis $\bar{k}_2 = 0.3$, level of significance 1 percent. (k) Test the hypothesis $\bar{k}_3 = 0.5$, level of significance 1 percent.

3 The following data refer to Austria for the period 1948–1955. x_{1t} is the logarithm of the quantity of pork consumed per capita; x_{2t} is the logarithm of the retail price of pork, in constant schillings; x_{3t} is the logarithm of real per capita disposable income.

Year	1948	1949	1950	1951	1952	1953	1954	1955
x_{1t}	10	10	13	13	14	14	14	14
x_{2t}	6	7	5	6	6	6	6	6
x_{3t}	30	31	31	31	31	31	32	32

(a–e) Proceed as in problem 2. (f) Make the assumption of normal and independent deviations and compute the square of the multiple correlation coefficient. Test it at the 1 percent level of significance. (g) Test the significance of the constant k_0 and the regression coefficients k_2 and k_3, level of significance 1 percent. (h) Compute the 95 percent confidence limits for the regression coefficients k_2 and k_3. (i) Test the hypothesis $\bar{k}_2 = -1$, level of significance 5 percent. (j) Test the hypothesis $\bar{k}_3 = 1$, level of significance 5 percent.

4 The following data come from United States statistics for 1919–1941. The number of observations is $N = 23$. x_{1t} is the quantity of meat consumed per capita, x_{2t} the real retail price of meat, x_{3t} the real cost of production of meat, and x_{4t} the real cost of agricultural production. The arithmetic means of the variables are $\bar{x}_1 = 166$, $\bar{x}_2 = 92$, $\bar{x}_3 = 88$, $\bar{x}_4 = 102$. The sums of squares and products of the deviations of the variables from their arithmetic means are $S_{11} = 1370$, $S_{12} = -353$, $S_{13} = -536, S_{14} = 984, S_{22} = 1581, S_{23} = 850, S_{24} = 1236, S_{33} = 2535$, $S_{34} = 731$, $S_{44} = 2627$. (a) Estimate the following supply function for meat by the method of least squares: $x_{1t} = k_0 + k_2x_{2t} + k_3x_{3t} + k_4x_{4t}$. (b) Predict x_{1t} if $x_{2t} = 90$, $x_{3t} = 95$, $x_{4t} = 100$. (c) Compute the elasticity of supply with respect to price if all variables have the values of their arithmetic means. (d) Assume normality and independence of the deviations. Compute the square of the multiple correlation coefficient R^2 and test it, level of significance 5 percent. (e) Test the significance of the constant k_0 and the regression coefficients k_2, k_3, k_4, level of significance 1 percent. (f) Compute the 95 percent confidence limits for the regression coefficients k_2, k_3, k_4. (g) Test the hypothesis $\bar{k}_2 = +1$, level of significance 5 percent. (h) Test the hypothesis $\bar{k}_4 = -1$, level of significance 5 percent.

**5 Given that

$$Q = \sum_{t=1}^{N} (x_{1t} - \hat{x}_{1t})^2,$$

with $\hat{x}_{1t} = k_0 + k_2x_{2t} + k_3x_{3t}$; assume normality and independence of the deviations $x_{1t} - \hat{x}_{1t}$. They are normally and independently distributed with mean zero and variance σ^2. (a) Show that the likelihood function (probability of the occurrence of the sample values) is

$$L = \frac{e^{-Q/2\sigma^2}}{2\pi^{N/2}\sigma^N}.$$

(b) Prove that the method of maximum likelihood (L maximum) is equivalent to the method of least squares (Q minimum). (HINT: Use log L.) (c) Find the normal equations by partial differentiation of L and Q. Use the sums of squares and products of the deviations of the variables from their arithmetic means S_{ij} ($i, j = 1, 2, 3$). (d) Show that the constant k_0 may be estimated by the same formula by the method of least squares and the method of maximum likelihood.

6 Consider the following German data (Menges):

Year	Income of Entrepreneurs in a Given Year (Q_t)	Income of Entrepreneurs of the Previous Year (Q_{t-1})	Productivity (R_t)
1950	26.30	21.0	100
1951	33.4	26.3	108
1952	32.9	33.4	112
1953	33.5	32.9	119
1954	36.5	33.5	126
1955	41.3	36.5	134
1956	44.2	41.3	139
1957	46.9	44.2	150

(a) Find the multiple regression $Q_t = k_0 + k_2 Q_{t-1} + k_3 R_t$. (b) Predict Q_t if $Q_{t-1} = 46.9$ and $R_t = 155$. (c) Test the regression coefficients, level of significance 5 percent. (d) Compute the multiple correlation coefficient. (e) Test the multiple correlation coefficient, level of significance 1 percent.

124 IDENTIFICATION

The identification problem may be formulated as follows: An economic model is a set of functional or stochastic relationships between a certain number of variables. Is it possible to estimate each one of these assumed equations if the sample is large enough? We will discuss here only linear models, and we assume also that errors in the variables (errors of observation) are absent. Then we obtain a set of linear stochastic relations; there is no reason that we should have functional relations which are strictly deterministic.

We distinguish first two classes of variables. We have *endogenous* variables, whose number must be equal to the number of linear relations in the system. Let G be the number of linear equations and also of the endogenous variables. We denote them by $Y_1, Y_2, \cdots, Y_G$. These are the really economic variables that are interdependent, such as prices and quantities of different commodities, income, interest rates, and so on.

The second class of variables are those that are *predetermined*. They influence the system but are not influenced by it. They are truly *exogenous* variables such as time, weather, and so on, but also *lagged* values of endogenous variables, for example, the price of the previous year. Let K be the number of predetermined variables. We denote them by Z_1, Z_2, $\cdots$, Z_K.

Under these assumptions, we present our model as follows:

$$b_{10} + b_{11}Y_1 + b_{12}Y_2 + \cdots + b_{1G}Y_G + c_{11}Z_1 + c_{12}Z_2 + \cdots + c_{1K}Z_K$$
$$= \Sigma_1,$$
$$b_{20} + b_{21}Y_1 + b_{22}Y_2 + \cdots + b_{2G}Y_G + c_{21}Z_1 + c_{22}Z_2 + \cdots + c_{2k}Z_K$$
$$= \Sigma_2,$$
$$\cdots$$
$$b_{G0} + b_{G1}Y_1 + b_{G2}Y_2 + \cdots + c_{GG}Y_G + c_{G1}Z_1 + c_{G2}Z_2 + \cdots + c_{GK}Z_K$$
$$= \Sigma_G.$$

The terms Σ_1, Σ_2, $\cdots$, Σ_G on the right-hand sides of these equations are random variables and represent errors in the equations. We make the following assumptions about them: Their mean values (mathematical expectations) are zero: $E\Sigma_i = 0$, $i = 1, 2, \cdots , G$. There is an unknown constant matrix of their variances and covariances: $E\Sigma_i \Sigma_j = \sigma_{ij}$ ($i, j = 1, 2, \cdots , G$). We also assume that the errors or deviations Σ_i are independent over time. It is also simplest to assume that their distribution is normal.

The identification problem is now whether there is a large enough sample of the observable variables Y_1, Y_2, $\cdots$, Y_G, Z_1, Z_2, $\cdots$, Z_k to permit us the estimation of the unknown parameters b_{10}, b_{11}, $\cdots$, b_{GG}, c_{11}, c_{12}, $\cdots$, c_{GK}. The importance of this problem is the fact that the system of equations represented above consists of *structural equations* that have economic meaning. Such structural equations are demand functions, supply functions, consumption functions, and so on. The unknown parameters are then structural parameters such as elasticities, marginal productivities, marginal propensities to consume, and so on.

A necessary condition for identification is that the total number of (endogenous and predetermined) variables *absent* in a given equation must be at least $G - 1$. In the equation we want to identify we need at least $G - 1$ zero coefficients.

If there are exactly $G - 1$ absent variables, we say the equation is *just identified*. If there are more than $G - 1$ zeros, we have an over-identified equation. If there are not at least $G - 1$ variables absent, the equation is not *identified* and cannot be estimated in the given system.

EXAMPLE 1

We have the following linear model with three equations, containing three endogenous variables, Y_1, Y_2, Y_3, and two predetermined variables, Z_1 and Z_2:

$$b_{10} + b_{11}Y_1 + b_{12}Y_2 + b_{13}Y_3 + c_{11}Z_1 \qquad\qquad = \Sigma_1,$$
$$b_{20} + b_{21}Y_1 + b_{22}Y_2 \qquad\qquad\qquad + c_{22}Z_2 = \Sigma_2,$$
$$b_{30} \qquad\quad + b_{32}Y_2 + b_{33}Y_3 \qquad\qquad\qquad = \Sigma_3.$$

Note that the coefficients c_{12}, b_{23}, c_{21}, b_{31}, c_{31}, and c_{32} are *a priori* assumed to be zero. Since we have $G = 3$ endogenous variables (and also a system consisting of three linear equations), the necessary condition for identification is the absence of at least $G - 1 = 3 - 1 = 2$ variables (which might be endogenous or predetermined) from a given equation. Hence the first equation is not identified, since only one variable (Z_2) is absent. The second equation is just identified, since exactly two variables (Y_3 and Z_1) are not included in this equation. The third equation is over-identified, since more than two variables (Y_1, Z_1, Z_2) are not in this equation.

For *just identified equations* the method of estimation is the classical method of least squares, explained in Section 118. Suppose we denote the endogenous variables in the equation we want to estimate by X_1, X_2, $\cdots$, X_H $(H \leq G)$. Further, we denote by U_1, U_2, $\cdots$, U_F the predetermined variables in the equation to be estimated. Then this equation might be written

$$b_0 + b_1X_1 + b_2X_2 + \cdots + b_HX_H + c_1U_1 + c_2U_2 + \cdots$$
$$+ c_FU_F = \Sigma.$$

But there are also now $K - F = D$ predetermined variables in the system, but not in the equation we want to estimate. We denote them by

$$V_1, V_2, \cdots, V_D.$$

We utilize now the method of least squares in order to compute the *reduced-form equations*. These are the linear relations between each one of the endogenous variables in the equation to be estimated $(X_1, X_2, \cdots, X_H)$ and *all* the predetermined variables, both those in the equation $(U_1, U_2, \cdots, U_F)$ and those in the system but not in the equation $(V_1, V_2, \cdots, V_D)$:

$$\hat{X}_1 = A_{10} + A_{11}U_1 + A_{12}U_2 + \cdots + A_{1F}U_FB_{11}V_1$$
$$+ B_{12}V_2 + \cdots + B_{1D}V_D,$$
$$\hat{X}_2 = A_{20} + A_{21}U_1 + A_{22}U_2 + \cdots + A_{2F}U_F + B_{21}V_2$$
$$+ B_{22}V_2 + \cdots + B_{2D}V_D,$$
$$\cdots$$
$$\hat{X}_H = A_{H0} + A_{H1}U_1 + A_{H2}U_2 + \cdots + A_{HF}U_F + B_{H1}V_1$$
$$+ B_{H2}V_2 + \cdots + B_{HD}V_D.$$

Since the equation to be estimated is just identified, we have
$F + H = G + K - (G - 1) = K + 1; K - F = D; H - 1 = D$.
From the system of H reduced-form equations given above, we might eliminate $H - 1 = D$ variables. These are the last D variables, namely, $V_1, V_2, \cdots, V_D$, the predetermined variables that do not appear in our equation. By eliminating them we obtain a linear relationship between the endogenous variables in our equation $(X_1, X_2, \cdots, X_H)$ and the predetermined variables in the equation $(U_1, U_2, \cdots, U_F)$, which is just the relationship we desire to estimate.

EXAMPLE 2

We want to estimate the following relationship:

$$b_0 + b_1 X_1 + b_2 X_2 + cU = \Sigma$$

in a system that contains three endogenous variables and two predetermined variables, U and V. This is the case of equation 2 in Example 1. This equation is just identifiable $(H - 1 = D)$.

We have $G = 3$, $H = 2$, $K = 2$, $F = D = 1$. Now we utilize the method of least squares to compute the reduced-form equations:

$$\hat{X}_1 = A_{10} + A_{11}U + B_{11}V,$$
$$\hat{X}_2 = A_{20} + A_{21}U + B_{21}V.$$

Since our equation is just identified, we eliminate the variable V (a predetermined variable which does not appear in the equation) from this system. We obtain

$$(B_{11}A_{20} - B_{21}A_{10}) + B_{21}X_1 - A_{12}X_2 + (B_{11}A_{21} - B_{21}A_{11})U = 0,$$

and this is the equation we wanted to estimate:

$$b_0 = B_{11}A_{20} - B_{21}A_{10},$$
$$b_1 = B_{21},$$
$$b_2 = B_{11},$$
$$c = B_{11}A_{21} - B_{21}A_{11}.$$

We show the necessary calculations by an example. Suppose we have the following data: Number of observations: $N = 20$; arithmetic means: $\bar{X}_1 = 1$, $\bar{X}_2 = 2$, $\bar{U} = 3$, $\bar{V} = 4$; sums of squares and cross products of the variables: $\Sigma X_1 U = 70$, $\Sigma X_1 V = 85$, $\Sigma X_2 U = 132$, $\Sigma X_2 V = 168$, $\Sigma U^2 = 200$, $\Sigma UV = 245$, $\Sigma V^2 = 330$. The sums of the squares and products of deviations of our variables from their arithmetic means are given by

$$S_{1U} = \Sigma(X_1 - \bar{X}_1)(U - \bar{U}) = 70 - (20)(1)(3) = 10,$$
$$S_{1V} = \Sigma(X_1 - \bar{X}_1)(V - \bar{V}) = 85 - (20)(1)(4) = 5,$$
$$S_{2U} = \Sigma(X_2 - \bar{X}_2)(U - \bar{U}) = 132 - (20)(2)(3) = 12,$$
$$S_{2V} = \Sigma(X_2 - \bar{X}_2)(V - \bar{V}) = 168 - (20)(2)(4) = 8,$$
$$S_{UU} = \Sigma(U - \bar{U})^2 = 200 - (20)(3)^2 = 20,$$
$$S_{UV} = \Sigma(U - \bar{U})(V - \bar{V}) = 245 - (20)(3)(4) = 5,$$
$$S_{VV} = \Sigma(V - \bar{V})^2 = 330 - (20)(4)^2 = 10.$$

The normal equations are the following for the first reduced-form equation:

$$\bar{X}_1 = A_{10} + A_{11}\bar{U} + B_{11}\bar{V},$$
$$S_{1U} = S_{UU}A_{11} + S_{UV} + B_{11},$$
$$S_{1V} = S_{UV}A_{11} + S_{VV}B_{11}.$$

The normal equations for the second reduced-form equation are

$$\bar{X}_2 = A_{20} + A_{21}\bar{U} + B_{21}\bar{V},$$
$$S_{2U} = S_{UU}A_{21} + S_{UV}B_{21},$$
$$S_{2V} = S_{UV}A_{21} + S_{VV}B_{21}.$$

We note that the equations for the determination of A_{11} and B_{11} and those for the calculation of A_{21} and B_{21} have the same coefficients. Hence the computations might be most conveniently arranged with the help of the Crout method (Table 1).

Table 1

		I		
20.000000	5.000000	10.000000	12.000000	47.000000
5.000000	10.000000	5.000000	8.000000	28.000000

		II		
20.000000	0.250000	0.500000	0.600000	2.350000
5.000000	8.750000	0.285714	0.571428	1.857142

	III			
0.428571	0.285714			
0.457143	0.571428			
1.885714	1.857142			

We write in Table 1 first the common coefficients of the normal equations, the matrix

$$\begin{bmatrix} S_{UU} & S_{UV} \\ S_{UV} & S_{VV} \end{bmatrix} = \begin{bmatrix} 20 & 5 \\ 5 & 10 \end{bmatrix}.$$

Next we write the column of the constants of the first set:

$$\begin{bmatrix} S_{1U} \\ S_{1V} \end{bmatrix} = \begin{bmatrix} 10 \\ 5 \end{bmatrix}.$$

Next we write the column of the constants of the second set:

$$\begin{bmatrix} S_{2U} \\ S_{2V} \end{bmatrix} = \begin{bmatrix} 12 \\ 8 \end{bmatrix}.$$

The last column gives a check. Part III gives us in the first line the solutions of the first set of normal equations:

$$A_{11} = 0.428571, \qquad B_{11} = 0.285714.$$

The second line of part III gives us the solutions of the second set of normal equations:

$$A_{21} = 0.457143, \qquad B_{21} = 0.571428.$$

Finally, we have for the determination of A_{10} and A_{20},

$$A_{10} = 1 - (3)(0.428571) - (4)(0.285714) = -1.428569,$$
$$A_{20} = 2 - (3)(0.457143) - (4)(0.571428) = -1.657141.$$

The reduced-form equations are

$$\hat{X}_1 = -1.428569 + 0.428571U + 0.285714V,$$
$$\hat{X}_2 = -1.657141 + 0.457143U + 0.571428V.$$

Eliminating V from these two equations, we obtain the estimate of our just identified equation:

$$b_0 = (0.285714)(-1.657141) - (0.571428)(-1.428569)$$
$$= 0.342856,$$
$$b_1 = 0.571428,$$
$$b_2 = -0.285714,$$
$$c = (0.285714)(0.457143) - (0.571428)(0.428571)$$
$$= -0.114285.$$

Hence

$$0.342856 + 0.571428X_1 - 0.285714X_2 - 0.114285U = 0.$$

EXERCISES 124

1   Let Y_1 and Y_2 be two endogeneous variables and Z_1, Z_2, Z_3 three predetermined variables. Consider the system

$$b_{10} + b_{11}Y_1 + b_{12}Y_2 + c_{11}Z_1 + c_{12}Z_2 + c_{13}Z_3 = \Sigma_1,$$
$$b_{20} + b_{21}Y_1 + b_{22}Y_2 + c_{21}Z_1 + c_{22}Z_2 + c_{23}Z_3 = \Sigma_2.$$

Determine whether each equation is underidentified, just identified, or overidentified under these assumptions: (a) no coefficient is zero; (b) $c_{12} = c_{13} = 0$;   (c) $c_{12} = c_{13} = c_{21} = c_{23} = 0$;   (d) $c_{11} = c_{12} = c_{13} = c_{21} = c_{23} = c_{22} = 0$.

2   With the same notation as in problem 1, consider the system

$$b_{10} + b_{11}Y_1 + b_{12}Y_2 + c_{11}Z_1 = \Sigma_1,$$
$$b_{20} + b_{21}Y_1 + b_{22}Y_2 + c_{22}Z_2 = \Sigma_2.$$

(a) Show that each equation is just identified. (b) Find the reduced-form equations with the following data: $\bar{Y}_1 = 1$, $\bar{Y}_2 = 3$, $\bar{Z}_1 = 3$, $\bar{z}_2 = 2$, $\Sigma(Y_1 - \bar{Y}_1)(Z_1 - \bar{Z}_1) = 4$, $\Sigma(Y_1 - \bar{Y}_1)(Z_2 - \bar{Z}_2) = 0$, $\Sigma(Y_2 - \bar{Y}_2)$ $(Z_1 - \bar{Z}_1) = 6$, $\Sigma(Y_2 - \bar{Y}_2)(Z_2 - \bar{Z}_2) = 2$, $\Sigma(Z_1 - \bar{Z}_1)^2 = 10$, $\Sigma(Z_1 - \bar{Z}_1)(Z_2 - \bar{Z}_2) = 2$, $\Sigma(Z_2 - \bar{Z}_2)^2 = 2$. (c) Estimate the equations with the help of the reduced-form equations.

3 The following data are taken from United States statistics for 1919–1941. The number of observations is $N = 23$. Let Y_1 be the quantity of meat, Y_2 the price of meat, Z_1 disposable income, and Z_2 the cost of producing meat. The model is

$$b_{10} + b_{11}Y_1 + b_{12}Y_2 + c_{11}Z_1 = \Sigma_1,$$
$$b_{20} + b_{21}Y_1 + b_{22}Y_2 + c_{22}Z_2 = \Sigma_2.$$

The first equation is the demand function, the second the supply function of meat. (a) Show that both equations are just identified. (b) Find the reduced-form equation with the help of the following data:

$\bar{Y}_1 = 166$, $\bar{Y}_2 = 92$, $\bar{Z}_1 = 496$, $\bar{Z}_2 = 88$.
$\Sigma(Y_1 - \bar{Y}_1)(Z_1 - \bar{Z}_1) = 3672$, $\Sigma(Y_1 - \bar{Y}_1)(Z_2 - \bar{Z}_2) = -536$,
$\Sigma(Y_2 - \bar{Y}_2)(Z_1 - \bar{Z}_1) = 2355$, $\Sigma(Y_2 - \bar{Y}_2)(Z_2 - \bar{Z}_2) = 850$,
$\Sigma(Z_1 - \bar{Z}_1)^2 = 83434$, $\Sigma(Z_1 - \bar{Z}_1)(Z_2 - \bar{Z}_2) = 3612$,
$$\Sigma(Z_2 - \bar{Z}_2)^2 = 2535.$$

(c) Estimate both equations from the reduced-form equations.

4 (*Two-stage least squares*). Assume we want to estimate the relationship $x_{1t} = b_0 + b_2x_{2t} + c_1u_{1t}$, where x_1 and x_2 are endogenous variables and u_1 is a predetermined variable in the equation to be estimated. But we know that there are two other predetermined variables, v_{1t} and v_{2t} in the system but not in the equation. The equation to be estimated is overidentified. Assume that we have the following data:

t	x_{1t}	x_{2t}	u_{1t}	v_{1t}	v_{21}
1	40	10	3	9	25
2	50	9	7	1	15
3	70	8	6	5	30
4	30	12	5	3	10
5	60	11	4	7	20

With two-stage least squares we proceed as follows: (a) Estimate by the method of least squares the relationship

$$\hat{x}_{2t} = A_{20} + A_{21}u_{1t} + B_{21}v_{1t} + B_{22}v_{2t}.$$

(b) Compute the values of $\hat{x}_{2t}$ for $t = 1, 2, 3, 4, 5$. (c) Estimate by the method of least squares the desired relation:

$$\hat{x}_{1t} = b_0 + b_2\hat{x}_{2t} + c_1u_{1t}.$$

Chapter 28

Aggregation and
Index Numbers

125 LINEAR AGGREGATION

In microeconomics we analyze the behavior of each individual and each firm in order to establish their characteristic relations. The *aggregation problem* represents an effort to go from these individual relations to relations that describe the behavior of all the individuals and forms in a total economy. We proceed from microeconomics to macroeconomics.

In general, this is a very difficult problem. We will discuss here only linear relations between the individuals, but we will find similar difficulties for the goods consumed.

Consider an economy in which there are n individuals ($i = 1, 2, \cdots, n$). Let us define y_i as the demand of individual i for a commodity A and designate by m_i the individual's money income. The *Engel curves* assumed to be linear have the equation $y_i = a_i m_i + k_i$. The constants a_i and k_i are characteristic for the individual i. We interpret a_i *as the marginal propensity to consume* of the individual i for commodity A. Now we look for a macroeconomic relation of the form $y = am + k$. This is an Engel curve for the total economy. Again, a and k are constants and the relation is assumed to be linear. Here a is the marginal propensity to consume of the total economy in relation to commodity A.

Total demand for commodity A is evidently the sum of all the individual quantities demanded:

$$y = \sum_{i=1}^{n} y_i.$$

Hence the global relationship might be written

$$y = \sum_{i=1}^{n} a_i m_i + \sum_{i=1}^{n} k_i.$$

407

We want to write this relation in the form $y = a\mu k$. Hence we have to define total money income μ in a way that is the weighted arithmetic mean of the individual money incomes m_i. The weights are the ratio of the individual propensities to consume, a_i, divided by the average propensity to consume $\bar{a}$:

$$\mu = \sum_{i=1}^{n} \left(\frac{a_i}{\bar{a}}\right) m_i, \qquad \bar{a} = \frac{\sum_{i=1}^{n} a_i}{n}.$$

These definitions permit us to write

$$y = \bar{a}\mu + k, \qquad k = \sum_{i=1}^{n} k_i.$$

But the definition of average money income is artificial. There is a different approach that bases itself upon a statistical analysis of the problem.

Define now in a natural way total demand (y) as the sum of all the individual quantities demanded (y_i) and total money income (m) as the sum of individual money incomes (m):

$$y = \sum_{i=1}^{n} y_i, \qquad m = \sum_{i=1}^{n} m_i.$$

Assume now that we have a sample of observations of the n individuals over the period $t = 1, 2, \cdots, T$. We utilize the method of least squares to fit linear relations of the type

$$\hat{m}_{it} = A_i m_t + K_i \ (i = 1, 2, \cdots, n).$$

The individual Engels curves are given by

$$y_{it} = a_i \hat{m}_{it} + k_i = a_i A_i m_t + a_i K_i + k_i.$$

If we aggregate these relations, we derive the global Engel curve,

$$y_t = \sum_{i=1}^{n} (a_i A_i) m_t + \sum_{i=1}^{n} (a_i K_i + k_i),$$

which now has the derived form $y = am + k$:

$$a = \sum_{i=1}^{n} a_i A_i, \qquad k = \sum_{i=1}^{n} a_i K_i + k_i.$$

Now we transform this expression for the global parameters a and k. We use the classical idea of covariance:

$$\text{cov}(X, Y) = \left(\frac{1}{N}\right) E[(X - EX)(Y - EY)] = \left(\frac{1}{N}\right)[EXY - (EX)(EY)],$$

where N is the size of the sample. We write it in the form

$$EXY = (EX)(EY) + N \text{ cov } (X, Y).$$

Assume now that each of the parameters a_i, k_i, K_i, A_i has a probability distribution independent of the individual i. Hence the individual i appears as a random drawing from the probability distribution of money income and consumption of commodity A. We can now write

$$a = \sum_{i=1}^{n} a_i A_i = E(a_i A_i) = (Ea_i)(EA_i) + n \text{ cov } (a_i, A_i),$$

$$k = \sum_{i=1}^{n} (a_i K_i) = \sum_{i=1}^{n} k_i + E(a_i K_i) = \sum_{i=1}^{n} k_i + E(a_i)E(K_i) + n \text{ cov } (a_i, K_i).$$

What are now the mathematical expectations of the parameters a_i, A_i K_i? We consider the relations

$$\hat{m}_{it} = A_i m_t + K_i,$$

which might be written

$$\hat{m}_{it} = A_i m_t + K_i + \Sigma,$$

where Σ is an error or deviation with mathematical expectation zero. Hence we have

$$E(\hat{m}_{it}) = E(A_i m_t) + E(K_i) + E(\Sigma).$$

We assume

$$E(\Sigma) = 0,$$
$$E(A_i m_t) = n m_t E(A_i),$$
$$E(\hat{m}_{it}) = \sum_{i=1}^{n} \hat{m}_{it} = m_t.$$

Hence,

$$m_t = n E(A_i) m_t + E(K_i),$$

and, finally,

$$E(A_i) = \frac{1}{n}, \qquad E(K_i) = 0.$$

We know that

$$E(a_i) = \sum_{i=1}^{n} a_i = n \bar{a}.$$

The global parameters are then

$$a = \frac{n \bar{a}}{n} + n \text{ cov } (a_i A_i),$$

$$k = \sum_{i=1}^{n} k_i + n \bar{a}(0) + n \text{ cov } (a_i, K_i).$$

Hence,

$$a = \bar{a} + n \text{ cov } (a_i, A_i),$$

$$k = \sum_{i=1}^{n} k_i + n \text{ cov } (a_i, K_i).$$

Hence these parameters will not assume their "natural" values,

$$a = \bar{a}, \qquad k = \sum_{i=1}^{n} k_i,$$

except if the joint distribution of the parameters a_i, A_i and K_i are such that in the population the following covariances are zero:

$$\text{cov } (a_i, A_i) = 0, \qquad \text{cov } (a_i, K_i) = 0.$$

It is easy to see that in general the application of the natural formula

$$y = \bar{a}m + \sum_{i=1}^{n} k_i$$

leads to contradictions. Assume that the individual money incomes m_i are changed by quantities Δm_i. Then the total income is given by

$$\Delta m = \sum_{i=1}^{n} \Delta m_i.$$

The global change in consumption is given by

$$\Delta_1 y = \sum_{i=1}^{n} \Delta y_i = \sum_{i=1}^{n} a_i \Delta m_i.$$

But if we use the assumed global relationship, the total change in consumption is given by

$$\Delta_2 y = \bar{a}\Delta m = \bar{a} \sum_{i=1}^{n} \Delta m_i.$$

The two estimates $\Delta_1 y$ and $\Delta_2 y$ are in general different, except if all the changes in individual money incomes Δm_i are equal.

EXERCISES 125

1   The following are German data for the years 1927–1928 (Allen and Bowley): Workers ($n_1 = 896$ families), white collar workers ($n_2 = 542$ families), employers ($n_3 = 498$ families). Engel curves for food: Workers, $y_1 = a_1 m_1 + k_1 = 0.36 m_1 + 284.85$; white collar workers, $y_2 = a_2 m_2 + k_2 = 0.27 m_2 + 348.16$; employers, $y_3 = a_3 m_3 + k_3 = 0.23 m_3 + 591$.

Aggregate, using total income $y = n_1y_1 + n_2y_2 + n_3y_3$ and

$$\mu = \frac{n_1a_1m_1 + n_2a_2m_2 + n_3a_3m_3}{n_1a_1 + n_2a_2 + n_3a_3}.$$

2 Proceed as in problem 1, but use the Engel curves for clothing. Workers, $y_1 = 0.18m_1 = 158.25$; white collar workers, $y_2 = 0.15m_2 - 108.80$; employers, $y_3 = 0.15m_3 - 49.25$.

3 The following data are for Sweden for 1923 (Allen and Bowley): Workers ($n_1 = 747$ families); employers ($n_2 = 445$ families); middle class ($n_3 = 208$ families). Engel curves for meat: $y_1 = 0.31m_1 - 0.588$; $y_2 = 0.275m_2 - 0.225$; $y_3 = 0.36m_3 - 1.080$. Proceed as in problem 1.

4 The following data refer to a community of two individuals:

t	y_1	m_1	y_2	m_2
1	5	10	10	15
2	15	15	20	20
3	10	10	25	20
4	20	20	10	10
5	10	10	15	15

Put $y = y_1 + y_2$ and $m = m_1 + m_2$. (a) Fit by the method of least squares the relations: $\hat{m}_1 = Am + K_1$ and $\hat{m}_2 = A_2m + K_2$. (b) Fit by the method of least squares $\hat{y}_1 = a_1m_1 + k_1$, $\hat{y}_2 = a_2m_2 + k_2$. (c) Show that $A_1 + A_2 = 1K_1 + K_2 = 0$. (d) Fit with the help of the method of least squares the global relation $\hat{y} = am + k$. (e) Compare

$$\Delta_1 y = a_1\Delta m_1 + a_2\Delta m_2,$$
$$\Delta_2 y = a(\Delta m_1 + \Delta m_2).$$

126 INDEX NUMBERS

Index numbers are supposed to measure the value of money. The way in which they are constructed, which commodities are included, and so on, depend largely upon the purpose for which they are to be used.

One important purpose of index numbers is the measurement of the standard of living. If the consumption of a well-defined group of people is known, theoretical limits can be established (under certain conditions), and, under more restrictive conditions, the change in the cost of living can actually be estimated.

Formulas

If the quantities consumed or sold are not known, there are two important formulas that are employed rather frequently. Denote the price at the base period as p_0 and at the period for comparison by p_1.

The number of commodities in the index is n. Then

$$S = \frac{\Sigma p_1/p_0}{n} \quad \text{(Sauerbeck)},$$

$$G = \sqrt[n]{\Pi\left(\frac{p_1}{p_0}\right)},$$

where p_1/p_0 is the price ratio for each commodity and Π denotes multiplication. The summation Σ and the multiplication Π are extended over all the commodities. Moreover, S is the arithmetic mean and G is the geometric mean of the n price ratios.

If the quantities consumed are known, we denote by q_0 the quantity consumed or bought in the base period and by q_1 the quantity in the period of comparison. We have the following formulas:

$$L = \frac{\Sigma p_1 q_0}{\Sigma p_0 q_0} \quad \text{(Laspeyre)}.$$

$$P = \frac{\Sigma p_1 q_1}{\Sigma p_0 q_1} \quad \text{(Paasche)}.$$

$$I = \sqrt{LP} \quad \text{(Fisher's ideal index)}.$$

The summations are extended over all commodities. It can be shown under somewhat restrictive conditions, and if there is no change in taste, that Laspeyre's index number gives the upper limit and Paasche's the lower limit of the "true" change in the cost of living. Under still greater restrictions Fisher's ideal index number I, which is the geometric mean of L and P, gives an approximation to the "true" cost of living index.

EXAMPLE

We give an example for only two commodities:

Commodity	A	B
p_0	1	2
q_0	5	10
p_1	2	3
q_1	1	5

We have by the use of the above formulas

$$S = \frac{\Sigma(p_1/p_0)}{n} = \frac{(2/1) + (3/2)}{2} = \frac{2 + 1.5}{2} = \frac{3.5}{2} = 1.75$$
$$= 175 \text{ percent}$$

$$G = \sqrt[n]{\Pi\left(\frac{p_1}{p_0}\right)} = \sqrt{\left(\frac{2}{1}\right)\left(\frac{3}{2}\right)} = \sqrt{3} = 1.73 = 173 \text{ percent}$$

Taking the quantities q into account, as required by the formulas of Laspeyre, Paasche, and Fisher, we get

$$L = \frac{\Sigma p_1 q_0}{\Sigma p_0 q_0} = \frac{(2)(5) + (3)(10)}{(1)(5) + (2)(10)} = \frac{10 + 30}{5 + 20} = \frac{40}{25} = 1.6$$

$$= 160 \text{ percent.}$$

$$P = \frac{\Sigma p_1 q_1}{\Sigma p_0 q_1} = \frac{(2)(1) + (3)(5)}{(1)(1) + (2)(5)} = \frac{2 + 15}{1 + 10} = \frac{17}{11} = 1.55$$

$$= 155 \text{ percent.}$$

Finally: $I = \sqrt{LP} = \sqrt{(1.6)(1.55)} = 1.57 = 157$ per cent.

These values of L and P are much closer than is common. As a general principle, the "true" index of the cost of living is regarded as between P and L; it may be approximated by the geometric mean of these two indexes, which is I.

EXERCISES 126

1   Consider the following data:

Commodity	A	B	C	D	E	F
p_0	1	2	7	6	1	6
q_0	10	8	6	7	1	9
p_1	1.5	3	8	8	8	7
q_1	5	6	3	6	0	5

Compute the index number according to (a) Sauerbeck's formula; (b) the geometric mean; (c) Laspeyre's formula; (d) Paasche's formula; (e) Fisher's ideal formula. (f) Establish limits for the "true" index of cost of living. (g) Estimate the "true" index of cost of living.

2   Consider the following data:

Commodity	A	B	C	D	E	F	G	H
p_0	2	5	10	1	2.7	1	5	6.9
q_0	20	9	4	6	10	8	9	7
p_1	1.5	4	9	0.8	2.5	0.6	4	6.8
q_1	25	10	5	8	11	9	9.5	7.2

(a) Compute the change in the value of money according to Sauerbeck; (b) the geometric mean; (c) Laspeyre; (d) Paasche; (e) Fisher. (f) Give limits for the "true" cost of living index. (g) Estimate the "true" cost of living index.

3   Consider the following data:

Commodity	Corn	Wheat	Oats	Potatoes	Sugar	Tobacco
Price 1926	0.75	1.45	0.41	1.42	0.043	0.182
Quantity 1926	2,692	831	1,247	354	12,952	1,298
Price 1930	0.84	0.87	0.39	0.90	0.034	0.144
Quantity 1930	2,060	858	1,278	333	13,169	1,635

Compute the increase in the cost of living according to (a) Sauerbeck's index number; (b) the geometric mean; (c) Laspeyre; (d) Paasche; (e) Fisher. (f) Estimate the limits for the "true" increase in the cost of living. (g) Estimate the increase in the cost of living.

4   Consider the following data:

Commodity	A	B	C
p_0	1	5	8
q_0	10	12	5
p_1	1.5	6	10
q_1	8	10	2

Compute the increase in the cost of living using (a) Sauerbeck's index; (b) the geometric mean; (c) Laspeyre's; (d) Paasche's; (e) Fisher's ideal index formula. (f) Establish limits for the increase in the cost of living. (g) Estimate the "true" cost of living index.

**5   Consider the definition of Laspeyre's index number. Assume that we compute $L = 1.20$. Show that a person whose income in time 0 was $100 will be not worse off in time 1 with an income of $120. (HINT: Consider the commodities which he bought in time 0 and which he could buy with his increased income in time 1.)

6   Consider the following data:

Commodities	A	B
p_0	1	1
q_0	10	5
p_1	2	x
q_1	5	2

Find x if the following indexes have the value 1.5: (a) Sauerbeck's; (b) the geometric mean; (c) Laspeyre's; (d) Paasche's; (e) Fisher's.

7   Use the data in problem 3 for the following commodities: corn, wheat, oats, potatoes to compute the increase in the cost of living between 1926 and 1930 according to the following formulas: (a) Sauerbeck's; (b) the geometric mean; (c) Laspeyre's; (d) Paasche's; (e) the ideal.

8 Use the data in problem 3 for the commodities sugar and tobacco to compute the increase in the cost of living according to the following formulas: (a) Sauerbeck's; (b) the geometric mean; (c) Laspeyre's; (d) Paasche's; (e) the ideal.

9 Consider the following data:

Year	Beef Consumption (million lb.)	Retail Price (cents per lb.)
1939	7,159	36.0
1942	8,104	29.3
1943	6,434	30.2

Year	Pork Consumption (million lb.)	Retail Price (cents per lb.)
1939	8,474	30.4
1942	8,139	41.4
1943	9,380	40.3

Year	Lamb Consumption, (million lb.)	Retail Price (cents per lb.)
1939	868	28.2
1942	948	35.3
1943	865	40.3

Year	Butter Consumption (million lb.)	Retail Price (cents per lb.)
1939	1,782	32.5
1942	1,764	34.8
1943	1,673	37.7

Year	Cheese Consumption (million lb.)	Retail Price (cents per lb.)
1939	537	25.3
1942	603	34.8
1943	753	37.7

Year	Oranges Production (million boxes)	Retail Price (cents per lb.)
1939	70	28.9
1942	272	35.7
1943	297	44.3

Year	Potatoes Production (million bu.)	Retail Price (cents per lb.)
1939	342	2.5
1942	433	3.4
1943	611	4.6

	Sugar	
Year	Disappearance (1,000 Short Tons)	Retail Price (cents per lb.)
1939	7,078	5.4
1942	5,974	6.8
1943	6,664	6.9

Use the formulae for Laspeyre's, Paasche's, and Fisher's indexes to compute the increase or decrease in food price (a) from 1939 to 1942; (b) from 1939 to 1943; (c) from 1942 to 1943.

**10   Investigate the various price index formulas for homogeneity with respect to the prices. Check by using the Euler theorem. (See Sections 81 and 82.)

Appendix A
Suggestions for
Further Study

It has been the purpose of this book to introduce the student of economics to some mathematical methods useful in mathematical economics, econometrics, and operations research. For the student who wishes to gain greater proficiency in these areas, the following readings are suggested.

A comprehensive survey of modern algebra, which covers topics not treated in this book, is Garret Birkhoff and Saunders MacLane, *A Survey of Modern Algebra* (New York: The Macmillan Company, 1941). We also recommend Taro Yamane, *Mathematics for Economists* (Englewood Cliffs, N.J. Prentice Hall, Inc., 1962); Louis O. Kattsoff and Albert J. Simone, *Foundations of Contemporary Mathematics* (New York: McGraw-Hill Book Company, Inc., 1967); and J. G. Kemeny, J. L. Snell, and G. L. Thompson, *Introduction to Finite Mathematics* (Englewood Cliffs, N.J.: Prentice-Hall, Inc., 1957).

The theory of matrices, so important in modern econometrics, is treated in R. A. Frazer, W. J. Duncan, and A. R. Collar, *Elementary Matrices* (New York: The Macmillan Company, 1946), and also in an appendix to the Tintner's book, *Econometrics* (New York: John Wiley & Sons, Inc., 1952). Topics in game theory are treated in the famous book by J. von Neumann and O. Morgenstern, *Theory of Games and Economic Behavior* (Princeton, N.J. Princeton University Press, 1944). We also recommend R. D. Luce and H. Raiffa, *Games and Decisions* (New York: John Wiley & Sons, Inc., 1957).

A more rigorous treatment of many topics found in this book is given in K. O. May, *Elementary Analysis* (New York: John Wiley & Sons, Inc., 1952), and in J. C. Mathews and C. E. Langenhop, *Discrete and Continuous Methods in Applied Mathematics* (New York: John Wiley & Sons, Inc., 1966). The two books by R. G. D. Allen, *Mathematical Analysis for Economists* (New York: The Macmillan Company, 1939) and *Mathematica Economics*, 2d ed. (London: The Macmillan Company, 1963), are especially written for economists.

W. Baumol, *Economic Dynamics*, 2d ed. (New York: The Macmillan Company, 1959), presents material useful in the treatment of problems of nonstatic economics. Linear programming and input-output analysis as well as related topics are discussed in R. Dorfman, P. A. Samuelson, and R. M. Solow, *Linear Programming and Economic Analysis* (New York: McGraw-Hill Book Company, Inc., 1958). An excellent introduction to the modern treatment of many of these problems is contained in T. C. Koopmans, *Three Essays on the State of Economic Science* (New York: McGraw-Hill Book Company, Inc., 1957).

For a more extensive study of econometrics see the following books: G. Tintner, *Econometrics* (New York: John Wiley & Sons, Inc., 1952); L. R. Klein, *Introduction to Econometrics* (Englewood Cliffs, N.J. Prentice Hall, Inc., 1962); C. F. Christ, *Econometric Models and Methods* (New York: John Wiley & Sons, Inc., 1966); A. S. Goldberger, *Econometric Theory* (New York: John Wiley & Sons, Inc., 1964); J. Johnston, *Econometric Methods* (New York: McGraw-Hill Book Company, Inc., 1963); E. Malinvaud, *Statistical Methods of Econometrics* (Amsterdam: North Holland, 1966).

For a more detailed treatment of probability see W. Feller, *An Introduction to Probability Theory and Its Applications*, Vol. I, 2d ed. (New York: John Wiley & Sons, Inc., 1957), and his *Probability Theory and Mathematical Statistics*, 3d ed. (New York: John Wiley & Sons, Inc., 1963). More information about statistics may be obtained in R. L. Anderson and T. A. Bancroft, *Statistical Theory in Research* (New York: McGraw-Hill Book Company, Inc., 1952), and in A. M. Mood and F. A. Graybill, *Introduction to the Theory of Statistics*, 2d ed. (New York: McGraw-Hill Book Company, Inc., 1963). More advanced books are S. S. Wilks, *Mathematical Statistics* (New York: John Wiley & Sons, Inc., 1962), and M. G. Kendall and A. Stuart, *The Advanced Theory of Statistics*, 3 vols. (New York: Hafner, 1958, 1961, 1966).

Answers to
Selected Problems

Exercises 1

1 (a)

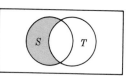

(c)

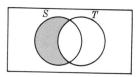

3 $\{a\}, \{b\}, \{c\}, \{a, b\}, \{a, c\}\ \{b, c\}\ \{a, b, c\}, \varphi$ φ is a subset of all sets
5 $V - T \subset V - S.$

Exercises 2

1 (a) $\{X, Y\}$ (c) $\{1, 2\}$
3 a, b, c

Exercises 3

1 $15P_a$
   $_4C_4 \cdot {}_4C_4 \cdot {}_4C_4 \cdot {}_{40}C_1$
5 $13 \cdot {}_4C_3 \cdot 12 \cdot {}_4C_2$
7 $4 \cdot {}_5C_2$

Exercises 4, 5, 6

1 (a) is reflexive and transitive   (c) is transitive
3 $f(0) = 3;$ $f(-2) = 13;$ $f(5) = 18;$ $f(-1) = 0$
5 $f(0) = a;$ $f(a) = a + ab;$ $f(a/b) = 2a;$ $f(-a/b) = 0$

Exercises 9

1 $-\frac{2}{3}$ **3** $1\frac{7}{5}$ **5** $\frac{7}{5}$ **7** $\frac{1}{6}$

Exercises 10

1 (a) $y = -2x + 2$ (b) $y = -2$ (c) $y = 5x$ (d) $y = -x + 5$
3 (a) $y = -x + 2$ (b) $y = 2x + 5$ (c) $y = 5x + 8$ (d) $y = 3$
5 (a) $-1, 0$ (b) $-4, -3$ (c) $3, -7$ (d) $4, 6$

Exercises 11

1 (a) 10   (b) 16.8   (c) 15   (d) 5   (e) 50   (f) 95
   (g) 100   (h) 20
3 (a) 9   (b) 6   (c) 18.75   (d) 4   (e) 12   (f) 32
   (g) 40   (h) 10
5 (a) 0.333   (b) 1.111   (c) 5.051   (d) 4.625   (e) 10.25
   (f) 11.375   (g) 5.56   (h) 12.5
7 (a) 3.4   (b) 2.725   (c) 4.9   (d) $4\frac{2}{3}$ (e) 13.2   (f) 10.13
   (g) 6.4   (h) 21.33
9 (a) 0.68   (b) 0.53   (c) 0.455   (d) 48   (e) 38   (f) 28
   (g) 0.88   (h) 88
11 (a) $\frac{5}{3}$ (b) $\frac{5}{2}$ (c) $D = \dfrac{5 - 3p}{2}$

Exercises 12

1 (a) 3   (b) 19   (c) 199   (d) $5\frac{1}{2}$ (e) 13   (f) 50.5
   (g) $\frac{1}{2}$
3 (a) 4   (b) 6   (c) 22   (d) 32   (e) 5   (f) 17.50
   (g) 40   (h) 2
5 (a) 1.0   (b) 0.818   (c) 0.546   (d) 8.7   (e) 6.5   (f) 4.41
   (g) 0.091
7 (a) m (b) $10m$ (c) m^2 (d) $\frac{1}{3}$ (e) $8/m$ (f) $6/m$
   (g) 1   (h) $5/m^2$ (i) 0
9 (a) 75   (b) 15   (c) $5\frac{7}{15}$ (d) 11   (e) 5

Exercises 13

1 (a) $2\frac{1}{5}$ (b) $3\frac{2}{5}$
3 (a) $4\frac{4}{9}$ (b) $3\frac{8}{9}$
5 (a) 7   (b) 14
7 (a) $1\frac{2}{3}$ (b) 5
9 (a) $(A + N)/(B + M)$ (b) $(AM - BN)/(B + M)$
11 (a) $1\frac{1}{13}$ (b) 1.1
13 0.355, 0.09

Exercise 14

1 (a) $10\frac{2}{5}, 4\frac{4}{5}$ (b) $5\frac{2}{5}, 9\frac{1}{5}, 9\frac{1}{5}$ (c) 6, 8, 16   (d) 5.1, 9.8, 4.9
   (e) 4.2, 11.6, 11.6   (f) 4.65, 10.7, 2.68

3   (a) 9.02, 6.96, 0.35   (b) 9.03, 6.93, 0.69   (c) 9.17, 6.67, 3.34
    (d) 8.99, 7.01, 0.14   (e) 8.92, 7.16, 1.79
5   (a) $\frac{5}{8}$ subsidy   (b) 2.5 tax   (c) 5 tax
7   (a) $(a + m)/(b + n)$, $(an - bm)/(b + n)$
    (b) $(an - bm - bnt)/(b + n)$, $(a + m + nt)/(b + n)$
    with $-t$ for a subsidy, t for a tax
    $(ant - bmt - bnt^2)/(b + n)$ for a tax,
    $(ant - bmt + bnt^2)/(b + n)$ for a subsidy
9   (a) Price rises 0.9, quantity decreases by 1.8
    (b) Price decreases by 1.2, quantity increases by 2.4

Exercises 15

1   2.08, 9.4
3   2.62, 17.36
5   4.73, 157.9
7   3.2, 219.3
9   5, 20
11   2.24, 6.67

Exercises 16

1   47, -19
3    $1\frac{6}{23}$, $\frac{6}{23}$
5   0.0
6    $-\frac{1}{2}$, -1, 1
8   1, -1, 2

Exercises 17

1   (a) $\frac{1}{2}$, 4   (b) $1\frac{1}{2}$, $1\frac{1}{2}$
3   (a) 1, 2   (b) 9, 14
5   (a) 5.399, 1.524, 13.308   (b) 60.0, 70.0, 7.0
7    $(h - a)(g - n) - c(m - e)/(b - k)(g - n) - fc$,
     $f(h - a) - (m - e)(b - k)/fc - (g - n)(b - k)$
9   2, 1, 3, and 18, 27, 8

Exercises 18

1   1, 3
3   3, 2, 4
5   8, 32, 4
7   Only 1 independent equation and 2 unknowns
9   10, 10, 5, 3

Exercises 19

1    $x_1 = 1$, $x_2 = 2$, $x_3 = 0$

Exercises 20

1 (a) 7,248   (b) 1,050   (c) 3,359,300   (d) 38,092
   (e) 120,870,000   (f) 8,267,600   (g) 382,240   (h) 86,214,000
   (i) 462,170,000
3 (a) 3,053   (b) 1,516   (c) 50   (d) 3,779,500   (e) 20
   (f) 20,833,000   (g) 2,303,400   (h) 42,571
5 (a) 6091   (b) 991,780   (c) 4,247,700   (d) 34   (e) 395
   (f) 3,903,500   (g) 1,121,500   (h) 260,010   (i) 11,199,000
   (j) 29,660   (k) 4,808
7 (a) a/K^b (b) $a/10^{5b}$ (c) $(a/100)^{1/b}$ (d) $(a/10)^{1/b}$
   (e) $a(t^b - s^b)/s^b t^b$ (f) $a(3_b - 1)/(15 \times 10^5)^b$
9 (a) 1,000   (b) 444   (c) 31.62   (d) 141.42   (e) 3   (f) 22
11 (a) 0.00013   (b) 0.000055   (c) 0.216

Exercises 21

1 (a) 0.098   (b) 1.024   (c) 1,286.1   (d) $3,125 \times 10^{12}$
   (e) 1.585   (f) 0.833   (g) 2.886   (h) 8.027
3 (a) 0.177   (b) 0.380   (c) 1.06   (d) 55.49   (e) 0.657
   (f) 0.04   (g) 0.833   (h) 66.267
5 (a) 32.64   (b) 27.68   (c) 20.84   (d) 20.06   (e) 81.50
   (f) 26.02   (g) 18.84   (h) 12.56
7 (a) 27.46   (b) 65.42   (c) 108.05   (d) 4,071.5   (e) 473.21
   (f) 4.57   (g) 4.402   (h) 4.200   (i) 4.733   (j) 4.975
9 (a) $(1/5)^{1/b}$ (b) $a^{1/6}$ (c) a (d) $a^{1/b}$
11 (a) 20   (b) 100   (c) 4   (d) 100   (e) 50   (f) 100
13 $p = 4.056$, $q = 18.02$

Exercises 22

1 (a) 14   (b) 23   (c) 452
3 (a) 40   (b) 10   (c) −9890
5 (a) 0, 10   (b) 90   (c) 240
7 (a) −2.5   (b) 7.5   (c) 13
9 4

Exercises 23

1 (a) 140   (b) 150   (c) −900
3 (a) 94   (b) 325   (c) 16,750
5 $2an + n(n - 1)d/2$
7 (a) 120, −40   (b) −240   (c) 120
9 $a = Am(m - 1) - Bn(n - 1)/mn(m - n)$
   $d = 2(Am - Bn)/mn(n - m)$

Exercises 24

1 (a) 400   (b) 650   (c) 2,450   (d) 1,100
3 (a) 200   (b) 8th year   (c) 2,700

5   (a) 50   (b) 700   (c) 950
7   (a) 960   (b) −240   (c) 240   (d) 2,160
9   159

Exercises 25

1   (a) 80   (b) 5,120   (c) 163,840
3   (a) 125   (b) 3,125   (c) 1,953,125
5   (a) 10   (b) 100,000   (c) 10,000,000,000
7   $a = \dfrac{A^{\,m-1/m-n}}{B^{\,n-1/m-n}},\qquad r = \left(\dfrac{B}{A}\right)^{1/(m-n)}$
9   $a = 8,\qquad r = 1$

Exercises 26

1   (a) 21   (b) 341   (c) 21,845
3   (a) 35   (b) 155   (c) 635
5   (a) $5\frac{5}{7}$ (b) $\frac{5}{28}$ (c) $11\frac{1}{4}$
7   ar^n. This is y_{n+1}.
9   (a) $\left[\dfrac{B-A}{A}\right]^{1/m}$ (b) $\dfrac{\left[\left(\dfrac{B-A}{A}\right)^{1/m} - 1\right]}{B - 2A}\,A^2$

Exercises 27

1   (a) 1,060   (b) 1,124   (c) 1,690   (d) 7.96 years
    (e) 1.166 years   (f) 12.9 years
3   (a) 228,220   (b) 4.66 percent   (c) 376,560   (d) 543,230
    (e) 10.4 years   (f) 18.2 years   (g) 5.6 years
5   (a) 0.7 percent   (b) 123,880,000   (c) 128,330,000
    (d) 131,080,000   (e) 141,680,000   (f) 157,530,000
7   (a) 3,438,800,000   (b) 535,080,000   (c) 203,990,000
    (d) 113,140,000   (e) 92,814,000
9   (a) 3.8 percent   (b) 27,380,000   (c) 33,060,000
11 156,200,000

Exercises 28

1   (a) $10.816   (b) $14.801   (c) $71.06
3   (a) $525.50   (b) $638.14   (c) $805.24   (d) $500.00
5   (a) 4.1 percent   (b) 1.6 percent   (c) 0.4 percent
7   (a) $1,104,600   (b) $1,280,000   (c) $1,628,900
9   (a) 35 years   (b) 81.3 years   (c) 116.3 years
11 (a) $284,000,000,000   (b) $314,000,000,000   (c) $419,000,000,000

Exercises 29

7   $ad = bc$
9   The determinant appearing in the numerator equals zero and the determinant in the denominator is not equal to zero.

11 (a) $\begin{vmatrix} 2 & 4 \\ 1 & 2 \end{vmatrix} = 2 \cdot 2 - 4 \cdot 1 = 0$ (b) $x = k$ $y = -k/2$ and k is any

number, so an infinite number of solutions is possible

13 (a) $\lambda = 4, 1$ (b) $y = 2k$ when $\lambda = 4$ $y = -k$ when $\lambda = 1$
where k is an arbitrary number

Exercises 30

1 (a) -46 (b) 19 (c) -39

3 $6x + 45$

5 abc

7 $40, 40$

Exercises 31

1 $-5,$ $-5.5,$ -10.5

3 $1,$ $-1, 2$

5 $-21\tfrac{3}{2}2,$ $-21\%_{11},$ $55\%_{2}2$

7 $\begin{vmatrix} a & b \\ c & d \end{vmatrix} = ad - bc = - \begin{vmatrix} c & d \\ a & b \end{vmatrix}$

Exercises 32

1 (a) -5 (b) -3 (c) 10 (d) -48

Exercises 33

1 $-5 \geqq x$:

$$\underset{\quad -5\ -4\ -3\ -2\ -1\quad O}{\longleftarrow\!\!\!\!\rule{2cm}{0.4pt}\!\!|\!\!-\!\!|\!\!-\!\!|\!\!-\!\!|\!\!-\!\!|}$$

3

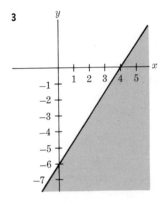

5

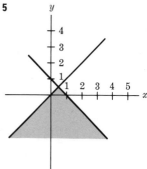

7

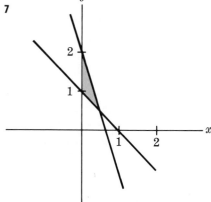

Exercises 34

1 15
3 (a) 0   (b) 2

Exercises 35

1 $x_1 = 0,$ $x_2 = 6,$ $f = 18$
3 $x_1 = 64{,}347,$ $x_2 = 0,$ $f = 100{,}382.60$
5 $x_1 = 5{,}365.37,$ $x_2 = 0,$ $f = 8{,}837$

Exercises 36

1 $x_1 = 10,$ $x_2 = 0,$ $x_3 = 0,$ $f = 30$
2 $z = 10,$ $x_1 = 10,$ $x_2 = x_3 = 0$
3 $z = 8830.19$
5 $z = 23\frac{1}{3}$

Exercises 37

1 (b) $\begin{vmatrix} 0 & 1 & 2 & 3 \\ 2 & 0 & 2 & 4 \end{vmatrix}$ (c) $\begin{vmatrix} 0 & \frac{1}{4} & \frac{1}{2} \\ \frac{2}{3} & 0 & \frac{1}{2} \\ \frac{1}{3} & \frac{3}{4} & 0 \end{vmatrix}$

(d) $x_2/x_1 = \frac{2}{3}$, $x_3/x_1 = \frac{4}{3}$

(f) $x_1 = 1 \cdot 2y_1 + 0 \cdot 3y_2$; $x_2 = 0 \cdot 8y_1 + 1 \cdot 2y_2$

(g) $x_1 = 2 \cdot 4$, $x_2 = 3 \cdot 6$

Exercises 38

1 (a) $\begin{bmatrix} 10 & -5 & -2 \\ -1 & 1 & 0 \\ 8 & -5 & -1 \end{bmatrix}$ (b) $\begin{bmatrix} -8 & 5 & 0 \\ -1 & -1 & 4 \\ -2 & 5 & -1 \end{bmatrix}$

(c) $\begin{bmatrix} 2 & 0 & -2 \\ -2 & 0 & 4 \\ 6 & 0 & -2 \end{bmatrix}$ (d) $\begin{bmatrix} -27 & 15 & 3 \\ 0 & -3 & 6 \\ -15 & 15 & 0 \end{bmatrix}$

(e) $\begin{bmatrix} 29 & -15 & -5 \\ -2 & 3 & -2 \\ 21 & -15 & -2 \end{bmatrix}$ (f) $\begin{bmatrix} 4 & -5 & 4 \\ 5 & 1 & -12 \\ -10 & -5 & 5 \end{bmatrix}$

Exercises 39

1 (a) $\begin{bmatrix} 8 & 1 & -1 \\ 1 & 3 & -1 \\ 24 & 1 & 11 \end{bmatrix}$ (b) $\begin{bmatrix} 3 & 11 & 4 \\ -5 & -1 & 4 \\ 2 & 1 & 8 \end{bmatrix}$ (c) $\begin{bmatrix} 2 & 2 & 1 \\ -6 & 6 & 1 \\ 2 & 1 & 2 \end{bmatrix}$

(d) $\begin{bmatrix} 8 & 5 & -5 \\ 4 & -7 & 1 \\ 20 & 5 & -5 \end{bmatrix}$ (e) $\begin{bmatrix} 4 & 7 & -4 \\ 5 & -1 & 4 \\ 12 & 23 & -20 \end{bmatrix}$ (f) $\begin{bmatrix} 4 & 1 & 3 \\ 24 & 19 & -1 \\ 10 & -5 & 0 \end{bmatrix}$

3 (a) $\begin{bmatrix} \frac{3}{5} & -\frac{2}{5} \\ -\frac{1}{5} & \frac{4}{5} \end{bmatrix}$ (b) $\begin{bmatrix} 2 & 1 \\ \frac{1}{2} & \frac{3}{2} \end{bmatrix}$ (c) $\begin{bmatrix} \frac{3}{5} & -\frac{1}{5} \\ -\frac{2}{5} & \frac{4}{5} \end{bmatrix}$

(d) $\begin{bmatrix} 2 & \frac{1}{2} \\ 1 & \frac{3}{2} \end{bmatrix}$

Exercises 40

1 (a) $\begin{bmatrix} \frac{4}{5} & -\frac{3}{5} \\ -\frac{1}{5} & \frac{2}{5} \end{bmatrix}$ (b) $\begin{bmatrix} 3 & 2 \\ 2 & 1 \end{bmatrix}$ (c) $\begin{bmatrix} \frac{1}{4} & 0 \\ 0 & 1 \end{bmatrix}$ (d) $\begin{bmatrix} -1 & 0 \\ 0 & -\frac{1}{5} \end{bmatrix}$

3 (a) $\begin{bmatrix} 2 & 1 \\ -1 & 3 \end{bmatrix}\begin{bmatrix} x_1 \\ x_2 \end{bmatrix} = \begin{bmatrix} 3 \\ 18 \end{bmatrix}$ (b) $\begin{bmatrix} \frac{3}{7} & -\frac{1}{7} \\ \frac{1}{7} & \frac{2}{7} \end{bmatrix}$

(c) $\begin{bmatrix} x_1 \\ x_2 \end{bmatrix} = \begin{bmatrix} \frac{3}{7} & -\frac{1}{7} \\ \frac{1}{7} & \frac{2}{7} \end{bmatrix} \cdot \begin{bmatrix} 3 \\ 18 \end{bmatrix} = \begin{bmatrix} -\frac{9}{7} \\ \frac{39}{7} \end{bmatrix}$

Exercises 41

1 (a) $y(x) = (10)(5)^x$ (b) 6,250   (c) 1,550,000

3 (a) $y(x) = (10,000)(\frac{1}{10})^x$ (b) 100   (c) $\frac{1}{10}$

5 $A(x+1) - 1.05A(x) = 0$

7 b/a is positive

9 $-1 < \dfrac{b}{a} < 0$

11 (a) 114.6   (b) 146.2

Exercises 42

1 (a) 8   (b) 8   (c) 8   (d) $8 - \frac{1}{2}(8) = 4$

3 (a) $y(x) = (-2)^x(15) + 1$ (b) 61, -119

5 (a) 13,315.36   (b) 17,546.68

7 (a) $a\left[km^{x+1} + \dfrac{c}{c+b}\right] + b\left[km^x + \dfrac{c}{c+b}\right] = c$

(b) $akm^{x+1} + bkm^x = 0$ (c) $k + n = K$

9 175, 199, $231\frac{1}{256}$

11 (a) 1.101×10^9 (b) 1.134×10^9

13 (a) $p(x) = 5(-\frac{1}{6})^x + 60$ $D(x) = 20 - 10(-\frac{1}{6})^x$

(b) $5(-\frac{1}{6})^x + 60 = 70 - \frac{1}{2}[20 - 10(-\frac{1}{6})^x]$

$5(-\frac{1}{6})^x + 60 = 70 - 10 + 5(-\frac{1}{6})^x$

$5(-\frac{1}{6})^x + 60 = 60 + 5(-\frac{1}{6})^x$

$20 - 10(-\frac{1}{6})^x = \frac{1}{3}[5(-\frac{1}{6})^{x+1} + 60]$

$\qquad = \frac{2}{6}[5(-\frac{1}{6})^{x+1} + 60]$

$\qquad = (-10)(-\frac{1}{6})(-\frac{1}{6})^{x-1} + 20 = 20 - 10(-\frac{1}{6})^x$

(c) 60, 20

15 (a) $p(x) = 4 + 2(-2)^x$ $D(x) = 8 - 2(-2)^x$

(b) $4 + 2(-2)^x = 12 - [8 - (2)(-2)^x]$

$8 - 2(-2)^x = 2[4 + 2(-2)^{x-1}] = 8 - 2(-2)^x$

17 7.93026

Exercises 43

1 (a) Sum is (4, 0); product is (7, 4); quotient is $(-\frac{1}{5}, -\frac{8}{5})$

(c) Sum is (5, 5); product is (0, 25); quotient is (0, -1)

3 $(x, y) \cdot (u, v) = r(\cos \theta + i \sin \theta) \cdot s(\cos \phi + i \sin \phi) = rs\,[\cos \theta \cos \phi - \sin \theta \sin \phi + i(\sin \theta \cos \phi + \cos \theta \sin \phi)] = rs\,[\cos(\theta + \phi) + i \sin(\theta + \phi)]$

Exercises 44

1 (a) $y_t = 2^t$ (b) $y_t = (\frac{5}{6})3^t - (\frac{1}{6})(-3)^t$

(c) $y_t = (1.732)^t(0.732 \sin(35.3t) + 0.268 \cos(35.3t))$

(d) $y_t = 2 - (\frac{1}{6})5 - (\frac{5}{6})(-1)^t$

(e) $y_t = 2 + (3.606)^t(-3 \cos 56.3t + 2 \sin 56.3t)$

(f) $y_t = \frac{1}{2} + 5^t(\frac{1}{5}) \cos 90t + (\frac{3}{10}) \sin 90t$

3 $y_t = c^{t/2}(a \cos st + b \sin st)$, $\cos s = c$, $\sin s = 1 - c$

5 $y_t = 2.381v_0 + 0.7616^t(A \sin 40.4t + B \cos 40.4t)$

7 $\text{Lim}_{t \to \infty} m_i{}^t = 0$ if $|m_i| < 1$

9 $y_t = 636.30 + 0.664^t(A \sin 64.5t + B \cos 64.5t)$

Exercises 45

1 (a) $y = \sqrt{\dfrac{5x + 5}{2}}$, $y = -\sqrt{\dfrac{5x + 5}{2}}$, domains are both

$\{x|x \geq -1\}$, ranges are $\{y|y \geq 0\}$ and $\{y|y \leq 0\}$, respectively
(c) $y = x/3$; domain, range all real numbers
(e) $y = -x + 1$, $y = -x - 1$; domain, range all real numbers

2 (a) $f^{-1}(x) = \sqrt[3]{x/3 + 3}$; domain, range all real numbers
(c) $f^{-1}(x) = x$
(e) $f^{-1}(x) = x^2 + 1$; domain [2, ∞), range [3, ∞)

(f) $f^{-1}(x) = \left\{ \left(x, \dfrac{1 \pm \sqrt{8x - 7}}{2} \right) \right\}$; domain $\{x|x \geq \frac{7}{8}\}$, range [¼, ∞).

Exercises 46

1 (a) $p = 5 - 3D/2$ (b) $R = 5D - 3D^2/2$ (c) $3\frac{1}{2}$ (d) 1.25
(e) 3.8675 (f) 2.90625 (g) 3.72656 (h) 1.5 (i) 0
3 (a) $p = \sqrt{100 - 5D}$ (b) $R = D\sqrt{100 - 5D}$ (c) 7.071
(d) 9.487 (e) 3.873 (f) 24.685 (g) 31.967 (h) 1.249
5 (a) $p = 24/\log D$ (b) $R = 24D/\log D$ (c) 24 (d) 79.727
(e) 18.94 (f) 240 (g) 171.681 (h) 200.521
7 (a) $p = 1 + \sqrt{11 - D}$ (b) $R = D + D\sqrt{11 - D}$ (c) 4.2404
(d) 4.3015 (e) 4.3164 (f) 4.0822 (g) 19.996 (h) 1.0697
9 (a) $p = 0.11/D^{1.4}$ (b) $R = 0.11/D^{0.4}$ (c) 0.00248
(d) 0.00166 (e) 0.00339 (f) 0.04379 (g) 0.04071
(h) 0.03724
11 (a) $p = 116.3/D^{2.56}$ (b) $R = 116.3/D^{1.56}$ (c) 116.3
(d) 19.71 (e) 6.98 (f) 13.37 (g) 20.95
13 (a) $p = 20.72/D^{0.833}$ (b) $R = 20.72D^{0.167}$ (c) 11.63
(d) 23.26

Exercises 47

1 (a) $C = D^2 + 2D$ (b) $A = D + 2$ (c) 168 (d) 24
(e) 15 (f) 8 (g) 13 (h) 7
3 (a) $C = 3D + 10\frac{9}{5}$ (b) $A = \frac{9}{5} + 100/5D$ (c) 20
(d) 21.8 (e) 23.6 (f) 20.6 (g) 2.6
5 (a) $C = \sqrt{5D^2 + D + 45}$ (b) $A = \sqrt{5D^2 + D + 45}/D$
(c) 6.7082 (d) 23.55844 (e) 223.93 (f) 7.1414
(g) 2.64575 (h) 2.295 (i) 3.21455
7 (a) $C = 2D\sqrt{2D}$ (b) $A = 2\sqrt{2D}$ (c) $16\sqrt{2}$
(d) $640\sqrt{10}$ (e) $2000\sqrt{2}$ (f) $2\sqrt{2}$ (g) $10\sqrt{2}$
9 (a) $C = 24\log D$ (b) $A = (24/D)\log D$ (c) 0
(d) 7.22472 (e) 48 (f) 96 (g) 64.77528 (h) 0.48
(i) 1.34202 (j) 0.0012
11 (a) $A = 10,485/D + 6.75 - 0.0003D$ (b) 13,407 (c) 19,215
(d) 25,296.75 (e) 21,793.9425 (f) 3.153 (g) 3.011
(h) 3.08570

Exercises 48

1 (a) $(\Delta x)^2 + \Delta x(3x + 2) + 3x^2 + 4x$ (b) 96   (c) $89°24'$
3 (a) $2x + 3 + \Delta x$ (b) $-\frac{5}{2}$
5 (a) $3x^2 + 3x\Delta x + (\Delta x)^2$ (b) $-0.6997, -0.16967$
7 (b) $3x^2 + 3x\Delta x + (\Delta x)^2$ (c) $19, 86°59'$ (d) $12.61, 85°28'$
   (e) $12.0601, 85°16'$ (f) $12,00060001, 85°14'$
9 1   3   5
11 1   1   1   1   1

Exercises 49

1 (a) $\frac{3}{4}$ (c) 4   (e) 0   (g) 0.

Exercises 50

1 (a) $6x + 3\Delta x - 5$ (b) $6x - 5$ (c) 25   (d) $87°43'$
3 (a) $3x^2 + 3x\Delta x + (\Delta x)^2$ (b) $3x^2$ (c) 12   (d) $85°14'$
   (e) ± 0.76
5 (a) $6x - 6 + 3x\Delta x$ (b) $6x - 6$ (c) $-6, 99°27'$
   (d) $-36, 91°35'$ (e) $6, 80°33'$ (f) 1.04466   (g) 0.90379
7 (a) $-3x^2 - 3x\Delta x - (\Delta x)^2$ (b) $-3x^2$ (c) $-3, 108°26'$
   (d) $-0.76, 0.76, 0.438976, -0.438976$
9 (a) $\frac{1}{12}, \frac{1}{24}$ (b) $-\frac{1}{12}, \frac{1}{24}$
11 0.57

Exercises 51

1 (a) $C' = 1$ (b) 1   (c) 1   (d) 1
3 (a) $C' = 2D + 2$ (b) 22   (c) 2   (d) 6   (e) 32   (f) 8
5 $C' = 2 + 2D$ (a) 4   (b) 12   (c) 22
7 $C' = 56$ (a) 56   (b) 56
9 (a) $C' = m + 2nD$ (b) $m + 2n$ (c) m (d) $m + 10n$
   (e) $m + 2mn$ (f) $m + 2n^2$
11 $C' = 0.8$ (a) 0.8   (b) 0.8   (c) 0.8   (d) 0.8   (e) 0.8

Exercises 52

1 (a) $10D - 3D^2$ (b) $10 - 6D$ (c) 4   (d) 10   (e) -8
   (f) -10
3 (a) $16D - D^3/2$ (b) $16 - 3D^2/2$ (c) 14.5   (d) -21.5
   (e) 14.25156
5 (a) $p = 12 - 0.1D$ (b) $12D - 0.1D^2$ (c) $12 - 0.2D$
   (d) 1   (e) 4   (f) -2
7 (a) $p = 26.5 - 5D$ (b) $26.5D - 5D^2$ (c) $26.5 - 10D$
   (d) -3.5 (e) -13.5 (f) -8.5 (g) 5.5
9 (a) $kD/b - aD^2/b$ (b) $k/b - 2aD/b$ (c) k/b (d) $k - 2a/b$
   (e) $k - 2a^2/b$ (f) $k(1 - 2a)/b$

Exercises 53

1 (a) $5x^4$ (b) 5

3 $7x^2$

5 (a) $6x^5$ (b) 0   (c) $(-0.69883, 0.11647)$

7 $20x^{19}$

9 (a) $4x^3$ (b) $-32, 91°47'$

Exercises 54

1 (a) $24x^5$ (b) -24 (c) 0

3 (a) $16x^3$ (b) 0   (c) $(-.39685, 0.09922)$

5 $-12x^3$

7 $-30x^5$

9 $-8x; 92°23'$

Exercises 55

1 (a) $4 - 4x$ (b) 4

3 (a) $4x - 15x^2 + 4x^3$ (b) 0   (c) -100

5 (a) $4x^3 - 6x$ (b) $-20; 92°52'$

7 (a) $1,000D - 2D^2 - 3D^3$ (b) $1,000 - 4D - 9D^2$ (c) 987
   (d) -344 (e) 652   (f) 674.04

9 (a) $8D - D^2$ (b) $8 - 2D$ (c) -2 (d) 6   (e) 0
   (f) -5

11 (a) $76D - 73D^2$ (b) $76 - 146D$ (c) 17.60   (d) -4.30
   (e) 22.71   (f) 38.77

13 (a) $15D - 2D^2$ (b) $15 - 4D$ (c) 13   (d) 11   (e) 14.2
   (f) 12   (g) 11.20

Exercises 56

1 $-2 + 10x$

3 (a) $2 + 2x$ (b) 4   (d) -6 (e) -0.81802
   (f) $(-1.8661, 0.85013)$

5 (a) 10   (b) 0   (c) 0   (d) 0   (e) 0   (f) 0

7 (a) 3   (b) 3   (c) 3

9 (a) $6.75 - 0.0006D$ (b) 3.75   (c) 2.55   (d) 2.85

11 (a) $1.052 - 0.004D$ (b) 0.932   (c) 0.452   (d) 0.652
   (e) 0.752

Exercises 57

1 $6x^2 - 20x - 11$

3 $-5 + 6x + 21x^2 - 20x^3 - 20x^4$

5 $7x^6 - 24x^5 - 10x^4 + 72x^3 - 87x^2 + 92x + 30$

7 (a) $-7x^6 + 48x^5 - 85x^4 + 128x^3 - 81x^2 + 70x - 33$
   (b) 40, 88°34'   (c) $-4865, 90°1'$

9 (a) $2D^4 - 10D^3 - 40D^2 + 200D$ (b) $8D^3 - 30D^2 - 80D + 200$
   (c) -78 (d) -94 (e) 98   (f) -62.5

Exercises 58

1 $12x^2 + 12x/(2x + 1)^2$

3 $-4x^2 - 2/(x^3 + 2x)^2$

5 (a) $0.366, -1.366; 1.63394, 3.36605$

(b) $0.69067, -1.69067; 1.01644, 3.12989$

(c) $-1.51447, 0.51447; 2.16985, 1.7607$

7 (a) $10D/1 + 5D$ (b) $10/(1 + 5D)^2$ (c) $^{10}\!\!/\!\!_{36}$ (d) $^{10}\!\!/\!\!_{2601}$

9 (a) $40/(20 - 3D)^2$ (b) $^{40}\!\!/\!\!_{289}$ (c) $^{8}\!\!/\!\!_{5}$

Exercises 59

1 $15(3x - 2)^4$

3 (a) $50D(1 + 5D^2)^4$ (b) $64,800$ (c) $19,448,100$

(d) $671,618,400$

5 $\dfrac{dy}{du} \cdot \dfrac{du}{dx} = \dfrac{dy}{dx} \qquad q \cdot u^{q-1}\dfrac{du}{dx} = px^{p-1}$

$\therefore \dfrac{du}{dx} = \dfrac{px^{p-1}}{qu^{q-1}} = \dfrac{p}{q}\left[\dfrac{x^{p-1}}{(x^{p/q})^{q-1}}\right] = \dfrac{p}{q}\left[\dfrac{x^{p-1}}{x^{p-p/q}}\right]$

$= \dfrac{p}{q}\,(x^{p/q-1}) = nx^{n-1} \text{ where } n = \dfrac{p}{q}$

7 (a) $\dfrac{1}{\sqrt{1 + 2D}}$ (b) $\dfrac{1}{\sqrt{3}}$ (c) $\tfrac{1}{2}$ (d) $\tfrac{1}{3}$

9 (a) $D\sqrt{10 - 2D}$ (b) $\dfrac{10 - 3D}{\sqrt{10 - 2D}}$ (c) $\tfrac{1}{2}$ (b) -3.5

11 (a) $-1/x^2$ (b) $-7/x^8$ (c) $-20/(2x + 1)^2$ (d) $\dfrac{-12}{\sqrt[3]{x^2}}$

13 (a) $\dfrac{12,800}{D^{0.3}}; - \dfrac{-3,840}{D^{1.3}}$ (b) -78.16 (c) -37.76

(d) -27.24 (e) -23.75 (f) -46.14

15 (a) $R = 2,180/D, R' = -2,180/D^2$ (b) -60.56 (c) -200.18

(d) -51.60 (e) -482.77 (f) -196.57

17 (a) $x = g(y) = \sqrt{y} \qquad x^2 = y \qquad \therefore y = x^2 = f(x)$

(b) $2x, \dfrac{1}{2\sqrt{y}}$ (c) $(8)\left(\dfrac{1}{2\sqrt{16}}\right) = 1$ (d) $(6)\left(\dfrac{1}{2\sqrt{9}}\right) = 1$

(e) $(20)\left(\dfrac{1}{2\sqrt{100}}\right) = 1$ (f) $f'(x) \cdot g'(y) = \dfrac{dy}{dx} \cdot \dfrac{dx}{dy} = 1$

19 $\dfrac{dx}{dy} = 2y, \dfrac{dy}{dx} = \dfrac{1}{2y} = \dfrac{1}{2\sqrt{x}} = \dfrac{1}{2}\,x^{-\frac{1}{2}}$

21 $x = y^n, \qquad \dfrac{dx}{dy} = ny^{n-1},$

$\dfrac{dy}{dx} = \dfrac{1}{ny^{n-1}} = \dfrac{1}{n[x^{1/n}]}\,n - 1 = \dfrac{1}{nx^{n-1/n}} = \dfrac{1}{n(\sqrt[n]{x^{n-1}})} = \dfrac{1}{n}\,x^{1/n-1}$

Exercises 60

1 (a) 2.48832   (b) 2.5936

Exercises 61

1 (a) 1   (b) 0   (c) 6   (d) $\frac{1}{3}$ (e) $\frac{5}{4}$ (f) -1
   (g) -6 (h) -2 (i) $-\frac{1}{4}$ (j) $-\frac{3}{2}$ (k) $-\frac{9}{6}$
4 (a) 2   (b) 10   (c) 6   (d) 60   (e) 115   (f) 6.9   (g) 3.5

Exercises 62

1 $10/x$;   10;   2.5
3 $2 + 2 \log_e x$;   2;   4;   6.96982
5 $4(\log_e x)^3/x$;   0; $32/e^2$;   4.71453.
7 (a) $100D/\log_e D$ (b) $100 \log_e D - 100/(\log_e D)^2$ (c) 23.53
   (d) -63.87
9 (a) $5/D$ (b) 5   (c) 1   (d) $5/e^2$
11 (a) $(20 - 3D + 3D \log_e D)/(20 - 3D)^2$ (b) 0.06920
   (c) $20/(20 - 3e)^2$ (d) 1.16567

Exercises 63

1 $-4/1 + 4x$
3 $2x + 3/x^2 + 3x - 7$.
5 $5x^2 - 12x - 5/(5x - 6)^2$
7 $2(1 + x)(1 - 2x)^3/(x^2 - 5)^2 - 6(1 + x)^2(1 - 2x)^2/(x^2 - 5)^2$
   $- 4x(1 + x)^2(1 - 2x)^3/(x^2 - 5)^3$
9 (a) $18/1 + 3D$ (b) 18   (c) 4.5   (d) $18\frac{9}{19}$

Exercises 64

1 $-2e^{-2x}$
3 $-5/4e^{5x}$
5 $5e^x/(2 + 3e^x)^2$
7 $(10^x)(2.30259)$
9 (a) $100D - De^D$ (b) $100 - e^D(D + 1)$ (c) $100 - 2e$
   (d) $100 - 4e^3$
11 (a) $50e^{5D}$ (b) $50e^5$ (c) $50e^{50}$ (d) $50e^{35}$

Exercises 65

1 (a) $2x - 2x^2/1 + 2x - x^2$ (b) 0   (c) ∞ (d) $26\frac{4}{7}$
   (e) $22\frac{2}{9}$
3 (a) 3   (b) 3   (c) 3
5 (a) $5x$ (b) 5   (c) 0   (d) 6   (e) 25   (f) 10
7 $bx/a + bx$
9 $(x/u)(du/dx) = Eu/Ex$

11 $\dfrac{uEu/Ex + vEv/Ex}{u + v}$

13 $(au/au + bv)Eu/Ex + (bv/au + b_v)Ev/Ex$

15 $Eu/Ex - Ev/Ex$

Exercises 66

1 (a) $10 - 3D/-3D$ (b) $-2\frac{1}{3}$ (c) $-\frac{1}{3}$ (d) $-1\frac{2}{9}$
   (e) $-5\frac{2}{3}$

3 $Dp^a = b$ $p = [b/D]^{1/a}$

$ED/Ep = \dfrac{[b/D]^{1/a}}{D} \cdot \dfrac{1/-b^{1/a} \cdot D^{-(a+1/a)}}{a} = -1/D^{a+1/a} \cdot aD^{a+1/a} = -a$

5 $ED/Ep = a/D[1/0] = a/0 = \infty$

7 dp/dD is the slope of the tangent (p, D) and for demand curves which fall from left down to the right this slope is negative

9 $(8 - D)/(-D)$ (a) -7 (b) -0.60 (c) -0.143 (d) -3

11 $(76 - 73D)/(-73D)$ (a) -1.082 (b) -0.388 (c) -1.603
   (d) -1.314 (e) -1.975

13 $-\frac{1}{3}$

15 -0.5

17 $(15 - 2D)/(-2D)$ (a) -6.5 (b) -8.375 (c) -10.538

Exercises 67

1 $ED/Ep = 1,000 - 2D - 3D^2/D(1/-2 - 6D)$
   $R' = (1,000 - 2D - 3D^2)[1 + (-2D - 6D^2)/(1,000 - 2D - 3D^2)]$
   $= 1,000 - 2D - 3D^2 - 2D - 6D^2$
   $= 1,000 - 4D - 9D^2$

3 $ED/Ep = 6/D(2 + 3D)(2 + 3D)^2/-18 = (6/-18D)(2 + 3D)$
   $R' = 6/2 + 3D[1 + (-18D)/6(2 + 3D)]$
   $= 6/2 + 3D[12 + 18D - 18D/6(2 + 3D)]$
   $= 12/(2 + 3D)^2$

5 $ED/Ep = 100 - 3 \log_e D/D[D/-3] = 100 - 3 \log_e D/-3$
   $R' = 100 - 3 \log_e D[1 + (-3/100 - 3 \log_e D)]$
   $= 97 - 3 \log_e D$

7 $R' = p + p/\infty = p + 0$ $\therefore R' = p$

9 $ED/Ep = (76 - 73D)(-73D)$
   $R' = (76 - 73D)[1 - 1/(76 - 73D)/(-73D)]$
   $= 76 - 146D$

11 $ED/Ep = -1\frac{1}{2}$ $R' = -2180D^{-2}$

Exercises 68

1 (a) Increasing   (b) Increasing   (c) Increasing   (d) Increasing

3 Monotonically increasing

5 Increasing for $b > 0$ Decreasing for $b < 0$

7 (a) $R' = 1 - 2D$ Increasing for $D < \frac{1}{2}$ Decreasing for $D > \frac{1}{2}$
(b) $R' = 10 - 6D$ Increasing for $D < 1\frac{2}{3}$
Decreasing for $D > 1\frac{2}{3}$ (c) $R' = 20 - 10D$ Increasing for $D < 2$ Decreasing for $D > 2$ (d) $R' = 100 - 6D^2$ Increasing for $D < 10/\sqrt{6}$ Decreasing for $D > 10/\sqrt{6}$
(e) $R' = 20D - 3D^2$ Increasing for $D < 2\frac{0}{3}$ Decreasing for $D > 2\frac{0}{3}$
9 $R' = 76 - 146D$ Increasing for $D < 0.521$ Decreasing for $D > 0.521$
11 (a) $-0.51e^{-0.11t}/(1 + 0.51e^{-0.11t})^2$
(b) $(0.00012342 - 0.51e^{-0.11t})e^{-0.11t}/(1 + 0.51e^{-0.11t})^3$

⑤ Exercises 69

1 (a) $10, 0, 0$ (b) $5 - 2x + 5x^4, -2 + 20x^3, 60x^2$
(c) $xe^x + e^x, xe^x + 2e^x, xe^x + 3e^x$
(d) $1 - \log_e x/x^2, -3x + 2x \log_e x/x^4, 11 - 6 \log_e x/x^4$
3 (a) $1/x, -1/x^2, 2/x^3, -6/x^4$ (b) $(-1)^{m+1}(m - 1)!x^{-m}$
5 $y^{(s)} = (-1)^s[m + (s - 1)]!/(m - 1)!x^{m+s}$
7 $y^{(n)} = a^n e^{ax}$
9 $y' = 8x^7 - 14x^6 + 3x^2,$ $y'' = 56x^6 - 84x^5 + 6x,$
$y''' = 336x^5 - 420x^4 + 6,$ $y^{iv} = 1{,}680x^4 - 1{,}680x^3,$
$y^v = 6{,}720x^3 - 5{,}040x^2,$ $y^{vi} = 20{,}160x^2 - 10{,}080x,$
$y^{vii} = 40{,}320x - 10{,}080,$ $y^{viii} = 40{,}320$

Exercises 70

1 (a) Concave upward   (b) Concave upward
(c) Concave downward   (d) Concave downward
(e) Since $y'' = 6x$ the curve is concave upward for positive x and concave downward for negative x
3 (a) Concave downward   (b) Concave downward
(c) Concave downward   (d) Concave downward
(e) Concave downward
(f) Since $y'' = -2$ the curve is concave downward for all values of x
5 (a) Concave upward for all values of x
(b) Concave upward for all values of x
(c) Concave downward for all values of x
(d) Concave upward for $x > -2$, concave downward for $x < -2$
7 Concave upward for $x > \frac{2}{3}$, concave downward for $x < \frac{2}{3}$

Exercises 71

1 (a) $50{,}000 - 600D + 3D^2$ (b) $-600 + 6D$
(c) Increasing marginal costs for $D > 100$, decreasing marginal costs for $D < 100$ and constant marginal cost for $D = 100$

3 (a) $40 - 24D + 3D^2$ (b) $-24 + 6D$

   (c) Increasing marginal costs for $D > 4$, decreasing marginal costs for $D < 4$ and constant marginal costs for $D = 4$

5 (a) $1,000 - 48D + 12D^2 + 4D^3$ (b) $-48 + 24D + 12D^2$

   (c) Increasing marginal costs for $D > 1.236068$, decreasing marginal costs for $D < 1.236068$ and constant marginal costs for $D = 1.236068$

7 Constant marginal costs for all values of D

9 Constant marginal costs for all values of D

Exercises 72

1 Critical points: 0.264, -1.264
   Minimum at $x = 0.264$, maximum at $x = -1.264$

3 Critical points, $\frac{2}{3}$, $-\frac{2}{3}$. Maximum at $x = \frac{2}{3}$, minimum at $x = -\frac{2}{3}$

5 Critical points: 0, -1, -3. Minimum at $x = 0$, maximum at $x = -1$, minimum at $x = -3$

7 Critical point $1/e$ a minimum

9 Critical points: 3, -3, 2, -2. A minimum at $x = 3$, a maximum at $x = -3$, a maximum at $x = 2$, a minimum at $x = -2$

Exercises 73

1 (a) $3D$ (b) 3 (c) $10D - 5D^2$ (d) $10 - 10D$
   (e) $7D - 5D^2$ (f) $D = \frac{7}{10}$ (g) $-10 < 0$
   (j) 6.5, 4.55, 2.1, 1.95

3 (a) $D = 1$ (b) $D > -\frac{1}{2}$ (c) 9; 9; 2; 7

5 (a) $D = \frac{1}{2}$ (b) $R'' = -20/e \cdot C'' = 0$ $\therefore R'' < C''$

7 (a) $D = \frac{1}{3}$ (b) $-150 < 0$

9 (a) $2.34D - 1.34D^2$, $1 - 0.83D + 0.85D^2$, $-1 + 3.17D - 2.19D^2$
   (b) $D = 0.724$ (c) $R'' = -2.68$, $C''' = 1.70$ $\therefore R'' < C'''$
   (d) 1.370; 0.992; 0.845; 0.147
   (e) Competitive: $D = 1.043$, $p = 0.942$
      Monopoly: $D = 0.724$, $p = 1.370$

Exercises 74

1 (a) $D = 3$ (b) $C' = 11 = A$

3 (a) $D = 1$ (b) $C' = 9 = A$

5 (a) $D = 0$ (b) $C' = 2 = A$

7 (a) $D = 1/e$ (b) $C' = 1 - 1/e = A$

9 (a) $5 - 3D + 2D^2$ (b) $D = \frac{3}{4}$ (c) $5 - 6D + 6D^2$
   (d) $C' = 3\frac{7}{8} = A$

Exercises 75

1 Concave upward for $x > \frac{1}{6}$, concave downward for $x < \frac{1}{6}$
   (b) Point of inflection at $(\frac{1}{6}, -\frac{1}{54})$ (c) $-\frac{1}{6}$

3 This curve has no inflection point, but a maximum at $x = \frac{3}{2}$, so concave downwards

5 $y' = 4x^3$ $y'' = 12x^2$ Since $y'' = 12x^2$ this is positive for all values of x other than 0 and the concavity of the curve does not change so there is no inflection point
   (b) $y' = 5x^4$ $y'' = 20x^3$ $y = x^5$ then has an inflection point at $x = 0$ since the concavity changes at that point

7 $50D - 8D^2 + D^3$ (a) $D = 2\frac{2}{3}$
   (b) $C' = 50 - 16D + 3D^2$ $C'' = -16 + 6D = 0$ $\therefore D = 2\frac{2}{3}$
   $C''' = 6$, so a minimum at $D = 2\frac{2}{3}$, which is the inflection point on C

9 $C = f(D)$ $C' = f'(D)$ $C'' = f''(D) = 0$ is the inflection point on C, but at the same time gives critical points on C', in our case minima

Exercises 76

1 (a) 0   (b) 6   (c) $\frac{3}{2}$ (d) 3
3 (a) -6 (b) 11   (c) -3 (d) $-6a + 1$
5 (a) 1   (b) 0   (c) $-a$
7 (a) 0   (b) 11   (c) $3a^2 + 4a$
9 (a) -1 (b) -31 (c) $-a^2$

Exercises 77

1 (a) $2x + y^2 - 2, 2xy + 5$ (b) 4, 9
3 (a) $2 + 3y - z, 3x, -x$ (b) $7, 0, 0 - xye^{-x}$
5 (a) $1 + \log_e xy, x/y$ (b) 1, 1
7 (a) $-4.0848p^{-1.040}\pi^{0.939}Q^{-1.023} - 184.704Q^{-0.023}\pi^{0.939}p^{-2.040}$,
   $166.7664Q^{-0.023}p^{-1.040}\pi^{-0.061}$ (b) $43.334; 0.95836; 0.94215$
9 (a) $54.0144Q^{-0.928}p^{-0.513}\pi^{0.513}, -384.8526Q^{0.072}p^{-1.513}\pi^{0.513}$,
   $384.8526Q^{0.072}p^{-0.513}\pi^{-0.487}$ (b) $0.78226; 0.23696; 4.4518$

Exercises 78

1 (a) $10 - 2a + b; a$ (b) 12; 2
3 (a) $100 - 2a - 5b + 3c; 200 - 4b - 5a - c; 50 - 6c + 3a - b$
   (b) 103; 182; 21
5 (a) $0.64L^{-0.36}C^{0.36}; 0.36L^{0.64}C^{-0.64}$ (b) $0.57239; 0.43905$
7 (a) $0.58L^{0.43}C^{-0.42}; 0.43L^{-0.57}C^{0.58}$ (b) $0.55079; 0.45938$
9 (a) $31.056; 12.755; 4.4366; 12.571; 24.401$
11 (a) $2.13a^{1.13}b^{0.34}, 0.34a^{2.13}b^{-0.66}$ (b) $4.9107; 0.66628$

Exercises 79

1 (a) $\dfrac{-1.9p_A}{63.3 - 1.9p_A + 0.2p_B + 0.5p_C}, \dfrac{0.2p_B}{63.3 - 1.9p_A + 0.2p_B + 0.5p_C},$
   $\dfrac{0.5p_C}{63.3 - 1.9p_A + 0.2p_B + 0.5p_C}$ (b) $-0.28571; 0.02406; 0.05263$

3 (a) $\dfrac{0.1p_A}{10.3 + 0.1p_A + 0.1p_B - 0.3p_C}$, $\dfrac{0.1p_B}{10.3 + 0.1p_A + 0.1p_B - 0.3p_C}$,

$\dfrac{-0.3p_C}{10.3 + 0.1p_A + 0.1p_B - 0.3p_C}$ (b) $0.094; 0.118; -0.424$

5 (a) $\dfrac{-0.02p_A}{49.07 - 0.02p_A - 0.36p_B - 0.03p_C + 0.03p_D}$

$\dfrac{-0.36p_B}{49.07 - 0.02p_A - 0.36p_B - 0.03p_C + 0.03p_D}$

$\dfrac{-0.03p_C}{49.07 - 0.02p_A - 0.36p_B - 0.03p_C + 0.03p_D}$

$\dfrac{0.03p_D}{49.07 - 0.02p_A - 0.36p_B - 0.03p_C + 0.03p_D}$

  (b) $-0.0004; -0.0149; -0.0019; 0.0006$

7 (a) $\dfrac{0.1p_B}{24.2 + 0.1p_B - 0.6p_C - 0.3p_D}$, $\dfrac{-0.6p_C}{24.2 + 0.1p_B - 0.6p_C - 0.3p_D}$,

$\dfrac{-0.3p_D}{24.2 + 0.1p_B - 0.6p_C - 0.3p_D}$ (b) $0.004; -0.026; -0.013$

9 $0.538; -0.717; 0.717$

11 $0.317; -0.38; 0.327$

13 (a) $\dfrac{11.2K}{11.2K - 8.6P - 379}$ (b) $\dfrac{-8.6p}{11.2K - 8.6P - 379}$

  (c) $1.46214; -0.50522$

17 (a) $-1.32; 0.4$

19 $0.097P/Q; \quad -0.236Y/Q$

21 (a) $-2.27, 1.31$ (b) $0.324, -0.512$

23 (a) -2.75 (b) -0.005787

Exercises 80

1 (a) $\dfrac{-184}{69}$ (b) -1 (c) -1 (d) -0.62350

3 (a) $-\tfrac{3}{2}$ (b) $D^2 = p^{-3}, 2D\dfrac{\partial D}{\partial p} = -3p^{-4}$,

$\dfrac{ED}{Ep} = \dfrac{-3p}{2D} \cdot \dfrac{p}{D} = \dfrac{-3p^{-3}}{2p^{-3}} = \dfrac{-3}{2}$

5 (a) $-x/z; -y/z$ (b) $-x/z; -y/z$

7 (a) $-\tfrac{3}{2}; -\tfrac{1}{2}$ (b) $-\tfrac{3}{2}; -\tfrac{1}{2}$

9 $-1; -1$

11 $\dfrac{dp}{da} = f_D\dfrac{dD}{da} + f_a, \quad \dfrac{dp}{da} = g_D\dfrac{dD}{da}.$ Solving for $\dfrac{dD}{da}$;

$\dfrac{dD}{da} = \dfrac{f_a}{f_D - g_D}$ which is $< 0.$ $\dfrac{dp}{da} = g_D\dfrac{dD}{da}$ which is < 0

13 $1/1 - b$

Exercises 81

1 $k = 3$

3 $k = 1$

5 (a) $D_A = \dfrac{50(tp_B)}{(tp_A)} = t^0 \dfrac{50p_B}{p_A}$, $k = 0$. Similarly for D_B

   (d) The demand for A and B is unchanged if all prices change by the same percent   (e) 30; 166⅔.

7 Homogeneous of degree 1

9 Homogeneous of degree 0

11 yes, 1.03

13 (a) 1.053   (b) 0.015; 0.250; 0.350; 0.408; 0.030

Exercises 82

1 (a) Homogeneous of degree 4   (b) $x(8x^3) - y(16y^3) = 4u$.

3 (a) Homogeneous of degree 2   (b) $x(2x) + y(2y) = 2u$.

5 Yes, $L[(1.01)(0.75)L^{-0.25}C^{0.25}] + C[(1.01)(0.25)L^{0.75}C^{-0.75}]$
   $= 1.01L^{0.75}C^{0.25}(0.75 + 0.25) = 1.01L^{0.75}C^{0.25}$ $2x$

7 No, $L[0.43L^{-0.57}C^{0.58}] + C[0.58L^{0.43}C^{-0.42}]$
   $= L^{0.43}C^{0.58}(0.43 + 0.58) = 1.01L^{0.43}C^{0.58}$

9 Not linear homogeneous. $a[(100)(0.28)a^{-0.72}b^{0.23}c^{0.04}d^{0.17}f^{0.18}] +$
   $b[(100)(0.23)a^{0.28}b^{-0.77}c^{0.04}d^{0.17}f^{0.18}] +$
   $c[(100)(0.04)a^{0.28}b^{0.23}c^{-0.96}d^{0.17}f^{0.18}] +$
   $d[(100)(0.17)a^{0.28}b^{0.23}c^{0.04}d^{-0.83}f^{0.18}] +$
   $f[(100)(0.18)a^{0.28}b^{0.23}c^{0.04}d^{0.17}f^{-0.82}]$
   $= x[0.28 + 0.23 + 0.04 + 0.17 + 0.18] = 0.90x$

11 No

Exercises 83

1 $12x^2$; $-30xy$; $-15y^2 + 6$

3 0; $-x/y^2$; $1/y$

5 $6x, 0, -2, -1, 4, 0$

7 (a) $0; \dfrac{2x}{y^3}; \dfrac{-1}{y^2}$ (b) $0; \dfrac{-1}{54}; \dfrac{-1}{36}$

9 (a) $6x, 0, 0, 12u^2z, -z, -y, 0, -x, 0, 4u^3$
   (b) $6, 0, 0, 0, 0, 1, 0, -1, 0, 32$

Exercises 84

1 Minimum at $(-1, -\frac{1}{2}, -1\frac{1}{4})$

3 Minimum at $(6, 13\frac{1}{2}) \cdot -218.25$

5 The determinant is <0 so neither a maximum nor minimum

7 Determinant $= 0$ so neither a maximum nor a minimum

9 (a) $a < 0, c < 0, b^2 < ac$ (b) $a > 0, c > 0, b^2 < ac$ (c) $b^2 > ac$

11 Minimum at $(0, 0, 0, 0, 0)$.

Exercises 85

1 (a) $D_A = 3$; $D_B = 1$ and $-8 < 0$; $-10 < 0$ (b) 19, 20, 24, 53
3 (a) $D_A = 2$, $D_B = 3$; $-2 < 0$ and $-6 < 0$ (b) 7, 20, 37, 37
5 (a) $D_A = \frac{5}{6}$, $D_B = 1\frac{4}{6}$, $D_C = 3\frac{6}{7}$ (b) $7\frac{1}{2}$, 11, 33, 40.9095, 112.4214
7 (a) $D_A = 9.80517$, $D_B = 6.69637$, $D_C = 1.4098$, $D_D = 4.10416$
   (b) 121.94830; 56.51815; 51.5412; 21.79168; 345.72347; 1390.5661

9 (a) $D_A = \dfrac{a(2d + 2n) - cq}{(2d + 2n)(2b + 2m) - q^2}$, $D_B = \dfrac{c(2b + 2m) - aq}{(2d + 2n)(2b + 2m) - q^2}$,
   $b > -m$, $d > -n$
   (b) $p_A = \dfrac{2a(d + n)(b + 2m) - aq^2 + bcq}{4(d + n)(b + m) - q^2}$,
   $p_B = \dfrac{2c(b + m)(d + 2n) - cq^2 + adq}{4(d + n)(b + m) - q^2}$

Exercises 86

1 $(2\frac{1}{2}, \frac{5}{6})$, $25\frac{5}{12}$
3 $(16\frac{2}{3}, 8\frac{1}{3}, 8\frac{1}{3}) \cdot 833\frac{1}{3}$
5 $\left(\dfrac{-5\sqrt{5}}{3}, \dfrac{-2\sqrt{5}}{3}\right) \cdot 9\sqrt{5}$
7 $\left(\frac{5}{3}, \dfrac{-10}{9}, \dfrac{10}{3}\right) \cdot \dfrac{-500}{81}$
9 $x = \dfrac{-k(2mc - bn)}{2(bmn - m^2c - an^2)}$, $y = \dfrac{-k(2an - bm)}{a(bmn - m^2c - an^2)}$,
   $\dfrac{k^2(b^2 - 4ac)}{4(bmn - m^2c - an^2)}$
11 $f_x - \lambda g_x = 0$, $f_y - \lambda g_y = 0$, $\therefore \dfrac{f_x}{g_x} = \lambda = \dfrac{f_y}{g_y}$ $\therefore \dfrac{f_x}{f_y} = \dfrac{g_x}{g_y}$,
   $\dfrac{f_x}{f_y} = \dfrac{g_x}{g_y}$ By implicit differentiation: $0 = f_x + f_y \dfrac{dy}{dx}$
   $\therefore \dfrac{dy}{dx} = \dfrac{-f_x}{f_y}$,   Similarly $\dfrac{dy}{dx} = \dfrac{-g_x}{g_y}$ from $g(x,y) = 0$.

Exercises 87

1 5; $2\frac{1}{2}$
3 $x = 1152.155$, $y = 1225.307$
5 4; $1\frac{1}{2}$
7 (a) 5; $\dfrac{5}{q}$ (b) -1 (c) -1
9 (a) $\dfrac{J}{2}, \dfrac{J}{4}$ (b) 1; 1   (c) 1, 1
11 $\dfrac{y}{1} = \dfrac{x}{2}$,   But $x = 5$, $y = 2\frac{1}{2}$ $\therefore \frac{5}{2} = \frac{5}{2}$

13 $\dfrac{\partial V}{\partial x} = \dfrac{2U\partial U}{\partial x} = 2Uy + \lambda = 0, \qquad \dfrac{\partial V}{\partial y} = \dfrac{2U\partial U}{\partial y} = 2Ux + 2\lambda = 0$

Eliminating λ and using the restriction gives the same result as in problem 1. $\quad \dfrac{\partial W}{\partial x} = \dfrac{5U^4\partial U}{\partial x} = 5U^4y + \lambda = 0,$

$\dfrac{\partial W}{\partial y} = \dfrac{5U^4\partial U}{\partial y} = 5U^4x + 2\lambda = 0, \qquad$ which gives the same result

$\dfrac{\partial z}{\partial x} = \dfrac{1}{U}\dfrac{\partial U}{\partial x} = \dfrac{1}{U}y + \lambda = 0, \qquad \dfrac{\partial z}{\partial y} = \dfrac{1}{U}\dfrac{\partial U}{\partial y} = \dfrac{1}{U}x + 2\lambda$ which gives the same result

15 $U(x,y) + \lambda[xp_x + yp_y - I], \dfrac{\partial U}{\partial x} + \lambda p_x = 0, \dfrac{\partial U}{\partial y} + \lambda p_y = 0$

$\therefore \dfrac{(\partial U)/(\partial x)}{p_x} = \dfrac{-\lambda}{1} = \dfrac{(\partial U)/(\partial y)}{p_y} \qquad \therefore -\lambda$ is the marginal utility of money

Exercises 88

1 $1, \frac{1}{4}, 3\frac{1}{2}, 4$

3 $3, \frac{3}{2}, 11, 90$

5 $-2a^{-3} < 0, -2b^{-3} < 0, 4a^{-3}b^{-3} > 0, -\frac{5}{2} - \frac{5}{2},$

$\dfrac{-3a^{-\frac{5}{2}}}{4} < 0, \dfrac{-3b^{-\frac{5}{2}}}{4} < 0, (\frac{9}{16})ab > 0, -6a^{-4} < 0,$

$-6b^{-4} < 0, 4a^{-3}b^{-3} > 0, -2a^{-3} < 0, -2b^{-3} < 0, 4a^{-3}b^{-3} > 0$

7 $\pi = xp_x - ap_a - bp_b + \lambda g(x,a,b) \qquad \pi_a = -p_a + \lambda g_a = 0$
$\pi_b = -p_b + \lambda g_b = 0 \qquad \pi_x = p_x + \lambda g_x = 0$
$\therefore \dfrac{g_a}{p_a} = \dfrac{g_b}{p_b} = \dfrac{-g_x}{p_x} = \dfrac{1}{\lambda}$

9 (a) $a = \frac{1}{2}, b = \sqrt[3]{\frac{1}{4}}, -2a^{-3} < 0, -6b^{-4} < 0, 12a^{-3}b^{-4} > 0$
(b) $\frac{1}{2}, \sqrt[3]{\frac{1}{4}}, 15.48, 42.20$

11 (a) $\log_e x = \log_e a + b \log_e L + c \log_e K; (\partial x/\partial L)/x = b/L;$
$\partial x/\partial L = bx/L; \partial x/\partial K = cx/K; \partial^2x/\partial L^2 = b(b-1)x/L^2;$
$\partial^2x/\partial K^2 = c(c-1)x/K^2; \partial^2x/\partial L\partial K = bcx/LK;$
$\partial P/\partial L = p_x(\partial x/\partial L) - p_L = p_x(bx/L) - p_L = 0;$
$\partial P/\partial K = p_x(\partial x/\partial K) - p_K = p_x(cx/K) - p_K = 0;$
(b) $\partial^2P/\partial L^2 = p_x(\partial^2x/\partial L^2) = p_x[b(b-1)]x/L^2 < 0;$
$\partial^2x/\partial L^2 = p_xc(c-1)x/K^2 < 0; (\partial^2x/\partial L^2)(\partial^2x/\partial K^2) -$
$(\partial^2x/\partial L\partial K)^2 = p_x[b(b-1)]x/L^2c(c-1)x/K^2 - (bcx/LK)^2 > 0$

13 (a) $0.63x/L = p_L/p_x; 0.30x/K = p_K/p_x$
(b) $0 \le 0.63 \le 1; 0 \le 0.30 \le 1 \qquad 0.63 + 0.30 < 1$

Exercises 89

1 $x - x^2 + x^4/4 + c$

3 $10 \ln x + e^x + c$

5 $17x^{\frac{2}{3}}(\frac{3}{2}) + c$

7 $\frac{3}{2}e^{2x} + \frac{5}{6}x^{\frac{9}{5}} + c$

Exercises 90

1 (a) $150\frac{2}{3} + D + 50D^2 - \dfrac{5D^3}{3}$ (b) $\dfrac{150\frac{2}{3}}{D} + 1 + 50D - \dfrac{5D^2}{3}$

3 (a) $2D + 5e^D + 95$ (b) $2 + \dfrac{5e^D}{D} + \dfrac{95}{D}$

  (c) $5e^{60} + 215;\ 2 + 5e^{60};\ \dfrac{43 + e^{60}}{12}$

5 (a) $20\frac{2}{3}D^{3/2} - 1780$ (b) $\dfrac{200}{3}D^{1/2} - \dfrac{1780}{D}$

  (c) $2486\frac{2}{3};\ 25;\ 1555\frac{5}{12}$

7 (a) $200\sqrt{D} - 700$ (b) $\dfrac{\sqrt{200}}{D} - \dfrac{700}{D}$ (c) $1300;\ 10;\ 13$

9 $6.75D - 0.0003D^2 - 10{,}485,\ 6.75 - 0.0003D - \dfrac{10{,}485}{D}$

11 $1.052D - 0.002D^2 + 16.8,\ 1.052 - 0.002D + \dfrac{16.8}{D}$

Exercises 91

3 8
5 (a) $41\frac{1}{3}$ (c) 3   (e) -4
9 $a + b/2$ The area under the curve from $x = 0$ to $x = 1$

Exercises 92

1 (a) $20\frac{1}{4}$ (b) $12\frac{1}{4}$ (c) $6\frac{1}{4}$ (d) 75
3 (a) 567   (b) 531.40271   (c) 576.02495
5 (a) 469.71661   (b) 4661   (c) 453.1821
7 (a) 0.351   (b) 0.729   (c) 2.043
9 (a) 1.92667   (b) 0.80667   (c) 1.30667   (d) 1.79307
  (e) 3.52667   (f) 2.82907
11 (a) 1.210   (b) 1.204   (c) 1.178   (d) 1.229   (e) 1.242
13 (a) $P = 0.415,\ Q = 0.081$ (b) 0.052726

Exercises 93

1 (a) $(x^2/2) + 1$ (b) e^{2x} (c) $(x^2 + 1)^{1/2}$ (d) No such function

3 (a) $y = e^2\,\dfrac{(e^{-3x+1} - e^{1+x})}{-e^4 + 1}$ (b) $y = xe^{4x-4}$ (c) $y = xe^{1-x}$

Exercises 94

1 $x = e^{(x-1)/2} + e^{(1-x)/2}$
3 $p = M + N_1 e^{(d/g)t} + N_2 e^{-(d/g)t}$;

  $M = \dfrac{bd(B + Da) - (1 - Db) \cdot (c + ad + bcd)}{2bd^2(1 - Db)}$;

  N_1 and N_2 are determined by initial conditions

Exercises 95

1   Sample space $\{K, i, n, d\}$
2   (a) $_{52}C_5$ (b) $_4C_2 \cdot {}_4C_2 \cdot {}_{44}C_1$ (c) $_4C_4 \cdot {}_{48}C_1$
3   (a) $\{(h, h, h)\ (h, h, t),\ (h, t, h),\ (t, h, h),\ (t, t, h),\ (t, h, t),\ (h, t, t),\ (t, t, t)\}$
    (b) $\{(h, h, h),\ (h, h, t),\ (h, t, h),\ (t, h, h)\}$
    (c) $\{(h, h, t),\ (h, t, h),\ (t, h, h)\}$
    (d) $\{(h, h, h),\ (h, h, t),\ (h, t, h),\ (h, t, t)\}$
    (e) $\{(h, h, h),\ (h, t, h)\}$
5   (a) $\frac{1}{6}$ (b) $\frac{1}{6}$ (c) $\frac{1}{6}$ (d) $\frac{1}{6}$ (e) 0   (f) 0   (g) 0
    (h) 0   (i) $\frac{1}{3}$ (j) $\frac{1}{3}$ (k) No
7   (a) $\frac{1}{3}$ (b) $\frac{1}{3}$ (c) $\frac{1}{3}$ (d) 0   (e) 1   (f) 0
9   (a) $\frac{23}{60}$ (b) $\frac{1}{4}$ (c) $\frac{1}{2}$ (d) Probability with a true die $= \frac{1}{2}$
11 (a) 0.51333   (b) 0.51334   (c) 0.51332

Exercises 96

1   (a) $\frac{1}{3}$ (b) $\frac{1}{2}$ (c) $\frac{1}{2}$ (d) $\frac{1}{2}$ (e) $\frac{5}{6}$ (f) 1
3   $p + q = 1$
5   (a) $\frac{5}{36}$
7   (a) $\frac{1}{8}$ (b) $\frac{1}{8}$ (c) $\frac{1}{8}$ (d) $\frac{27}{512}$
9   (a) $\frac{1}{32}$ (b) $\frac{1}{32}$ (c) $\frac{1}{32}$ (d) $\frac{1}{32}$
11 (a) $\dfrac{1}{6^n}$ (b) $\dfrac{1}{6^n}$
13 $\frac{1}{4}$

Exercises 97

1   0.3
3   0.25

Cumulative Distribution

x	p
1	0.25
2	0.75
3	1.00

5   (a) $\frac{1}{2} + \frac{1}{2} \cdot \frac{1}{2} + \frac{1}{2} \cdot \frac{1}{2} \cdot \frac{1}{2} - - = \dfrac{\frac{1}{2}}{1 - \frac{1}{2}} = 1$ (b) $\frac{1}{16}$
    (c) $\frac{1}{128}$ (d) $\frac{1}{4}$
7   (a) $p(1) = 0.4;\ p(2) = 0.3;\ p(3) = 0.2;\ p(4) = 0.1$
    (b) $0.4 + 0.3 + 0.2 + 0.1 = 1$

9

x	p
0	$\frac{1}{8}$
1	$\frac{3}{8}$
2	$\frac{3}{8}$
3	$\frac{1}{8}$

Cumulative Distribution

x	p
0	$\frac{1}{8}$
1	$\frac{1}{2}$
2	$\frac{7}{8}$
3	1.0

11

x	p		Cumulative	
			x	p
2	$\frac{1}{36}$		2	$\frac{1}{36}$
3	$\frac{2}{36}$		3	$\frac{3}{36}$
4	$\frac{3}{36}$		4	$\frac{6}{36}$
5	$\frac{4}{36}$		5	$\frac{10}{36}$
6	$\frac{5}{36}$		6	$\frac{15}{36}$
7	$\frac{6}{36}$		7	$\frac{21}{36}$
8	$\frac{5}{36}$		8	$\frac{26}{36}$
9	$\frac{4}{36}$		9	$\frac{30}{36}$
10	$\frac{3}{36}$		10	$\frac{33}{36}$
11	$\frac{2}{36}$		11	$\frac{35}{36}$
12	$\frac{1}{36}$		12	1.00

Exercises 98

1 1.8
3 2.0
5 1.0
7 $1\frac{1}{2}$
9 2.0

Exercises 99

1 (a) 12   (b) 24   (c) 9   (d) 18   (e) 14   (f) 2   (g) -20
(h) 49   (i) 48   (j) 240   (k) 58   (l) -16
3 (a) 3   (b) $4\frac{1}{2}$ (c) $7\frac{1}{2}$ (d) $-1\frac{1}{2}$ (e) $-16\frac{1}{2}$ (f) 12.5
(g) $13\frac{1}{2}$
5 (a) 1   (b) 8.5   (c) -5.5
7 (a) 1.8   (b) 0   (c) 15.4   (d) 100

Exercises 100

1 (a) 31.62; 0.63; 632.46   (b) 14.14; 0.45; 400
(c) 2.24; 0.045; 894.43
3 (a) $\frac{2}{3}$ (b) $\frac{8}{3}$ (c) $\frac{7}{3}$ (d) $2a/3$ (e) $(a + 2b)/3$
(f) $1 - 1/\sqrt{3}$ (g) $ab - (a/\sqrt{3b})$

Exercises 101

1 73.8; 9.0
3 6.0; 70.8
5 1.5; 8.5
7 3.0; 6.75
9 0.1; 0.4; 0.4; 0.1
11 $\dfrac{b^{k+1} - a^{k+1}}{(k + 1)(b - a)}$

Exercises 102

1 0.56; 0.5536; 0.57920
3 2.0; 0; 6.8

5 $\frac{1}{2}$; 0

7 0.56; 0.748

9 $E(x - \mu)^3 = Ex^3 - 3\mu Ex^2 + 3(\mu)^2 Ex - \mu^3 = \mu_3' - 3\mu_1'\mu_2' + 2(\mu_1')^3$
$= Ex^3 - 3Ex \cdot Ex^2 + 2(Ex)^3 = Ex^3 - 3\mu Ex^2 + 2(\mu)^3$

11 2.0; 0; 6.8

Exercises 103

1 (a) $\frac{4}{9}$ (b) $^{80}\!\!/_{243}$ (c) $\frac{1}{243}$ (d) $\frac{8}{27}$ (e) $^{1611}\!\!/_{2187}$
   (f) $^{1808}\!\!/_{2187}$

3 (a) $\frac{1}{2}$ (b) $^{15}\!\!/_{64}$ (c) $\frac{1}{16}$ (d) $1 - (25)10^{-19}$ (e) 0.00369

5 (a) 0.08192   (b) 0.06606   (c) 0.8192   (d) 0.32212

7 (a) 0.000003960   (b) 0.000000002058   (c) 0.99860
   (d) 0.02967

9 (a) 0.45941/10   (b) 0.17097   (c) 0.72531   (d) 0.000001217

11 $p_0 = 0.0466$ $p_1 = 0.1866$ $p_2 = 0.3110$ $p_3 = 0.2765$
   $p_4 = 0.1382$ $p_5 = 0.0369$ $p_6 = 0.0041$

13 (a) $e^{-L}(1 + L/1! + L^2/2! + \cdots) = e^{-L} \cdot e^L = 1$
   (b) $e^{-L}(L + L^2/1! + L^3 2! + \cdots)$
   $= e^{-L}L(1 + L/1! + L^2/2! + \cdots) = e^{-L}Le^L = L$

Exercises 104

1 0.8450

3 0.1615

5 (a) 0.8950   (b) 0.3272   (c) 0.2082   (d) 0.0569   (e) 0.9525
   (f) 0.0764   (g) 0.2420   (h) 0.8023

7 (a) 0.1859   (b) 0.3219   (c) 0.0227   (d) 0.1587   (e) 0.2119
   (f) 0.9192   (g) 0.9192   (h) 0.0139

9 $p_0 = 0.0492$ $p_1 = 0.1696$ $p_2 = 0.3053$ $p_3 = 0.2893$
   $p_4 = 0.1361$ $p_5 = 0.0352$ $p_6 = 0.0046$

11 $P = \left(\dfrac{1}{\sigma\sqrt{2\pi}}\right) e^{-(x-\mu)^2/2\sigma^2}$

$\dfrac{dP}{dx} = \left(\dfrac{1}{\sigma\sqrt{2\pi}}\right) (e^{-(x-\mu)^2/2\sigma^2}) \cdot \left[\dfrac{-2(x-\mu)}{2\sigma^2}\right] = 0 \qquad -x + \mu = 0,$

$x = \mu \qquad \dfrac{d^2P}{dx^2} = -1/\sigma^3\sqrt{2\pi} < 0,$ so P is a maximum

13 0.3977

Exercises 105

1 $\log_e P_x(t) = -Lt + x(\log_e L + \log_e t)$;
   $dP_x(t)/P_x(t) = -Ldt + xdt/t$;
   $P_{x-1}(t) = e^{-L}(Lt)^{x-1}/(x - 1)! = P_x(t)x/t$

3 11.2;   225.6

Exercises 106

1 (a) $(\frac{2}{3})(\frac{1}{3})^n$ (b) 1

Exercises 107

1 $Ez = E\left[\sum_{i=1}^{n} x_i\right] = \sum_{i=1}^{n} E(x_i) = n\mu$

3 $\dfrac{\sum_{i=1}^{n}(x_i - \bar{x})^2}{n-1} = \dfrac{1}{n-1}\left[\sum_{i=1}^{n}\left(x_i - \dfrac{\sum_{i}^{n} x_i}{n}\right)^2\right]$

$= \dfrac{1}{n-1}\left[\sum_{i=1}^{n}\left\{x_i^2 + \left(\dfrac{\sum x_i}{n}\right)^2 - 2x_i\dfrac{\sum_{i=1}^{n} x_i}{n}\right\}\right]$

$= \dfrac{1}{n-1}\left[\sum_{i=1}^{n} x_i^2 + n\left(\dfrac{\sum x_i}{n}\right)^2 - 2n\left\{\dfrac{\sum_{i=1}^{n} x_i}{n}\right\}^2\right]$

$= \dfrac{1}{n-1}\left[\sum_{i=1}^{n} x_i^2 - n\bar{x}^2\right]$

5 (a) $L = \dfrac{1}{(2\pi)^{n/2}} exp.\left\{-\tfrac{1}{2}\sum_{i=1}^{n}(x_i - a)^2\right\}$

(b) $\dfrac{dL}{da} = \left[\dfrac{1}{(2\pi)^{n/2}} exp.\left\{-\tfrac{1}{2}\sum_{i=1}^{n}(x_i - a)^2\right\}\right]\sum_{i=1}^{n}(x_i - a) = 0$

$\therefore \sum_{i=1}^{n} x_i = na \quad a = \sum_{i=1}^{n} x_i/n = \bar{x}$

7 $E(Z) = 1/n\left[\sum_{i=1}^{n} E(x_i - \mu)^2\right] = \dfrac{n\sigma^2}{n} = \sigma^2$

W is the estimated variance, Z is the actual variance, and from 6 W is a biased estimate of σ^2.

Exercises 108

1

	Class Limits	Frequency		Class Limits	Frequency
(a)	0–4	1.0	(b)	0–5	2.5
	4–8	3.5		5–10	3.0
	8–12	1.5		10–15	0.5
	12–16	0.0		15–20	2.5
	16–20	2.5		20–25	2.0
	20–24	1.5		25–30	0.5
	24–28	1.0		30–35	0.0
	28–32	0.0		35–40	1.0
	32–36	1.0			

	Class Limits	Frequency
(c)	0–10	5.5
	10–20	3.0
	20–30	2.5
	30–40	1.0

3

Class Limits	Frequency
0–10	4.5
10–20	4.5
20–30	3.0
30–40	2.0
40–50	3.0

5 (a) 32 (b)

Class Limits	Frequency
4–14.67	6.0
14.67–25.34	5.0
25.34–36.01	1.0

(c)

Class Limits	Frequency
4–12	6.0
12–20	2.5
20–28	2.5
28–36	1.0

7 (a) 45 (b)

Class Limits	Frequency
0– 7.5	2.0
7.5–15	3.0
15–22.5	4.0
22.5–30	3.0
30–37.5	1.0
37.5–45	4

Exercises 109

1 27; 173.3; 13.16
3 11.0; 28.8; 5.37
5 11.5; 32.2; 5.67
7 2,146.5; 2,902,857; 1704
9 (b) 31.72; 416.63; 20.41
11 (a) 5 (b) 13.5

Exercises 110

1 165, 12.85
3 27.47, 5.24
5 30.1, 5.49
7 414.55, 20.36

Exercises 111

1 8.97; 20.53
3 15.90; 29.38

5 18.85; 35.15
7 9.24; 13.36
9 485,988; 495,972

Exercises 112

1 Rejected
3 Rejected
5 (a) Accepted   (b) Accepted   (c) Accepted   (d) Accepted
7 Rejected
9 4.27; 4.93

Exercises 113

1 Accepted
3 Accepted
5 Accepted
7 Rejected
9 $\dfrac{\bar{x} - \mu}{s_{\bar{x}}}$ is distributed as t with $(n - 1)$ degrees of freedom

The values of t being from the t tables with $(n - 1)$ degrees of freedom
The confidence limits are: $\bar{x} - s_{\bar{x}}t_{(n-1)(0.05)}$ $\bar{x} + s_{\bar{x}}t_{(n-1)(0.05)}$
11 8.14, 13.86; 7.05, 14.95

Exercises 114

1 Nonsignificant
3 Nonsignificant
5 (a) Nonsignificant   (b) Nonsignificant   (c) Nonsignificant
7 (a) Nonsignificant   (b) Significant   (c) Significant
9 $\dfrac{d - \mu_d}{\sigma_d}$ is normal with mean 0 and variance 1, where $\mu_d = (\mu_1 - \mu_2)$

(a) $d - 1.96\sigma_d$, $d + 1.96\sigma_d$ (b) $d - 2.57\sigma_d$, $d + 2.57\sigma_d$
(c) $-\infty$, $+\infty$ (d) $d - 1.65\sigma_d$, $d + 1.65\sigma_d$
11 (a) Nonsignificant   (b) Nonsignificant

Exercises 115

1 (a) $\bar{x} = 27$, $s = 13.16$

Upper Limits (Standardized)	Cumulative Probability	p	Np
-1.24	0.1075	0.1075	10.75
0.31	0.6217	0.5142	51.42
1.86	0.9686	0.3469	34.69

3 (a) 11.3; 4.71

Upper Limits (Standardized)	Cumulative Probability	p	Np
-1.34	0.0901	0.0901	1.80
-0.70	0.2420	0.1519	3.04
-0.06	0.4761	0.2341	4.68
0.57	0.7157	0.2396	4.79
1.21	0.8869	0.1712	3.42
1.85	0.9678	0.0809	1.62

5 (a) 45.7; 17.34

Upper Limits (Standardized)	Cumulative Probability	p	Np
−1.48	0.0694	0.0694	4.86
−0.33	0.3707	0.3013	21.09
0.82	0.7939	0.4232	29.62
1.98	0.9762	0.1823	12.76

7 (a) 31.72; 20.41

Upper Limits (Standardized)	Cumulative Probability	p	Np
−1.31	0.0951	0.0951	12.74
−1.06	0.1446	0.0495	6.63
−0.82	0.2061	0.0615	8.24
−0.57	0.2843	0.0782	10.48
−0.33	0.3707	0.0864	11.58
−0.08	0.4681	0.0974	13.05
0.16	0.5636	0.0955	12.80
0.41	0.6591	0.0955	12.80
0.65	0.7422	0.0831	11.14
0.90	0.8159	0.0737	9.88
1.14	0.8729	0.0570	7.64
1.39	0.9177	0.0448	6.00
1.63	0.9485	0.0308	4.13
1.88	0.9700	0.0215	2.88
2.12	0.9830	0.0130	1.74
2.52	0.9941	0.0111	1.49

9 (a) 1837; 641.3

Upper Limits (Standardized)	Cumulative Probability	p	Np
−1.31	0.0951	0.0951	1,962,198
−0.53	0.2981	0.2030	4,188,499
0.25	0.5987	0.3006	6,202,280
1.03	0.8485	0.2498	5,154,123
1.81	0.9649	0.1164	2,401,681

Exercises 116

1 (a) $\bar{x} = 27$, $s = 13.16$

Upper Limits (Standardized)	Cumulative Probability	p	Np
−1.29	0.0985	0.0985	0.98
0.53	0.2981	0.1996	2.00
0.23	0.5910	0.2929	2.93
0.99	0.8389	0.2479	2.45
1.75	0.9599	0.1210	1.21

Nonsignificant

3 Significant

5 Nonsignificant

7 $\bar{x} = 7$, $s = 2.83$

Upper Limits (Standardized)	Cumulative Probability	p	Np
-1.06	0.1446	0.1446	1.16
0.35	0.6368	0.4922	3.94
1.78	0.9625	0.3257	2.61

Nonsignificant

Exercises 117

1 Significant
3 Nonsignificant
5 Nonsignificant
7 Nonsignificant

Exercises 118

1 (a) $3a^2 - 32a + 110$ (b) $a = 5\frac{1}{3}$ (c) $\bar{x} = 5\frac{1}{3}$

3 $Q = \sum_{i=1}^{n} (\log x_i - \log G)^2$, $\dfrac{dQ}{dG} = -2 \sum_{i=1}^{n} (\log x_i - \log G)/G = 0$,

$\sum_{i=1}^{n} \log x_i = n \log G$, $\log G = \dfrac{\sum_{i=1}^{n} \log x_i}{n}$

5 $s^2 = \dfrac{\sum_{i=1}^{n} (x_i - \bar{x})^2}{n-1}$ is the sample variance,   so $Q = (n-1)s^2$, where s^2 is the sample variance

7 3.9831
9 5.7349

Exercises 119

1 (a) $\hat{y} = 40.2 + 2x$ (b) 42.6   (c) 43   (d) 43.8   (e) 48.2
   (f) 50.2   (g) 51.0

3 (a) $\hat{y} = 47.285 + 5.43x$ (b) 59.231   (d) 61.403   (e) 62.489
   (f) 69.005   (g) 83.123

5 (a) $\hat{y} = 116.75 - 6.25x$ (c) 104.25   (d) 99.25   (e) 93.0
   (f) 90.5

7 (a) $\hat{y} = 70.774 + 2.088x$, $\hat{y} = 58.55 + 2.994x$, $\hat{y} = 69.1 + 1.917x$,
   $\hat{y} = 76.557 + 1.68x$ (c) 81.214; 73.520; 78.685; 84.957
   (d) 89.57; 85.496; 86.353; 91.677   (e) 104.182; 106.454; 99.772;
   103.437

9 $\dfrac{\partial F}{\partial a} = -2\left[\displaystyle\sum_{i=1}^{n} y_i - an - b\sum_{i=1}^{n} x_i^2\right] = 0$

$\dfrac{\partial^2 F}{\partial a^2} = 2n > 0$

$\dfrac{\partial F}{\partial b} = 2\left[-\displaystyle\sum_{i=1}^{n} x_i y_i + a\sum_{i=1}^{n} x_i + b\sum_{i=1}^{n} x_i^2\right] = 0$

$\dfrac{\partial^2 F}{\partial b^2} = 2\displaystyle\sum_{i=1}^{n} x_i^2 > 0$

Necessary and sufficient conditions for a minimum are met

11 $\hat{y} = 2.0 + 0.3x$

13 (a) $\hat{y} = 109.5625 - 6.25x + 1.4375x^2$ (c) 103.81   (d) 103.33
(e) 106.57   (f) 108.67

15 (a) $\log \hat{y} = 2.01608 + 0.06056x$ (c) 111.25   (d) 131.53
(e) 135.25   (f) 150.48

17 (a) $\log \hat{y} = 1.85352 + 0.02119x$ (b) 78.687   (c) 79.458
(d) 81.818   (e) 86.758   (f) 92.886

19 (a) $\log \hat{y} = 1.65641 + 0.05608x$ (c) 60.227   (d) 63.419
(e) 65.077   (f) 75.985   (g) 106.31

21 $G = \displaystyle\sum_{i=1}^{n} (x_i - A - By_i)^2,$

$\dfrac{\partial G}{\partial A} = 2\displaystyle\sum_{i=1}^{n} (x_i - A - By_i)(-1) = 0,$

$\therefore \displaystyle\sum_{i=1}^{n} x_i = An + B\sum_{i=1}^{n} y_i,$

$\dfrac{\partial G}{\partial B} = 2\displaystyle\sum_{i=1}^{n} (x_i - A - By_i)(-y_i) = 0,$

$\displaystyle\sum_{i=1}^{n} x_i y_i = A\sum_{i=1}^{n} y_i + B\sum_{i=1}^{n} y_i^2$

23 (a) Cumulative Probability
0.36278
0.93556
0.99262
1.00000
(b) $\log \hat{y} = 8.93768 - 0.6223 \log x$ (c) 4,323,200   (d) 3,340,800
(e) 8,207,000   (f) 848,000   (g) 96.000

25 (a) Cumulative Probability
0.27130
0.51667
0.71328
0.90664
1.00000

(b) $\log \hat{y} = 8.46854 - 0.59016 \log x$ (c) 2,905,400
(d) 2,201,600   (e) 50,900   (f) 158,800

Exercises 120

1   (a) $\hat{y} = 0.4 + 0.9x$, $\hat{x} = 0.97 + 0.305y$ (c) 4.0   (d) 1.89
3   (a) $\hat{y} = 2.86 - 0.30x$, $\hat{x} = 3.44 - 0.28y$ (c) -0.14 (d) 2.74
5   (a) $\hat{y} = -14.25 + 1.42x$, $\hat{x} = 68.58 + 0.12y$ (c) 113.6
    (d) 82.98
7   (b) $\hat{y} = 4.14 - 0.028x$, $\hat{x} = 77.8 - 10.0y$ (c) 2.46   (d) 62.8
9   (b) $\hat{y} = 13.84 + 1.23x$, $\hat{x} = -1.43 + 0.70y$ (c) 136.84
    (d) 33.57
11 (a) $\hat{y} = 40.92 + 80.68x$, $\hat{x} = 0.225 + 0.011y$ (b) 847.72
    (c) 11.225

Exercises 121

1   0.524; 0.275; nonsignificant; -0.70, 3.42
3   -0.291; 0.085; nonsignificant; -1.305, 0.697
5   0.409; 0.167; nonsignificant; -4.412, 7.268
7   -0.532; 0.283; nonsignificant; -0.110, 0.056
9   0.932; 0.869; significant; 0.84, 1.62
11 (a) $C_t = -7.412 + 0.118y_t$ (b) 16.118   (c) Significant
    (d) 0.995   (e) Significant

Exercises 122

1   (a) $\hat{y} = 133.4 - 1.20x$, $\hat{x} = 59.09 - 0.12y$ (b) 73.4   (c) 48.3
    (d) -0.382 (e) 0.146   (g) Nonsignificant   (h) Nonsignificant
    (i) $\log \hat{y} = 2.1393 - 0.1771 \log x$ (j) -4.916, 2.522
3   (a) $\hat{y} = 48.88 + 1.31x$, $\hat{x} = 28.40 + 0.056y$ (b) 101.28
    (c) 32.88   (d) 0.2697   (e) 0.0727   (g) Nonsignificant
    (h) -0.116, 0.424   (i) $\log \hat{y} = 1.1216 + 0.5389 \log x$,
    $\log \hat{x} = 1.0754 + 0.2259 \log y$ (j) 0.3487   (k) Nonsignificant
    (l) Nonsignificant
5   (a) $\hat{y} = 6.755 + 0.1293x$, $\hat{x} = 1.7234 + 3.0569y$ (b) 17.008
    (c) 14.514   (d) 0.629   (e) 0.3956   (g) Significant
7   (a) $\hat{y} = -5.0632 + 1.1279x$, $\hat{x} = 24.092 + 0.7187y$ (b) 107.727
    (c) 131.897   (d) 0.9005   (e) 0.8109   (g) Nonsignificant
    (h) -0.527, 2.783
9   (a) $\hat{y} = 73.3955 + 0.2898x$ (c) 108.1715   (d) 98.0285
    (e) 103.8245   (f) 0.3811   (g) Nonsignificant   (h) 0.1452
    (i) $\hat{y} = 87.77581 + 0.14096x$ (k) 101.87181   (l) 105.39581
    (m) 99.47549   (n) 0.2010   (o) Nonsignificant   (p) 0.0404

Exercises 123

1   (a) 10, 5, 20   (b) 1.25, 0.625, 2.5   (c) 20, 6, 29, 7, 12, 62
    (d) 7.5, -0.25, 4, 3.875, -0.5, 12

(e) $x_1 = 0.432434 - 0.021622x_2 + 0.332432x_3$ (f) 1.697296

(g) $0.178F = 0.541$, not significant

(h) $t_0 = 0.872$, $t_2 = -0.038$, $t_3 = 1.032$, not significant

(i) -2.296, 2.252; -0.966, 1.671   (j) $t = 3.508$, not significant

(k) $t = 14.496$, significant

3 (a) 102, 48, 249   (b) 12.75, 6, 31.125

(c) 1322, 609, 3180, 290, 1494, 7753   (d) 21.5, -3, 5.25, 2, 0, 2.875

(e) $x_1 = -35.087 - 1.5x_2 + 1.826087x_3$

(f) $R^2 = 0.655$, $F = 7.746$, not significant   (g) $t_0 = -28.822$, significant; $t_2 = -0.780$, not significant; $t_3 = 1.139$, not significant

(h) $t = 0.26$, not significant   (i) -6.447, 3.447; -2.295, 5.947

(j) $t = 0.515$, not significant

5 (a) $p_t = e^{-(x_{1t}-k_0-k_2x_{2t}-k_3x_{3t})^2/2\sigma^2}/\sqrt{2\pi}\,\sigma$;

$$L = p_1 \cdot p_2 \cdots p_N = e^{-\sum_{t=1}^{N}(x_{1t}-k_0-k_2x_{2t}-k_3x_{3t})^2/2\sigma^2}/(2\pi)^{N/2}\sigma^N$$

$$= e^{-Q/2\sigma^2}/(2\pi)^{N/2}\sigma^N$$

(b) $\text{Log } L = -Q/2\sigma^2 - N/2 \log 2\pi - N \log \sigma$;

$\partial \log L/\partial k_i = -(\partial Q/\partial k_i)/2\sigma^2 = 0$

(c) $$\sum_{t=1}^{N}(k_2x_{2t} + k_3x_{3t}) = \sum_{t=1}^{N} x_{1t}; \qquad \sum_{t=1}^{N}(k_2x_{2t} + k_3x_{3t})x_{2t} = \sum_{t=1}^{N} x_{1t}x_{2t};$$

$$\sum_{t=1}^{N}(k_2x_{2t} + k_3x_{3t})x_{3t} = \sum_{t=1}^{N} x_{1t}x_{3t} \qquad \text{From } s_{ij} = \sum_{t=1}^{N} x_{it}x_{jt} - N\bar{x}_i\bar{x}_j$$

follow the normal equations   (d) Divide the first equation under (c) by N and use the other normal equations

Exercises 124

1 (a) Both not identified   (b) First overidentified, second not identified

(c) Both just identified   (d) Both not identified

3 (a) Both equations are just identified since Z_2 is lacking in the first, Z_2 in the second

(b) $Y_1 = 163.608 + 0.056660Z_1 - 0.292171Z_2$,
$Y_2 = 28.674 + 0.091252Z_1 + 0.205285Z_2$

(c) $Y_1 = 204.418 - 1.423Y_2 + 0.187Z_1$,
$Y_1 = 145.805 + 0.621Y_2 - 0.420Z_2$

Exercises 125

1 $y = 896y_1 + 542y_2 + 498y_3$. $M = 0.553M_1 + 0.250M_2 + 0.197M_3$,
$y = 0.30M + 738,246.32$

3 $y = 747y_1 + 445y_2 + 208y_3$. $M = 0.450M_1 + 0.285M_2 + 0.175M_3$,
$y = 306.3M - 764$

Exercises 126

1 (a) 244%   (b) 178%   (c) 130%   (d) 127%   (e) 129%
(f) 127% − 130%   (g) 129%

3 (a) −19%   (b) −21%   (c) −13%   (d) −15%
(e) −14%   (f) −13% to −15%   (g) −14%

5 $L = \dfrac{\Sigma p_1 q_0}{\Sigma p_0 q_0} = 1.2$ But $\Sigma p_0 q_0 = 100$, and $\Sigma p_1 q_0 = 120$, so that with
an income of 120 in time 1 a person may buy the same amounts of commodities, at the new prices, as he bought with 100 at the prices in time 0; so is no worse off.

7 (a) −17%   (b) −20%   (c) −11%   (d) −13%
(e) −12%

9 (a) 11% 9%; 10%   (b) 12%; 15%; 13%   (c) 2%; 1%; 1.4%

Appendix C
Sources of
Numerical Examples

The numerical examples given in the text are taken from the following publications:

Cobb, Charles W., and Paul H. Douglas, "A Theory of Production," *American Economic Review*, XVIII (Supplement) (1938), pp. 139–156.

Davis, H. T., *The Analysis of Economic Time Series*, Cowles Commission for Research in Economics, Mono. 6. Bloomington, Ind.: Principia Press, 1941.

———, *The Theory of Econometrics*. Bloomington: Principia Press, 1941.

Dean, Joel, "Department Store Cost Functions," *Studies in Mathematical Economics and Econometrics; In Memory of Henry Schultz*. Chicago: University of Chicago Press, 1942, pp. 222–254.

———, "The Relation of Cost to Output for a Leather Belt Shop," *Technical Paper 2*. New York: National Bureau of Economic Research, 1941.

———, "Statistical Cost Functions of a Hosiery Mill," *Studies in Business Administration*, XI, No. 4. Chicago: University of Chicago Press, 1941.

Derksen, J. B. D., and A. Rombouts, "The Demand for Bicycles in the Netherlands," *Econometrica*, V (1937), pp. 295–300.

Douglas, Paul H., *The Theory of Wages*. New York: The Macmillan Company, 1934.

———, and M. Bronfenbrenner, "Cross-Section Studies in the Cobb-Douglas Function," *Journal of Political Economy*, XLVII (1939), pp. 761–785.

———, and Patricia Daly, "The Production Function for Canadian Manufactures," *Journal of the American Statistical Association*, XXXIX (1943), pp. 178–186.

———, Patricia Daly, and Ernest Olson, "The Production Function for the United States, 1904," *Journal of Political Economy*, LI (1943), pp. 61–65.

———, and Grace T. Gunn, "Further Measurement of Marginal Productivity," *Quarterly Journal of Economics*, LIV (1940), pp. 399–428.

———, and Grace T. Gunn, "The Production Function for American Manufacturing for 1914," *Journal of Political Economy*, L (1942), pp. 595–602.

———, and Grace T. Gunn, "The Production Function for American Manufacturing in 1919," *American Economic Review*, XXXI (1941), pp. 67–80.

———, and Grace T. Gunn, "The Production Function for Australian Manufacturing," *Quarterly Journal of Economics*, LVI (1941), pp. 108–129.

———, and Marjorie H. Handsaker, "The Theory of Marginal Productivity Tested by Data for Manufacturing in Victoria," *Quarterly Journal of Economics*, LII (1937), pp. 1–36, 214–254.

Haavelmo, T., "Methods of Measuring the Marginal Propensity to Consumer," *Journal of the American Statistical Association*, XLII (1947), pp. 105–122.

Leontief, W., *The Structure of the American Economy in 1919–1939; An Empirical Application of Equilibrium Analysis*, 2nd ed. Cambridge: Harvard University Press, 1941.

Nichols, W. H., *Labor Productivity Functions in Meat Packing*. Chicago: University of Chicago Press, 1948.

Nordin, J. A., "Note on a Light Plant's Cost Curve," *Econometrica*, XV (1947), p. 231 *ff*.

Pabst, W. R., Jr., *Butter and Oleomargarine; An Analysis of Competing Commodities. (Studies in History, Economics and Public Law, No. 427.)* New York: Columbia University Press, 1937.

Roos, C. F., and Victor von Szeliski, "Factors Governing Changes in Domestic Automobile Demand," in *General Motors Corporation: The Dynamics of Automobile Demand*. Detroit: 1939.

Samuelson, Paul A., "A Statistical Analysis of the Consumption Function," in A. H. Hansen, *Fiscal Policy and the Business Cycle*. New York: W. W. Norton & Company, Inc., 1941, pp. 250–260.

Schultz, Henry, *Statistical Laws of Demand and Supply with Special Applications to Sugar*. Chicago: University of Chicago Press, 1928.

———, *The Theory and Measurement of Demand*. Chicago: University of Chicago Press, 1938.

Stone, Richard, "The Analysis of Market Demand," *Journal of the Royal Statistical Society*, CVIII (1945), pp. 286–382.

———, *The Role of Measurement in Economics*. (The Newmarch Lectures, 1948–1949.) Cambridge, England: Cambridge University Press, 1951.

Szeliski, Victor von, "Frequency Distribution of National Income," Report of the Meeting of the Econometric Society in Philadelphia, *Econometrica*, II (1934), pp. 215 *ff*.

———, and L. J. Paradiso, "Demand for Shoes As Affected by Price Levels and National Income," *Econometrica*, IV (1936), pp. 338–355.

Tintner, Gerhard, "An Application of the Variate Difference Method to Multiple Regression," *Econometrica*, XII (1944), pp. 97–113.

———, *Econometrics*. New York: John Wiley & Sons, Inc., 1952.

———, "Multiple Regression for Systems of Equations," *Econometrica*, XIV (1946), pp. 5–36.

———, "A Note of the Derivation of Production Functions from Farm Records," *Econometrica*, XII (1944), pp. 26–34.

———, "Some Applications of Multivariate Analysis to Economic Data," *Journal of the American Statistical Association*, XLI (1946), pp. 472–500.

———, and O. H. Brownlee, "Production Functions Derived from Farm Records," *Journal of Farm Economics*, XXVI (1944), pp. 566–571.

Whitmann, R. H., "The Statistical Law of Demand for a Producer's Goods As Illustrated by the Demand for Steel," *Econometrica*, IV (1936), pp. 138–152.

Wold, Herman, *Demand Analysis; A Study in Econometrics*. New York: John Wiley & Sons, Inc., 1953.

Yntema, T. O., "United States Steel Corporation," *TNEC Papers*. New York: United States Steel Corporation, Vol. I, 1940.

Tables

Table 1

10.0—Four-Place Common Logarithms of Numbers—54.9

N	0	1	2	3	4	5	6	7	8	9
10	0000	0043	0086	0128	0170	0212	0253	0294	0334	0374
11	0414	0453	0492	0531	0569	0607	0645	0682	0719	0755
12	0792	0828	0864	0899	0934	0969	1004	1038	1072	1106
13	1139	1173	1206	1239	1271	1303	1335	1367	1399	1430
14	1461	1492	1523	1553	1584	1614	1644	1673	1703	1732
15	1761	1790	1818	1847	1875	1903	1931	1959	1987	2014
16	2041	2068	2095	2122	2148	2175	2201	2227	2253	2279
17	2304	2330	2355	2380	2405	2430	2455	2480	2504	2529
18	2553	2577	2601	2625	2648	2672	2695	2718	2742	2765
19	2788	2810	2833	2856	2878	2900	2923	2945	2967	2989
20	3010	3032	3054	3075	3096	3118	3139	3160	3181	3201
21	3222	3243	3263	3284	3304	3324	3345	3365	3385	3404
22	3424	3444	3464	3483	3502	3522	3541	3560	3579	3598
23	3617	3636	3655	3674	3692	3711	3729	3747	3766	3784
24	3802	3820	3838	3856	3874	3892	3909	3927	3945	3962
25	3979	3997	4014	4031	4048	4065	4082	4099	4116	4133
26	4150	4166	4183	4200	4216	4232	4249	4265	4281	4298
27	4314	4330	4346	4362	4378	4393	4409	4425	4440	4456
28	4472	4487	4502	4518	4533	4548	4564	4579	4594	4609
29	4624	4639	4654	4669	4683	4698	4713	4728	4742	4757
30	4771	4786	4800	4814	4829	4843	4857	4871	4886	4900
31	4914	4928	4942	4955	4969	4983	4997	5011	5024	5038
32	5051	5065	5079	5092	5105	5119	5132	5145	5159	5172
33	5185	5198	5211	5224	5237	5250	5263	5276	5289	5302
34	5315	5328	5340	5353	5366	5378	5391	5403	5416	5428
35	5441	5453	5465	5478	5490	5502	5514	5527	5539	5551
36	5563	5575	5587	5599	5611	5623	5635	5647	5658	5670
37	5682	5694	5705	5717	5729	5740	5752	5763	5775	5786
38	5798	5809	5821	5832	5843	5855	5866	5877	5888	5899
39	5911	5922	5933	5944	5955	5966	5977	5988	5999	6010
40	6021	6031	6042	6053	6064	6075	6085	6096	6107	6117
41	6128	6138	6149	6160	6170	6180	6191	6201	6212	6222
42	6232	6243	6253	6263	6274	6284	6294	6304	6314	6325
43	6335	6345	6355	6365	6375	6385	6395	6405	6415	6425
44	6435	6444	6454	6464	6474	6484	6493	6503	6513	6522
45	6532	6542	6551	6561	6571	6580	6590	6599	6609	6618
46	6628	6637	6646	6656	6665	6675	6684	6693	6702	6712
47	6721	6730	6739	6749	6758	6767	6776	6785	6794	6803
48	6812	6821	6830	6839	6848	6857	6866	6875	6884	6893
49	6902	6911	6920	6928	6937	6946	6955	6964	6972	6981
50	6990	6998	7007	7016	7024	7033	7042	7050	7059	7067
51	7076	7084	7093	7101	7110	7118	7126	7135	7143	7152
52	7160	7168	7177	7185	7193	7202	7210	7218	7226	7235
53	7243	7251	7259	7267	7275	7284	7292	7300	7308	7316
54	7324	7332	7340	7348	7356	7364	7372	7380	7388	7396
N	0	1	2	3	4	5	6	7	8	9

10.0—Four-Place Common Logarithms of Numbers—54.9

55.0—Four-Place Common Logarithms of Numbers—99.9

N	0	1	2	3	4	5	6	7	8	9
55	7404	7412	7419	7427	7435	7443	7451	7459	7466	7474
56	7482	7490	7497	7505	7513	7520	7528	7536	7543	7551
57	7559	7566	7574	7582	7589	7597	7604	7612	7619	7627
58	7634	7642	7649	7657	7664	7672	7679	7686	7694	7701
59	7709	7716	7723	7731	7738	7745	7752	7760	7767	7774
60	7782	7789	7796	7803	7810	7818	7825	7832	7839	7846
61	7853	7860	7868	7875	7882	7889	7896	7903	7910	7917
62	7924	7931	7938	7945	7952	7959	7966	7973	7980	7987
63	7993	8000	8007	8014	8021	8028	8035	8041	8048	8055
64	8062	8069	8075	8082	8089	8096	8102	8109	8116	8122
65	8129	8136	8142	8149	8156	8162	8169	8176	8182	8189
66	8195	8202	8209	8215	8222	8228	8235	8241	8248	8254
67	8261	8267	8274	8280	8287	8293	8299	8306	8312	8319
68	8325	8331	8338	8344	8351	8357	8363	8370	8376	8382
69	8388	8395	8401	8407	8414	8420	8426	8432	8439	8445
70	8451	8457	8463	8470	8476	8482	8488	8494	8500	8506
71	8513	8519	8525	8531	8537	8543	8549	8555	8561	8567
72	8573	8579	8585	8591	8597	8603	8609	8615	8621	8627
73	8633	8639	8645	8651	8657	8663	8669	8675	8681	8686
74	8692	8698	8704	8710	8716	8722	8727	8733	8739	8745
75	8751	8756	8762	8768	8774	8779	8785	8791	8797	8802
76	8808	8814	8820	8825	8831	8837	8842	8848	8854	8859
77	8865	8871	8876	8882	8887	8893	8899	8904	8910	8915
78	8921	8927	8932	8938	8943	8949	8954	8960	8965	8971
79	8976	8982	8987	8993	8998	9004	9009	9015	9020	9025
80	9031	9036	9042	9047	9053	9058	9063	9069	9074	9079
81	9085	9090	9096	9101	9106	9112	9117	9122	9128	9133
82	9138	9143	9149	9154	9159	9165	9170	9175	9180	9186
83	9191	9196	9201	9206	9212	9217	9222	9227	9232	9238
84	9243	9248	9253	9258	9263	9269	9274	9279	9284	9289
85	9294	9299	9304	9309	9315	9320	9325	9330	9335	9340
86	9345	9350	9355	9360	9365	9370	9375	9380	9385	9390
87	9395	9400	9405	9410	9415	9420	9425	9430	9435	9440
88	9445	9450	9455	9460	9465	9469	9474	9479	9484	9489
89	9494	9499	9504	9509	9513	9518	9523	9528	9533	9538
90	9542	9547	9552	9557	9562	9566	9571	9576	9581	9586
91	9590	9595	9600	9605	9609	9614	9619	9624	9628	9633
92	9638	9643	9647	9652	9657	9661	9666	9671	9675	9680
93	9685	9689	9694	9699	9703	9708	9713	9717	9722	9727
94	9731	9736	9741	9745	9750	9754	9759	9763	9768	9773
95	9777	9782	9786	9791	9795	9800	9805	9809	9814	9818
96	9823	9827	9832	9836	9841	9845	9850	9854	9859	9863
97	9868	9872	9877	9881	9886	9890	9894	9899	9903	9908
98	9912	9917	9921	9926	9930	9934	9939	9943	9948	9952
99	9956	9961	9965	9969	9974	9978	9983	9987	9991	9996
N	0	1	2	3	4	5	6	7	8	9

55.0—Four-Place Common Logarithms of Numbers—99.9

Table 2
Natural Trigonometric Functions for Decimal Fractions of a Degree

Deg.	Sin	Tan	Ctn	Cos	Deg.	Deg.	Sin	Tan	Ctn	Cos	Deg.
0–	.00000	.00000	—	1.00000	90–	6–	.10453	.10510	9.5144	.99452	84–
.1	.00175	.00175	572.96	1.00000	.9	.1	.10626	.10687	9.3572	.99434	.9
.2	.00349	.00349	286.48	0.99999	.8	.2	.10800	.10863	9.2052	.99415	.8
.3	.00524	.00524	190.98	.99999	.7	.3	.10973	.11040	9.0579	.99396	.7
.4	.00698	.00698	143.24	.99998	.6	.4	.11147	.11217	8.9152	.99377	.6
.5	.00873	.00873	114.59	.99996	.5	.5	.11320	.11394	8.7769	.99357	.5
.6	.01047	.01047	95.489	.99995	.4	.6	.11494	.11570	8.6427	.99337	.4
.7	.01222	.01222	81.847	.99993	.3	.7	.11667	.11747	8.5126	.99317	.3
.8	.01396	.01396	71.615	.99990	.2	.8	.11840	.11924	8.3863	.99297	.2
.9	.01571	.01571	63.657	.99988	.1	.9	.12014	.12101	8.2636	.99276	.1
1–	.01745	.01746	57.290	.99985	89–	7–	.12187	.12278	8.1443	.99255	83–
.1	.01920	.01920	52.081	.99982	.9	.1	.12360	.12456	8.0285	.99233	.9
.2	.02094	.02095	47.740	.99978	.8	.2	.12533	.12633	7.9158	.99211	.8
.3	.02269	.02269	44.066	.99974	.7	.3	.12706	.12810	7.8062	.99189	.7
.4	.02443	.02444	40.917	.99970	.6	.4	.12880	.12988	7.6996	.99167	.6
.5	.02618	.02619	38.188	.99966	.5	.5	.13053	.13165	7.5958	.99144	.5
.6	.02792	.02793	35.801	.99961	.4	.6	.13226	.13343	7.4947	.99122	.4
.7	.02967	.02968	33.694	.99956	.3	.7	.13399	.13521	7.3962	.99098	.3
.8	.03141	.03143	31.821	.99951	.2	.8	.13572	.13698	7.3002	.99075	.2
.9	.03316	.03317	30.145	.99945	.1	.9	.13744	.13876	7.2066	.99051	.1
2–	.03490	.03492	28.636	.99939	88–	8–	.13917	.14054	7.1154	.99027	82–
.1	.03664	.03667	27.271	.99933	.9	.1	.14090	.14232	7.0264	.99002	.9
.2	.03839	.03842	26.031	.99926	.8	.2	.14263	.14410	6.9395	.98978	.8
.3	.04013	.04016	24.898	.99919	.7	.3	.14436	.14588	6.8548	.98953	.7
.4	.04188	.04191	23.859	.99912	.6	.4	.14608	.14767	6.7720	.98927	.6
.5	.04362	.04366	22.904	.99905	.5	.5	.14781	.14945	6.6912	.98902	.5
.6	.04536	.04541	22.022	.99897	.4	.6	.14954	.15124	6.6122	.98876	.4
.7	.04711	.04716	21.205	.99889	.3	.7	.15126	.15302	6.5350	.98849	.3
.8	.04885	.04891	20.446	.99881	.2	.8	.15299	.15481	6.4596	.98823	.2
.9	.05059	.05066	19.740	.99872	.1	.9	.15471	.15660	6.3859	.98796	.1
3–	.05234	.05241	19.081	.99863	87–	9–	.15643	.15838	6.3138	.98769	81–
.1	.05408	.05416	18.464	.99854	.9	.1	.15816	.16017	6.2432	.98741	.9
.2	.05582	.05591	17.886	.99844	.8	.2	.15988	.16196	6.1742	.98714	.8
.3	.05756	.05766	17.343	.99834	.7	.3	.16160	.16376	6.1066	.98686	.7
.4	.05931	.05941	16.832	.99824	.6	.4	.16333	.16555	6.0405	.98657	.6
.5	.06105	.06116	16.350	.99813	.5	.5	.16505	.16734	5.9758	.98629	.5
.6	.06279	.06291	15.895	.99803	.4	.6	.16677	.16914	5.9124	.98600	.4
.7	.06453	.06467	15.464	.99792	.3	.7	.16849	.17093	5.8502	.98570	.3
.8	.06627	.06642	15.056	.99780	.2	.8	.17021	.17273	5.7894	.98541	.2
.9	.06802	.06817	14.669	.99768	.1	.9	.17193	.17453	5.7297	.98511	.1
4–	.06976	.06993	14.301	.99756	86–	10–	.17365	.17633	5.6713	.98481	80–
.1	.07150	.07168	13.951	.99744	.9	.1	.17537	.17813	5.6140	.98450	.9
.2	.07324	.07344	13.617	.99731	.8	.2	.17708	.17993	5.5578	.98420	.8
.3	.07498	.07519	13.300	.99719	.7	.3	.17880	.18173	5.5026	.98389	.7
.4	.07672	.07695	12.996	.99705	.6	.4	.18052	.18353	5.4486	.98357	.6
.5	.07846	.07870	12.706	.99692	.5	.5	.18224	.18534	5.3955	.98325	.5
.6	.08020	.08046	12.429	.99678	.4	.6	.18395	.18714	5.3435	.98294	.4
.7	.08194	.08221	12.163	.99664	.3	.7	.18567	.18895	5.2924	.98261	.3
.8	.08368	.08397	11.909	.99649	.2	.8	.18738	.19076	5.2422	.98229	.2
.9	.08542	.08573	11.664	.99635	.1	.9	.18910	.19257	5.1929	.98196	.1
5–	.08716	.08749	11.430	.99619	85–	11–	.19081	.19438	5.1446	.98163	79–
.1	.08889	.08925	11.205	.99604	.9	.1	.19252	.19619	5.0970	.98129	.9
.2	.09063	.09101	10.988	.99588	.8	.2	.19423	.19801	5.0504	.98096	.8
.3	.09237	.09277	10.780	.99572	.7	.3	.19595	.19982	5.0045	.98061	.7
.4	.09411	.09453	10.579	.99556	.6	.4	.19766	.20164	4.9594	.98027	.6
.5	.09585	.09629	10.385	.99540	.5	.5	.19937	.20345	4.9152	.97992	.5
.6	.09758	.09805	10.199	.99523	.4	.6	.20108	.20527	4.8716	.97958	.4
.7	.09932	.09981	10.019	.99506	.3	.7	.20279	.20709	4.8288	.97922	.3
.8	.10106	.10158	9.8448	.99488	.2	.8	.20450	.20891	4.7867	.97887	.2
.9	.10279	.10334	9.6768	.99470	.1	.9	.20620	.21073	4.7453	.97851	.1
6–	.10453	.10510	9.5144	.99452	84–	12–	.20791	.21256	4.7046	.97815	78–
Deg.	Cos	Ctn	Tan	Sin	Deg.	Deg.	Cos	Ctn	Tan	Sin	Deg.

Natural Trigonometric Functions for Decimal Fractions of a Degree

Natural Trigonometric Functions for Decimal Fractions of a Degree

Deg.	Sin	Tan	Ctn	Cos	Deg.
12–	.20791	.21256	4.7046	.97815	**78–**
.1	.20962	.21438	4.6646	.97778	.9
.2	.21132	.21621	4.6252	.97742	.8
.3	.21303	.21804	4.5864	.97705	.7
.4	.21474	.21986	4.5483	.97667	.6
.5	.21644	.22169	4.5107	.97630	.5
.6	.21814	.22353	4.4737	.97592	.4
.7	.21985	.22536	4.4373	.97553	.3
.8	.22155	.22719	4.4015	.97515	.2
.9	.22325	.22903	4.3662	.97476	.1
13–	.22495	.23087	4.3315	.97437	**77–**
.1	.22665	.23271	4.2972	.97398	.9
.2	.22835	.23455	4.2635	.97358	.8
.3	.23005	.23639	4.2303	.97318	.7
.4	.23175	.23823	4.1976	.97278	.6
.5	.23345	.24008	4.1653	.97237	.5
.6	.23514	.24193	4.1335	.97196	.4
.7	.23684	.24377	4.1022	.97155	.3
.8	.23853	.24562	4.0713	.97113	.2
.9	.24023	.24747	4.0408	.97072	.1
14–	.24192	.24933	4.0108	.97030	**76–**
.1	.24362	.25118	3.9812	.96987	.9
.2	.24531	.25304	3.9520	.96945	.8
.3	.24700	.25490	3.9232	.96902	.7
.4	.24869	.25676	3.8947	.96858	.6
.5	.25038	.25862	3.8667	.96815	.5
.6	.25207	.26048	3.8391	.96771	.4
.7	.25376	.26235	3.8118	.96727	.3
.8	.25545	.26421	3.7848	.96682	.2
.9	.25713	.26608	3.7583	.96638	.1
15–	.25882	.26795	3.7321	.96593	**75–**
.1	.26050	.26982	3.7062	.96547	.9
.2	.26219	.27169	3.6806	.96502	.8
.3	.26387	.27357	3.6554	.96456	.7
.4	.26556	.27545	3.6305	.96410	.6
.5	.26724	.27732	3.6059	.96363	.5
.6	.26892	.27921	3.5816	.96316	.4
.7	.27060	.28109	3.5576	.96269	.3
.8	.27228	.28297	3.5339	.96222	.2
.9	.27396	.28486	3.5105	.96174	.1
16–	.27564	.28675	3.4874	.96126	**74–**
.1	.27731	.28864	3.4646	.96078	.9
.2	.27899	.29053	3.4420	.96029	.8
.3	.28067	.29242	3.4197	.95981	.7
.4	.28234	.29432	3.3977	.95931	.6
.5	.28402	.29621	3.3759	.95882	.5
.6	.28569	.29811	3.3544	.95832	.4
.7	.28736	.30001	3.3332	.95782	.3
.8	.28903	.30192	3.3122	.95732	.2
.9	.29070	.30382	3.2914	.95681	.1
17–	.29237	.30573	3.2709	.95630	**73–**
.1	.29404	.30764	3.2506	.95579	.9
.2	.29571	.30955	3.2305	.95528	.8
.3	.29737	.31147	3.2106	.95476	.7
.4	.29904	.31338	3.1910	.95424	.6
17.5	.30071	.31530	3.1716	.95372	**72.5**
Deg.	**Cos**	**Ctn**	**Tan**	**Sin**	**Deg.**

Deg.	Sin	Tan	Ctn	Cos	Deg.
17.5	.30071	.31530	3.1716	.95372	**72.5**
.6	.30237	.31722	3.1524	.95319	.4
.7	.30403	.31914	3.1334	.95266	.3
.8	.30570	.32106	3.1146	.95213	.2
.9	.30736	.32299	3.0961	.95159	.1
18–	.30902	.32492	3.0777	.95106	**72–**
.1	.31068	.32685	3.0595	.95052	.9
.2	.31233	.32878	3.0415	.94997	.8
.3	.31399	.33072	3.0237	.94943	.7
.4	.31565	.33266	3.0061	.94888	.6
.5	.31730	.33460	2.9887	.94832	.5
.6	.31896	.33654	2.9714	.94777	.4
.7	.32061	.33848	2.9544	.94721	.3
.8	.32227	.34043	2.9375	.94665	.2
.9	.32392	.34238	2.9208	.94609	.1
19–	.32557	.34433	2.9042	.94552	**71–**
.1	.32722	.34628	2.8878	.94495	.9
.2	.32887	.34824	2.8716	.94438	.8
.3	.33051	.35020	2.8556	.94380	.7
.4	.33216	.35216	2.8397	.94322	.6
.5	.33381	.35412	2.8239	.94264	.5
.6	.33545	.35608	2.8083	.94206	.4
.7	.33710	.35805	2.7929	.94147	.3
.8	.33874	.36002	2.7776	.94088	.2
.9	.34038	.36199	2.7625	.94029	.1
20–	.34202	.36397	2.7475	.93969	**70–**
.1	.34366	.36595	2.7326	.93909	.9
.2	.34530	.36793	2.7179	.93849	.8
.3	.34694	.36991	2.7034	.93789	.7
.4	.34857	.37190	2.6889	.93728	.6
.5	.35021	.37388	2.6746	.93667	.5
.6	.35184	.37588	2.6605	.93606	.4
.7	.35347	.37787	2.6464	.93544	.3
.8	.35511	.37986	2.6325	.93483	.2
.9	.35674	.38186	2.6187	.93420	.1
21–	.35837	.38386	2.6051	.93358	**69–**
.1	.36000	.38587	2.5916	.93295	.9
.2	.36162	.38787	2.5782	.93232	.8
.3	.36325	.38988	2.5649	.93169	.7
.4	.36488	.39190	2.5517	.93106	.6
.5	.36650	.39391	2.5386	.93042	.5
.6	.36812	.39593	2.5257	.92978	.4
.7	.36975	.39795	2.5129	.92913	.3
.8	.37137	.39997	2.5002	.92849	.2
.9	.37299	.40200	2.4876	.92784	.1
22–	.37461	.40403	2.4751	.92718	**68–**
.1	.37622	.40606	2.4627	.92653	.9
.2	.37784	.40809	2.4504	.92587	.8
.3	.37946	.41013	2.4383	.92521	.7
.4	.38107	.41217	2.4262	.92455	.6
.5	.38268	.41421	2.4142	.92388	.5
.6	.38430	.41626	2.4023	.92321	.4
.7	.38591	.41831	2.3906	.92254	.3
.8	.38752	.42036	2.3789	.92186	.2
.9	.38912	.42242	2.3673	.92119	.1
23–	.39073	.42447	2.3559	.92050	**67–**
Deg.	**Cos**	**Ctn**	**Tan**	**Sin**	**Deg.**

Natural Trigonometric Functions for Decimal Fractions of a Degree

Natural Trigonometric Functions for Decimal Fractions of a Degree

Deg.	Sin	Tan	Ctn	Cos	Deg.
23–	.39073	.42447	2.3559	.92050	**67–**
.1	.39234	.42654	2.3445	.91982	.9
.2	.39394	.42860	2.3332	.91914	.8
.3	.39555	.43067	2.3220	.91845	.7
.4	.39715	.43274	2.3109	.91775	.6
.5	.39875	.43481	2.2998	.91706	.5
.6	.40035	.43689	2.2889	.91636	.4
.7	.40195	.43897	2.2781	.91566	.3
.8	.40355	.44105	2.2673	.91496	.2
.9	.40514	.44314	2.2566	.91425	.1
24–	.40674	.44523	2.2460	.91355	**66–**
.1	.40833	.44732	2.2355	.91283	.9
.2	.40992	.44942	2.2251	.91212	.8
.3	.41151	.45152	2.2148	.91140	.7
.4	.41310	.45362	2.2045	.91068	.6
.5	.41469	.45573	2.1943	.90996	.5
.6	.41628	.45784	2.1842	.90924	.4
.7	.41787	.45995	2.1742	.90851	.3
.8	.41945	.46206	2.1642	.90778	.2
.9	.42104	.46418	2.1543	.90704	.1
25–	.42262	.46631	2.1445	.90631	**65–**
.1	.42420	.46843	2.1348	.90557	.9
.2	.42578	.47056	2.1251	.90483	.8
.3	.42736	.47270	2.1155	.90408	.7
.4	.42894	.47483	2.1060	.90334	.6
.5	.43051	.47698	2.0965	.90259	.5
.6	.43209	.47912	2.0872	.90183	.4
.7	.43366	.48127	2.0778	.90108	.3
.8	.43523	.48342	2.0686	.90032	.2
.9	.43680	.48557	2.0594	.89956	.1
26–	.43837	.48773	2.0503	.89879	**64–**
.1	.43994	.48989	2.0413	.89803	.9
.2	.44151	.49206	2.0323	.89726	.8
.3	.44307	.49423	2.0233	.89649	.7
.4	.44464	.49640	2.0145	.89571	.6
.5	.44620	.49858	2.0057	.89493	.5
.6	.44776	.50076	1.9970	.89415	.4
.7	.44932	.50295	1.9883	.89337	.3
.8	.45088	.50514	1.9797	.89259	.2
.9	.45243	.50733	1.9711	.89180	.1
27–	.45399	.50953	1.9626	.89101	**63–**
.1	.45554	.51173	1.9542	.89021	.9
.2	.45710	.51393	1.9458	.88942	.8
.3	.45865	.51614	1.9375	.88862	.7
.4	.46020	.51835	1.9292	.88782	.6
.5	.46175	.52057	1.9210	.88701	.5
.6	.46330	.52279	1.9128	.88620	.4
.7	.46484	.52501	1.9047	.88539	.3
.8	.46639	.52724	1.8967	.88458	.2
.9	.46793	.52947	1.8887	.88377	.1
28–	.46947	.53171	1.8807	.88295	**62–**
.1	.47101	.53395	1.8728	.88213	.9
.2	.47255	.53620	1.8650	.88130	.8
.3	.47409	.53844	1.8572	.88048	.7
.4	.47562	.54070	1.8495	.87965	.6
28.5	.47716	.54296	1.8418	.87882	**61.5**
Deg.	Cos	Ctn	Tan	Sin	Deg.

Deg.	Sin	Tan	Ctn	Cos	Deg.
28.5	.47716	.54296	1.8418	.87882	**61.5**
.6	.47869	.54522	1.8341	.87798	.4
.7	.48022	.54748	1.8265	.87715	.3
.8	.48175	.54975	1.8190	.87631	.2
.9	.48328	.55203	1.8115	.87546	.1
29–	.48481	.55431	1.8040	.87462	**61–**
.1	.48634	.55659	1.7966	.87377	.9
.2	.48786	.55888	1.7893	.87292	.8
.3	.48938	.56117	1.7820	.87207	.7
.4	.49090	.56347	1.7747	.87121	.6
.5	.49242	.56577	1.7675	.87036	.5
.6	.49394	.56808	1.7603	.86949	.4
.7	.49546	.57039	1.7532	.86863	.3
.8	.49697	.57271	1.7461	.86777	.2
.9	.49849	.57503	1.7391	.86690	.1
30–	.50000	.57735	1.7321	.86603	**60–**
.1	.50151	.57968	1.7251	.86515	.9
.2	.50302	.58201	1.7182	.86427	.8
.3	.50453	.58435	1.7113	.86340	.7
.4	.50603	.58670	1.7045	.86251	.6
.5	.50754	.58905	1.6977	.86163	.5
.6	.50904	.59140	1.6909	.86074	.4
.7	.51054	.59376	1.6842	.85985	.3
.8	.51204	.59612	1.6775	.85896	.2
.9	.51354	.59849	1.6709	.85806	.1
31–	.51504	.60086	1.6643	.85717	**59–**
.1	.51653	.60324	1.6577	.85627	.9
.2	.51803	.60562	1.6512	.85536	.8
.3	.51952	.60801	1.6447	.85446	.7
.4	.52101	.61040	1.6383	.85355	.6
.5	.52250	.61280	1.6319	.85264	.5
.6	.52399	.61520	1.6255	.85173	.4
.7	.52547	.61761	1.6191	.85081	.3
.8	.52696	.62003	1.6128	.84989	.2
.9	.52844	.62245	1.6066	.84897	.1
32–	.52992	.62487	1.6003	.84805	**58–**
.1	.53140	.62730	1.5941	.84712	.9
.2	.53288	.62973	1.5880	.84619	.8
.3	.53435	.63217	1.5818	.84526	.7
.4	.53583	.63462	1.5757	.84433	.6
.5	.53730	.63707	1.5697	.84339	.5
.6	.53877	.63953	1.5637	.84245	.4
.7	.54024	.64199	1.5577	.84151	.3
.8	.54171	.64446	1.5517	.84057	.2
.9	.54317	.64693	1.5458	.83962	.1
33–	.54464	.64941	1.5399	.83867	**57–**
.1	.54610	.65189	1.5340	.83772	.9
.2	.54756	.65438	1.5282	.83676	.8
.3	.54902	.65688	1.5224	.83581	.7
.4	.55048	.65938	1.5166	.83485	.6
.5	.55194	.66189	1.5108	.83389	.5
.6	.55339	.66440	1.5051	.83292	.4
.7	.55484	.66692	1.4994	.83195	.3
.8	.55630	.66944	1.4938	.83098	.2
.9	.56775	.67197	1.4882	.83001	.1
34–	.55919	.67451	1.4826	.82904	**56–**
Deg.	Cos	Ctn	Tan	Sin	Deg.

Natural Trigonometric Functions for Decimal Fractions of a Degree

Natural Trigonometric Functions for Decimal Fractions of a Degree

Deg.	Sin	Tan	Ctn	Cos	Deg.		Deg.	Sin	Tan	Ctn	Cos	Deg.
34–	.55919	.67451	1.4826	.82904	56–		39.5	.63608	.82434	1.2131	.77162	50.5
.1	.56064	.67705	1.4770	.82806	.9		.6	.63742	.82727	1.2088	.77051	.4
.2	.56208	.67960	1.4715	.82708	.8		.7	.63877	.83022	1.2045	.76940	.3
.3	.56353	.68215	1.4659	.82610	.7		.8	.64011	.83317	1.2002	.76828	.2
.4	.56497	.68471	1.4605	.82511	.6		.9	.64145	.83613	1.1960	.76717	.1
.5	.56641	.68728	1.4550	.82413	.5		40–	.64279	.83910	1.1918	.76604	50–
.6	.56784	.68985	1.4496	.82314	.4		.1	.64412	.84208	1.1875	.76492	.9
.7	.56928	.69243	1.4442	.82214	.3		.2	.64546	.84507	1.1833	.76380	.8
.8	.57071	.69502	1.4388	.82115	.2		.3	.64679	.84806	1.1792	.76267	.7
.9	.57215	.69761	1.4335	.82015	.1		.4	.64812	.85107	1.1750	.76154	.6
35–	.57358	.70021	1.4281	.81915	55–		.5	.64945	.85408	1.1708	.76041	.5
.1	.57501	.70281	1.4229	.81815	.9		.6	.65077	.85710	1.1667	.75927	.4
.2	.57643	.70542	1.4176	.81714	.8		.7	.65210	.86014	1.1626	.75813	.3
.3	.57786	.70804	1.4124	.81614	.7		.8	.65342	.86318	1.1585	.75700	.2
.4	.57928	.71066	1.4071	.81513	.6		.9	.65474	.86623	1.1544	.75585	.1
.5	.58070	.71329	1.4019	.81412	.5		41–	.65606	.86929	1.1504	.75471	49–
.6	.58212	.71593	1.3968	.81310	.4		.1	.65738	.87236	1.1463	.75356	.9
.7	.58354	.71857	1.3916	.81208	.3		.2	.65869	.87543	1.1423	.75241	.8
.8	.58496	.72122	1.3865	.81106	.2		.3	.66000	.87852	1.1383	.75126	.7
.9	.58637	.72388	1.3814	.81004	.1		.4	.66131	.88162	1.1343	.75011	.6
36–	.58779	.72654	1.3764	.80902	54–		.5	.66262	.88473	1.1303	.74896	.5
.1	.58920	.72921	1.3713	.80799	.9		.6	.66393	.88784	1.1263	.74780	.4
.2	.59061	.73189	1.3663	.80696	.8		.7	.66523	.89097	1.1224	.74664	.3
.3	.59201	.73457	1.3613	.80593	.7		.8	.66653	.89410	1.1184	.74548	.2
.4	.59342	.73726	1.3564	.80489	.6		.9	.66783	.89725	1.1145	.74431	.1
.5	.59482	.73996	1.3514	.80386	.5		42–	.66913	.90040	1.1106	.74314	48–
.6	.59622	.74267	1.3465	.80282	.4		.1	.67043	.90357	1.1067	.74198	.9
.7	.59763	.74538	1.3416	.80178	.3		.2	.67172	.90674	1.1028	.74080	.8
.8	.59902	.74810	1.3367	.80073	.2		.3	.67301	.90993	1.0990	.73963	.7
.9	.60042	.75082	1.3319	.79968	.1		.4	.67430	.91313	1.0951	.73846	.6
37–	.60182	.75355	1.3270	.79864	53–		.5	.67559	.91633	1.0913	.73728	.5
.1	.60321	.75629	1.3222	.79758	.9		.6	.67688	.91955	1.0875	.73610	.4
.2	.60460	.75904	1.3175	.79653	.8		.7	.67816	.92277	1.0837	.73491	.3
.3	.60599	.76180	1.3127	.79547	.7		.8	.67944	.92601	1.0799	.73373	.2
.4	.60738	.76456	1.3079	.79441	.6		.9	.68072	.92926	1.0761	.73254	.1
.5	.60876	.76733	1.3032	.79335	.5		43–	.68200	.93252	1.0724	.73135	47–
.6	.61015	.77010	1.2985	.79229	.4		.1	.68327	.93578	1.0686	.73016	.9
.7	.61153	.77289	1.2938	.79122	.3		.2	.68455	.93906	1.0649	.72897	.8
.8	.61291	.77568	1.2892	.79016	.2		.3	.68582	.94235	1.0612	.72777	.7
.9	.61429	.77848	1.2846	.78908	.1		.4	.68709	.94565	1.0575	.72657	.6
38–	.61566	.78129	1.2799	.78801	52–		.5	.68835	.94896	1.0538	.72537	.5
.1	.61704	.78410	1.2753	.78694	.9		.6	.68962	.95229	1.0501	.72417	.4
.2	.61841	.78692	1.2708	.78586	.8		.7	.69088	.95562	1.0464	.72297	.3
.3	.61978	.78975	1.2662	.78478	.7		.8	.69214	.95897	1.0428	.72176	.2
.4	.62115	.79259	1.2617	.78369	.6		.9	.69340	.96232	1.0392	.72055	.1
.5	.62251	.79544	1.2572	.78261	.5		44–	.69466	.96569	1.0355	.71934	46–
.6	.62388	.79829	1.2527	.78152	.4		.1	.69591	.96907	1.0319	.71813	.9
.7	.62524	.80115	1.2482	.78043	.3		.2	.69717	.97246	1.0283	.71691	.8
.8	.62660	.80402	1.2437	.77934	.2		.3	.69842	.97586	1.0247	.71569	.7
.9	.62796	.80690	1.2393	.77824	.1		.4	.69966	.97927	1.0212	.71447	.6
39–	.62932	.80978	1.2349	.77715	51–		.5	.70091	.98270	1.0176	.71325	.5
.1	.63068	.81268	1.2305	.77605	.9		.6	.70215	.98613	1.0141	.71203	.4
.2	.63203	.81558	1.2261	.77494	.8		.7	.70339	.98958	1.0105	.71080	.3
.3	.63338	.81849	1.2218	.77384	.7		.8	.70463	.99304	1.0070	.70957	.2
.4	.63473	.82141	1.2174	.77273	.6		.9	.70587	.99652	1.0035	.70834	.1
39.5	.63608	.82434	1.2131	.77162	50.5		45–	.70711	1.00000	1.0000	.70711	45–
Deg.	Cos	Ctn	Tan	Sin	Deg.		Deg.	Cos	Ctn	Tan	Sin	Deg.

Natural Trigonometric Functions for Decimal Fractions of a Degree

Table 3
1.00—Four-Place Natural Logarithms—5.59

N	.00	.01	.02	.03	.04	.05	.06	.07	.08	.09
1.0	0.0000	0.0100	0.0198	0.0296	0.0392	0.0488	0.0583	0.0677	0.0770	0.0862
1.1	0.0953	0.1044	0.1133	0.1222	0.1310	0.1398	0.1484	0.1570	0.1655	0.1740
1.2	0.1823	0.1906	0.1989	0.2070	0.2151	0.2231	0.2311	0.2390	0.2469	0.2546
1.3	0.2624	0.2700	0.2776	0.2852	0.2927	0.3001	0.3075	0.3148	0.3221	0.3293
1.4	0.3365	0.3436	0.3507	0.3577	0.3646	0.3716	0.3784	0.3853	0.3920	0.3988
1.5	0.4055	0.4121	0.4187	0.4253	0.4318	0.4383	0.4447	0.4511	0.4574	0.4637
1.6	0.4700	0.4762	0.4824	0.4886	0.4947	0.5008	0.5068	0.5128	0.5188	0.5247
1.7	0.5306	0.5365	0.5423	0.5481	0.5539	0.5596	0.5653	0.5710	0.5766	0.5822
1.8	0.5878	0.5933	0.5988	0.6043	0.6098	0.6152	0.6206	0.6259	0.6313	0.6366
1.9	0.6419	0.6471	0.6523	0.6575	0.6627	0.6678	0.6729	0.6780	0.6831	0.6881
2.0	0.6931	0.6981	0.7031	0.7080	0.7129	0.7178	0.7227	0.7275	0.7324	0.7372
2.1	0.7419	0.7467	0.7514	0.7561	0.7608	0.7655	0.7701	0.7747	0.7793	0.7839
2.2	0.7885	0.7930	0.7975	0.8020	0.8065	0.8109	0.8154	0.8198	0.8242	0.8286
2.3	0.8329	0.8372	0.8416	0.8459	0.8502	0.8544	0.8587	0.8629	0.8671	0.8713
2.4	0.8755	0.8796	0.8838	0.8879	0.8920	0.8961	0.9002	0.9042	0.9083	0.9123
2.5	0.9163	0.9203	0.9243	0.9282	0.9322	0.9361	0.9400	0.9439	0.9478	0.9517
2.6	0.9555	0.9594	0.9632	0.9670	0.9708	0.9746	0.9783	0.9821	0.9858	0.9895
2.7	0.9933	0.9969	1.0006	1.0043	1.0080	1.0116	1.0152	1.0188	1.0225	1.0260
2.8	1.0296	1.0332	1.0367	1.0403	1.0438	1.0473	1.0508	1.0543	1.0578	1.0613
2.9	1.0647	1.0682	1.0716	1.0750	1.0784	1.0818	1.0852	1.0886	1.0919	1.0953
3.0	1.0986	1.1019	1.1053	1.1086	1.1119	1.1151	1.1184	1.1217	1.1249	1.1282
3.1	1.1314	1.1346	1.1378	1.1410	1.1442	1.1474	1.1506	1.1537	1.1569	1.1600
3.2	1.1632	1.1663	1.1694	1.1725	1.1756	1.1787	1.1817	1.1848	1.1878	1.1909
3.3	1.1939	1.1969	1.2000	1.2030	1.2060	1.2090	1.2119	1.2149	1.2179	1.2208
3.4	1.2238	1.2267	1.2296	1.2326	1.2355	1.2384	1.2413	1.2442	1.2470	1.2499
3.5	1.2528	1.2556	1.2585	1.2613	1.2641	1.2669	1.2698	1.2726	1.2754	1.2782
3.6	1.2809	1.2837	1.2865	1.2892	1.2920	1.2947	1.2975	1.3002	1.3029	1.3056
3.7	1.3083	1.3110	1.3137	1.3164	1.3191	1.3218	1.3244	1.3271	1.3297	1.3324
3.8	1.3350	1.3376	1.3403	1.3429	1.3455	1.3481	1.3507	1.3533	1.3558	1.3584
3.9	1.3610	1.3635	1.3661	1.3686	1.3712	1.3737	1.3762	1.3788	1.3813	1.3838
4.0	1.3863	1.3888	1.3913	1.3938	1.3962	1.3987	1.4012	1.4036	1.4061	1.4085
4.1	1.4110	1.4134	1.4159	1.4183	1.4207	1.4231	1.4255	1.4279	1.4303	1.4327
4.2	1.4351	1.4375	1.4398	1.4422	1.4446	1.4469	1.4493	1.4516	1.4540	1.4563
4.3	1.4586	1.4609	1.4633	1.4656	1.4679	1.4702	1.4725	1.4748	1.4770	1.4793
4.4	1.4816	1.4839	1.4861	1.4884	1.4907	1.4929	1.4951	1.4974	1.4996	1.5019
4.5	1.5041	1.5063	1.5085	1.5107	1.5129	1.5151	1.5173	1.5195	1.5217	1.5239
4.6	1.5261	1.5282	1.5304	1.5326	1.5347	1.5369	1.5390	1.5412	1.5433	1.5454
4.7	1.5476	1.5497	1.5518	1.5539	1.5560	1.5581	1.5602	1.5623	1.5644	1.5665
4.8	1.5686	1.5707	1.5728	1.5748	1.5769	1.5790	1.5810	1.5831	1.5851	1.5872
4.9	1.5892	1.5913	1.5933	1.5953	1.5974	1.5994	1.6014	1.6034	1.6054	1.6074
5.0	1.6094	1.6114	1.6134	1.6154	1.6174	1.6194	1.6214	1.6233	1.6253	1.6273
5.1	1.6292	1.6312	1.6332	1.6351	1.6371	1.6390	1.6409	1.6429	1.6448	1.6467
5.2	1.6487	1.6506	1.6525	1.6544	1.6563	1.6582	1.6601	1.6620	1.6639	1.6658
5.3	1.6677	1.6696	1.6715	1.6734	1.6752	1.6771	1.6790	1.6808	1.6827	1.6845
5.4	1.6864	1.6882	1.6901	1.6919	1.6938	1.6956	1.6974	1.6993	1.7011	1.7029
5.5	1.7047	1.7066	1.7084	1.7102	1.7120	1.7138	1.7156	1.7174	1.7192	1.7210
N	.00	.01	.02	.03	.04	.05	.06	.07	.08	.09

$\log_e .1 = .6974-3$ $\log_e .01 = .3948-5$ $\log_e .001 = .0922-7$
1.00—Four-Place Natural Logarithms—5.59

5.50—Four-Place Natural Logarithms—10.09

N	.00	.01	.02	.03	.04	.05	.06	.07	.08	.09
5.5	1.7047	1.7066	1.7084	1.7102	1.7120	1.7138	1.7156	1.7174	1.7192	1.7210
5.6	1.7228	1.7246	1.7263	1.7281	1.7299	1.7317	1.7334	1.7352	1.7370	1.7387
5.7	1.7405	1.7422	1.7440	1.7457	1.7475	1.7492	1.7509	1.7527	1.7544	1.7561
5.8	1.7579	1.7596	1.7613	1.7630	1.7647	1.7664	1.7681	1.7699	1.7716	1.7733
5.9	1.7750	1.7766	1.7783	1.7800	1.7817	1.7834	1.7851	1.7867	1.7884	1.7901
6.0	1.7918	1.7934	1.7951	1.7967	1.7984	1.8001	1.8017	1.8034	1.8050	1.8066
6.1	1.8083	1.8099	1.8116	1.8132	1.8148	1.8165	1.8181	1.8197	1.8213	1.8229
6.2	1.8245	1.8262	1.8278	1.8294	1.8310	1.8326	1.8342	1.8358	1.8374	1.8390
6.3	1.8405	1.8421	1.8437	1.8453	1.8469	1.8485	1.8500	1.8516	1.8532	1.8547
6.4	1.8563	1.8579	1.8594	1.8610	1.8625	1.8641	1.8656	1.8672	1.8687	1.8703
6.5	1.8718	1.8733	1.8749	1.8764	1.8779	1.8795	1.8810	1.8825	1.8840	1.8856
6.6	1.8871	1.8886	1.8901	1.8916	1.8931	1.8946	1.8961	1.8976	1.8991	1.9006
6.7	1.9021	1.9036	1.9051	1.9066	1.9081	1.9095	1.9110	1.9125	1.9140	1.9155
6.8	1.9169	1.9184	1.9199	1.9213	1.9228	1.9242	1.9257	1.9272	1.9286	1.9301
6.9	1.9315	1.9330	1.9344	1.9359	1.9373	1.9387	1.9402	1.9416	1.9430	1.9445
7.0	1.9459	1.9473	1.9488	1.9502	1.9516	1.9530	1.9544	1.9559	1.9573	1.9587
7.1	1.9601	1.9615	1.9629	1.9643	1.9657	1.9671	1.9685	1.9699	1.9713	1.9727
7.2	1.9741	1.9755	1.9769	1.9782	1.9796	1.9810	1.9824	1.9838	1.9851	1.9865
7.3	1.9879	1.9892	1.9906	1.9920	1.9933	1.9947	1.9961	1.9974	1.9988	2.0001
7.4	2.0015	2.0028	2.0042	2.0055	2.0069	2.0082	2.0096	2.0109	2.0122	2.0136
7.5	2.0149	2.0162	2.0176	2.0189	2.0202	2.0215	2.0229	2.0242	2.0255	2.0268
7.6	2.0281	2.0295	2.0308	2.0321	2.0334	2.0347	2.0360	2.0373	2.0386	2.0399
7.7	2.0412	2.0425	2.0438	2.0451	2.0464	2.0477	2.0490	2.0503	2.0516	2.0528
7.8	2.0541	2.0554	2.0567	2.0580	2.0592	2.0605	2.0618	2.0631	2.0643	2.0656
7.9	2.0669	2.0681	2.0694	2.0707	2.0719	2.0732	2.0744	2.0757	2.0769	2.0782
8.0	2.0794	2.0807	2.0819	2.0832	2.0844	2.0857	2.0869	2.0882	2.0894	2.0906
8.1	2.0919	2.0931	2.0943	2.0956	2.0968	2.0980	2.0992	2.1005	2.1017	2.1029
8.2	2.1041	2.1054	2.1066	2.1078	2.1090	2.1102	2.1114	2.1126	2.1138	2.1150
8.3	2.1163	2.1175	2.1187	2.1199	2.1211	2.1223	2.1235	2.1247	2.1258	2.1270
8.4	2.1282	2.1294	2.1306	2.1318	2.1330	2.1342	2.1353	2.1365	2.1377	2.1389
8.5	2.1401	2.1412	2.1424	2.1436	2.1448	2.1459	2.1471	2.1483	2.1494	2.1506
8.6	2.1518	2.1529	2.1541	2.1552	2.1564	2.1576	2.1587	2.1599	2.1610	2.1622
8.7	2.1633	2.1645	2.1656	2.1668	2.1679	2.1691	2.1702	2.1713	2.1725	2.1736
8.8	2.1748	2.1759	2.1770	2.1782	2.1793	2.1804	2.1815	2.1827	2.1838	2.1849
8.9	2.1861	2.1872	2.1883	2.1894	2.1905	2.1917	2.1928	2.1939	2.1950	2.1961
9.0	2.1972	2.1983	2.1994	2.2006	2.2017	2.2028	2.2039	2.2050	2.2061	2.2072
9.1	2.2083	2.2094	2.2105	2.2116	2.2127	2.2138	2.2148	2.2159	2.2170	2.2181
9.2	2.2192	2.2203	2.2214	2.2225	2.2235	2.2246	2.2257	2.2268	2.2279	2.2289
9.3	2.2300	2.2311	2.2322	2.2332	2.2343	2.2354	2.2364	2.2375	2.2386	2.2396
9.4	2.2407	2.2418	2.2428	2.2439	2.2450	2.2460	2.2471	2.2481	2.2492	2.2502
9.5	2.2513	2.2523	2.2534	2.2544	2.2555	2.2565	2.2576	2.2586	2.2597	2.2607
9.6	2.2618	2.2628	2.2638	2.2649	2.2659	2.2670	2.2680	2.2690	2.2701	2.2711
9.7	2.2721	2.2732	2.2742	2.2752	2.2762	2.2773	2.2783	2.2793	2.2803	2.2814
9.8	2.2824	2.2834	2.2844	2.2854	2.2865	2.2875	2.2885	2.2895	2.2905	2.2915
9.9	2.2925	2.2935	2.2946	2.2956	2.2966	2.2976	2.2986	2.2996	2.3006	2.3016
10.0	2.3026	2.3036	2.3046	2.3056	2.3066	2.3076	2.3086	2.3096	2.3106	2.3115
N	.00	.01	.02	.03	.04	.05	.06	.07	.08	.09

$\log_e .0001 = .7897-10$ $\log_e .00001 = .4871-12$ $\log_e .000\ 001 = .1845-14$

5.50—Four-Place Natural Logarithms—10.09

Table 4
Areas of the Normal Probability Curve

$$\int_o^u \phi(t)dt$$

μ	0.00	0.01	0.02	0.03	0.04	0.05	0.06	0.07	0.08	0.09
0.0	.0000	.0040	.0080	.0120	.0160	.0199	.0239	.0279	.0319	.0359
0.1	.0398	.0438	.0478	.0517	.0557	.0596	.0636	.0675	.0714	.0753
0.2	.0793	.0832	.0871	.0910	.0948	.0987	.1026	.1064	.1103	.1141
0.3	.1179	.1217	.1255	.1293	.1331	.1368	.1406	.1443	.1480	.1517
0.4	.1554	.1591	.1628	.1664	.1700	.1736	.1772	.1808	.1844	.1879
0.5	.1915	.1950	.1985	.2019	.2054	.2088	.2123	.2157	.2190	.2224
0.6	.2257	.2291	.2324	.2357	.2389	.2422	.2454	.2486	.2517	.2549
0.7	.2580	.2611	.2642	.2673	.2704	.2734	.2764	.2794	.2823	.2852
0.8	.2881	.2910	.2939	.2967	.2995	.3023	.3051	.3078	.3106	.3133
0.9	.3159	.3186	.3212	.3238	.3264	.3289	.3315	.3340	.3365	.3389
1.0	.3413	.3438	.3461	.3485	.3508	.3531	.3554	.3577	.3599	.3621
1.1	.3643	.3665	.3686	.3708	.3729	.3749	.3770	.3790	.3810	.3830
1.2	.3849	.3869	.3888	.3907	.3925	.3944	.3962	.3980	.3997	.4015
1.3	.4032	.4049	.4066	.4082	.4099	.4115	.4131	.4147	.4162	.4177
1.4	.4192	.4207	.4222	.4236	.4251	.4265	.4279	.4292	.4306	.4319
1.5	.4332	.4345	.4357	.4370	.4382	.4394	.4406	.4418	.4429	.4441
1.6	.4452	.4463	.4474	.4484	.4495	.4505	.4515	.4525	.4535	.4545
1.7	.4554	.4564	.4573	.4582	.4591	.4599	.4608	.4616	.4625	.4633
1.8	.4641	.4649	.4656	.4664	.4671	.4678	.4686	.4693	.4699	.4706
1.9	.4713	.4719	.4726	.4732	.4738	.4744	.4750	.4756	.4761	.4767
2.0	.4773	.4778	.4783	.4788	.4793	.4798	.4803	.4808	.4812	.4817
2.1	.4821	.4826	.4830	.4834	.4838	.4842	.4846	.4850	.4854	.4857
2.2	.4861	.4864	.4868	.4871	.4875	.4878	.4881	.4884	.4887	.4890
2.3	.4893	.4896	.4898	.4901	.4904	.4906	.4909	.4911	.4913	.4916
2.4	.4918	.4920	.4922	.4925	.4927	.4929	.4931	.4932	.4934	.4936
2.5	.4938	.4940	.4941	.4943	.4945	.4946	.4948	.4949	.4951	.4952
2.6	.4953	.4955	.4956	.4957	.4959	.4960	.4961	.4962	.4963	.4964
2.7	.4965	.4966	.4967	.4968	.4969	.4970	.4971	.4972	.4973	.4974
2.8	.4974	.4975	.4976	.4977	.4977	.4978	.4979	.4979	.4980	.4981
2.9	.4981	.4982	.4983	.4983	.4984	.4984	.4985	.4985	.4986	.4986
3.0	.4987	.4987	.4987	.4988	.4988	.4989	.4989	.4989	.4989	.4990
3.1	.4990	.4991	.4991	.4991	.4992	.4992	.4992	.4992	.4993	.4993
3.2	.4993	.4993	.4994	.4994	.4994	.4994	.4994	.4995	.4995	.4995
3.3	.4995	.4995	.4996	.4996	.4996	.4996	.4996	.4996	.4996	.4997
3.4	.4997	.4997	.4997	.4997	.4997	.4997	.4997	.4997	.4997	.4998
3.5	.4998	.4998	.4998	.4998	.4998	.4998	.4998	.4998	.4998	.4998
3.6	.4998	.4998	.4999	.4999	.4999	.4999	.4999	.4999	.4999	.4999
3.7	.4999	.4999	.4999	.4999	.4999	.4999	.4999	.4999	.4999	.4999
3.8	.4999	.4999	.4999	.4999	.4999	.4999	.4999	.4999	.4999	.5000
3.9	.5000	.5000	.5000	.5000	.5000	.5000	.5000	.5000	.5000	.5000
μ	0.00	0.01	0.02	0.03	0.04	0.05	0.06	0.07	0.08	0.09

Areas of the Normal Probability Curve

Table 5
Student's t-Distribution

Degrees of Freedom	5 percent	1 percent
1	12.706	63.657
2	4.303	9.925
3	3.182	5.841
4	2.776	4.604
5	2.571	4.032
6	2.447	3.707
7	2.365	3.499
8	2.306	3.355
9	2.262	3.250
10	2.228	3.169
11	2.201	3.106
12	2.179	3.055
13	2.160	3.012
14	2.145	2.977
15	2.131	2.947
16	2.120	2.921
17	2.110	2.898
18	2.101	2.878
19	2.093	2.861
20	2.086	2.845
21	2.080	2.831
22	2.074	2.819
23	2.069	2.807
24	2.064	2.797
25	2.060	2.787
26	2.056	2.779
27	2.052	2.771
28	2.048	2.763
29	2.045	2.756
30	2.042	2.750
40	2.021	2.704
50	2.008	2.678
Degrees of Freedom	5 percent	1 percent

Student's t-Distribution

Table 6

χ^2 Probability Scale

Values of χ^2 Corresponding to Certain Chances of Exceeding χ^2

Degrees of Freedom	$P = .90$	.70	.50	.30	.20	.10	.05	.02	.01
1	0.02	0.15	0.45	1.07	1.64	2.71	3.84	5.41	6.63
2	0.21	0.71	1.39	2.41	3.22	4.60	5.99	7.82	9.21
3	0.58	1.42	2.37	3.66	4.64	6.25	7.81	9.84	11.34
4	1.06	2.19	3.36	4.88	5.99	7.78	9.49	11.67	13.28
5	1.61	3.00	4.35	6.06	7.29	9.24	11.07	13.39	15.09
6	2.20	3.83	5.35	7.23	8.56	10.64	12.59	15.03	16.81
7	2.83	4.67	6.35	8.38	9.80	12.02	14.07	16.62	18.47
8	3.49	5.53	7.34	9.52	11.03	13.36	15.51	18.17	20.09
9	4.17	6.39	8.34	10.66	12.24	14.68	16.92	19.68	21.67
10	4.86	7.27	9.34	11.78	13.44	15.99	18.31	21.16	23.21
11	5.58	8.15	10.34	12.90	14.63	17.27	19.67	22.62	24.72
12	6.30	9.03	11.34	14.01	15.81	18.55	21.03	24.05	26.22
13	7.04	9.93	12.34	15.12	16.98	19.81	22.36	25.47	27.69
14	7.79	10.82	13.34	16.22	18.15	21.06	23.68	26.87	29.14
15	8.55	11.72	14.34	17.32	19.31	22.31	25.00	28.26	30.58
16	9.31	12.62	15.34	18.42	20.46	23.54	26.30	29.63	32.00
17	10.08	13.53	16.34	19.51	21.61	24.77	27.59	30.99	33.41
18	10.86	14.44	17.34	20.60	22.76	25.99	28.87	32.35	34.80
19	11.65	15.35	18.34	21.69	23.90	27.20	30.14	33.69	36.19
20	12.44	16.27	19.34	22.77	25.04	28.41	31.41	35.02	37.57
21	13.24	17.18	20.34	23.86	26.17	29.61	32.67	36.34	38.93
22	14.04	18.10	21.34	24.94	27.30	30.81	33.92	37.66	40.29
23	14.85	19.02	22.34	26.02	28.43	32.01	35.17	38.97	41.64
24	15.66	19.94	23.34	27.10	29.55	33.20	36.41	40.27	42.98
25	16.47	20.87	24.34	28.17	30.67	34.38	37.65	41.57	44.31
26	17.29	21.79	25.34	29.25	31.79	35.56	38.88	42.86	45.64
27	18.11	22.72	26.34	30.32	32.91	36.74	40.11	44.14	46.96
28	18.94	23.65	27.34	31.39	34.03	37.92	41.34	45.42	48.28
29	19.77	24.58	28.24	32.46	35.14	39.09	42.56	46.69	49.59
30	20.60	25.51	29.34	33.53	36.25	40.26	43.77	47.96	50.89
Degrees of Freedom	$P = .90$	.70	.50	.30	.20	.10	.05	.02	.01

χ^2 Probability Scale

For larger degrees of freedom, let $t = \sqrt{2\chi^2} - \sqrt{2n - 1}$, where $n = $ degrees of freedom. Then, approximately,

$$P = \frac{1}{2} - \int_0^t \varphi(t)\, dt$$

and Table 4 may be used.

This table is taken from Fisher: *Statistical Methods for Research Workers*, published by Oliver & Boyd, Limited, Edinburgh and by permission of the author and publishers.

Table 7
Values of F and t
5% (Lightface) and 1% (Boldface) Points

Degrees of Freedom for Lesser Mean Square	Degrees of Freedom for Greater Mean Square																				Values of t
	1	2	3	4	5	6	7	8	9	10	12	16	20	30	40	50	75	100	200	∞	
1	161 / **4,052**	200 / **4,999**	216 / **5,403**	225 / **5,625**	230 / **5,764**	234 / **5,859**	237 / **5,928**	239 / **5,981**	241 / **6,022**	242 / **6,056**	244 / **6,106**	246 / **6,169**	248 / **6,208**	250 / **6,258**	251 / **6,286**	252 / **6,302**	253 / **6,323**	253 / **6,334**	254 / **6,352**	254 / **6,366**	12.706 / **63.657**
2	18.51 / **98.49**	19.00 / **99.01**	19.16 / **99.17**	19.25 / **99.25**	19.30 / **99.30**	19.33 / **99.33**	19.36 / **99.34**	19.37 / **99.36**	19.38 / **99.38**	19.39 / **99.40**	19.41 / **99.42**	19.43 / **99.44**	19.44 / **99.45**	19.46 / **99.47**	19.47 / **99.48**	19.47 / **99.48**	19.48 / **99.49**	19.49 / **99.49**	19.49 / **99.49**	19.50 / **99.50**	4.303 / **9.925**
3	10.13 / **34.12**	9.55 / **30.81**	9.28 / **29.46**	9.12 / **28.71**	9.01 / **28.24**	8.94 / **27.91**	8.88 / **27.67**	8.84 / **27.49**	8.81 / **27.34**	8.78 / **27.23**	8.74 / **27.05**	8.69 / **26.83**	8.66 / **26.69**	8.62 / **26.50**	8.60 / **26.41**	8.58 / **26.35**	8.57 / **26.27**	8.56 / **26.23**	8.54 / **26.18**	8.53 / **26.12**	3.182 / **5.841**
4	7.71 / **21.20**	6.94 / **18.00**	6.59 / **16.69**	6.39 / **15.98**	6.26 / **15.52**	6.16 / **15.21**	6.09 / **14.98**	6.04 / **14.80**	6.00 / **14.66**	5.96 / **14.54**	5.91 / **14.37**	5.84 / **14.15**	5.80 / **14.02**	5.74 / **13.83**	5.71 / **13.74**	5.70 / **13.69**	5.68 / **13.61**	5.66 / **13.57**	5.65 / **13.52**	5.63 / **13.46**	2.776 / **4.604**
5	6.61 / **16.26**	5.79 / **13.27**	5.41 / **12.06**	5.19 / **11.39**	5.05 / **10.97**	4.95 / **10.67**	4.88 / **10.45**	4.82 / **10.27**	4.78 / **10.15**	4.74 / **10.05**	4.68 / **9.89**	4.60 / **9.68**	4.56 / **9.55**	4.50 / **9.38**	4.46 / **9.29**	4.44 / **9.24**	4.42 / **9.17**	4.40 / **9.13**	4.38 / **9.07**	4.36 / **9.02**	2.571 / **4.032**
6	5.99 / **13.74**	5.14 / **10.92**	4.76 / **9.78**	4.53 / **9.15**	4.39 / **8.75**	4.28 / **8.47**	4.21 / **8.26**	4.15 / **8.10**	4.10 / **7.98**	4.06 / **7.87**	4.00 / **7.72**	3.92 / **7.52**	3.87 / **7.39**	3.81 / **7.23**	3.77 / **7.14**	3.75 / **7.09**	3.72 / **7.02**	3.71 / **6.99**	3.69 / **6.94**	3.67 / **6.88**	2.447 / **3.707**
7	5.59 / **12.25**	4.74 / **9.55**	4.35 / **8.45**	4.12 / **7.85**	3.97 / **7.46**	3.87 / **7.19**	3.79 / **7.00**	3.73 / **6.84**	3.68 / **6.71**	3.63 / **6.62**	3.57 / **6.47**	3.49 / **6.27**	3.44 / **6.15**	3.38 / **5.98**	3.34 / **5.90**	3.32 / **5.85**	3.29 / **5.78**	3.28 / **5.75**	3.25 / **5.70**	3.23 / **5.65**	2.365 / **3.499**
8	5.32 / **11.26**	4.46 / **8.65**	4.07 / **7.59**	3.84 / **7.01**	3.69 / **6.63**	3.58 / **6.37**	3.50 / **6.19**	3.44 / **6.03**	3.39 / **5.91**	3.34 / **5.82**	3.28 / **5.67**	3.20 / **5.48**	3.15 / **5.36**	3.08 / **5.20**	3.05 / **5.11**	3.03 / **5.06**	3.00 / **5.00**	2.98 / **4.96**	2.96 / **4.91**	2.93 / **4.86**	2.306 / **3.355**
9	5.12 / **10.56**	4.26 / **8.02**	3.86 / **6.99**	3.63 / **6.42**	3.48 / **6.06**	3.37 / **5.80**	3.29 / **5.62**	3.23 / **5.47**	3.18 / **5.35**	3.13 / **5.26**	3.07 / **5.11**	2.98 / **4.92**	2.93 / **4.80**	2.86 / **4.64**	2.82 / **4.56**	2.80 / **4.51**	2.77 / **4.45**	2.76 / **4.41**	2.73 / **4.36**	2.71 / **4.31**	2.262 / **3.250**
10	4.96 / **10.04**	4.10 / **7.56**	3.71 / **6.55**	3.48 / **5.99**	3.33 / **5.64**	3.22 / **5.39**	3.14 / **5.21**	3.07 / **5.06**	3.02 / **4.95**	2.97 / **4.85**	2.91 / **4.71**	2.82 / **4.52**	2.77 / **4.41**	2.70 / **4.25**	2.67 / **4.17**	2.64 / **4.12**	2.61 / **4.05**	2.59 / **4.01**	2.56 / **3.96**	2.54 / **3.91**	2.228 / **3.169**
11	4.84 / **9.65**	3.98 / **7.20**	3.59 / **6.22**	3.36 / **5.67**	3.20 / **5.32**	3.09 / **5.07**	3.01 / **4.88**	2.95 / **4.74**	2.90 / **4.63**	2.86 / **4.54**	2.79 / **4.40**	2.70 / **4.21**	2.65 / **4.10**	2.57 / **3.94**	2.53 / **3.86**	2.50 / **3.80**	2.47 / **3.74**	2.45 / **3.70**	2.42 / **3.66**	2.40 / **3.60**	2.201 / **3.106**
12	4.75 / **9.33**	3.88 / **6.93**	3.49 / **5.95**	3.26 / **5.41**	3.11 / **5.06**	3.00 / **4.82**	2.92 / **4.65**	2.85 / **4.50**	2.80 / **4.39**	2.76 / **4.30**	2.69 / **4.16**	2.60 / **3.98**	2.54 / **3.86**	2.46 / **3.70**	2.42 / **3.61**	2.40 / **3.56**	2.36 / **3.49**	2.35 / **3.46**	2.32 / **3.41**	2.30 / **3.36**	2.179 / **3.055**
13	4.67 / **9.07**	3.80 / **6.70**	3.41 / **5.74**	3.18 / **5.20**	3.02 / **4.86**	2.92 / **4.62**	2.84 / **4.44**	2.77 / **4.30**	2.72 / **4.19**	2.67 / **4.10**	2.60 / **3.96**	2.51 / **3.78**	2.46 / **3.67**	2.38 / **3.51**	2.34 / **3.42**	2.32 / **3.37**	2.28 / **3.30**	2.26 / **3.27**	2.24 / **3.21**	2.21 / **3.16**	2.160 / **3.012**

Values of F and t
5% (Lightface) and 1% (Boldface) Points

Degrees of Freedom for Greater Mean Square

Degrees of Freedom for Lesser Mean Square	1	2	3	4	5	6	7	8	9	10	12	16	20	30	40	50	75	100	200	∞	Values of t
14	4.60 **8.86**	3.74 **6.51**	3.34 **5.56**	3.11 **5.03**	2.96 **4.69**	2.85 **4.46**	2.77 **4.28**	2.70 **4.14**	2.65 **4.03**	2.60 **3.94**	2.53 **3.80**	2.44 **3.62**	2.39 **3.51**	2.31 **3.34**	2.27 **3.26**	2.24 **3.21**	2.21 **3.14**	2.19 **3.11**	2.16 **3.06**	2.13 **3.00**	2.145 **2.977**
15	4.54 **8.68**	3.68 **6.36**	3.29 **5.42**	3.06 **4.89**	2.90 **4.56**	2.79 **4.32**	2.70 **4.14**	2.64 **4.00**	2.59 **3.89**	2.55 **3.80**	2.48 **3.67**	2.39 **3.48**	2.33 **3.36**	2.25 **3.20**	2.21 **3.12**	2.18 **3.07**	2.15 **3.00**	2.12 **2.97**	2.10 **2.92**	2.07 **2.87**	2.131 **2.947**
16	4.49 **8.53**	3.63 **6.23**	3.24 **5.29**	3.01 **4.77**	2.85 **4.44**	2.74 **4.20**	2.66 **4.03**	2.59 **3.89**	2.54 **3.78**	2.49 **3.69**	2.42 **3.55**	2.33 **3.37**	2.28 **3.25**	2.20 **3.10**	2.16 **3.01**	2.13 **2.96**	2.09 **2.89**	2.07 **2.86**	2.04 **2.80**	2.01 **2.75**	2.120 **2.921**
17	4.45 **8.40**	3.59 **6.11**	3.20 **5.18**	2.96 **4.67**	2.81 **4.34**	2.70 **4.10**	2.62 **3.93**	2.55 **3.79**	2.50 **3.68**	2.45 **3.59**	2.38 **3.45**	2.29 **3.27**	2.23 **3.16**	2.15 **3.00**	2.11 **2.92**	2.08 **2.86**	2.04 **2.79**	2.02 **2.76**	1.99 **2.70**	1.96 **2.65**	2.110 **2.898**
18	4.41 **8.28**	3.55 **6.01**	3.16 **5.09**	2.93 **4.58**	2.77 **4.25**	2.66 **4.01**	2.58 **3.85**	2.51 **3.71**	2.46 **3.60**	2.41 **3.51**	2.34 **3.37**	2.25 **3.19**	2.19 **3.07**	2.11 **2.91**	2.07 **2.83**	2.04 **2.78**	2.00 **2.71**	1.98 **2.68**	1.95 **2.62**	1.92 **2.57**	2.101 **2.878**
19	4.38 **8.18**	3.52 **5.93**	3.13 **5.01**	2.90 **4.50**	2.74 **4.17**	2.63 **3.94**	2.55 **3.77**	2.48 **3.63**	2.43 **3.52**	2.38 **3.43**	2.31 **3.30**	2.21 **3.12**	2.15 **3.00**	2.07 **2.84**	2.02 **2.76**	2.00 **2.70**	1.96 **2.63**	1.94 **2.60**	1.91 **2.54**	1.88 **2.49**	2.093 **2.861**
20	4.35 **8.10**	3.49 **5.85**	3.10 **4.94**	2.87 **4.43**	2.71 **4.10**	2.60 **3.87**	2.52 **3.71**	2.45 **3.56**	2.40 **3.45**	2.35 **3.37**	2.28 **3.23**	2.18 **3.05**	2.12 **2.94**	2.04 **2.77**	1.99 **2.69**	1.96 **2.63**	1.92 **2.56**	1.90 **2.53**	1.87 **2.47**	1.84 **2.42**	2.086 **2.845**
21	4.32 **8.02**	3.47 **5.78**	3.07 **4.87**	2.84 **4.37**	2.68 **4.04**	2.57 **3.81**	2.49 **3.65**	2.42 **3.51**	2.37 **3.40**	2.32 **3.31**	2.25 **3.17**	2.15 **2.99**	2.09 **2.88**	2.00 **2.72**	1.96 **2.63**	1.93 **2.58**	1.89 **2.51**	1.87 **2.47**	1.84 **2.42**	1.81 **2.36**	2.080 **2.831**
22	4.30 **7.94**	3.44 **5.72**	3.05 **4.82**	2.82 **4.31**	2.66 **3.99**	2.55 **3.76**	2.47 **3.59**	2.40 **3.45**	2.35 **3.35**	2.30 **3.26**	2.23 **3.12**	2.13 **2.94**	2.07 **2.83**	1.98 **2.67**	1.93 **2.58**	1.91 **2.53**	1.87 **2.46**	1.84 **2.42**	1.81 **2.37**	1.78 **2.31**	2.074 **2.819**
23	4.28 **7.88**	3.42 **5.66**	3.03 **4.76**	2.80 **4.26**	2.64 **3.94**	2.53 **3.71**	2.45 **3.54**	2.38 **3.41**	2.32 **3.30**	2.28 **3.21**	2.20 **3.07**	2.10 **2.89**	2.04 **2.78**	1.96 **2.62**	1.91 **2.53**	1.88 **2.48**	1.84 **2.41**	1.82 **2.37**	1.79 **2.32**	1.76 **2.26**	2.069 **2.807**
24	4.26 **7.82**	3.40 **5.61**	3.01 **4.72**	2.78 **4.22**	2.62 **3.90**	2.51 **3.67**	2.43 **3.50**	2.36 **3.36**	2.30 **3.25**	2.26 **3.17**	2.18 **3.03**	2.09 **2.85**	2.02 **2.74**	1.94 **2.58**	1.89 **2.49**	1.86 **2.44**	1.82 **2.36**	1.80 **2.33**	1.76 **2.27**	1.73 **2.21**	2.064 **2.797**
25	4.24 **7.77**	3.38 **5.57**	2.99 **4.68**	2.76 **4.18**	2.60 **3.86**	2.49 **3.63**	2.41 **3.46**	2.34 **3.32**	2.28 **3.21**	2.24 **3.13**	2.16 **2.99**	2.06 **2.81**	2.00 **2.70**	1.92 **2.54**	1.87 **2.45**	1.84 **2.40**	1.80 **2.32**	1.77 **2.29**	1.74 **2.23**	1.71 **2.17**	2.060 **2.787**
26	4.22 **7.72**	3.37 **5.53**	2.98 **4.64**	2.74 **4.14**	2.59 **3.82**	2.47 **3.59**	2.39 **3.42**	2.32 **3.29**	2.27 **3.17**	2.22 **3.09**	2.15 **2.96**	2.05 **2.77**	1.99 **2.66**	1.90 **2.50**	1.85 **2.41**	1.82 **2.36**	1.78 **2.28**	1.76 **2.25**	1.72 **2.19**	1.69 **2.13**	2.056 **2.779**

Reproduced by permission from *Calculation and Interpretation of Analysis of Variance* by George W. Snedecor, © 1934 by The Iowa State University Press.

Values of F and t

5% (Lightface) and 1% (Boldface) Points

Degrees of Freedom for Greater Mean Square

Degrees of Freedom for Lesser Mean Square	1	2	3	4	5	6	7	8	9	10	12	16	20	30	40	50	75	100	200	∞	Values of $t*$
27	4.21 **7.68**	3.35 **5.49**	2.96 **4.60**	2.73 **4.11**	2.57 **3.79**	2.46 **3.56**	2.37 **3.39**	2.30 **3.26**	2.25 **3.14**	2.20 **3.06**	2.13 **2.93**	2.03 **2.74**	1.97 **2.63**	1.88 **2.47**	1.84 **2.38**	1.80 **2.33**	1.76 **2.25**	1.74 **2.21**	1.71 **2.16**	1.67 **2.10**	2.052 **2.771**
28	4.20 **7.64**	3.34 **5.45**	2.95 **4.57**	2.71 **4.07**	2.56 **3.76**	2.44 **3.53**	2.36 **3.36**	2.29 **3.23**	2.24 **3.11**	2.19 **3.03**	2.12 **2.90**	2.02 **2.71**	1.96 **2.60**	1.87 **2.44**	1.81 **2.35**	1.78 **2.30**	1.75 **2.22**	1.72 **2.18**	1.69 **2.13**	1.65 **2.06**	2.048 **2.763**
29	4.18 **7.60**	3.33 **5.42**	2.93 **4.54**	2.70 **4.04**	2.54 **3.73**	2.43 **3.50**	2.35 **3.33**	2.28 **3.20**	2.22 **3.08**	2.18 **3.00**	2.10 **2.87**	2.00 **2.68**	1.94 **2.57**	1.85 **2.41**	1.80 **2.32**	1.77 **2.27**	1.73 **2.19**	1.71 **2.15**	1.68 **2.10**	1.64 **2.03**	2.045 **2.756**
30	4.17 **7.56**	3.32 **5.39**	2.92 **4.51**	2.69 **4.02**	2.53 **3.70**	2.42 **3.47**	2.34 **3.30**	2.27 **3.17**	2.21 **3.06**	2.16 **2.98**	2.09 **2.84**	1.99 **2.66**	1.93 **2.55**	1.84 **2.38**	1.79 **2.29**	1.76 **2.24**	1.72 **2.16**	1.69 **2.13**	1.66 **2.07**	1.62 **2.01**	2.042 **2.750**
32	4.15 **7.50**	3.30 **5.34**	2.90 **4.46**	2.67 **3.97**	2.51 **3.66**	2.40 **3.42**	2.32 **3.25**	2.25 **3.12**	2.19 **3.01**	2.14 **2.94**	2.07 **2.80**	1.97 **2.62**	1.91 **2.51**	1.82 **2.34**	1.76 **2.25**	1.74 **2.20**	1.69 **2.12**	1.67 **2.08**	1.64 **2.02**	1.59 **1.96**	2.037 **2.738**
34	4.13 **7.44**	3.28 **5.29**	2.88 **4.42**	2.65 **3.93**	2.49 **3.61**	2.38 **3.38**	2.30 **3.21**	2.23 **3.08**	2.17 **2.97**	2.12 **2.89**	2.05 **2.76**	1.95 **2.58**	1.89 **2.47**	1.80 **2.30**	1.74 **2.21**	1.71 **2.15**	1.67 **2.08**	1.64 **2.04**	1.61 **1.98**	1.57 **1.91**	2.032 **2.728**
36	4.11 **7.39**	3.26 **5.25**	2.86 **4.38**	2.63 **3.89**	2.48 **3.58**	2.36 **3.35**	2.28 **3.18**	2.21 **3.04**	2.15 **2.94**	2.10 **2.86**	2.03 **2.72**	1.93 **2.54**	1.87 **2.43**	1.78 **2.26**	1.72 **2.17**	1.69 **2.12**	1.65 **2.04**	1.62 **2.00**	1.59 **1.94**	1.55 **1.87**	2.028 **2.720**
38	4.10 **7.35**	3.25 **5.21**	2.85 **4.34**	2.62 **3.86**	2.46 **3.54**	2.35 **3.32**	2.26 **3.15**	2.19 **3.02**	2.14 **2.91**	2.09 **2.82**	2.02 **2.69**	1.92 **2.51**	1.85 **2.40**	1.76 **2.22**	1.71 **2.14**	1.67 **2.08**	1.63 **2.00**	1.60 **1.97**	1.57 **1.90**	1.53 **1.84**	2.024 **2.711**
40	4.08 **7.31**	3.23 **5.18**	2.84 **4.31**	2.61 **3.83**	2.45 **3.51**	2.34 **3.29**	2.25 **3.12**	2.18 **2.99**	2.12 **2.88**	2.07 **2.80**	2.00 **2.66**	1.90 **2.49**	1.84 **2.37**	1.74 **2.20**	1.69 **2.11**	1.66 **2.05**	1.61 **1.97**	1.59 **1.94**	1.55 **1.88**	1.51 **1.81**	2.021 **2.704**
42	4.07 **7.27**	3.22 **5.15**	2.83 **4.29**	2.59 **3.80**	2.44 **3.49**	2.32 **3.26**	2.24 **3.10**	2.17 **2.96**	2.11 **2.86**	2.06 **2.77**	1.99 **2.64**	1.89 **2.46**	1.82 **2.35**	1.73 **2.17**	1.68 **2.08**	1.64 **2.02**	1.60 **1.94**	1.57 **1.91**	1.54 **1.85**	1.49 **1.78**	2.018 **2.698**
44	4.06 **7.24**	3.21 **5.12**	2.82 **4.26**	2.58 **3.78**	2.43 **3.46**	2.31 **3.24**	2.23 **3.07**	2.16 **2.94**	2.10 **2.84**	2.05 **2.75**	1.98 **2.62**	1.88 **2.44**	1.81 **2.32**	1.72 **2.15**	1.66 **2.06**	1.63 **2.00**	1.58 **1.92**	1.56 **1.88**	1.52 **1.82**	1.48 **1.75**	2.015 **2.693**
46	4.05 **7.21**	3.20 **5.10**	2.81 **4.24**	2.57 **3.76**	2.42 **3.44**	2.30 **3.22**	2.22 **3.05**	2.14 **2.92**	2.09 **2.82**	2.04 **2.73**	1.97 **2.60**	1.87 **2.42**	1.80 **2.30**	1.71 **2.13**	1.65 **2.04**	1.62 **1.98**	1.57 **1.90**	1.54 **1.86**	1.51 **1.80**	1.46 **1.72**	2.012 **2.687**
48	4.04 **7.19**	3.19 **5.08**	2.80 **4.22**	2.56 **3.74**	2.41 **3.42**	2.30 **3.20**	2.21 **3.04**	2.14 **2.90**	2.08 **2.80**	2.03 **2.71**	1.96 **2.58**	1.86 **2.40**	1.79 **2.28**	1.70 **2.11**	1.64 **2.02**	1.61 **1.96**	1.56 **1.88**	1.53 **1.84**	1.50 **1.78**	1.45 **1.70**	2.010 **2.682**

Values of F and t

5% (Lightface) and 1% (Boldface) Points

Degrees of Freedom for Greater Mean Square

Each cell shows the 5% (lightface) value over the 1% (boldface) value.

Degrees of Freedom for Lesser Mean Square	1	2	3	4	5	6	7	8	9	10	11	16	20	30	40	50	75	100	200	∞	Values of t*
50	4.03 / **7.17**	3.18 / **5.06**	2.79 / **4.20**	2.56 / **3.72**	2.40 / **3.41**	2.29 / **3.18**	2.20 / **3.02**	2.13 / **2.88**	2.07 / **2.78**	2.02 / **2.70**	1.95 / **2.56**	1.85 / **2.39**	1.78 / **2.26**	1.69 / **2.10**	1.63 / **2.00**	1.60 / **1.94**	1.55 / **1.86**	1.52 / **1.82**	1.48 / **1.76**	1.44 / **1.68**	2.008 / **2.678**
55	4.02 / **7.12**	3.17 / **5.01**	2.78 / **4.16**	2.54 / **3.68**	2.38 / **3.37**	2.27 / **3.15**	2.18 / **2.98**	2.11 / **2.85**	2.05 / **2.75**	2.00 / **2.66**	1.93 / **2.53**	1.83 / **2.35**	1.76 / **2.23**	1.67 / **2.06**	1.61 / **1.96**	1.58 / **1.90**	1.52 / **1.82**	1.50 / **1.78**	1.46 / **1.71**	1.41 / **1.64**	2.003 / **2.668**
60	4.00 / **7.08**	3.15 / **4.98**	2.76 / **4.13**	2.52 / **3.65**	2.37 / **3.34**	2.25 / **3.12**	2.17 / **2.95**	2.10 / **2.82**	2.04 / **2.72**	1.99 / **2.63**	1.92 / **2.50**	1.81 / **2.32**	1.75 / **2.20**	1.65 / **2.03**	1.59 / **.93**	1.56 / **1.87**	1.50 / **1.79**	1.48 / **1.74**	1.44 / **1.68**	1.39 / **1.60**	2.000 / **2.660**
65	3.99 / **7.04**	3.14 / **4.95**	2.75 / **4.10**	2.51 / **3.62**	2.36 / **3.31**	2.24 / **3.09**	2.15 / **2.93**	2.08 / **2.79**	2.02 / **2.70**	1.98 / **2.61**	1.90 / **2.47**	1.80 / **2.30**	1.73 / **2.18**	1.63 / **2.00**	1.57 / **1.90**	1.54 / **1.84**	1.49 / **1.76**	1.46 / **1.71**	1.42 / **1.64**	1.37 / **1.56**	1.996 / **2.653**
70	3.98 / **7.01**	3.13 / **4.92**	2.74 / **4.08**	2.50 / **3.60**	2.35 / **3.29**	2.23 / **3.07**	2.14 / **2.91**	2.07 / **2.77**	2.01 / **2.67**	1.97 / **2.59**	1.89 / **2.45**	1.79 / **2.28**	1.72 / **2.15**	1.62 / **1.98**	1.56 / **1.88**	1.53 / **1.82**	1.47 / **1.74**	1.45 / **1.69**	1.40 / **1.62**	1.35 / **1.53**	1.994 / **2.648**
80	3.96 / **6.96**	3.11 / **4.88**	2.72 / **4.04**	2.48 / **3.56**	2.33 / **3.25**	2.21 / **3.04**	2.12 / **2.87**	2.05 / **2.74**	1.99 / **2.64**	1.95 / **2.55**	1.88 / **2.41**	1.77 / **2.24**	1.70 / **2.11**	1.60 / **1.94**	1.54 / **1.84**	1.51 / **1.78**	1.45 / **1.70**	1.42 / **1.65**	1.38 / **1.57**	1.32 / **1.49**	1.990 / **2.638**
100	3.94 / **6.90**	3.09 / **4.82**	2.70 / **3.98**	2.46 / **3.51**	2.30 / **3.20**	2.19 / **2.99**	2.10 / **2.82**	2.03 / **2.69**	1.97 / **2.59**	1.92 / **2.51**	1.85 / **2.36**	1.75 / **2.19**	1.68 / **2.06**	1.57 / **1.89**	1.51 / **1.79**	1.48 / **1.73**	1.42 / **1.64**	1.39 / **1.59**	1.34 / **1.51**	1.28 / **1.43**	1.984 / **2.626**
125	3.92 / **6.84**	3.07 / **4.78**	2.68 / **3.94**	2.44 / **3.47**	2.29 / **3.17**	2.17 / **2.95**	2.08 / **2.79**	2.01 / **2.65**	1.95 / **2.56**	1.90 / **2.47**	1.83 / **2.33**	1.72 / **2.15**	1.65 / **2.03**	1.55 / **1.85**	1.49 / **1.75**	1.45 / **1.68**	1.39 / **1.59**	1.36 / **1.54**	1.31 / **1.46**	1.25 / **1.37**	1.979 / **2.616**
150	3.91 / **6.81**	3.06 / **4.75**	2.67 / **3.91**	2.43 / **3.44**	2.27 / **3.14**	2.16 / **2.92**	2.07 / **2.76**	2.00 / **2.62**	1.94 / **2.53**	1.89 / **2.44**	1.82 / **2.30**	1.71 / **2.12**	1.64 / **2.00**	1.54 / **1.83**	1.47 / **1.72**	1.44 / **1.66**	1.37 / **1.56**	1.34 / **1.51**	1.29 / **1.43**	1.22 / **1.33**	1.976 / **2.609**
200	3.89 / **6.76**	3.04 / **4.71**	2.65 / **3.88**	2.41 / **3.41**	2.26 / **3.11**	2.14 / **2.90**	2.05 / **2.73**	1.98 / **2.60**	1.92 / **2.50**	1.87 / **2.41**	1.80 / **2.28**	1.69 / **2.09**	1.62 / **1.97**	1.52 / **1.79**	1.45 / **1.69**	1.42 / **1.62**	1.35 / **1.53**	1.32 / **1.48**	1.26 / **1.39**	1.19 / **1.28**	1.972 / **2.601**
400	3.86 / **6.70**	3.02 / **4.66**	2.62 / **3.83**	2.39 / **3.36**	2.23 / **3.06**	2.12 / **2.85**	2.03 / **2.69**	1.96 / **2.55**	1.90 / **2.46**	1.85 / **2.37**	1.78 / **2.23**	1.67 / **2.04**	1.60 / **1.92**	1.49 / **1.74**	1.42 / **1.64**	1.38 / **1.57**	1.32 / **1.47**	1.28 / **1.42**	1.22 / **1.32**	1.13 / **1.19**	1.966 / **2.588**
1000	3.85 / **6.66**	3.00 / **4.62**	2.61 / **3.80**	2.38 / **3.34**	2.22 / **3.04**	2.10 / **2.82**	2.02 / **2.66**	1.95 / **2.53**	1.89 / **2.43**	1.84 / **2.34**	1.76 / **2.20**	1.65 / **2.01**	1.58 / **1.89**	1.47 / **1.71**	1.41 / **1.61**	1.36 / **1.54**	1.30 / **1.44**	1.26 / **1.38**	1.19 / **1.28**	1.08 / **1.11**	1.962 / **2.581**
∞	3.84 / **6.64**	2.99 / **4.60**	2.60 / **3.78**	2.37 / **3.32**	2.21 / **3.02**	2.09 / **2.80**	2.01 / **2.64**	1.94 / **2.51**	1.88 / **2.41**	1.83 / **2.32**	1.75 / **2.18**	1.64 / **1.99**	1.57 / **1.87**	1.46 / **1.69**	1.40 / **1.59**	1.35 / **1.52**	1.28 / **1.41**	1.24 / **1.36**	1.17 / **1.25**	1.00 / **1.00**	1.960 / **2.576**

* Some of these values of t were determined by graphical interpolation.

INDEXES

INDEX OF NAMES

INDEX OF MATHEMATICAL
AND STATISTICAL TERMS

INDEX OF ECONOMIC TERMS